Understanding the Interactive Digital Media Marketplace:

Frameworks, Platforms, Communities and Issues

Ravi S. Sharma
Nanyang Technological University, Singapore

Margaret Tan
Nanyang Technological University, Singapore

Francis Pereira
University of Southern California, USA

Information Science
REFERENCE

Managing Director:	Lindsay Johnston
Senior Editorial Director:	Heather Probst
Book Production Manager:	Sean Woznicki
Development Manager:	Joel Gamon
Development Editor:	Michael Killian
Acquisitions Editor:	Erika Gallagher
Typesetter:	Christopher Shearer
Print Coordinator:	Jamie Snavely
Cover Design:	Nick Newcomer

Published in the United States of America by
Information Science Reference (an imprint of IGI Global)
701 E. Chocolate Avenue
Hershey PA 17033
Tel: 717-533-8845
Fax: 717-533-8661
E-mail: cust@igi-global.com
Web site: http://www.igi-global.com

Library of Congress Cataloging-in-Publication Data

Understanding the interactive digital media marketplace: frameworks, platforms, communities and issues / Ravi S. Sharma, Margaret Tan and Francis Pereira, editors.
    p. cm.
 Includes bibliographical references and index.
 ISBN 978-1-61350-147-4 (hbk.) -- ISBN 978-1-61350-148-1 (ebook) 1. Digital media. 2. Electronic industries. 3. Internet industry. 4. Computer industry. I. Sharma, Ravi, 1961- II. Tan, Margaret. III. Pereira, Francis, 1961-
 HD9696.A2.U45 2012
 381'.45302231--dc22
                              2011013918

British Cataloguing in Publication Data
A Cataloguing in Publication record for this book is available from the British Library.

All work contributed to this book is new, previously-unpublished material. The views expressed in this book are those of the authors, but not necessarily of the publisher.

Editorial Advisory Board

Table of Contents

Section 2
Technology Platforms

Section 3
Digital Communities

Section 4
Regulatory and Policy Issues

Preface

UNDERSTANDING THE INTERACTIVE DIGITAL MEDIA MARKETPLACE: FRAMEWORKS, PLATFORMS, COMMUNITIES, AND ISSUES

This book is targeted at an audience of researchers in the area of Interactive Digital Media (IDM), which includes a wide range of applications using multimedia content, delivered over a broadband network such as the Internet. Examples are software as a service, music, movies, news-on-demand, online games, archived digital art and books, sharable educational material, e-government services, electronic health records, and so on. The book is the result of an on-going research programme at the Special Interest Group on Interactive Digital Enterprise (SIGIDE) funded by Singapore's National Research Foundation.

The primary objective of SIGIDE is to serve as "intellectual venture capitalists" to IDM incubators and start-ups in Singapore as they take the necessary steps "to reach the next billion" users. The first phase was a 3 year project which began in December 2007, hosted within the Nanyang Technological University. In its anticipated 2nd phase SIGIDE will take a more international and industry facing dimension.

Through its industry-oriented, action-research programme, and leveraging on its network of international and industry partners, SIGIDE has developed expertise and capabilities that covered the four pillars of the IDM marketplace – (I) Business Frameworks; (II) Technology Platforms; (III) Digital Communities; and (IV) Regulatory & Policy Issues. Key outcomes were research publications, industry whitepapers, manuals and workshops, capability development, and advisory services.

This book outlines some of the research findings of SIGIDE's work in IDM. As an overview, the 34 chapters are organized as follows: there is an introductory chapter on the ADVISOR framework and about 5-7 specialised chapters for each pillar. Each chapter has been written by different authors coming from a wide ranging set of perspectives. As a whole, this book seeks to uncover usable business models, market strategies, and policy frameworks for the emerging global digital economy. It will be a useful read for graduate students and other researchers exploring the area as well as entrepreneurs considering their strategic and tactical options.

This first section of the book overviews the business frameworks necessary to start and grow an IDM firm. By business framework, we mean a model that encompasses the structures, relationships, and resources in order to determine an optimal and sustaining method of revenue generation. El-Sawy & Pereira begin the discussion of business frameworks in Chapter 1 with a description of the ADVISOR model (an extension of their earlier work) for what they term as networked digital industries. This model serves to predict what the parameters of success could be and therefore guide IDM businesses in the design of business models. Chapter 2 is a review of pricing strategies by Lei, Shi, & Iqbal, leading to a summary of their understanding in the form of a case study of online music. In Chapter 3, Bansal,

Manoher, & Shantani focus on variable pricing and conclude that adverse reaction of consumers to unfair price discrimination is the greatest hindrance to the effective application of variable pricing schemes. Verma, Gupta, & Keshav continue the discussion on more specific pricing schemes in Chapter 4 with an analysis of how the pricing decision of bundling vs. à la carte is resolved using the case of cable television. Chapter 5 by Budi, Wang, & Wang is a comparative analysis of digital products and services studied from the perspective of key marketing processes such as promotion, sale, and distribution. Ng, Arias, & Koh discuss the concept, nature, and implications of freemium content and consider the problems caused by the rise of this phenomenon in an otherwise flourishing digital marketplace in Chapter 6. In Chapter 7, Goh, Tan, & Wang consider the question of whether to bundle or unbundle an IDM service offer and conclude after case studies of two leading players that the most effect option depends on market conditions more than other factors. Chapter 8 by Nizam, Kumar, & Jayaraman focuses on how enterprises can profit from radical and incremental innovations in the IDM marketplace by factoring the roles played, importance, and impact of the two types of innovations. Completing this part of the book is Chapter 9 by Tan, Ge, & Rajkumar, which considers the strategic issue of fragmentation in mobile platforms and the current on-going industry solutions that address the problems associated with this, such as non-compliance and niche segments. The above chapters may not have comprehensively covered all IDM business issues but suggest that while pricing is critical, other factors such as strategic marketing tactics contribute significantly to business modeling.

Section 2 of the book overviews the technology platforms necessary for the launch and delivery of IDM products and services. In a digital eco-system, technology platforms refer to the servers, devices, networks, as well as the management services (for production, delivery, payment, access security, digital rights, etc.). Designing the platform or configuring one that brings about a strategic advantage for the business is the theme of this section. Arguably, the most fundamental of these strategic platform considerations concerns whether to deploy an open platform or closed one. Wu, Khan, & Serraf discuss this in Chapter 10 with the proviso that each is more effective than the other under certain market conditions. Chapter 11 on the same key question takes a contrary view with Alexander, Ho, & Arasu conclude that it is more than market conditions such as new entrants vs. dominant incumbents, presence and significance of complementors, et cetera, that give competitive advantage with an open or closed platform superiority. Another popular topic in IDM technology is the ubiquitous IPTV platform. Yang, Chua, & Li discuss in Chapter 12 how value emerges from the platform characteristics of IPTV in order to compete in a crowded market. Following this, Chapter 13 by Huang, Tan, & Buyi considers the broader notion of interactive TV platforms as disruptive innovation and how the chasm (of user adoption) may be crossed. Peer-to-Peer (P2P) networks are clearly a post-modernist platform for a myriad of IDM applications. However they are fraught with controversies relating to digital rights and their protection. Chapter 14 by Mansukhani, He, & Ma show how digital rights management may be enforced on P2P networks. In Chapter 15, Morales-Arroyo, Foo, Lim, & Kwek configure, use and evaluate eight web-scraping spiders for their functionality in order to determine their suitability for IDM competitive intelligence. The deployment of such a technology, they suggest, should be a vital component of the platforms of start-ups and established firms alike. Shwe, Gao, & Chia, in Chapter 16, describe the general architecture and specific design features of mobile operating systems and their connection to value creation. Chapter 17 by Yeo, Jing, Khin, & Fan explores and discuss the issues and opportunities centered around the centralization and integration of platforms in order to secure dominant market share. Chapter 18 by Tan, Chua, & Kaung closes the section with an analysis of social networks and their impact on the marketing of (particularly) digital goods where word-of-mouth prevails over conventional advertising and promotion. Whereas we may conjecture that the technology platform is a tactical play centered on efficiency objects, the set of chapters in this part of the book seem to suggest that the platform is equally a strategic component of the IDM business.

Section 3 of the book covers user communities and markets for IDM services and applications. Continuing from where Section 2 left off, and delving deeper into the notion of e-Word-of-Mouth, Chapter 19 by Bhatt, Chang, & Wang makes a case for the effect use of social networks in viral marketing. Next, Azeharie reviews virtual worlds and their economies using Second Life as an exemplar in Chapter 20. Machill, Gerstner, & Class, in Chapter 21, describe the results of an empirical study in Germany which revealed the use of online videos and other content by the community of journalists who participated in the study. Chapter 22 by Stephanie, Srinivasan, & Lawale reviews the use of IDM in healthcare, the first of three communities covered in this book, and suggest that it is very much in its infancy despite the longstanding activities. In a reflective, personal account, Jones in Chapter 23 narrates his use of blended learning in the context of university education and concludes that its success very much depends of the effect mix of technology and face-to-face teaching. Chapter 24 by Li, Shen, & Tan describe the third of the IDM communities covered, with a description of online games for children and how such services may be exploited by users. In Chapter 25, Lai & Lee evaluate several models and frameworks for the assessment of e-government services using case-studies of Iraq, Zambia, Malaysia, and Canada in order to validate their findings. A macro level perspective of eWord-of-Mouth is that such messages combine into a "wisdom of the crowds," which in turn influences collective behavior; this is the subject of Zhang & Yang's Chapter 26 which is the last of section 3. With these chapters, we may concede that the theme of community is too vast to bottle into a comprehensive set of frameworks. Nevertheless, it is useful to consider such systemic studies of such communities so as to better serve them and draw some lessons for IDM in general.

The final section of the book comprises chapters which discuss regulatory and policy issues that ostensibly promote the growth of the IDM sector(s) and safeguard the interests of the public. But as the chapters in the section reveal, this is no easy matter and involves trade-offs that affect both segments negatively. In Chapter 27, Mahizhnan captures one aspect of this policy dilemma of balancing between the inevitable need for some kind of regulation with the essentially uncontrollable nature of the architecture and function of new media, concluding that self-control of the user communities seems more critical to the outcome than externally imposed control regimes. More specifically, Chapter 28 by Lim, Lu, & Tan attempts to show that the game industry, parents, and society at large should be more participative in influencing the direction of game content development and regulating violence in massively multiplayer online role playing games. In Chapter 29, Balgayev, Phng, & Kaung ask whether DRM is the great spoiler in the IDM marketplace and show that the advantages brought by DRM to firms go beyond what would be needed for the efficient distribution of digital goods. Chapter 30, by Wildman & Chew, describes current trends in the internet television market and traditional television industry players' efforts to respond to the opportunities and threats posed by new media. Again on Internet television, Wong, Chow, & Chua propose a modified product life cycle for radio and TV broadcasting in Chapter 31 in which its decline phase is replaced by an evolution phase due to disruptions from the Internet. Chapter 32, by Xu, Xu, & Zeng, ponders over the future of television (and audiences) using a myriad of frameworks to determine how television in the future may create value, seize value, and add value into the interactive services and products they provide. Lee, Ismail, & Ma examine the future of the printed book in Chapter 33 and note that shift of physical books into digital form has resulted in a significant change in perspectives of business models within the publishing and affected players in its eco-system. Ending Section 4 and the book is Chapter 34 by Kurniawan, Kok, & Zhang, which similarly examines the future of newspapers and prescribes key areas and conceptual models of future newspapers' strategy framework and supply chain management. The sum total of takeaways from the chapters in this section of the book suggest that IDM regulatory policy ought to take greater economic than political tones in order to be effective. Both the industry and regulatory agencies would better serve consumers with such an agenda.

Therefore, in a nutshell, we posit that understanding the IDM marketplace requires first in-depth studies on business frameworks, technology platforms, user communities, and regulatory policies. This book is an attempt to do just this.

Ravi S. Sharma
Nanyang Technological University, Singapore

Margaret Tan
Nanyang Technological University, Singapore

Francis Pereira
University of Southern California, USA

Acknowledgment

SIGIGE's IDM research program has been funded by the National Research Foundation of Singapore. We are grateful to the authors of the chapters for working with us in of our journey. We are also grateful to the institutions involved – NTU, USC, SMU, MSU, Leipzig University, MMTC (Jonkoping) – for allowing us the discretion to pursue what were then the lonely by-ways of new media research. Our delightful undergraduate assistants – Alyssa Lee and Ma Vengmov – are deeply thanked for their patience and persistence with proofreading and formatting the documents. As SIGIDE moves into its second phase of active industry and international engagements, we welcome contact with likeminded researchers in the IDM eco-system.

Ravi S. Sharma
Nanyang Technological University, Singapore

Margaret Tan
Nanyang Technological University, Singapore

Francis Pereira
University of Southern California, USA

Section 1
Business Frameworks

Chapter 1
Disruptions and Value in the Interactive Digital Media Marketplace

Omar El-Sawy
University of Southern California, USA

Francis Pereira
University of Southern California, USA

ABSTRACT

This introductory chapter explains business modeling in the context of interactive digital products and services. The ADVISOR framework is presented as a useful means of articulating value. A review of other approaches suggests that business modeling is all about determining value and the ADVISOR framework is a valid one.

INTRODUCTION

The Interactive Digital Media (IDM) marketplace is not entirely new. Even before the current popularity of MMORPG, online music stores, IPTV and a host of social network applications, the digitization of content had been driven by the convergence of web services with telecommunications networks and devices. Today's ubiquity of the broadband (and often wireless) Internet is at the centre of how this content is produced,

consumed, repackaged and traded. In such content delivery networks, there are various roles played by producers, consumers, syndicators, aggregators and distributors in the emerging marketplace. Topical examples of Interactive Digital Media include music, movies, games, software, books, social content on devices as diverse as networked TV sets, home and car entertainment systems, mobile communications devices, and online games consoles.

Whereas networks, content or services, and regulatory regimes have made progress through media, network and industry convergence, busi-

DOI: 10.4018/978-1-61350-147-4.ch001

ness models are only beginning to re-engineer themselves to the current realities of (dis-) intermediation. Much of this is due to the legacy cost-plus pricing of telcos, licensing of broadcasters and the subscription based revenue streams of the media industry. Content owners, on the other hand, are understandably concerned with digital rights management (DRM) and how business models and pricing strategies might affect piracy. Advertising revenue streams are lucrative but work differently in the online marketplace than they would in traditional practice, moreover, there is no demarcated difference between vendors who own the content and those that have access to the customers.

Technological advancement and globalization has caused the rise of a new type of media which is networked and interactive. The new media are basically cultural objects which utilize digital computer technology for distribution as well as exhibition (Manovich, 2001). The emergence of new technology, specifically the broadband and wireless Internet, associated services and devices, is another contributor to the disruptions to the underlying business models of the IDM industry by reducing the distribution cost digitization of content, and creating new possibilities (Anderson, 2008). Such a phenomenon is distinct from the term disruptive innovation used by Christensen (1997) to describe simpler and cheaper to use versions of existing products that target low-end or entirely new customers. Disruptions to the IDM marketplace are radical transformations of existing lines of business with a future-oriented and risk-taking strategy that cannibalizes current revenue streams with online substitutes. Business include music album sold in CDs to individual tracks sold online and revenue streams are perhaps declining. This is similar to the notion of radical innovation introduced by Chandy and Tellis (1998).

Meisel (2007) pointed out two effects that technology had impeded upon the IDM marketplace. First, the growth in broadband penetration has made the Internet a viable alternative of distribution platform. Secondly, the convergence of technology that allows the transfer of all types of data, video, audio, images and text among different physical platforms leads to media convergence. These impacts had opened (or leveled) the playing fields in IDM for new players who are able to capitalize on the technological advancement.

The distribution cost of digital content depends on bandwidth, storage, and processing. The costs of these technologies have been reduced dramatically in the last 40 years, which makes the distribution costs of digital content close to zero (Anderson, 1002). Hence the prevalence of free Internet services with unlimited storage for e-mail, video, images, maps, music and even software. The reduction in cost and peer-to-peer technology has additionally introduced the power of network effects to this platform.

With increasing competition, technological growth, and increasingly universal appeal of the Internet, the industry structure is changing and business convergence is taking shape. For example, television has progressed to a time-shifted format (in other words, to be watched at the convenience of individual viewers), music and movies are sold or leased online, and games are massively multiplayer with the possibility of customized roles and background music. Such vulnerable markets are characterized by the following conditions: (1) easy to enter; (2) attractive to attack; and (3) difficult to defend (Clemons, 2002). When a marketplace become vulnerable, new strategies are constructed and new players emerge, disrupting the existing ecosystem as well as the revenue apportionment among the players. As new players enter, the existing players which have been dominated by incumbents in the music, movie and games industries such as Universal and Sony-BMG; DreamWorks and Warner Brothers; Sony, Nintendo, and Microsoft, respectively, are forced to change their strategy to be able to maintain their profitability. This, however, is not easy as evidenced by the failure of several celebrated attempts.

The uncertainties and disruptions that are happening in the IDM industries posess a critical need to be understood in order for incumbents and new entrants to profit from the opportunities. Figure 1 depicts a simple work-flow of the IDM ecosystem. Digital media is produced or packaged by a number of sources from online games developers, movie and animation studios, music producers, publishers of books and magazines, and a host of digital paraphernalia such as ring-tones, screensavers and images. Typically, the IDM marketplace comprises of three groups of intermediaries who come between the producers and consumers of digital media products and services.

The significant IDM players take on one or more of the roles of syndicators, aggregators, and distributors. Aggregation is the collection of content from a variety of sources, often repackaged or archived to facilitate catalog search and browsing. Syndication is the proactive streaming of such content, especially after a launch period window to alternate and repeat consumer segments. Traditionally, content has been syndicated in newspapers and TV, it is however possible to syndicate digital services like background music rights, images and avatars, movie clips and perhaps even bill-board space in virtual worlds in emerging digital ecosystem. Distribution is the conveying of digital content to the devices of consumers and this includes the aspects of billing and collection aspects.

The roles of syndicator, aggregator, or distributor are complex and their respective duties may overlap. There is no established understanding of what precisely these roles are (cf. Picard 2002; Vogel 2007). Picard considers distribution to be the entire process of taking media products from the producer to the consumer and in some instances direct distribution. Vogel defines syndication as the process where previously exhibited material is reused to a new collection of buyers such as broadcasters. In some scenarios, some or all of these roles may even be redundant such as in the case of YouTube movies or in music being sold or given away on the websites of artistes. Each intermediary plays a different role; and the producers are the creators of initial value of digital content or services. And there are hence many intermediary issues among the players of the IDM marketplace that remain unresolved. Major IDM sectors are transforming from high price, low volume (niche) to lower price, higher volume (mass). User generated content is also increasingly in-vogue. A key issue is hence how value can be generated in the IDM marketplace and how it will be rewarded. AD-VISOR framework for analyzing the Digital Media business to determine the notion of adding value is used in this chapter. The framework will be described in the next section, followed by an analysis of three typical scenarios. We conclude by summarizing the key disruptions in the IDM marketplace and suggest a conceptual platform

Figure 1. The digital media business eco-system

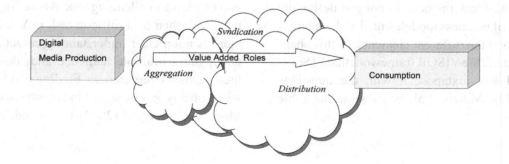

that brokers the contributions and interests of the players in the IDM eco-system.

VALUE FRAMEWORKS

The concept of business models started to gain its reputation as a part of venture creation literature in the 1990s. These models were developed to help in opportunity evaluation and business planning (Mäkinen & Seppänen, 2007). There have been many definitions of business models, but in general it has been defined from economic, operational, and strategic perspectives. Morris et al. (2005) summed the three perspectives and defined business models as "a concise representation of how an interrelated set of decision variables in the areas of venture strategy, architecture, and economics are addressed to create sustainable competitive advantage in defined markets." Picard (2007) defines a business model as the description of various business activities, roles, potential benefits for the players and the sources of revenues.

With these definitions in mind, the next step to making business models useful is to evaluate opportunities and plan businesses is to define what elements will be used to represent business models. There have also been many different suggestions on what the elements of business models are. As Table 1 depicts however, elements like value, interface, revenue, and network constantly appear.

These components of business models are usually generic for different companies in various industries. However, with the emergence of the Networked Digital Industry (NDI), however El Sawy (2005) saw the need to not just define the elements of business models but also the interactions among the different elements. In this chapter, we extend the VISOR framework that El Sawy proposed and juxtapose it with the questions proposed by Morris et al. as shown in the Table 2.

EFFICIENCY AND FAIRNESS IN THE MARKET

What creates revenue? The answer is simple. Audiences are willing to pay for content that they are interested in, in this case, digital content. However, building an audience has never been an easy task. Pricing the content has been a challenge in the digital ecosystem. Music Consumers reject the idea of paying for song they do not want nor are they willing to pay a price equivalent to CDs.

What then does an audience demand from digital entertainment? Typically, an audience wants good content (Gianopulus, 2008), variety of choices (Vogel, 2007), easy access, easy to find (Anderson, 2004), convenience, friendly interface, capacity to enjoy entertainment in different technological platforms and easy to transfer content from one into another (Jobs, 2008), control about where, when, and how to enjoy digital content, security in their transactions with the content distributors. However, the content quality remains the pertinent factor of all. Table 3 summarizes the essential differences between traditional and new media.

Technology has made it possible to reach disperse communities, and get revenue from them. For example, Nexnnn can deliver Indian films in a disperse community in the USA. However, identifying and reaching the audience is not an easy task in the digital ecosystem. For example, YouTube has a huge amount of content, and a probable vast range of different audiences. The quality of content varies, and finding something without having the title of the video or the provider makes a challenging task. Attracting advertisers will then be a difficult task in YouTube as there is not a clear understanding about how to target these multiple audience and identifying their needs and preferences. Finding good content will probably require some kind of intermediation. Moreover, as Vogel (2007) has found, after an

Table 1. Business model components (adapted from Boehnke, 2007)

Source	Business Models Elements
Alt & Zimmermann (2001)	1. Mission: Vision, strategic goals, value proposition 2. Structure: Actors and governance, strategic focus 3. Processes: Value creating activities 4. Revenues 5. Legal environment: Beneficial and constraining regulations 6. Technological environment: Opportunities and limitations
Bieger et al (2002)	1. Value system: Customers, products and services 2. Communication concept: Marketing position 3. Revenue concept 4. Growth concept: Margin, market share 5. Configuration of competences: Core competences 6. Organization: Firm boundaries 7. Cooperation concept: Value partners 8. Coordination concept: Governance across firm boundaries
El Sawy (2005)	1. Value proposition 2. Interface experience 3. Service platforms 4. Organizing model 5. Revenue/cost models
Hedman & Kalling (2003)	1. Customers 2. Competitors 3. Offering: Products and services, marketing strategy 4. Activities and organization 5. Resources: Human, physical, organizational 6. Supply of factors and production inputs 7. Longitudinal process component: Dynamics over time, scope of management
Morris et al. (2005)	1. Factors related to the offering: Products and services, value chain architecture 2. Market factors: Customer target groups 3. Internal capability factors: Core competences 4. Competitive strategy factors 5. Economic factors: Revenues, margins 6. Personal/investor factors: Time, scope and size ambitions
Osterwalder et al. (2005)	1. Product: Value proposition 2. Customer interface: Target customer, distribution channel, relationship 3. Infrastructure management: Value configuration, core competence, partner network 4. Financial aspects: Cost structure, revenue model
Shafer et al. (2005)	1. Strategic choices: Customer, value proposition, competences, revenue/ pricing, competitors, offering, strategy, branding, differentiation, mission 2. Create value: Resources, processes 3. Value network: Suppliers, customer information/relationship, information flows, product/ service flows 4. Capture value: Cost, financial aspects, profit
Stähler (2002)	1. Value proposition 2. Products or services 3. Value architecture: Market design, internal and external value architecture 4. Revenue model

extensive analysis of the media and entertainment industry, audiences' preferences change over time. Word of mouth (and its electronic or Internet equivalent) will continue playing an important role in the creation of audiences. Technology will provide huge opportunities to multiplex advertising, product placement, subscription and other revenue opportunities in the same time frame. Different revenue strategies can be put in place:

Table 2. AD-VISOR business model framework

Elements	LEST Questions
V **(Value Proposition for Targeted Customer Segment**: This proposition is usually accompanied by a good story about why particular customer segments would value an enterprise's products and services and be willing to pay a premium price for them.)	How do we create value? (select from each set) • Offering: primarily products/primarily services/heavy mix • Offering: standardized/some customization/high customization • offering: broad line/medium breadth/narrow line/long tail • Offering: deep lines/medium depth/shallow lines • Offering: access to product/ product itself/ product bundled with other firm's product • Offering: internal manufacturing or service delivery/ outsourcing/ licensing/ reselling/ value added reselling • Offering: direct distribution/indirect distribution (if indirect: single or multichannel) How do we competitively position ourselves? (select one or more) • Image of operational excellence /consistency/ dependability/ speed • Product or service quality/selection/features/availability • Innovation leadership • Low cost/efficiency • Intimate customer relationship/experience
I **("Wow" Interface Experience**: The success of delivery of a product or service is heavily predicated on the user interface experience in terms of the ease of use, simplicity, convenience, and positive energy that it generates. A great value proposition with a rickety user interface experience is not viable, and similarly a great user interface can significantly alter the value proposition.)	Who do we create value for? • Type of organization: b-to-b/b-to-c/ both • Local/regional/national/international • Broad or general market/multiple segment/niche market • Transactional/relational How are factors like the eases of use and navigation as well as simplicity and security of payment system factors addressed?
S **(Service Platforms to Enable Delivery**: These IT platforms enable, shape, and support the business processes and relationships that are needed to deliver the products and services, as well as improve the value proposition. Enabling service platforms becomes an increasingly critical component in IT-intensive environments. In the NDI, the commonality of platforms across partners joining to deliver a service is a critical enabler.	What is our source of competence? (select one or more) • Production/operating systems • Selling/marketing • Information management/mining/packaging • Technology/R&D/creative or innovative capability/intellectual • Financial transactions/arbitrage • Supply chain management • Networking/resource leveraging How can we execute our product service strategy efficiently, effectively?
O **(Organizing Model for Processes and Relationships**: This model describes how an enterprise or a set of partners will organize business processes, value chains, and partner relationships to effectively and efficiently deliver products and services.)	Who are our suppliers, consumers, substitutors, and complementors? What are the rules governing the relationship? What are our time, scope, and size ambitions? (select one) • Subsistence model • Income model • Growth model • Speculative model

continued on the following page

Cross subsidy, ad-supported for distribution of digital content, versioning, labor exchange etc.

This hence leads us to evaluate and come up with models that determine the efficiency and fairness constraints that considers multiple buyers – multiple suppliers (combination of network operators, content owners and advertising agencies) scenarios.

Table 2. Continued

Elements	LEST Questions
R (**Revenue/Cost Model Calculations for All Partners**: In a good business model, the combination of the value proposition, the way that offerings are delivered, and the investments in IT platforms are such that revenues exceed costs. Furthermore, if there are many partnering organizations involved, then the revenue agreement should be attractive to all partners. Finally, the risk of errors in forecasted revenues and costs should be manageable, and the revenue/ cost margin robust.)	How do we make money? (not mutually exclusive) • Pricing and revenue sources: fixed/mixed/flexible • Operating leverage: high/medium/low • Volumes: high/medium/low • Margins: high/medium/low
A (**Adoption by Society**: Converging technologies have caused industry boundaries to shift and blur. Customers are increasingly able and willing to get their own combination of products/services. Hence, it is highly important to adapt to what the customers desire, or in other word to co-create the products/services with customers, Prahalad, 2003)	Where is customer in value chain? (select one or more) • upstream supplier/ downstream supplier/ government/ institutional/ wholesaler/ retailer/ service provider/ final consumer What new possibilities/benefits are brought to consumers? Who are our customers anyway?
D (**Disruptive Innovation**: This is typically cheaper, simpler to use versions of existing products that target low-end or entirely new customers, Christensen, 1997)	How can the disruptions help make the competition irrelevant? (Blue ocean strategy) What new fields/areas have the disruptions caused, and which new consumers may be attracted? (Greenfield opportunities) When should we enter a market?

Table 3. AD-VISOR perspective on traditional vs. interactive digital media

	Traditional	IDM
A	Hierarchic	Networked
D	Linear	Compounded
V	Scarcity	Abundance
I	Mass media	Internet Connectivity and Devices
S	Stores, warehouses, shipping	Infomediaries
O	Retailers, subscribers, libraries	Syndication, aggregation, distribution
R	Sales, subscriptions, advertising	Prosumer behaviour

RESEARCH CHALLENGES

Efficiency in the online market has been created by intensive competition, content variety and availability (the i.e. long tail effect), and information technology infrastructure (Brynjolfsson et al., 2003). Given the nature of information goods, they can be divided into pieces that allow fragmented distribution, can be standardized. This includes business rules, such as, usage rights that can be passed between organizations along with the content (Werbach, 2000). The previous elements permit limitless virtual inventory and convenient access, reduced search and transaction costs, greater hit rates or finding relevant content, and the elimination of manufacturing and shelf space costs. Hence the distribution of content over digital networks have an extremely reduced marginal cost and have made possible disintermediation (Clemons et al, 2002), serve disperse audiences, and satisfy the needs of multiple niche markets. The criteria of profitability include not only popular content, but also those less appealing to the mass market (Brynjolfsson et al., 2003) and have affected market size and the price that consumers are willing to pay (Werbach, 2000). Some research themes worthy of study are:

- Analysis of competition, bargaining, and strategies in the IDM Marketplace and how they influence the amount of value created and its distribution among market participants including consumers, network operators, content suppliers, advertisers and the a host of new and emerging intermediaries.
- The stability of the music, movie, books, games, software industries.
- Development of parameters for a model which shows the value of matching consumer interest with the placement of advertisements in order to better influence certain behavior (purchasing or brand recall). There is also the issue of piracy.

Within the context of our AD-VISOR framework:

1. **Value:** How do the various intermediaries add value to the digital media networks? Is there a volume vs. cost trade-off regardless of how long the tail becomes?
2. **Interface:** How are the interfaces best designed in the digital networks, particularly the most critical ones to the consumer? Are

digital gatekeepers and viral marketing conducive?
3. **Service Platform:** How is sharing and distribution carried out such that costs are less than the marginal costs of production? What is the role of DRM? How may consumption be promoted with mobility, re-purposing and the like?
4. **Organizing Model:** How are alliances and vertical and horizontal integration structured? What protection is there against piracy and free-riding?
5. **Revenues:** How can the revenues from the network be allocated in an optimal and fair manner? What are some pricing strategies (e.g. Pay per view, DRM-free, sell-through, syndication)? What is the effect of additional revenue streams such as advertising and ongoing syndication?
6. **Adoption:** How, when and why do societies or communities adopt IDM services and what is their feedback?
7. **Disruptions:** What are some of the key disruptions (to existing markets and revenues streams) that appear in the horizon and how do players strategize for these disruptions?

The issue of differences in online and mobile prices is an anomalous one worthy of further study. How could MNOs (or more generically online sellers) get away with premium pricing in the face of competition which is merely several clicks away or within the set of hits returned by the search engine. Brynjolfsson and Smith (2000) in an interesting study of price dispersion in e-tailing, "we expect to see only a small degree of price dispersion on the Internet. With regard to product heterogeneity, we have intentionally selected products—books and CDs—whose physical characteristics are entirely homogeneous. Considering search costs, as noted above, we expect lower search costs on the Internet than in conventional channels. Similarly, we expect the role of informed and uninformed consumers to be less of a factor in dispersion among Internet prices than it is among conventional prices." [p 574]. However, "posted prices vary as much as 47% across Internet retailers. Furthermore, the retailers with the lowest prices do not make the most sales." [p 580]. They concluded that these price disparities were attributable to awareness, trust and branding.

However this introduces the notion of bias in the search and matching process and may erode the credibility of such mechanisms in the long run. As Brewer (2003) suggests that "there are at least three kinds of admitted bias in search engines today: advertisements, paid placement, and paid inclusion. Ads are the most visible and the most similar to other media; there's always an implicit issue about how the ad dollars affect the integrity' of the publication (or engine). Paid placement is the practice of selling top placement in search engine results. A pioneer in this space – Overture, now part of Yahoo - shows how much the buyer paid for the placement alongside the result. Although biased, the bias is made clear to the user. Paid inclusion is when content owners pay search engines for better coverage, but not better placement." He concludes that although such bias seem to have minor and sometimes even positive effects on the search quality. He continues that the best way around bias is simply to maintain a diversity of engines, just as reading a diversity of sources provides less bias as a group.

The marketplace for digital media is large and complex. Media players both traditional as well as new have yet to seize the opportunities that have come about in the syndication, aggregation and distribution spaces of this market. For one, telecommunications network operators are continually clutching at straws in their attempts to profit from and add value to the IDM lines of business. It is worth recapping that in a recent, comprehensive study, Berman et al. (2007) suggests ten specific recommendations that are supplied for incumbent media companies as they face the immediate threat from new entrants and eventual collisions with traditional partners:

1.   Put consumers at the center of your business and boardroom.
2.   Convert consumer data into competitive advantage.
3.   Give control to get share.
4.   Deliver experiences, not just content.
5.   Leverage virtual worlds.
6.   Innovate business models.
7.   Invest in interactive, measurable advertising services and platforms
8.   Redefine partnerships, while mitigating fallout.
9.   Shift investment from traditional business to new models.
10.   Create a flexible business design.

The findings of an extensive study by Gantz et al.. 2007 state that: In 2006, the amount of digital information created, captured, and replicated was 1,288×1018 bits. In computer parlance, that's 161 exabytes or 161 billion gigabytes. This is about 3 million times the information in all the books ever written. Between 2006 and 2010, the information added annually to the digital universe will increase more than six fold from 161 exabytes to 988 exabytes. Three major analog to digital conversions are powering this growth – film to digital image capture, analog to digital voice, and analog to digital TV. Images, captured by more than 1 billion devices in the world, from digital cameras and camera phones to medical scanners and security cameras, comprise the largest component of the digital universe. They are replicated over the Internet, on private organizational networks, by PCs and servers, in data centers, in digital TV broadcasts, and on digital projection movie screens.

Adding to this complexity, IDC predicts that by 2010, while nearly 70% of the digital universe will be created by individuals, organizations which includes businesses of all sizes, agencies, governments, associations, etc. will be responsible for the security, privacy, reliability, and compliance of at least 85% of that same digital universe. This rapidly expanding prosumer behaviour will put pressure on existing computing operations and drive organizations to develop more information-centric computing architectures. IT managers will see the span of their domains considerably enlarged – as VoIP phones come onto corporate networks, building automation and security migrates to IP networks, surveillance goes digital, and RFID and sensor networks proliferate. In 2007 the amount of information created will surpass, for the first time, the storage capacity available.

The message is hence clear. New media will require a level of added value like never before in the traditional markets. As such, producers, consumers, syndicators, aggregators and distributors have to be relentless in seeking out opportunities and being dynamic in their business relationships. Is there room for convergence in the business models? Is there is framework to analyze who may be winners and losers? These are some of the questions to be explored further in this book.

REFERENCES

Anderson, C. (2004). The long tail. *Wired Magazine, 10*(12), 171–177.

Anderson, C. (2008, March). Why $0.00 is the future of business. *Wired*.

Berman, S. J., Abraham, S., Battino, B., Shipnuck, L., & Neus, A. (2007). *Navigating the media divide: Innovating and enabling new business models. Executive Brief.* IBM Institute for Business Value.

Brandenburger, A. M., & Nalebuff, B. J. (1995). The right game: Use game theory to shape strategy. *Harvard Business Review, 73*(4), 57–71.

Brandenburger, A. M., & Stuart, H. W. (1996). Value-based business strategy. *Journal of Economics & Management Strategy, 5*(1), 5–24. doi:10.1111/j.1430-9134.1996.00005.x

Brynjolfsson, E., Hu, Y. J., & Smith, M. D. (2003). Consumer surplus in the digital economy: Estimating the value of increased product variety at online booksellers. *Management Science, 49*, 1580–1596. doi:10.1287/mnsc.49.11.1580.20580

Brynjolfsson, E., & Smith, M. D. (2000). Frictionless commerce? A comparison of Internet and conventional retailers. *Management Science, 46*(4), 563–585. doi:10.1287/mnsc.46.4.563.12061

Chandy, R. K., & Tellis, G. J. (1998). Organizing for radical product innovation: The overlooked role of willingness to cannibalize. *JMR, Journal of Marketing Research, 35*, 474–487. doi:10.2307/3152166

Clemons, E. K., Gu, B., & Lang, K. R. (2002). Newly vulnerable markets in an age of pure information products: An analysis of online music and online news. *Proceedings of the 35th Annual Hawaii International Conference on Systems Sciences* (HICSS), (pp. 2949-2958).

Dennis, E. E., Warley, S., & Sheridan, J. (2006). Doing digital: An assessment of the top 25 U.S. media companies and their digital strategies. *Journal of Media Business Studies, 3*(1), 33–51.

El Sawy, O., Fife, E., & Pereira, F. (2005). *The VISOR framework: Business model definition for new marketspaces in the networked digital industry*. CTM Research Brief, Marshall School of Business, University of Southern California, November.

Gantz, I., Reinsel, D., Chute, C., Schlichting, W., McArthur, J., Minton, S., et al. (2007). *The expanding digital universe–A forecast of worldwide information growth through 2010*. An IDC White Paper sponsored by EMC.

Kim, H. W., & Xu, Y. (2007). Drivers of price premium in e-markets. *Communications of the ACM, 50*(11), 91–95. doi:10.1145/1297797.1297803

Mahadevan, B. (2000). Business models for Internet-based e-commerce: An anatomy. *California Management Review, 42*(4), 55–69.

Morris, M., Schindehutte, M., & Allen, J. (2005). The entrepreneur's business model: Toward a unified perspective. *Journal of Business Research, 58*(6), 726–735. doi:10.1016/j.jbusres.2003.11.001

Osterwalder, A. (2004). *The business model ontology: A proposition in a design science approach.* Doctoral Thesis, Universite de Lausanne.

Picard, R. (2000). Changing business models of online content services - Their implications for multimedia and other content producers. *The International Journal on Media Management, 2*(2), 60–68. doi:10.1080/14241270009389923

Shafer, S. M., Smith, H. J., & Linder, J. C. (2005). The power of business models. *Business Horizons, 48*(3), 199–207. doi:10.1016/j.bushor.2004.10.014

Shapiro, C., & Varian, H. R. (1999). *Information rules: A strategic guide to the network economy.* Boston, MA: Harvard Business School Press.

Sterne, J. (2005). Digital media and disciplinarity. *The Information Society, 21*(4), 249–256. doi:10.1080/01972240591007562

Swatman, P. M. C., Krueger, C., & van der Beek, K. (2006). The changing digital content landscape. *Internet Research, 16*(1), 53–80. doi:10.1108/10662240610642541

Varian, H. R. (2000). Buying, sharing and renting information goods. *The Journal of Industrial Economics, 48*(4), 473–488. doi:10.1111/1467-6451.00133

Vogel, H. L. (2007). *Entertainment industry economics: A guide for financial analysis.* Cambridge University Press. doi:10.1017/CBO9780511510786

Werbach, K. (2000). Syndication: The emerging model for business in the internet era. *Harvard Business Review, 78*(3), 85–93.

Werbach, K. (2000). Syndication: The emerging model for business in the internet era. *Harvard Business Review, 78*, 85–93.

Chapter 2
A Comparison of Pricing Strategies for Digital Goods

Peng Lei
Nanyang Technological University, Singapore

Kristy Shi
Nanyang Technological University, Singapore

Tahani Iqbal
National University of Singapore, Singapore

ABSTRACT

This chapter is a review of pricing strategies for digital goods. The basis for a number of such strategies is analysed. Using the case of online music, some lessons for the practice of digital pricing are derived.

INTRODUCTION

The world of media business has entered into an era of Interactive Digital Media (IDM) marketplace. The significant increase in possibilities for inter-activity especially over large distances brought by the broadband internet boosted the thriving interactive digital media. Digital goods such as e-books, online music, movies, and multiplayer role playing games are produced, consumed, repackaged and traded via the Internet (Garcia, 2006).

Digital goods that are categorized as information product grow rapidly with the penetration of Internet and the advancement of info-com-munication technology. As the Internet platform becomes more open and interactive with Web 2.0 technologies, the traditional distributional channels are being disrupted and restructured. With the movement from previous dedicated distribution channels to today's P2P or social networks, consumers can easily obtain their online digital products and services at very competitive prices, or even for free (Anderson, 2004).

Moreover, as digital media products possess unique cost structures and characteristics, it is neither feasible nor optimal to adopt the traditional pricing strategy, cost plus. Evolution in digital media and changes in consumer demand have affected current business models. As an important

DOI: 10.4018/978-1-61350-147-4.ch002

aspect of market strategies and business plans, pricing strategies are targeted and investigated in this chapter.

BACKGROUND

IDM Market

The fast development and wide coverage of broadband networks has become a catalyst for the growth of interactive digital media. Today children as young as two years old learn new words and play online games to accelerate their learning curve. IDM has penetrated into people's life at their much earlier age. For adults, social networking platforms such as Facebook, My spaces and Twitter, have gained a huge popularity among people. It helps them look for missing old friends, and network with people from all around the world. Within such a virtual network, people communicate freely and interactively through sending messages, sharing photos, videos, and playing games together. The success of Facebook not only lies on being a social networking tool, but also in continuously adding interesting interactive new applications to improve the user experience.

Interactive digital media deals with digitized goods such as e-books, online music, movies, and multiplayer role playing games. Digital goods refer broadly to anything that can be digitalized (Krishnamurthy, 2002). Choi and Whinston (2000)

defined digital goods as any knowledge-based and knowledge-enhanced products which include various forms of human creation such as information, knowledge, news, databases, software, literature, and arts, etc. Moreover, digital goods not only include products but also include something what can be called as "services" in the traditional market. However, IDM is very general in concept and is not restricted to entertainment industry only. In Singapore, the IDM R&D Programme Office has identified four key focus areas: Education, Animation, Games & Effects, Media Intermediary Services, and "On-the-Move" Technologies (National Research Foundation). Increasing lifestyle services such as e-learning, e-health, e-banking and government services have become dependent on IDM for its advanced efficacy.

In the IDM eco-system, there are typically five players which are classified into three groups: producer, intermediaries (including syndicator, aggregator and distributor) and consumers. A generalized IDM eco-system is depicted in Figure 1.

In the first stage, producers such as game developers, movie and animation studios, music artists, book publishers and etc produce digital goods. Next, these digital goods will undergo aggregation; syndication and are finally distributed to customers. This is a process of adding values to services and goods before their final delivery to end-users. Aggregators perform a specific distribution role in which the same intermediary distributes content from different provid-

Figure 1. IDM eco-system (adopted from Morales-Arroyo & Sharma, 2009)

ers. For syndication, it is a type of distribution in which limited rights are given for the media content which is sold to various distributors (Hjelm, 2008).

As an overall picture of IDM market has been shown, the development of interactive digital media is highly correlated to the information and communication technologies. Based on current fast adoption rate in gaming, advertising and multimedia, the demand of interactive digital media will undergo continuously increase to meet the needs of users.

Digital Goods: Characteristics and Pricing

Pricing is a key factor of revenue. It is one of the most difficult yet important issues businesses must address. Due to the ease of replication and distribution of electronic data (Kehal & Singh, 2005), traditional pricing schemes (Price=Marginal Cost) become obsolete (Varian, 1996). The basic objective of every pricing strategy is to capture as much consumer surplus as possible and convert it into additional profit for the firm. Generally, a good pricing strategy should help the firm capture as much as profit which comes from consumer surplus (Shapiro & Varian, 1999). To maximize revenues, providers of digital information goods are experimenting with different pricing schemes. There are various pricing schemes for digital goods providers to maximize the revenues.

Information products, especially digital goods which are encoded as a stream of bits, possess unique cost structure and features (Carl, 1999):

- Fixed cost is substantially high but marginal cost is negligible.
- Sunk costs to produce the first copy can hardly be recovered.
- Per-unit cost tends to be a constant, regardless of the volume of production.
- There are no capacity limits for additional copies.

When digital goods are distributed through the Internet, the variable cost becomes negligible. Because the products are not in the physical forms, there is comparatively less cost for manufacturing, packaging, distribution etc. These characteristics of information goods have important implications for competitive pricing strategy. Simply put, survival in a digital media market, where the marginal cost of products or services can be negligible, price should be set according to the customer value, but not according to the cost.

The basic strategy depends on which market structure the information goods belong to. If it is a differentiated products industry, the strategy is to add value to the raw information, therefore distinguishing them from the competition. More specifically, if aiming to sell information goods in a differentiated products industry, the crucial pricing strategy is to add value to the raw information. The more the firm can do, the better it can distinguish its products from the competitors' (Shapiro & Varian, 1999). In a dominant firm industry, the strategy should be to achieve cost leadership through economics of scale and scope, meaning in quantity as well as quality.

As the Internet has made it possible to repackage content by using the following approaches - bundling, site licensing, subscriptions, rentals, differential pricing and pay-per-use fees (Hjelm, 2008), these pricing strategies can be considered as examples of aggregation or disaggregation of information products along some dimension.

Media Divide: Clash between the Traditional and the New Media

The new media world has spread quickly into virtually every consumer segment, and it is also starting to encroach on the traditional media. Indeed, the new media is also starting to take up the territory owned by traditional media. There are two aspects of change leading to the clash between the traditional and the new media:

- Change in distribution means: Traditional closed and proprietary distribution channels are disrupted. Open distribution platforms emerge without the need for dedicated access providers or devices.
- Change in content production: Due to low production cost and the ease of technology, content can be created not only by professionals but also by the mass public. Consumers can also play the role as producers, hence a multiple-role called prosumer. They are not only interested in consuming content, but they too want to create, manipulate and mash it." (Berman et al., 2007, p.11-13)

Due to these trends, a conceptual framework is developed to reveal the old business models and the resulting new ones (Tan & Morales-Arroyo, 2009). As Figure 2 shows, four business models coexist in near future based on two dimensions: the ownership of intellectual property and market distribution platforms.

As shown in Figure 2, the vertical axis represents intellectual property ranging from 'private' to 'public', IP is described from a full control of one's copyright to a situation where contents are contributed by the mass community, hence it is difficult to entitle the copyright to anyone for the legal possession of the creations. The horizontal axis depicts how products are distributed and delivered to customers. Distribution channels evolve from the physical and dedicated market place, towards an open online platform as the chart goes from left to right. The traditional distribution pattern is disrupted under the new digital media economics (Sparrow, 2006).

With these two dimensions, a four-business model framework is developed to reveal the situation of IDM market for current and near future. It is anticipated that these four models will coexist for at least the next 3-5 years (Tan & Morales-Arroyo, 2009). In reality, the marketplace will not simply be in any purest form but be full of combinations. Some companies appear in the extreme corners of this framework, while some other with a more mixed model will operate near the intersecting lines. To support the business models adopted by a company, it is essential for it to target the specific market segment, set clear the market position, and develop featured products and services. The rising popularity of user-created content and the move toward open distribution platforms call for innovation on business models and pricing techniques.

Figure 2. A conceptual framework for IDM business models. (adopted from: Tan and Morales-Arroyo, 2009)

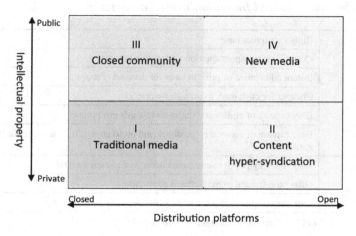

REVIEW OF PRICING STRATEGIES

Pricing is always one of the biggest strategic challenges facing businesses. There is never a fixed formula to calculate the exact price for a product. Price can be set in either a structured or an unstructured manner. There have been a variety of existing pricing strategies developed from the past. It is the manager's job to decide which one would best fulfill the company's objectives and would maximize profit.

Old pricing methods are not sustainable any more, and new categories of pricing tools are created for surviving in the new-economy environment. 'Interactivity' and 'individualization' are the two forces of the Internet, which have affected the pricing patterns (Mohammed, Fisher, Jaworski & Paddison, 2003), resulting in more dynamic pricing strategies. The effects caused by each force are listed in Table 1.

When analyzing pricing strategies, it is good to employ the economic law which states that a company should price at the point where marginal cost equals marginal revenue. However, in a dynamic market, more sophisticated analyses are required to take into account the competitors' reactions. The following section will review those most frequently used pricing techniques in the digital media era. There are six pricing schemes to be discussed: free, subscription, pay per view / item, bundling, auction (dynamic pricing) and versioning (price discrimination).

Free

The broadband network has enabled consumers to access large amount of business information easily, and has made the transactions much more transparent. As consumers become more globalized, they are not restricted by geography when making purchase decisions. They are also free to switch between a number of providers for cheaper and higher qualified goods and services. IDM is a highly efficient market, in which the differences between products and pricing will diminish. The intense competition causes companies to compete mainly on price.

As a result, digital goods such as music, games, and data have been given away to customers at comparatively low price. This simply works in accordance with the economics law: the product is sold at its marginal cost at zero. However, the rationale behind this "free strategy" is to capture a loyal customer base, and hopefully monetize the base (Mohammed, Fisher, Jaworski & Paddison, 2003). A good example for this practice is Amazon.com. The company was established in 1994 and started with the business as online

Table 1. The effects of Interactivity and Individualization on pricing

Interactivity	Bigger customer base
	Cost-efficient implementation of dynamic pricing
	Instant adjustment of price to cater for demand changes
	Cheaper for customers to investigate prices
	Easy capture of customers' reactions towards promotions
	Easy capture of customers' feedback and preference which facilitate the adoption of price discrimination
Individualization	Easy to covey prices to customers according to their interests
	Offer targeted and individualized promotions
	Easy for customers to participate in the dynamic pricing process

(©2003 Rafi A Mohammed, Robert J Fisher, Bernard J Jaworski & Gordon Paddison)

bookstore. It was operated with no profit until the fourth quarter in 2001.

Of course, a free strategy does not really mean offering products for nothing. There must be sound business logic behind such a free offer. As in common practices, the free versions are offered only when they are likely to achieve the following goals (Shapiro & Varian, 1998):

- Building awareness
- Boosting follow-on sales
- Creating a network effect
- Attracting eyeballs
- Gaining competitive advantage

For most companies, the strategy is to retain some level of free services and then stimulate their consumers to purchase an upgraded version. For example, Adobe is well known for its PDF viewing application. It allows everyone to download the software and open PDF files for free. However, if professionals need to create their own PDF documents, Adobe charges for that service by providing an additional creation function.

Especially for internet based companies, information and digital products are "experience goods". For a unique game or new branded anti-virus software, consumers won't know whether the new product is worthy or not until they have tried it. Thus, free offers provide an attractive chance for them to test out the digital goods.

Subscription

Subscription is a way of pricing where customers pay a periodic, monthly, yearly or seasonal fee to gain access to the product or service. This model was pioneered by magazines and newspapers, but is now widely adopted by many online websites and digital media businesses. Many music and movie portals based on P2P networks have utilized this pricing method.

Subscription can take on several forms:

- Users subscribe for a fixed set of products and services, such as a copy of periodic publications.
- Users subscribe for unlimited use for goods and services, such as listen to unlimited on-demand music online (streaming).
- Users subscribe for basic access to goods and services, with additional charge for advanced and more sophisticated functions.

This pricing scheme is most advantageous in the sense that it assures companies a steady revenue stream for the duration of the subscriber's agreement. It reduces uncertainty and the riskiness for the enterprise, and companies are usually guaranteed with payment in advance. Moreover, producers are driven to ensure and improve the quality of their goods, in order to keep the customers.

To enjoy the benefits brought by the subscription model, both customers' and producers' goals should be satisfied. These two parties will benefit only if the customer receives value from the subscription. As long as customers perceive value and trust that it is worthy of investment, they are likely to renew with the same provider and even accept an increased rate.

Pay Per View or Item

Pay per view or per item is also known as "a la carte" which means paying for each ordered item. Price is set in such a direct way that charging a proper amount of money for each item becomes a big challenge. This strategy can be found commonly applied in online music portals such as iTunes and this is especially successful in television and broadcasting industries.

Pay-per-view (PPV) requires cable TV subscribers to pay a pre-defined fee for the single movie or event viewed. In the last couple of years, a new type of service called Video on Demand (VOD) was introduced, which allows customers to access some of the best programs whenever they want. The program can be paused, fast forwarded, and rewound just like a DVD. The innovation makes PPV such a success that it would appear firmly in place in the future. One cable executive labelled PPV as a "marketing-intensive business" that relies on an "impulse buy" strategy to attract subscriber (The Museum of Broadcast Communications, 2010).

Bundling or Packaging

There are two types of bundling or packaging strategies: pure bundling and mixed bundling. Pure bundling means the company provides its products only as part of a bundle. For example, a firm can bundle new products with established products to attract customers; or it can bundle complementary products to stimulate consumer demand. Mixed bundling refers to goods that can be sold both individually and in bundles. Of course the bundle price will be generally less than the sum of the price of the individual items. This strategy is particularly effective and profitable for Internet digital goods.

Bundling is viewed as the best suited pricing strategies for Internet products (Mohammed, Fisher, Jaworski & Paddison, 2003). Companies are used to differentiating their offerings by bundling products and services. Services such as purchase suggestions, delivery or payment options, and customer support are bundled to products at the time of selling them. Consumers will value these features differently according to their preferences and criteria. Moreover, the Internet helped speed up the evolution for bundling. Customers are now able to create their own way of bundling things together. Dell allows individuals to assemble their unique computer by selecting components for themselves; online bookstores enable users to choose their favourite books into a 2-item bundle, which is then sold at a discount. Bundling gives consumers a high degree of freedom to purchase goods at a bargain, and at the same time, it boosts sales for providers.

Dynamic Pricing: Auction

The Internet has changed the ordinary way of pricing goods, resulting in a dynamic pricing strategy. As the name suggests, dynamic pricing is such a pricing environment in which prices are not fixed but are fluid. For digital goods traded on the Internet, it is very convenient and virtually costless to change product prices. Therefore, firms are able to adjust their label prices duly according to the fast changing demand and supply conditions.

As part of the dynamic pricing, auction is considered to be a key pricing strategy in the new economy. Auction creates a competitive environment in which customers willingly bid for goods up to the highest price they would like to pay. Providers will then benefit from this process because they can then capture as much value as possible. There is a wide variety of auction types. Some common ones and how each is implemented will be briefly introduced in Table 2.

Auctions have different forms and some can be very complex to implement. Nevertheless, they are indeed efficient pricing tools that would benefit both consumers and providers. As the number of bidders increase, each party will maximize their goals by obtaining and selling goods at more optimal prices.

Differential Pricing: Versioning

The extremely low marginal cost of digital goods rule out most traditional pricing strategies such as cost-plus. It is ideal to set prices according to the maximal value a customer places on the product, which means charging each customer different prices for the same goods. However in reality, it is not feasible because there is no way to know exactly how much each person would like to pay. Fortunately a practical way has been found to achieve this price discrimination without incurring high costs or offending customers, to offer different versions of the same product which would appeal to different types of customers.

Table 2. Auction types and implementations

Type	Implementation
English /Ascending Auctions	Buyers successively raise their prices until only one buyer remains.
Reverse-Price English Auctions	Potential suppliers bid to serve customers. The firm with the lowest price will win.
Dutch Auctions	Decrease the pre-announced price slowly until a bidder accepts it.
New-Economy Dutch Auctions	The highest bidders purchase the products at the price offered by the lowest winner bidder. The number of the products is limited.
First-Price Sealed-Bid Auctions	Each buyer's bidding price is unknown and the highest bidder will win.
Reverse First-Price Sealed-Bid Auctions	Potential suppliers submit the sealed price only one; lowest bidder will win.

(©2003 Rafi A Mohammed, Robert J Fisher, Bernard J Jaworski & Gordon Paddison)

This strategy called versioning falls into a concept of differential pricing. The theory was proposed by the economist A.C. Pigou (Varian, 1989). He introduced three degrees of price discrimination:

1. **Personalized pricing:** Charge the individual a price equals to his or her willingness to pay.
2. **Group pricing:** Set different prices to different groups of consumers which are categorized by some observable characteristics.
3. **Versioning:** Offer a product line and customers choose the one that would fit them best.

Price discrimination provides a useful framework for developing new ways to pricing. It is especially flexible and powerful for goods produced digitally, because digital data are less costly and less time consuming to manipulate. With the Internet, the market can approach much larger and more diverse consumers. Versioning takes its effects as it creates multiple price points for potential buyers, hence increasing the chance of selling a product that can meet different customers' needs at the same time. The most important concern when firms design their own versioning is to identify how to best distinguish the different versions of their products. They need to determine which features are highly valued by a group of consumers but of little value to others. Then the

right number of versions and the price charged for each can be properly decided.

CASE OF PRICING STRATEGIES FOR ONLINE MUSIC

The music industry went through dramatic changes brought by the high penetration of broadband Internet and development of info-communication technology. Figure 3 provides a simple model of the pricing strategy for online music in the early years. The vertical continuum represents the progression of payment mechanisms for online music, from free music to pay-per-play or pay-per-download, and fixed subscriptions. The horizontal continuum indicates the move from peer-to-peer or P2P (unorganized) networks on one end and organized social networks on the other. Using this structure, we map out the online music industry in its early years (circa 2000-2005) and as it is at present (circa 2006-2009).

Free and Illegal Distribution of Online Music

The proliferation of online music gained prominence in the late 1990s, when Napster surfaced on the Internet. This software, the first of its kind, enabled the sharing of music and other files, freely, among members over a peer-to-peer (P2P)

Figure 3. Pricing strategy for online music in the early years

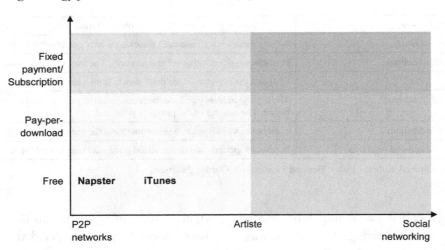

network. This development had drastic effects on the global music industry and "by letting friends swap MP3 tracks, perfect digital copies of music, Napster made the casual copying and exchanging of music among friends into a global, automated and simple process that threatened the music industry, whose business model was in no way geared, or even prepared, for the digital online age" (Waters, 2009).

Within a short span of time, Napster had become the most popular means through which music was distributed and downloaded online. However, given the impact it had on the legal distribution of music, Napster was sued and forced to shut down its network (Wilde & Schwerzmann, 2004). Napster was based on a centralized P2P network which made it vulnerable to legal action.

The distribution of online music however, did not cease with the shutting down of Napster. In fact, it led to the development of many other P2P networking programmes based on distributed networks, which the courts could not block. These networks function in a manner similar to a search engine and therefore made it difficult for recording companies to take legal action. Furthermore, the number of such networks that were created and established across the world, in a short space of

time, obscured the suppression of illegally distributed music online. Among the most popular P2P networks that still exist are Kazaa, Morpheus, and Grokster (Wilde & Schwerzmann, 2004).

A more recent development based also on P2P networks and enabling free distribution of media is BitTorrent. This software allows for larger chunks of data transfer making it easy to download a movie and whole music albums all at once. Given that this software is also based on a distributed network means that there is very little legal action that can be taken. Figure 4 shows the pricing strategy for online music in the current times.

Move to Legal Distribution of Music

Following the advent of Napster and the like, the global music industry found the need to address the growing move to access and acquire music online. As a result the recording companies and even independent artists decided to permit the legal distribution of their music in return for an agreed fee. There has been a push for several new business models to be adopted by service providers, each attempting to create a sustainable stream of profits for the service provider and the content producers like the recording companies

Figure 4. Pricing strategy for online music today

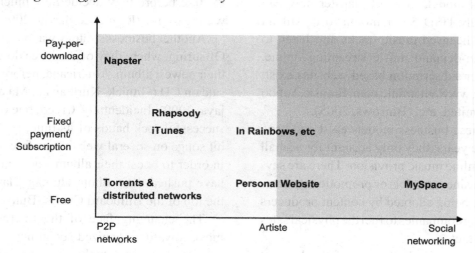

and artistes. The most common and seemingly viable forms for legal online music provision by far, are currently the pay-per-download or pay-per-play and subscription based payment schemes. There are hundreds, if not more, websites that provide music online, in cooperation with the larger recording companies like BMG, Sony, etc.

iTunes is one of the most well known services for obtaining legal music downloads. The company, run by Apple, initially provided licensed music for free, in order to pique the interest of keen music lovers, looking for quality in their downloads. Apple iPod users were able to download these tunes and put them on a single iPod, due to the copy protection restrictions embedded within each music track or MP3 available for download. However, in order to make money through this scheme, iTunes changed their payment policies and imposed charges on its music, at approximately US$0.79 per song downloaded and approx. US$ 8 for a whole album. In addition to this, they removed the copyright protections on their MP3s, allowing users to copy the downloaded music onto as many iPods or CDs or other recording media as they wished. The success of this model indicates that consumers are willing to pay for music if they are allowed access to good quality music, from a

variety of labels and content producers, with no copy protection restrictions, over a trusted source (Erik Wilde, Jacqueline Schwerzmann, 2004).

The second type of "pay-per" or "variable" type payment mechanism is that of the streaming, where users pay for each song they listen to online. Recording artistes and companies prefer this means of accessing their music as it encourages users to purchase the physical product if they like the music enough. However, this is not the most optimal option for music lovers, who are more likely to opt for obtaining copies of the song on to their own hard disks, to copy on to their iPods and other music players. Additionally, users require high bandwidth connections in order to stream high quality music in real time. RealNetworks' Rhapsody is one such example of this type of online and legal distributor of music. Users pay a monthly fee and are able to listen to as many songs as they want to – downloading is optional but has incremental charges (Warton Business School, 2003).

Subscription based music models are the next level in acquiring music from online distributors. Since its closure, Napster was bought by Roxio, Inc. and has now moved into the legal distribution of online music. Based on a subscription fee payment model, users of Napster now pay approximately USD 5 per month to download a total of 5 licensed music tracks and listen to unlimited on-demand music streaming online. Several other subscription based websites exist; for example, www.vitaminic.com, Emusic, Yahoo Music Unlimited, etc. (Burrows, 2005).

While these business models exist and have survived the years, they only account for a small portion of online music provision. There are several other business models or promotional strategies that are being adopted by content producers and recording companies to fuel the physical sales of their products.

With the growing influence of the Internet and coupled with decreasing margins earned by recording companies as well as the content producers, the singers, composers, the artists have opted to "go solo". The Internet has empowered these individuals to promote their music on their personal websites, and even get in touch with their fans on a more direct and personal level. Musicians have had to develop various promotional strategies and "marketing ploys", catering to online music listeners and downloaders, in order to increase or sustain their record sales in order to make some money.

Initially, this type of marketing and self-promotion succeeded for established artists who already had a large fan following, who lapped up any records made by the artist. One such ploy was the one utilized by Radiohead, who released their most recent album – In Rainbows – on their own website and asked users to pay what they wanted to, even if they paid nothing (O'Hear, 2007).

This spurred the development of several online music providers whose business models were based on the "pay-what-you-want" model. Magnatune, is a good example of such a site, but does not allow users to download music and pay nothing, unlike in the case of Radiohead's album promotion. Instead, users are able to choose between US$ 5-18 for the licensed albums available for sale; they are allowed to listen to the music for free before they decide how much they are willing to pay (Regner & Barria, 2008).

Another business strategy was adopted by The Offspring, where they offered free downloads of their newest album, Americana, before it went on sale on CD (Gitnick, Kurniawan, Ma & Milawijaya, 2000). Incidentally, Creed, one of the most successful rock bands of its time, released their hit songs on several websites as free downloads in order to boost their album sales and this may have pushed their album Human Clay to reach the top of the Billboard Charts (Buhse, 2001a).

The changing face of the Internet and its move towards organized social networks in the recent years has meant that content producers will increasingly try to leverage these innovations in order to build their online fan bases and entice them to purchase their music legally. Contrary to perception that only established artistes could succeed without the backing of a label or recording company, many independent and little known artistes have been able to successfully promote their music on their own self-made personal websites and social networking sites.

The popularity of MySpace, a social network site, has grown among artists, both independent and those with labels, as it has opened up the market for music in terms of sourcing new talent and promoting their music. There are several success stories of young and upcoming musicians who put their music online first and built a fan base without any external help. Some have continued to produce their music independently and have been able to sustain their passion by obtaining touring contracts and sponsorships. Others have been offered contracts by the big recording companies and have gone on to become as famous as their peers who did not start out on the Internet traditional musicians for example. Artistes such as Lilly Allen, Colbie Caillat, Panic! At the Disco, Kate Nash, Taylor Swift, and more, owe much to MySpace, as they have become overnight sensations through these means.

The strategy that most of these artistes have followed is to initially stream their music online for free but not for download, and later sell the licenses to these songs on other websites such as iTunes, Rhapsody, etc, and sell them on CDs and other media, once they become sought after.

In a more recent development, UK Internet Service Provider (ISP), Virgin, and Universal have signed a deal through which the ISP subscribers gain access to unlimited music available on Universal (BBC news, 2009). This partnership enables Universal to promote its music online as real sales dwindle, and it also helps Virgin to police the illegal download of music on its networks. Another development, also in the UK, is that the Weekly Top 40 is considering including the numbers of songs streamed when compiling its ranked list (BBC news, 2009). This is a clear indication that the music industry is accepting the increasing use of online play of music.

CONCLUSION

This chapter overviewed the emerging IDM market, and the transformation taken in this marketplace. The wide spread of broadband network act as a catalyst for the new economy, in which the traditional distribution system has been disrupted, goods are digitally produced but less in physical form, and consumers are more interactively involved, etc. Old business models are challenged and innovations on them are urgently needed.

As part of the market strategy, pricing for goods in the new economy gains lots of attention and concerns. The low marginal costs of production and distribution allowed an increased commoditization of the IDM market. Companies should be innovative and dynamic in designing new pricing schemes, at the same time they should provide differentiated products and services to attract customers. At the end of day, it is the product's quality and unique features that add the value placed by consumers.

REFERENCES

Anderson, C. (2004). The long tail. *Wired Magazine, 10*(12), 171–177.

Berman, S. J., Abraham, S. A., Battino, B., Shipnuck, L., & Neus, A. (2007). *Navigating the digital divide: Innovating and enabling new business models*. IBM Institute of Business Value. Retrieved March 18, 2010, from http://www-935. ibm.com/services/us/gbs/bus/pdf/g510-6579-03-mediadivide.pdf

Buhse, W. (2001). Implications of digital rights management for online music – A business perspective. In Sander, T. (Ed.), *Security and privacy in digital rights management* (pp. 201–212). Philadelphia.

Burrows, P. (2005, May 19). Online music: Rewriting the story. *Business Week*, News Analysis.

Carl, S. (1999). *Information rules: A strategic guide to the network economy*. Boston, MA: Harvard Business School Press.

Garcia, D. (2006). *Disruptive technologies boast Internet advertising*. Gartner Report.

Gitnick, A., Kurniawan, F., Ma, P., & Milawijaya, P. (2000). *E-business impact on retail in the music industry. Class Project Report, Fall 2000*. Berkeley, Berkeley: University of California.

Hjelm, J. (2008). *Why IPTV? – Interactivity, technologies and services*. UK: Wiley.

Kehal, H. S., & Singh, V. P. (2005). Digital products on the web: Pricing issues and revenue models. In Kehal, H., & Singh, V. P. (Eds.), *Digital economy: Impacts influences and challenges*. Hershey, PA: Idea group Publishing.

Krishnamurthy, S. (2002, June). Cave or community? An empirical examination of 100 mature open source projects. *First Monday, 7*(6). Retrieved March 1, 2010, from http://www.firstmonday. org/issues/issue7n 6/krishnamurthy/index.html

Mohammed, R. A., Fisher, R. J., Jaworski, B. J., & Paddison, G. (2003). *Internet marketing: Building advantage in a networked economy*. McGraw Hill.

Morales-Arroyo, M., & Sharma, R. S. (2009). Deriving value in digital media networks. *International Journal of Computer Science and Security*, *3*(2), 126–137.

National Research Foundation. (2010). *Singapore government*. Retrieved January 8, 2010 from https://rita.nrf.gov.sg/IDM/IDM/default.aspx

News, B. B. C. (June 2009). Anti-piracy music deal for Virgin. *BBC News*. Retrieved February 12, 2010, from http://news.bbc.co.uk/2/hi/technology/8100394.stm

O'Hear, S. (2007, October 11). *Music industry: Five alternative business models*. Retrieved March 16, 2010, from http://www.last100.com/2007/10/11/music-industry-five-alternative-business-models/

Regner, T., & Barria, J. (2008, September 4). *Magnatune – A voluntary-based model for online music*. Retrieved March 16, 2010, from http://www.indicare.org/tiki-read_article.php?articleId=147

Shapiro, C., & Varian, H. R. (1998, June). Versioning: The smart way to sell information. *Harvard Business Review*, *76*(6), 106–114.

Shapiro, C., & Varian, H. R. (1999). Pricing information . In Shapiro, C., & Varian, H. R. (Eds.), *Information rules. A strategy guide to the network economy*. Boston, MA: Harvard Business Press.

Sparrow, A. P. (2006). *Music distribution and the Internet*. England: Gower Publishing.

Tan, M., & Morales-Arroyo, M. (2009). *Disruption of the digital media distribution*. Singapore: Institute for Media Innovation, Nanyang Technological University.

The Museum of Broadcast Communications. (June 2010). *Pay per view*. Retrieved from http://www.museum.tv/eotvsection.php?entrycode=payperview

Varian, H. (June 1996). *Differential pricing and efficiency*. SIMS working paper, Berkeley.

Varian, H. R. (1989). Price discrimination . In Armstrong, M., & Porter, R. (Eds.), *Elsevier handbook of industrial organization, I* (pp. 597–654).

Waters, D. (2009, June 8). Napster: 10 years of change. *BBC News*, Technology.

Wharton Business School. (2003). Online music's winners and losers. *CNET News*. Retrieved March 16, 2010, from http://news.cnet.com/2030-1027_3-5133561.html

Wilde, E., & Schwerzmann, J. (2004). *When business models go bad: The music industry's future*. International Joint Conference on E-Business and Telecommunications, 1, 48-54.

Youngs, I. (2009). Top 40 faces new digital shake-up. *BBC News*. Retrieved February 3, 2010, from http://news.bbc.co.uk/2/hi/entertainment/8109267.stm

Chapter 3
The Case for Variable Pricing of IDM

Ankit Bansal
Nanyang Technological University, Singapore

Desai Mayura Manohar
Nanyang Technological University, Singapore

S. Shantani
Nanyang Technological University, Singapore

ABSTRACT

This chapter proposes different variable pricing strategies that can be implemented in IDM market-places to increase revenues and consumption of IDM content. Adverse reaction of consumers to price discrimination, where they consider it unfair, is the greatest hindrance to successful application of variable pricing schemes.

INTRODUCTION

Media is being increasingly delivered through and consumed on the Internet via both legal and illegal means in this digital age. Most popular information portals in the initial years of the Internet provided free content and generated revenues through advertising. On the other hand, media companies opposed this practice of providing content for free, with the exception of a few select services like Internet radio. Some industries, like the music industry, were late in embracing the Internet as a mainstream means of distribution and failed to legally provide content online. Consequently, music industry suffered lost sales opportunities due to piracy and illegal file sharing.

Many research studies claim that online consumers are not used to making payments online and that it is better to earn revenues through advertising. Advertising however, especially in recessionary times, is not adequate to cover costs of producing content and yet leave a profit.

While it is difficult to generate revenues online, Internet also offers unprecedented opportunities

DOI: 10.4018/978-1-61350-147-4.ch003

for employing different pricing schemes (Leyland et al., 2001) to maximize revenue generation. Media companies can use pricing as a strategic tool that can help them build and sustain competitive advantage and protect areas of vulnerability (Stern, 1989). In contrast to other strategic moves, such as new product development or new market penetration, change in pricing schemes requires little investment and can generate quick results.

Media companies have always employed creative pricing techniques to extract maximum possible revenues from consumers. One such technique is the bundling of different items of content (singles for music, articles for newspaper) to cover production and distribution costs. Such an approach helps increase revenues as different consumers place different value on different items in the bundle (Viswanathan & Anandalingam, 2005). Another technique is the use of 'release windows' where the price of content is reduced with the passage of time. This is often legitimized by offering content in a different medium. An example of this practice is the release of books in hardback forms which have a higher price tag compared to paperbacks which are released much later.

Although pricing models for digital media content delivered through internet have evolved considerably from yesteryears when content was delivered through physical media, they still do not fully exploit the opportunities offered by online delivery mechanisms (Waterman, 2001). Many services delivering interactive digital media (IDM) content online are still using fixed or relatively fixed pricing schemes used in the era gone by.

BACKGROUND (PRICING OF IDM CONTENT)

Flat Pricing

Flat rate or fixed pricing schemes refer to charging all the consumers the same price for the me-

dia goods. Sometimes, even different items are charged at the same price. An example of such flat rate pricing is the price of 99 cents per music single offered by iTunes music store till 2008. It later moved to a simple variable pricing structure with three price points.

The major drawback of flat pricing schemes is the lack of price segmentation, i.e. not charging different prices to different user segments. Flat pricing drives away some potential consumers whose prices are higher than they are willing to pay and leaves money on the table in case of high value customers for whom the price is lower than what they are willing to pay.

Variable Pricing

Variable pricing can be defined as a pricing strategy where prices change over time, across consumers, and/or across product bundles (Jayaraman & Baker, 2003). In the e-marketplace, usage related factors such as purchase & usage history and WebPages visited, are used to vary the prices of products (Avlonitis & Indounas, 2006).

Variable pricing is particularly apt for information goods such as IDM as the value derived by consumers is significantly different for different consumers for the same type of content (Viswanathan & Anandalingam, 2005). Variable pricing enables revenue maximization by charging different consumers different prices based on the differences in the value derived by them or their willingness to pay. Variable pricing can also be the weapon against loss of revenues due to piracy, since charging consumers based on their willingness to pay reduces the incentive to resort to illegal means.

Extreme forms of variable pricing in IDM content have become possible due to possibilities offered by online delivery mechanisms:

- **Economics of abundance:** Unlike tangible goods, media content does not deplete with consumption and with falling technology prices, the marginal cost of storage and distribution of content through online means is almost zero. This creates opportunities for unbundling content and selling discrete pieces at no additional marginal cost (when compared to *bundled* content).

- **Mass customization:** Internet not only enables serving niche content to niche consumers but also provides opportunities for mass customization to create unique value for each consumer. In the case of IDM content, unique value can be created by helping consumers find the content they desire, providing different versions/qualities of content and charging prices acceptable to them.

- **Ease of profiling consumers:** Price discrimination depends upon the ability of sellers to gather personal information about their buyers as well as monitor their purchasing habits to segment them according to their willingness to pay. The costs of acquiring this information are prohibitive in bricks and mortar businesses. E-tailing, however, enables sellers to acquire rich consumer data at a minimal cost (Narahari et al., 2005).

- **Ease of changing prices:** The time, cost and effort associated with changing prices quickly for the entire product range are quite low for online stores (Leyland et al., 2001). Online stores can even employ algorithms that automatically change prices displayed on website depending upon user profile and past history of purchases.

- **Transaction costs:** Micro-payment systems on the internet allow consumers to make a multitude of purchases in a convenient and secure fashion, thereby supporting unbundling of content (Waterman, 2001).

FOCUS: FRAMEWORK FOR COMPARING DIFFERENT SCHEMES

As employing variable pricing techniques helps to increase revenue, we devise a framework, shown in Figure 1, which depicts the potential to increase revenues by using a particular pricing scheme against the degree to which the scheme is variable in nature. There are two dimensions to the framework – the degree of variableness and the potential increase in revenue. The *degree of variableness* is defined as the extent to which the price of each transaction differs from the rest. In other words, the higher the dispersion between price of transactions, the higher the degree of variableness. This further depends upon the extent to which the following variables are taken into account to vary the prices:

- **Content:** Prices vary across different items, bundles of items or quantum of purchase.
- **Consumer profile:** Consumers can be profiled based on their demographic profile, past purchase patterns, ratings, website navigation behavior etc. This practice of charging different consumers different prices is known as differential pricing or price discrimination.
- **Time of consumption:** Prices can be varied frequently over time based on the total demand and elasticity of demand. This practice is called temporal price dispersion (Narahari et al., 2005).

PRICING STRATEGY

Pay what you Want

In this scheme, users are free to make any amount of payment for each discrete item of IDM content they have downloaded. This altruistic model automatically takes into account the consumer's

Figure 1. Framework for analyzing various schemes

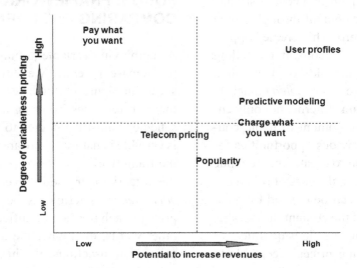

willingness to pay and revokes the age old concept of patronage. An example of this pricing strategy is the music album, *In Rainbows*, released by *Radiohead* in 2007. A modification to this scheme may insist upon consumers to pay a minimum floor price.

In theory, 'Pay what you want' is the most dynamic scheme of all as each transaction can have any price point. It is also likely to be highly effective in combating piracy and building a loyal base of customers. It's biggest disadvantage however, is that it may not lead to increase in revenues as high value users would be unwilling to shell out enough to cover the lower contributions from low value users. Generally, consumers would tend to be unwilling to part with a majority of their surplus – the gap between the free market price and the price they are willing to pay.

Charge what you Want

The e-tailer serves as a distribution platform and prices are decided and changed over time by content providers as often as they please. An example of such pricing is lulu.com that enables independent authors to publish & sell their books

at any price they like (above a minimum floor price to cover production and distribution costs). The e-tailer may however, restrict the content providers to charge within a price band.

This model does not vary prices for different users but allows a high degree of variation across time and across different types of content. Such a model if applied to online music and video stores, would enable movie studios and record labels to charge and change prices based on their analysis of consumer demand for each item.

Predictive Modeling

Predictive modeling employs use of analytical tools to predict future demands based on past purchase patterns. Prices are changed so that revenue is maximized for the forecasted demand curve. Such pricing can be restricted to selection of a prefixed price points within a price band. This technique was employed by Pass Along Networks, a media player platform provider to online music stores.

This pricing strategy exploits the different prices customers are willing to pay at different times. It increases the prices with a likelihood of increase in demand and adjusts prices downward when demand is expected to fall. This pricing can lead to a high increase in revenues if there is a significant variation in demand for content over relatively short periods of time. It measures relatively low on the degree of variableness as prices are varied only across the dimension of time. Its biggest disadvantage is that continuously changing prices can frustrate consumers and can also provoke them to consider other means of acquiring content.

Popularity

Under this strategy, each piece of content is offered to consumers at a fixed floor price which is common to all items. Later, the price of this item is increased and fixed depending upon its popularity during the initial short period of sale. Popularity is calculated using three criteria

- Cumulative and average user ratings
- Quantum of usage - e.g. number of times a music song is played, time spent and pages flipped for an e-book or online journal
- Average daily sales for the initial period

Amie Street (acquired by Amazon in 2010) is an example of a music store that employed user ratings to fix price of music singles. One major advantage of this scheme over others is that it explicitly makes pricing of content a 'democratic' process and hence consumers are likely to accept increased prices.

User Profiles

This scheme is the ultimate in price discrimination as it takes into account a multitude of factors. The profile of users in terms of their past purchase patterns, friends in social network, ratings, location and web analytics is used to offer different prices to each one of them. Such pricing is highly variable as it takes into account all the three variables Vis-à-vis content, user profile and time of consumption. If effectively employed, it can generate maximum possible revenue streams among all.

One huge disadvantage of this scheme however is that it is extremely difficult to implement as it raises privacy issues and makes consumers feel that they are being cheated. Amazon had once used such price discrimination on its website by offering different prices to different login accounts. Consumers revolted and Amazon quickly removed the differential pricing system, later refunding the extra money to consumers who paid higher prices.

Telecom Pricing

Here, consumers pay a monthly subscription fee which varies depending upon usage level as well as the consumer segment. The monthly subscription gives access to the entire library of content with the condition of consumption of limited items per month, e.g. databases providing academic journals charge different subscription fees to students, academic institutions and corporate users. The subscription price per unit of item usually falls with increasing price plans. This scheme does not rate high on degree of variableness as it does not change pricing with the passage of time and distinguishes between consumer segments alone (rather than individuals) and levels of usage (rather than exact usage). However, it automatically takes into account a user's willingness to pay as it is based on the concept of bundling.

We have not included the auction model, although it is quite popular in e-marketplaces. The reason for this is that auctions works best when there is a limited supply of goods. Therefore, there is no incentive with the seller to create an artificial scarcity and use auction pricing models. Even if auctioning is attempted, it would end up taking the shape of schemes such as 'pay what you want' or 'predictive modeling'.

CONCLUSION

Variable pricing enhances value for all the players in IDM value network. Digital medium of delivery of IDM content makes variable pricing strategies both feasible and highly effective in increasing sales of IDM content. Pricing of goods in accordance with consumers' willingness to pay helps to increase the reach of content to a wider audience. For instance, higher payments from fans of a specific music band enable lowering prices for mass audiences.

The different pricing schemes mentioned need not be implemented in isolation. A hybrid of different schemes can be far more effective than individual ones. For example, 'popularity' scheme technique can be used to set a base price for a 'pay what you want' scheme. Pricing of customized bundles based on 'popularity' can leverage 'user profiles' by providing recommendations to drive further sales. Such bundling would also help in obscuring prices to consumers and make it difficult for them to gauge the prices for individual components (Nalebuff 2003) and hence prevent them from retaliating in response to price discrimination.

The retaliation from consumers to price discrimination is a major hindrance to the application of variable pricing. Price discrimination is hugely unpopular as it tarnishes the reputation of e-tailer permanently by making people feel cheated. Therefore it is recommended that sellers implementing variable pricing that discriminate among different users should make the variables taken into account for changing prices be made known to users. Another reason for the unpopularity of variable pricing is that they make it difficult for consumers to make purchase decisions by making comparisons and hence causing inconveniences. Another factor that can hinder success of a variable pricing strategy is the prevalence of opportunities for arbitrage among consumers such that lower price paying consumers are able to trade or share the media item with high value potential consumers

(Reinartz, 2001). This concern is already being addressed using DRM technologies to restrict usage of content on authorized devices only.

It is difficult for market followers to use variable pricing strategies if market leaders employ fixed schemes. This is because consumers can easily compare prices of media content across e-marketplaces and opt for stores offering lowest price. As a result, sellers using variable pricing schemes will be left only with low value customers, a phenomenon known as *adverse selection*. This barrier to using variable pricing schemes can be addressed if sellers can differentiate their service experience and reduce the incentive for consumers to go to rival stores. Recommendations systems can be an enduring source of differentiation to sellers as they are based on past purchase patterns as well as network of social friends and hence cannot be replicated by rivals overnight (Kambil & Aggarwal, 2001). Another technique is to add additional attributes to content thereby 'attaching' legitimacy to the practice of charging different prices. For example in the case of online music different qualities of music can be charged at different prices, even though the cost of production & distribution is nearly the same.

In essence, variable pricing must be employed considering the response from consumers. Some consumers may not respond positively to variable pricing which could either be due to the difficulty faced in making purchase decisions or if the variable pricing appears unfair. In such cases, sellers should stick to either flat pricing strategies or use tiered pricing models such as 'telecom pricing'.

Variable pricing also enables sharing of revenues among content providers and intermediaries in a fair and transparent manner. Schemes that inherently rely on tracking the exact usage of each consumer can enable estimation of fair compensation of content creators. For example Kachingle.com is a paid blog site which distributes subscription fee received from users to blog writers based on the user's activity i.e. blogs visited, time spent etc. Since most e-tailers share a percentage of their revenues with players in media industry value chain, variation in prices across content and time would also vary their share in revenues. This would reflect a fair & performance based sharing of revenues rather than averaging across different items consumed.

We suggest conducting further studies to investigate change in consumer behavior in response to the variable pricing schemes mentioned in the chapter. This can be done most effectively by running pilot tests and simulations. Another area of investigation is to determine the manner in which trust can be built among consumers for pricing strategies employing price discrimination.

REFERENCES

Anderson, C. (2008). *Why $0.00 is the future of business* (pp. 140–149). Wired.

Avlonitis, G. J., & Indounas, K. A. (2006). Pricing practices of service organizations. *Journal of Services Marketing, 20*(5), 346–356. doi:10.1108/08876040610679954

Bhattacharjee, S. (2003). *Economic of online music*. ICEC.

Dolan, R. J., & Moon, Y. (1999). Pricing and market making on the Internet. *Harvard Business Review*.

He, S., Cattelan, R. G., Jain, K., & Kirovski, D. (2007). *Offline viral economies for digital media*. (Technical Report MSR-TR-2007-167 December 2007). Microsoft Research.

Jayaraman, V., & Baker, T. (2003). The internet as an enabler for dynamic pricing of goods. *IEEE Transactions on Engineering Management, 50*(4), 470–477. doi:10.1109/TEM.2003.820134

Kambil, A., & Agrawal, V. (2001). *E-commerce: The new realities of dynamic pricing*. The Outlook.

Nalebuff, B. (2003). *Bundling, tying and portfolio effects*. DTI Economics Paper I, Dept. of Trade & Industry.

Narahari, Y., Raju, C., Ravikumar, K., & Shah, S. (2005). Dynamic pricing models for electronic business. *Sadhana, 30*, 231–256. doi:10.1007/BF02706246

Pitt, L. F., Berthon, P., & Watson, R. T. (2001). Pricing strategy and the Net. *Business Horizons*.

Reinartz, W. J. (2001). *Customizing prices in online markets*. European Union Business Forum.

Stern, A. (1989). Pricing and differentiation strategies. *Strategy and Leadership, 17*(5), 30–34. doi:10.1108/eb054271

Viswanathan, S., & Anandalingam, G. (2005). Pricing strategies for information goods. *Sadhana, 30*, 257–274. doi:10.1007/BF02706247

Waterman, D. (2001). *Internet TV: Business models and program content*. Annual TPRC Research Conference on Information, Communication, and Internet Policy, Washington, DC, October 27-29.

Zhu, K., & MacQuarrie, B. (2003). The economics of digital bundling. *Communications of the ACM, 46*(9), 264–270. doi:10.1145/903893.903946

Chapter 4
Buffet or à la Carte:
Pricing Digital Goods

Deepti Verma
Nanyang Technological University, Singapore

Gaurav Gupta
Nanyang Technological University, Singapore

Kamat Keshav
Nanyang Technological University, Singapore

ABSTRACT

Pricing strategy plays a key role in most organizations. The pricing decision of bundling or à la carte in the case of cable television industry is a long debated one. While consumers seem to favor the à la carte option, operators are persistent in continuing with the bundling options. In this chapter, we explore both sides of the argument. We then discuss several factors affecting the players in the eco-system of cable television industry; these include the subscriber-operator relationship, operator-distributor relationship, and the role of government policies affecting their decisions. In concluding we use these factors to conceptualize a framework that seeks to assist the players in the cable television industry in choosing an adequate pricing model.

INTRODUCTION

Pricing takes a key role in most of the organizations as it determines the turnover and achieved returns (Lehmann & Buxmann, 2009). The concept of network effects (Shy, 2001) and the lowered costs of reproduction play a dominant role in digital media industry that makes the pricing strategies different from other industry types. With the

DOI: 10.4018/978-1-61350-147-4.ch004

increase in choices, consumers today can decide what to opt for. Instead of purchasing an entire music album, a consumer is able to pick his favorite song through i-Tunes. Similarly, customers might want to view movies at home based on their preferences rather than the ones offered by the distributor. On the other hand an office executive might prefer a bundled Microsoft Office suite for all his document needs. Likewise a consumer of a new PC might not mind adding a little price to buy a package consisting of a mouse, mouse pad and a maintenance kit. Hence it becomes critical for organizations to understand when to bundle the products in a package and when to offer an à la carte option for the consumers.

The cable television rates have increased tremendously over the years on the assumption of improvements in the quality and the increase in the number of channels offered (Buckley, 2008). Crawford et al. (Crawford, Kwerel, & Levy, 2008) report that the unadjusted cable prices increased by 84.1% over the period from 1997-2005, quality improvements by 50.5% in comparison while the consumer price index by 18.8%. However several consumer groups feel that the fact that subscribers generally do not watch all the added channels is ignored (Prices, 2004). They argue that bundling practiced by the cable TV operators has led to a steep increase in the prices (Chen, 2009). The report states that the cable television operators abuse their market power by claiming that despite the massive cost production increase, the consumers are getting a greater value for their dollar. The operators on the other hand believe that bundling helps them lower the transaction costs, realize economies of scale and simplify the decision process for the consumer. A la carte option would simply increase the prices for the consumer (Crawford & Yurukoglu, 2009). The situation is further worsened by the ambiguous stand of US Government's Federation Communication Commission (Rennhoff & Serfes, 2008). The November 2004 report by the Commission states that using an à la carte option would increase the prices and thereby limit the benefits to the consumers while their February 2006 report take a completely opposite stand (Chen, 2009). This leaves both the operators and the consumers confused.

There is hence a need to understand the basis of arguments in each case that will help understand what is suitable. Although there have been research done on this case of the cable television, it is still not clear how the option of à la carte would benefit customers. In this chapter, we use the case

of cable television to compare the pros and cons of à la carte or bundling or otherwise known as a buffet system as strategies for pricing. We first explore both sides of the coin by researching the recent trends and then consider several factors that impact the pricing options. At the end of it, we propose a conceptual framework that seeks to help the concerned people in the eco-system of cable television industry understand the suitability of each pricing option.

BACKGROUND

The stand on whether the cable television operators should offer channels on an individual (or à la carte) basis as opposed to the bundled options that are offered presently, has been a long debated one. While customers seem to prefer the individual options, there must be a reason why operators favor the bundled option. In this section, we see both the sides of the coin and then use the research materials to compare the two.

Literature Review

Emergence and growth of the Internet has not only created new opportunities for pricing the digital goods but also made the firms re-consider their pricing models and strategies (Bakos & Brynjolfsson, 1997). The ability to create and distribute electronic goods at minimal cost has brought a change in the old pricing model of price being equal to marginal costings. However, the pricing in organizations is often plagued by rationality deficits in the form of ad hoc or arbitrary decisions (Florissen, 2008). Internet has made possible, the monitoring and micro payment, making it more feasible to sell small units of information, which may be used for limited time, by limited people and in limited situations; which has given rise to the concept of on-demand (Bakos & Brynjolfsson, 1997) consumption.

Venkatesh and Chatterjee (2006) examine the three predominant ways in which products in digital market can be offered. The first one is pure bundling where the products are offered as a single bundle without any choice for the consumers to select from. The second type is pure components where the products are offered individually. As per Geng, Stinchcombe, & Whinston (2005), pure bundling is one of the simplest pricing strategies that an organization can adopt. In this model, all the goods are sold in a single package at a single price. The optimality of pure bundling of information goods depends upon a number of factors and one of these factors is consumers' values. If the consumers' values do not decrease rapidly then is bundling approximately optimal. However, if the consumers' values to subsequent goods decrease too quickly, bundling is then expected to be suboptimal (Geng, Stinchcombe, & Whinston, 2005). Chen (2009) shows that pure bundling leads to lesser advertisements, higher consumer surplus and therefore higher profits for the monopolist. When there is inadequate information available about preference of individual customer's, bundling is the efficient way for the firm to increase their profits from the consumers' willingness to pay (Linde, 2009). For the digital goods, there is a negligible marginal cost of adding another good to the bundle. It is worth noting what Linde (2009) mentions "[b]undling is a worthwhile variant of price discrimination". The bundle price is based on the willingness to pay and it is not the sum of unit prices of the goods. The third type is mixed bundling where a good or a service is offered both as a bundle as well with the option to let the user choose on à la carte basis. This option is considered a good strategy in a market of competition (Chen, 2009).

The Pro à la Carte Position

The proponents of the à la carte in cable television argue that the bundling system cause a price inflation as the subscribers are forced to pay for channels that they do not consume (Buckley, 2008). This perspective is based on the idea that the market place should be influenced by customer preferences so that there is an increased competition leading to a better customer service. According to a study (Consumers Union Cable TV Issues Survey, 2004), two thirds of the subscribers would only pay for selected channels while 60% would prefer to select fewer channels. This means that à la carte is considered as a popular idea by the cable TV subscribers. Several groups such as the Parental Television Council state their argument that customers need not pay for programs of offensive nature. For example, parents who subscribe to Nickelodeon for their kids should not be forced to subscribe to the MTV channel as well if they are against it (Buckley, 2008).

The Pro Bundling Position

The opponents of à la carte system argue that it would lead to higher prices and decreased programming diversity (Buckley, 2008). They also believe that the customer's choice would decline with the addition of more channels. The supporters of bundling also believe that there is no consensus on the regulatory effects of à la carte (Crawford & Yurukoglu, 2009). As per a numerical simulation study on the possible outcome of à la carte regulation, the increase in consumer surplus tends to reduce the cable operator profit (Gregory & Joseph, 2007). A study by Rennhoff & Serfes (2008) shows also similar results with the exception of an additional factor: influences of advertising. The proponents of bundling state that the family objectionable channels also support smaller family and religions, stations and without the support of whom, these family friendly channels might cease to survive (Buckley, 2008). These studies hence show the reluctance on the part of cable TV operators to consider à la carte as an option.

Comparison of Bundling and Unbundling

After considering various costs involved with bundling and unbundling, Bakos and Brynjolfsson (1997) mentioned that low cost of transaction and distribution makes unbundling a good option for sellers, whereas low marginal costs of production makes bundling an attractive alternative. When the inter-network effects are small or large but equi-proportional, bundling is preferred; whereas when network effects are large and skewed, unbundling is preferred.

Bundling is a value-based pricing strategy. It has many advantages in terms of revenue management and seems to meet the challenges of pricing information goods (Rautio, 2007). Offering product bundles is useful in generating more profits when the revenues and margins are more than that by offering stand alone products. The predictive value of bundling enables firms to mine more value from any given goods (Bakos & Brynjolfsson, 2000). It also helps a bundler enter new market and capture it from a present firm who does not bundle, giving the bundler a chance for innovation. Bundling helps to speed-up the circulation of information goods. Lowly priced packages with additional offers make it interesting and easy for the customer to at least take a trial and the consumer can get a feel and experience of the product (Linde, 2009). Bakos & Brynjolfsson

(2000) also mentions that large-scale bundlings creates a barrier to entry for competitors, favors price discrmination. On average, it increases demand and favors innovation (see Table 1).

In the next section, we would explore the factors affecting the players in order to help conceptualize our framework that can be used to understand the pricing decisions in the cable television eco-system.

DISCUSSION

In this section we shall analyze the different relationships among the players and discuss the factors affecting each relationship. We shall also include the government regulations and other factors that influence tpricing decisions. At the end of the discussion, we shall use these factors to put together a conceptual framework that we opine, affects the choices of à la carte and bundling for players in cable TV industry.

Subscribers: Cable TV Operators

Adding a new product to form a bundle could be beneficial to few subscribers, but Crawford and Cullen (2007) observe that the benefits are normally overshadowed by losses incurred to existing customer. Among others, we consider four main factors that affect the pricing options

Table 1. Comparison of bundling and à la carte options

Criteria	Bundling	à la carte
Costs	Lower transaction & maintenance costs for operators, customers pay more than what they consume.	Higher transaction & maintenance costs for operators, costs might be lower for customers (unclear).
Competitors	Creates a barrier for competitors.	Easier entry for new entrants.
Customers	Simplifies Customer choice/preference.	Caters to the long tail.
Network Effects	Small or Large, but well proportioned.	Large and Skewed.
Product Goal	Long Term Benefits	Short Term Benefits
Demand	Demand Increases for the same price.	Demand is affected by Dead Weight Loss and Customer Surplus.

in this relationship. These are the willingness to pay, consumer preferences, economies of scale and the subscription fee.

Willingness to Pay

The discrimination of price in digital goods is formed on the basis that consumers, even with a low level of willingness to pay would purchase the goods due to low variable cost of digital goods (Lehmann & Buxmann, 2009). In short, willingness to pay refers to the tendency of households to purchasing a network that they view frequently (Crawford & Cullen, 2007). For example the willingness to pay for channels such as Nickelodeon and Disney Channels are estimated to be higher for family households than non family households (Crawford & Yurukoglu, 2009). If the cable TV operators are able to discriminate using prices, then it can use the option of willingness to pay within the subscribers to charge different prices to each and every individual consumer (Bakos & Brynjolfsson, 1997). As per Chen (2009), advertising leads to a location effect that increases the viewers' willingness to pay and increases the profitability of pure bundling as compared to mixed bundling. Bundling has been proven to reduce the effective heterogeneity of the consumer's willingness to pay, thus a single price can be efficiently used to sell goods to them (Bakos & Brynjolfsson, 1997). The willingness to pay also has an effect on the number of viewers. An increase in the willingness to pay increases the viewers in a multiple demand group (Chen, 2009). The combination of the degree of interrelatedness of complements, substitutes and the level of marginal costs with respect to willingness to pay determines the optimal strategy (Venkatesh & Chaterjee, 2006). Individuals will also seek to maximize utility by considering each price schedule till marginal willingness to pay becomes exactly equal to the marginal price of that quality (Anstine, 2004).

Consumer Preferences

The choice of à la carte or bundling the products depends upon how heterogeneous the consumer choices are. Bundling can significantly reduce the heterogeneity of choices because it provides the consumers with a variety of components at a lower price which is not possible with the individual price of the components (Crawford G. S., 2008). It is difficult to measure this heterogeneity in the cable industry because watching a particular program restricts the consumer from watching another program. Bundling strategy will be beneficial only if they have several combinations of cables at different prices. Consumer will be ready to pay only for the pricing option which has channels that they value strongly (Anstine, How Much Will Consumers Pay? A Hedonic Analysis of the Cable Television Industry, 2001). The increasing prices in the channel bundles that the cable industry offers have triggered the research of discovering the benefits of the unbundling strategy against bundling (Rennhoff & Serfes, 2008). It has been found that majority of the consumers are interested in group options as compared to individual options. For e.g. if a consumer is interested in sports he will be more interested in the pricing options which offers him all the sports channels. Hence measuring channel utility in contrast to bundle utility will help the cable industry to reduce the options in the bundling and hence the overall price associated with it. This strategy will prove to be beneficial to both consumers and producers (Byzalov, 2008).

Subscription Fees

Subscription fee, in its simplest terms, refers to the payment made by the viewers for the content and the service that they receive from the operators. A single subscription fee can lead to greater efficiency in an argument of bundling and site licensing (Bakos & Brynjolfsson, 1997). In the absence of pricing flexibility, a cable television operator will be very cautious of raising his sub-scription fee (Chen, 2009). Under mixed bundling, an operator can take advantage of the viewers' willingness to pay to increase the subscription fees. In pure bundling however an operator has much lesser freedom in setting the subscription fees (Chen, 2009). For individual pricing, it is still not clear how the operators would influence the subscription fees. Thus it is vital to consider the usage of subscription fee to understand the provi-sion of these services by operators to cover their costs and how it would help to provide alternate services (Brousseau & Penard, 2007).

Cable TV Operators: TV Network Distributors

Bundling increases the profits on the cost of exploiting the preferences of the consumers com-pared to a` la carte, further proving encouragement to offer more TV networks (Crawford & Cullen, 2007). In the relationship between the TV opera-tors and the TV network distributors, we chose to consider the following factors.

Network Externalities or Economies of Scale

Economies of scale help in creation of distribu-tion channels, pricing of goods and consumer's awareness about the product's existence (Bakos & Brynjolfsson, 1999). Bundling might not always be a motive to extract consumer surplus for the cable TV operators, but may be the intention of utilizing economies of scale in the TV distribution (Chae, 1992). Bundling helps in reducing admin-istrative costs and favors interoperability which creates positive network externalities (Bakos & Brynjolfsson, 1997). According to Chen (2009) the advocates of cable TV believe that bundling reduces the transaction costs and achieves econo-mies of scale, further providing the consumers with simplified options to make choices. They believe that the à la carte option would increase

the prices and affect the consumers. Cable TV operators need to utilize the concepts of market penetration provided by Lehmann and Buxmann (2009) where they mention that the initial objec-tive must be market penetration by providing low price. Over a period of time economies of scale would cause a reduction in the marginal costs as the number of subscribers grows to a large extent (Owen, Wildman, & Greenhalgh, 1986). Even in the absence of network externalities the channel TV providers may use bundling to attract the TV network providers (Brousseau & Penard, 2007). After reaching the critical mass and having net-work effects and economies of scale, the cable TV operators may have the liberty to increase the prices. A similar phenomenon is explained by Bakos and Brynjolfsson (1999) wherein it is beneficial to bundle low marginal goods when the economies of scale exist. On the contrary, Brous-seau & Penard (2007) mention that in absence of economies of scale and network externalities, bundling of channels provides a competitive advantage to the cable TV providers in terms of price discrimination, barriers for competitors, re-moval of small players and luring of TV network providers to provide more channels.

Transaction Costs

Transaction costs are generated because the cable operators have to deal with TV networks and the consumers (Brousseau & Penard, 2007). In the digital market, the transaction costs are declining as are the marginal costs of production and distribution. Bakos & Brynjolfsson (1997) states that the lower transactional and distribu-tion costs favors unbundling while on the other hand the lower marginal costs makes bundling a good option. Bundling is a strategy to reduce consumer heterogeneity and also helps in reducing the distribution and the transaction costs which in turn favors flexible pricing mechanisms and models (Lehmann & Buxmann, 2009). For most of the cable TV operators the transaction cost is almost the same, so it does not make a remarkable difference in pricing decisions for the consumers (Bakos & Brynjolfsson, 1999).

License Fees

TV networks make their earnings in the two-sided market by revenues from advertising and licensing fees. Network effects tend to maximize the license fee which also has an effect on the price and frequency of advertising (Chen, 2009). In bundling, cable operators would have to pay license fees for all the subscribers irrespective of number of viewers for any channels (Chen, 2009). Byzalov (2008) has analyzed a few factors that would cause an increase in the license fees upon unbundling the channels. The first is due to massive drop in the number of consumer for most of the channels because it would no more be compulsory for consumers to pay for the unwanted channel as part of bundle. This disturbance of channel viewers would have an effect on the advertising rates (Crawford & Cullen, 2007). Unbundling would be a cause of increased competition in the market where every TV network would be forced to compete for subscribers. Although the amount is not known, the license fee is bound to go up upon unbundling (Byzalov, 2008) (Hamilton, 2004). Chen (2009) states that the license fee varies depending on who has power to determine it – the TV network providers or the cable TV operators, which therefore has a major influence on bundling or unbundling of the channels. Although many authors believe that unbundling would increase the license fee, Rennhoff and Serfes (2008) propose that the à la carte model changes the demand and pricing of each TV network which helps in reduction of the licensing fees for the cable operators. This would mean a lesser revenue for the TV networks. If they try to compensate for this by increasing the license fee, the consumers would be badly affected (Byzalov, 2008).

Government Directives

In the absence of government regulations, a downstream cable operator can choose to offer any pricing options that he desires (Chen, 2009). As an example, the downstream price of cable bundle for news channel is approximated to be US$6.96 as compared to the satellite bundle price of US$4.95 with no government regulations in place (Rennhoff & Serfes, 2008). However, there is no significant evidence to calculate the approximate value with a government regulation supporting the à la carte option (Crawford & Yurukoglu, 2009) as anti-bundling regulations have not been implemented. Rennhoff and Serfes (2008) in their study note that all networks experience a demand reduction relative to the pre-regulation demand. They too go on to state that these regulations have a significant impact on the downstream and upstream effects. A study by Crawford and Yurukoglu (2009), predict that regulations in favor of à la carte decrease the total welfare even though the households that are not served by bundling are partially served under à la carte. Thus are government regulations and policies factors the viewers, operators and distributors cannot ignore.

Other Factors

Other factors such as technical costs and collaboration also play a vital role in the pricing decisions of the cable television industry. The technical costs include the installation and equipment such as satellite dish and receiver (Byzalov, 2008). These also include the costs incurred due to promotional activities and quality of improvement (Crawford & Yurukoglu, 2009). The profits of the cable television operators are also affected by the costly technical upgrades. Thus any calculation of social surplus requires a reasonable estimate of these technical costs (Rennhoff & Serfes, 2008). As with any other industry, collaboration of the cable television industry with the network distributors and amongst themselves will also help in subsidizing costs to a greater degree (Goyal & Joshi, 2003).

Using these factors, we propose the conceptual framework as shown in Figure 1.

FUTURE RESEARCH DIRECTIONS

The tradeoff between customers seeking to have their preferences delivered and the cable TV operators favoring the bundling option to maximize their profits has been a long debated topic. In our model, we attempt to explore certain factors that the concerned parties in the cable television industry might have to consider before it can reach a consensus on the next course of action. This model however does not focus on the type of market, its pre-conditions and post-conditions. More so, we have not accounted separately for the options for mixed bundling and pure bundling. Further research might focus on the type of market, its conditions and volatility thereby adding a dynamic perspective to this analytic framework.

The pricing models of an industry are also affected by the technological advances. As far as the TV industry goes, several people are demanding the television services to be delivered as a utility. Our model does not incorporate the newer technological ways people prefer to purchase

the services of cable television. Thus, our model assumes the conventional method of delivering the television services by the cable television to the viewers. The future research might consider the technological improvements for the delivery of services, having implications on the total costs, in-turn having a direct effect on the pricing model to be adopted.

CONCLUSION

In this chapter, we have attempted to compare the options of à la carte and bundling options in the ecosystem of cable television industry. Using the literature available, we have first tried to explore both sides of the coin. We have then used different relationships among the players of the eco-system to understand the different factors affecting the pricing model. Among other factors, willingness to pay has a major effect on the number of users wishing to adopt a service while bundling is favorable to reach the economies of scale. The government regulations and policies are also proven to significantly impact the pricing decisions, although there is no substantial evidence as to how à la carte regulations would impact pricing simply because there aren't any. Since the license fees, transaction costs along and technical costs of the operators directly translate

Figure 1. Framework for pricing option decision in the cable TV ecosystem

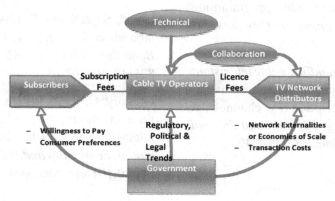

to the subscription fees, changes in these will ultimately lead to a change in how a customer is billed. Using these factors, we have finally made an attempt to conceptualize a framework that seeks to understand the pricing decisions that the players have to consider in the cable television industry.

REFERENCES

Anstine, D. B. (2004). How much will consumers pay? A hedonic analysis of the cable television industry. *Review of Industrial Organization*, *19*(2), 129–147. doi:10.1023/A:1011111329176

Bakos, Y., & Brynjolfsson, E. (1997). Aggregation and disaggregation of information goods: Implication for bundling, site licencing and micropayment systems. In B. Kahin, & H. R. Varian (Eds.), *Internet publishing and beyond: The economics of digital information and intellectual property* (pp. 114-137). MIT Press, 2000.

Bakos, Y., & Brynjolfsson, E. (1999). Bundling information goods: Pricing, profits, and efficiency. *Management Science*, *45*(12), 1613–1630. doi:10.1287/mnsc.45.12.1613

Brousseau, E., & Penard, T. (2007). The economics of digital business models: A framework for analyzing the economics of platforms. *Review of Network Economics*, *6*(2), 81–114. doi:10.2202/1446-9022.1112

Buckley, C. T. (2008). À la carte v. channel bundling: The debate over video programming distribution. *Loyola Consumer Law Review*, *20*(4), 413–437.

Byzalov, D. (2008). *Unbundling cable television: An empirical investigation*. Philadelphia.Chae, S. (1992). Bundling subscription TV channels: A case of natural bundling. *International Journal of Industrial Organization*, *10*, 213–230.

Chen, M. (2009). *Bundling and a la carte pricing in a two-sided market*. Philadelphia: Bennett S. LeBow College of Business, Drexel University, Department of Economics and International Business.

Consumers Union. (2004, May 25). *Cable TV issues survey*. Retrieved April 10, 2010, from http://www.hearusnow.org/fileadmin/sitecontent/052504_CUCableChoicePoll.pdf

Crawford, G. S., & Cullen, J. (2007). Bundling, product choice, and efficiency: Should cable television networks be offered à la carte? *Information Economics and Policy*, *19*, 379–404. doi:10.1016/j.infoecopol.2007.06.005

Crawford, G. S., Kwerel, E., & Levy, J. (2008). Economics at the FCC: 2007-200. *Review of Industrial Organization*, *33*(3), 187–210. doi:10.1007/s11151-008-9196-6

Crawford, G. S., & Yurukoglu, A. (2009). *The welfare effects of bundling in multi-channel television markets*. Working Paper, University of Warwick, New York University, Department of Economics.

Florissen, A. (2008). Preiscontrolling – Rationalitätssicherung im Preismanagement. *Zeitschrift für Controlling und Management*, *52*(2), 85–90. doi:10.1007/s12176-008-0027-2

Geng, X., Stinchcombe, M. B., & Whinston, A. B. (2005). Bundling information goods of decreasing value. *Management Science*, *51*(4), 662–667. doi:10.1287/mnsc.1040.0344

Goyal, S., & Joshi, S. (2003). Networks of collaboration in oligopoly. *Games and Economic Behavior*, *43*(1), 57–85. doi:10.1016/S0899-8256(02)00562-6

Gregory, C. S., & Joseph, C. (2007). Bundling, product choice, and efficiency: Should cable television networks be offered a la carte? *Information Economics and Policy*, *19*(3-4), 379–404. doi:10.1016/j.infoecopol.2007.06.005

Hamilton, B. A. (2004). *The a la carte paradox: Higher consumer costs and reduced programming diversity.* National Cable & Telecommunications Association.

Lehmann, S., & Buxmann, P. (2009). Pricing strategies of software vendors. *Business & Information Systems Engineering, 1*(6), 452–462. doi:10.1007/s12599-009-0075-y

Linde, F. (2009). Pricing information goods. *Journal of Product and Brand Management, 18*(5), 379–384. doi:10.1108/10610420910981864

Owen, B. M., Wildman, S. S., & Greenhalgh, P. R. (1986). Competitive considerations in cable television franchises. *Contemporary Economic Policy, 4*(2), 69–79. doi:10.1111/j.1465-7287.1986.tb00843.x

Prices, R. (2004). *The continuing abuse of market power by the cable industry: Rising prices, denial of consumer choice and discriminatory access to content.* Consumer Federation of America. Consumers Union.

Rautio, T. (2007). Bundling of information goods: A value driver for new mobile TV services. *International Journal of Revenue Management, 1*(1), 45–64. doi:10.1504/IJRM.2007.011193

Rennhoff, A. D., & Serfes, K. (2008). *Estimating the effects of a la carte pricing: The case of cable.* Working Paper, Drexel University, Middle Tennessee State University.

Shy, O. (2001). *The economics of network industries.* Cambridge University Press. doi:10.1017/CBO9780511754401

Venkatesh, R., & Chaterjee, R. (2006). Bundling, unbundling, and pricing of multiform products: The case of magazine content. *Journal of Interactive Marketing, 20*(2), 21–40. doi:10.1002/dir.20059

ADDITIONAL READING

Beard, R. T., Ford, G. S., & Koutsky, T. M. (2006). A La Carte and Family Tiers as a Response to a Market Defect in the Multichannel Video Programming Market. *CommLaw Conspectus, 31*, 1–65.

Berry, S. T. (1994). Estimating Discrete-Choice Models of Product Differentiation . *The Rand Journal of Economics, 25*(2), 242–262. doi:10.2307/2555829

Chae, S. (1992). Bundling subscription TV channels: A case of natural bundling. *International Journal of Industrial Organization, 10*, 213–230. doi:10.1016/0167-7187(92)90016-R

Chipty, T. (1995). Horizontal integration for bargaining power: Evidence from the cable television industry. *Journal of Economics & Management Strategy, 4*(2), 375–397. doi:10.1111/j.1430-9134.1995.00375.x

Chipty, T. (2001). Vertical Integration, Market Foreclosure, and Consumer Welfare in the Cable Television Industry . *The American Economic Review, 91*(3), 428–453. doi:10.1257/aer.91.3.428

Chipty, T. (2001). Vertical integration, market foreclosure, and consumer welfare in the cable television industry. *The American Economic Review, 91*(3), 428–453. doi:10.1257/aer.91.3.428

Chu, C. S., Leslie, P., & Sorensen, A. (2006). *"Incomplex Alternatives to Mixed Bundling",* mimeo. Stanford University.

Evans, D. S., & Salinger, M. (2005). Why do firms bundle and tie? Evidence from competitive markets and implications for Tying Law. *Yale Journal on Regulation, 22*(1), 37–89.

Evans, D. S., & Webster, K. L. (2007). Designing the right product offerings. *MIT Sloan Management Review, 49*(1), 44–50.

FCC. (2003, 2002) Report on Cable Industry Prices", Discussion paper, Federal Communications Commission. Available at http://www.fcc.gov/mb/csrptpg.html.

GAO (2003). Issues related to competition and subscriber rates in the cable television industry. Discussion paper, General Accounting Office, GAO-04-8.

Goolsbee, A., & Petrin, A. (2004). The Consumer Gains from Direct Broadcast Satellites and Competition with Cable TV . *Econometrica, 72*(2), 351–381. doi:10.1111/j.1468-0262.2004.00494.x

Kagan Media Research. (2005). À la Carte pricing makes great theory, but tv channel bundling tough to beat. Kagan Media Research, December 2005. Available at _HYPERLINK "http://www.ncta"_http://www.ncta_. com/IssueBrief.aspx?contentId=15.

Liebowitz, S. J., & Margolis, S. E. (2008). Bundles of Joy: The Ubiquity and Efficiency of bundles in new technology markets. *Journal of Competition Law & Economics, 5,* 1–47. doi:10.1093/joclec/nhn013

McAfee, P., & Schwartz, M. (1994). Opportunism in Multilateral Vertical Contracting: Nondiscrimination, Exclusivity and Uniformity . *The American Economic Review, 84,* 210–230.

Nalebuff, B. (2004). Bundling as an entry barrier. *The Quarterly Journal of Economics, 119*(1), 159–187. doi:10.1162/0033553304772839551

Noam, E. M. (1985). Economics of scale in cable television: A multiproduct analysis . In Noam, E. M. (Ed.), *Video Media Competition: Regulation, Economics, and Technology*. Columbia University Press.

Owen, B. M. (2008). The Temptation of Media Regulation. *Regulation, 31*(1), 8–12.

Thompson, A. (2006). NFL v. cable is turning into a real nailbiter. Wall Street Journal.

Wildman, S. (2006). A Case for A La Carte and Increased Choice? An Economic Assessment of the FCCs Further Report, Discussion Paper, Michigan State University.

Wildman, S., & Owen, B. (1985). Program competition, diversity, and multichannel bundling in the New Video Industry . In Noam, E. M. (Ed.), *Video Media Competition: Regulation, Economics, and Technology*. Columbia University Press.

Xiao, P., Chan, T., & Narasimhan, C. (2006). *Product bundles under three-part tariffs*. Research Memorandum, Washington University.

KEY TERMS AND DEFINITIONS

À la Carte: Goods are priced and sold individually rather than being bundled. This is also known as unbundling.

Bundling: Clubbing and offering similar products together as a single unit.

Network Externalities: It is related to increase in the value of the goods being used by the increasing number of users. It is also termed as 'Network Effects'.

Willingness to Pay: The maximum amount a user would like to pay for a good. It is related to the perceived value of the good by the user.

Chapter 5
IDM Products vs. Services:
A Comparative Analysis

Aditya Budi
Nanyang Technological University, Singapore

Mi Wang
Nanyang Technological University, Singapore

Tianyuan Wang
Nanyang Technological University, Singapore

ABSTRACT

In today's increasingly competitive market, marketing a product or a service is getting tougher than before, especially in the industry domain of interaction digital media (IDM), which produces completely different types of digital goods. Knowing the key differences between them is vital, as it will allow IDM companies to position resources more effectively. Moreover, it will help get more profits from investments. Unfortunately, research done on this topic is still rare and inadequate. This chapter aims to give a comparative analysis between the digital products and services study from the perspective of marketing, in a bid to better understand their differences and similarities. The comparative analysis is divided into different stages according to the new digital goods development process. We use two case studies to support the points of view: WSJ.com and PayPal. Directions for future research are discussed at the end of this chapter.

INTRODUCTION

A good marketing plan for every company is undoubtedly significant to the success of their business. It helps to ensure that the company reaps the most optimum benefits in the shortest possible time with minimal expenditure. In today's increasingly competitive market, however, marketing for a product or a service is not an easy, and this gets tougher especially in interactive digital media (IDM) industry.

DOI: 10.4018/978-1-61350-147-4.ch005

IDM products used to be easy to differentiate by quality. However, due to improved information technology, most products can meet acceptable quality levels. IDM services are more competitive and therefore require a good enough reason to be purchased by consumers. Thus, the company needs to have different approaches and plans to marketing products and services. Looking at the comparative analysis between digital products and services before launching a business can help companies improve their commercial success rates in the future. Knowing the key differences between the different kinds of marketing will allow IDM companies position resources more effectively to obtain more returns from investments.

Unfortunately, we found that previous research on this topic is still rare and inadequate in the IDM domain. In order to better understand their differences and similarities, this chapter aims to give a comparative analysis between the digital products and services study from the perspective of marketing. And the comparative analysis is divided into six stages according to the new digital goods development process (see Figure 1): user study stage, productizing stage, pricing stage, distribution stage, promotion stage, and selling stage. In addition, to support the points of view in this chapter we will use two case studies: WSJ. com and PayPal. Directions for future research are discussed at the end of this chapter.

BACKGROUND

Varian, H. (2000), among others, defines digital products which can be transmitted via the Internet, as essentially information products. Digitized books, pictures and online newspaper are good examples. Digital services, on the other hand, are defined as information which can be processed over the Internet. This includes services that provide access to useful resources like server connections as well as online utilities that assist users in accomplishing specific tasks. Online banking and security transactions are example of such services (Wang, 2001).

The largest and most respected paid online newspaper subscription is World Street Journal (WSJ). It focused on selling subscription as well generating advertising revenue from their print version. In 2005 itself, WSJ has more than 712.000 paid subscriptions in the United States only and 60% of their paid subscription is not subscription to the print version (Scott, 2005). Since it was bought over by News Corp for $5.6 billion, they increased free content as well as video clips which are being supplied from News Corp's Fox news television channel (Red Herring, 2008).

PayPal is a popular method of payment on the Internet, used for person-to-person payments by more than 1.5 million business websites. By 2002, PayPal had more than ten millions accounts (Prabalad, 2002) and in 2008, PayPal had more than sixty millions accounts with accounting for 9% of global online commerce (MarketWatch,

Figure 1. Framework for comparative analysis of the IDM products and services

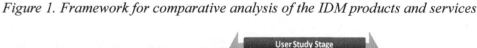

2008). PayPal is the world's fastest growing global currency exchange, and it is clear that PayPal is creating the new standard in online payments.

THE DIFFERENCES AND SIMILARITIES BEWEEN IDM PRODUCTS AND SERVICES

User Study Stage

We found that value creation in digital products lies inside its content or information. In order to formulate the winning strategy in digital production we need to have a deep understanding the economic production of information goods. When the digital products delivered over a network the cost can disappear almost completely. Indeed the initial cost of digital product is huge, yet the reproduction is small (Shapiro, 1998). On the other hand, protection scheme is becoming popular on digital content. For online services the value is inside in the interaction from the users with the firm. Thanks to the technology in web 2.0 which gets users to be more engaged on the Internet, this will in turn benefit the company to tap on this kind of engagement to generate revenue. (Manyika, 2008)

Wall Street Journal (WSJ) provides various subscription plans in order to enjoy their content. According to News Corp Chief Executive Rupert Murdoch, not all online Wall Street Journal content will be free. (Red Herring, 2008). Meanwhile, PayPal is looking to be in partnership with financial services to provide one whole eco-system as payment solution. Many financial services look to PayPal for success in online commerce has become an assets to banks. (Schatt, 2009)

Production and Deliverable Stage

In general digital product sellers can deliver products by two means. They can either deliver the full product at one time through Internet downloads or they can deliver the product interactively on a continual basis. Digital products are often downloadable, as they are by and large the digital counterparts of their physical goods. When the product is delivered via download, the value of the product is transferred to customers in a relatively clear-cut fashion. Conversely, for online services, interaction between the customers and the service provider via the Internet is often needed during the transaction. Therefore, the functions or the values of the products are provided in a piecemeal fashion and in an interactive mode (Wang, 2001).

Pricing Stage

Digital product providers face new challenges. With the revolution in internet technology, they need lots of efforts to get more online customers in order to be generate a stable revenue stream. Providing an easy to use to be able to read the news at ease online comes with a price. nAdweekMedia and Harris Poll conducted a survey in early 2010, which explained that the masses have not stopped reading newspapers, with 59 percent between 18 – 34 years of age at least read either printed or online versions of newspapers (Dolliver, 2010). Another recent study from BMRB internet in 2008 found out that the online newspaper users are younger and more up market as compared to the average online user. It mentioned that 67% of users said that they trust their online newspaper which makes national newspaper websites the perfect environment for connecting with consumers online. It also shown that young people in the UK aged between 15 – 24 years old with more online experience are spending more time as well money in the internet. The report also showed that online newspaper users who do make purchases online had spent an average of £688 online in the previous six months, which was £45 more than online users who do not use online newspapers. (Campaign [UK], 2009) WSJ Subscription in Asia's fee is USD 1.99 per week, totaling up to USD 103.98 per year. This is a price premium for an all-access account to all of WSJ world edition and its own subsidiary contents.

Distribution Stage

Distribution is the fundamental bridge between producers and consumers. The link to producer provided by distributors allows consumers to consume content. Without it, content may never reach the user. Compared with traditional market, digital distribution is the distribution of content using digital, as opposed to analog delivery platforms. Content must be digitally formatted to enable distribution on these platforms (Anshin, P, 2006). Digital distribution is immediate, breaking the traditional delivery barriers of time and space. There are typically two ways of digital distribution, the 'pull' approach allows people to access the website and the 'push' approach is based on user's interest, providing customized information via e-mail.

Wall Street Journal Online News Distribution Model

For the online Wall Street Journal, it is a digital newspaper that can replicate the printed newspaper in content and organization or be made to look like a traditional newspaper. It can also offer interactive multimedia content tailored to the individual customer in a manner different from that of traditional newspapers.

As we can see from Figure 2, all news from WSJ is distributed via these websites, in which they are owned by Dow Jones & Company. Therefore, in the stage of WSJ's digital distribution, direct channels are used to establish brand identity and preference. However, WSJ is a very special example, because it provides both free news and fee-payable news. For the free news, readers can get full access from other websites, such as Google, which means that WSJ news can be distributed via other platforms. For the essential fee-paying news, audiences need to subscribe and

Figure 2. The digital distribution of WSJ news (direct channel)

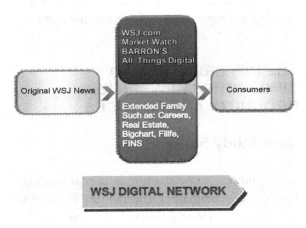

go directly to the WSJ. WSJ is one example only for the traditional media; there are other business models for distributing pure information products (Table 1).

PayPal Service Distribution Model

PayPal aims to enable consumers to shop where they want, when they want, in whatever format they want, which means PayPal service can be delivered to end-user easily. A subsidiary of eBay Inc., PayPal's service can reach to consumers directly via PayPal shops and eBay's website. Except for these direct channels, PayPal has established powerful partnership with many companies in almost 190 markets with 24 currencies around the

Table 1. Main business model in the online news industry

Model	Value Chain	Examples
Model 1 Traditional Media	Creation to distribution	WSJ, New York Times,
Model 2 Distribution intermediaries	Distribution	Google News, Yahoo News,
Model 3 Web content aggregators	Content packaging & Distribution	News Hub, My News Online,

world (Figure 3). For instance, PayPal, in partnership with Master-Card, issues a co-branded debit card. Therefore, PayPal registered users are able to spend money from their online PayPal accounts at any of the 19 million MasterCard accepting merchants all over the world. They also can get funds from their PayPal accounts at MasterCard affiliated ATMs worldwide. This means that users can get PayPal service from MasterCard platform around the global. From PayPal's website, there are more than 5263 websites that accept PayPal payment, and by cooperating with these brands, PayPal publicizes its services and promotes its brand.

According to the analysis of these two cases, it is not difficult to see that both digital products and digital services are distributed via more than one platform. In this stage, choosing valuable partners is important, which is also a key point in the e-business strategy. Finally, there is a trend to distribute products and services through the mobile devices, these mobile platforms can make great conveniences for consumers to achieve digital goods and services anytime anywhere.

Promotion Stage

Promotion includes the activities of advertising and merchandising the product. Promoting prod-

ucts or services can take place through customer incentives or by providing related products or services information (Palmer, 1999). No matter how good your product or service is, without effective promotion, it may not succeed. For digital products and services, the promotion process is almost the same (Table 2).

In terms of promotion, there are seven communication tools, such as traditional media advertising, public relationship, direct mail, trade show seminars, catalog lists & manual, telemarketing and salesperson. And each of them can be used for promoting digital goods and services. In the B2B marketing, it is totally differentiated from consumer marketing, that is the B2C, because the business buyers are not consuming the products themselves, but they are acting as intermediaries. For instance, when WSJ and PayPal promote their sales to customers, they expect instantaneous direct sales, if customers like their products or service, and hopefully long term relationship can be built. However, for B2B marketing, the standard of measurement is based on the loyal relationship rather than immediate economic benefits. The successful B2B strategy is to help the customer to be loyal and supportive to the firm and its products (Alvarez, 2005). When a B2B marketer and a B2C marketer want to develop strategy driven promotion that motivate each of their

Figure 3. Market share of the top Web e-payment technologies

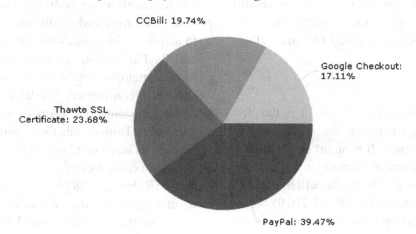

Table 2. Promotion process for digital products and services

Promotion Process	Digital Goods	Digital Services
Identify target users' characteristics	✓	✓
Determine cost-effective media channels	✓	✓
Design and test promotion program	✓	✓
Implement promotional campaign	✓	✓

customers, B2B marketer has a more complex problem than B2C marketer.

The segmental market of each service will be then be taken to explain the different promotion strategy. When PayPal does promotion to individuals, they know clearly who their end users are, it does not need to formulate a promotion plan for each customer, only draw one plan for the target market to launch it. But when WSJ as a B2B marketer, they have to solve the first key question, who is the true decision-maker at the target company and what excites the decision-maker, when this question have been answered the type of promotional strategy can be chosen. The promotional advertisements for B2B in WSJ's website however cannot be found. Therefore is it safe to assume that the promotion methods they used to business clients are different from individual clients. In brief, in order to develop a successful promotional strategy, a clear definition of the target market must be identified. (Alvarez, 2005)

Selling Stage

The stage of selling is crucial as it is the first transactional stage between the seller and the prospective customers. It is an art of persuasion in getting the potential consumer to buy the product or service, which may benefit him or her, and closing the transaction (Ward, 2010). Thus, for sellers, whatever product or service they are selling, it needs to concentrate the selling efforts on communicating the benefits of the product or service to potential consumers, that is to say, what value they can achieve, otherwise the product or service will not sell without value experience. When selling products, they should focus on the benefits to the buyer concerning how they can help customers achieve the desired benefits. The selling of services is more like concept selling for companies. To differentiate themselves, and to build their brands, services companies must market a point of view concerning how they can help customers solve problems and achieve the desired benefits.

Understanding that customers tend to compare carefully the quality of goods, it is easy to compare the quality of different IDM products. For example, the act of differentiating between the quality of digital books and different digital library is easy. However, it is much more difficult to evaluate the quality of similar IDM services that are provided, simply because it is harder to judge the intangible value of the service than the product. For instance, PayPal and Alipay; which is better? The company's brand image has a great influence on consumer behavior (Edvardsson, 2003). To illustrate this, we take PayPal for example. The association with eBay for Paypal has undoubtedly benefitted the brand. However, when the brand was first established, retailers and customers were not so keen to engage their services with a non-bank payment service provider. The trust and credibility crisis continued to affect the business with phishing emails and anti-PayPal website. In order to build its trust, PayPal attempts to reduce scams in order to boost consumer confidence. PayPal also realizes that its brand extension is a way of growing to target customers. To make sure that consumers keep buying into its service, it built on its reputation as the dominant consumer payment system in the online world (Roberts, 2008). Even after the initial payment transactions, there are still contacts required to service the after-sale stage. For example, after buying a PayPal account, a customer will use it for different business online transactions. In order to keep the customers, the company needs to continue marketing and interacting with them. Besides handling the relationship with customers, the guarantee is different between products and services. If the customer is not satisfied with the product, it is often returnable whereas services are not. It is harder to guarantee a service, while it is fairly easy to guarantee a product.

CONCLUSION

The commercialization of the Internet has seen it being deployed for facilitating trading activities, an increasing number of organizations have migrated products and services from physical world to the virtual world. When organizations do the market strategy, they must consider the nature of digital products and digital service as well as its impact on consumer behavior. We have interpreted the differences of digital products and digital services in an online strategy with two cases: WSJ online and PayPal. We also give suggestions for doing different marketing plans for the 6 stages: user study stage, production stage, pricing stage, distribution stage, promotional and selling stage. However, we should mentioned here that we have found that unlike the distinctive differences in the physical world, the difference between products and services become increasingly blurred and both take on an entirely new set of common characteristics.

REFERENCES

Alvarez, A. B., & Casielles, R. V. (2005). Consumer evaluations of sale promotion: The effect on brand choice. *European Journal of Marketing, 39*(1), 54–70. doi:10.1108/03090560510572016

Anshin, P., & Shiizuka, H. (2006). Getting closer to the consumer: The digitization of content distribution. *Lecture Notes in Computer Science, 4253*, 988–996. doi:10.1007/11893011_125

Campaign, U. K. (2009). *The online newspaper user* (pp. 28–29). Campaign, UK: Retrieved from Business Source Premier Database.

Datamonitor. (2008). PayPal: 10 years of successful operation highlight the potential threat to card issuers. *MarketWatch: Global Round-up, 7*(8), 134.

Dolliver, M. (2010). Pay for online newspaper? Hah! *Adweek, 51*(2), 17.

Edvardsson, B., Johnson, M. D., Gustafsson, A., & Strandvik, T. (2003). The effects of satisfaction and loyalty on profits and growth: products versus services. *Total Quality Management & Business Excellence, 11*(7), 917–927.

Hui, K. L., & Chau, P. Y. K. (2002). Classifying digital products. *Communications of the ACM, 45*.

Manyika, J., Roberts, R., & Sprague, K. (2008). Eight business technology trends to watch. *The McKinsey Quarterly, 1*, 60–71.

Powers, W. C. Jr. (1998). *Distinguishing between products and services in strict liability.*

Prabalad, C., & Ramaswamy, V. (2004). *The future of competition: Co-creating unique value with customers.* Boston, MA: Harvard Business School Press.

Reuters News. (2008). Murdoch Won't Make All WSJ.com Content Free. *Red Herring*, 5.

Roberts, J. (2008). *Case study - PayPal: Plug and pay* (p. 20). Brand Strategy.

Schatt, D. (2009). Two deals by eBay unit to enable banks to support PayPal payments. *Cards & Payments, 22*(11), 10–11.

Scott, D. M. (2005). *Cashing in with content: How innovative marketers use digital information to turn browsers into buyers.* New Jersey: Cyber Age Books.

Tapscott, D. W., & Anthony, D. (2006). *Wikinomics: How mass collaboration changes everything.* New York, NY: Portfolio Hardcover.

Ward, S. (2010). *Selling.* The New York Times Company. Retrieved April 13, 2010, from http://sbinfocanada.about.com/od/marketing/g/selling.htm

Werbach, K. (2000). Syndication: The emerging model for business in the internet era. *Harvard Business Review, 78*, 85–93.

ADDITIONAL READING

Baker, W., Lin, E., Marn, M., & Zawada, C. (2001). Getting prices right on the Web. McKinsey Quarterly, (2), 54-63. Retrieved from Business Source Premier database.

Benjamin, R., & Wigand, R. (1995). Electronic markets and virtual value chains on the information superhighway. *Sloan Management Review, 36*(2), 62–72.

Black, J. Web Radio Pioneers Sing the blues. Business Week. (June 21, 2001).

Buhalis, D. (2004). eAirlines: Strategic and tactical use of ICTs in the airline industry. *Information & Management, 41*, 805–825. doi:10.1016/j.im.2003.08.015

Burt, D. (1976). Getting the Right Price with the Right Contract. [Retrieved from Business Source Premier database.]. *Management Review, 65*(5), 24.

Byrne, T. (2003). Content Syndication: Ready for the Masses? E-content, June. Retrieved 26 April 2010, from /http://www.econtentmag.com.

Chircu, A. M., & Kauffman, R. J. (1999). Strategies for internet middlemen in the Intermediation/dis-intermediation/reintermediationcycle. Electronic Markets—The International Journal of Electronic Commerce and Business Media, 9(2), 109–117.

Clemons, E. K., Gu, B., & Lang, K. R. (2002). Newly vulnerable markets in an age of pure information products: An analysis of online music and online news. *Journal of Management Information Systems, 19*(3), 17–41.

Davenport, T. H., & Dickson, T. (Eds.), *Mastering information management* (pp. 197–201). London: Pearson.

Dedrick, J. and Kraemer, K. The impacts of information technology, the Internet and electronic commerce on firm and industry structure: The personal computer industry. CRITO Report (July 2002), University of California, Irvine.

Forsyth, J., Lavoie, J., & McGuire, T. (2000). Segmenting the e-market. McKinsey Quarterly, (4), 14-18. Retrieved from Business Source Premier database.

Fox, M. & Wrenn, B. A broadcasting model for the music industry. Journal of Media Management 3, 2 (2001), 112–119

Goldsborough, R. (2010). Plotting PayPal's Progress and Problems. [Central New York]. *Business Journal, 24*(8), 8.

Hammer, M. (1990). Re-engineering work: Don't automate, obliterate. *Harvard Business Review*, (July–August): 104–112.

Havick, J. (2000). The impact of the Internet on a television-based society. *Technology in Society, 22*, 273–287. doi:10.1016/S0160-791X(00)00008-7

Heizer, J., & Render, B. (1999). *Operations management* (5th ed.). Englewood Cliffs, NJ: Prentice-Hall.

Johns, K. (2010). Paid Vs Free. B&T Magazine, 60(2712), 16-19. Retrieved from Business Source Premier database.

Johnson, R. (2010). E-Newspaper Mimics Broadsheet Touch and Feel. Electronic Engineering Times (01921541), (1576), 29. Retrieved from Business Source Premier database.

Koufaris, M., & Hampton-Sosa, W. (2004). The development of initial trust in an online company by new customers. *Information & Management, 41*, 377–397. doi:10.1016/j.im.2003.08.004

Koufaris, M., Kambil, A., & LaBarbera, P. A. (2002). Consumer behavior in web-based commerce: An empirical study. *International Journal of Electronic Commerce, 6*(2), 115–138.

May, B., & Singer, M. (2001). Unchained melody. *The McKinsey Quarterly, 1*, 128–137.

Meuter, M. L., Ostrom, A. L., Roundtree, R. I., & Bitner, M. J. (2000). Selfservice technologies: A critical incident investigation of technology based service encounters. *Journal of Marketing, 64*(3), 50–64. doi:10.1509/jmkg.64.3.50.18024

Parasuraman, A. (2000). Technology Readiness Index (TRI), a multiple-item scale to measure readiness to embrace new technologies. *Journal of Service Research, 2*(4), 307–320. doi:10.1177/109467050024001

Parry, T. (2010). Alternative payment methods gain acceptance. [Retrieved from Business Source Premier database.]. *Multichannel Merchant, 6*(3), 36–38.

Rust, R. T., & Kannan, P. K. (2002). *E-Service: New Directions in Theory and Practice*. Armonk, New York, NY: ME Sharpe.

Sarkar, M., Butler, B., Steinfield, Ch. "Intermediaries and Cybermediaries: A Continuing Role for Mediating Players in the Electronic Marketplace", JCMC - Journal of Computer-Mediated Communication, No. 3, 1995.

Varian, H. (2000). Buying, Sharing and Renting Information Goods. [Retrieved from Business Source Premier database.]. *The Journal of Industrial Economics, 48*(4), 473–488. doi:10.1111/1467-6451.00133

W.D. Nazareth, D.L. (eds.): Proceedings of the Fifth Americas Conference on Information Systems (AMCIS' 99), Milwaukee, WI, August 13-15, 1999.

KEY TERMS AND DEFINITIONS

B2B Commerce: Generated by businesses providing other businesses with products and services.

B2C Commerce: Generated by businesses providing good and services to consumers.

Digital Products: Items that can be ordered and delivered directly to a computer over the Internet.

Online Newspaper: A newspaper that available virtually in the internet which allow user to have an interaction with the content.

Online Service: Providers who provide access to useful interaction over the internet that will bring benefits for customer.

Payment Gateway: A combination of hardware and software interface to support commerce transaction over the internet.

PayPal: Account based for secure transaction over the internet, which allow people to send and receive money using credit card or bank transfer.

Chapter 6
The Problem with Free Web Content

Ping Seng Ng
Nanyang Technological University, Singapore

Diego Fernando Vergara Arias
Nanyang Technological University, Singapore

Mei-En Elizabeth Koh
Nanyang Technological University, Singapore

Ravi Sharma
Nanyang Technological University, Singapore

ABSTRACT

This chapter will discuss the concept, nature and implications of free web content; with a focus on the problems caused by the rise of this phenomenon in the recent and rapidly flourishing digital age. A pricing strategy will also be proposed as part of our solution to regulate the use of free web content. As part of the proposed recommendation, a case study on Singapore Press Holdings has been conducted to assess to a certain extent, the impact of free web content on a traditional business model. This will determine if the organization is making correct judgment calls, media changes and business decisions, which helps to assimilate the new digital model, and hence, establish a possible guideline to the correct method in which businesses should be heading towards in order to succeed in this digital age.

INTRODUCTION

In the late 1990's when the Internet boom caused the saturation of the dot-com companies, business models were focused on targeting users at zero revenue. Market strategy consisted in investing in all the effort in technology and developers to build platforms on the web in order to attract more and more customers; however the concern of gaining profits was placed in the background (Wikipedia, 2010).

Dot-com companies like *Hotmail* and *Nupedia* did not get any profit in their first years of operations. While Hotmail spent capital on extending

DOI: 10.4018/978-1-61350-147-4.ch006

its users adepts by granting email accounts for free, *Nupedia* struggled to invest lots of capital in professionals - editors, writers and academics. This will maintain constant updates of their free online encyclopedia updated (Geuss, 2010). These events led to the prejudices we know as the dot-com bubble whereby many companies went to bankruptcy like *Nupedia*, others had to be sold out like *Hotmail* and the rest were forced to reconsider their business model. Perhaps this was the first catastrophe registered on the Internet caused by the impact of "free content" phenomenon. Consequently some survivors to the bubble bust like Google, Amazon and Microsoft would apply different strategies to maintain their life on the network but not precisely giving everything for free.

This chapter seeks to discover the consequences of the distribution of free content in the digital media market on the web, based on the perspective of the players (customers, authors and media companies) and the application of the concept of "free".

Literature Review

The term "free-content" as by suggested Anderson (2008) implies two different concepts of free. The first involves giving away some products or services to one set of customers, while selling to another set, where the free products are bundled with other products that that have a price; for instance cell phones given for free but bundled with a very expensive monthly plan. The second approach is the utilization of the low or almost no cost of the digital network to distribute products or services almost gratis, where online newspapers, radio stations, music, videos, books are involved.

This low cost of the digital network is attributable to Web being able to target anyone, in any place of the globe, at any time, and deliver content rapidly is superior to any other existing distribution channel. The concept of free requires the following four conditions (Freedom Defined Organization, 2008):

- Free to use the work and enjoy the benefits of using it.
- Free to study the work and to apply knowledge acquired from it
- Free to make and redistribute copies, in whole or in part, of the information or expression.
- Free to make changes and improvements, and to distribute derivative works.

When some of these conditions are not applicable in content, then the concept of free is lost.

How Free-Content Works

Various strategies are implemented by online content providers in order to apply the concept of free by not getting profits from the content itself. Some of these strategies are explained below.

Free in Exchange for Advertising

The majority of online services are free. Users do not need to pay to use them. Content providers, on the other hand, generate revenue from the promoters who wish to advertise on their website (Iskold, 2008). In this manner more customers will come to the site to get their contents for free, and more advertisers will be pleased with the increased traffic of patrons. More advertisements will then be put up and the website which in turn generates more revenues. An example of this strategy is implemented by Google, as it promotes services or products through ads called "AdWords", which are shown in its search engine via its powerful platform (Google, 2010). Consequently promoters pay Google based on the numbers of times their ad was clicked, a pay-per-click model and Google in exchange gets substantial revenues to provide free and fast search results to its users.

Free in Exchange for Personal Data

This is perhaps one of the first concepts of free-content created on the web. Customers are provided email accounts, membership to web sites, photos or readings for free. In exchange, they must provide personal information to feed the databases of content providers, who will then subsequently sell the data to big corporations. The data is then that will used for marketing purposes as segmentation, advertisements, researches, etc. According to research conducted by Computer World, 89% of Internet users have at some point gladly given away personal details online (Skinner, 2008). However what most of them do not know is that their data will be spread to advertisers for marketing purposes.

Free in Exchange for Marketing Side Effects

Digital content on the internet is moving from peer to peer sites; music, videos, books and others are disseminated for free on the Web with or without legal permissions, as the distribution on the network is basically at no cost. Therefore, some artists give away their music online when they realize their core business does not focus on selling CDs, MP3 or Videos; instead they gather revenues from concert, merchandise or licenses (Anderson, 2008). This is a good strategy when the authors themselves authorize their content to be provided for free, knowing that will attract more people who can be potential customers of some others goods that they have to pay for. The English rock band "Radiohead" is one of the examples of this free concept. The group let fans decide what to pay for the 10 MP3 files - from *nothing* to £100 (BBC News, 2007). This strategy seemed to fit very well with the band as they generated a fan base with only three albums so far.

Free in Exchange for Collective Knowledge

Beyond the benefits of marketing, the focus of this free concept is basically to offer content at zero cost in exchange of collective knowledge to produce goods or services that contribute to the welfare of organizations or people. This means that organizations stand in the schema of seeking the ROI (Return of Investment) in social capital instead of financial benefits, which is also called Non-profit Organizations. Among this schema, FSF (Free Software Foundation) provides software and even entire operating systems (GNU/Linux) for free. FSF receives very little funding from corporations or grant-making foundations but relies on support from individuals (FSF, 2010). However volunteers developers contribute on the source code to build entire systems. One more sample of collective knowledge for free is Wikipedia. It provides free knowledge to everyone in the world; its content can be read or edited for free (Wikipedia, 2010). Wikipedia Foundation is a non-profit organization therefore also relies on public donations to keep their projects running.

WHEN FREE BECOMES A PROBLEM

Violation of Intellectual Property

Artist and authors like Radiohead have the power to authorize the distribution of their hits on the Internet. Software communities like GNU also distribute their operating system (Linux) for free to anyone, implying that they grant the rights for anyone to distribute, use, update, research their operating system (OS). This is possible because Radiohead and GNU collect revenues from other activities and not from the sale of their content. However, for the authors, artists, managers and rental stores, the sale of every single song or video is the main revenue generator in the market. Here is where free becomes a problem and this affects not only the direct creators of the content but the thousands of people who work for an artist or company that are being fed from those earnings. For instance, the biggest movie, music and games rental store, *Blockbuster* is struggling against its possible bankruptcy. With more than 7000 stores over the world (Blockbuster, 2010), they closed hundreds of stores in the past few years, sales have declined by 20%, and profits are plummeting (Cinematical, 2010). This once profitable company has been threatened with the advent of online piracy. It has faced difficulties in competing against the free movies distributed through the Web, triggering a dramatic fall that places Blockbuster near to bankruptcy. The problem seems to be uncontrollable; the force behind online content distribution either from broadcasting or peer-to-peer is so powerful that laws, morality and ethics, DRM, and every other barrier to piracy that the labels can think of have failed (Anderson, 2008).

Customers' Misperception of "Free"

It has been demonstrated that unfairness of price have made customers abandon relationships with their sellers (Lan, Monroe & Cox, 2004). Consequently, buyers are forced to break relationship with their vendors and some of the times demand free content that gives a perception of fairness. However, what most of the online users do not realize is that what they are getting is not 100% free; instead they are paying with personal information, time attention and reception of advertising. Specifically, this becomes dangerous when the customer is not made aware what the vendors will do with the submitted personal data and information. If the use of personal information is not handled properly it can cause problems, leading to unfair denial of employment, housing, benefits, credit or a place at college (ICO, 2010). The social network, Facebook has been accused several times of violating the users' privacy. It has been reported that Facebook collects sensitive

information about its users and shares it without their permission. Moreover it does not alert users about how they use this information and does not destroy user data after accounts are closed (BBC News, 2008).

Free is not Sustainable for the Business

This problem has been faced for most of the paper-based media companies like news papers, magazines and journals. Information given away freely is a big challenge for these companies, as companies invest lots of capital on journalists, researches, professional analysts and general staff to bring high quality information which is not compensated by the price advertisers pay. The New York Times, a very prestigious news paper; has received a lot of attention for its plan to begin charging a fee for access to some of its web content by 2011 (Financial Edge, 2010), as its internet paper business were not as successful as its traditional paper business equivalent. This maybe a simplistic view of the drastic changes that media industry must implement to survive in the market, with users' willingness to pay for content continues to decrease.

Model of Free Content Online

The concept of free and repercussions it implies are summarized in Figure 1.

Four different concepts of free have been identified, among these concepts the different implications of free content have been discussed:

- **Misuse of personal information:** Facebook is an example where users submit their personal data in exchange of obtaining an account to share content, applications and build social groups. However users do not know how Facebook uses their data.

Figure 1. Model of free content and its implications

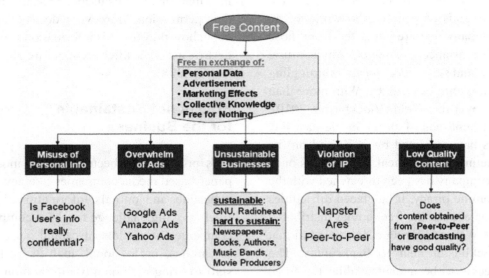

- **Overwhelming advertisements:** Some users get free email accounts, free web sites, free search engines but receive an overwhelming amount of advertisements that sometimes saturate their mails or the pages they visit.
- **Unsustainable business models:** Examples like Radiohead and GNU who have different, sustainable business models, can give away content because their core businesses do not focus on selling products. Nevertheless book sellers, newspapers and other music brands will find it difficult to survive if they release their products free because their products are the source of most of the revenue.
- **Violation of intellectual property:** The law in the web environments is still weak in terms of protecting authors' rights; therefore some peer-to-peer tools spread music, videos and other multimedia content for free, while producers lose revenues due to this "online piracy".
- **Low quality content:** Users' experiences also is a factor, because some of the content they get for free is usually junk infor-

mation being downloaded on their computers, or content of low quality, and thus low levels of consumer satisfaction.

CASE STUDY: SINGAPORE PRESS HOLDINGS LTD

Background

Incorporated in 1984, Singapore Press Holdings Ltd (SPH) publishes 17 newspaper titles in four languages. It has captured the majority of readership (79%) in Singapore for all news publications, and it also produces more than 100 magazine titles in Singapore and the region, ranging from lifestyle to information technology. The English newspaper, The Straits Times, is often considered the national paper and serves as a medium for dissemination of government policies.

The business model of SPH has remained largely unchanged over the years since its early inception. It is the primary print media publisher and producer in Singapore and the region. However, the Internet has brought about significant changes to the marketplace in the past few years. For example, unlike in the past, people no longer just consume information through printed media but instead, more consumers are flocking to the Internet for the latest news updates that is happening around the world.

Financial Performance of Newspapers and Magazines

The revenue trend of the printed newspapers and magazines business division, based on the annual financial reports since 2002, is illustrated in Figure 2.

As shown, from 2002, revenue has grown from about S$808 million to about S$892 million in 2009, with a peak recorded at slightly over S$1 billion in 2008. This represents a growth rate of 9.4% over a period of 8 years but which translates to a mere 1.25% compounded annual growth rate. By comparing to growth of the Singapore economy in the same 8 year period, Singapore's GDP enjoyed a growth rate of 62%, which is an annualized rate of 6.29% (Singapore Government, 2010) Clearly, from a purely business point of view, this growth statistic is far from ideal for SPH. It is the management's top priority to tackle this issue, in order to continually grow the SPH business.

New Media Developments

As the Internet becomes more and more prevalent in Singapore, in order to keep up with other developed world, the new media national initiative has served as a key driving force for the change of consumer habit. The Internet has penetrated almost every household in Singapore, and this is why SPH understands that there is a need to re-examine its business strategy. The Internet editions of SPH newspapers have been one of the SPH's products from the early 1990s, and have served 14 million unique visitors every month. However, it must be noted that most of the Internet editions of SPH newspapers, e.g. The Straits Times Digital (StraitsTimes.com), employs a subscription-based business model, and charges a monthly fee ranging from S$4.25 to S$12 a month.

Figure 2. Revenue of newspapers and magazines in SGD against year

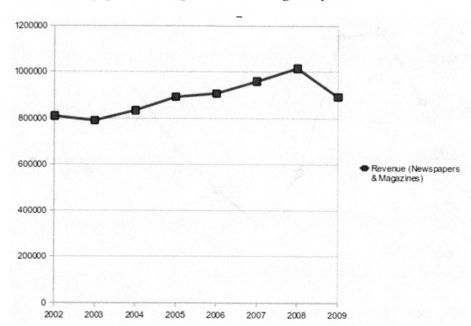

Lately, the emerging trend of Web 2.0 technologies like blogs, RSS, has further propelled Internet adoption into the mainstream. In 2006, SPH launched Stomp, the highly popular citizen-journalism website with user-generated material. At the same time, SPH launched ST701, an online portal offering classified advertisement ranging from jobs, cars, to properties, and acquired the popular Hardwarezone, a web portal specialized in technology products and gadgets. 2006 can be considered the time when SPH was starting to make a big push into the new media marketplace. In 2007, SPH launched Omy.sg (Online Mobile for the Young), the first bilingual news and interactive web portal targeted at online users from 18 to 35 years old.

2008 marked another milestone for SPH, as it launched 4 brand new web initiatives, namely the ST701 Shops, Razor TV, SoShiok.com, and Rednano.sg. It acquired ShareInvestor.com - the investment portal for Singapore and region. ST701 Shops is an extension of the existing online classified portal, which it tries to emulate the success story of Amazon.com from the Unites States. Razor TV serves as an online television service with a strong emphasis on local content. SoShiok.com is SPH's attempt to provide an online portal for all things food-related in Singapore, and Rednano.sg is the company's first attempt to create a localized search and directory engine. As can be observed, SPH has been extremely proactive in the realm of New Media Marketplace, with over 9 products launched in a short span of 3 years.

Financial Performance of Internet Media

Based on the financial reports of the past 8 years, we compiled the revenues generated from the Internet Media, and this is shown in Figure 3.

It should be noted that the amount presented in *Figure 2prior to 2005* includes the revenue from the previously owned broadcasting arm of SPH, Channel U, which was absorbed into MediaCorp in 2004. Therefore, we see a sharp drop in the revenues in 2005 and 2006. Hence, for more

Figure 3. Revenue from Internet media in SGD against year

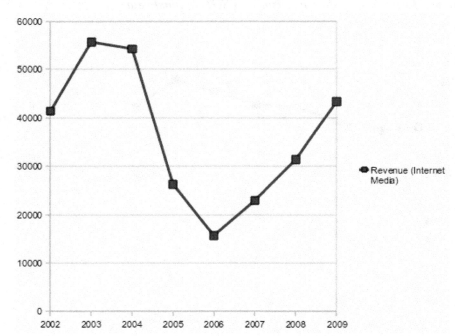

accuracy in the analysis, we only consider the revenues from 2006 onwards, which was also the period of time where SPH started its massive push for online initiatives.

For a period of 4 years, from 2006 to 2009, the revenues from Internet media grew at a impressive rate of 176% (from $156 million to S$433 million) which translates to an annualized growth rate of 28.98%. In contrast to the earlier analysis on the revenues of newspapers and magazines, the various investments into the web initiatives by SPH are paying off at an exponential rate.

Other Businesses

Apart from the media industry, SPH has also channeled some of its investment into and focus on the property market in Singapore. SPH owns and manages the Paragon, a retail and office complex in the heart of Orchard Road, which provides it with a recurring income from the commercial rental market. A new property project, called Sky@Eleven, was also scheduled to be completed in year 2010, which again brings in additional revenues for the company. The revenues generated from the property arm increased from S$53 million in 2002, to S$365 million in 2009, which is an astounding 588% increase.

ANALYSIS AND DISCUSSION

We can see that the exponential growth of the Internet has prompted a radical change in the market dynamics of the traditional news industry. This is largely due to the speed of this new distribution channel and the ease of which one can obtain information – in this case news – at a much faster pace and of a greater variety. The appeal of news via the Internet is the speed of access, and consumers in this digital age are demanding and refusing to settle for anything less than constant improvement to their user experience. Hence, to stay afloat in this rapid-paced and continuously

evolving market, the pressure is on news organizations such as Singapore Press Holdings to adapt to this new medium and to mold their business model in response to this new trend.

As seen from Figure 2 and Figure 3, there has been a decline in revenue from newspapers and magazines, the traditional forms of news media. This is a signal to the news industry that consumers are no longer willing to pay for content that they can easily obtain online at no cost. This is the point where prudent companies should start transforming their business model to provide what the consumer demands.

A crucial threat to the traditional news industry is the emergence of Web 2.0 tools, such as the general weblog, RSS feeds, and especially micro-blogging tools like Twitter; which are fast replacing traditional media as the best news distribution channels. Twitter trends go viral rapidly and news is disseminated in a matter of minutes, or sometimes even seconds. Newspapers which are published daily, cannot conceivably come close to matching that cycle time. Hence, the best way for companies to address these trends is to utilize this new media to one's advantage by making use of these Web 2.0 tools, and at the same time marrying the concept of free content and the new distribution channels, with the old traditional model of paying for content.

Another recommendation for companies in this precarious position is to look for additional revenue streams to complement their traditional mainstream. This could be offering free content, bundled with other regenerating product or service, or offering limited free content, after which additional content has to be paid for. SPH has proven to be quite successful in accomplishing this, and even capitalizing on this new media and the consumer's need to be a part of the content dissemination process. This can be seen from their launch of Stomp, which promotes and thrives on citizen-journalism, by solely using user-generated free content. This has proved to be highly popular with consumers and has brought in an alternative revenue stream for SPH in the form of advertisements which are aided by the high traffic to the Stomp website.

SPH has also launched many other online ventures; each targeted at a certain area and has hence made great progress within the Interactive Digital Media marketplace.

Pricing of content to generate revenue is also an important and is a challenging issue as the nature of free content seems to render these considerations obsolete and places companies into a difficult position. However, SPH's strategy here is excellent, as not only have they ensured a constant, stable stream of revenue from advertisements on their online websites, they have also succeeded in revamping their news distribution methods and pricing them accordingly.

This method involves providing short excerpts of articles online, on their main news site, and directing consumers to those online articles via Twitter news updates or RSS feeds. This free content is digested by significant number of consumers daily, who get bite-sized pieces of news that is just enough to spark their interest. Once consumers have read the gist of that piece of news and wish to know more, access to the full article is gained via a paid subscription to the news site or the purchase of the traditional paper. This is a much better strategy then simply charging a subscription fee to consumers across the board.

Using these methods, SPH has managed to not only traverse these new waters of the Interactive Digital Media Marketplace by adapting quickly to new trends of information delivery and the problem of free content. To succeed in doing so, which can be seen in Figure 2 where the revenue generated by SPH's ventures have made a sharp increase.

CONCLUSION

This chapter has provided some understanding of the concept, nature and implications of the new emerging trend of free web content. It has also listed the problems faced by consumers and businesses dealing with the shift from the traditional models to this new trend as well as the proliferation of digital distribution and discussion tools.

From analysis of the case study, we can also see that SPH's successful strategy was not to oppose the new media. Instead it embraced the arrival of new media in the form of Web 2.0 and the rising trend of free content, and adapt its traditional business model towards a two-fold approach of generating new revenue streams and pricing paid content to incorporate free content.

This prudent strategy has enabled them to transit relatively smoothly into the new digital era with all its accompanying trends and consumer demands. Hence, for information-based organizations to be able to deal appropriately with the problem of free web content in the interactive digital media marketplace, our team would recommend the solution of SPH.

REFERENCES

Anderson, C. (2008). Why $0.00 is the future of business. *Wired*, 140-149.

Blockbuster News. (2010). *Blockbuster's company overview*. Retrieved April 17, 2010, from http://www.blockbuster.com/corporate/news

Cinematical. (2010). *Has Blockbuster finally gone bankrupt*? Retrieved April 17, 2010, from http://www.cinematical.com/2010/03/19/has-blockbuster-finally-gone-bankrupt/

Financial Edge. (2010). *Free online content: Can it last?* Retrieved April 17, 2010, from http://financialedge.investopedia.com/financial-edge/0210/Free-Online-Content-Can-It-Last.aspx

Freedom Defined Organization. (2006). *Free cultural works*. Retrieved April 10, 2010, from http://freedomdefined.org/Definition

Geuss, M. (2010, March). The dotcom boom-10 years after. *Wired Magazine.*

Google. (2010). *What is Google AdWords?* Retrieved April 10, 2010, from https://adwords.google.com/support/aw/bin/answer.py?hl=en&answer=6084

Information Commissioner's Office. (2010). *Your personal information.* Retrieved April 17, 2010, from http://www.ico.gov.uk/for_the_public/your_personal_information.aspx

Iskolk, A. (2008). The danger of free. Retrieved April 0, 2010, from http://www.readwriteweb.com/archives/the_danger_of_free.php

Keenan, F. (2003). The price is really right. *Business Week,* 62-67.

Lan, X., Monroe, K., & Cox, J. (2004). The price is unfair. A conceptual framework of price fairness perceptions. *Journal of Marketing, 68,* 1–15. doi:10.1509/jmkg.68.4.1.42733

News, B. B. C. (2007). Radiohead album set free on web. *BBC News.* Retrieved April 05, 2010, from http://news.bbc.co.uk/2/hi/7037219.stm

News, B. B. C. (2008). Facebook violates privacy laws. *BBC News.* Retrieved April 18, 2010, from http://news.bbc.co.uk/2/hi/7428833.stm

Project, G. N. U. (2010). *What is the Free Software Foundation?* Retrieved April 11, 2010, from http://www.gnu.org/

Singapore Government. (2010). *Department of Statistics website.* Retrieved April 5, 2010, from http://www.singstat.gov.sg/stats/themes/economy/hist/gdp2.html

Singapore Press Holdings. (2010). *Annual report.* Retrieved April 5, 2010, from http://www.sph.com.sg/annual_report.shtml

Skinner, C. (2008). *Majority of Web users share personal data online.* Retrieved April 10, 2010, from http://www.computerworld.com/s/article/9112302/Majority_of_Web_users_share_personal_data_online

Wikipedia. (2010). *Dot-com bubble.* Retrieved April 10, 2010, from http://en.wikipedia.org/wiki/Dot-com_bubble

Wikipedia. (2010). *About Wikipedia.* Retrieved April 10, 2010, from http://en.wikipedia.org/wiki/Help:About

Zettelmeyer, F., Scott, F., & Silva, J. (2006). How the Internet lowers prices: Evidence from matched survey and auto transaction data. *JMR, Journal of Marketing Research, 43,* 168–181. doi:10.1509/jmkr.43.2.168

Chapter 7
Bundling Strategy in the IDM Marketplace

Goh Kok Min
Info Sys, Singapore

Kelvin Tan Yuean Soo
Info Sys, Singapore

Wang Geng
Info Sys, China

ABSTRACT

In recent years, many local telecommunication firms are selling their interactive digital media (IDM) services such as broadband and Pay Television in the form of a bundle to their customers. On the other hand, many IDM firms (e.g. Apple iTunes) have chosen to sell their IDM services to customers in an unbundled manner. This chapter studies the effect of bundling and unbundling of any type of information goods which can be digitized. We will discuss the four factors which encourage IDM firms to choose either bundling or unbundling strategy in their marketing of digital goods. The four factors are customer, environmental, firm, and product. This chapter concludes by emphasising that bundling or unbundling might not be necessarily good or bad. The choice boils down to the market segment – the value that customers perceive from the products. It is also important to take into account the overall marketing strategy that the firm is embarking on and to also consider the market situation at the point in time.

INTRODUCTION

Singapore's telecommunication sector is entering into a more competitive phase. SingTel has been leveraging on its paid TV segment and uses a bundling strategy to stay ahead of M1 and StarHub. It appears that SingTel has a head start

DOI: 10.4018/978-1-61350-147-4.ch007

based on its latest financial results. SingTel reported a 24-per-cent rise in its 2009 third quarter net profit to $991 million, which was driven by strong performances in its Singapore, Australia and regional associates. In order to make better profits, carriers would need to bundle services and cross-sell. SingTel and StarHub are better positioned to bundle services for the consumer market compared to M1, said Mr Foong King

Yew, research director for Carrier Operations & Strategies at Gartner (TodayOnline, 2010).

On the other hand, the unbundled age seems to be ushering its way in. The latest sign of this comes from Kevin J. Martin, the chairman of the Federal Communications Commission, who suggested that consumers might be better off if they could buy cable television fare channel-by-channel – instead of cable packages. Although cable providers are not happy about this, Charles F. Dolan, the independent-minded chairman of Cablevision Systems, supported the idea. Broadband Internet connections and companies like Apple Computer are already making it possible for consumers to download one television show at a time. Another form of unbundling is found within record albums. Sites like iTunes from Apple offer music song by song, and many users are cherry-picking their favourites. Again, this can be seen in books in which they are being unbundled. Google is digitizing mountains of books and including them in its search engine, allowing users to read modest segments online. In addition, Amazon.com says it will start selling access to some books a page at a time. Currently, Amazon users are allowed restricted viewing of book pages. (The New York Times, 2010)

With this distinct phenomenon, this chapter aims to understand what contributed to bundling and unbundling of digital information goods for SingTel and iTunes respectively. The next section will set the context of the discussion of this chapter by providing the definitions of the key terms used as well as providing two literature reviews, which will provide knowledge on bundling and unbundling of digital information goods based on past research.

BACKGROUND

Bundling has been adopted by many enterprises for a long time, but there have been no consensus among scholars on the definition of bundling.

Literatures reviewed in this area had revealed that bundling have two types, namely broad, and narrow. Broad bundling refers to two or more products or services being sold together. For example, earlier studies on bundling done by Adams and Yellen (1976) defined bundling as 'goods sold in the form of the number of packages'. Guiltinan (1987) defined bundling as 'special pricing to the overall sales of two and more products and services '. Yadav and Monroe (1993) defined bundling as 'selling two or more products or services at one price'.

Narrow bundling on the other hand is two or more different products or services are sold together in one price. For example, Stremersch and Tellis (2002) defined bundling as "the combine sales of two or more independent products" and "Independent Product" is defined as "each individual product has existence in the market ".

As the theme of the paper circles around bundling of information goods, it is important to understand the characteristics of information goods. Information goods are anything that can be digitised – a book, a movie, a record, a telephone conversation etc. Information goods have three general characteristics. Firstly, it provides an experience. You must experience information good before you know what it is. Secondly, it returns to scale. Information typically has a high fixed cost of production but a low marginal cost of reproduction. Thirdly, information goods are public goods. Information goods are sometimes non-rival and sometimes non-excludable. (Hal R. Varian, 1998).

Literature Review 1: Economies of Aggregation

Millions of digital information goods can be distributed at almost zero cost via emerging information infrastructure today. By bundling and aggregating these large numbers of unrelated information goods, which are increasingly available on the Internet and selling them on a fixed price

Figure 1. Cost and demand chart (Shaded areas are profit). Demands of bundles 1, 2, and 20 distribution goods. Bakos and Brynjolfsson (2000).

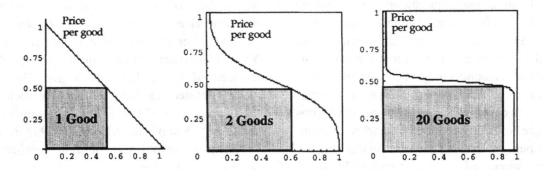

can be surprisingly profitable. Recent emergence of such new large-scale bundling strategies can create "economies of aggregation" for information goods if their marginal costs are very low, even in the absence of network externalities or economies of scale or scope. It is easier for a seller to predict how a customer will value a collection of goods than it is to value any goods individually. As a result, a seller can typically extract more value from each information good when it is part of a bundle than when it is sold separately. At the optimal price, more consumers will find the bundle worth buying than buying the same goods sold separately. Because of the predictive value of bundling, large aggregators will often be more profitable than small aggregators, including sellers of single goods.

Also as the number of goods in the bundle increases, total profit and profit per good increases. This is shown in Figure 1. The profit-maximizing

price per good for the bundle steadily approaches the per-good expected value of the bundle to consumers. As the items in the bundles increases, the deadweight loss per good decreases, and the seller's profit per good increases to its maximum value. The number of goods necessary to make bundling desirable and the speed at which deadweight loss and profit coverage to their limiting value depends on the actual distribution of consumer valuation separately (Bakos & Brynjolfsson, 2000). In addition, Figure 2 shows the competitive advantage by creating economies of aggregation.

Competing for Upstream Content and Downstream Consumer

When competing for upstream content, larger bundlers are able to outbid smaller ones when all else is equal. This is because the predictive value

Figure 2. Creating the economies of aggregation with bundling strategy

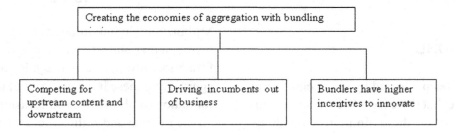

of bundling enables bundlers to extract more value from any given good. The larger bundler will always be willing to spend the most to develop a new good to add to its bundle or pay the most to purchase any new good that becomes available from third parties. Large-scale bundling strategies may provide an advantage in the competition for upstream content

When competing with downstream consumers, the act of bundling information goods makes an incumbent seem "tougher" to single-product competitors selling similar goods. The resulting equilibrium is less profitable for potential entrants and can discourage entry in the bundler's market. From Figure 3, it shows competition between a Single Good (A) and a Bundle (B). Single good providers can only charge a lower price, and be limited to a lower market share

Driving Incumbents out of Business

By simply adding information good to an existing bundle, a bundler maybe able to profitably enter a new market and dislodge an incumbent who does not bundle, capturing most of the market share from the incumbent firm, and even driving the incumbent out of business.

Bundling can achieve a positive effect from external. Products can be priced with bundle price using bundling strategy. This bundle pricing methodology could develop market share. The

Figure 3. Competition between a single good (A) and a bundle (B), i.e. font package, Bakos and Brynjolfsson (2000)

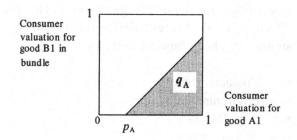

larger the user base for basic products, the more value can be obtained by users. This will stimulate more potential users to buy the product. At same time, the greater the user base of basic products, the more ancillary products other companies will provide. This will further increase the effectiveness of use on basic products. Consequently number of "positive feedback" is increased. The product becomes the market leader as well as the market standard. This becomes a "winner takes all" situation.

Bundling strategy does not only offer price discounts for consumers, but also enhance the value of the product from user perspective. For the entry-level users, bundling reduces the cost that users incur in searching and using for complex products. Therefore product value to customer is improved. For example, telecomm operators introduced free Modem and installation services as part of the bundle packages. Bundling also lowered consumer search costs, especially when basic products and bundled products are strongly complimentary to each other, the cost reduction become more obvious. After all consumers only need to make one transaction for all products or services that are bundled together.

Bundlers Have Higher Incentives to Innovate

A bundler can potentially capture a large share of profits in new markets, and hence, single-product firms may have lower incentives to innovate and create such markets. At the same time, bundlers may have higher incentives to innovate (Bakos & Brynjolfsson, 2000).

Literature Review 2: When to Bundle or Unbundle Products

Although this chapter is not specifically written on digital goods, it provides a generic view of when bundling is desirable or undesirable and it is equally applicable to digital goods (Paun, 1993).

This chapter articulates the bundling decision that companies make and emphasized that it is not final or irreversible. The factors affecting the choice of bundling or unbundling strategy can be grouped as follows:

- Customer factors
- Environmental factors
- Firm factors
- Product factors

Customer Factors

This group of factors looks at how customers think, how they behave and perceive the value of bundling products. For example, issues like all most customers have similar needs will encourage bundling since buying product A will most likely require him to buy product B. Putting this concept into the context of Singapore digital market place, we can see how SingTel provides bundling services for its mobile plans. Understandably, in this 21st century, iPhone users are not only making calls with their phone but they will also be using the service of short message service (SMS) and data on the go. This had led the telco to come up with bundled mobile plans, which include the three basic features (i.e. voice, SMS and data) into one plan.

Environmental Factors

Environmental factors look at the organisation's competitors and the operating environment that could include physical location. Physical location could affect bundling due to government regulations or economy of the country. Examples in the digital world of unbundling could be seen again from how different telcos react to bundling. SingTel first started unbundling of its mobile plan with the introduction of Hi-Card. This captures a different market segment such as foreigners. This inevitably leads to the introduction of pay per use of unbundle calls by other telcos.

Firm Factors

This particular area of factors is targeted at firm's strategy and/or other issues relating to the firm. It could be issues of proprietary control after bundling or cost advantage for bundling due to economies of scale. For example, in cable television, it is common to see how StarHub has bundled the different channels together instead of selling individual channels to users. Such a move will provide for economies of scale, which he/she can negotiate for better pricing with the content provider as well as advertisers.

Product Factors

Finally, product factors looks at the following questions:

- Are the bundled products complements?
- Does bundling provide a new and different product offering?
- Does bundling optimize product performance? Design, manufacture and service of all parts of the bundle is controlled by the firm may also optimize performance.

The questions consider the viability of bundling the product. For example, Xbox has bundled games with its console for selling. The console and the games complements each other very well and cannot do without the other.

CASE STUDIES AND DISCUSSION

According to the second literature review, factors affecting a firm's choice of bundling or unbundling strategy can be grouped as follows:

- Customer factors
- Environmental factors
- Firm factors
- Product factors

Figure 4. Factors affecting the choice of bundling or unbundling strategy

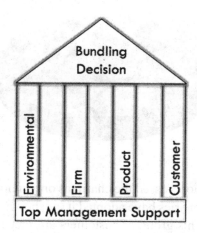

The following discussion on the case studies will be based on Figure 4, adapted from the 4 factors above. Case study one will assess how these four factors encourages SingTel to adopt the bundling strategy and in case study two, we will assess how these four factors encourages Apple iTunes to adopt the unbundling strategy.

Case Study 1: SingTel's Bundling Strategy

Introduction

SingTel introduced Mio TV service on 20 Jul 2007 to compete with StarHub, which was the only cable TV provider in Singapore then. As a new entrant to the pay TV market, SingTel introduced bundling strategy by packaging TV programs. The following will explore how each of the four factors had made bundling a feasible strategy for SingTel.

Customer Factors

Table 1 shows contents exclusive to SingTel MioTV. In addition to winning the Barclays Premier League (BPL) rights, SingTel has also secured exclusive broadcast rights to a suite of sports networks and services from ESPN Star Sports (ESS) for MioTV starting from mid-2010(Media Asia, 2009).

Besides these exclusive contents, ESPN Star Sports and SingTel officially launched ESPNews on November 2009. This is a first 24/7 sports news channel dedicated to Asian sports fans, which will be aired on SingTel's MioTV platform. The channel consists of highlights, scores, updates and comprehensive sports information, and delivers content from local, regional and international sporting events in a viewer-friendly format (Marketing Interactive, 2009). All these services are offered to their customers in a bundle.

Selling the information goods in a bundle adds value as it helps its customers save substantial time and money in this one-stop shopping. Research shows that non- monetary cost, such as time, effort and search are a pivotal concern of consumers (Paun 1993). By bundling the various sports channel into a package it will increase the overall value that the customer perceived.

Moreover, if customer needs are similar, the offering of one bundled product that satisfies those needs becomes a feasible strategy for the firm. SingTel customers who subscribe to the BPL might find the UEFA Champions League equally important since it is also featuring soccer matches. Therefore bundling the two content together is feasible strategy for Singtel MioTv.

Table 1. Exclusive content for SingTel. Chua (2010)

Channels	Shows Include	Exclusive until
BPL		2013
UEFA Champions League		2012
ESS, Star Sports, Star Cricket	F1, Wimbledon, Australian and US Open, etc.	Between 2013 and 2015
Season Pass US TV Series (video-on-demand)	Vampire Diaries, Miami Medical	

Environment Factors

For the Pay-TV industry in Singapore, StarHub has been selling its TV content in a bundle since its merger with Singapore Cable Vision (SCV). In addition, StarHub in recent years has used the bundling strategy to bundle its pay TV, voice, data and mobile services (BNET, 2002). Therefore, SingTel's pay TV service is expected to be bundled together with its broadband and voice offerings, rather than launched as a stand-alone service (OnScreen Asia, 2007).

The bundling strategy favours the SingTel MioTV because such a strategy is often attractive when the industry consists of competitors selling only a bundled product as no competition exists from unbundled competitors who specialize in providing parts of the bundle on more favourable terms. In addition, continuing to offer only bundled products in an industry may present formidable barriers to entry, thus inhibiting the entrance of new unbundled competitors(Paun 1993). This is because the act of bundling information goods makes an incumbent seem "tougher" to single-product competitors selling similar goods. The resulting equilibrium is less profitable for potential entrants and can discourage entry into the bundler's market.

Firm Factors

These are intrinsic to SingTel and were not observable.

Crossing the Chasm

SingTel's Mio TV is relatively new to the pay TV scene, as its operations started only in July 2007. Today the incumbent of Pay TV in Singapore is StarHub Cable. Figure 5 shows that StarHub and SingTel having 83% and 17% market share of Pay TV respectively. With a small percentage of 17% market share, it means that SingTel Mio

Figure 5. SingTel and StarHub market share in pay TV industry (ZDNet Asia, 2009)

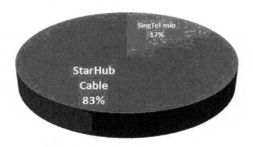

TV has not crossed the chasm as only innovators and visionaries have adopted it (as shown in Figure 6). This group of customers are focusing on perceived value. They are technology enthusiasts and visionaries. SingTel has identified a beach head, which is to serve the sports fans and meeting their changing needs. They do not however have enough partners to provide content, which can make Mio TV a whole Product. According to Geoffrey Moore, high –tech companies cannot cross the chasm without a whole product.

Therefore, SingTel Mio TV needs to develop the complete product. SingTel is currently trying to achieve this by partnering multiple content providers (i.e. BPL), ESPN Star Sports (ESS), etc) and bundling them as 1 product.

Creating Competitive Advantage

In October 2009, SingTel announced that it has won the bid for the rights to the Barclays Premier League (BPL) matches for three years commencing from August 2010. Frost and Sullivan estimated that SingTel's winning bid came at a price range of S$300 million (US$215.19 million) to S$400 million (US$286.92 million). StarHub holds the exclusive broadcast rights for the current BPL season, which will end in May 2010. The rights will be for Mio TV, as well as the Internet and mobile. In addition to winning the Barclays Premier League rights, SingTel has

Figure 6. Adoption and diffusion of innovation

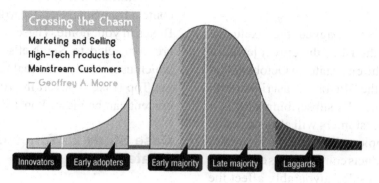

secured exclusive broadcast rights to a suite of sports networks and services from ESPN Star Sports (ESS) for Mio TV starting from mid-2010. The channels include ESPN, Star Sports and Star Cricket, which feature sporting events including the FA Cup, AFC, Formula One, the Australian Open, Wimbledon, The Open Championship for golf and the US Open Golf Championship. ESPNEWS, a brand new 24-hours sports news channel, is also set to premiere on Mio TV in November 2009 with other exclusive sports services that would be unveiled soon (Media Asia, 2009).

SingTel Mio TV offers the above exclusive contents to its customers in a bundled form. The appropriateness of a given bundling strategy centers on whether a competitive advantage is created. First, the strongest case can be made for bundling when competitors cannot duplicate the bundle because of the firm's proprietary control that is, the firm has a "license" to create a new and different product (Paun 1993). The exclusive content gives SingTel Mio TV a competitive advantage. This is because its competitors like StarHub cannot duplicate the bundle because of the SingTel's proprietary control.

SingTel "will not make a profit" from winning the rights to broadcast the BPL, but it can prove to be a critical tool to boost subscriber numbers for its Mio TV service and will boost SingTel's Mio TV to become the "number one sports offering in Singapore". Hence, allowing SingTel to compete

more aggressively with the Singapore's dominant cable TV provider StarHub, which currently has 83 percent share of the country's pay TV market. This recent content coup will enable SingTel to double its ARPU (average revenue per user) to reach S$45 (US$34.43) by 2013, coming close to StarHub's current ARPU for its cable TV service. It is predicted that SingTel is expected to add 231,000 subscribers in 2010 alone, with sports fan tuning into mio TV to catch the BPL. These numbers include 90,000 subscribers who are expected to switch from StarHub, 100,000 subscribers who will retain their StarHub subscriptions and the rest are anticipated to be new subscribers to pay TV service (source: interview with Adeel Najam, Market Analyst for Asia-Pacific ICT, Frost & Sullivan).

Although SingTel may not be making profit from BPL, its pay TV service may still be profitable. This is due to bundling of other products, which will contribute, to increase in profits and hence enabling the firm to gain a cost advantage. A bundled product is, in essence, a standardized product that costs less to produce than several customized products. Shared economies of scale can be reached as all parts of the bundle are guaranteed equivalent volume (Paun, 1993). In addition, the objective of SingTel Mio TV is not profit but rather, winning over the 83% market shares incumbent StarHub holds at the moment.

Product Factors

As mentioned, SingTel bagged the exclusive broadcast rights to the BPL, the crown jewel of pay-TV content in the city-state, in October 2009 and quickly bundle the BPL broadcast rights with other Mio TV offerings. By subscribing to BPL, it is highly likely the customers will also subscribe to the UEFA Champions league. It is important that the bundled products complements each other where one product's sales favourably affect the sales of another. Bundled products that are complements make the inherent cross-selling/buying a much simpler task (Paun, 1993). Therefore the sales of BPL subscription will also enhance the subscriptions sales of UEFA Champions league.

By bundling contents may also optimize product performance because the design, manufacture, and service of all parts of the bundle is controlled by the firm, thus ensuring that components will interface easily and work properly (Paun, 1993). SingTel Mio TV bundled its content and deliver to its customers using its SingNet Network and Mio TV Set-Top boxes in their home. Since SingTel controls all the delivery and interface of the bundle content, it is easier for both consumer and SingTel to ensure that it works properly. The following is an illustration of how Mio TV works. Multimedia content from SingNet is fed to the Mio TV Set-Top Boxes in your home. These IP HD Set-top Boxes are connected to SingNet's ADSL2+ network, which uses your residential telephone line. Your Set-Top Boxes convert the IP signals so that the content can be viewed on TV (Figure 7).

Case Study 2: iTunes Unbundling Strategy

Introduction

Case study 1 has provided a view of how bundling in digital good can be useful for various reasons and how SingTel has employed such strategy to its advantage. In the following section, however, we take a look at the flip side of the coin, how can unbundling be useful for the marketing of digital goods? Factors from "When to bundle or unbundle Products" by Dorothy Paun will again be used to examine the case of Apple iTunes.

iTunes Music Store is a software-based online digital media store operated by Apple Inc. Since the introduction of the iTunes store, songs are sold to customers by piecemeal at an affordable price of 99 cents per song. Recently Apple has changed

Figure 7. SingTel, 2010

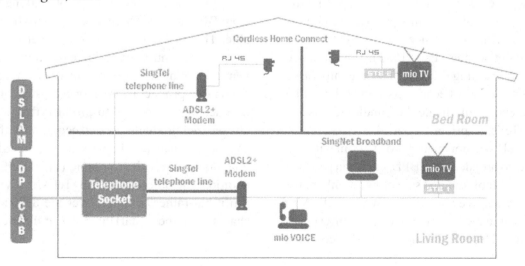

it strategy to provide a 3-tier pricing depending on the quality and age of the song.

According to an NPD MusicWatch Survey done in April 2008, iTunes Music Store is the number-one music vendor in the United States. On 24 February 2010, Apple announced that the store served its 10 billionth song download, having reached this major milestone in only seven years since being replaced online.

The shift from selling albums to selling individual songs, a new model embarked by Apple, has changed the entire industry and provides an interesting area of study where consumers prefer the unbundling instead of the bundled products.

Sections below provide analysis on how unbundling of the selling of music had contributed to the success of Apple's iTunes Store.

Customer Factors

One of the key customer factors affecting buying bundled products is the question, are customer needs diverse? Observably, customers' needs are diverse with the different types of music genre available such as pop to metallic. Although albums sold are normally packaged with songs from the same artist and similar type of music, not all songs by the same artist appeals to individuals even if they are of same genre. The sale of albums serves to be favourable for a segment of the population as it is normally the fans of the artist who will buy the entire album for collection purpose. Mainstream consumers will however prefer to buy only songs that appeal to them. With the presence of such strong customers factors of diverse needs, unbundling is inarguably the direction to follow.

Environmental Factors

Music house have controlled the selling of piecemeal music in the past. With intense competition from illegal downloading of music and the medium shifting away from compact discs, there is a strong push factor for the music sales at more affordable price. Music albums were selling at an average of US$10-20, which has given users the rationalization to download illegal songs instead for free. However, with the introduction of per song purchase at affordable price of about US$1, users are now prompted to switch to legal means of getting songs instead of downloading them illegally. This psychological change of behaviour by consumers could be explained using the fraud triangle as shown in Figure 8.

Using the 3 factors from the above triangle to make a decision on downloading illegally or legally, it is obvious that the legal option will be chosen. With opportunity and pressure staying in the status quo, rationalizing the cost and benefits, with a low cost single piece music would encourage users to legally download instead.

Firm Factors

With the iTunes store being a new entrant to the music industry, it will need to have a value proposition for its success for its launch of a music store. Unbundling in this case will increase the market size in serving new and emerging segments, particularly the segments of people who download illegally. In addition, unbundled music would also woe customers over from buying albums.

Figure 8. Fraud triangle

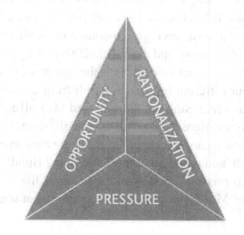

How is the cost affected by unbundling? This was also one of the important considerations that led Apple to make a decision to unbundle. The unbundling of music does not affect the cost of the product since this music is produced digitally and has very low cost. This leverage on the concepts of unit one cost, where the first song produced was expensive and each additional unit will be very low cost.

Product Factors

With the introduction of unbundled products, new and different products offerings are created. Users are now given the choice of lower absolute cost of buying songs they like instead of buying an entire album which they may only want certain tracks.

With little factors inhibiting the unbundling and understanding the different factors affecting the music industry, unbundling of music from albums to piecemeal has indeed proven to be a successful model to Apple.

Bundled vs. Unbundled Service

Based on our analysis from the 2 cases above, there is indeed no 1 size fits all solution. An organisation has to analyse closely the 4 factors to justify its marketing strategy of bundling or unbundling. However, advantages of the bundling outcome should be customer focused.

For example, in bundling information goods, the possible efficiencies from bundling can be marginal cost savings, customer convenience, or both (Evans and Salinger, 2005). Why will customers want to deal with the hassle of three or four different bills each month from different vendors (e.g. SingTel, StarHub and M1), all coming in at different times, all due on different dates when you can get one bill at the same time every month, and pay it all at the same time? Bundling of information goods make consumer life a lot easier. Moreover, consumers are likely get some

discount by having more than one service on the same bill. (Articlesbase, 2008).

On the other hand, for unbundling, the likely advantage to a customer is cost. For example in the case of iTunes, with an unbundled of music, one will pay only what he or she enjoys rather than paying addition money for music that he/she dislikes.

By increasing customer's perceived value will eventually lead to increase in firm's value. Hence, among the four factors discussed, the most important factor is the customer factor and company should take additional steps in ensuring that customers' needs are met during the process of bundling or unbundling of information goods.

Having said so this does not mean that the rest of the factors are not important. In fact, the other factors should be taken into consideration when the customer factors support the bundling or unbundling decision. This is extremely important. For example, it does not make sense to bundle at the expense of the bottom line in the long run (Firm Factor). After all, if a company is not profitable it may lead to a going concern and nothing beats the importance of a company's survival.

CONCLUSION

In summary, the study from this chapter has provided a comprehensive understanding of bundling and unbundling in the interactive digital market. The results provide readers with a good sense of when to bundle or unbundle. In a concluding note, there is a need to emphasise that bundling or unbundling might not be necessary good or bad. The choice voices down to the market segment – the value that customer perceive from the products. In addition, it is also important to take into account the overall marketing strategy that the firm is embarking on and finally considering the market situation at the point in time.

The results have also prompted a new area of study: "Will hybrid of bundling and unbundling of products work in IDM?" For example, SingTel is currently partially using such strategy. They offer users a bundled product such as SuperSaver English in their pay TV and move on to provide add-on channels (unbundled products) to the existing bundled products. Proposed methodology for such a study could include qualitative survey.

Another possible hypothesis for future research could be "In similar nature of information goods, consumers' perceived value is higher for lead information good than for secondary bundled information good." Taking pay TV as an example, similar channels such as HBO and Star Movies bundled in a package may lead to consumer's perception of the 2nd channel provided as lower value comparing to the first since both are of similar genre. However, this study should be executed with care during the selection of control for the study. This is because the perceived value stated in the hypothesis is unlikely to be true with certain information good such as sports channel. For example being able to watch BPL does not necessarily reduce the value of one watching World Cup though both are soccer matches.

Future studies mentioned above could be of interest to many organisations in understanding the concepts behind the perceived value of consumers in bundling and unbundling of information goods and leveraging on such concepts to bring marketing of information goods to higher level.

REFERENCES

Articlesbase. (2008). *Phone, TV, Internet bundled vs unbundled service*. Retrieved from http://www. articlesbase.com/computers-articles/phone-tv-internet-bundled-vs-unbundled-service-681817. html#ixzz0mHLuXbhw

Bakos, Y., & Brynjolfsson, E. (1999). Bundling information goods: Pricing, profits, and efficiency. *Management Science, 45*(12), 1613–1630. doi:10.1287/mnsc.45.12.1613

Bakos, Y., & Brynjolfsson, E. (2000). Bundling and competition on the Internet. *Marketing Science, 19*(1), 63–82. doi:10.1287/mksc.19.1.63.15182

BNET. (2002). *Duopoly rising - News analysis - Singapore's StarHub and Singapore Cablevision plan merger.* Retrieved from http://findarticles. com/p/articles/mi_m0FGI/is_7_13/ai_90427740/

Chua, H. H. (2010, April 9). Still two set-up boxes needed for good shows. The Straits Times, p. G2.

Evans, D. S., & Salinger, M. (2005). Why do firms bundle and tie - Evidence from competitive markets and implications for tying law. *Yale Journal on Regulation, 22*(1).

Hanson, W., & Martin, K. (1990). Optimal bundle pricing. *Management Science, 36*(2), 155–174. doi:10.1287/mnsc.36.2.155

Interactive, M. (2009). *ESPNews launches on SingTel's Mio TV.* Retrieved from http://www. marketing-interactive.com/news/16439

McAdams, D. L. (1997). *Multiproduct monopoly bundling. Mimeo Graduate School of Business.* Stanford, CA: Stanford University.

Media Asia. (2009). *SingTel clinches exclusive rights to Barclays Premier League- ESS moves to mioTV.* Retrieved from http://www.media.asia/ searcharticle/SingTel-clinches-exclusive-rights-to-Barclays-Premier-League-ESS-moves-to-mioTV/2008/37342?src=related

Media Asia. (2009). StarHub, SingTel squabble over Premier League content proposal. Retrieved from http://www.media.asia/searcharticle/StarHub-SingTel-squabble-over-Premier-League-content-proposal/2008/37879?src=related

Mooney, E. V. (2001). Vivendi points out its strength in European market. *RCR Wireless News, 20*(41), 26.

Moore, G. (1999). *Crossing the chasm: Marketing and selling high-tech products to mainstream customers* (rev. edition). New York, NY: Harper-Collins Publishers.

Net Asia, Z. D. (2009). *SingTel launches cloud platform*. Retrieved from http://www.zdnetasia.com/singtel-launches-cloud-platform-62055983.htm

Net Asia, Z. D. (2009). SingTel's EPL win not profitable, but ups ante. Retrieved from http://www.zdnetasia.com/singtel-s-epl-win-not-profitable-but-ups-ante-62058563.htm

OnScreen Asia. (2007). *SingTel expected to bundle new pay TV service*. Retrieved from http://www.onscreenasia.com/article-1220-singtelexpectedtobundlenewpaytvservice-onscreenasia.html

Paun, D. (1993). When to bundle or unbundle products. *Industrial Marketing Management, 22*, 29–34. doi:10.1016/0019-8501(93)90017-2

Point-Topic. (2010). SingTel. Retrieved from http://point-topic.com/content/operatorSource/profiles2/singapore-telecom.htm

SingTel. (2010). *How does MioTv work?* Retrieved from http://mio.singtel.com/miotv/about_getting-started.asp

The New York Times. (2010). *On the contrary: Unbundles of joy*. Retrieved from http://query.nytimes.com/gst/fullpage.html?res=9501E4DC1131F932A25751C1A9639C8B63

TodayOnline. (2010). *SingTel widens telco lead*. Retrieved from http://www.todayonline.com/Business/EDC100210-0000078/SingTel-widens-telco-lead

Varian, H. R. (1998, October). *Markets for information goods*. SIMS, UC Berkeley.

ADDITONAL READING

Arora, R. (2008). Price bundling and framing strategies for complementary products. *Journal of Product and Brand Management, 17*(7), 475–484. doi:10.1108/10610420810916371

Arun, S. (2004). Nonlinear Pricing of Information Goods. *Management Science, 50*(12), 1660–1673. doi:10.1287/mnsc.1040.0291

Bakos, Y., & Brynjolfsson, E. (2000). Bundling and Competition on the Internet. *Marketing Science, 19*(1), 63–82. doi:10.1287/mksc.19.1.63.15182

Bennett, R. J., & Robson, P. J. A. (2001). Exploring the market potential and bundling of business association services. *Journal of Services Marketing, 15*(3), 222–239. doi:10.1108/08876040110392498

Bratton, W. J., & Bennett, R. J. (2003). Critical mass and economies of scale in the supply of services by business support organizations. *Journal of Services Marketing, 17*(7), 730–752. doi:10.1108/08876040310501278

Christoph, B. (2006). *Estimation of willingness-to-pay: theory, measurement, application*. Germany: DUV.

Docters, R., & Reopel, M. (2004). Pricing for boom or bust: smart moves for maximum flexibility. *The Journal of Business Strategy, 25*(1), 39–44. doi:10.1108/02756660410516001

Docters, R., & Schefers, B. (2006). Bundles with sharp teeth: effective product combinations. *The Journal of Business Strategy, 27*(5), 10–16. doi:10.1108/02756660610692653

Gomes, P. J., & Dahab, S. (2010). Bundling resources across supply chain dyads: The role of modularity and coordination capabilities. *International Journal of Operations & Production Management, 30*(1), 57–74. doi:10.1108/01443571011012370

Heeler, R. M., & Nguyen, A. (2007). Bundles = discount? Revisiting complex theories of bundle effects. *Journal of Product and Brand Management, 16*(7), 492–500. doi:10.1108/10610420710834940

Herrmann, A., & Huber, F. (1997). Product and service bundling decisions and their effects on purchase intention. *Pricing Strategy and Practice, 5*(3), 99–107. doi:10.1108/09684909710171873

John, C., & Marvin, S. (1999). Optimal bundling strategy for digital information goods: network delivery of articles and subscriptions. *Information Economics and Policy, 11*(2), 147–176. doi:10.1016/S0167-6245(99)00008-6

K, J. (2009). "Bundling vertically differentiated communications services to leverage market power." info 11(3): 64 - 74.

Kevin, Z., & Bryan, M. (2003). The economics of digital bundling: the impact of digitization and bundling on the music industry. *Communications of the ACM, 46*(9).

Legarreta, J. M. B., & Miguel, C. E. (2004). Collaborative relationship bundling: a new angle on services marketing. *International Journal of Service Industry Management, 15*(3), 264–283. doi:10.1108/09564230410540935

Linde, F. (2009). Pricing information goods. *Journal of Product and Brand Management, 18*(5), 379–384. doi:10.1108/10610420910981864

Lorin, H., & Pei-Yu, C. (2003). Bundling with Customer Self-Selection: A Simple Approach to Bundling Low Marginal Cost Goods, available at: http://grace.wharton.upenn.edu/~lhitt/bundling.pdf

Michael, A., & Flemming, P. (2006). *Discount Business Strategy: How the New Market Leaders are Redefining Business Strategy.* England: Wiley.

Michael, P. (2000). *Competitive advantage: creating and sustaining superior performance: with a new introduction.* New York: Free Press.

Modell, S. (2009). Bundling management control innovations: A field study of organisational experimenting with total quality management and the balanced scorecard. *Accounting, Auditing & Accountability Journal, 22*(1), 59–90. doi:10.1108/09513570910923015

Mourdoukoutas, P., & Mourdoukoutas, P. (2004). Bundling in a semi-global economy. *European Business Review, 16*(5), 522–530. doi:10.1108/09555340410556602

Munger, J. L., & Grewal, D. (2001). The effects of alternative price promotional methods on consumers' product evaluations and purchase intentions. *Journal of Product and Brand Management, 10*(3), 185–197. doi:10.1108/10610420110395377

Ralph, F. (2010). *Optimal Bundling: Marketing Strategies for Improving Economic Performance.* Germany: Springer.

Skiera, B. O. (2000). *T* (*Vol. 52*). The Benefits of Bundling Strategies. Schmalenbach Business Review.

Vithala, R. (2009). *Handbook of Pricing Research in Marketing.* United Kingdom: Edward Elgar Publishing Limited.

KEY TERMS AND DEFINITIONS

Aggregation: It refers to syndicating Web contents into a single location for easy transaction or viewing.

Broad Bundling: It refers to two or more products or services sold together.

Bundling: It is defined as selling two or more products or services at one price.

Competitive Advantage: It refers to company gaining an advantage by doing more than its competitors by producing more values to its customers.

Information Goods: They are public good that are digitized where one must experience it before know what it is.

Public Goods: It means that consumption by one person does not affect the consumption of others (e.g. free-to-air television, national defense).

Unbundling: It refers to goods and services sold separately.

Chapter 8
Profiting from IDM Innovations:
Learning from Amazon.com and iTunes

Bakrudeen Hyder Ali Nizam
Nanyang Technological University, Singapore

Senthil Kumar Praveen Kumar
Nanyang Technological University, Singapore

Trichy Ranganathan Jayaraman
Nanyang Technological University, Singapore

ABSTRACT

This chapter focuses on how enterprises can profit from radical and incremental innovations in the IDM marketplace. It describes the roles played, importance, and impact of the two innovations in the business ecosystem. Using the ADVISOR Framework, we analyze the case study of iPhone for radical innovation and various examples such as Google, Microsoft applications, and Amazon.com for incremental innovation. We also outline the business model achieved by making a comparison between radical and incremental innovations.

INTRODUCTION

It is accepted that the long-term success of firms is linked with the ability to innovate by making improvements and introducing new market growths. This creates a rapid growth and high return on investment. This chapter discusses the radical innovation in the IDM market that will lead to such successes and profiteering.

DOI: 10.4018/978-1-61350-147-4.ch008

Radical innovation can be compared with incremental innovation; the former being concerned with the exploration of new technology, the latter with the exploitation of existing technology. Radical innovation is a product, process or service with either unprecedented performance features or familiar features that offer potential for significant improvements in performance and cost. It creates such a dramatic change in processes, products, or services that they transform existing markets or industries, or create new ones. Steve Jobs, on the subject of radical innovation, once said: "My experience has been that creating a compelling new technology is so much harder than you think it will be that you're almost dead when you get to the other shore".

Radical innovation requires organizations to move into unknown territories and experiment with new processes that largely elude systemization. In reality, there are a number of organizational factors that leverage the human side of making radical innovation happen. These factors could be utilized more broadly for greater radical innovational success and corporate profiteering when viewed systematically. Radical, breakthrough, discontinuous, step out, game changing innovations are all labels adopted in the academic literature and management practice to identify projects whose objectives are to create new to the world offerings and, concomitantly, whole new lines of business for companies. They are distinguished not only by the promise of reward they offer, which is not only large in scope and strategically important to the corporation's organizational renewal, but also by the risk and uncertainty that accompanies their potential outcome. Radical or breakthrough innovation is increasingly relevant in today's technologically competitive environment for the growth, renewal and even long term survival of most firms. Radical innovation is even more difficult due to higher levels of uncertainty stemming from long development times, conformist decision making cultures and the potential confusion of roles. Radical innovation is an underdeveloped capability that requires better understanding.

BACKGROUND

According to Robert B. Tucker (2002), product innovation is the result of a life that satisfies the needs of the customer problem through new product, which benefits both the customer and the company. Radical innovation has the capacity to destroy the fortunes of firms (Fosters 1986;

Tushman & Anderson 1986). Costly innovations that were made for many years by an organization suddenly become useless because of new innovative products taking over the market. Usually the small and medium sized organizations succeed in the competitive market by means of radically innovative products (Chandy & Tellis, 1998).

There is an overall general opinion about radical innovation that they usually provide a disproportionate contribution towards the profitability of an organization. This fact can be best understood with the help of its definition. Firstly, radical innovation provides significant improvements over the existing alternatives in the aspects of need satisfaction and thereby triggers towards higher demand. Secondly, radical innovation is usually based on new and complex technology which is usually difficult to imitate (Terziovski, 2002).

Radical innovation remains as the factor that has the greatest influence on economic growth. It has the capacity to create, merge or even destroy the existing markets. It can transform the small firms into market leaders and can destroy markets that fail to innovate (Srinivasan, Lilien, & Rangaswamy 2002; Chandy & Tellis 2000; Utterback 1994). Companies adopting the radical innovation, lead the world markets while promoting its competitiveness (Tellis & Golder 2001; Atuahene-Gima 2005). A nation's economic growth, company's success and the market growth are all driven by adical innovations (Sood & Tellis 2005; Landes 1998; Sorescu, Chandy, & Prabhu, 2003). The advantages of radical innovation signify its importance to companies all over the world. (Yadav, Prabhu, & Chandy, 2007; Measuring Innovation in the 21st Century Economy Advisory Committee 2008; Zhou, Yim, & Tse 2005).

Innovative companies with a range of differing attitudes such as positive orientation towards the future market or tolerance towards the risks faced during the innovation period prove to be the driving forces behind radical innovation. Apple Inc. is one such company that has proven to possess such attitudes and hence shine at radical innovation

(Tellis & Golder 2001). There is no need for this type of companies to count the number of patents or the number of research engineers, but the best way to achieve such a strong position in the market is by possessing good corporate cultures as driving forces (Business Week 2005). Companies in different countries have experienced that such corporate culture remains the driving force for innovations, though there are also other driving forces (Govindarajan & Kopalle 2004; Chandy & Tellis 1998; Nelson 1993; Kortum 2004). Companies having greater positive financial support for their innovations produce more value for their innovations and tend to be the most innovative (Sorescu, Chandy, & Prabhu 2003).

The characteristics of radical innovation vary in different countries (Furman, Porter, & Stern 2002; Andes 1999). Innovation of new products cannot happen with just a normal input (Griliches 1990; Acs & Audretsch, 1987). The companies will not be guaranteed with the monetary value they expect (von Hippel, 2005). The conversion of the inputs to the most valuable expected output still remains without any proper consideration (Hauser, Tellis, & Griffin, 2007; Chandy et al., 2006). Mairesse (quoted in Kortum, 2004, p. 358) pointed out recently that, "We have exhausted all we can get from our old data sets on R&D, patents, citation counts."

Figure 1 shows different product types with respect to how the newness of the product dif-

ferentiates itself from the existing products. It differentiates both at the level of technology newness and its level of uniqueness between the existing technology and the adapted one. Table 1 briefly describes in varying aspects between incremental and radical innovations.

FRAMEWORK

In this section we briefly discuss a minor variation of the ADVISOR framework (adaptation instead of adoption) and use it to analyze how revenue is generated in a business ecosystem.

Adaptation

Adapting to new environment i.e. technology and business for the better performance. In terms of business, companies adapt themselves to the new market by changing its business strategy to suit well to the local market with products that cater to new and existing consumers in a competitive market.

Disruption

Its tool or method which results in positive outputs and responses to the challenges that other competitors lack in the sector, creates a whole new technology or business strategy in a new

Figure 1. Managing new products (Source: Kuczmarski, 2002)

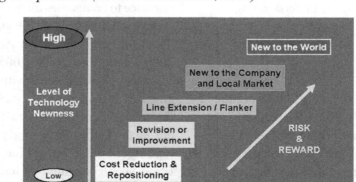

Table 1. Incremental vs. radical innovation

Focus	Incremental Innovation	Radical Innovation
Intervals of time	Short time interval which ranges between 6 months – 24 months.	The time interval is long, which will be more than 10 years in normal cases.
Strategy used for development	There will be higher levels of certainty, as there will be step by step development strategy.	The development strategy will not be continuous with a higher uncertainty.
Recognition for opportunities and generation of concepts	There will be higher levels of expectation for critical events with continuous incremental improvements.	The purpose and the scope can change at any time of the development and the unexpected sources can bring out great ideas.
Processes Involved	The processes will be formal with different stages for each process.	Unstructured processes.
Production of business cases	The reaction of customers will not be known, whereas business cases can be output at any required time.	Business case will be evolving throughout the development stage, whereas it is hard to know customer reactions.
Players involved	The roles will be assigned with the cross-functional team.	Skill areas are often concentrated with the assignment varying with the time.
Structure used in development	The assigned team, which can be cross-functional in nature, will operate within a business unit.	This will originate from the research and development team and will be dependent on individual.
Requirements in resources and expertise	All the required resources will be allocated with standard processes within the project team.	The skill requirements cannot be predicted early.
Involvement by the different operational teams	Different units of operation will be involved from the starting stage.	Operational units will not be involved at the initial stages, as this will lead to the shrinking of great ideas.

market ecosystem. It is also described as disruptive technology as technologies that have long shelf lives pushing technological companies to re-evaluate their products. Benefits generated would be in terms of revenue growth, customer value and high returns on investment.

Value Proposition

In the consumer segments value proposition is determined from the product or services provided by the company and creating the consumer's willingness to pay a premium price. The willingness to pay is further measured into value creation and value substitution. Value creation is concerned with meeting the end-user demand and value substitution is related to provide an alternative access to an existing application or service for the end-user.

Interface

User interface derives the success of a product or service on the basis of the ease of usage, simplicity, convenience and positive energy, all of which in turn generate a fantastic experience.

Service Platform

Value proposition improves when an IT platform is enabled, shaping and supporting the business process, well delivering the relationship associated with its product and services.

Organizing Model

For effective and efficient delivery of products and services, an enterprise or set of partners should have good organization business processes, value chains and partner relationships.

Revenue Model

To exceed revenue over cost, a good business model should have the combination of Value proposition, the way offers are delivered and good investments in IT platform.

ANALYSIS OF INCREMENTAL INNOVATION USING ADVISOR FRAMEWORK

To maintain consistent foothold by facing marketing challenges, an entrepreneur should understand the nature of the innovation, which in turn depends on technologies designed from the R&D department and commercialization into the market.

Incremental innovation is more evolutionary in nature as it is an extension from an existing product or process. Comparatively, stakeholders related to the business ecosystem, such as the supplier and consumer know *what value is generated as the end result*. This creates demand from the consumer towards the supplier side, which in turn motivates the supplier to provide more to satisfy the consumer's needs. For instance, the users of Microsoft Office 2003 needed more features relating to interface, to which Microsoft had in turn introduced "MS-Office 2007".

However, it is unjustified to state that all incremental innovations have an easy start. When a new innovation is created and aimed at large market potential, the manufactures have a higher risk of uncertainty while crossing the chasm in the "Categories of Adopters". Take for instance, the Microsoft products consumers of 'Windows Vista' and 'Office 2007' versus its predecessor, the Windows XP and Office 2003. The producers had failed to level out the gap in the technological interface, thus leading to lack of consumers who were able to appreciate the later versions of Microsoft's technologies. Fortunately for Microsoft, consumers gradually accepted the changes, which in turn generated a slow profit for Microsoft for their investments (see Figure 2 and Figure 3).

Incremental Innovation in the business model is as important. A good part of management tools are intended to facilitate this type of innovation. Quality control techniques enable companies to constantly improve quality, financial analysis helps identify mistakes to move forward, market research provides information to better target customer needs, and supply chain management are intended to increase the efficiency of the supply chain by removing non-value added activities. In some cases, the business processes have not been turned up for long periods of time and a more dramatic refinement is required –such as restructuring and reengineering processes. While incremental innovation may sound like a minor piece in the equation, it is, in fact, its cornerstone. It is extremely valuable in providing protection from the competitive corrosion that eats away at market share, profitability, or both. By providing small improvements via change in both technology and the business model, a company can sustain its product market share and profitability for a longer time, providing better cash flow and payback on its development and commercialization investments. Gillette, for instance, has done an admirable job of its incremental improvements to its razor technologies since 2000.

In new market niches, business models help create a common language and framework, define the factors necessary for success, and are useful to help determine the viability of a new business offering. ADVISOR defines seven variables that

Figure 2. Ribbon menu in Microsoft's Office 2007 suite

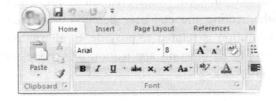

Figure 3. Related searches on the Google search page

can be used to assess the viability of any service offering (see Figure 4): We apply ADVISOR framework on Amazon.com's business model.

Adaptation

Amazon.com's DRM-free music store is a rather welcomed move by a major industry player, fore-telling the death of DRM, and its move to a new business model. Partnership approach of Amazon. com is another breakthrough in their business. This partnership approach is to let another firm bear the risk of selling products that had unique problems and share in the potential upside from such a venture. Amazon.com has three partners, (1) Large partners (2) Small partners and (3) Trusted partners. Amazon.com announced that enrolment in its Associates program had reached 15 000 online booksellers. This associate program itself has been quite successful with Amazon.com

Figure 4. Using the ADVISOR framework

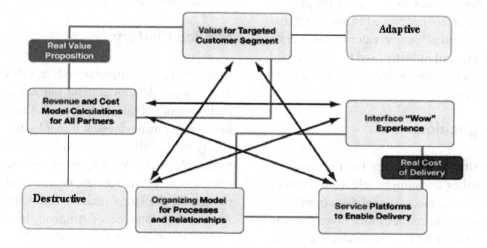

reporting signage up to at least 800,000 associates at that time. At this point, the vast majority of online retailers have an associate program.

Disruption

Amazon.com is the pioneer of the e-commerce and leader of online shopping because of its successful and well defined website. Amazon sells a lot of items online to its customers over 40 categories and Amazon attempts to customize buyer experience. Primarily because it is such an outstanding electronic communication resource, Amazon.com sets the standards, which others follow (Baxley, 2003, pp.382). Amazon has provided a platform for its customers to sell their personal belongings. Amazon has got partnership and alliances with other companies and it enables its customers to buy directly from those companies. Amazon's shipping system is better compared to their competitors, as they have customized targeted advertising and carry almost everything. Amazon has also created its own "product Wikipedia" called Amapedia, where shoppers share information about products in a wiki-based setting. Amazon also has the tagging system in place so that one can add tags to products or sort products out by the tags. With the help of the latest technological advancements ie. Web2.0, Amazon has created API's and systems that generate revenue by empowering smaller entities to gain online sales exposure. A simple and user friendly interface has played an important role in helping Amazon achieve greater profit than its competitors in retail industry, and this has forced its competitors to create value added services to its customers free.

Value Proposition

Value proposition summarizes the reasons why a business makes consumers select products or choose a kind of services. It applies to marketing statement that could attract more consumers to select the particular service or products that pro-

vided better solutions or more values than other offerings. It is very important for firms to use this statement in targeting consumers which will help in reflecting their strongest decision – making drivers and make companies in market succession. Amazon.com is a very good example of using value propositions to achieve success in targeting the customer-focused products and the required services. It runs as a huge on-line superstore that sells products and provides services in various categories such as food, stationeries and cosmetic products. Other than a traditional superstore, it has expanded to be a business which provides services such as advertising and even the source of producing new innovations by combined Internet technologies and superstore services.

Interface

The interface which is provided by Amazon to its customers is simple but is very user-friendly. It enables a e-commerce platform which is connected to a huge database for its customers to browse and purchase items from over forty categories, such as Electronics, Gourmet Food and Furniture's, and even provides variety sources of Digital Downloads, both within Amazon itself and to outside retail partners' contacts. All the distinguished attributes in its interface has played a important role in helping Amazon with achieving greater profit than its competitors in retail industry.

Service Platform

Amazon uses e-commerce web services platform between the developers and partner retailers in fueling innovations. As one of Amazon.com's fastest growing businesses, it enabled the solid reliability and stability for its e-commerce services by Systinet's WASP(Web Applications and Services Platform) to exchange new sources and information about the latest product line with updating the existing database of Amazon. It enables the ability of Amazon.com in dealing the flowing of the information between multi-vendors and Amazon by using C++, C# and SOAP envelopes as the backdrop and delivering of its service platforms.

Organizing Model

Business Processes are cross departmental and often cross-company related coordination of work that create and deliver value to customers. Business processes address the need of the new knowledge driven economy to integrate business process thinking with strategy. Also it addresses organizational structure and people issues. Organizations improve the business process to drive productivity higher and compete more efficiently. Multiple value chain participants must involve in process analysis and design because they must collaborate to deliver value. Amazon has built up its business into a multi-channel retailer by interacting with customers using Call Centres, Catalogs, Web Portals and Email Contact Centers. Amazon has built up its business into a multi-channel retailer by interacting with customers using Call Centres, Catalogs, Web Portals and Email Contact Centers. Even though sales kiosks are placed in its various partner stores, Amazon has a significant presence in its bricks and mortar channel. When the business process changes, the services supporting it must change as well. Visibility is an important value regarding customer satisfaction. For example, customers want to know the status of their orders. Therefore enabling visibility in the business process is an important factor. Amazon has built a new business by outsourcing in a relatively short period, selling goods on behalf of other merchants. Amazon increases its revenue by collecting commission on those third party transactions. Therefore the service oriented approach delivers strategic advantage that simply breaks apart conventional business models. Three operational strategies have helped Amazon.com to enhance its competitive advantage. (Saunders, 2001, pp.122-123) The 3 strategies are (1) Cost Leadership (2) Customer Differentiation and (3) Focus Strategy.

Revenue

Amazon.com has survived during the technology bubble burst unlike many of its e-commerce counterparts. Moreover, it has become a profitable company during these years and has made itself an undisputed leader in the e-commerce business. Its business model has helped the company to grow into a multibillion dollar business. Amazon was the first worldwide community which was built online. The communities of more than 40 million customers have thus been supporting the company to retain its lead over its competitors. Amazon added more product categories to sustain its growth and increase its revenue. Amazon found new ways on better managing all the merchandise it carried by developing new set of rules to solve the problem that exists from delivering packages sorted by geographical location to postal hubs and analyzing the relationship between items that customers buy from them. With the help of this analysis, the items could be grouped in the same warehouse. Amazon has expanded its revenue by selling other companies warehouse products. Amazon has transformed itself into an online shopping portal, Amazon Auctions, from its original role of specialty retailer for competing against Ebay. Amazon's revenue has increased by adding merchandise from other small retailers in its zShops. Even though the profits from the sales of products that belong to third-party vendors are smaller compared to its overall revenue, the margins are comparatively higher. Amazon has embarked itself into new technology developments and these developments enhance customer experience and satisfaction. Amazon has largely expanded its geographic footprint into the world's major e-commerce markets and it has acquired a significant growth from its International businesses. Figure 5 show Amazon's illustrious growth.

ANALYSIS OF RADICAL INNOVATION USING ADVISOR FRAMEWORK

In this section iPhone, a product of Apple.inc in US Market, is taken as a case study for radical innovation; and analyzed with ADVISOR Framework. As iPhone is a breakthrough in booth technological and business aspects, it is a consumer benefit in terms of interface, technological support, and entertainment and communication device. In the framework below we show the appliance of Apple as a product and AT&T as mobile service provider contributing to consumer satisfaction and profiting from their investments.

Adaptation

iPhone adapted the smart touch screen technology which is a breakthrough and cutting edge compared to its competitors. However this made its consumer to adapt to the revolutionary interface compared to the traditional key storks or buttons with the existing functions of device and features like 3G, Wi-Fi.

Disruption

"iPhone is disruptive technology because it has created a pocket desktop for users and forced laptop makers to give buyers more for their money" ("The iPhone as a disruption? For tech execs, yes"). By innovating iPhone in the mobile industry, Apple not only disrupted the other competitors, but also cannibalized one of its own product 'iPod Touch'. iPod Touch had most of the features in the current iPhone, but lacked communication services.

Value Proposition

iPhone created a value by integrating entertainment media and communication network together making consumers willing to buy the product. e.g. iTunes which can download songs using Wi-Fi

Figure 5. Long march of Amazon.com (Source: http://online.barrons.com)

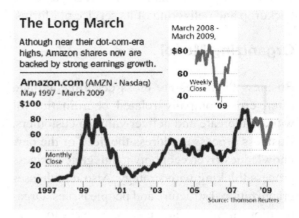

network directly from Apple Music Store without plug-in to any PC, as other mobile devices do. This is one of the features that had made consumers willing to buy the iPhone.

Interface

The success of delivery of iPhone and service from AT&T was heavily predicted on the user interface experience Smart phone touch screen technology for ease, Simplicity in terms of design and Convenience in terms of communication and interaction with the applications. The whole concept of iPhone was successful, because they had understood the consumer needs and made conscious effort to design upon consumer control over its interface and services plans. The development of Apps and Selection of Apps from iTunes Store in terms of interface and choosing the Plans from the consumer point of view and their willingness to pay for subscription fees where provided by AT&T.

Service Platforms

AT&T is the network service provider and Apple is the technical support to the iPhone. If a consumer is having a problem he/she can go to either one of the stores to rectify, which is convenient for the consumer. A consumer can either call the hotline or visit the website for technical support. The other new concept innovated by Apple is to allow consumers to become contributors to the iPhone, where a consumer develops an application and posts upon approval from the technical developer of Apple in the iTunes store. Therefore, iPhone acts as a platform where an independent developer develops applications for interested consumer to download, enabling peer-peer sharing of apps in iTune store for iPhone (see Table 2).

Organizing Model

Apple and AT&T are partners in the distribution of product and services by direct sale through their online stores and distribute through authorized dealers in U.S. The relationship between Apple & AT&T is that of a Partnership based on contract, where AT&T is the only one authorized Service provider in U.S who has licenses to sell iPhone. If a consumer in U.S. plans to buy an iPhone through Apple on-line store, he/she will be forwarded to AT&T site for the final purchase within the network service.

Table 2. Architecture and configuration of iPhone 3G and 3G-S

Type: Candy bar Smartphone
Operating system: iPhone OS 2.2.1 (Build 5H11) with
CPU: 620 MHz ARM 1176,[4] under clocked to 412 MHz[5]
Storage capacity: Flash memory (Original: 4, 8, & 16 GB; 3G: 8 & 16 GB)
Memory 128 MB DRAM [7]
Camera: 2.0 megapixels
Connectivity: Quad band GSM 850 900 1800 1900 GPRS/ EDGE
3G also includes: Tri band UMTS/HSDPA 850, 1900, 2100, A-GPS[8]
Dimensions Original: 3G: 4.5 in (115.5 mm) (h) 2.4 in (62.1 mm) (w) 0.48 In (12.3 mm) (d)
Weight Original: 3G: 133 g (4.7 oz)

(Source: www.apple.com)

Revenue/Cost Sharing

Cost sharing between Apple & AT&T was based on advertising the product and services provided by them. AT&T has agreed to a revenue sharing plan with Apple where the iPhone maker would receive a small portion of each subscriber's monthly service fees. According to the company's vice president of iPod and iPhone product marketing; since its launch, Apple has sold a total of 17 million iPhones—including sales of both the original iPhone and iPhone 3G. (PCworld.com, March 21, 2009).

Profits from iPhone and AT&T

Figure 6 shows that growth in the integrated mobile device contributes to good profits in returns and iPhone being the key contributor compared to its competitors in the Integrated Device Service.

CONCLUSION

An innovation always creates benefits for every actor on a market. However, the importance of its shares depends on the strategy decided by the innovator. Innovation is the successful exploitation of new ideas. Innovation should not be confused with technology. Innovation is the way to stay ahead of the competition. If well exploited, it will improve business survivability and lead to increased profits. Usually the small and medium sized organizations succeed in the competitive market by means of radically innovative products. Radical innovation is crucial to the growth of firms and economies. Radical innovation has the capacity to destroy the fortunes of firms. Costly innovations that were made for many years by an organization suddenly becomes useless because of new innovative products taking over the market. Radical innovation provides significant improvements over the existing alternatives in the aspects of need satisfaction and thereby triggers towards

Figure 6. Integrated device growth

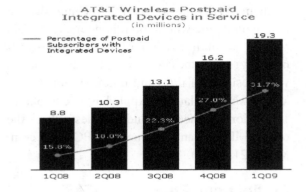

higher demand. Radical innovation is usually based on new and complex technology which is usually difficult to imitate.

In new market spaces with new products and services, new partners, and new IT-based delivery platforms, the search for viable business models is a critical activity. It is therefore especially important to better articulate and define the elements of a business model and their interactions in order to be able to (1) get a common language and framework that can be used to have intelligent conversations; (2) use the framework to assess the viability of new business propositions; and (3) understand the multiple elements that have to be in place for a business model to be successful in a niche business ecosystem. The success of delivery of a product or service is heavily predicated on the user interface experience in terms of ease of use, simplicity, convenience, and positive energy that it generates. A great value proposition with a rickety user interface experience is not viable. Similarly a great user interface can significantly alter the value of proposition.

Most of the online businesses depend crucially on IT for its competitiveness. Amazon.com has emerged in the e-commerce business in various ways and many of the ways are holding

significant promises. Amazon.com is profiting from electronic procurement with its high quantity of buying activity from the customers. Organizing Model, IT Platforms and Service Platforms are critical components in IDM environments. These components enable, shape and support the business processes which are important to improve the value proposition. Companies should find new ways to attract customers by offering better value propositions than their competitors. It is not only in the terms of price. It has to find better ways to successfully compete and increase its market share. If the companies play by the rules they create in the market then it is not easy to successfully compete against large and more established competitors. A firm has to reconsider and optimize its business model, processes and supporting systems for all value creation systems. Creation of new ideas to organize activities to increase market offering, usage of current technologies and setting new performance standards is crucial for it to become a market leader. It is possible to create a new business value creation source to gain sustaining advantages in the market by altering major business principles.

Considering the iPhone as the radical innovation and analyzing with the 'ADVISOR'

Framework, we highlighted the role of partnership between Apple and AT&T and focus on their business strategy on targeting the consumer segment by consumer needs, control and satisfaction over their investments. This in turn yields to profits for Apple and AT&T in the long run.

REFERENCES

Acs, Z., & Audretsch, D. (1987). Innovation, market structure, and firm size. *The Review of Economics and Statistics, 69*(4), 678–690. doi:10.2307/1935950

Aestebro, T., & Dahlin, K. (2005). Opportunity knocks. *Research Policy, 34*, 1404–1418. doi:10.1016/j.respol.2005.06.003

Ahuja, G., & Lampert, C. M. (2001). Entrepreneurship in the large corporation: A longitudinal study of how established firms create breakthrough inventions. *Strategic Management Journal, 22*, 521–543. doi:10.1002/smj.176

Ally Insider. (2008). Amazon Kindle a $750 million iPod-like business by 2010. Retrieved May 27, 2008, from www.allyinsider.com

Atuahene-Gima, K. (2005). Resolving the capability—rigidity paradox in new product innovation. *Journal of Marketing, 69*(4), 61–83. doi:10.1509/jmkg.2005.69.4.61

Business Week. (2005, September 6). Apple's other legacy: Top designers. *Business Week Online.* Retrieved from www.businessweek.com/technology/content/sep2005/tc2005096_1655_tc210.htm

Chandrasekaran, D., & Tellis, G. J. (2007). A critical review of marketing research on diffusion of new products. *Review of Marketing Research,* (pp. 39-80). (Marshall School of Business Working Paper No. MKT 01-08). Available at SSRN: http://ssrn.com/abstract=969775.

Chandrasekaran, D., & Tellis, G. J. (2008). The global takeoff of new products: Culture, wealth, or vanishing differences. *Marketing Science, 27*(1), 1–17.

Chandy, R., Hopstaken, B., Narasimhan, O., & Prabhu, J. (2006). From invention to innovation: Conversion ability in product development. *JMR, Journal of Marketing Research, 43*(3), 494–508. doi:10.1509/jmkr.43.3.494

Chandy, R., & Tellis, G. (2000). The incumbent's curse? Incumbency, size and radical product innovation. *Journal of Marketing, 64*(July), 1–17. doi:10.1509/jmkg.64.3.1.18033

Chandy, R., & Tellis, G. J. (1998). Organizing for radical product innovation: The overlooked role of willingness to cannibalize. *JMR, Journal of Marketing Research, 35*(4), 474–488. doi:10.2307/3152166

Dewar, R. D., & Dutton, J. E. (1986). The adoption of radical and incremental innovations: An empirical analysis. *Management Science, 32*(11), 1422–1433. doi:10.1287/mnsc.32.11.1422

Ettlie, J. E., Bridges, W., & O'Keefe, R. (1984). Organizational strategy and structural differences for radical vs. incremental innovation. *Management Science, 30*, 682–695. doi:10.1287/mnsc.30.6.682

Feldstein, J., & Flanagan, C. (2000). Handspring: Partnerships. In Kraemer et al. (Eds.), *Refining and extending the business model with Information Technology: Dell Computer Corporation. Information Society, 16*, 5-21.

Finnegan, A. (2009, January 9). *The iPhone as a disruption? For tech execs, yes.* Retrieved from lasvegassun.com

Foster, V. (1986). *Innovation: The attacker's advantage.* New York, NY: Summit Books.

Freeman, C., & Soete, L. (1997). *The economics of industrial innovation* (3rd ed.). Cambridge, MA: MIT Press.

Furman, J. L., Porter, M. E., & Stern, S. (2002). The determinants of national innovative capacity. *Research Policy, 31,* 899–933. doi:10.1016/S0048-7333(01)00152-4

Govindarajan, V., & Kopalle, P. (2004). *How legacy firms can introduce radical and disruptive innovations: Theoretical and empirical analyses.* Working paper, Dartmouth College.

Griliches, Z. (1990). Patent statistics as economic indicators. *Journal of Economic Literature, 28,* 1661–1707.

Hauser, J., Tellis, G., & Griffin, A. (2007). Research on innovation and new products: A review and agenda for marketing science. *Marketing Science, 25*(6), 687–717. doi:10.1287/mksc.1050.0144

Innovation Metrics. (2007). *Measuring innovation in the 21st century: Economy Advisory Committee, meeting transcript.* Retrieved from http://www.innovationmetrics.gov

Kortum, S. S. (2004). An R&D roundtable. *Economics of Innovation and New Technology, 13*(4), 349–363. doi:10.1080/10438590410001629034

Landes, D. (1999). *The wealth and poverty of nations: Why some are so rich and some so poor.* New York, NY: W.W. Norton.

Nelson, R. R. (1993). *National innovation systems: A comparative analysis.* Oxford, UK: Oxford University Press.

Saunders, R. (2001). *Business: The Amazon.com.* UK: Capstone Publishing Limited.

Sood, A., & Tellis, G. J. (2005). Technological evolution and radical innovation. *Journal of Marketing, 69*(3), 152–168. doi:10.1509/jmkg.69.3.152.66361

Sorescu, A., Chandy, R., & Prabhu, J. (2003). Sources and financial consequences of radical innovation: Insights from pharmaceuticals. *Journal of Marketing, 67*(4), 82–101. doi:10.1509/jmkg.67.4.82.18687

Srinivasan, R., Lilien, G. L., & Rangaswamy, A. (2002). Technological opportunism and radical technology adoption: An application to e-business. *Journal of Marketing, 66*(3), 47–60. doi:10.1509/jmkg.66.3.47.18508

Tellis, G. J., & Golder, P. (2001). *Will and vision: How latecomers grow to dominate markets.* New York, NY: McGraw-Hill.

Tellis, G. J., Stremersch, S., & Yin, E. (2003). The international takeoff of new products: Economics, culture and country innovativeness. *Marketing Science, 22*(2), 161–187. doi:10.1287/mksc.22.2.188.16041

Terziovski, M. (2002). *Portfolios of interfirm agreements in technology-intensive markets: Consequences for innovation and profitability. Measuring business excellence.* Retrieved from www.emeraldinsight.com

Tucker, R. B. (2008). *Driving growth through innovation: How leading firms are transforming their futures.*

Tushman, M., & Anderson, P. (1986). Technological discontinuities and organization environments. *Administrative Science Quarterly, 31,* 604–633. doi:10.2307/2392832

Utterback, J. (1994). *Mastering the dynamics of innovation.* Cambridge, MA: HBS Press.

von Hippel, E. (2005). *Democratizing innovation.* Cambridge, MA: MIT Press.

Yadav, M., Prabhu, J. C., & Chandy, R. J. (2007). Managing the future: CEO attention and innovation outcomes. *Journal of Marketing, 71*(4), 84–101. doi:10.1509/jmkg.71.4.84

Zhou, K. Z., Yim, C. K. B., & Tse, D. K. (2005). The effects of strategic orientations on technology- and market-based breakthrough innovations. *Journal of Marketing, 69*(2), 42–60. doi:10.1509/jmkg.69.2.42.60756

Chapter 9
The Issue of Fragmentation on Mobile Games Platforms

Tan Keng Tiong
Nanyang Technological University, Singapore

Ge Tianyi
Nanyang Technological University, Singapore

Rajkumar Sopra
Nanyang Technological University, Singapore

Ravi Sharma
Nanyang Technological University, Singapore

ABSTRACT

The rapid growth of mobile device usage in recent years has given rise to the problem of fragmentation in mobile platforms. In this chapter, we address the background of the rise in mobile devices and their platforms. We then look at the issue of fragmentation in mobile platforms and the effects of it on the parties in the mobile services ecosystem. We conclude by discounting the solutions that the industry has implemented to resolve this issue of fragmentation.

INTRODUCTION

In present times, mobile devices have become the fastest growing consumer products in terms of adoption. There have been more phones shipped each year than automobiles and personal computers combined (Mahatanankoon et al. 2005; Clarke & Madison, 2001). It is thus not surprising that the market value of the mobile game, which is only 0.46 billion Euros in 2003, had soared to 1.65 billion euros in 2006 (Mobile, 2006). In addition, the mobile game market is expected to grow to 9 billion euros by 2011(Jordan, 2007).

Mobile games have quite a few advantages compared to PC and console games. Mobile games are ubiquitous and portable; allowing people to game anywhere, anytime. In addition, they can serve as a practical alternative to PC-based games (Okazaki et al., 2007). While mobile games could be played with mobile phones or other hand-held gaming devices, this chapter focuses solely on games that are being played on mobile phones.

DOI: 10.4018/978-1-61350-147-4.ch009

The fast growing mobile game industry has a prominent role in the area of mobile technology development. Games, similar to the experiences with Internet shows, are among the few network data services which consumers are willing to pay for (Nokia, 2004). Since mobile phones are being rapidly embedded with software platforms, which are capable of supporting gaming, many handset manufacturers, operators and game developers have come to recognize the opportunities in mobile games.

In the current market, there are 5 significant mobile platforms - Android, iPhone OS, J2ME, Symbian OS and Windows Mobile - all of which make up close to 100% of the market. These popular platforms offer extensive middleware support, to help developers create rich mobile applications rapidly. This includes allowing a developer access to different platform resources, such as the underlying operating system, middleware components, useful libraries and tools, etc. An example is the Linux-based open-source platform that Android provides to third-party developers which allows them to create and port their applications, while at the same time making use of services like search, Gmail and Google Maps. Similarly, Nokia S60, iPhone OS offer their own application development environments. Most platforms also provide applications with interfaces that allow them to access an abundance of information on the mobile handset. Information, such as user contact, calendar, geographic location, as well as functionalities like making calls, sending SMSs, using the camera, and so on. By combining application logic with these platform interfaces, richer applications may be created. For example, using the location information available on the mobile phone, one can design a number of location-based applications.

However these mobile platforms are not interoperable as each differs in their interfaces and service access points. This is due to the portability of mobile applications across multiple platforms. This fragmentation of mobile platforms has become a problem that cannot be ignored (Fasli & Michalakopoulos, 2008) particularly in the mobile gaming area with its massively parallel community. In the remainder of this chapter, we discuss how this problem of fragmentation affects the parties in the mobile game application market, and offer some recommendations on how to achieve standardization of mobile gaming platform.

The Development of Mobile Devices

In 1946, the first global mobile network was introduced by the USA and it could only be used nationally today for it was mainly developed for military purposes. However, it was not until the end of the 1950's that the Analog network (A-network) replaced this technique. In 1973, Motorola launched a prototype of the first cellular telephone in the world. It was approximately 12 inches long, weighted 2 pounds, costed US$3995. This cell phone, which became commercially available in 1983, could provide one hour of talk time and could store up to 30 phone numbers. Within a year, 300,000 people from all over the world sought to claim ownership of this phone. This hardly crossed the chasm but the steadily declining price of the mobile phone has brought about a striking market growth and a plethora of applications.

In 1982 the Finnish handset manufacturer Nokia launched its first mobile phone, "Mobira Senator" which looked much like a portable radio weighing 21 pounds. Bell South/IBM released the first cell phone with PDA features in 1993. It included applications and capability such as phone and pager functionalities, calendar and calculator as well as electronic mail and fax. The weight was about 18 pounds and it was sold for $900. Motorola's "StarTac" launched in 1996, was integrated with both aesthetic design and usability. It was much lighter than the previous phones by at least 3.1 pounds. Kyocera introduced its mobile phone QCP6035 in 2000 and was the first widely available Palm OS-based phone. In

2002, the Danger Hiptop launched the T-Mobile Sidekick. It can be said to be one of the first mobile devices with the integration of a Web browser, reliable e-mail access and instant messaging. The Motorola product-RAZRv3 then led a trend towards ultra-thin, stylish phones, which is still influences today's smart phones. It was the first mobile device that attracted people from all walks of life, mainly, because of its style, ease of use and cost. It is still one of the most popular mobile phones today.

In 2007, Apple released the ultimate market success with its design of a strong technology, interface and applications with the iPhone family of smart-phone (Speckmann, 2008). To date, it remains the dominant market leader with a third of smart-phones across the globe being Apple.

The Development of Mobile Game Platforms

Along with the development of mobile devices, the mobile platform also developed with what was used to create mobile games. In the early stages, mobile phones were equipped with simple features, and monotonous screen color, what handset manufacturers could do was to add simple, built-in games into mobile phones. Usually these games were developed on manufacturers' own proprietary platforms, and built into the devices that manufacturers launch for themselves, which user could not add and delete (Isakow & Shi, 2008). Nokia can be said to be the first vendor to launch mobile phones with "value-added" applications such as the pioneering "Snake" (Robert & Gupta, 2007). A number of other mobile manufacturers then followed the trend; adding games to their newly launched mobile phones, such as "Tetris" in the small screen of an Ericsson T28.

As consumers wanted more services in mobile gaming, Sun released J2ME in 1999. Java version 2 Mobile Edition can be understood simply as a stripped down version of Java which required a very thin client. The MIDP (Mobile Information Device Profile) framework is designed especially for handheld devices such as mobile phones and PDA. Since J2ME technology is advanced and can run cross platforms, it was instantly supported by many manufacturers and even became an important technical criterion for users purchasing mobile devices. Within game application platforms of mobile phone, mobile phones that support J2ME platforms are the highest in number until the recent iPhone phenomenon. J2ME software developers have also been increasing; J2ME has become the mainstream mobile gaming platform since the second half of 2002. In particular, based on JSR184 standard on Mobile 3D Graphics API for J2ME, 3D games began to emerge, and new mobiles phones, such as Sony Ericsson S700/K700/Z500 and Siemens S65, started to support 3D Java games running on mobile phones (Shivas, 2006).

Other software platforms are also emerging as more mobile device producers enter the market. In particular, Apple Inc's iPhone have risen rapidly to dominate the industry. In June 2007, the iPhone OS was introduced as the primary operating system of the iPhone. Initially, Apple had no plans to release a software development kit (SDK) for the OS, which meant that the only third-party applications with official support were web applications. In 2008, the first beta version of the iPhone SDK was released to allow developers to create mobile applications in particular games (AdMob, 2010). As of April 2010, there were more than 185,000 applications available for the iPhone OS with over four billion downloads (Apple Inc 2010). The iPhone OS 4.0 announced in April 2010 introduces multitasking as well as a slew of business-oriented features, including encryption for email and attachments.

Mobile Platform Interoperability Issues

As the mobile applications industry developed, there are many issues and problems that remain unresolved. One of the most pressing issues is the lack of interoperability (Fasli & Michala-kopoulos, 2008). With different types of mobile platforms which differ from each other in syntax and semantics, usage of specific data structures and properties, handling of platform specific exceptions, and characterized by inconsistencies in implementation by different vendors. This fragmentation of mobile platforms is a similar problem that also faces much of the IT (or automobile, for that matter) world. In the recent past, a few solutions had been proposed and implemented for the IT world. For example, standardization approaches such as POSIX, have been success-ful in providing uniform APIs for accessing OS services. Similarly, programming techniques such as abstraction through models aim to hide hetero-geneity in a manner that makes the applications easily portable. Although attempts are being made to apply similar techniques in the mobile setting, they fall short due to various unique characteristics of the mobile domain:

- Tight coupling of the application develop-ment and deployment model to platform middleware,
- Strong desire by vendors to offer differen-tiated API functionality to developers, and
- Rapidly evolving platforms and arrival of new ones.

As we have seen in recent times, mobile phones had been so readily accepted that more phones are shipped each year than personal computers (Mahatanankoon et al., 2005; Clarke & Madison, 2001). By the end of 2005, there were over 2 billion mobile subscribers worldwide compared to only 1.2 billion fixed landline phones. During 2005, mobile phones accounted for half of the world's telecommunications service revenues, and 40% of the world's telecom equipment sales. The mobile phone market dwarfs the volume of other consumer electronics.

More than a third of all existing subscribers bought a new phone within the year, as indicated by the 825 million phones sold in 2005 (Figure 1). In 2006, an estimated 930 million phones were sold, an increase of around 12%. This translates to a steady expansion of over 100 million additional phones every year. Much of the unit growth is happening in emerging markets such as India and China, where entry level mobile phones are cheaper than installing a fixed phone line. In the US, Europe, and Japan, growth is appearing in mobile device sophistication; an increasing number of the nearly one billion phones sold each year now fit the description of smart phones. The US is just catching up to the rest of the developed world in the adoption of smart phones. With such an alarming rate of growth, it is not surprising to see that more emphasis will be put on the problem of interoperability between the mobile platforms. It is apparent that the same problems of interoper-ability and fragmentation that had plagued the IT world will also plague the mobile world. What inhibited cloud computing 30 years ago will also inhibit ubiquitous mobility today.

Value Analysis of Players

The focus of this chapter is to look at the stake-holders involved in the industry and how they are affected by the problem of fragmentation. Figure 2 shows that the industry is divided into 5 categories and we will look at how they are affected by the problem of fragmentation. The suppliers consist of the mobile phone hardware producers, the companies that manufacture the hardware for the companies to sell, for example HTC. The complementors are the mobile applica-

Figure 1. IDC mobile sales estimate

tion developers, which can be split into 2 groups – in-house developers and third party developers. The third party developers can be further split into 2 sub-groups – large application development companies (e.g. Square Enix) and individual application developers. Next, the Company will be the firms that combine the mobile platform with the mobile phone hardware to sell as a product, for example Apple Inc. The substitutors are the direct competitors. The last group in the ecosystem are the customers, people who purchase the mobile devices.

Using the value net shown in Figure 2, we can now take a look at who actually benefits from this issue of fragmentation. The first group is the hardware suppliers of mobile devices. Take for example, Sony Ericsson; they were initially involved in the fragmentation of the mobile platform, as they had their own unique (and closed) one. However they decided to scrape it in favor of using an open platform, in particular J2ME, Symbian S60, Window Mobile and most recently Android. The strategy allows them more time to concentrate on creating new hardware without worrying about the software portion. It will also increase their market share of the industry as they can appeal to more users. An example is HTC, which is currently using Window Mobile and Android as its base platform.

The next group in the eco-system that benefits from this is the company itself. Fragmentation in the mobile platform allows the company to create a close environment where they have full control. This, in turn, will allow them to market their applications more effectively and also to provide better support for their products. The close environment allows the company to cut off the challenge from competitors and to allow them to have an advantage when dealing with third party application developers. An example of such a company is Apple Inc, with its iPhone OS and iTune app store (Johnson et al., 2008).

However, just as there are beneficiaries, there are also those who are affected by the problems of fragmentation. The first group in the ecosystem that will be negatively affected are the competitors. In this case we view competitors as companies with a sizable portion of the market but their market share is considerably lower than the leading company in the ecosystem. An example of this is Google Android, which owns a sizable share of the market, but when its market share as compared to Apple's iPhone OS or Nokia's Symbian S60 can be considered small (AdMob, 2010). Hence, competitors are affected directly in their profit margin by this fragmentation issue. This is because new users are more willing to use the products by the companies with the major market share as there will be more support in terms of

Figure 2. Value net

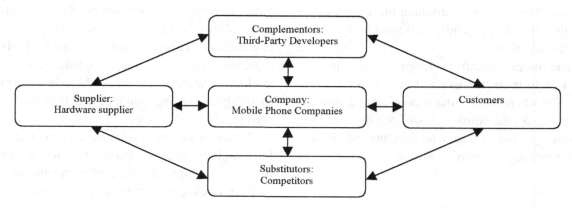

applications and accessories for them. In addition, existing customers of the competitors would be incentivized to switch over to the companies with the major market share.

The complementors, or the third party application developers in particular, are the other group of stakeholders in the ecosystem to be affected by the issue. The individual third party developers as well as the large application development companies will be affected differently. For the individual third party developers, the closed environment created by the fragmentation issue will limit their creativity and also the profitability of the applications, as they will have to obey the rules set by the major market shareholders. As for the large third party application development companies, they will be affected in terms of their business planning, as they have to wait and see if the platform to be released has sufficient users to sustain their profit. Moreover, should they want to distribute their application to other platforms, they will incur additional costs to their operations as their applications will not be portable and needs to be reprogrammed.

The last group of stakeholders that we will look at is the customers, who basically are not evenly affected by this issue. The effect of the fragmentation issue on this group of stakeholders will only be the reduction of the number of choices of companies customers can get mobile applications from. However there will be a group of customers who might be adversely affected by this issue of fragmentation. These are the customers who have become individual third party application developers, and are affected in the way mentioned earlier.

The mobile platform fragmentation issue can lead to protectionism and may also reach a situation where one company dominates and sets directions for the whole industry. Whilst there is a growing trend of fragmentation, the creativity of the industry remains un-stifled.

Ongoing Solutions

After examining the impact that the mobile platform fragmentation will have on the industry, we will now look at some of the solutions that have already been suggested and implemented. Standardization seems to be the obvious solution; though it is highly unlikely that a complete standardization of Mobile Platform will occur, despite a similar situation in the desktop world where there is a common standard within the different platforms for compromise.

How can such standardization be done in the Mobile Platform world? Currently there are three different ways of standardization. The first is the creation of one overall standard via the collaboration of all parties in the market. Google attempted by founding the Open Handset Alliance, a consortium of 65 hardware, software, and telecom companies devoted to advancing open standards for mobile devices (Android Wiki, 2010). It is a step towards the creation of an open standard that will be portable at least among most of the available Mobile Platforms. The second method of standardization is via third party or middleware. While there has been little research on such a solution, currently Adobe Flash seeks to be such a de-facto third party. However things are not smooth sailing for Adobe as Apple is trying to block such a move (Rawson, 2010) since it threatens the competitive advantage Apple has over Adobe. However it seems that Apple had overlooked a certain area that might still take away its competitive advantage. Apple had recently allowed for HTML5 to access its function (Chen, 2009). This is actually the third method of standardization that is being implemented in the market: standardization of the Mobile Platform by using an existing standard that is commonly used by all.

Although these methods have been successfully implemented to a certain extent, it will not be possible to completely standardize the platforms. At best, market players may agree to achieve a point where the playing field is level for all the parties in the ecosystem.

CONCLUSION

The increased usage of mobile device and games has pushed the problems of mobile platform fragmentation into the forefront and made it impossible for the industry to ignore. The issue is not a simple one to resolve, as we can see from the desktop world. However the problem has not reached the point that any of the parties in the ecosystem is in a serious disadvantage. The dynamism and creativity of the industry had not been stifled. It should not be allowed to reach such a point though. The industry is taking measures to resolve the issue, even though the reason for resolving the issue might be monetary. Some parties like Apple in the ecosystem will continue to resist such a change, as it will remove their existing advantage of capturing value. The movement to standardize the mobile platform will continue to a point similar to the desktop world where the different platforms are interoperable to a certain extent while maintaining their uniqueness.

REFERENCES

AdMob. (2010). *AdMob Mobile metrics: Our insights on the mobile ecosystem*. Retrieved from http://metrics.admob.com/.

Android Wiki. (2010). *Wikipedia entry on Android*. Retrieved from http://en.wikipedia.org/wiki/Android_(operating_system).

Apple Inc. (2010). *Apple Previews iPhone OS 4*. Retrieved from http://www.apple.com/pr/library/2010/04/08iphoneos.html.

Barbagallo, R. (2002). *Wireless game development in C/C++ with brew*. Wordware Publishing.

Chen, B. X. (2009). *Will the mobile Web kill off the App Store?* Retrieved from http://www.wired.com/gadgetlab/2009/12/firefox-mobile-vs-app-stores/.

Clarke, I., & Madison, J. (2001). Emerging value proposition for m-commerce. *The Journal of Business Strategy, 18*(2), 133–148.

Fasli, M., & Michalakopoulos, M. (2008). e-Game: A platform for developing auction-based market simulations. *Decision Support Systems, 44*(2), 469–481. doi:10.1016/j.dss.2007.06.003

Forum Nokia. (2004). *Multiplayer mobile games: Business challenges and opportunities*. Forum Nokia 2005.

Gruber, J. (2010). *New iPhone developer agreement bans the use of Adobe's Flash-to-iPhone compiler*. Retrieved from http://daringfireball.net/2010/04/iphone_agreement_bans_flash_compiler.

Ho, V. (2009). *Mobile interoperability to remain pipe dream*. Retrieved from http://www.zdnetasia.com/mobile-interoperability-to-remain-pipe-dream-62055375.htm.

Isakow, A., & Shi, H. (2008). Review of J2ME and J2ME-based mobile applications. *International Journal of Computer Science and Network Security, 8*(2).

Johnson, G., Lee, S. J., Middleton, M., Ngai, N., & Palmeri, G. (2008). *iTunes case study - Apple Inc.* Retrieved from http://www.plu.edu/~johnsogd/doc/itunes-case.doc.

Jordan, J. (2007). *Who knows how the mobile games market will grow?* Steel Media Ltd.

Leavitt, N. (2003). Will wireless gaming be a winner? *Computer, 1*, 24–28. doi:10.1109/MC.2003.1160050

Liang, X., & Zhao, Q. (2009). A point-based rendering approach for real-time interaction on mobile devices. *Science in China Series F: Information Sciences, 52*(8), 1335–1345. doi:10.1007/s11432-009-0144-3

Mahatanankoon, P., & Wen, H. J. (2005). Consumer-based m-commerce: Exploring consumer perception of mobile applications. *Computer Standards & Interfaces, 27*, 347–357. doi:10.1016/j.csi.2004.10.003

Malik, O. (2009). *How big is the Apple iPhone app economy? The answer might surprise you.* Retrieved from http://gigaom.com/2009/08/27/how-big-is-apple-iphone-app-economy-the-answer-might-surprise-you/.

Nakajima, K., & Hori, M. (2009). *How to integrate mobile technologies with an e-learning system.*

Net Mobile, Z. D. (2006). *Mobile games market report.* Retrieved from http://www.zdnet.com/.

Okazaki, S., & Skapa, R. (2007). Global youth and mobile games: Applying the extended technology acceptance model in the USA, Japan, Spain, and Czech Republic - Cross-cultural buyer behavior. *Advances in International Marketing, 18*, 253–270. doi:10.1016/S1474-7979(06)18011-4

Rawson, C. (2010). *iPhone OS 4.0 dev agreement blocks using Flash or Unity as IDEs?* Retrieved from http://www.tuaw.com/2010/04/08/iphone-os-4-0-dev-agreement-blocks-using-flash-or-unity-as-ides/.

Robert, M., & Gupta, S. (2007). *Nokia and mobile gaming.* M.S Thesis, Simon Fraser University, Burnaby, Canada.

Sanneblad, J., & Holmquist, L. E. (2004). The GapiDraw platform: High-performance cross-platform graphics on mobile devices. *Proceedings of the 3rd International Conference on Mobile and Ubiquitous Multimedia* (pp. 47-53). College Park, MD: ACM.

Shivas, M. (2006, August 9). *J2ME Game Optimization Secrets.* Retrieved from http://www.microjava.com/articles/techtalk/optimization.

Speckmann, B. (2008). *The Android mobile platform.* Unpublished M.S Thesis, Eastern Michigan University, United States.

Wilcox, J. (2010). *Apple's problem with Flash is mobile applications competition.* Retrieved from http://www.betanews.com/joewilcox/article/Apples-problem-with-Flash-is-mobile-applications-competition/1266602742.

Section 2
Technology Platforms

Chapter 10
Deriving Value from Platforms in IDM

Wu (Harley) and Sze Wei
Nanyang Technological University, Singapore

Niazi Babar Zaman Khan
Nanyang Technological University, Singapore

Satish Kumar Sarraf
Nanyang Technological University, Singapore

ABSTRACT

In this chapter, we will discuss what value is and how a firm in the Interactive Digital Marketplace may garner it with a fundamental technology option. Firms often come to a crossroad, choosing whether to keep a platform open or closed. This decision is never direct or ever simple. We explore the various value propositions that a firm may derive by keeping the platform open versus closed and see how the firm has to look both ways, inwards and outwards, to arrive at a solution. Market forces, though invisible, are strongly felt by the firm. This chapter also investigates how these forces affect this decision. Lastly, we propose an overarching framework that we hope may prove useful in aiding the reader with this difficult decision.

INTRODUCTION

As we approach the turn of the first decade in the new millennia, not only does the Internet provide businesses, institutions and individuals with an additional channel to disseminate information on existing goods, products or services it also enables geographically-separated computers and its peripherals to work together as well. External

network effect relates to the effect in which the usage of a good or service brings value to other users (Mohr et al., 2005). As businesses, institutions and individuals alike begin to leverage on the computational capacity of multi-core networked-computers, the information and value contained within the network increases along with the network effect accrued to each user. When caught in this dilemma between the introduction and the generation of closed and open platforms, a firm must choose whether to open or close the

DOI: 10.4018/978-1-61350-147-4.ch010

platforms and decide on how value can be derived from it. We will take the view of value from a firm's perspective.

INTERACTIVE DIGITAL MARKETPLACE

For the purpose of this chapter, we define the Interactive Digital Marketplace (IDM) as a landscape in which high technology digital products are traded, sold or exchanged. We continue this assertion with a notion that the landscape is based on the Internet and its underlying networking infrastructure. According to Mohr et al. (2005), several definitions of "high technology" exist and for the purpose of our discussion, we define high technology products in IDM in terms of their common characteristics. This is summarized in Table 1.

The Competitive Landscape

The competitive landscape in which an IDM firms plays a crucial part in influencing the strategies and decisions the firm partakes in. D'Aveni (1996) proposed a 7S framework in which we feel encapsulates the nature of the competitive landscape in which an IDM firm today resides in. This is shown in Figure 1.

The Global Virtual Landscape

Competitive advantages that arise from geographical proximity between a firm and its suppliers or customers are almost non-existent in the IDM landscape. The electronic network in which an IDM firm sits in erases the boundaries between firms along the value chain (Amit & Zott, 2001). As boundaries between firms blur, business processes are increasingly being shared between firms in different industries in such an efficient manner that it is generally not noticed by the end customers (Amit & Zott, 2001).

As information processing costs continue to fall (The Economist, 2003) and the increase of transmission throughput over the networks (IDA, 2009), an increased level of information goods with increased levels of functions and granularity will eventuate (Amit & Zott, 2001). The instant gratification nature of IDM products and services coupled with the increasing amounts of information goods transmitted over the network results in the dis-intermediation of traditional businesses and information brokers (Amit & Zott, 2001). This change resulted in traditional firms exiting

Table 1. A high technology product (Mohr et al., 2005)

Term	Definition	Examples
Market uncertainty	Ambiguity about the type and extent of customers needs that can be satisfied by any particular technology	Toshiba's HD DVD and Sony's Blu-ray disc
Technological uncertainty	Not knowing whether the technology can deliver on its promise to meet specific needs	Mars Exploration Rover, Hubble Space Telescope.
Competitive volatility	Changes in the competitive landscape, the products delivered and tools used to make these products	Amazon.com and Expedia.com versus traditional bookstores like Barnes & Noble.
Unit-one costs	Situation when the costs of producing the first unit are high relative to the costs of re-production.	Software creation are expensive but relatively inexpensive to duplicate and re-produce
Tradability problems	Underlying know-how represents portion of the value of the product or service.	Latitudes and longitudes coordinates of a particular location.
Knowledge spillovers	Synergies in creation and distribution of know-how further enrich the pool of existing knowledge.	Human Genome Project helps pharmaceutical companies to develop ace-inhibitors.

Figure 1. D'Aveni's hypercompetition model (D'Aveni, 1996)

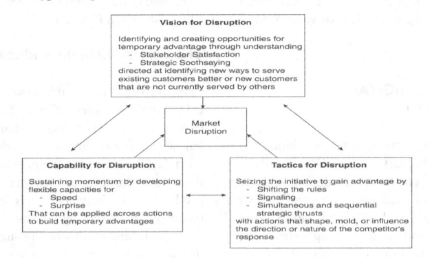

the market but also created new opportunities for others (Amit & Zott, 2001), affecting the way value is interpreted in a firm.

The Notion of Value

In order to appreciate the value that a product or an innovation brings to an IDM firm, we must first look at Porter and Millar's (1985) value chain model, shown in Figure 2, to discover how Information Technology can bring value to a traditional firm. Porter and Millar (1985) define value as "the amount of money buyers are willing to pay for a particular good or service". They believe that value can only be created solely by product differentiation. Product differentiation may be done along every component of the value chain towards a lower buying cost or higher level of performance. Information Technology in this aspect, garner value only by supporting differentiation strategies.

In the parlance of economists, a firm competing in perfect competition is a price taker and accepts the price set by the market while a firm in monopoly sets the price and hence the possibility for profit. The biggest difference between these two firms is product differentiation and competition (barriers to entry). With differentiation comes

Figure 2. The value chain of a traditional firm (Porter & Millar, 1985)

the likelihood of sustainable profits. We believe Porter and Millar's (1985) approach to value creation within a firm to be congruent with the economists' notion of using product differentiation to shift the firm away from a homogenous product in perfect competition market to a differentiated one in Monopoly. However, unlike traditional businesses with clear and distinct components in the value chain, lines separating the various components in an IDM firm are often blurred (Amit & Zott, 2001).

High Tech Supply Chain

The blurred lines between the various components that exist in an IDM firm is the result of inherent differences between an IDM firm and a traditional one. Porter and Millar's value chain analysis provides us with an internal perspective of the various activities in a firm. However, the notion of how an IDM firm works with others is also equally important. A value chain framework emphasizes the activities of an individual firm. In order to get a holistic view of value within an IDM firm, we have to look outwards as well. We believe that the high tech supply chain framework of Mohr et al (2005: 253) shown in Figure 3 gives us a good view of where an IDM firm resides in the GVL as well as the interactions it has with its suppliers and customers.

This framework clearly presents us with a holistic view of the various market segments that an IDM firm may operate in. Here, an IDM firm may play the role of a distributor.

Value Creation and Value Added

Value is created when a firm adds value to a product or service above and beyond the costs needed to produce it. Hence, value added is defined as "the additional value of a commodity over the cost of commodities used to produce it from the previous stage of production" (Porter & Millar, 1985).

Figure 3. High tech supply chain (Mohr et al., 2005, p 253)

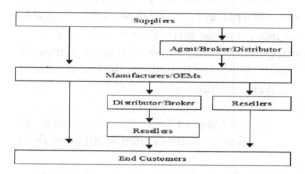

Example 1: Take the main dish of Filet Mignon which consists of a generous cut of seasoned tenderloin beef with a side of broccoli and potatoes. Let us assume the monetary cost to prepare this dish to be X amount of dollars, while Y dollars is the amount the restaurant charges on its menu, where Y is greater than X. The value added by the Chef is thus the amount, ($Y-$X) dollars.

Brandenburger and Stuart (1995) proposed a simple mathematical formula:

Value Created = Willingness to Pay – Opportunity Cost

Willingness to pay is the amount of money that a buyer is willing to part with in exchange for a certain quantity of goods and services (Brandenburger & Stuart, 1996). In the above example, this would be the amount $Y. Although opportunity cost is defined in conventional economics as "the next best alternative forgone", opportunity cost in the above formula is seen as the suppliers' willingness to part with its resources for a given amount of dollars. In the example, this would be the amount of money that the suppliers to the restaurant received for the constituents for the dish, $X.

Added Value

Unlike value creation or value addedness which looks at value created from a product point-of-view, added-value looks at the value that a firm creates from an industry perspective. The added value of a player is "*equal to the value created by all players in the vertical chain minus the value created by all other players*" (Brandenburger & Stuart, 1996). The formula for the added value of a player is as follows:

Added Value of firm = Value created by all firms – Value created by all other firms

The added-value measure provides a basis to answer how value is divided between various firms in the market. As we have covered the framework in which a firm derives value, the next few sections, we will attempt to discover value from an open and close platform as well as make a comparison between the two.

PLATFORMS

In a traditional computing environment, a platform is a specific implementation of a hardware and or software architecture that enables software and or applications to be run on. This traditional perspective defines a platform from a user's perspective. For the purpose of this discussion, we broaden the notion of the aforementioned platform to include participants. A platform-mediated network, hereinafter platform, is defined as a platform that "encompasses distinct types of participants who use, develop and propagate its use" (Eisenmann et al., 2008).

The roles participants may play fall under one or more of the four types:

1. demand-side platform users – "end users";
2. supply-side platform users, who offer complements used by demand-side platform users;
3. platform providers who serve as users' primary point of contact with the platform;

4. platform sponsors who exercise property rights and for determining who may use and partake in its development (Eisenmann et al., 2008).

These are analogous to suppliers, customers, substitutions and complementors suggested by Brandenburger and Stuart (1996) in their notion of a Value-Net. The interactions between the users are subjected to network effects and the network value depends on the number of other users (Eisenmann, 2008).

Open and Closed Platforms

The decision between an open and closed and hence proprietary or shared control occurs as firms develop new platforms (Eisenmann, 2008). According to Eisenmann (2008), these two models often square off against each other, so managers must gauge which model is more attractive. Table 2 summarises the key disfferences. Proprietary and shared platforms may also coexist permanently in some markets (Eisenmann, 2008). There are varying levels of openness to a platform; an open platform is one with the following characteristics: (1) no restrictions placed on participation in its development, commercialization or use; or (2) restrictions, if any, are reasonable and non-discriminatory in nature (Eisenmann et al., 2008).

There are management challenges that the platform provider may encounter as they create new platforms but the paramount challenge lies in finding the right formula for creating value for its users (Eisenmann, 2008).

Considering Platforms

Table 3 shows the matrix at that provides a model in which we can use to decide whether a firm should favor an open or closed platform based on the availability of the following information; (1) who serves as the platform sponsor; (2) who

Table 2. A comparison of openness by role in platforms; adapted from Eisenmann et al., 2008

Roles	Linux	Windows	Macintosh	iPhone
Demand-side User (End User)	Open	Open	Open	Open
Supply-side User (Application Developer)	Open	Open	Open	Closed
Platform Provider (Hardware / OS Bundle)	Open	Open	Closed	Closed
Platform Sponsor (Design & IP Rights Owner)	Open	Closed	Closed	Closed

Table 3. Models for organizing platforms (Eisenmann, 2008)

One Firm as Platform Sponsor One Firm as Platform Provider	Closed
One Firm as Platform Sponsor Many Firms as Platform Providers	Licensed
Many Firms as Platform Sponsor One Firm as Platform Provider	Joint Venture
Many Firms as Platform Sponsor Many Firms as Platform Provider	Open

serves as the platform provider and (3) the competitive landscape.

Platform providers mediate users' interactions and serve as their primary point of contact while platform sponsors do not deal directly with users. Instead, they hold rights to modify the platform's technology and may decide who may participate in the network, either as a provider or user. A platform sponsor and provider roles may be filled up by one or two multiple firms.

Considerations in a Licensed Framework

A licensed framework is a closed framework where a single firm develops or sponsors the platform's technology and then licenses other firms as providers (Eisenmann, 2008). In many platforms, sponsors may grant licenses to users in order to collect more revenue or to ensure transaction

quality is met (Eisenmann, 2008). However it should be noted that licenses should be granted to the platform providers rather than directly to the user. This is because granting directly to the user would mean that the Platform Sponsor becomes the Platform Provider as well which may eventually come into conflict between other Platform Providers. An IDM firm which decides on this strategy may use the framework given in Figure 4 to capture additional value to its product.

Deriving Value from Syndicators, Aggregators, and Distributors

The platform sponsor may license its products to a variety of syndicating, aggregating or distributing firms. These channel operators become platform providers and they serve as the point of primary contact as well as mediate its use. According to Eisenmann (2008), three factors may motivate sponsors to license multiple providers;

1. licensees may have unique capabilities;
2. sponsors may leverage on licensees marketing clout;
3. multiple licensees may reduce bottlenecks and increase the availability of product supply.

All three factors account for value that each Platform Provider brings to the product.

Figure 4. Value added through syndication, aggregation, and distribution

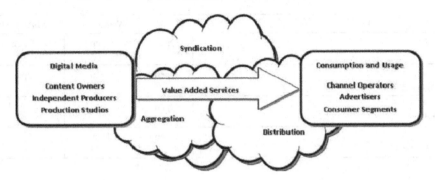

Consideration in a Joint-Venture Framework

A joint venture is a version of a closed platform where several firms or sponsors cooperate in developing the platform, but a single entity serves as its sole provider (Eisenmann, 2008). A firm may choose to deploy a joint venture framework in a situation where many firms own the Intellectual Property Rights while a single entity deals with the customers. With only one provider serving the entire market, it is important that an underlying level of coordination and commitment exists between the sponsors.

Although having numerous providers can help ease bottlenecks in supply and increase the available of the product, firms or sponsors may choose to use this framework if one capable firm or a provider is able to bring a greater value to the sponsors than the numerous providers combined. An example of this situation is given below:

Example 2: Nokia Siemens Networks is one of the largest telecommunications solutions suppliers in the world; the company consists of 2 main sponsors, Nokia and Siemens with the new company Nokia Siemens Networks serving as the sole provider.

We have seen how a single provider, as opposed to many providers, bring value to the sponsors but why should sponsors cooperate in the first place? In order to understand their reason for collusion, it is important to know the market dynamics and

the competitive landscape. When many firms are evenly matched, the opportunities by preempting patents or by attaining scarce resources are limited (Eisenmann, 2008). Many evenly matched firms are able to serve a new platform market. When a first mover launches a new platform, it will typically face rivals quickly. There are two factors that provide impetus for collusion;

1. Will building a new platform require significant investments that others can capitalize on?
2. Is the market likely to be served by a single platform over the long run?

Considerations in a Closed Framework

A closed framework is one where the platform sponsors retain with them at their sole discretion the ability to select providers and participants for their platform. A closed platform sponsor may select who it wishes to use, manage, administer, manufacture and provide peripherals for the platform. A firm may select a closed framework where there is only one sponsor and one provider in the market.

Unlike a product of incremental innovation, where a new product is based on an existing one, a product of radical innovation often consists of breakthrough methods or technology that puts the firm and its product in abovementioned market position. Although such a position favors the firm in terms of few rival sponsors and competitors, important considerations must be taken into consideration.

A penguin problem is defined as *"two actions that each depends on the other being completed first"* (Eisenmann, 2008). This penguin problem often exists for products of radical innovation where a platform provider often subsidizes network users in terms of free use or bundling in order to achieve its short term goals such as positive feedback or positive network externalities. However, in order to achieve long term business viability, new users are charged with fees in order to recover the subsidies offered to the first group of users.

In Figure 5, we see the large void between the early adopters and early majority. This void is known as the chasm. The 5 groups of users shown in Figure 5 are;

1. Innovators, people who are fundamentally committed to new technology;
2. Early adopters, the first group of people who bring real money to the table;
3. Early majority, people who make the bulk of all technology infrastructure purchases;

4. Late majority, customers who are pessimistic about their ability to gain any value;
5. Laggards, not a huge potential opportunity (Mohr et al., 2005).

In order to appropriately handle the penguin problem, it is evident from the above diagram that a firm must be aware of the fact that these various categories of adopters exist. They should consider to which category of users subsidies should be given to as well as when and from whom they should be recovered from. It is paramount to cross the chasm that exists between the early adopters and early majority. Recovering the subsidies too early may result in the form not being adopted by the main stream cliental.

Penetration Pricing

To address the penguin problems, platform provider may choose to permanently subsidize the early adopters by reducing their upfront payment. By reducing their upfront payments, this will increase the users' willingness to pay among later adopters due to the underlying network externalities in effect (Eisenmann, 2008). A firm may then increase its price once the network achieves its critical mass later.

Figure 5. The chasm that exists between the types of adopters (Mohr et al., 2005, p 177)

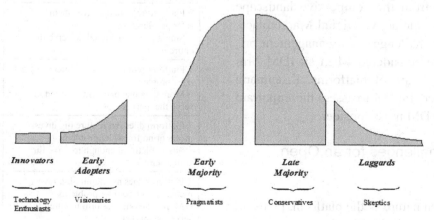

Exclusivity

An IDM firm may wish to drive early network growth by limiting the parties whom many other users wish to interact with. This exclusive access may resolve penguin problems by increasing users' willingness to pay in order to achieve this interaction (Eisenmann, 2008).

Example 3: DirecTV's "Sunday Ticket" package offers exclusive access to every NFL game which boosts the subscriber base.

Permanent Subsidies

Platform providers may subsidize a certain group of users permanently in order to derive a higher willingness to pay on the "paying" group of users. The provider should subsidize the more price sensitive side and charge the side which most strongly value growth in the number of transacting partners on the platform (Eisenmann, 2008).

Considerations in an Open Framework

An open framework is one where numerous competing platform sponsors vie for the same market segment by way of numerous platform providers. Unlike a firm who deploys a closed framework, an IDM firm deploying an open framework is largely dependent on market considerations especially those coming from the competitive landscape inherent in the Interactive Digital Marketplace. Both strategic challenges and management priorities must be considered when an IDM firm considers the nature of platforms. Eisenmann (2008) proposed Table 4 to assess the important issues that an IDM must consider.

Strategic Challenges for an Open Platform

Due to the open nature of the platform, platform sponsors face the difficulties in trying to cap-

ture value for its providers (Eisenmann, 2008). Platform architects should ensure that providers have the propensity to earn enough for continual participation. A provider may switch to another open platform if long term profitability for the provider is affected.

A sponsor can mitigate this problem by the following methods;

1. Restricting entry to the provider pool. This actively limits the number of providers as well as maintains the level of value each participating brings to the pool;
2. License IP to providers. A sponsor can capitalize on the amount of clout and value that a provider brings by licensing the rights directly to them;
3. Profit from Implementation. A sponsor or its providers may use this method as a basis to create revenue by providing expertise such as consulting and implementation know-how.

Management Priorities for an Open Platform

Timing is crucial. An IDM firm should time technical proposals in order to avoid moving into

Table 4. Contingencies favoring closed versus open platforms (Eisenmann et al., 2008)

+ Platform require big investments + free rider problems + Single platform enough to serve the entire market	Closed preferred
+ Platform require big investments + free rider problems + More than one platform required to serve the market	Closed preferred
+ Platform does not require big investments or no free rider problems + Single platform enough to serve the entire market	Open preferred
+ Platform does not require big investments or no free rider problems + More than one platform required to serve the market	Open and Closed often coexist

the market either too early or too late. A firm is unable to maximize its profits should the market be unwilling or unable to accept the new platform.

Example 4: In terms of moving too early, a platform that relies on a sustained minimum transmission rate of a 5Mbps would move into the market too early if the average transmission rates are 512Kbps. In terms of moving too late, entering into the market with an average transmission rates of 5Mbps amidst other competitors which come in at 3Mbps.

The open nature of platform dictates a necessity to licensing strategies, patent pools as well as disclosure policies in order to shield the sponsor from IP-related (Eisenmann, 2008). A firm should also rely on diplomacy and balance of power strategies to ensure coordination between the sponsors and peers. In this high tech market, the influence that a firm relies both an individual delegate's technical capability as well as the firm's power in the market (Eisenmann, 2008). Firms and managers must groom and retain highly capable engineers because they are the same ones who have a huge influence on others.

Making the Choice of Platform

From Table 4, choosing the favored platform type often predicates upon knowing the investment outlay required by the firm as well as the level of free riders that may capitalize on the platform. When a platform does not require big investments or where no free rider problems exist, a firm should be inclined towards the open framework. This is due to the positive network externalities that the platform enjoys as the total value of the network increases by more than the value added by that one individual participant.

When a high capital outlay is expected from a firm coupled with the possibility of free rider problems, firms are inclined towards choosing the closed frame as the basis for their platform. In this manner, the firm is able to generate value both in the short and long run in an attempt to

recover the high investment. It is important to understand that as with an IDM, this framework is not a static one. An IDM using this framework must understand that market conditions do change, the favorable position that a firm enjoys today do not necessarily equate to guaranteed profitability in the future. A firm must always change just before the market does.

An IDM firm competes on a hypercompetitive playing field that is global in nature. Competition and new entrants may not necessarily come from within the country as it is with potential clients. This very nature dictates constant vigilance over current position, future prospects and the global competitive landscape. To the reader, an IDM firm may use the framework understand the considerations in making the decision of whether to keep the innovation on a closed or open platform. One has to remember that the global nature of platform may expose the platform to its competitors worldwide but at the same time garner positive network externalities that a firm can enjoy in the long run.

CONCLUSION

We have seen what value is and how an IDM firm may create and capture it. We also made the distinction between value-added and added-value. In this hyper competitive playing field, firms often arrive at the difficult choice on whether to keep a platform open or closed. Moreover, we have also seen that it is never direct and or simple despite the recurring nature of this choice.

The IDM firm's competitive landscape is one of highest level of competition and it is no wonder that the contingencies favoring platform selection is largely based on having competition in mind. When a high level of investment is involved, the framework favors a closed platform structure in order to capture both short-term and long-term gains. A firm using a closed platform may then select providers who are able garner the greatest value-add to the firm.

However, if a large amount of investment is not required, this framework then favors an open nature in order to both capture the positive network externalities as well as provide avenues for revenues from consulting and implementation expertise. By creating a strong irreplaceable added-valueness to the industry, the firm may continue to profit both in the short and long run as well.

REFERENCES

Amit, R., & Zott, C. (2001). Value creation in e-business. *Strategic Management Journal, 22,* 493–520. doi:10.1002/smj.187

Brandenburger, A. M., & Stuart, H. W. (1996). Value-based business strategy. *Journal of Economics & Management Strategy, 5*(1), 5–24. doi:10.1111/j.1430-9134.1996.00005.x

Cavanaugh, M. (2008). The Evolution of Online Media. *strategy+business,* 1-3.

D'Aveni, R. (1996). *Hypercompetition: Managing the dynamics of strategic maneuvering.* New York, NY: Free Press.

Eisenmann, T., Parker, G., & Alstyne, M. V. (2008). *Opening platforms: How, when and why?* Harvard Business School.

Eisenmann, T. R. (2008). Managing proprietary and shared platforms. *California Management Review, 50*(4), 31–53.

Infocomm Development Authority. (2009). *Statistical charts: Telecommunications.* Retrieved April 28, 2009, from http://www.ida.gov.sg/Publications/20070822130650.aspx.

Mohr, J., Sengupta, S., & Slater, S. (2005). *Marketing of high-technology products and innovations* (2nd ed., p. 11). Pearson Prentice Hall.

Porter, M. E., & Millar, V. E. (1985). How information gives you competitive advantage. *Harvard Business Review, 63*(4), 149–160.

The Economist. (2003). A survey of the new economy. *The Economist,* (p. 6).

Chapter 11
Deriving Value in the IDM Market:
Open vs. Closed Platforms

Nisha Alexander
Nanyang Technological University, Singapore

Ho Wei Ching
Nanyang Technological University, Singapore

Arasu Prem Kumar
Nanyang Technological University, Singapore

ABSTRACT

Faced with different market contexts and changing circumstances, businesses in the IDM marketplace often find themselves in a dilemma with respect to whether to make their platforms open or closed. This chapter presents the Open vs. Closed Value Analysis Framework Model that identifies, describes, and categorizes considerations for IDM platform owners deciding whether, where, when, and how to make their platforms more open or closed. We focused on platform-mediated networks commonly found in the IDM marketplace. We have found that there are generally no clear-cut rules of thumb that point clearly to whether a platform should be open or closed. Various factors like new industry entrants vs. dominant incumbent platforms, the presence and significance of complementors giving competitive advantage, and platform superiority weigh in on the decision.

INTRODUCTION

The IDM Ecosystem

The IDM marketplace typically comprises producers and consumers of digital media products and services and various intermediaries in between, as illustrated in Figure 1. These intermediaries are the content aggregators, syndicators and distributors. These players typically interact with each other in platform-mediated networks. Digital media is created or packaged by sources such as online games developers, movie and animation studios. Aggregation involves collection or repackaging of content from various sources. Syndication is the proactive streaming of content to alternate and

DOI: 10.4018/978-1-61350-147-4.ch011

Figure 1. IDM ecosystem (Source: Dharmawirya et al, 2008)

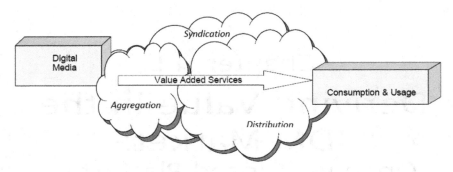

repeat consumer segments, may be after a certain window period. Distribution is the conveying of digital content to consumers. In reality, these roles may be redundant or overlapping. (Dharmawirya et al., 2008).

Platform and Platform Mediated Networks

A platform comprises various components such as hardware, software, networks, rules and policies that govern their use and coordinate users' activities. A platform facilitates interaction between two parties in the manner they wish to interact (Rochet & Jean, 2004). In platform mediated networks, interactions occur in a triangular manner. Supply side and demand side users transact with each other, and also with platform providers (Eisenmann et al., 2008). Platform mediated networks comprise several players: demand side users, supply side users, platform providers, and platform sponsors. This is illustrated in Figure 2.

The Question: Open or Closed?

Businesses in the Interactive Digital Media (IDM) market are caught in a dilemma between going for open vs. closed platforms business models. The challenge here is to find a balance between openness and control (The Economist, 2008). To adapt to changing market trends, firms tend to

gravitate towards adopting a mixed open-closed approach to their business strategy (Eisenmann et al., 2008). A good example is the iPhone which was initially launched as a closed platform. Apple recently opened it to developers subject to strict licensing conditions.

The trend of adoption of open or closed platforms is found to be different in different markets. For example in the mobile market, the same firm might provide both open and closed platforms. As an example, some high end Nokia phones come with S60 software, which runs on mobile phones with Symbian OS, which allows installation of third party applications. But lower end phones from Nokia are closed. No installation of third party applications is allowed. Whereas the enter-

Figure 2. Elements of a platform mediated network and their interaction

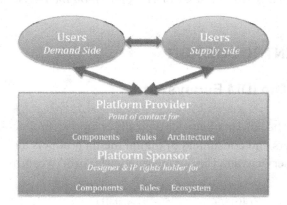

prise applications software market is dominated by closed products like SAP and PeopleSoft (Tag, 2008). Furthermore, closed and open platforms are often found to coexist in some markets. For example, among PC operating systems, both Apple's proprietary Macintosh platform and the open Linux platform are gaining share and popular (Eisennman et al., 2008).

Kende (1998) analysed conditions under which open and closed systems are profitable. He concluded that an open system is more profitable than a closed system when preference for variety in complementary goods is strong, when demand for the system is elastic, and when the budget share of the core platform itself is high. He further found that a closed platform enables manufacturers to earn profits on sales of both the core platform itself, as well as the complementary goods. For open platforms, high competition in the production of complementary goods results in lower prices, and greater variety compared to a closed platform (Kende, 1998).

Firms hence have several compelling reasons to adopt open or closed platform for their products. Open platforms tend to attract more customers and complementors, thereby promoting innovation and tapping the skills of the mass market. However firms need exercise greater control over how people use their products to ensure security and protect intellectual property. This means moving towards a more closed platform (Tag, 2008). Excessive control can be detrimental and risky as it stifles the innovativeness offered by the penetration of technology awareness into the mass market.

How then do firms decide whether to make their platforms open or closed? Under what circumstances should they open or close their platforms? And how do they actually go about making their platforms open or closed? In this chapter, we explain the Open vs. Closed (OvC) Value Analysis Framework Model that identifies and describes the factors and considerations that

firms should take in to account, when deciding on the above questions.

Background Concepts

This section defines and explains some core concepts necessary to the development and understanding of the theoretical framework to be introduced in the next section.

Open vs. Closed Platforms

According to Eisenmann et al, (2008), an open platform has the following 2 characteristics:

1. No restriction is placed on participation in the platform's development, commercialization or use, OR
2. Restrictions exist on the above, but are reasonable and applied in a non-discriminatory manner to all potential platform participants.

Eisenmann further explains that, in a platform-mediated network, common among businesses in the IDM marketplace, all the participants may be categorized into 4 distinct roles, namely:

1. Demand-side platform users
2. Supply-side platform users
3. Platform providers
4. Platform sponsors

Demand-side platform users refer to the end users or the consumers of IDM content, products and services. Supply-side platform users refer to those businesses that offer products or services that enrich, enhance, specialize, or otherwise complement the platform. Platform providers refer to those businesses that offer users access to the platform. Platform sponsors are those businesses and entities that own, control, and develop the platform.

For each of these four roles, a business may choose to open or close its platform. For example,

Android is an Open Source operating system designed for mobile phones. By virtue of its Open Source license, it is freely available for download and use by end-users. Developers may also freely build applications that run on top of it. Businesses may also freely bundle and distribute Android together with their other offerings. And lastly, developers have free access to the source code of Android and may freely modify it. In other words, Android as a platform is opened to all four roles. In contrast, the Google Maps service is freely available for end users to access and use. Developers, after requesting for an application key from Google, may freely build applications that make use of Google Maps functionality and/ or the data. However, Google Maps as a service is only offered by Google Inc. No other business or entity may commercialize it. And lastly, the Google Maps copyright ownership, source code, and full control are retained by Google Inc. Hence, Google Maps as a platform is opened to end-users; the demand-side users and third party application developers or the supply-side users, but is closed to the platform provider and platform sponsor roles.

Indeed, the same business may choose to offer both open and closed platforms as part of its range of products and services. For example, Nokia's N95 mobile phone model allows the installation of 3rd party applications, but the 1600 model is sold as-is and no application can be installed.

Value Added vs. Added Value

Eisenmann (2008) describes a platform's added-value as "the difference between: the value derived by the users of the platform; and the value from users' next best alternative". In other words, the concept of added-value for a platform refers to how a platform measures up compared to its many competitors and rivals. It is an indication of the relative competitive advantage or disadvantage of that platform in the context of the whole market.

In contrast, value-added refers to the extra satisfaction or value derived by users because of

what the platform owner has done. This can be in terms of additional functionality, ease of use, lower prices, or new innovative features. For example, by adding friendly-search functionality to an online social networking web service, the platform owner has increased the value-added of the service to its user-base.

Horizontal vs. Vertical Strategy

As suggested by the Value Net model from Brandenburger and Nalebuff (1995), the course of any market is influenced by four main groups, its customers, suppliers, competitors and complementors (Figure 3). A vertical market is one which serves the need of a particular industry; where as a horizontal market serves the needs across industries. The vertical market players are customers and suppliers, the horizontal market players are competitors and complementors (Brandenburger & Nalebuff, 1995).

The next section introduces and explains the OvC Value Analysis framework model.

THE OVC VALUE ANALYSIS FRAMEWORK

The OvC (Open vs. Closed) Value Analysis framework is a conceptual model that aids to identify, describe and organize the various factors

Figure 3. Value net framework (source: Brandenburger & Nalebuff, 1995)

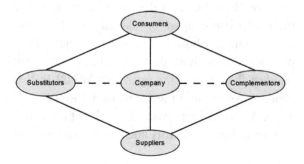

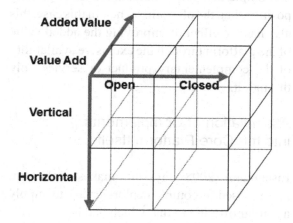

Figure 4. OvC value analysis framework model

and considerations IDM platform owners need to think about when deciding whether, where, when, and how to implement open or closed platforms in order to increase their derived business value. Figure 4 shows the three dimensions in the OvC model.

The OvC framework model organizes the open vs. closed factors and considerations into 4 quadrants for easy reference. The 4 quadrants are:

- **Quadrant 1:** open platform considerations in vertical market strategy
- **Quadrant 2:** closed platform considerations in vertical market strategy
- **Quadrant 3:** open platform considerations in horizontal market strategy
- **Quadrant 4:** closed platform considerations in horizontal market strategy

Quadrant 1 and 2: Open vs. Closed Platform Considerations in Vertical Market Strategy

Platform sponsors and providers whose platforms support significant numbers of supply-side users, third party application develops for instance, offering complementary products and services consumed by demand-side users, face complex choices about whether, where, when, and how to

open or close their platforms (Eisenmann et al., 2008). They must decide whether to:

- Support backward compatibility when developing and rolling out new versions of their platforms.
- Grant exclusive access rights to selected complementors.
- Assimilate certain critical complements into the core platform itself.

Backward Compatibility

This is an important consideration faced by IDM platform owners with a large supply-side user community when planning for their next-generation platform upgrade. Not supporting backward compatibility with previous versions of the platform is equivalent to making the platform more closed (Eisenmann et al., 2008). This is equivalent to adding new restrictions on platform access to existing complementors.

For platforms that enjoy significant competitive advantage due to their complementors, supporting backward compatibility would preserve the platforms' added value vis-à-vis the competitors. In cases where the new generation platform is vastly superior to the previous version, this added value may actually increase, widening the competitive advantage over its rivals. Of course, the decision depends on how much of this added value, platform owners can capture. Ideally, the majority of users choose to pay a premium and upgrade to the next generation non-backward-compatible platform due to great improvement in platform functionality or performance. When improvements are modest, it may be better to offer backward compatibility in the new platform version (Choi, 1994).

For platforms that do not enjoy significant competitive advantage from their complementors, and assuming that the new non-backward-compatible platform version is significantly superior compared to the previous version, users would likely be encouraged to upgrade to the new platform version. The cost-savings from not supporting backward compatibility can also be passed on by platform owners to users in the form or lower prices, thus improving the platform value added.

Platform and Category Exclusivity

This refers to special agreements between selected complementors and the platform sponsors and/or providers, allowing the complementors exclusive access to the platform in terms of development, commercialization or use. Eisenmann et al, (2008) describe two aspects of these types of special agreements:

- Platform exclusivity
- Category exclusivity

Platform exclusivity refers to whether platform owners would "allow" complementors' offerings to also support rival platforms. For example the Integrated Development Environment Eclipse supports Linux as well as Windows operating systems. In contrast, Microsoft Visual Studio only runs on Windows. Imposing platform exclusivity has the effect of closing up rival platforms, but also increases the added value of the platform especially in cases where the complementary offering is highly sought after by consumers. In cases where the complementary offering is actually a critical part of the way consumers interact with or use the platform, this may also shut out potential new platform entrants to the market.

Category exclusivity refers to platform owners allowing only certain selected complementors to supply specific add-ons or complementary offerings. For example, the Firefox Internet browser has agreements with Google to supply the browser extensions for search. In general, category exclusivity benefits the complementor and does almost nothing for the platform owner. However, such an agreement is sometimes accompanied by platform exclusivity agreements, especially in cases where,

the complementor firm holds a weaker bargaining position than the platform owner. In this case, this also has the effect of improving the added value of the platform through the exclusive availability of the complementary product or service only through it.

Assimilation of Complements into the Core Platform Itself

Eisenmann (2008) says this makes a platform more closed to complementors trying to supply a similar offering to that which had been assimilated and is currently being offered as part of the core platform. When much sought after or critical complements are assimilated this way, users may find it more convenient since whatever they need is already part of the core platform itself and they do not need to look around for some other add-on. This has the effect of improving the value addedness of the platform for users in the form of the additional functionality or feature. This may also improve the added value of the platform when the assimilation vastly improves the platform usability and convenience to users over its rivals. Eisenmann et al. (2008) gives the example of Microsoft Windows assimilating other complementary software that started out initially as third party extensions. Such things as disk management tools and desktop games like Solitaire, are now part of the Windows core offering, making it more convenient for consumers who only need a single installation of Windows to get all these functionality and features.

Assimilation of complements work best in situations where the complements are much sought after by platform users, or where multiple varieties of generally undifferentiated complements exist. Assimilation has the effect of commoditizing the complement, making it part of the "basic" offering (Eisenmann, 2008). It also allows the bundling of several related complements together with the core platform into a customized offering geared to consumers with specific needs. For example, the Windows Small Business Server (SBS) is a bundle of the Windows Server operating system, Microsoft Outlook, and several other complementary software that are particularly geared towards small and medium business consumers. This has the effect of increasing the added value of the platform over and above its rivals.

In certain cases where the assimilated complements are highly innovative and have the potential to be disruptive to the core business of the platform owners, the act of assimilating them also removes potential threats to the business, in addition to providing consumers with an even more innovative and useful platform. An example is the tendency of Google to buy smaller web companies with innovative products and services, and then to try to integrate the offerings as part of the entire Google value offering to consumers. YouTube is a prime example of this behavior.

Quadrant 3 and 4: Open vs. Closed Platform Considerations in Horizontal Market Strategy

According to Eisenmann (2008), the considerations in these two quadrants are as follows:

- Interoperability
- Licensing new platform providers
- Broadening platform sponsorship

Interoperability

Katz and Shapiro (1985) and Farrell and Saloner (1992) define interoperability as allowing "cross-platform transactions between their respective users". Interoperability improves the openness of a platform as restrictions for participation of end users and complementors are reduced. Interoperability opens the platform with respect to demand-side users, supply-side users and platform providers.

For a platform that is newly entering a market where established offerings dominate, supporting interoperability with the dominating platforms generally improves the added value of the new platform for users since they are able to try out the new platform while still retaining their ability to operate with other more established platforms. In this case, interoperability may even become the major competitive advantage and selling point for the new platform (Katz & Shapiro, 1992; Matutes & Regibeau, 1996).

Conversely, for an incumbent dominating platform, supporting interoperability with newer platforms may result in a decrease in its added value since users are now able to try out the newer platforms while still retaining their ability to interoperate with the existing platform (Katz & Shapiro, 1992; Matutes & Regibeau, 1996).

Licensing New Providers

The effect of this opens up the platform with respect to platform providers. Eisenmann et al. (2008), state that this is "most attractive when new providers can offer innovative versions of platform products, rather than just simply creating clones". This has the effect of improving the added value of the platform compared to its rivals. This is because new platform providers may be able to share the collective load for customizing the platform to cater to customers in specific segments with special needs. The side effect of licensing new providers may be the appearance of free-riding by the new providers on the marketing and channel sales development efforts by the original provider.

Broadening Sponsorship

This refers to the opening up of the platform to development by other parties (Eisenmann et al., 2008). In cases where this results in a sharing of the load for research, development and maintenance of the platform, this may produce cost savings that can be passed on to platform providers and users, thus increasing value added for them.

Where new development participants bring new expertise and knowledge into the platform design and development, this may also result in platform added value over the long term for users.

CONCLUSION

Faced with different market contexts and changing circumstances, businesses in the IDM marketplace often find themselves in a dilemma with respect to whether to make their platforms open or closed. We have described the OvC Value Analysis Framework that identifies, describes and categorizes some of the considerations relevant to IDM firms when deciding whether to have open or closed platforms. The considerations are classified in terms of their influence on horizontal and vertical market strategies.

Through the development of the model, we have found that there are generally no clear-cut rules of thumb that point clearly to whether a platform should be open or closed. Various factors like new industry entrants vs. dominant incumbent platforms, the presence and significance of complementors giving competitive advantage, and platform superiority, weigh in on the decision. Due to the influence of these myriad factors, we expect that different firms would likely end up with mixed platform models with varying degrees of openness or closeness for different platform stakeholders. The theoretical model is based heavily on references from Eisenmann's research which focuses on mature markets. As such, it may not be as useful when used to describe platform considerations for new and emerging markets.

REFERENCES

Choi, J. (1994). Network externality, compatibility choice, and planned obsolescence. *The Journal of Industrial Economics*, *42*, 167–182. doi:10.2307/2950488

Eisenmann, T. (2008). Managing proprietary and shared platforms. *California Management Review*, *50*(4), 31–53.

Eisenmann, T., Geoffrey, P., & Marshall, V. A. (2008). *Opening platforms: How, when and why?* Harvard Business School Entrepreneurial Management (Working Paper No. 09-030).

Farrell, J., & Saloner, G. (1992). Converters, compatibility, and the control of interfaces. *The Journal of Industrial Economics*, *40*(1), 9–35. doi:10.2307/2950625

Hagiu, A. (2006). *Proprietary vs. open two-sided platforms and social efficiency*. American Enterprise Institute-Brookings Joint Center (Working paper 06-12).

International Telecommunications Union. (2009). *ITU information and communication technology statistics*. Retrieved from http://www.itu.int/ITUD/ict/statistics/ict/index.html

Katz, M., & Shapiro, C. (1985). Network externalities, competition, and compatibility. *The American Economic Review*, *75*, 424–440.

Katz, M., & Shapiro, C. (1992). Product introduction with network externalities. *The Journal of Industrial Economics*, *40*, 55–83. doi:10.2307/2950627

Kende, M. (1998). Profitability under an open versus a closed system. *Journal of Economics & Management Strategy*, *7*(2), 307–326. doi:10.1162/105864098567434

Matutes, C., & Regibeau, P. (1996). A selective review of the economics of standardization: Entry deterrence, technological progress and international competition. *European Journal of Political Economy*, *12*, 183–209. doi:10.1016/0176-2680(95)00013-5

Nalebuff, B. J., & Brandenburger, A. M. (1995). The right game: Use game theory to shape strategy. *Harvard Business Review*, 57–71.

Parker, G., & Alstyne, M. V. (2005). Two-sided network effects: A theory of information product design. *Management Science, 51*, 1494–1504. doi:10.1287/mnsc.1050.0400

Rey, P., & Salant, D. (2007). *Abuse of dominance and licensing of intellectual property*. IDEI Working Paper.

Rochet, J., & Tirole, J. (2004, March). *Two-sided markets: An overview*. Toulouse, France: Industrial Economic Institute.

Tag, J. (2008). *Open versus closed platforms*. Research Institute of Industrial Economics, IFN Working Paper No. 747

Tag, J. (2008). *Efficiency and the provision of open platforms*. Research Institute of Industrial Economics, (IFN Working Paper 748).

The Economist. (2008, August 15). Who holds the key? The struggle to balance openness and control. *The Economist Online*. Retrieved April 28, 2009, from http://www.economist.com/science/displaystory.cfm?story_id=11919515

Chapter 12
Can IPTV Survive in Singapore's Small and Over-Crowded Market?

Yang Yi
Nanyang Technological University, Singapore

Li Lin
Nanyang Technological University, Singapore

Chua Bee Hoon
Nanyang Technological University, Singapore

ABSTRACT

IPTV is a new technology that uses Internet Protocol technology to allow people to view high definition, time-shifted TV program. In this chapter we will discuss the definition and overview of IPTV, the current IPTV status, and popularity in different countries. We will focus on the Singapore market to discuss how IPTV can survive in Singapore's small but over-crowded marketplace by analyzing and comparing current operations and situations of four IPTV services in Singapore and corresponding suggestions and improvements.

INTRODUCTION

What is IPTV?

The Internet Protocol (IP) technology and broadband being applied to TV services had created a new emerging market called IPTV – Internet Protocol Television. IPTV covers the transmission of television programming taking the form of either full scheduled channels and/or video-on-demand content to households via a broadband connection using Internet protocol. Using the IPTV network, service providers can also offer rich interactivity and services such as television commerce, Voice-over-IP, video conferencing and gaming. Instead of delivering the program channel through traditional broadcast cable format, channels are encoded into IP format and deliver

DOI: 10.4018/978-1-61350-147-4.ch012

through the technologies, the IP protocol, used for computer networks.

IPTV services often offer both live TV programs, which are multicasting streaming, live as well as Video-On-Demand (VOD), which basically content is stored and played based on consumer selection or combination of these two. Some of the typical services of IPTV might include VOD service, personal video recording (PVR) service, etc. Features and services can differ from the service provider.

With the IPTV, the quality of the video streaming is much better and clearer than the traditional analogue TV. The features such as Video-On-Demand and Personal-Video-Recording make IPTV more interactive. For IPTV, what you need is just broadband connection, a PC or a traditional TV with set up box which is normally provided by service provider to convert the data back to television signal.

Global Review of IPTV Development

Currently, IPTV is under the limelight of global TV market in terms of subscription growth. At the end of 2008, there was 21.7 million subscribers to IPTV services worldwide at the end of 2008, which was an increase of 63% compared with the end of 2007,[1] of which nearly 10.4 million were in Western Europe and a further 884,000 in Eastern Europe, giving the region 51.4 percent of the worldwide market. (See Table 1)

Western Europe remains the predominant sole region for IPTV. To be more specific, France enjoys the biggest domestic market so far, representing over half of Western Europe's 10.2 million subscribers. This is largely due to the competitive carrier Free's policy of providing CPE which includes an IPTV set-top box to all of its subscribers. All those served by an unbundled line can access some TV services without an extra charge, with on-demand services available for extra fees.

On the other hand, there have been a couple of IPTV service closures. Volny IPTV in the

Table 1. IPTV subscribers by region

Region	IPTV subscribers at the end of 2008	IPTV subscribers at the end of 2007
Western Europe	10,388,000	7,045,860
Eastern Europe	884,466	465,223
North America	3,835,544	1,774,671
South & East Asia	3,615,000	1,840,000
Asia/Pacific	3,082,182	2,199,828
Latin America	21,495	8,991
Mideast & Africa	10,000	10,000
Global total	21,836,687	13,344,573

Source: Broadband Forum/Point Topic

Czech Republic and Tiscali IPTV in Italy have both closed TV operations recently. Both failed to grow in the face of strong competition in their respective markets. These examples, however, are very much exceptions to an overall picture of steady growth in most markets.

In US market, the perception is that the large carriers have been playing IPTV catch-up with Western Europe and Asia. During 2008, North American IPTV did a lot of catching up. For AT&T, a significant milestone was passed in the fourth quarter of 2008. The US operator passed the 1 million mark for IPTV subscribers, joining Verizon.

This increase helped to give North America the largest percentage growth over the quarter, an increase of 19%. In North America, the rollout of fiber has been crucial to the deployment of IPTV.

Although the build-out of fiber took time to reach significant subscriber numbers, it has now reached a position where it provides a large number of homes with an alternative to cable offerings. And in the near future, innovative services could appear that will really differentiate IPTV from cable or satellite TV, such as targeted advertising or location-dependent information like weather and traffic reports for your postal or ZIP code area.

This has led to an expansion in IPTV numbers, as viewers who had previously only been using catch-up services or Web-TV services can now watch full-IPTV. Korea Telecom also offers IPTV via the Sony PlayStation 3 gaming console, although only a small minority of viewers uses this. SK Broadband (formerly Hanaro), Korea Telecom and LG Dacom's myLGtv service had a total of around 1.6 million subscribers at the end of 2008. Japan has been relatively slow to see IPTV subscriber growth. This situation partly reflects a cautious regulatory approach for TV. There is potentially however, a great scope for development. NTT is installing fiber with a target of 30 million FTTH subscribers by 2010.NTT's Plala ISP, servicing Fiber customers, says that it provides IPTV to 'hundreds of thousands' of homes. Its Hikari, meaning 'light', TV service is the first major IPTV deployment to use IPv6. This is important for the future because it addresses the problem of a diminishing supply of addresses available in IPv4.

Although most other markets are nowhere near that the potential exists. For example, Hong Kong, a place tailor-made for IPTV with short distances between exchanges and homes, and around a quarter of broadband subscribers are already on fiber. The subscribers will expand exponentially with the improvement of infrastructure and market strategy and so will the situation in Singapore (see Table 1).

IPTV in Singapore

Television was introduced in Singapore in 1963. Along with the constant changes in technological development, it has evolved from analogue to digital to interactive.

Singapore's broadcast regulator, The Media Development Authority (MDA), takes a proactive role in encouraging the growth of the TV industry by establishing various guidelines to ensure high programme standards as well as creates opportunities for growth. One of the potential growths is digital TV, which is the complete digitization of TV signals from transmission to reception. The MDA views this new technology as an exciting and dynamic medium, and has adopted the European DVB-T (Digital Video Broadcasting-Terrestrial) standard, which is widely adopted by many countries worldwide.

In order to encourage more development of innovative applications that will further enhance the potential of digital TV, the MDA has proposed some funds such as Digital Broadcasting Development Fund to support the development of digital content and service. Moreover, the MDA collaborates with the National Digital TV Committee to publish about the successful deployment of digital TV in Singapore to encourage more companies to entry to the IPTV market.

The MDA has developed a business friendly and technology neutral license framework in order to facilitate the growth of IPTV service in Singapore, as well as to bring the best experience to Singaporeans. Thus, all media service operators are required to obtain a license from the MDA, in order to offer any IPTV services or any form of subscription TV services, in or from Singapore.

The MDA has created two types of licenses for IPTV: niche and nationwide, with a desire to boost the growth of the IPTV market:

- **Niche subscription TV license:** This facilitates the entry of new niche players offering IPTV services which have a limited reach and impact of 100,000 subscribers or less. The licensee would be subject to a lighter license framework. (MDA, 2009)
- **Nationwide subscription TV license:** Players providing services that have wide reach and impact of over 100,000 subscribers. They will be awarded a Nationwide License, similar to that for a mass market pay TV operator. (MDA,2009)

Until July 2008, the MDA has issued 8 licenses to the IPTV/VOD service providers. However, in this chapter, we will be only looking into 4 major IPTV services provider in Singapore. They are the Video-on-demand (VOD) of Starhub, mio TV of SingTel, Mediacorp Online Broadband Television (MOBTV) of Mediacorp and Razor TV of the Singapore Press Holdings (SPH).

Starhub was a monopoly pay-TV operator in Singapore until the arrival of mio TV by SingTel. Due to this competition, Starhub decided to launch the VOD in June 2007. Currently, it has 508,000 subscribers.

In July 2007, Singapore's Internet service provider Singapore Telecommunications (SingTel) launched the IPTV services, mio TV. It has a monthly subscription fee of S$29.96 and it has 45,000 subscribers.

MOBTV was launched in August 2008 and was Singapore's first subscription-based video-on-demand service that enables the viewers with access to various TV programs via immediate digital streaming or download from an internet connection.

Razor TV by SPH, an interactive web television service mainly focused on local content was launched on 22 Feb 2008. It offers both live and video-on-demand programs. It targets Net-consumers in the 18 to 40 age group and its emphasis is more on the local news and events to appeal to local audiences.

BACKGROUND

Theoretical Framework

In our chapter we will use the simplified VISOR model (El Sawy et al., 2005) combined with Value Net (Brandenberger et al., 1996) framework to analyze and discuss the current situation as well as the future of IPTV. We will first begin with an overview of the VISOR framework and Value Net framework.

The VISOR framework intends to help organization make responds on the customers' need, and thus adding the greatest value to the product and service according to customers' needs and requirement in a most profitable and sustainable manner, therefore making the greatest profit. Companies use VISOR framework should keep the five components aligned and balance in order to increase willing to buy of consumers and gener-

Figure 1. VISOR framework

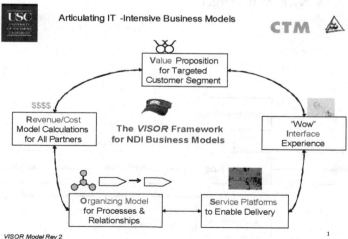

ate the maximum profit. The VISOR framework consists of five components (see Figure 1).

Value Proposition

Value proposition addresses what the value of your product/service is to your target customer segment. Why target customer segment would appreciate the product/service and hence be willing to pay for the product/service. In order to increase the level of customers' willing to pay, organization should keep practice to add and create vale to the product and service to meet latent target consumer demand or become a substation that provide an alternative way form target customer.

Interface Experience

Consumer interface plays a very important way of presenting product or service to the customers. A good interface should offer ease of use, simplicity, convenience and give consumers a satisfyingly great experience.

Service Platforms

Service platform refers to IT infrastructure which may including hardware, software and network. A good service platform can support the business process and relationships which are needed to deliver the products and services to the target group of customers. It can also help to achieve the value proposition.

Organizing Model

Organizing model focuses mainly on how a organization and a set of partners will organize the whole business process, strategy, value chain to deliver the product or service to the target group of customers.

In the analysis of the organizing model of IPTV, we will apply value net to further discuss the whole partnership and alliance in the supply chain. Please refer Figure 2 about Value Net.

Value net consists of five components besides the company (Mohr, Sengupta, & Slater, 2005): Suppliers, Complementors, Competitors, Distributors and Customers. Most of the components are easy to understand. Complement ion normally means another product/service increase the attractiveness of the product.

Revenue/Cost Sharing

In a successful organization, the pricing of the product/service, the value proposition, the delivery of product/service and as well as the investment on the IT infrastructure would allow revenue exceed the cost and give more attractive profit.

Figure 2. Value net

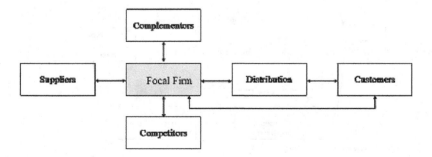

ANALYSIS AND DISCUSSION

First of all, we will compare the four major IPTV in Singapore which are MioTV, MobTV, DemandTV and Razor TV. Table 2 is the summary of the comparisons according to VISOR framework.

From the description mentioned above, we can conclude that in the current Singaporean market, there are two different kinds of IPTV business models. Mio TV, Mob TV and TV on demand are in one category and Razor TV is in the other category. Thus, in the following session, we will compare these two categories in detail based on VISOR framework. Through VISOR

analysis, we have a glimpse of the current 4 major IPTV in Singapore Market. From added-value perspective, we found that each IPTV has its own competitive advantage.

Value Proposition

Demand TV: Widest Range of Channels and Programmers for Time-Shifted Experience

Starhub Demand TV offers Video-On-Demand Title as well as On Demand Channels. Starhub Demand TV offers large variety of programs and

Table 2. Comparisons between 4 major IPTV service providers

	Mio TV	MobTV	DemandTV	RazorTV
Value Proposition	1. Next generation of TV that combines both broadcast channels and true video on demand. 2. The widest range of true HD programmer. 3. Mobile version of Mio TV enables you to view programmers anytime and anywhere	1. Review of TV drama in advance. 2. Media corp. channels and animeTrix channels, which cater for the taste of Cartoons fans.	1. Provide wide variety and time-shifted TV programs	1. Another source of broadcasting new for SPH, with new feature which provide free interactive web TV
Interface Experience	1. Easy to use, Movable	1.Mob TV interface is more complicated than Mio TV and Demand TV 2.Interactive forum to get feedback from the audience	1. Simple, Organized easy to use	1. Develop a new genre of TV with live web studio streaming and real time audience interactivity.
Service Platform	1.SingTel Telephone line 3G mobile platform for mio TV in mobile	1. A PC with windows XP system and windows media player version 9 at least and accessible to the Internet	1.Offer record and play and high-definition output through Hub Station	1.Allow Third-party developers to create innovative applications to enhance the website for a more engaging Web 2.0 experience
Organizing Model	1.Recording TV free of charge for 9 months 2.Recording TV 30 in advance and remote control 3. Bundling service: no basic tier subscription and no extra cost for HD box Mio TV on mile.	1. People can stream or download from an Internet connection. 2.A 14-day online review is available	1.Refer details below (1.2.4)	1. With CoreMedia's future-driven Content Management technology, Supporting implementation partner is Ufinity, who will be the technology partner delivery the infrastructure for RazorTV. There are funding from the MDA to support and promote research and development in innovative services.
Revenue / Cost Sharing	1. Pay per view price for 10 minutes 2.Monthly subscription	1.Pay per view-for each content 3 Packages for monthly subscription based on various languages channels	1. Pay per use model combined with monthly subscription model	1. Free subscription

high definition time shifted TV program, which allow consumers to watch whatever TV show they want to watch at any one time. With Demand TV, you can also personalize your way of playing by pause, fast forward and rewind. Demand TV also can fulfill consumers who want to catch the latest release of TV shows/programs which even have not been released in the Starhub Cable TV.

In current Singapore IPTV market, Starhub Demand TV provides the widest selection of Video-On-Demand Title (TV series, movies and sport program) and On Demand Channels. Starhub Demand TV offers six On Demand Channels which are: HBO On Demand, BPL On Demand, Disney Channel @ Play, VV Drama On Demand, TVBJ On Demand and Ruyi Hokkien Channel On Demand (http://www.starhub.com/). With these On Demand Channels, customers can enjoy the same show/program in the normal non-demanding TV whenever you want to watch, which means, if you have HBO On Demand, you can watch all the shows in HBO channels with your own timing preference. . Demand TV also provides playing function like pause, fast forward and rewind function which personalized the way of watching programs to meet different customers' needs and requirement, while MioTV and MobTV also have the similar functions.

In this regard, Demand TV enjoys the largest data base compared to its local competitors.

MioTV-Dual Platforms with Movable Characters and Exclusive Content and Feedback Forum

SingTel, the distributor of Mio TV, as the largest telecom company in Singapore launched a Mio TV in traditional version and mobile version. In Mobile version, the subscribers can enjoy their favorite movie clips anytime and experience movable entertainment content.

As for Mobile TV part, the potential incremental as opposed to substitution nature of the audience for these services arises principally from the nature

of the platform itself, which enables customers to consumer TV content at times when they would otherwise be unable to do so, such as on a train. A further factor helps to be re-purposed clips and additional "made for mobile" materials rather than a re-versioned form of the entire original content. Mob TV has exclusive content with appealing price package to grasp the niche market.

Besides programmers offered by MediaCorp., there is a special channel on Cartoon released to the anime fans, which cannot be accessed otherwise. Since MediaCorp. is both the content provider and distributor, the subscription fee is lower as compared to other IPTV in Singapore. Also, the special channel pack designed deliberately to meet certain people's taste will grasp the niche market in the future. Besides that, there is an online feedback forum in Mob TV, where the audiences can communicate ideas, exchange information on content and submit timely feedback so that a user-friendly and interactive consuming environment has been established. Although the role and influence of this forum in the Mob TV remain to be seen, we believe the forum per se indicates a way of direct communication and interactivity in and beyond audience, which will be the mainstream of future entertainment industry.

Razor TV-Rich News Media Delivery in Digital Form

Unlike Starhub Demand or SingTel MioTV, Razor TV of SPH (Figure 3) was another new media breakthrough in digital media market. It broadcasts "live" news and lifestyle content through "live" streaming. It enables live interaction between the studio and audience through web, whereby audience are able to send feedbacks and comments "live" online while watching the programmes.

Room for Improvement

The increasingly high paced lives in recent years has seen a reduction in the amount of time allocated

Figure 3. Screenshot of Razor TV

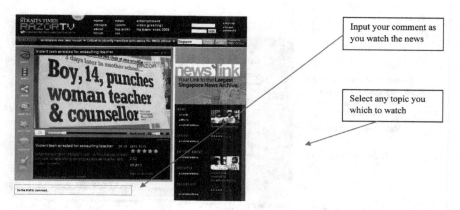

for watching TV at home. Time shift TV like Mio, mob and on-demand, has provide customers the opportunities to watch TV program whenever they like. However, people now feel that purely watching TV program anytime is not enough for them. They now look to options of watching TV program anytime and anywhere, as well as being able to interact and transact with what they are watching, which is similar to what Razor TV offers. With the popularity of mobile devices and mobile computing, there is an uprising trend to develop the Demand TV on mobile handset to give consumer more flexibility. As for Mio TV, there is already the presence of a mobile version that has monopolized the mobile TV market. Thus, with more entrants coming into this new market, the price will reduce and the service quality will improve for sure to grasp a bigger market share.

Therefore, the number of high definition program and channel should be increased to fulfill customers' needs for enjoyment of auditory and visual experiment.

Interface Experience

In general, the overall interface experiences of all IPTV services are pretty simple and easy to use for both novice and experts. We will take Starhub Demand TV as an instance to analyze the interface experience.

To access Demand TV portal, simply press PPV.VOD button on the remote control. The main catalog page of Demand TV is shown in Figure 4. The design and layout of the catalog page is pretty simple and well structured and organized. The left hand side shows the categories while the right hand side shows the content overview. Navigation functions locate at the bottom of the page. The overall design of Demand TV is clear and easy to use. Consumers can easily find the functions/programs they desire. Figure 4 is a screenshot from StarHub Demand TV.

For Razor TV, it is just like browsing any website, click at any topics you would like to view and post your comments/feedback as you watch the programmes.

SOLUTIONS AND RECOMMENDATIONS

The current interface of Demand TV is quite consumer friendly with very high usability standard. There is a need to maintain the high standard in the future for different platform other than mobile devices and new features/functions that provides real time audience interactivity.

Another suggestion would be to design the interface in such a way that the consumer can access the content in the same way as they shop

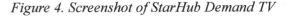

Figure 4. Screenshot of StarHub Demand TV

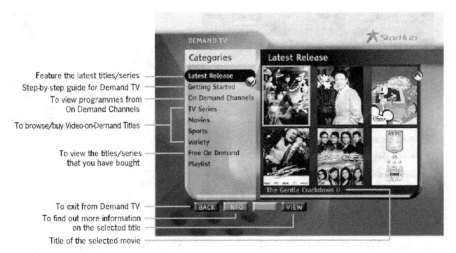

for goods and services in the web. Contents will be priced based on the quality, scarcity and timeliness of content being supplied. The consumer can select the content they want and when they required. If they want something earlier, they will need to pay extra for the special delivery.

Service Platform

Singapore per se is a multi-media hub with solid technological infrastructure and high penetration rate of Internet and mobile service. As reported by IDA, the newly released data stated that there are 4,883,700 internet broadband subscribers and 6,375,500 mobile subscribers. The IPTV industry thus has a huge potential to expand further. Moreover, each IPTV we analyzed here requires various service platform and technology requirement to achieve the value proposition.

Demand TV: Hub Station

In order to use Demand TV service, customers need to have Hub Station that provides record and play functions. Not only is Hub Station a high definition set up box but also a digital video recorder and cable modem. Current Hub Station provides large amount of hard disk, which is 160GB which allow

consumers to record down the programs for the future viewing. Hub Station provides high quality of both audio and video output which provides high definition delivery to customers.

MioTV: SingTel Telephone Line and 3G Mobile

The dual service platform is a unique characteristic of Mio TV. For the traditional TV version, a SingTel telephone line is required to do TV subscription.

As for the mobile version of Mio TV, the subscribers should meet the following requirements:

1. A SingTel 3G mobile subscribers,
2. Have a supported handset and now it is only confined to some models of Nokia and Samsung.

MobTV: Internet Browser and Media Players

The technological barrier for the subscribers to enjoy Mob TV is quite low and almost every Singaporean with Internet can meet its requirement and experience Mob TV easily. Table 3 is the basic computer requirement for subscriptions.

The current compatibility level of Mob TV is low. From its compatibility chart (Table 4), it is evident that improving the content transmission technology and diversifying the content distributing platform will definitely profit both the Mob TV and audience.

Mob TV with normal PC infrastructure requirement paved the road to successful expanding market from early adopters to common family. The accessible way to IPTV without extra charges and investment in infrastructure will appeal a lot of potential audience.

Razor TV: Web 2.0 Technology Driven Platform

For Razor TV, it adopts the Web 2.0 technologies like AJAX and Flash so as to enable the viewers to rate, comment and vote in polls in real-time as the show is being webcasted LIVE. Beside this, an advanced Web Content Management system is used to catalog all shows and provide them as VODs so that the viewers can enjoy the shows later.

Room for Improvement

More types of terminals besides TV such as laptop computers, mobile devices should be supported to fulfill the customers' demand.

Demand TV currently uses Hub Station to transmit the IPTV computer signal to analogue signal so that it can be played on TV. Hub Station also plays the role of Video Recorder to support the Record and Play service. Customers need to pay for the additional Hub Station in order to enjoy Demand TV service. So if they do the transmission of analogue signal in the backend server, and store consumers' record data in the database server, Hub Station can be eliminated.

With the potential of further growth in the numbers of the subscriber base for IPTV services, there is a need for the service providers to invest and improve their technologies, such as reliable bandwidth with high quality of service to support peak demand. The reason is that most of the family comes back from work or school during the evening time between 7pm and 11pm which is when they spend their time in front of the TV.

Moreover, the next generation web 2.0 technologies will include high-level user tools such as Rich Internet application techniques which will enable the IPTV service providers to develop greater interactivity and connectivity with other platforms.

In Singapore, MDA encourage new IPTV service providers to enter the market with innovative and diverse programming content by providing

Table 3. Basic computer requirements for subscriptions

Computer IP Address	Singapore User
Computer Operating System	Windows XP
Windows Media Player	Windows Media Player version 9
Browser	Internet Explorer V6 and above, Firefox 1.5 and above and Netscape 4.75 and above

Source: http://www.mobtv.sg/TestVideo.aspx

Table 4. Mob TV compatibility chart: A circle represents that the device is compatible and tested

Windows XP-based PC	O
Mac OS	X
Archos AV500	O
Archos AV700	O
Zen Portable Media Center	X
Creative Zen Vision W	X
Creative Zen Vision	X
iPOD	X
iPOD U2	X

Source: http://www.mobtv.sg/Faq.aspx

funds to support the service providers to upgrade their technologies and this will in return help them to reduce their investment cost and in return provide better quality and content to the consumers.

Organizing Model

For the discussion of organizing model, we will adopt the Value Net to look into details about the customers, distributors, suppliers, competitors and complementors. Table 5 gives a summary of the organizing model of IPTV service providers:

Customers

Most of the IPTV customers are from the existing cable TV subscribers. For examples, customers of Demand TV is mainly on the existing Starhub Cable TV subscribers who are willing to watch TV program for their own timing preference, or catch the latest release even before it shows in Starhub Cable TV. There are also a small amount of customers who are not existing Starhub Cable TV subscribers. While the target user group for Razor TV is a bit different from others. Razor TV

targeted to those age between 18-40 internet users who more interested on News.

Distributors

The distributors of IPTV in Singapore are their funders, such as SingTel, Starhub, Mediacorp and SPH.

Suppliers

The suppliers of IPTV in Singapore are mostly content providers, program/content producers. For example, Demand TV offers both Video-On-Demand service as well as Demand Channel. So the suppliers of Demand TV include content producers/distributors such as Disney Channel which support Demand Channel, media producers like movie producer and distributors, such as Mediacorp which support Video-On-Demand. Another supplier is the hardware (set up box - Hub Station) software and the whole process supplier which is by Motorola, Inc who provide end-to-end Demand TV delivery solution to the customers.

Table 5. Summary of organizing model of IPTV service providers

	MioTV	**MobTV**	**Demand TV**	**Razor TV**
Customers	TV subscribers Mobile entertainment fans	Cable TV subscribers	Cable TV subscribers who want to watch demand TV	Aged 18 – 40 years old Net Users
Distributors	**SingTel**	**Mediacorp**	**Starhub**	**SPH**
Suppliers	Content producers from domestic and overseas	Mediacorp and other media content producers, mainly are program channels overseas	Program channels/content producer/distributors, media producers and hardware/software suppliers	Strait Times, solution provider – Ufinity Pte Ltd
Competitors	Other IPTV in Singapore	Other IPTV in Singapore	Other IPTV in Singapore, Internet TV, DVD rental Store, Cinema, etc	Other IPTV in Singapore having the Niche Subscription TV licensee
Complementors	Mobile Phone supplier – Nokia, Samsung, NEC, etc	Personal Computer Supplier – HP, Dell, Acer, etc	Mobile Phone supplier – Nokia, Samsung, NEC, etc	Newspaper

Competitors

The current IPTV in Singapore are competitors to each others. There are also threat from other competitors like Internet TV, DVD rental store, and cinema. Some Internet TV is also a strong competitor of Demand TV. Some of Internet TV providers also provide video on demand service. DVD rental store and cinema are also competitors to Demand TV. So how does Demand TV gain competitive advantages among those competitors? We will discuss this in the next section.

Complementors

The complementors for Mio TV and Demand TV are the mobile phone suppliers as we could bundle the services together with the purchase of the mobile phone, while for Mob TV, it could partner with hardware vendor such as the HP, Dell to bundle services with the purchase of any personal computers. Razor TV is unique as it is a free subscription. A way to add further value to its service would be to partner it with the newspaper to promote the service by publish interesting topic to be discussed and announcement of inviting famous actors or singers to Razor TV to encourage youngest to logon to Razor TV.

Room for Improvement

The IPTV providers must master the trick of finding the right market segment in which they need to understand the consumer needs and what they actually want from the services. With this information, they will be able to position their business such that they can deliver them in a rapid, flexible, and truly personalized manner. For instance, to offer the right content to the consumer and provide a compelling content which includes its timing, pricing, quality and availability.

As the market dynamics keep changing, consumers will benefit the most with wider options and better content. They can enter into a richer digital experience with more interactive engagement. IF IPTV could pull through in capturing consumers and provide a wider content, advertisers can benefit from another viable media option.

IPTV provider can offer features that have advantage to the advertisers, for instance, a feature whereby consumer could pause the programme he is watching and request for further information of the product and purchase the product. With a more interactive media, we are able to capture more precise statistic by analyzing the activity of the consumer interacting with adverts. Thus, the IPTV providers are able to liaise with the right advertisers to provide the right product and services to the consumers.

Finally, to be able to sustain in the competitive market, there is a need to differentiate themselves from their competitors. One way is to partner with other technology giants to widen the compatibility of MobTV content and enhance the video experience for consumer and at the same time create opportunity to the developer in the IP convergence space.

Revenue/Cost Sharing

For the existing IPTV, there are two categories in terms of revenue. One is profitable and the other is free. As Razor TV belongs to the latter, we could only analyze the different profit models among Mio TV, Mob TV and On Demand TV.

Demand TV

In order to enjoy the Demand TV service, the basic charge is the monthly rental fee of the Hub Station. Demand TV has 2 types of services which are Video-On-Demand and Demand Channel. Video-On-Demand services like TV series, movies and sports charge per use. The price varies according to the popularity of the show and that of the duration of the show also. As for Demand Channel service, it charges either a fix amount of monthly subscription fee e.g. RUyi Hokkien

Table 6. Screenshot of service price

Channel / Title	Price
HBO On Demand (Channel)	Free to HBO PAK subscribers
Disney Channel @ Play (Channel)	S$4.28 per month for Kids Basic Group subscribers
Ruyi Hokkien Channel On Demand (Channel)	S$6.42 per month
Speech of Silence (TV Series)	S$17.10
April Fool's Day (Movie)	S$5.0
WrestleMania 25 (Sports)	S$12.0

Source: www.starhub.com

Channel On Demand, or better price e.g. Disney Channel @ Play or even free e.g. HBO On Demand for existing Starhub cable TV subscribers. Table 6 is some of the screenshot of the service price:

Mio TV

It offers two platforms to the audience, that is, Mio TV and Mio TV on mobile. For Mio TV, people can pay for content or for channels. For channels subscriptions there are three price packages for different languages channels. Under each pack, all the channels have been categorized into 5 parts: lifestyle/variety, kids / family, news, education and music.

Beyond that, Mio TV corporate its U.S. Counterparts to launch a Season Pass plan, which means SingTel's latest tie-up with Disney-ABC international Television. Twentieth Century Fox

Table 7. Price structure of on demand content

On demand	Pay per view Price/clip
Mobisodes: Sorority Forever	$0.50
Korean: The Legend	Free
Sports	$0.50

Source: http://mio.singtel.com/miotv/mio-tv-on-mobile_price-plan.asp

and Warner Bros International Television Distribution, so the audiences can watch the latest season of shows as early as 24 hours after their USA telecast. For this timely package, the price will be much higher than other programmers, ranging from $16.05 to $ 214.0 (see Table 7).

Currently, there is a price reduction promotion in Mio TV. The Mio TV market may cross the chasm from the early adaptors to mass market stages, due to the ample contents with cheap pricing.

Mob TV

There is a little difference in Mob TV, in which MediaCorp. is the distributor and mainly content provider. Mob TV subscribers enjoy fewer programmers compared to the other two TV in the same category. On the other hand, MediaCorp as a content provider, it takes advantage to offer its audience exclusive content, such as cartoon channel: ANIMETRIX. Because of its limited content options, the price is the lowest one among three charged IPTV. Its subscription period is shorter than those of others, for one and three month respectively (see Table 8).

Room for Improvement

Bundling of similar types of TV program together is a way for promoting. Bundling might include bundling similar interest movie and program together, for example, bundle all Jacky Chan's

Table 8. Promotion packages for Mob TV

Channel packages	Price
Media Corp Channel Pack	$16/per month or $30/ three month
Asian China Pack	$9.90/ per month or $19.90/ three month
AnimeTrix Package	$5/ per month or $10/ three month

Source: http://www.mobtv.sg/Promotions/PromotionsDetail.aspx?contentid=EDC070430-0000001

movie for a promotion price. Bundle IPTV with other services, such as mobile subscription or Cable TV subscription.

CONCLUSION

There are four major IPTV service providers in Singapore despite having a small market place. Is it over-crowded? Can we have another one more IPTV service provider in Singapore? In this chapter we argue that it is still possible to have one more IPTV service provider in Singapore as long as they have the competitive advantage. Though four IPTV may seem a bit crowded for the small market Singapore, each IPTV has its own USP, such like Mio TV's mobility, Demand TV's wide variety of programs and MobTV web/Internet platform. Each IPTV service providers have their own customer base, like Starhub existing cable TV customers will choose DemandTV as the IPTV service provider instead of MioTV, because of the customer loyalty and valuable package offered for existing Starhub customers.

In order to survive in the highly competitive market, the IPTV service providers needs to first listen to the market trend and customer voice, change and build their value proposition, and make necessary changes on business strategy to better fulfill the customers' current and feature needs. Secondly, the IPTV service providers need to closely observe and adopt new technology to improve the interface design and service platform infrastructure, to give customers better and more flexible experience. Lastly, the IPTV service providers need to carefully examine the parties involved in the supply chain, optimize the supply chain to retrieve higher quality services and produce more revenues from supply chain as well as the cost and promotion strategies.

REFERENCES

Kulow., T. (2008). Singapore's first WebTV portal with CoreMedia, The Straits Times Razor TV, stays in tune. *Straits Times*. Retrieved from http://www.coremedia.com/en/130970/singapores-first-webtv-portal-with-coremedia/

Light, C., & Lancefield, D. (2007). *Show me the money: Strategies for success in IPTV*. London, UK: PricewaterhouseCoopers.

MDA. (2009). *MDA websites*. Retrieved from http://www.mda.gov.sg

Mio, T. V. (2009). *MioTV on mobile price*. Retrieved from http://mio.singtel.com/miotv/mio-tv-on-mobile_price-plan.asp

Mob, T. V. (2009). *Mob TV promotion plan*. Retrieved from http://www.mobtv.sg/Promotions/PromotionsDetail.aspx?contentid=EDC070430-0000001

Mob, T. V. (2009). *Mob TV compatibility chart*. Retrieved from http://www.mobtv.sg/Faq.aspx

Mob, T. V. (2009). *MobTV wizard*. Retrieved from http://www.mobtv.sg/TestVideo.aspx

Mohr, J., Sengupta, S., & Slater, S. (2005). *Marketing of high-technology products and innovations* (2nd ed.). Pearson Prentice Hall.

Razor, T. V. (2009). *Servlet segment*. Retrieved from http://www.razor.tv/site/servlet/segment/main

Starhub. (2009). *On demand TV*. Retrieved from http://www.starhub.com/DemandTV/pdf/HStatnConsumerG_DenamdTVpages.pdf

ENDNOTE

[1] *IPTV subscribers up 63%*, http://mybroadbanc.co.za/news/General/7495.html

Chapter 13
Disruptions in the IDM Marketplace:
Time–Shifted TV

Huang Jian
Nanyang Technological University, Singapore

Daniel Tan Dezheng
Nanyang Technological University, Singapore

Ren Buyi
Nanyang Technological University, Singapore

ABSTRACT

The proliferation of digital video content and the diffusion of broadband Internet networks have resulted in the growth of online video and video on demand as forms of time-shifted television. This chapter examines time-shifted-television as a disruptive influence to traditional broadcast television. The conceptual framework of syndicators, aggregators, and distributors (SAD Framework) is used to analyze the market for time-shifted television. This chapter examines the issues and challenges faced by time-shifted television to cross the chasm and gain adoption in the mainstream market. Finally, using the VISOR framework, we also examine the business models which could enable time-shifted television to cross the chasm.

INTRODUCTION

The growth of digital media and diffusion of broadband internet networks have resulted in a growth of online video, video on demand and Internet Protocol television (IPTV). Consumers now watch television programs on alternative

DOI: 10.4018/978-1-61350-147-4.ch013

platforms and devices, which have the potential to offer consumers more choice and flexibility. This innovation disrupts interactive the traditional broadcast television markets. It is also known as time-shifted television.

Time-shifted television consists of products and services, which enable viewers to watch television programs on demand. The convergence of digital technology and media has created new opportunities for creating value in the market place with digital content. Consumers can enjoy more choice and flexibility as to when and how they want to watch the television programs. Time-shifted television can also provide value added services, such as advertisement-free television programmes, which provide consumers with enhanced viewing experiences.

This chapter begins by providing an overview of time-shifted television as a disruptive innovation in the IDM marketplace. This is followed by a market overview for time-shifted television, which illustrates how time-shifted television has yet to cross the chasm and enter the mainstream market (Moore, 1991), despite having the potential to be a truly disruptive innovation. Subsequently, the business eco-system for time-shifted television is analyzed by using the SAD framework introduced by Sharma et al (2008) and the VISOR framework described by El Sawy et al (2005). Based on our analysis of the market, opportunities and challenges for time-shifted television, we will examine business models which can help time-shifted television to cross the chasm.

BACKGROUND

Time-Shifted Television

Time-shifted television consists of a new products and services which enable viewers to watch television programs on demand and in expanded time slots. Figure 1 illustrates the greater flexibility in viewing time slots which time-shifted television offers compared to traditional television. These services include video on demand and IPTV. In the traditional television, programmes are broadcasted linearly in pre-determined time slots. Viewers who are unable to watch the television programmes will need to wait for re-runs (Motorola, 2007).

On the other hand, time-shifted television services such as video-on-demand and IPTV en-

Figure 1. Expanded viewing timeslots for time-shifted television

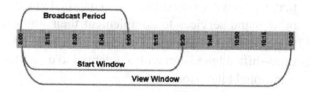

able consumers to enjoy their favourite content with greater flexibility and choice. IPTV which delivers the digital content on demand over Internet Protocol allow consumers to download video content on multiple network connected devices such as mobile phone, computers, high-definition television sets, game consoles or digital video recorders. The consumer can then enjoy the video content anytime and anywhere. Time-shifted television also can provide consumers with other value-added services not found in traditional broadcast television, such as advertisement-free programmes, personalization of content, exclusive programming and a more interactive experience (Palmer, 2006, p 28). While time-shifted television has the potential to be a major disruption to the IDM marketplace and traditional broadcast television, time-shifted television services such as video-on-demand and IPTV have yet to cross the chasm and gain wide-spread adoption by the mainstream market.

Consumer research by the Leitchman Research Group (2009) has shown that while the usage of online video has grown, the time spent watching traditional broadcast television has remain largely unchanged. Based on a survey of 1,250 households in the US in 2008, it was found that 34% of adults viewed online videos weekly. There is an increase from 31% which was reported in the previous year. However, 93% of adults spend at least an hour a day on average watching traditional television, while 35% of adults spend at least four hours watching television each day. Based on the research from Leitchman Research Group, online video has had little impact on traditional television viewing. However, the report suggests that TV viewers may subscribe to bundled video on demand services to complement their traditional television content. This may be a form of time-shifted television with a potential to disrupt traditional television.

According to the North American Technographics Technology, Media and Marketing Benchmark Survey conducted by Forrester Research in the third quarter of 2007, 47% of US consumers have either not heard of video-on-demand or have heard of video-on-demand but do not know what it is, as shown in Figure 2 (Graves, 2008). The survey also revealed that only 15% of US consumers have used video-on-demand, thereby indicating that the adoption of video-on-demand has yet to achieve widespread adoption in the US. A lack of awareness of time-shifted television and its benefits over traditional television may be a barrier to overcome if time-shifted television is to cross the chasm.

In Hong Kong, mobile television delivered to mobile phones over mobile 3G networks is a form of time-shifted television, which has been introduced into the market. Like video-on-demand in the US, early adopters of technology and not the mainstream market have mainly adopted mobile television in Hong Kong. In February 2007, only

11% of mobile users in Hong Kong subscribed to 3G services which include mobile television (Wang, 2007). In Singapore, the IPTV has also yet to enjoy widespread adoption from the mainstream market. The Singapore IPTV service Mio TV reported 59,000 subscribers (IPTV News, 2009). Similarly other offerings from Razor TV and Mob TV have yet to enjoy widespread adoption in Singapore.

Time-shifted television is an emerging technology with the potential to change the way people watch television and video content. Despite its advantages to both consumers, advertisers and producers, time-shifted television has yet to achieve adoption in the mainstream market. The various players in the IDM business eco-system play various interdependent and overlapping roles which have the potential to add value to digital content (Dharmawirya et al., 2008), and provide consumers with better products and services through time-shifted television. In order for market players to succeed in bringing time-shifted television to the market and capturing value from the market, sound business strategies which create value in the market and enable the market players to profit from this created value are necessary (Amit & Zott, 2001). These strategies need to be implemented with a business model (Shafer et al, 2005). In the following section, value net analysis, the SAD framework, and the VISOR model, which refines the value net for the market for digital content, will be introduced. The SAD framework will then be used to analyze the market for time-shifted television and the VISOR model will be used to examine business models which can enable time-shifted television to cross the chasm.

Frameworks for Analysis

In this section we present several frameworks for analyzing the business eco-system for time-shifted television. Value net analysis will be described, followed by the SAD framework which refines the value net analysis for the market for digital content

Figure 2. Familiarity with video-on-demand in the US

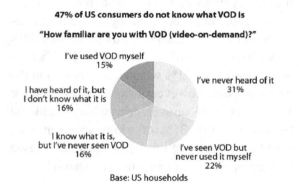

such as time-shifted television. Subsequently the VISOR model, a framework for analyzing business models will be described.

Value Net Analysis

Value Net Analysis adopts a game-theoretical approach to analyzing business. The marketplace for time-shifted television consists of several players who take on value adding roles. These include the firm, substitutors, complementors, suppliers and consumers. Brandenburger and Nalebuff (1995) and Brandenburger and Stuart (1996) proposed the firm's value net as a framework for describing the players in the marketplace and analyzing their interdependent relationships. The Value Net map in Figure 3 illustrates the interdependent relationships among players in the marketplace for IDM and time-shifted television.

The Value Net map focuses on four main groups which influence a company's business environment, namely, customers and suppliers along the vertical axis and substitutors and complementors along the horizontal axis. The company, its suppliers, substitutors and complementors are players in the marketplace whose roles are to add value to the products and services which they are producing (Brandenburger & Nalebuff, 1995). Interactions occur along the vertical dimension where consumers interact with the company, which interacts with suppliers. In these interactions, the company typically acts as a distributor of the

Figure 3. Value net map

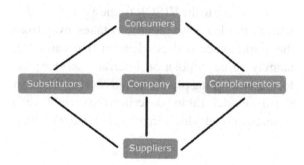

product or service. Along the horizontal dimension, the company interacts with substitutors and complementors. Substitutors offer consumers and suppliers products and services which are alternatives to those which the company is offering, while complementors offer products and services which augment those offered by the company.

The Value Net of a company can be used to analyze the company's business strategy. To succeed, the company needs to analyze the game of business which it is engaged in and seek strategic partnerships which allow it to gain a competitive advantage in the market. In general, the analysis involves identifying game players, describing the added value of the various players, and finally identifying rules, tactics and the scope of the game of business. This analysis can then be used to shape the company's business strategy

The SAD Framework (Syndicators, Aggregators, Distributors)

The Value Net map depicts a company-centric perspective of the marketplace. The SAD framework introduced by Dharmawirya et al (2008), refines the interdependent relationships among the players in the marketplace, which are illustrated in the Value Net map. These interactions add value to the digital content which is created by producers and deliver the digital content to consumers.

The production of time-shifted television involves a number of players in the market. There are 3 value adding processes between the production of the digital media for time-shifted television and the consumption of time-shifted television by consumers. The value adding processes are syndication, aggregation and distribution. These roles are played by the company, suppliers, complementors and substitutors depicted in the value net map. Figure 4 illustrates the chain of syndicators, aggregators and distributors (SAD) which exist between the producers of digital media for time-shifted television and consumers who purchase and consume the digital media.

Figure 4. The SAD framework

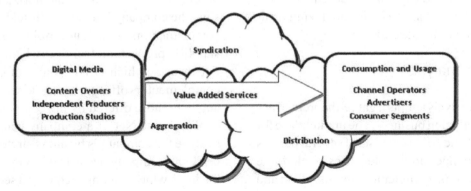

The intermediaries in the SAD chain have different roles to play and add value to the digital content in different ways. Figures 5 to 7 illustrate the various interactions which occur between producers or suppliers of digital content, the intermediaries and consumers.

Syndicators take digital content from suppliers, may integrate with other offerings, and sell the content to various customers segments, including some distribution channels and other syndicators. Figure 5 illustrates the relationships and interactions between producers of digital content, syndicators and consumers.

Aggregators collect digital content from a variety of sources. The content may be repackaged or bundled with other similar content, before reaching consumers. Figure 6 illustrates the relationships and interactions between the producers of digital content, aggregators and consumers.

Figure 5. Syndicator and the syndication map

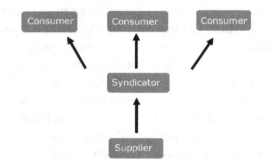

Distributors deliver the digital content to the consumers, often with aspects of billing and payment receiving. Figure 7 illustrates the relationships between producers of digital content, distributors and consumers

While Value Net analysis and the SAD framework can help a company to identify market players and the relationships among the players, they do not systematically assist players to operationalize this analysis into a business model to implement the company's business strategy. The next section will introduce the VISOR model, a model for analyzing business models.

The VISOR Model

The VISOR Model, described by El Sawy et al (2005) is a conceptual framework for analyzing business models for IDM marketplace. The model defines five aspects of a business model for firms seeking to create value in the market, and profit from this value.

According to the VISOR framework, the value which a market player adds to or takes away from the marketplace is dependent on five variables, namely, value proposition, interface, service platforms, organizing platform, and revenue and cost sharing model. Table 1 describes the variables of a business model which create value in the market.

Figure 6. *Aggregator and the aggregation map*

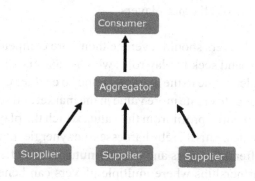

Figure 7. *Distributor and the distribution map*

The SAD framework, together with the VISOR model will be used to analyze the marketplace for time-shifted television and to examine business models, which can help time-shifted television to cross the chasm, thus allowing the various market players to profit from the value created in the market. The SAD framework identifies and examines the roles of producer, syndicator, aggregator, distributor and consumer, which are adopted by players in the market. The VISOR framework will then be used to analyze the value created by the various market players for time-shifted television.

KEY FINDINGS AND TAKEAWAYS

In this section, key findings from our analysis are presented. The marketplace of time-shifted television is analyzed using the SAD framework and a business models for time-shifted televisions will be examined using the VISOR framework.

SAD Framework Analysis

Table 2 describes the roles which the various players or stakeholders in the market for time-shifted television add value in the marketplace.

From our analysis, there are various roles which players can adopt in the business ecosystem for time-shifted are overlapping and interdependent. A single player may play multiple roles and create value in a variety of ways. For example, television studios create value by producing the television programmes. In addition, the television studios may syndicate the digital content which they create to a variety of distribu-

Table 1. *Components of value for the VISOR model (Source: El Sawy et al., 2005)*

Component of Value	Description
Value Proposition	The value proposition offered to the targeted customer segment by the product or service
Interface	The user interface used to deliver the product or service to the customer, and the experience which is created for the customer
Service Platform	The platform to sell, aggregator and distribute the product and service to the customer
Organizing Model	How market players organize business process, use of standards or proprietary technology. How the market players relate to each other in the form of strategic alliance and partnerships so that the value created by market players as a whole is greater than the sum of their value each player creates.
Revenue and Cost Sharing Model	Revenue and cost calculations for each market player. The revenues which are generated from the delivery of the products and services and IT investment should exceed the costs and each player should be rewarded for the added value which they create in the market.

Table 2. SAD framework analysis of the market for time-shifted television

Role	Stakeholder
Digital Content Producer	• Television studios • Movie studios • Independent content producers • News and media companies
Syndicator	• Telecommunications companies • Television studios • Movie studios • Independent content producers • News and media companies
Aggregator	• Telecommunications companies • Television studios • Movie studios • Independent content producers • Cable television providers • IPTV providers • Video-on-demand providers • Internet video websites • News and media companies
Distributor	• Telecommunications companies • Internet Service Providers • Digital device producers • Advertisers • Cable television providers • IPTV providers • Video-on-demand providers • Internet video websites • News and media companies
Consumer	Consumers of digital content via time-shifted television

tors such as video-on-demand services, IPTV service providers and telecommunication companies who may subsequently bundle the digital content with other value added services such as expanded viewing timeslots, advertisement-free viewing or personalized recommendations for other similar content, and distribute the digital content to different or repeated market segments.

While it is possible for a player to play more than one value adding role in the supply chain, it is important for the player to identify its core competencies and how best it can contribute added value to the market. The added value that a player brings to the market is the total value which all players add to the market less the value which all other players add to the market (Brandenburger & Stuart, 1996). In other words,

Player's Added Value = Value of all players – Value of all other players

Players should leverage their core competencies and seek to play roles which maximize their added value to the market. Doing so enables each player to create more value in the market and subsequently, profit from the value, which the player creates. This thereby harnesses the synergies of the different players and creates mutually beneficial partnerships where multiple players can benefit from the value, which is created.

It is also interesting to note that some of the players identified as part of the marketplace for time-shifted television, such as television studios, movie studios and news and media companies, are also market players for traditional broadcast television. While time-shifted television has yet to cross the chasm and gain mainstream adoption, their involvement could be an indication that these players recognize and acknowledge the disruptive threat that time-shifted television poses to their current broadcast television. It also remains to be seen whether these major players from the broadcast televisions exercise visionary leadership and view their involvement in time-shifted television as a way to engage in creative destruction which will cannibalize their existing markets while helping themselves to ensure profitable markets in the future (Chandy & Tellis, 1998), or whether their core competencies of the past may become core rigidities, rendering them only capable of reacting to the disruptive and creative innovations which threaten their business (Schumpeter, 1976).

VISOR Model Analysis

With our analysis of the market place for time-shifted television using the SAD framework, we have identified the various roles which market players can take on to create value as digital content is produced and then delivered to the consumer for consumption. The VISOR framework will now be used to examine business models that can

Table 3. Business model analysis for time-shifted television using the VISOR model

Component of Value	Analysis
Value Proposition	Time-shifted television offers digital content of their choice to consumers, which can be viewed anytime, anywhere and on a variety of devices. This flexibility and choice of content and viewing timeslots enhances the viewing experience for consumers and differentiates time-shifted television from traditional linear broadcast television. It also offers value added services such as advertisement-free content, content recommendations based on consumer viewing preferences and exclusive content. For time-shifted television to cross the chasm and gain adoption in mainstream market, the communication and promotion of the time-shifted television's value proposition is important to gain awareness and brand equity. This is especially important due to the lack of market awareness of some time-shifted television offerings (Graves, 2008). Several forms of consumer-based time-shifted television such as digital video recorders are also similar to video on demand that many consumers are not able to differentiate between the two (Palmer, 2006, p 36), resulting in a lack of awareness of the forms of time-shifted television such as IPTV and video on demand. Again, promotion and creating awareness of the product and service is an important value-creating component of the business model. Time-shifted television can be marketed effectively through a variety of marketing strategies including viral marketing and bundling with existing digital content services such as broadband internet or cable television which consumers may be consuming.
Interface	Time-shifted television can be delivered to consumers through a variety of distribution channels and content can be played on a variety of devices such as networks high definition television sets, television box sets, computers and mobile phones. Interfaces for technology innovations like time-shifted television are especially important for providing consumers with enhanced and interactive viewing experiences (Palmer, 2006, p 34). Providing a good user experiences can help market players for time-shifted television build brand equity and creates value for consumers.
Service Platform	The service platform for time-shifted television consists of a variety of market player who provided added value to the digital content to which content producers create. These include syndicators, aggregators and distributors who play interdependent and overlapping roles to deliver digital content, together with the value added services which time-shifted televisions provides, from the producers to the consumers. The syndicators, aggregators and distributors can add value, not available in traditional television, for consumers such providing added a wider choice of digital content through bundling or flexibility in terms of expands viewing time slots. These value added services which enhance the digital content delivered to consumers via time-shifted television can help market players achieve market orientation.
Organizing Model	Due to the interdependent and overlapping roles, which the market players in the SAD chain for time-shifted television play, strategic alliances and partnerships are important for creating value in the market and ensuring win-win relationships between the various parties. The value adding activities which syndicators, aggregators and distributors perform in the process of delivering digital content from the producer to the consumer can help time-shifted television to achieve market orientation by delivering digital content viewing experiences which consumers want, through time-shifted television, thereby enabling time-shifted television to gain mainstream user adoption, and potentially cross the chasm.
Revenue and Cost Sharing Model	The pricing model is an important part of a business model to enable time-shifted television to cross the chasm. The consumer's willingness to pay is an important factor which influences pricing strategy. Digital content is especially vulnerable to zero-cost as the marginal cost of producing and distributing a unit of digital content is often close to zero after the first unit, due to economies of scale afforded by Moore's Law and the diffusion of digital networks. Market player also need to account for the technology paradox which leads to a rapid decline in prices of digital goods and services (Mohr et al, 2005). To counter these downward forces on prices and to enable time-shifted television to cross the chasm, market players should seek market orientation and adopt customer-oriented pricing. Strong brand equity is also important to pricing strategy (Mohr et al, 2005). Gaining strong brand equity can enable players to adopt captive pricing strategies. This can be relevant to time-shifted television as syndicators, aggregators and distributors deliver digital content to consumers with other value adding services which may be charged at a premium. The quality of the digital content offered also affects the price that consumers will be willing to pay for time-shifted television.

allow time shifted television to create value in the market, gain mainstream adoption, and thereby cross the chasm. Table 3 describes the various components of value for a business model for time-shifted television.

The ways in which the different market players can add value to the market are highlighted in the business model analysis for time-shifted television. It is important the business model that market players adopt creates value in the market and those individuals players are able to subsequently profit appropriately from their created value. This creates a sustainable and mutually beneficial partnership which allows the market time-shifted television to grow, achieve market orientation and gain mainstream market adoption, and thereby cross the chasm.

CONCLUSION

This chapter analyzed the market for time-shifted television market using the SAD framework. The VISOR model has been used to identify value-creating aspects of business models for time-shifted television. We have highlighted ways which players in the market for time-shifted television can create value in the market.

Though time-shifted television was in the market for some time, it has some way to go to cross the chasm and gain mainstream adoption. However, the rapid pace of technology advancement, and the continuous growth of viewing online video content, indicates that there is the potential for time-shifted television. While many companies are trying to enter this new and exciting market place, most of them are not able to achieve adoption in the mainstream market. It remains to be seen whether time-shifted television will be able to cross the chasm.

There are other factors that need to be considered when developing a good business strategy and model to enable time-shifted television to cross the chasm. These include marketing strategy, pricing strategy and how a company can gain market orientation. Future work can be done using other frameworks of analysis, besides Value Net analysis, the SAD framework and the VISOR model, which are relevant to pricing and marketing strategies to further analyze the pricing and marketing strategies of a business model, which can enable time-shifted television to cross the chasm.

REFERENCES

Amit, R., & Zott, C. (2001). Value creation in e-business. *Strategic Management Journal, 22*(6/7), 493–520. doi:10.1002/smj.187

Bernoff, J. (2005). *The real potential of Internet video*. Forrester Research.

Bradenburger, A. M., & Stuart, H. W. (1996). Value-based business strategy. *Journal of Economics & Management Strategy, 5*(1), 5–24. doi:10.1111/j.1430-9134.1996.00005.x

Brandenburger, A. M., & Nalebuff, B. J. (1995). The right game: Use game theory to shape strategy. *Harvard Business Review, 73*(4), 57–71.

Chandy, R. K., & Tellis, G. J. (1998). Organizing for radical product innovation: The overlooked role of willingness to cannibalize. *JMR, Journal of Marketing Research, 25*, 474–487. doi:10.2307/3152166

Dharmawirya, M., Morales-Arroyo, M., & Sharma, R. S. (2008). Adding value in digital media networks. In *Proceedings of the 17th Asian Media Information and Communication Centre (AMIC) Annual Conference*, Manila, 14-16 July 2008.

El Sawy, O., Fife, E., & Pereira, F. (2005). *The VISOR framework: Business model definition for new marketspaces in the networked digital industry*. Retrieved on April 30, 2009, from http://dblab.usc.edu/csci599/CTMVISORFramework.pdf

Graves, D. (2008). *Personal TV: The reinvention of television*. Forrester Research.

IPTV News. (2009, April 15). *Good times come to Singtel's mio TV*. Retrieved April 30, 2009, from http://www.iptv-news.com/iptv_news/april_09/good_times_comes_to_singtels_mio

Leitchman Research Group. (2009). *Online video usage continues to grow: Yet online video is having little impact on traditional TV viewing and services*. Leitchman Research Group.

Mohr, J., Sengupta, S., & Slater, S. (2005). *Marketing of high-technology products and innovations* (2nd ed.). Upper Saddle River, NJ: Pearson Prentice Hall.

Moore, G. (1991). *Crossing the chasm: Marketing and selling technology products to mainstream customers*. New York: HarperCollins.

Motorola. (2007). *Time-shifted television: Expanding the window of television*. Motorola.

Palmer, S. (2006). *Television disrupted: The transition from network to networked TV*. Boston, MA: Focal Press.

Schumpeter, J. A. (1976). *Capitalism, socialism & democracy*. Routledge.

Shafer, S. M., Smith, H. J., & Linder, J. C. (2005). The power of business models. *Business Horizons, 48*(3), 199–207. doi:10.1016/j.bushor.2004.10.014

Wang, G. (2007). *Mobile TV value chain and operator strategies*. Master's Thesis, School of Information and Communication Technology (ICT), Kungliga Tekniska Hogskolan, Finland.

Chapter 14
Exploiting P2P in New Media Distribution

Marcus Mansukhani
Nanyang Technological University, Singapore

He Ye
Nanyang Technological University, Singapore

Ma Zhaoran
Nanyang Technological University, Singapore

ABSTRACT

P2P is currently the most contentious area of Interactive Digital Media on the Internet. It continues to grow in popularity at a phenomenal rate while media producers are seemingly stuck in a cycle of who needs to be prosecuted to prevent this form of piracy, and the majority feel that content should be paid for either to own or to rent with a Digital Rights Management time bomb. An alternative method of paying for the licence to download is presented by two self styled media futurists, and they conclude that it is easier for the industry to adapt to a market based on something that continues to feel like free rather than trying to enforce a model that is clearly not working at the moment and brands hundreds of millions of Internet users criminals. One proposal is that a US$5 monthly licence would produce an income of US$3 billion to the music industry. We explore how this could be extended to the digital media.

INTRODUCTION

Although broadcasting media has been around for a long time, however, each new technology has seemed to disrupt the previous one to some extent. Television disrupted radio and cinema, colour TV disrupted black and white. New media is currently disrupting traditional broadcasting. As

the technology of new media improves the extent of this disruption and means of exploiting it for profit needs to be considered.

At any given time millions of users are using some type of Peer to Peer (P2P) streaming technology to deliver live multimedia content. Existing technologies allow end users to peer-exchange blocks which reduce the burden on the servers of content providers; this has made it possible to distribute legal multimedia of an 'acceptable'

DOI: 10.4018/978-1-61350-147-4.ch014

quality to end users. P2P media streaming typically relies on a mesh overlay topology which has been demonstrated to be more successful than tree-based technologies. Current P2P technologies use simple protocols that form a mesh by sharing lists of peers in order to locate the data (Chuan, Baochun, & Shuqiao, 2008). Overlay multicasting, often referred to as peer-casting, alleviates many of these performance limitations through decentralising the multicasting method as well as facilitating on-demand content delivery. Multicasting is problematic by its very nature and suffers from huge overheads such as duplicate data transfers, uneven load distribution and the unreliability of end hosts.

PeerCast, a proposed implementation of overlay multicasting, is designed to overcome this by being self-configuring, efficient and failure-resistant. Jianjun et al (2008) proposed that this network should have a "Internet-landmark signature technique to cluster the end hosts of the overlay network", be capacity aware to balance the demands of multicasting and they also proposed a dynamic passive replication scheme to overcome the reliability issues of peers. Peer-casting allows chunks to be streamed. With broadband speeds and available bandwidth increasing the number of customers who can download chunks with sufficient speed is rapidly increasing, which makes live high definition media broadcasting a realistic proposition. Although it has already been implemented on a small scale, current bandwidth limitations have meant that on slower connections near-live streaming is not yet possible (Jianjun et al., 2008). Peer-casting refers to multicasting a data stream through P2P technology without central server for distribution.

Currently there are many available architectural designs of P2P systems used for content distribution (Tsoumakos & Roussopoulos, 2003). Content distribution can be done either in distributed way like Gnutella, the "pure P2P system", or in a server mediated way like Napster, BitTorrent, the "Hybrid P2P", a hybrid client/server model

or even based on a pure client/server model like the World Wide Web (Erman, Ilie, & Popescu, 2005). All P2P applications have attracted great attention and applications like BitTorrent, Skype and PPlive had already become part of lifestyle (Li, 2008). The successes of those popular P2P applications have attracted more and more people to develop and invest in P2P which is the main reason behind developments in the technology.

Legal Constraints to Profit from P2P

Since the inception of P2P the issue of copyright has always been the most challenging obstacle for exploiting the technology[1]. A wave of litigation in response to booming global intellectual property rights has been triggered by the prosperity of the Internet; this is accelerated by the growth in popularity of Web 2.0 technologies substantially worsening the problem. P2P in its current implementation provides the biggest platform for distributing pirated media and other illegal content. For instance with P2P online TV most of the distributed content is done without the permission of content owner and often breaches the local laws of some countries as well as the content often being restricted in certain regions (ManyWorlds, 2002).

Generating revenue from digital media distributed through the Internet is a critical growth area for Interactive Digital Media. There are two possible options for generating income through *pay for content* or the proposed model of *pay for attention*. Pay for content uses a traditional model of renting content for a limited period of time while pay for attention sets a fixed fee for unlimited content downloading (Leonhard, 2009). Exploiting P2P for profit is a controversial area with many media producers currently favouring a pay for content model which would parallel the existing traditional media distribution model where customers pay to purchase a physical object such as a video cassette or DVD or pay to rent content from a video rental shop, watch in the cinema or, in recent times, pay for time restricted DRM protected downloads. Pay for attention, also known as collective licensing, is a proposed alternative model where a licence fee is paid by the customer and he is granted the licence to download P2P content with some legal constraints that presumes that Internet users will download content through the most convenient means and that they will disregard if such means is legal or not. The model compares Internet media usage to licensed television and radio and proposes that a media licence should be issued to allow users to legally download copyrighted content through P2P. It presumes that no matter what legislation is enacted users will continue to access pirated content so offers an opportunity to profit from that content rather than keep it illegal (Leonhard, 2009). This would essentially move P2P from being free content to being 'feels like free' content and would remove the stigmatism of it being illegal. One suggested means of revenue for this would be a global tax on Internet usage, von Lohmann (2008) however argues that this should not be a tax but an opt-in licence.

In China music is currently available for free downloads with Google lubricating the market with little concern about cannibalisation due to the lack of copyright legislation. This is a move towards a legal model, at present there is no obvious profit channel from this model with Google stating that "we can make money later"[2]. This is an example of a disruptive technology where the initial intent is to capture the market and then later exploit it for profit. P2P has already done that, the market is enormous but very little has been done to exploit it with the current focus of media producers being on how to restrict it.

Leonhard (2004, 2009) proposes a model for music distribution based on the Chinese model with a licence and advertising revenue method. Figure 1 shows how the nature of revenue incomes is changing with traditional retail being the worst affected area and licensing and music service projected to take over the majority of the

market. This model is scalable for other forms of digital media; he proposes that this method would mean that the content producers would be paid, usage data is made available, market data is made available and media creators are paid by download as a proportion of the collected revenue. Such a model would require significant legislative change in the nations that choose to adopt it.

FRAMEWORK FOR ANALYSIS

Table 1 shows the implicit/structural and explicit/personalization of the SAD framework and Leonhard's remuneration model.

Syndication

Collective Licensing

The battle between legal and illegal use of P2P has existed for several years. The fact is that illegal downloading is here to stay – people will continue to share and download copyrighted digital material on the Internet for free. New technologies

Figure 1. Revenue streams: Today and tomorrow for the music industry (Leonhard, 2004)

Revenue Streams : today and tomorrow

Table 1. Based on SAD framework and Leonhard's remuneration model (2009)

	Implicit/ Structural	Explicit/ Personalization
Syndication	Proactive marketing, content licensing options	Advertising
Aggregation	Collection of content	Media convergence, consumer participation, affiliation and syndication
Distribution	Streaming of content, legal aspects, technological solutions, channel management, partnerships,	Provide value, billing and collection, sales and support, monetisation, strategy blending, repurposed content, viral sharing, social recommendations, combating piracy

enable users to obtain and distribute copyrighted digital material easier and P2P continues to gain popularity. An alternative approach to transfer P2P into profit making is collective licensing where the copyright holders are paid through the P2P network. Users share and download any digital material legally. The concept of collective licensing originated from the Electronic Frontier Foundation (Lohmann, 2008). The concept of collective licensing is as follows:

- Copyright holders create websites to allow P2P users to share and download legally by making a reasonable payment every month.
- The monthly download fee is adjustable and depends on a number of factors that need to be agreed upon between legislators and content producers.
- After the users pay the download fee, they can continue downloading any music, software and movies which are considered legal downloads by local law so long they continue to pay a monthly fee.

However the number of users of P2P around the world is unknown but has been estimated as being in the hundreds of thousands. If each of those paid a few dollars for downloading, the copyright owners or authors would gain a significant source of revenue that would substantially counter the loss of income caused by piracy. The money collected from subscribers would be divided among resource providers based on the popularity of content and therefore the creator of media that is most popular would gain the greatest revenue. Users can share whatever they want and have the right to let others know which digital media they like and which software they find interesting. Therefore more users sharing and downloading digital media and software would result in a greater income for copyright owners. According to the Electronic Frontier Foundation (Lohmann, 2008), there are 60 million Americans who uses P2P sharing software. The Foundation suggests that US\$5 per month for each user would result in over US\$3 billion income annually to music industry. This would represent a significant income to the music industry. In 2006 the global retail value for recorded music was estimated as being approximately US\$30 billion of which 36% was in the USA (Wikström, 2009) representing just under a third of the income for recorded music from what would previously have been considered income lost due to piracy. However when factoring in digital media and software this amount becomes increasingly spread out therefore the actual rate would need extensive market research before being set.

In order to implement the Collective Licensing, the copyright holders, authors, ISPs and P2P software creators must be syndicated. They must work together to create a standard that everybody must follow. Music producers, movie makers and even game developers need to work together.

The advantages of new revenue from collective licensing are as follows:

1. **No CD or DVD required:** The producers can make a CD-less albums and DVD-less movies, so that there is no cost producing physical media. The cost of transportation also can be saved and best of all no stock is needed, once an album or software is created it can be downloaded unlimited times. This would dramatically reduce the cost of the first item.

2. **No advertisement required:** The cost of promoting digital media through advertising is very high. With the help of the P2P network, users are able to download any digital media and software they want. They know which files they desire most and user recommendation will be a key means of promotion.

3. **No online / physical retail store required:** Medium-less music and software can be sold in physical stores as well as online retail store, for example, Amazon.com. The users who require it can share music, software or movie via the P2P network. The cost of online or physical retail store can be saved although physical stores may choose to adapt to the market by producing customised media.

Collective licensing, however, is not perfect as it does have its weak points. The popularity of software, music and digital media is determined via different standards. For example, software is typically popular due to good functionality, easy to use and so on while music becomes popular due to the popularity of the artist or the reputation of the song.

Advertising

File sharing through P2P networks are still gaining in popularity nowadays, according to Tiversa[3] over 450 million P2P users are issuing 1.5 billion searches per day. Such a huge number of searches can generate new revenue for the P2P market. The new concept is known as 'advertising with P2P search engines'. The rationale of advertising with P2P search engines is to embed advertising functions into both the P2P search engine and the download tools. Figure 2 shows how this works .

When users type in the keyword they wish to search, the advertisement will appear below the search results. Many potential uses for the advertisement include promotion of new albums, movies, or to introduce a product. This could very useful for a company to promote their product or service within the established P2P communities. With 450 million unique users every day conducting on average just over three searches the strategic benefits of placing advertising is an easy option to attract more people to recognise a brand or buy a product or service. The advantage of this method is that the size of user group is huge. Many companies could make money from it and revenue generation from P2P advertising is a market that could be more effectively exploited in the near future. P2P advertising has many advantages but it has areas for improvement. First, advertisement providers must follow the rules and regulations as there is no control over the content that the advertisers put on the P2P networks and even executable files are not a problem. Second, the adverts inserted by the software are not listed as adverts in the search results[5]. Certain policies

Figure 2. P2P search engine with advertising[4]

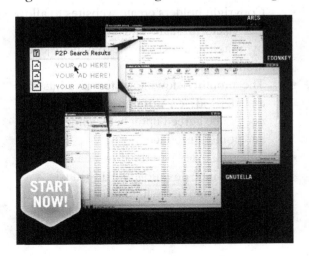

must be created to regulate the advertisement publishing. One of the risks of allowing unregulated advertising was demonstrated when the spam filters from Google resulted in user pages from Pirate Bay being blocked[6].

Aggregation

Collection of content is the main implicit requirement of aggregation. An individual media company would be primarily focused on aggregating its own content while an independent aggregator, such as Hulu.com, would be more interested in collecting media content from multiple sources[7]. Such syndication forms the basis of a structure for content distribution. External aggregation can be achieved through a number of methods including media convergence, consumer participation, affiliation and syndication. Media convergence can be achieved when content producers move beyond their traditional mediums and embrace different forms of media – for example the Straits Times in Singapore has started a RazorTV service where print journalists present commentary and conduct interviews[8]. The most famous case of consumer aggregation is through YouTube and modern digital media includes consumer generated work, Web 2.0 has empowered consumers and digital media is therefore driven by the consumer needs even more than traditional media. Due to its nature digital streaming of content through P2P methods such as peer-casting, it is substantially cheaper than through traditional methods and the costs incurred are mostly through aggregation of content rather than through distribution. This implies that consumer generated content is more feasible although this does strongly imply the need for regulation of content both for legal reasons and quality standards. The level of aggregation of consumer generated content is therefore dependent on the level of regulation. Affiliation and syndication are key methods of preserving quality, traditionally local broadcasters formed affiliations with regional and national broadcasters[9] who would

syndicate content for local distribution; with new media channels the concept of local broadcasting is countered with the option of an international audience although geographical restrictions can be put into place. Technically this would require the use of the existing Real-time Transport Protocol (RTP) and Real Time Control Protocol (RTCP) and the proposed Audio-Visual Profile with Feedback (AVPF) protocol (Johansson & Westerlund, 2009) where restrictions including geographical restrictions can be included.

Aggregated content using peer casting has the flexibility of using near live streams as well as time-shifted viewing without any additional technological change. A technological constraint is that less popular streams that are initially seeded from slower connections would only be available on a time shifted basis and this would restrict the broadcasting ability (Jianjun et al., 2008).

Distribution

Delivering restricted or non-copyrighted content is undeniably the most attractive factor in attracting a large number of users. However many media producers and aggregators suffer from the distribution of restricted and illegal content and have been accused by many organisations including the content owners, World Intellectual Property Organization (WIPO) and related monitoring authorities. More organisations have started to pay attention to protecting copyrighted content and fight to make the distribution of copyrighted content increasingly difficult. Digital Right Management systems have been developed to enhance the barrier of illegal distribution and legislation has been tightened globally in order to protect the legal rights of content owners. For instance the Digital Millennium Copyright Act (USA) and Copyright Amendments (Digital Agenda) Act (Australia) have been implemented and other similar acts are being developed all the time to meet the increasing demand. However, laws and regulations are unable to be the shelter of copyrighted content as technology has always developed faster and beyond the pace of completing legal codes as legal provision could seldom take initiatives in protecting copyrighted content but only can take passive countermeasures.

Potential Profiting Models for P2P

In order to seek the potential, business models of P2P marketers are advised to follow the steps[10]:

1. Be clear of the characteristics of P2P to locate the position of P2P in the industry chain.
2. Examine other nodes of the P2P industry chain and develop profiting possibilities.
3. Focus on the key profiting possibilities and seek potential opportunities.

The value chain of the P2P industry could be defined as Content→ Platform→ Technology→ Receiver.

*   **Content:** The content itself could not provide the distributor business value until the content was released and the purchase investment could be turned into profits. The profits could be derived from advertising, sponsor investment and so on.
*   **Platform:** The platform itself is the underpinning of distributing contents. Huge traffic volumes and information dissemination bring tremendous business advertising value and opportunities.
*   **Technology:** P2P technology occupies little business value except for selling the technology. Therefore it does not possess many potential opportunities for profiting. However peer casting is effectively more of a channel for media distribution and income can be derived through other sources.
*   **Receiver:** The huge amount of receivers is undeniably the crucial factor of developing peer casting. The number of receivers, consumption ability, online time, age

structure and the consumption preference of the receivers and many other characteristics could offer significant profit opportunities[11].

CONCLUSION

In order to exploit fourth generation P2P there are two possible revenue models. The content producers favour a model that parallels the retail industry with users being charged for each item either as a premium pay-to-own to parallel purchasing media or as pay-to-view to parallel renting of media. An alternative model is pay for attention or collective licensing where the consumer pays a fixed amount and can legally download unlimited amounts of media and software legally.

Collective licensing has the advantage that it retains the 'feels like free' feeling and mimics the actions of hundreds of millions of Internet users, the main disadvantage is that it would require some technological change and agreements of media content producers, software houses and legislative change and each of these could prove to be a bottleneck for implementation. Those who argue for this method claim that it would mean some revenue against no revenue from pirated material. One writer (Lohmann, 2008) argues that such a method should be voluntary opt-in rather than a tax although accepts that the opt-in could be done at ISP level rather than from individuals.

The technology behind PeerCasting is explored in some detail by Jianjun et al. (2008). The business models for exploiting P2P for profit through collective licensing are presented by Leonhard (2004, 2009) and Lohmann (2008). Background information is available through multiple sources and as the industry is changing so rapidly it is wise to continue to monitor the news and follow reports in publications such as CNet, Torrentfreak and various other sites that cover Interactive Digital Media and follow P2P news.

REFERENCES

Chuan, W., Baochun, L., & Shuqiao, Z. (2008). Exploring large-scale peer-to-peer live streaming topologies. *ACM Trans. Multimedia Comput. Commun. Appl., 4*(3), 1–23. doi:10.1145/1386109.1386112

Erman, D., Ilie, D., & Popescu, A. (2005). *Bittorrent session characteristics and models.* Paper presented at the 3rd International Working Conference on Performance Modelling and Evaluation of Heterogeneous Networks.

Jianjun, Z., Ling, L., Lakshmish, R., & Calton, P. (2008). PeerCast: Churn-resilient end system multicast on heterogeneous overlay networks. *Journal of Network and Computer Applications, 31*(4), 821–850. doi:10.1016/j.jnca.2007.05.001

Johansson, I., & Westerlund, M. (2009). *Support for reduced-size real-time transport control protocol (RTCP): Opportunities and consequences.* RFC 5506. Retrieved from http://tools.ietf.org/html/rfc5506

Leonhard, G. (2004). *The future of music - An introductory essay.*

Leonhard, G. (2009). *Music 2.0: Embracing business opportunities in the digital age: New compensation models new business paradigms.* MediaFuturist.

Li, J. (2008). On peer-to-peer (P2P) content delivery. *Peer-to-Peer Networking and Applications, 1*(1), 45–63. doi:10.1007/s12083-007-0003-1

Lohmann, F. v. (2008). A better way forward: Voluntary collective licensing of music file sharing ver. 2.1 [Electronic Version]. Retrieved from http://www.eff.org/files/eff-a-better-way-forward.pdf

ManyWorlds. (2002). *Can peer-to-peer processes produce profits?* Houston, TX: ManyWorlds, Inc.

Tsoumakos, D., & Roussopoulos, N. (2003). *A comparison of peer-to-peer search methods.* Paper presented at the International Workshop on the Web and Databases (WebDB).

Wikström, P. (2009). *A music business out of control.* Jönköping, Sweden: Media Management and Transformation Centre, Jönköping International Business School.

ENDNOTES

[1] http://tele.pconline.com.cn/live/0609/867595.html, Booming P2P industry struggling for profit models. Accessed 30/4/2009

[2] http://www.ft.com/cms/s/0/adaa5ca2-1e55-11de-830b-00144feabdc0.html Google forced to concede to Chinese way of thinking, Financial Times, 1/4/2009 as accessed 29/4/2009

[3] http://www.tiversa.com/ Homepage as accessed 30/4/2009

[4] http://www.brandassetdigital.com/#/introduction/ P2P Words – advertise your brand across P2P as accessed 30/4/2009

[5] http://b.www.mixx.com/cik6?campid=0&ssns=41& Adwords for P2P, Advertising Opportunity or Spamming Tool?, 23/11/2008 as accessed 30/4/2009

[6] http://torrentfreak.com/the-pirate-bay-user-pages-blocked-by-google-090315/ The Pirate Bay User Pages Blocked by Google, Firefox, 15/3/2009 as accessed 30/4/2009

[7] http://findarticles.com/p/articles/mi_m0EIN/is_2008_April_14/ai_n25151040/ Signiant Powers Digital Media Aggregation for Hulu, Business Services Industry, 14/4/2008 as accessed 29/4/2009

[8] http://www.razor.tv/site/servlet/segment/main/about/ About Us section on RazorTV website as accessed 29/4/2009

9   http://austv.hostforweb.com/cgi-bin/cgi2/
     index.rb?page=Affiliation&section=Glos
     sary/A&mode=0#sect1 Affiliation During
     Aggregation, Australian TV archive as ac-
     cessed 29/4/2009

10   http://comment.uuuso.com/show/Show.1
     236055.1.xhtml?NewsId=1236055 How
     to profit from P2P, 3/3/2009 as accessed
     29/4/2009

11   http://www.ccidconsulting.com/insights/
     content.asp?Content_id=16724 P2P New
     media is rich in profiting models, 30/7/2008
     as accessed 29/4/2009

Chapter 15
A Shop Bot for Web Market Intelligence

Miguel A. Morales-Arroyo
UNAM, Mexico

Foo Chee Yuan
Nanyang Technical University, Singapore

Lim Thian Muar
Nanyang Technical University, Singapore

Kwek Choon Hwee
Nanyang Technical University, Singapore

ABSTRACT

With the large amount of information available in the WWW, the ability to distinguish relevant from irrelevant data becomes a crucial factor. In this project, eight web scraping spiders were configured and evaluated for their functionality in order to determine their suitability for Interactive Digital media (IDM) start-ups to be utilized for competitive intelligence gathering. These spiders were chosen from the internet because of their availability and low cost. Each spider was configured and tested on two web sites. The evaluation process was first carried out individually to give a score to the spiders and then as a team to moderate the scores. The Web Info Extractor has the highest overall score as a web scraping spider while the Web Content Extractor has the best task analysis result. After the evaluation process, it is concluded that different spiders have varying capabilities and thus are suitable for different tasks. A spider that can handle more complex tasks is usually inherently more complex to configure and less-user friendly. Hence, in order to select the correct spider, companies should understand the tasks undertaken by their customers through basic task analysis as well as the knowledge of the amount of resources that they have at their disposal when it comes to configuring and operating the spiders.

DOI: 10.4018/978-1-61350-147-4.ch015

INTRODUCTION

In today's business environment, the competitiveness of a company will depend on the ability of the enterprise to gather information from their respective business market and transfer that information into their strategic plans and decision making processes. In addition, an appropriate plan can then be made in response to changes in the market environment. In the past, information was gathered manually through a tedious process. But with the advancement of computing technology and the vast amount of information in the World Wide Web (WWW), gathering large amount of information is now possible by the introduction of web crawlers or scrappers.

Enterprises use information and knowledge to generate their product and/or services. Besides, the know-how needed to understand the market, costumers, providers, competitors, their competitive advantages and weakness. Enterprises need to constantly monitor its environment to keep competitive. They need to scrutinize potential threats and to seek for opportunities. Consequently, they require to access to external sources of information.

Market intelligence is a set of methodologies and technologies that are used for gathering, storing, analyzing, and providing access to data that enable the decision makers to make better business decisions (Keyes, 2006). The goal is to transform data into knowledge. Web market intelligence is a subset of business intelligence whereby data comes solely gathered from the web for analyzing. Market intelligence is the acquisition of environmental information that allows enterprises to keep a competitive edge. In other words, market intelligence provides an apparent advantage to business organizations on their competition by identifying the position, strategies of their competition, users' preferences and dislikes by gathering and analyzing external sources of information. Once information and knowledge have been acquired, it needs to be categorized, processed, prepared, and distributed for analysis to users inside the organization. The objective is to ensure that all the required valuable knowledge and information in relation to the competition and consumers' preferences are available as an input for the decision-making process (Carpe, 2007).

With the arrival of the Internet, new external sources of information and knowledge are available. Inherently, social interaction could be mined to gather consumers' preferences in relation to the own enterprise products and services or the competition. The same technologies used to share knowledge and information in the Internet can be utilized inside of the organization to empower staff to participate in the business intelligence process as collectors, analyst, and decision makers. The internet is considered as a competitive source of information (Brabston & McNamara, 1998) and seen as a cheap and quick mean to collect information (Wood, 2001). Scanning the internet environment offers a gateway to vast and varied information that can assist the enterprise in seeking and using information (Pawar & Sharda, 1997).

It has been found that companies are not exploiting the full potential of the internet (Dutta & Segev, 1999). Another study had showed that companies only use the internet as a means of portraying the corporate image (Adam et al., 2002). When it comes to use the Internet as a knowledge resource, there is a surprising low usage.

Information source identification and information gathering use numerous sources and techniques to obtain knowledge and information required by enterprises. Some sources of information are easy to accessed and free, such as financial statements in public companies, but others are expensive like marketing reports. Some not distributed information may be very difficult or almost impossible to obtain, for example competitors' strategies. Potential sources of unpublished information could be providers, consumers, or governmental representatives that have interaction with the competition and the regulatory process (Calof & Wright, 2008).

Gathering information from the Internet is a reliable way to identify potential sources of unpublished information, call them potential informants. Networking sites could be a great source to identify people as a source of business intelligence. LinkedIn is an example of business social network, where users display their professional information. However, the process of making contact with potential informants and gathering data are frequently difficult and time consuming activity (Carpe, 2007).

Gathering information from the internet needs constant updates since web pages are constantly changing. RSS feeds are an alternative to keep updated when the content is added or changed. Some web sites, blogs, and other online resources are offering RSS feeds. These tools have the advantage to save time since the analyst does not have to visit everyday relevant online resources, just when there is relevant information. Other advantages include the reduction in costs and limited concerns about security (Johnson, 2006).

Market intelligence is a concept that has several interpretations, and this concept is addressed using different names like marketing intelligence, competitive intelligence, and costumer intelligence (Calof & Wright, 2008, Hannula & Pirttimäki, 2005, Thierauf, 2001). In this work, the authors consider market intelligence as a set tools and techniques used first to identify information and knowledge gaps with the intention to solve organizational problems related with their competition and consumers. Second, once the information and knowledge have been identified, these tools and techniques are used to gather, analyze, and process information and knowledge that will support the decision making process and strategic planning.

The business intelligence process initiates with the identification of information needs. It is not sufficient to identify information gaps in order to solve the problems organizations confront, but where and who needs relevant information. This information needs have to consider business strategies and organizational environment, and it cannot be considered in isolation. Not only it is important to gather and analyze the information needed, but also shared with the correct staff at the correct time (Turban et al., 2008).

Market intelligence is continual process of identification, gathering, analysis, synthesis, and once the decision making process has finished. A new cycle of market intelligence starts again. By using information and knowledge, a new understanding of the situation under study is achieved. The market intelligence process is not an isolated phenomenon, and it has to be associated with the rest of organizational processes (Choo, 2002, Gilad & Gilad, 1985).

Increasing high volumes of information are available for management from different types of databases (video, images, audio, and text), data warehouses, and information and knowledge repositories. There is a great need for tools that simplified the market business intelligence process. Among those tools, there are search engines, reporting systems, online analytical processing, decision support system, predictive analytics, executive information systems, data warehousing and data mining, Business Dashboards, and any management information systems (Foote & Krishnamurthi, 2001, Salomanna et al., 2005, Turban et al., 2008, Watson et al., 2006). In our particular case, we will study shop bots, also known as web scrappers, spider, or crawler. A web scrapper is a variant of the web crawler that search for certain specific information, for example prices of a particular product from online stores, and then aggregates it into a new set of information (Adams & McCrindle, 2008). With these web crawlers and scrappers, information on the web can be easily extracted.

The objective of this work is to evaluate various types of Shop Bots that are suitable for Interactive Digital Media (IDM) start-ups in order they can utilize the Shop Bots for competitive intelligence gathering. In this document, IDM refers to digital media that allows user to interact with the digital information, like digital video, digital music, etc that is available and IDM start-up refers to those businesses that involve in selling and buying digital products (i.e. music, video, computer games, et cetera).

The organization of this chapter is as follow: the next section will review the background literature in the area of web crawling and web data extraction. Evaluation strategy section will discuss the evaluation strategy follow by the Evaluation process section which focus on evaluation metrics and Section 5 which focuses on the task analysis for the web crawler. Section 6 discussed the evaluation process and then section 7 will present the result for the Shop Bots' evaluation. Section 8 will conclude the project and provide the scope for future works to be carried out in this area.

BACKGROUND

There are many terminologies used for web crawlers, namely ants, automatic indexers, bots, and worms or web spider, web robot, web scrapper, etc. In this chapter, the term Shop Bot will be used. Shop Bots are web crawlers that essentially help to gather price of product from different vendors. Smith and Brynjolfsson (2001) define Shop Bots and their functions as follow:

Shop Bots are Internet-based assistance that provides easy entry to products and services information their prices from many competitors. By doing so, they diminish purchase search costs. Shop Bots gather and present information on a diversity of product and/or service features, summarize information from known and unfamiliar vendors, and normally order the sellers based on a traits relevant to the buyer like price or delivery time. The comparative tabulations disclose discrepancies in price, product availability, delivery times and other features across sellers (Smith & Brynjolfsson, 2001). With the gathered information, customers' choice behavior can be observed and analyzed as they evaluate the listed alternatives and click on a particular product offer.

Architectures for Web Business Intelligence have been proposed. These process starts by retrieving information, follow by information extraction, and text processing. The process includes online analytical processing (OLAP), which is a way to rapidly reply multi-dimensional analytic queries. Relevance ranking, which is based specific criteria, in the case of Google – popularity indicated by the number of links. Pattern discovery uses different techniques and algorithms, like statistics, machine learning, and pattern recognition (Srivastava & Cooley, 2003). IBM developed Intelligent Miner Family describe their operation and techniques used are described by Tkach (1998). IBM made a detailed description of its functionality. The two most common kinds of information are structured data and text. Consequently, at the most basic level market intelligence includes data mining and text mining (Tkach, 1998).

It was found the use of term Web mining was confusing, and it was suggested three categories for Web mining, i.e. web content mining, web structure mining and web usage mining (Kosala & Blockeel, 2000). They define web content mining as the discovery of useful information from web pages but web content could encompass a very broad range of data. The attempts to find the model underlying the link structures of the web is classified as web structure mining. Finally, web usage mining tries to make sense of the data generated by the web crawling session.

An overview of the web data extraction tools has been provided based on their accuracy and robustness (Laender et al., 2002). The objective of these tools is to generate wrappers that are accurate and robust and at the same time required as little effort from the wrappers developer as possible. The paper mentioned previously in this paragraph address the issue - how the tools support some of the features that are important in generation of wrappers and the data extraction process.

In another study that focus on the major web data extraction alternatives. Three criteria are used to compare the different information extraction (IE) system, namely the task domain, the automation degree and the techniques used (Chang et al., 2006). The 'task domain' dimension is used to evaluate the difficulty of an IE task and why an IE system fails to handle some web sites. The 'automation degree' dimension measures how easy the IE system can be automated in the data extraction process. The 'techniques used' dimension looks into the type of extraction rules that are used in the IE system. These three criteria are applied to four different types of IE system: manual-constructed, supervised, semi-supervised and un-supervised, to determine how good they can perform the information extraction from the different web sites.

The literature review identifies that internet is a good source of information. However, it also reveals that there is a lack of use in web market information gathering by companies. The literature review also covers the recent research of web extraction tools.

EVALUATION STRATEGY

This section discusses the methodologies used in selecting and evaluating shop bots. The process followed in the evaluation. Defines shop bots selected and its features, the different strategies used during the evaluation. It also discussed the chosen website used for the evaluation.

Methodology

As IDM companies usually sell their products online as well as directly to consumers, it becomes obvious that the information to be gathered will come directly from monitoring and gathering from these websites which can be done by using suitable Shop Bots.

The authors adapted Jadhav and Sonar's (2009) proposed generic methodology in evaluation of suitable Shop Bots software packages (Jadhav &

Sonar, 2009). They suggested 7 stages in evaluation of software packages and these are determining the software needs, short listing the software candidates, eliminating unsuitable candidates, using an evaluation technique to evaluate the short listed candidates, obtaining trail copies to run pilot trials, negotiating prices and implementing the chosen software.

For this study, the last two stages are irrelevant as they deal with actual purchase of software and implementation. Hence they are disregarded and the final adapted steps are shown below.

- **Step 1: Identifying the IDM competitors' data to be gathered.** The data to be gathered have to be identified first. Since IDM players sell their products directly online, inventory, promotion, prices are likely to be made directly available to the public and hence all can be considered for gathering.
- **Step 2: Selecting the Shot Bots for evaluation.** A set of Shop Bots will be considered for evaluation based on the requirements as well as resources of a small IDM player.
- **Step 3: Selecting the websites for the Shop Bots evaluation.** A few major IDM players ecommerce website will be chosen for evaluation of the Shop Bots.
- **Step 4: Determining the Shop Bots evaluation technique and criteria.** The Shot Bots evaluation technique chosen is value based evaluation as introduced by Matthias Heindl et al. (2006). This methodology incorporates two rating models. The first model is the tool rating model whereby a neutral metrics evaluation criterion is used to compare the software. The evaluation metrics selected are listed in section 4. The second is tool value model whereby the software is being measured based on a task situation (Heindl et al., 2006). The criteria are listed in task analysis in section 5.

- **Step 5: Obtaining and evaluating the Shop Bots.** The Shop Bots are tested on the chosen web sites and evaluated based on the criteria chosen. For evaluation metrics, the authors based the evaluation process on previous research on web scraping software and on general software evaluation (Mehlführer, 2009, Vlahavas et al., 1999).

- **Step 6: Results moderation.** The results gathered will be moderated and the moderation technique used is explained later in the chapter. The main goal of this methodology is to suggest a mechanism to select a web shop tool. To achieve the previous goal, a tool selection process was defined. This selection procedure it is suggested for small companies in the interactive digital market. In order to suggest, the web shops, the study was carry by searching on two specific web sites.

Chosen Web Sites

Knowing how the Shop Bot crawl a web site will determine the web sites that would be used for the evaluation. Shop Bot typically crawls the web site by two methods, either breath first search or depth first search (Rappaport, 2008). Breath first search retrieves pages around the starting point before following links that are further away from the start point. Depth first search retrieves all pages that are linked from the first page before moving on to the second page.

In order to evaluate the two crawling methods, two web sites were chosen for their popularity. *7Digital* is chosen to evaluate depth first search and a "popular online retailer", which is referred in the images as zazx.ykt or zazx when needed. This popular retailer was chosen to evaluate breath first search. Figure 1 shows the screen shot of *7Digital*. Data are not shown on the first page. To get the data, one has to select the song title to go to the song detail page. Figure 2 shows the screen shot of the "popular online retailer." The Shop Bot can get all the data on the page.

Chosen Shop Bots

This sub-section gives a description of several Shop Bots that are chosen for the evaluation. The Shop Bots that are chosen have to be low cost as the start ups does not like to spend a lot on technology (Group, 2008). The Shop Bots must also be able to be easily purchased. Last but not least the installation of the Shop Bots must also be simple.

Figure 1. Screen shot of 7Digital

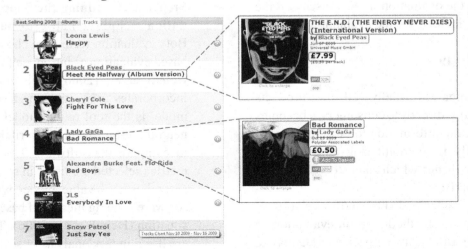

Figure 2. Screen shot of the "popular online retailer"

Screen shot of the Shop Bots' configuration and output are shown in Appendix B.

Bget

Bget (http://www.bget.com/) is fast and powerful web data extraction software. It supports web data mining, website content maintenance and web information monitoring. Although the software is powerful and it comes with an online help and has sample on the different scenarios, the author feels that the learning curve is steep. It requires substantial amount of time to become somehow proficient in the usage.

Vietspider

Vietspider (http://headvances.com/) is an open source crawler using HTML parsing as the means of crawling. Installation is easy as it is just a zip file containing its libraries. The crawler though a bit slow, has many advanced features such as database connectivity and GUI based configuration. It is also available for various platforms such as Linux as it is JAVA based. Though configuration is a bit complex as it has many features, the fact that it is zero cost and produce reasonable results make it a good choice for IDM start-up with little budget.

Web Content Extractor

Web Content Extractor (http://www.newprosoft.com/) is a low cost web data scraper which is relatively easy to use. It can handle complex tasks such as extracting from pop-up windows even if it is GUI based. Results though not clean can be filtered by end-user using criteria and scripts. Scraping speed is relatively fast.

Web Info Extractor

Web Info Extractor (http://www.webinfoextractor.com/) is a web scraper with advance features such as availability of child tasks being attached to main tasks as defined by user. It's multitasking, data filtering and database connections features are also very advanced. The interface is very clean and easy to understand and configuration is easy. Its only letdown is the pricing which is expensive for what it can do versus the other Shop Bots with similar features.

Visual Web Ripper

Visual Web Ripper (http://www.visualwebripper.com/) is an easy to use web site scraper as most of the steps that the user need to do in terms of configurations is done very the GUI. Complex operations such as script editing, creation of templates are also available for the users. This Shop Bot seems to take up much of the computer resources as some operations seem to make the software less responsive.

Happy Harvester

Happy harvester (http://www.happyharvester.com/) is a web scraper spider that uses parsing rules to extract data from web pages or text files. The sources can reside on local hard disk or on the internet. The user interface is designed to be intuitive and simple so as to allow easy customization

of the spider. It also has an advanced mode that can extract data from complex site structures by using script rules. Collected data can be exported to Excel or CSV format. Happy harvester also supports automatic scheduling.

Web Power Data Mining

Web power data mining (http://www.bitware-specialists.com) is a freeware that is design to be efficient in internet telemarketing, internet data mining, capturing data or links from the internet and web based emails. The application can be activated through the default user interface or DOS prompt. Web power data mining enable user to call via other application using the DOS prompt method, simplifying the integration process with other application. The data that is captured can be stored in text file, hypertext markup language or comma-separated values files. It also supports scheduling of jobs so that data can be captured at predefined timing.

Visual Web Task

Visual web task (http://www.lencom.com/VisualWTSite.html) allows user to configure the Shop Bots to negotiate logins, crawl proxies and security pages for data. It has an intuitive user interface and the Shop Bot's configuration is done using visual parsing. The data that is extracted can be stored in text files or ODBC databases. Visual web task also allows to be customized through Visual Basic.

Type of Shop Bots

Different types of Shop Bot employ different ways of data extraction, hence the configuration of such Shop Bots are also different. In the eight Shop Bots evaluated, the different configurations are listed below. Parsing is fundamental to identify words and syntactic, which is fundamental in the

Figure 3. Example of parsing rule algorithm

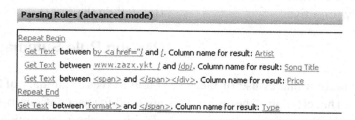

Figure 4. Example of words, phrases and sections excluded

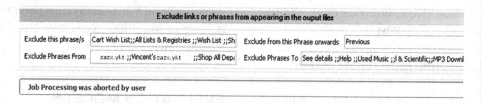

recognition of the basic elements for the discovery of information that is necessary to retrieve.

Parsing Rules

Shot Bot that uses parsing rules are represented by regular grammars to identify the beginning and end of the relevant data. Parsing rules are powerful for semi-structured web sites, since we usually find common tokens surrounding the data to be extracted (Chang et al., 2006). It requires user to have some understanding of how computer algorithm work. The user has to set a proper flow of execution for the parsing rules in order to extract the desire information from the web page. This method uses the HTML source code of the web page to set up the parsing algorithm and requires the user to locate the data (i.e. the first data record) to be extracted. It assumes all sequence data records have identical format as the first. Any differential may cause wrong information to be extracted. Figure 3 is an example of using the parsing rules to extract information, which is the process of analyzing a text, a sequence of words, to establish its grammatical construction.

Elimination

Shot bot will extract all information from the web page and producing it in an ad hoc format (Specialists, 2007). It then allows the users to eliminate the unwanted information base on the results obtain (Figure 4). The elimination process is carried by the Shop Bot when the user identifies the word, phrase and section of the web page that is to be left out during the crawling process. This requires multiply times of crawling before the

Figure 5. Example of HTML nodes for selection

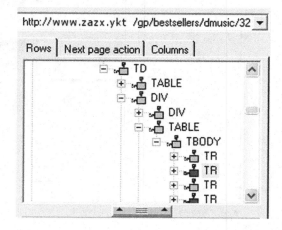

desire information can be obtained. This method of configuration is very primitive.

HTML Nodes

This method of configuration makes use of the HTML nodes (Figure 5). The selection of the desire data that is to be extracted is through the selection of node that contains the data in the web page. It is a quick and simply way of identifying the data for extraction (Kowalkiewicz et al., 2006a, Kowalkiewicz et al., 2006b).

Graphic User Interface (GUI) Based

Some Shop Bot uses extensive GUI to assist the users in the scraping process thereby hides the types of scraping techniques that they use underneath. GUI allows users to navigate and point to wanted data in order to build a scraping task for data extraction (Kowalkiewicz et al., 2006a, Kowalkiewicz et al., 2006b). The users basically follow through some wizard based process in

determining the data to be scraped and the Shop Bot will do the rest (Figure 6).

Parsing Rule Summary

Table 1 gives a summary of the parsing rules that are used for the configuration of the Shop Bot. It also gives a short description of the efficiency and the effectiveness of each method. These configuration traits have been identified in the literature as useful criteria when analyzing parsing behavior (Chang et al., 2006, Kosala & Blockeel, 2000, Kowalkiewicz et al., 2006a).

EVALUATION MODELS

Tool Rating Model (Evaluation Metrics)

For evaluation metrics, the authors based the evaluation process on previous research on web scraping software and on general software evalu-

Figure 6. Example of HTML nodes for selection

Table 1. Comparison of shop bot configuration

Method used for configuring Shop Bot	Efficiency (How fast is it to configure the Web Crawler)	Effectiveness (How good is the obtained result)	Remark
Parsing Rule	Medium	Good	Requires user to examine the source code
Elimination	Slow	Fair	Requires lots of work to remove unwanted data
HTML nodes	Fast	Good	Requires fairly little effort from user
GUI based	Fast	Good	What you see is what you get

ation (Mehlführer, 2009; Vlahavas et al., 1999). After the first round of evaluation of the Shop Bot, the criteria list was refined and finalized as shown in Table 2. These criteria operationalize the step 4 of the evaluation mythology used. For details on the criteria please refer to Appendix A.

Tool Value Model (Task Analysis)

This section discusses the tasks consumers do in the process of seeking information with regard to the digital media. To understand the consumers' information needs, it is important to simulate the thinking process of the consumers.

The authors assumed that companies will be interested in knowing the type of data that consumers will want to gather from the web sites of retailers and other competitors' website. Hence, by utilizing the Shop Bot the company can simulate the tasks the consumer go through as well as extract the competitive information needed.

In a 2008 survey conducted jointly by Krillion and the e-tailing group, it found that shoppers tend to use specific online sources to research product that is of their interest (Krillion and group, 2008). The numbers of participants in the survey are 1000 with 50% male and 50% female. The participants also purchase at least four times online and spend a minimum of $500 a year. The

Table 2. Evaluation metrics criteria

Criteria	Description
Configuration	How easily can the template be created to crawl the website for data? How good is the support for task administrative such as running task at specific timing?
Error Handling	When there is error, how well the Shop Bot handles it?
Crawling Standards	Can the Shop Bot crawl secure websites and popups? Can the Shop Bot handle cookies?
Navigation and Crawling	Does the Shop Bot support login to website and how does it generate links from user defined parameters for the URLs?
Selection	Is the Shop Bot able to crawl data from table, metadata, and websites that have Flash, Javascript, etc.?
Extraction	How easily can the user define the data to be extracted?
File	The output format is supported by Shop Bot.
Usability	How easy is the usage of the Shop Bot?
Efficiency	How much resources the Shop Bot consumes? How much does it cost?

Figure 7. Ranking of shopper preference of online source

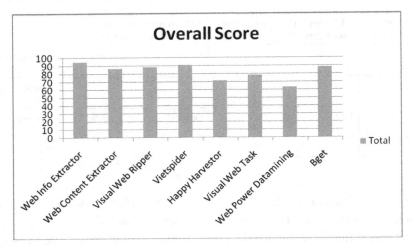

stringent selection of the participants makes it a good sampling of online shoppers. The result of the survey is shown in Figure 7.

Six online sources are preferred by shoppers in the information seeking process. These results can also be used as the shoppers' seeking behaviors towards the digital media. Knowing the shoppers information needs is critical for IDM start-up to formulate business strategy.

The authors surveyed a list of existing IDM, specifically digital music ecommerce websites, showed that most of these companies display their inventory and prices upfront to their customers. This presents a relatively easy task for IDM start-ups to utilize only some of the important features of the Shop Bots to collect web intelligence.

In order to re-rank the Shop Bots based on shoppers' behavior as well as IDM ecommerce websites product information availability, a subset of the evaluation criteria are extracted from the list of evaluation metrics (section 4) to form the new evaluation metrics. The new set of evaluation criteria will be used for the evaluation of the top three tasks. Table 3 shows the list of criteria chosen and the explanation. These are the criteria that the Shop Bots must have.

This section showed the characteristics of two evaluative models – metrics and task analysis. In the following section a synthesis of both models is achieved and applied in the evaluation process.

EVALUATION PROCESS

This section describes how the evaluation process of the Shop Bots is done. The evaluation process

Table 3. Criteria for task analysis

Criteria	Reason for inclusion
Configuration	This is an important criteria. It forms the bulk of the action the staff has to undertake in order to perform the data extraction.
Crawling Standards	This criteria is important in the sense that most of the ecommerce websites using secure connections and cookies handle the session. The Shop Bot also needs to have a masking ability as websites usually block Shop Bots.
Selection	The Shop Bots must be able to perform basic data extraction from the ecommerce sites.
Usability	This criterion is important because it is fundamental to software evaluation.

consists of two parts. The first part is the individual evaluation process. The second part is the moderation process.

Individual Evaluation Process

Prior to the evaluation, a demonstration of one of the Shop Bots is carried out in order to allow the evaluators to fully understand what each criteria means and how to look out for differences that will affect the Shop Bots scores.

Each Shop Bot is assigned to a single evaluator. The evaluator will configure the assigned Shop Bots to crawl the two selected websites mentioned in section 3.2. For each criterion, a score of 0-5 can be assigned. Shop Bots will get a result of "0", if they do not have any features that support a particular criterion. If the criterion is supported, the degree of support will be evaluated based on minimum support (scoring 1 point) to totally support (scoring 5 points). This stage is done based on the judgment of the single evaluator of the Shop Bots.

Moderation Process

Due to the fact that the evaluation process is based on individual evaluator's judgment, a moderation process is needed to prevent the judgment differences in each evaluator's scoring. After the individual evaluation process, all evaluators gathered together and each evaluator demonstrated the features of each Shop Bot to allow other evaluators to compare their own evaluated Shop Bots. Any perceived discrepancies in evaluation are pointed out and the scores are then moderated according to the agreement of all evaluators.

Solutions and Recommendations

Discuss solutions and recommendations in dealing with the issues, controversies, or problems presented in the preceding section.

Results

This section shows the evaluation result of the Shop Bot. The first set of result is based on the evaluation metrics evaluation. The second set of result is based on the task analysis evaluation.

Table 4. Individual category score

	Bget	Happy Harvester	Vietspider	Visual Web Ripper	Visual Web Task	Web Content Extractor	Web Info Extractor	Web Power Data Mining
Configuration	14	13	16	14	17	17	11	9
Error Handling	5	6	5	8	4	2	7	3
Crawling Standards	9	5	9	6	6	11	9	4
Navigation and Crawling	7	10	7	11	12	8	15	6
Selection	8	6	8	7	9	10	9	10
Extraction	4	3	4	6	4	5	6	5
File	10	5	10	9	9	9	12	6
Usability	14	15	14	14	12	10	14	13
Efficiency	18	9	18	14	9	15	12	8
Total Score	89	72	91	89	82	87	95	64

The evaluation results are presented in the Table 4 and figures. Figure **8** shows the overall score of evaluation; the maximum score possible is 225. From the result, it is noted that *Web Info Extractor* has the highest overall score as a Shop Bot while the *Web Power Datamining* has the lowest overall score.

However, Table 4 and Figure 9 also show that certain Shop Bots excel in certain categories. For example, *Web Content Extractor* and *Visual Web Task* score well in the Configuration category while *Vietspider* and *Bget* score well in the efficiency category. From the Figure 10, *Web Content Extractor* is most suitable in simulating consumers' information gathering behavior.

(So What) You need to talk about the figures and table.

Figure 10 shows the result of the task analysis score based on the four criteria selected in section 5. The result shows that Web Content Extractor is most suitable in simulating consumers' information gathering behavior.

Figure 8. Overall score (maximum score is 255)

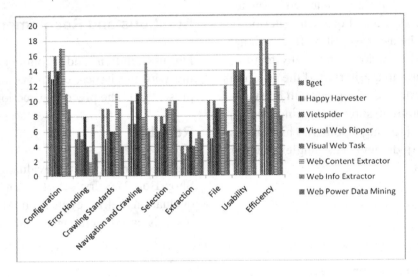

Figure 9. Individual category score

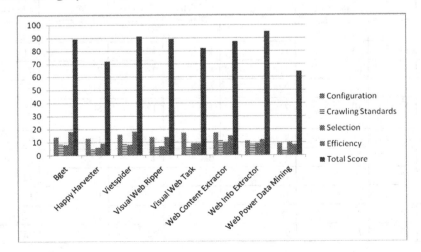

Figure 10. Task analysis score

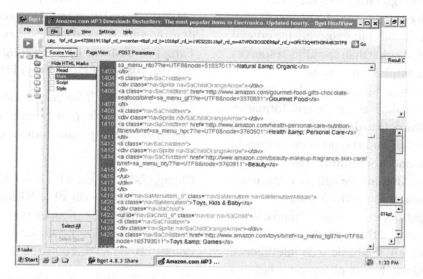

A general conclusion can be drawn from the results that the Shop bots evaluated are generally suitable for gathering data for business intelligence purpose regardless of whether the data in the website are structured in the breath or depth manner. This is due to their ability to crawl the two websites, the "popular online retailer" and *7Digital.com,* and return usable information.

CONCLUSION AND FUTURE RESEARCH

This research may provide a guide to practitioners and managers to help increase an understanding of how start-ups can use shop-bots. This research will provide the opportunity for small business to handle their customer relationships based on the information they collected from the market and keeping a competitive edge. By using new channels of information, small business could transform their business procedures.

A Web Crawler is a robot that starts at one point in the web and pursues chosen links. It could recover content entities of any kind, like HTML, text, images, audio, or video and stores them to the local file system for further processing. The Web Crawler could check Web-sites behavior and modifications to improve retrieval of content. We can discover applications for web crawlers in many areas of a business organization. Future has to address those challenges to gather data from many front business applications; such as help desk operations, contract management, e-mail processing, customer relationship management, and sales applications (Tkach, 1998).

The authors through this evaluation had learnt how to configure the eight Shop Bots to perform basic data extraction from the various web sites. Screenshot of the configuration of the Shop Bots are found in Appendix B.

After the evaluation process, the authors conclude that different Shop Bots have varying capabilities and thus are suitable for different tasks and that those Shop Bots that can handle more complex tasks are usually inherently more complex to configure and less user friendly.

Hence, in order to select an appropriate Shop Bot, IDM start-ups should understand the tasks undertaken by their customers through basic task analysis as well as have knowledge of how much resources they have in their disposal when it comes to configuring and operating the Shop Bots. For example, a small company may be better off with a simpler Shop Bot and start gathering the crucial information needed rather than spending resources on figuring out complex Shop Bots.

Although in most Shop Bots, the data can be collected in pre-defined tables and format or even uploading the data to databases, the data still need further analysis and should be presented in a meaningful manner for fruitful business intelligence purposes. An example will be data mining with captured data stored in the databases for the analysis of competitive environment trends. What the potential impact of these results is.

In this evaluation, the basic web intelligence can be performed purely by looking at the data that is extracted such as inventory, prices and promotions. This extraction also simulates what tasks end consumer will perform to gather the necessary information. However for more extensive intelligence on the competitors, the authors suggest that further work can be done in the utilization and analysis of the data collected.

REFERENCES

Adam, S., Mulye, R., Deans, K. R., & Palihawadana, D. (2002). E-marketing in perspective: A three-country comparison of business use of the internet. *Marketing Intelligence & Planning, 20,* 243–251. doi:10.1108/02634500210431649

Adams, A. A., & Mccrindle, R. (2008). *Pandora's Box: Social and professional issues of the information age.* Chichester, England: John Wiley & Sons.

Bitware Specialists. (2007). *Web power data mining.*

Brabston, M. E., & McNamara, G. (1998). The internet as a competitive knowledge tool for top managers. *Industrial Management & Data Systems, 98,* 158–164. doi:10.1108/02635579810219318

Calof, J. L., & Wright, S. (2008). Competitive intelligence: A practitioner, academic and inter-disciplinary perspective. *European Journal of Marketing, 42,* 717–730. doi:10.1108/03090560810877114

Carpe, D. (2007). *How the social internet simplifies source identification. Competitive Intelligence Magazine.* Strategic and Competitive Intelligence Professionals.

Chang, C.-H., Kayed, M., Girgis, M. R., & Shaalan, K. F. (2006). A survey of web information extraction systems. *IEEE Transactions On Knowledge And Data Engineering Archive, 18,* 1411–1428. doi:10.1109/TKDE.2006.152

Choo, C. W. (2002). *Information management for the intelligent organization: The art of scanning the environment.* Medford, NJ: Information Today.

DP Information Group. (2008). *SME development survey.* 2008 Media Development Conference.

Dutta, S., & Segev, A. (1999). Business transformation on the internet. *European Management Journal, 17,* 466–476. doi:10.1016/S0263-2373(99)00032-8

Foote, P. S., & Krishnamurthi, M. (2001). Forecasting using data warehousing model: Wal-Mart's experience. *Journal of Business Forecasting, 20,* 13–17.

Gilad, B., & Gilad, T. (1985). A systems approach to business intelligence. *Business Horizons, 28,* 65–70. doi:10.1016/0007-6813(85)90070-9

Hannula, M., & Pirttimäki, V. (2005). A cube of business information. *Competitive Intelligence and Management, 3,* 34–40.

Heindl, M., Reinisch, F., Biffl, S., & Egyed, A. (2006). Value-based selection of requirements engineering tool support. In *Proceeding of the 32nd Euromicro Conference on Software Engineering and Advanced Applications.* Cavtat/Dubrovnik, Croatia, IEEE Computer Society.

Jadhav, A. S., & Sonar, R. M. (2009). Evaluating and selecting software packages: A review source. *Information and Software Technology*, *51*, 555–563. doi:10.1016/j.infsof.2008.09.003

Johnson, T. (2006). Why is RSS important to you. *Competitive Intelligence Magazine*, *9*, 35–37.

Keyes, J. (2006). *Knowledge management, business intelligence, and content management: The IT practitioner's guide*. Boca Raton, FL: Auerbach Publications. doi:10.1201/9781420013863

Kosala, R., & Blockeel, H. (2000). Web mining research: A survey. *SigKDD Exploration: Newsletter Of The Special Interest Group (Sig) On Knowledge Discovery & Data Mining, 2,* 1-15.

Kowalkiewicz, M., Orlowska, M. E., Kaczmarek, T., & Abramowicz, W. (2006a). *Robust web content extraction*. The 15th International Conference on World Wide Web. Edinburgh, Scotland. New York, NY: ACM.

Kowalkiewicz, M., Orlowska, M. E., Kaczmarek, T., & Abramowicz, W. (2006b). *Towards more personalized web: Extraction and integration of dynamic content from the web*. The 8th Asia Pacific Web Conference APWeb 2006. Harbin, China.

Krillion Inc. (2008). New survey finds 67 percent of shoppers invest 30+ percent of their total shopping time researching what to buy.

Laender, A. H. F., Ribeiro-Neto, B. A., Silva, A. S. D., & Teixeira, J. S. (2002). A brief survey of web data extraction tools. *SIGMOD Record, 31,* 84–93. doi:10.1145/565117.565137

Mehlführer, A. (2009). *Web scraping: A tool evaluation. Fakultät Für Informatik Der Technischen Universität Wien*. Vienna: Vienna University Of Technology.

Pawar, B. S., & Sharda, R. (1997). Obtaining business intelligence on the internet. *Long Range Planning, 30,* 110–121. doi:10.1016/S0024-6301(96)00100-8

Rappaport, A. (2008). *How robots follow links to find pages*. Focuseek.

Salomanna, H., Dousa, M., Kolbea, L., & Brenner, W. (2005). Rejuvenating customer management: How to make knowledge for, from and about customers work. *European Management Journal, 23,* 392–403. doi:10.1016/j.emj.2005.06.009

Smith, M. D., & Brynjolfsson, E. (2001). Consumer decision-making at an internet shopbot: Brand still matter. *The Journal of Industrial Economics, 49,* 541–558. doi:10.1111/1467-6451.00162

Srivastava, J., & Cooley, R. (2003). Web business intelligence: Mining the web for actionable knowledge. *Journal on Computing, 15,* 191–207.

Thierauf, R. J. (2001). *Effective business intelligence systems*. Westport, CT: Quorum Books.

Tkach, D. S. (1998). *Information mining with the IBM intelligent miner family*. IBM White Paper.

Turban, E., Sharda, R., Aronson, J. E., & King, D. N. (2008). *Business intelligence: A managerial approach*. Upper Saddle River, NJ: Pearson Prentice Hall.

Vlahavas, I., Stamelos, I., Refanidis, I., & Tsoukiàs, A. (1999). Esse: An expert system for software evaluation. *Knowledge-Based Systems, 4,* 183–197. doi:10.1016/S0950-7051(99)00031-3

Watson, H. J., Wixom, B. H., Hoffer, J. A., Anderson-Lehman, R., & Reynolds, A. M. (2006). Real-time business intelligence: Best practices at Continental Airlines. *Information Systems Management, 23,* 7–18. doi:10.1201/1078.10580530/45769.23.1.20061201/91768.2

Wood, E. (2001). Marketing Information Systems in tourism and hospitality small and medium sized enterprises: A study of internet use for market intelligence. *International Journal of Tourism Research, 3,* 283–299. doi:10.1002/jtr.315

APPENDIX A

The below criteria are adapted from the research done by Andreas Mehlführer, (2009) on web scraping software and Vlahavas et al. (1999) on general software evaluation.

Configuration

- Creation / Modification of the data model
  - The Shop Bot should be able to allow the user to
    - Control the data output format such as tables and fields naming
    - Create the data model via a GUI
- Import/Export/Reuse of the data model
  - The Shop Bot should be able to allow the user to backup the data model and this is done via
    - Allowing the user to import the data model
    - Allowing the user to export the data model
    - Allowing the user to reuse the data model
- Creation/Modification of a scraping template
  - The Shop Bot should be able to allow the user to create scraping template via a GUI
- Import/Export/Reuse of a scraping template
  - The web scrapping spider should be able to allow the user to backup the scraping templates and this is down via
    - Allowing the user to import the scraping template
    - Allowing the user to export the scraping template
    - Allowing the user to reuse the scraping template
- Creation/Modification of URLs
  - The web scrapping spider should be able to allow the user to
    - Define various types of URLs such as fixtures or results
    - Use parameters to replace elements in URLs
- Standard configurations
  - The Shop Bot should come with some presets configurations for users to use
- Task administration
  - The Shop Bot should be able to allow the user to administer recurring tasks by setting the spider to run the recurring tasks at specified time intervals.

Error Handling

- Protocol function
  - The Shop Bot should be able to log important activities such as
    - Providing an overview of the extraction process
    - Exporting the log
    - Reporting time and type of errors encountered

- Notifications
  - The Shop Bot should be able to notify the user of
    - Error codes, dates, times, URLs, pages
- Notification administration
  - The Shop Bot should be able to produce the notifications via a GUI
- Visual debugging
  - The Shop Bot should be have visual debugging features that
    - Stops the processes user defined error points and wait for further instructions
    - Provides step by step process to debug

Crawling Standards

- User-Agent
  - The Shop Bot should be able to be configured to mask itself as user-defined web browsers such as Firefox
- Secure connections
  - The Shop Bot should be able to crawl secure web sites utilizing the HTTPS encryption
- Pop up windows
  - The Shop Bot should be able to scrape from data that are displayed in pop-up windows
- Cookies
  - The Shop Bot should be handle cookies sessions

Navigation and Crawling

- Recordable crawler navigation
  - The Shop Bot should be able to allow the user to record navigations to crawl data
- Log in
  - The Shop Bot should be able to allow the users to key in login details for websites that require authentication
- Parameterized crawling
  - The Shop Bot should be able to generate links from user defined parameters for the URLs
- Waiting periods
  - The Shop Bot should have configurations to allow for waiting periods to simulate human browsing
- Multitasking
  - The Shop Bot should be able to scrape more than one web sites at a time
- HTTP standard codes
  - The Shop Bot should be able to recognize standard HTTP codes such as 404
- Filling forms
  - The Shop Bot should be able to support web site forms filling for user defined data scraping

Selection

- Selection methods
  - The Shop Bot should be able to crawl for information using regular expressions
  - The Shop Bot should be able to support crawling using node attributes to gather information
- Tables
  - The Shop Bot should be able to extract data from a table from a HTML page
- Technologies
  - The Shop Bot should be able to navigate pages that use HTML, XHTML, Flash, Javascript
- Capturing meta data
  - The Shop Bot should be able to capture metadata of the a HTML page such as keywords, header information and description

Extraction

- Extraction condition
  - The Shop Bot should be able to allow user to define a filter to extract information when a condition is fulfilled
- Efficient extraction
  - The Shop Bot should be able to extract information based on data model or pre-defined rules such as page area and ignores the rest of the page for efficiency
- Validation
  - The Shop Bot should be able do handle simple validation by comparing the results gathered with the regular expressions defined.

File

- Unique name
  - The Shop Bot should be able to allow unique filenames to be used for different files created when the spider crawl the same site at different times.
- Standard file formats
  - The Shop Bot should be able to store the crawled data in the following standard formats for easy integration with databases
    - XML
    - CVS
    - TXT
    - ASCII
- Database connectivity
  - The Shop Bot should be able to store gathered data into standard databases such as those listed below
    - MySQL
    - Oracle

- Access
- PostgreSQL
- MS-SQL-Server

Usability

- Usability
  - The Shop Bot should have the following usability features to aid the users
    - Easily identifiable icons are used
    - The usage should be easy enough without the need for instructions
    - The interface is clear and consistent
    - The software provides undo function
    - The software provides preset configurations that allows the user to start using the software immediately
    - The user can save their preferred settings
    - Tutorials are provided
- Adaptability and expendability
  - The Shop Bot should be able to allow the user to customize the menu
  - The Shop Bot should be able to allow the user to add plug-ins or scripts to help with the data gathering
- Help functions and documentation
  - The Shop Bot should have off-line and on-line help provided
  - The Shop Bot should come with documentation
- Error handling
  - The Shop Bot should be able to create an error report when an error occur
  - The error message should be comprehensible to the user
- Installation
  - The software should have a automatic installation process with minimum user intervention
  - The user should be able to crawl within 10 minutes after installation

Efficiency

- System assumption
  - The Shop Bot should not use up too much of the system resources such as CPU cycles thus impeding the overall performance of other operations
- Platform independence
  - The Shop Bot should be able to operate in popular operating systems such as Windows, Macintosh and Linux
- Support
  - The Shop Bot should have some sort of support such as online forum or direct contact with developer via email or telephone.

- Effectiveness
  - The Shop Bot should be able to accomplish the tasks within a reasonable time
- Proxy server
  - The Shop Bot should be able to use proxy server if needed
- Price
  - The Shop Bot should have a reasonable price considering the features available
- Crawler traps
  - The Shop Bot should be able to prevent itself from falling into spider traps web sites that causes infinite loops and hence impedes crawling.

APPENDIX B

Bget Spider Screen Shot

Figure 11. Bget configuration

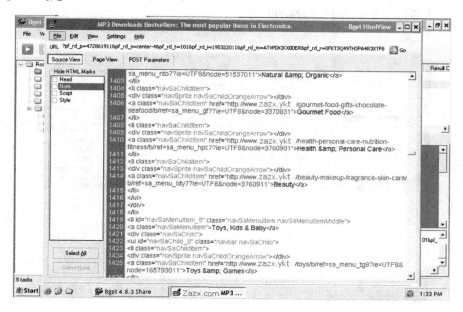

Figure 12. Bget output

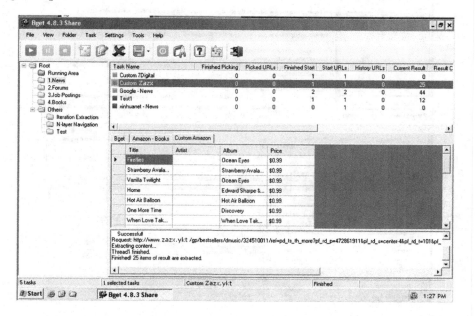

Happy Harvester Spider Screen Shot

Figure 13. Happy Harvester configuration

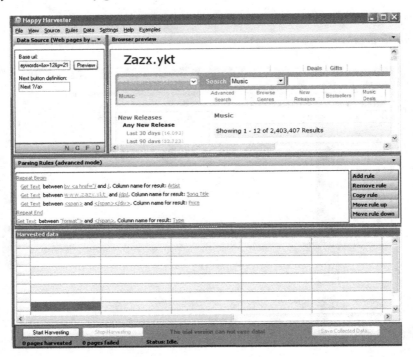

Figure 14. Happy Harvester output

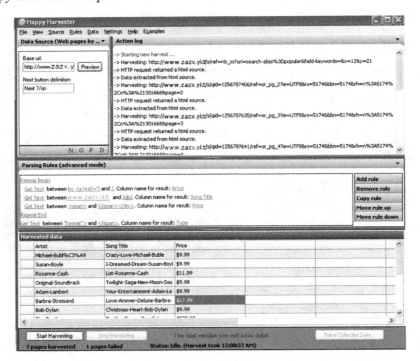

Visual Web Task Spider Screen Shot

Figure 15. Visual Web Task configuration

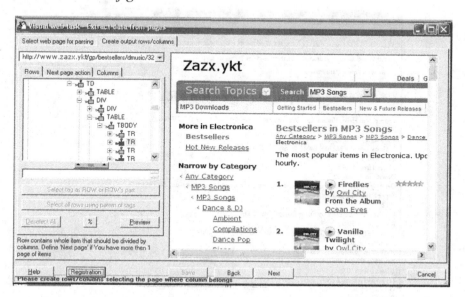

Figure 16. Visual Web Task output

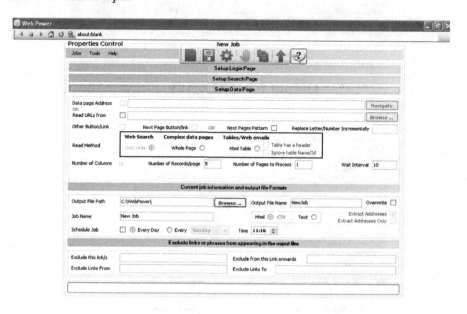

Web Power Data Mining Spider Screen Shot

Figure 17. Web Power Data Mining configuration

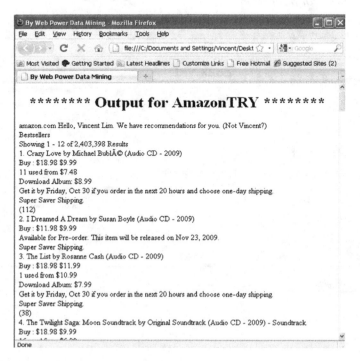

Figure 18. Web Power Data Mining output

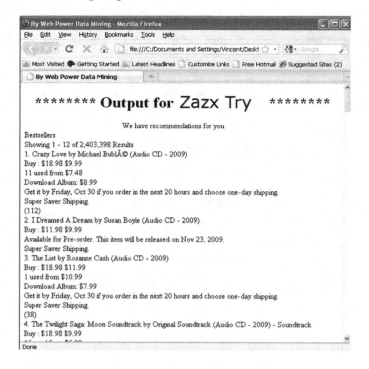

Web Info Extractor Spider Screen Shot

Figure 19. Web Info Extractor configuration

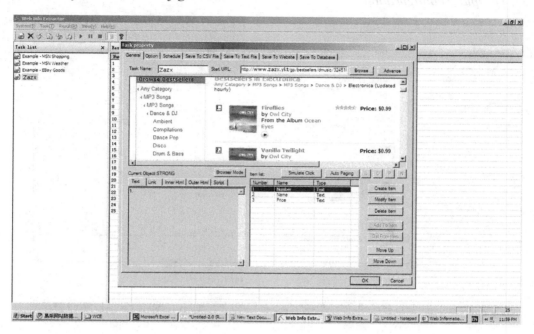

Figure 20. Web Info Extractor output

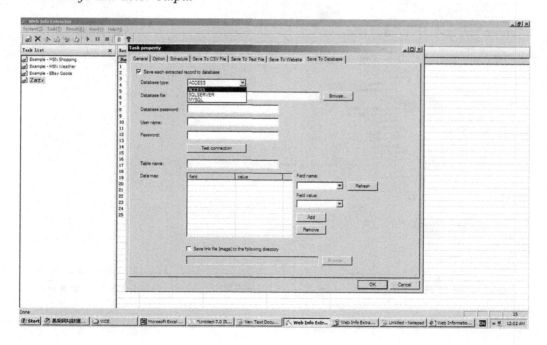

Vietspider Spider Screen Shot

Figure 21. Vietspider configuration

Figure 22. Vietspider output

VisualWebRipper Spider

Figure 23. VisualWebRipper configuration

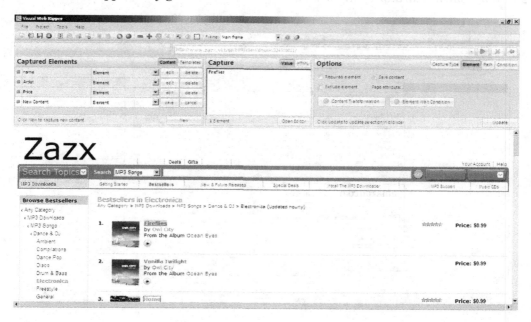

Figure 24. VisualWebRipper scheduling

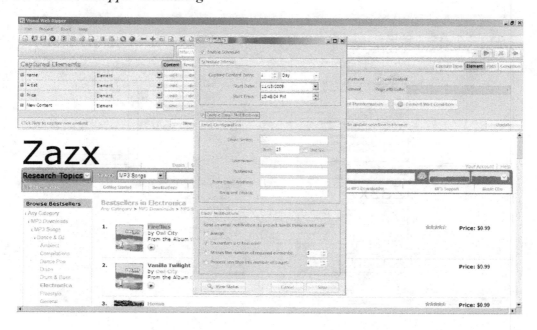

Web Content Extrator Spider

Figure 25. Web Content Extrator configuration

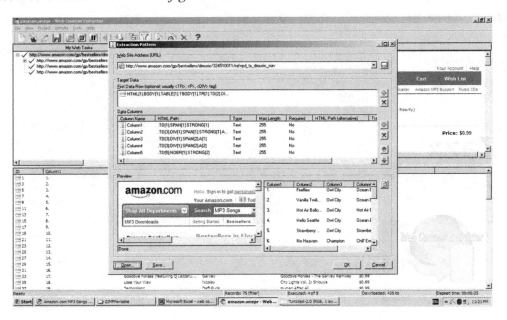

Figure 26. Web Content Extrator output

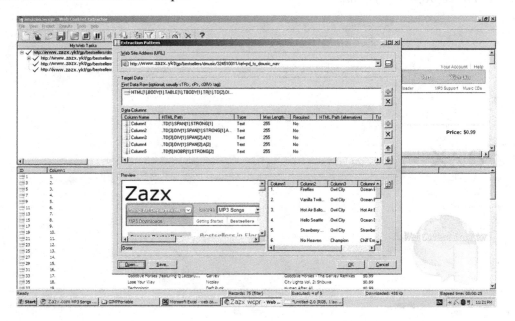

APPENDIX C

Bget

Figure 27. Bget table #1

	0	1	2	3	4	5	Subtotal	Remarks
Configuration								
Creation / Modification of the data model			√				2	
Import/Export/Reuse of the data model			√				2	
Creation/Modification of a scraping template		√					1	
Import/Export/Reuse of a scraping template		√					1	
Creation/Modification of URLs				√			3	
Standard configurations			√				2	
Task administration				√			3	
Subtotal					□		14	
Error Handling								
Protocol function			√				2	
Notifications Drop image files here to open them			√				2	
Notification administration		√					1	
Visual debugging	√						0	
Subtotal					□		5	
Crawling Standards								
User-Agent			√				2	
Secure connections			√				2	
Pop up windows				√			3	
Cookies			√				2	
Subtotal					□		9	

Figure 28. Bget table #2

Navigation and Crawling								
Recordable crawler navigation	√						0	
Log in			√				2	
Parameterized crawling			√				2	
Waiting periods	√						0	
Multitasking		√					1	
HTTP standard codes		√					1	
Filling forms		√					1	
Subtotal					□		7	
Selection				□				
Selection metho Drop image files here to open them				√			3	
Tables			√				2	
Technologies				√			3	
Capturing meta data	√						0	
Header Information	√						0	
Subtotal					□		8	
Extraction								
Extraction condition		√					1	
Efficient extraction			√				2	
Validation		√					1	
Subtotal					□		4	
File								
Unique name				√			3	
Standard file formats				√			3	
Database connectivity					√		4	
Subtotal					□		10	

Figure 29. Bget table #3

Usability								
Usability			√				2	
Adaptability and expendability				√			3	
Help functions and documentation		√					1	
Error handling				√			3	
Installation						√	5	
Subtotal					□		14	
Efficiency								
System assumption					√		4	
Platform independence		√					1	
Support			√				2	
Effectiveness				√			3	
Proxy server			√				2	
Price						√	5	
Crawler traps		√					1	
Subtotal					□		18	
Total Score							89	

Happy Harvester

Figure 30. Happy harvester table #1

	0	1	2	3	4	5	Subtotal	Remark
Configuration								
Creation / Modification of the data model		□	□		√		4	
Import/Export/Reuse of the data model	□			√			3	
Creation/Modification of a scraping template		√					1	
Import/Export/Reuse of a scraping template		√					1	Not supported
Creation/Modification of URLs		√	□				1	
Standard configurations	√						0	Not supported
Task administration				√			3	Not supported
Subtotal	□						13	
Error Handling								
Protocol function		□		√			3	
Notifications			□	√			3	
Notification administration	√						0	Not supported
Visual debugging	√						0	Not supported
Subtotal	□						6	
Crawling Standards								
User-Agent	□	□	√				2	
Secure connections	√						0	Not supported
Pop up windows		□	√				2	
Cookies		√					1	
Subtotal	□						5	

Figure 31. Happy harvester table #2

Navigation and Crawling								Score	Notes
Recordable crawler navigation	√							0	Not supported
Log in						√		4	
Parameterized crawling	√							0	Not supported
Waiting periods			□	√				3	
Multitasking	√							0	Not supported
HTTP standard codes	√							0	Not supported
Filling forms	□			√				3	
Subtotal	□							10	
Selection									
Selection methods		√	□					1	Use only parsing rules
Tables			√		□			2	
Technologies			√					2	
Capturing meta data	√							0	Not supported
Header Information		√	□					1	
Subtotal	□							6	
Extraction									
Extraction condition		√		□				1	
Efficient extraction			√					2	
Validation	√							0	Not supported
Subtotal	□							3	

Figure 32. Happy harvester table #3

File								Score	Notes
Unique name				√				3	
Standard file formats			√					2	Not available
Database connectivity	√							0	Not supported
Subtotal	□							5	
Usability									
Usability			√	□				2	
Adaptability and expendability			√					3	Not supported
Help functions and documentation			√					3	Not available
Error handling			□	√				3	
Installation						√		4	
Subtotal	□							15	
Efficiency									
System assumption						√		4	
Platform independence		√						1	Window
Support	√							0	Not available
Effectiveness			□	√				3	
Proxy server	√							0	Not supported
Price		√						1	Not available
Crawler traps	√							0	Not supported
Subtotal	□							9	
Total Score	□							60	

Vietspider

Figure 33. Vietspider table #1

	0	1	2	3	4	5	Subtotal	Remarks
Configuration								
Creation / Modification of the data model				√			3	
Import/Export/Reuse of the data model			√				2	
Creation/Modification of a scraping template		√					1	
Import/Export/Reuse of a scraping template		√					1	
Creation/Modification of URLs					√		4	
Standard configurations			√				2	
Task administration					√		4	
Subtotal					▫		16	
Error Handling								
Protocol function			√				2	
Notifications			√				2	
Notification administration		√					1	
Visual debugging	√						0	
Subtotal					▫		5	
Crawling Standards								
User-Agent			√				2	
Secure connections			√				2	
Pop up windows				√			3	
Cookies			√				2	
Subtotal					▫		9	
Navigation and Crawling								
Recordable crawler navigation	√						0	
Log in		√					1	
Parameterized crawling			√				2	
Waiting periods		√					1	
Multitasking			√				2	
HTTP standard codes		√					1	
Filling forms	√						0	
Subtotal					▫		7	

Figure 34. Vietspider table #2

Selection								
Selection methods				√			3	
Tables			√				2	
Technologies				√			3	
Capturing meta data	√						0	
Header Information	√						0	
Subtotal					□		8	
Extraction								
Extraction condition		√					1	
Efficient extraction			√				2	
Validation		√					1	
Subtotal					□		4	
File								
Unique name				√			3	
Standard file formats				√			3	
Database connectivity					√		4	
Subtotal					□		10	
Usability								
Usability			√				2	
Adaptability and expendability				√			3	
Help functions and documentation		√					1	
Error handling				√			3	
Installation						√	5	
Subtotal					□		14	
Efficiency								
System assumption		√					1	
Platform independence					√		4	
Support			√				2	
Effectiveness				√			3	
Proxy server				√			3	
Price						√	5	
Crawler traps	√						0	
Subtotal					□		18	
Total Score							91	

Visual Web Ripper

Figure 35. Visual web ripper table #1

	0	1	2	3	4	5	Subtotal
Configuration							
Creation / Modification of the data model			√				2
Import/Export/Reuse of the data model			√				2
Creation/Modification of a scraping template				√			3
Import/Export/Reuse of a scraping template				√			3
Creation/Modification of URLs		√					1
Standard configurations		√					1
Task administration			√				2
Subtotal							14
Error Handling							
Protocol function			√				2
Notifications				√			3
Notification administration			√				2
Visual debugging		√					1
Subtotal							8
Crawling Standards							
User-Agent			√				2
Secure connections			√				2
Pop up windows	√						0
Cookies		√					2
Subtotal							6
Navigation and Crawling							
Recordable crawler navigation	√						0
Log in		√					1
Parameterized crawling		√					1
Waiting periods				√			3
Multitasking			√				2
HTTP standard codes			√				2
Filling forms			√				2
Subtotal							11

Figure 36. Visual web ripper table #2

Selection							
Selection methods			√				2
Tables		√					1
Technologies					√		4
Capturing meta data	√						0
Header Information	√						0
Subtotal							7
Extraction							
Extraction condition			√				2
Efficient extraction			√				2
Validation			√				2
Subtotal							6
File							
Unique name				√			3
Standard file formats			√				2
Database connectivity				√			4
Subtotal							9
Usability							
Usability				√			3
Adaptability and expendability				√			3
Help functions and documentation				√			3
Error handling			√				2
Installation				√			3
Subtotal							14
Efficiency							
System assumption		√					1
Platform independence			√				2
Support				√			3
Effectiveness				√			3
Proxy server				√			3
Price		√					2
Crawler traps	√						0
Subtotal							14
Total Score							89

Visual Web Task

Figure 37. Visual web task table #1

	0	1	2	3	4	5	Subtotal	Remark
Configuration								
Creation / Modification of the data model		□			√		4	
Import/Export/Reuse of the data model	□		√	□			3	
Creation/Modification of a scraping template		□			√		4	
Import/Export/Reuse of a scraping template	√						0	Not supported
Creation/Modification of URLs			□		√		4	
Standard configurations	√		□				0	Not supported
Task administration			√		□		2	Can be started on commamd line
Subtotal			□		□		17	
Error Handling								
Protocol function		□	√				2	
Notifications			√				2	
Notification administration	√						0	Not supported
Visual debugging	√						0	Not supported
Subtotal			□		□		4	
Crawling Standards								
User-Agent	√						0	Not supported
Secure connections		□	□	√			3	Allow setting of password
Pop up windows			√				2	
Cookies		√					1	
Subtotal			□		□		6	
Navigation and Crawling								
Recordable crawler navigation	□				√		4	Click start recording
Log in	□			√			3	
Parameterized crawling	√						0	Not supported
Waiting periods	√						0	Not supported
Multitasking	□		√				2	
HTTP standard codes	√						0	Not supported
Filling forms	□			√			3	
Subtotal			□		□		12	

Figure 38. Visual web task table #2

	0	1	2	3	4	5	Subtotal	Remark
Selection								
Selection methods		□	□	√			3	Select by HTML node
Tables					√		4	
Technologies			√				2	
Capturing meta data	√						0	Not supported
Header Information	√						0	Not supported
Subtotal			□		□		9	
Extraction								
Extraction condition	√						0	Not supported
Efficient extraction			□		√		4	
Validation	√						0	Not supported
Subtotal			□		□		4	
File								
Unique name				√			3	
Standard file formats				√			3	TXT. HTML
Database connectivity	□			√			3	
Subtotal			□		□		9	
Usability								
Usability			√	□			2	
Adaptability and expendability	√						0	Not supported
Help functions and documentation			□	√	□		3	Help file readily available
Error handling			□	√			3	
Installation					√		4	
Subtotal			□		□		12	
Efficiency								
System assumption					√		4	
Platform independence			√				2	Window
Support	√						0	Not available
Effectiveness			□	√			3	
Proxy server	√						0	Not supported
Price	√						0	Not available
Crawler traps	√						0	Not supported
Subtotal			□		□		9	
Total Score							82	

Web Content Extractor

Figure 39. Web content extractor table #1

	0	1	2	3	4	5	Subtotal	Remarks
Configuration								
Creation / Modification of the data model					√		4	
Import/Export/Reuse of the data model				√			3	
Creation/Modification of a scraping template		√					1	
Import/Export/Reuse of a scraping template		√					1	
Creation/Modification of URLs				√			3	
Standard configurations			√				2	
Task administration				√			3	
Subtotal				▢			17	
Error Handling								
Protocol function		√					1	
Notifications		√					1	
Notification administration	√						0	
Visual debugging	√						0	
Subtotal				▢			2	
Crawling Standards								
User-Agent		√					1	
Secure connections				√			3	
Pop up windows					√		4	
Cookies				√			3	
Subtotal				▢			11	
Navigation and Crawling								
Recordable crawler navigation	√						0	
Log in			√				2	
Parameterized crawling	▢		√				2	
Waiting periods				√			4	
Multitasking	√						0	
HTTP standard codes	√						0	
Filling forms	√						0	
Subtotal				▢			8	

Figure 40. Web content extractor table #2

							Score	
Selection								
Selection methods				√			3	
Tables					√		4	
Technologies				√			3	
Capturing meta data	√						0	
Header Information	√						0	
Subtotal				□			10	
Extraction								
Extraction condition				√			3	
Efficient extraction			√				2	
Validation	√						0	
Subtotal				□			5	
File								
Unique name				√			3	
Standard file formats				√			3	
Database connectivity				√			3	
Subtotal				□			9	
Usability								
Usability				√			3	
Adaptability and expendability			√				2	
Help functions and documentation		√					1	
Error handling	√						0	
Installation					√		4	
Subtotal				□			10	
Efficiency								
System assumption				√			3	
Platform independence			√				2	
Support				√			3	
Effectiveness			√				2	
Proxy server			√				2	
Price				√			3	
Crawler traps								
Subtotal				□			15	
Total Score							87	

Web Info Extractor

Figure 40. Web info extractor table #1

	0	1	2	3	4	5	Subtotal	Remarks
Configuration								
Creation / Modification of the data model				√			3	
Import/Export/Reuse of the data model		√					1	
Creation/Modification of a scraping template	√						0	
Import/Export/Reuse of a scraping template	√			√			0	
Creation/Modification of URLs			√				2	
Standard configurations		√					1	
Task administration					√		4	
Subtotal					□		11	
Error Handling								
Protocol function		√					1	
Notifications				√			3	
Notification administration			√				2	
Visual debugging		√					1	
Subtotal					□		7	
Crawling Standards								
User-Agent			√				2	
Secure connections				√			3	
Pop up windows			√				2	
Cookies		√					2	
Subtotal					□		9	
Navigation and Crawling								
Recordable crawler navigation	√						0	
Log in		√					2	
Parameterized crawling				√			3	
Waiting periods				√			3	
Multitasking					√		4	
HTTP standard codes	√						0	
Filling forms				√			3	
Subtotal					□		15	

Figure 42. Web info extractor table #2

							Score	
Selection								
Selection methods				√			3	
Tables				√			3	
Technologies				√			3	
Capturing meta data	√						0	
Header Information	√						0	
Subtotal					□		9	
Extraction								
Extraction condition				√			3	
Efficient extraction				√			3	
Validation	√						0	
Subtotal					□		6	
File					□			
Unique name					√		4	
Standard file formats					√		4	
Database connectivity					√		4	
Subtotal					□		12	
Usability								
Usability					√		4	
Adaptability and expendability				√			3	
Help functions and documentation				√			3	
Error handling	√						0	
Installation					√		4	
Subtotal					□		14	
Efficiency								
System assumption					√		4	
Platform independence		√					1	
Support		√					1	
Effectiveness			√				2	
Proxy server				√			3	
Price		√					1	
Crawler traps								
Subtotal					□		12	
Total Score							95	

Web Power Data Mining

Figure 43. Web power data mining table #1

	0	1	2	3	4	5	Subtotal	Remark
Configuration								
Creation / Modification of the data model		√					1	
Import/Export/Reuse of the data model	√						0	Not supported
Creation/Modification of a scraping template		√					1	
Import/Export/Reuse of a scraping template	√						0	Not supported
Creation/Modification of URLs			√				2	
Standard configurations	√						0	Not supported
Task administration						√	5	Set schedule for crawling
Subtotal							9	
Error Handling								
Protocol function		√					1	
Notifications			√				2	
Notification administration	√						0	Not supported
Visual debugging	√						0	Not supported
Subtotal							3	
Crawling Standards								
User-Agent	√						0	Not supported
Secure connections		√					1	
Pop up windows			√				2	
Cookies		√					1	
Subtotal							4	
Navigation and Crawling								
Recordable crawler navigation	√						0	Not supported
Log in					√		4	
Parameterized crawling	√						0	Not supported
Waiting periods			√				2	For data page only
Multitasking	√						0	Not supported
HTTP standard codes	√						0	Not supported
Filling forms	√						0	Not supported
Subtotal							6	

Figure 44. Web power data mining table #2

	0	1	2	3	4	5	Subtotal	Remark
Selection								
Selection methods			√				2	Allow selection of link or whole page or table
Tables					√		4	
Technologies			√				2	
Capturing meta data	√						0	Not supported
Header Information			√				2	
Subtotal							10	
Extraction								
Extraction condition				√			3	Allow to exclude phrase or word
Efficient extraction			√				2	
Validation	√						0	Not supported
Subtotal							5	
File								
Unique name				√			3	
Standard file formats				√			3	CSV, TXT, HTML
Database connectivity	√						0	Not supported
Subtotal							6	
Usability								
Usability				√			3	
Adaptability and expendability	√						0	Not supported
Help functions and documentation			□		√		4	ON/OFF Help and Help file
Error handling			√				2	
Installation					√		4	
Subtotal							13	
Efficiency								
System assumption					√		4	
Platform independence			√				2	Window
Support	√						0	Not available
Effectiveness			√				2	
Proxy server	√						0	Not supported
Price	√						0	Not available
Crawler traps	√						0	Not supported
Subtotal							8	
	□							
Total Score							64	

Chapter 16
Value Creation in Mobile Operating Systems

Sander Myint Shwe
Nanyang Technological University, Singapore

Gao Xiuqing
Nanyang Technological University, Singapore

Katherine Chia
Nanyang Technological University, Singapore

ABSTRACT

Mobile OS embedded in mobile devices, such as smartphones, enables users to receive ever more mobility, flexibility and convenience. Value creation of mobile OS, regarded as the interaction between the business owners and users, not only bears the responsibility to create value for users, but also needs to achieve business owner's economic success. Various business models are created for the purpose of analyzing and improving value creation on behalf of both users and the value creators. One generic model of Osterwalder, Pigneur & Tucci (2005) is to explore the value creation by mobile OS. This chapter covers the general content and the objective of mobile OS as well as the specific design principles and value creation of two significant examples from Apple iPhone OS and Android OS.

INTRODUCTION

With the convergence of internet and mobile technologies, the consumer market is moving towards information mobility and open access. This means opportunities for innovation and marketing. With maturing development in functions and features of mobile phones, the market is now leaning towards the trend of smartphones, which has gained

DOI: 10.4018/978-1-61350-147-4.ch016

significant popularity and user conversion in the last 3 years (Schmidt et al., 2008). Product design aside, computing capabilities of mobile devices are now of considerable market and consumer interest. This has invariably resulted in a highly competitive environment among smartphones with different operating systems. The basis of smartphones is designed to achieve a range of informational objectives and personal productivity. It is a driving force for mobile / virtual offices and innovation as well as a consolidated platform for a wide range of high-end mobile phones. Nevertheless, there is a requirement of radical improvement for all mobile operating systems and software platforms to strive towards in this new Internet age. The objective of this chapter is to explore the value framework created by mobile operating systems, in terms of value creation and provision, using a generic business model of Osterwalder, Pigneur and Tucci (2005). The argument is that value can be obtained by analyzing value creation logic and profitable business can be transformed from potential business model. Mobile operating system firms are continuously pioneering approaches in the value framework. It is the ability to generate true value creation that eventually leads to their business success.

BACKGROUND

Conventional methods of connection, entertainment, and information exchange among people and sources have been radically reformed by the personal computers, Web 2.0 and advancement in mobile technologies, among which mobile operating system is the most significant one. A mobile system is a computer system which is able to be accessed regardless of time or location constraints. Mobility is the major concern of it (Speckmann, 2008). There are high demand for information mobility and network access on-the-go. In a bid to meet mobile accessibility, smartphones, like miniature computers running on complete mobile operating systems are invented. This is one of the key drivers that enable mobile OS to create value for its users. Keeney (1992) mentioned that value is the principle for evaluating the consequences of action, inaction or decision. Value proposition of mobile OS is the net value related to the benefits and costs associated with the adaptation and adoption of the mobile OS. Value creation in mobile OS is the strategy to improve the customer-driven interface and user satisfaction, and this is currently achieved through OS such as Symbian OS,

Blackberry OS, iPhone OS, Windows Mobile OS, Android, Palm Web OS, and Samsung Beta etc.

While considering the features of mobile OS, the market in which they are used should be taken into account. This chapter focuses on the usage of mobile OS in smartphone market. Among all the above mobile OS used by different smartphone manufacturers, they share the key features as follows:

1. **Mobility:** The mobile OS should be able to work normally as it is carried everywhere with the mobile phones.
2. **Connection:** Mobile OS on smartphones enables to connect to the wireless network, local computer and other devices.
3. **Innovation:** Mobile OS is derived from computer operating systems at first. Developers of mobile OS are striving for breakthrough innovation to make it "local" to smartphones.
4. **Open:** Mobile OS is working based on a open platform to inactivate the applications, which is developed by independent technology and software vendors (Morris, 2007).

PERSPECTIVE ON VALUE CREATION AND IMPACT ON BUSINESS

Value creation can be regarded as the interaction between business and customers. Value can be perceived in terms of monetary and non-monetary standards. On the other hand, value is also regarded as the trade-off between benefits and sacrifices. Appropriate assignment and creation of value rewards the provider not only in terms of profit, but also in forms of competence, market leadership and social reputation. The monetary benefits of larger market volume and economic profit are directly related to value creation function. While non-monetary benefits consist of reputation, manufacturer power and sustainable development in the long run. These are indirectly related to the value framework. Moreover, regardless of the various purchasing criteria of the consumer, the key criteria often lie in the fundamental value of the product and service, the degree of performance difference between a new and old or existing product, and time and cost savings and reduction (West & Mace, 2009).

Business models are commonly used for analyzing value creation in mobile OS. However, a business model should not only be established based on the value creation for OS users, but also emphasizes on capturing value on the part of the product manufacturer. A business model therefore needs to take into consideration of both the consumer and business owner. From the view of Chesbrough and Rosenbloom (2002), purposes of a business model should include the following points:

- Articulating the value proposition of a product
- Identifying the market segmentation of the firm
- Establishing the value creation for users as well as the value capture for the firm
- Envisioning the market position of the firm
- Formulating a sustainable and competitive strategy for the firm (Amant & Still, 2007).

While it is critical to create value for the market and consumers, it is also important to remember that in order to become a profitable business; the expectation of value captured by the business owner should be larger than the value created for its users. This will ensure efficiencies in innovation, production and marketing, and insure maximal profitability. The business model adapted from Osterwalder, Pigneur and Tucci (2005) fulfilled our criteria in the search for a suitable business model to base our evaluation on. It is based on four key elements that are integral in marketing and value appropriation of mobile OS. The four elements in this business model are: (1) Product Innovation, (2) Customer Relationship, (3) Infrastructure Operators, and (4) Financial Aspects.

Product Innovation

Product innovation is the result of bringing a new product or new service with a new working way to fulfill the customer's need and solve their problem. Value proposition is the explanation of overall product and service offered by the company, where typically the starting point is the innovation of a new product or idea. The consideration of value creation is closely linked to product innovation. If the value proposition is heading the right direction, there is no difficulty in the eventual implementation of the rest of the business model and in achieving desired success in the market upon launch.

Customer Relationship

Firstly, the value proposition in mobile OS is directly linked to the selection of the target users as in the example of the selection of a target developer group or a user community by product manufacturer. Secondly, to reach targeted market segment, distribution channels are established for strategic decision making. Mobile OS is currently at the fore most part of the mobile industry debate and act as brands to consumers in product comparison and evaluation. One of the main reasons in renewed interest in mobile OS stems from the current trend in application store, and the determinant to the success of the mobile OS relies on the developer community and ecosystem.

Infrastructure Operations

Understanding the plan and starting point to negotiate with the most suitable communities can utilize a successful business strategy, combined with collaboration and competencies in searches, evaluation, and negotiation. It should also contain an outline of sharing revenues and risks. The alliance of mobile OS with mobile operators and mobile phone manufacturers is one major determinant to profit making and value adding to mobile phone users. This alliance can offer cost reduction to subscribers by subsidies on costly handsets and capture other form of revenue opportunities, such as data subscription. An alliance on all fronts can ensure customer satisfaction and build brand equity.

Financial Aspects

The driving factor behind efficiency is the internal cost structure. The basis of the external cost structure is partners and consumers. The revenue model is then based on final value provision generated by the product or service in terms of the value it can render to its users (Osterwalder, et. al., 2005).

In this chapter, we will be studying the value frameworks of both Apple iPhone and Google Android and its market appropriation based on the above business model. Table 1 from Gartner Newsroom (2009), shows the worldwide sales of smartphones by OS and their respective market share percentage. According to the prescribed data, the sales figure and market share for iPhone are continuously increasing through the years while Android OS is enjoying accelerating sales and market share, albeit in its 'young' days. In summary, both Android and iPhone OS are the two fastest growing OS on an international scale and are key players in the OS market largely due to

their value frameworks and value alignment. This further illustrates that value creation (user) and value capture (business) are directly proportional to sales and market share (Gartner, 2009).

Values of mobile OS are usually not directly captured by users because mobile OS has been embedded into the smartphone as an integral and central part. Users are only able to capture the values through their interaction within the mobile OS interface and the experiences with the applications which are supported by the inbuilt mobile OS. Every mobile OS has its particular interface and mobile OS support different mobile applications in various ways, thus providing users with different experiences. However, there are still some common questions that the developers should always bear in mind while creating distinguishing values for mobile OS users (Chen, 2009).

- **Value object:** What is the focus of the mobile OS and what applications does it support?
- **Value content:** What kind of valuable experiences is intended for the users through the mobile OS applications?
- **Value delivery:** How is value created transferred by developers to the users?

Table 1. Worldwide smartphone sales by operating system in 2007 to 2009 (in 1000's of Units)

Mobile OS	2009		2008		2007	
	Units	Market Share %	Units	Market Share %	Units	Market Share %
Symbian	80,878.60	46.9	72,933.50	52.4	77,684.00	63.5
Research In Motion	34,346.60	19.9	23,149.00	16.6	11,767.70	9.7
iPhone	24,889.80	14.4	11,417.50	8.2	3,302.60	2.7
MS Windows Mobile	15,027.60	8.7	16,498.10	11.8	14,698.00	12
Linux	8,126.50	4.7	10,622.40	7.6	11,756.70	9.6
Android	6,798.40	3.9	640.5	0.5	NA	NA
Other Os	2,305.60	1.3	4,026.90	2.9	3,106.70	2.5
Total	172,373.10	100	139,287.90	100	122,315.60	100

- **Value feedback:** What feedback is expected from users and how can improvements be made accordingly?

ANALYSIS OF VALUE CREATION OF APPLE IPHONE AND ANDRIOD

We use the Apple iPhone OS and Google's Android OS as two leading representatives of current mobile platforms.

Apple iPhone OS

iPhone OS is a proprietary mobile operating system which Apple Inc. has developed and marketed aggressively and passionately in the smartphone market. While open platforms are being stressed every day, iPhone OS operates differently. Apple iPhone OS further creates a relatively closed and limited sharing kingdom. iPhone OS is a derivation of Mac OS hence it is UNIX-like, using no more than 500M of the mobile device's memory. iPhone OS thus has a reputation for its immediate response. Based on the "rich with possibilities" concept created by Apple, the iPhone as platform requires no special efforts to manipulate or interact with the mobile system. It also supports multi-touch gestures, such as swiping, tapping, pinching, and reverse pinching.

iPhone's Design Principles

The concrete difference of the highest potential impact on the design drives iPhone to hit the smartphone market and create a revolution in the mobile phone market for customization. The following design principles are found in iPhone OS that deliver significant intangible value to the user:

- **Compact screen size:** Small but high-resolution (480×320 pix) screen that can conveniently fit a pocket.

- **Limited memory:** Memory usage warning of cleaning up redundant information at a certain intervals.
- **One screen at a time:** Different screens will be shown sequentially but never simultaneously.
- **One application at a time:** "Incompatible" functions can be operated at the same time. If a new application is switched on, the previous application will be forced to quit.
- **Minimal user help:** iPhone mobile OS allows easy and standardized manipulation, and it provides an simple and straightforward information presentation style.

The above design principle can be further categorized into three application styles: productivity applications, usability applications and immersive applications. Together they help the user ascertain their needs based on visual presentations, behavioral characteristics, data model and experiences (Varnali & Toker, 2010). Productivity applications enable users' need based on information organization and system manipulation. Usability applications help the user to accomplish certain tasks with the least effort and user input. They tend to display the user's requested information on a flat screen despite the differences in information organization style and the depth of information from various sources. Immersive applications offer a full-screen, visually rich environment and multimedia display experience. They focused on users' feeling while using it. Immersion also emphasizes users' sense of entering the world that the applications bring to, instead of just accessing the interfaces of mobile devices (iPhone OS library, 2010).

Value Analysis of Apple iPhone Mobile OS Using the ADVISOR Model

Value

iPhone OS derives from its Mac OS. It well supports a lot of mobile applications thus making iPhone an internet-and multi-media-enabled smartphone. It is also a combination of a mobile phone, camera, a portable media player and an Internet client. It enables users to check emails and browse the web with a satisfactory response time, to download music wirelessly and to continue the social networking anytime anywhere. The App supported by the iPhone OS make iPhone act like a mini computer. It can load and view PDF, Word and Excel files and even has an audio notes feature that records details that cannot be input into the app. According to iPhone official advertisement, iPhone OS Software Update is free to all iPhone users and it is compatible with previous versions.

Interface

Apple places a lot of value on the user interface. It has a 3.5 inch touch screen with 320 *480 pix with scratch-free glass. The wide touch screen is not only fresh & fashionable to users but also provides users with aesthetic enjoyment. It satisfies all the important factors for a perfect interface, such as simplicity, convenience, intuitive nature, and aesthetics as well. It is fashionable, smart, colorful and also easy to use.

Service Platform

iPhone, iPod, iPad and iTunes share the same platform. Apple users who are already familiar with its platform require no extra effort is required to adapt to its services. Also, because of the shared platform among all Apple products, users do not need to worry about the storage space. They can listen directly to their music on iTunes through their mobile phone without downloading and storing onto the phone a second time. Apple has also successfully build up the barrier for user to switch from using Apple products & applications to other brands.

Organizing Model

Apple sells its products globally through its online stores, retail stores, direct sales force, third-party wholesalers, resellers and value-added resellers. On a global level, Apple stores feature a theatre for presentations and workshops, a studio for training with Apple products, and a Genius Bar for technical support and repairs. Apple stores also offer free workshops to the public.

Revenue/Cost Sharing

iPhone is designed with many technology innovations, and Apple is the first one in the market to develop such a multimedia mobile phone. Therefore, they are able to adopt a skim pricing strategy to make up their large R&D cost and maximize the profit. Moreover, iPhone, iPod, iPad and iTunes sharing the same platform not only enable s Apple to enjoy scale economies effect, but to also help cut down the operating and maintaining cost.

Adoption by Users

While developing iPhone, Apple not only developed the hardware themselves, but developed the mobile OS and other supporting software by themselves. Since Apple enjoys a super brand reputation and widely recognized by its users, users were confident about the newly invented iPhone mobile OS and accepted it without haste.

Disruptions

iPhone OS was derived from the Apple Mac operating system. In order to keep the secrecy of developing iPhone, Apple chose to develop the mobile OS for iPhone by themselves instead of purchasing from other suppliers.

Android Operating System

The Android OS is a mobile operating system that is applied on mobile devices, such as smartphones. Android OS was derived from Apple Mac operating system and thus it is Unix-like. It was initially developed by Android Inc. and then bought by Google. By using the Java libraries developed by Google and other Android tools, Android OS allows the application developers to program codes in Java, hence to control mobile device. Android OS as a mobile operating system is able to deliver a complete set of software for mobile devices: a unique operating system as well as other key mobile applications. The intention of Android's innovation is to revolutionize the mobile market with smartphones that support PC functionality. Google is also a major participant in the Android phone by offering its wide range of applications to Android OS. Since Google has established it reputation in worldwide market, Android is also quickly accepted by the large community of Google. The higher growth in the sales of Android implies that it has successfully delivered its values to users and is well accepted by them. In addition, the open sources on which Android based, supports a variety of customizations.

Android's Design Principles

- Optimizing the functionalities of mobile applications on it
- Basing on the open sources as well as customizing for users
- Improving mobile devices' supporting functions for 2D and 3D pictures
- Supporting developers using SQL for structured data storage
- Supporting common media, such as audio, video, pictures, text and movies etc

- Developing additional functionalities as Wi Fi cameras, GPS and compass
- Allowing further improvements in debugging tools, memory cards and other rich development environment (Android Developer, 2010)

Limitation and Challenges of Current Mobile OS

Security Issues

Security is always one of the utmost concerns from the perspective of value creation for users in mobile OS. According to the investigation results of the Top Ten IT Issues survey, the issue of security has left the top three spots since 2007. It even ranked top in 2008 (Agee, et. al, 2009). Although mobility is one of the most valuable characteristics of mobile OS, mobile OS are exposing themselves to more security challenges with smartphones and other mobile devices being carried everywhere, Security issues of operating systems are extremely important. Mobile phones are regarded as one of the commonly used portable storage devices and being accessed at a high frequency, they may also carry a lot of private information. For example, user may save the username and password of his online bank in his mobile OS in his phone. Should the phone be lost or stolen by accident, others will have the chance to access the mobile OS and further access the private information stored on the phone. Whatever viewing or modification of information may cause serious consequences for its previous owner.

Besides the concerns for the mobile OS itself, security impacts also the trust of data transmission on a mobile platform. Although mobility, flexibility and convenience to users is offered via the mobile OS and device, data transmission via a mobile platform is faces the threat of confidentiality. Unsafe data transmission on mobile OS can happen anytime anywhere without sufficient protection, and is vulnerable to be attacked (Mannino, 2007). Therefore, mobility and portability of mobile OS can only maximize the value creation for users if they can vouch for safety. The issues of security not only affect the value creation for users, but also the value capture by manufacturers.

Battery Life

Increased portability of mobile devices have been claimed to enable users to access it anytime anywhere, however, battery life limitation remains to be one of the major constraints. Once the battery runs out, the mobile device becomes nothing. Among complex reasons that are responsible for the battery life shortage, the large energy consumption of the mobile OS is one of the most important reasons. Mobile OS are energy-dependent and its high performance relies heavily on how much energy it can consume. There are usually several modes for users to choose, such as energy saving mode, sleeping mode, normal mode, and high performance mode. While Mobile OS under its higher performance mode gives significantly faster response to user requests, it also consumes much more energy than its normal mode or energy saving mode. Most of the power stored in the battery of a smart phone is consumed by the mobile phone's operating system. Due to the limited battery time, user activities may be affected. In other words, value creation is not fully realized.

Data Backup Supporting

As mobile devices become increasingly significant portable storage devices, people are able to carry and access data all the time. However, mobile devices faces big challenge of preventing data corruption and data loss. Thus data backup should be applied to mobile devices. However, not all mobile OS has the support to backup data by using an external storage card, such as a memory card. Even a mobile OS allows the user to use a memory card for data backup, incompatibility

problems occur on different mobile OS. If the backup data cannot be accessed on other devices with different mobile OS, the usability of data becomes compromised.

FINDINGS AND CONCLUSION

All problems and challenges that have been discussed earlier implies upon new direction for business owners to create value for users. Because of technological bottleneck, profitable concern or industrial standard, the current mobile OS manufacturers have not provided users values on these problematic aspects. Whatever the constraints, mobile OS providers as well as the supporting service providers should always bear their users' need in mind. For example, the solar battery can be used to replace the current energy providing system of mobile OS. Samsung has launched a new cell phone E1107 with solar battery in 2009. Solar battery may also be applied to other smartphones to solve the battery life limitation problem. Beyond the technical solutions, we see a tradeoff between value creation for users and economic concerns. It is paradoxical that the manufacturer wants to maximize the value creation for users and the economic profits of their own and compromise hence value creation of users in these situations. Therefore, a win win solution need to be created for the purpose of balancing the benefit of users and the manufacturers.

Mobile OS, as an integral part of many mobile devices nowadays, have been widely discussed about since its invention. In this chapter, we explored the mobile OS from the perspective of value creation for its users. Among many business models, we chose one generic model of Osterwalder, Pigneur and Tucci (2005), which is based on the elements of products innovation, customer relationship, infrastructure operators and financial aspects. Value creation is regarded as the interaction of manufacturers and users. For the manufacturers, they have to take into consideration both users' need and their own economic profit, in whatever value they are creating for users, thus creating a tradeoff between the two. The benefits towards the mobile phone users are sacrificed due to monetary concerns by manufacturers due to financial reasons to a certain degree, even though the manufactures have the technology to enhance the value creation. As with many other high-tech applications, value creation of mobile OS is indirectly captured by users since it is mainly captured through users' interactivities with the interfaces and their experience with mobile OS applications. Two outstanding representatives of current mobile OS, Apple iPhone OS and Android OS are analyzed and by examining their design principles and key values created for users, we see the overall value creation by mobile OS as well as the existing limitations of current mobile OS.

REFERENCES

Agee, A. S., & Yang, C. (2009). Top ten IT issues 2009. 2009 EDUCAUSE Current Issues Committee. *EDUCAUSE Review, 44*(4), 45–59.

Amant, K. S., & Still, B. (2007). *Handbook of research on open source software: Technological, economic, and social perspectives* (pp. 578–583). New York, NY: Information Science Reference. doi:10.4018/978-1-59140-999-1

Android Developer. (2010). *What is Android?* Retrieved on 25 April, 2010, from http://developer.android.com/guide/basics/what-is-android.html

Chen, Q. Y. (2009). A value-oriented framework of business models innovation: The case of Apple Inc. *Second International Symposium on Electronic Commerce and Security,* vol. 1, (pp. 426-430).

Gartner. (2009). *Gartner says worldwide smartphone sales grew 29 percent in first quarter of 2008.* Stamford, CT. Retrieved on 26 April, 2010, from http://www.gartner.com/it/page.jsp?id=688116

iPhone OS library (2010). *The iPhone OS platform: Rich with possibilities.* Retrieved on 30 April, 2010, from http://developer.apple.com/iphone/library/documentation/UserExperience/Conceptual/MobileHIG/DevelopingSoftware/DevelopingSoftware.html

Keeney, R. L. (1992). *Value-focused thinking.* Cambridge, MA: Harvard University Press.

Mannino, M. V. (2007). *Database design, application development, & administration* (3rd ed.). Boston, MA: McGraw-Hill.

Morris, B. (2007). *The Symbian OS architecture sourcebook: Design and evolution of a mobile phone OS.* Hoboken, NJ: John Wiley & Sons.

Osterwalder, A., Pigneur, Y., & Tucci, C. L. (2005). Clarifying business models: Origins, present, and future of the concept. *Communications of the Association for Information Systems, 16*(1).

Schmidt, A. D., Peters, F., Lamour, F., & Albayrak, S. (2008). *Monitoring smartphones for anomaly detection.* International Conference on Mobile Wireless Middleware, Operating Systems, and Applications (Mobileware), 2, (pp. 12-15).

Speckmann, B. (2008). *The Android mobile platform.* Unpublished Masters Dissertation, Eastern Michigan University, Ypsilanti, Michigan, United States.

Varnali, K., & Toker, A. (2010). Mobile marketing research: The-state-of-the-art. *Informational Journal of Information Management, 30,* 144–151.

West, J., & Mace, M. (2009). Browsing as the killer app: Explaining the rapid success of Apple's iPhone. *Telecommunications Policy, 33,* 10–11.

ADDITIONAL READING

Ansari, S., & Garud, R. (2009). Inter-generational transitions in socio-technical systems: The case of mobile communications. *Research Policy, 38*(2), 382–392. doi:10.1016/j.respol.2008.11.009

Antonini, P., Ippoliti, G., & Longhi, S. (2006). Learning control of mobile robots using a multiprocessor system. *Control Engineering Practice, 14*(11), 1279–1295. doi:10.1016/j.conengprac.2005.06.012

Balan, R. K., Ramasubbu, N., Prakobphol, K., Christin, N., & Hong, J. (2009). *mFerio: the design and evaluation of a peer-to-peer mobile payment system.* Paper presented at the Proceedings of the 7th international conference on Mobile systems, applications, and services.

Bayir, M. A., Demirbas, M., & Eagle, N. (in press). Mobility profiler: A framework for discovering mobility profiles of cell phone users. [*Corrected Proof.*]. *Pervasive and Mobile Computing.*

Bosch, J. (2009). *From software product lines to software ecosystems.* Paper presented at the Proceedings of the 13th International Software Product Line Conference.

Chang, Y. F., Chen, C. S., & Zhou, H. (2009). Smart phone for mobile commerce. *Computer Standards & Interfaces, 31*(4), 740–747. doi:10.1016/j.csi.2008.09.016

Goode, A. (2010). Managing mobile security: How are we doing? *Network Security, 2*(2), 12–15. doi:10.1016/S1353-4858(10)70025-8

Hall, S. P., & Anderson, E. (2009). Operating systems for mobile computing. *J. Comput. Small Coll., 25*(2), 64–71.

Herzberg, A. (2003). Payments and banking with mobile personal devices. *Communications of the ACM, 46*(5), 53–58. doi:10.1145/769800.769801

IsIklar, G., & Büyüközkan, G. (2007). Using a multi-criteria decision making approach to evaluate mobile phone alternatives. *Computer Standards & Interfaces, 29*(2), 265–274. doi:10.1016/j.csi.2006.05.002

Lin, F., & Ye, W. (2009). *Operating System Battle in the Ecosystem of Smartphone Industry.* Paper presented at the Proceedings of the 2009 International Symposium on Information Engineering and Electronic Commerce.

Lockton, D., Harrison, D., & Stanton, N. A. (2010). The Design with Intent Method: A design tool for influencing user behaviour. *Applied Ergonomics, 41*(3), 382–392. doi:10.1016/j.apergo.2009.09.001

Mallat, N., Rossi, M., & Tuunainen, V. K. (2004). Mobile banking services. *Communications of the ACM, 47*(5), 42–46. doi:10.1145/986213.986236

Mallat, N., Rossi, M., & Tuunainen, V. K. (2008). An empirical investigation of mobile ticketing service adoption in public transportation. *Personal and Ubiquitous Computing, 12*(1), 57–65. doi:10.1007/s00779-006-0126-z

Nah, F. F.-H., Siau, K., & Sheng, H. (2005). The value of mobile applications: a utility company study. *Communications of the ACM, 48*(2), 85–90. doi:10.1145/1042091.1042095

Oliver, E. (2008). A survey of platforms for mobile networks research. *SIGMOBILE Mob. Comput. Commun. Rev., 12*(4), 56–63. doi:10.1145/1508285.1508292

Oren, M. A., Seth, U., Huang, F., & Kang, S. (2009). *Cross-Cultural Design and Evaluation of the Apple iPhone.* Paper presented at the Proceedings of the 3rd International Conference on Internationalization, Design and Global Development: Held as Part of HCI International 2009.

Qiuying, C. (2009). *A Value-Oriented Framework of Business Models Innovation.*

Saif, U. (2006). *Opportunistic File-Associations for Mobile Operating Systems*. Paper presented at the Proceedings of the Seventh IEEE Workshop on Mobile Computing Systems & Applications.

Shih, G., Lakhani, P., & Nagy, P. (2010). Is Android or iPhone the Platform for Innovation in Imaging Informatics. *Journal of Digital Imaging, 23*(1), 2–7. doi:10.1007/s10278-009-9242-4

Sousa, J. P. (2008). *Challenges and architectural approaches for authenticating mobile users*. Paper presented at the Proceedings of the 1st international workshop on Software architectures and mobility.

Varnali, K., & Toker, A. (2010). Mobile marketing research: The-state-of-the-art. *International Journal of Information Management, 30*(2), 144–151. doi:10.1016/j.ijinfomgt.2009.08.009

Walker, G. H., Stanton, N. A., Jenkins, D. P., & Salmon, P. M. (2009). From telephones to iPhones: Applying systems thinking to networked, interoperable products. *Applied Ergonomics, 40*(2), 206–215. doi:10.1016/j.apergo.2008.04.003

West, J., & Mace, M. (in press). Browsing as the killer app: Explaining the rapid success of Apple's iPhone. [*Corrected Proof.*]. *Telecommunications Policy*.

Whipple, J., Arensman, W., & Boler, M. S. (2009). *A public safety application of GPS-enabled smartphones and the android operating system*. Paper presented at the Proceedings of the 2009 IEEE International Conference on Systems, Man and Cybernetics.

KEY TERMS AND DEFINITIONS

Android OS: A mobile operating system for mobile devices, which was developed by Android Inc., and then purchased by Google Inc.

Business Model: A model describes how an organization creates, captures and delivers values.

iPhone OS: A mobile operating system developed and market by Apple Inc. It derives from Mac operating system, thus is Unix-like.

Mobile OS: Mobile OS is also known as mobile operating system or a mobile platform, which is the operating system that controls a mobile device.

Smartphones: A mobile phone with part of PC's functions. It runs on mobile operating systems providing a standardized interface.

Value Creation: Benefits created by manufacturer and then transfer to users.

Value Proposition: A quantified review of benefit and cost that manufacturers create and deliver to users within the outside of the organization.

Chapter 17
Smartphone Application Wave and Trends on Different Platforms

Irvine Yeo
Nanyang Technological University, Singapore

Jing Cong
Nanyang Technological University, Singapore

Khin Mu Yar Soe
Nanyang Technological University, Singapore

Fan Jing
Nanyang Technological University, Singapore

ABSTRACT

Smartphones have experienced exponential growth and this in itself changes the way consumers use mobile communications. Traditionally, a phone is used only for communicating via voice but the Smartphone has extended the functions to include music player, camera, web browsing and executing of other applications. This wave of change has affected the traditional business model of telecommunication companies as well as creates new opportunities for platform owners to gear towards full integration. This chapter seeks to explore and discuss these issues and opportunities revolving around the platform, trends, problems and opportunities.

INTRODUCTION

In the recent years, we have witnessed the rising popularity of mobile handheld devices such as smartphone and personal digital assistants (PDAs). Numerous applications have been developed for those devices including navigation maps, daily news, games, fashion guides et cetera. The ability to utilise the equivalent of a mini computer from virtually anywhere, and the convergence of web and application technologies offer an unprecedented level of flexibility and convenience, particularly for ubiquitous information access

DOI: 10.4018/978-1-61350-147-4.ch017

through these mobile devices. However, the platform of these mobile handheld devices both open and proprietary also present challenges for both developers and consumers to take advantage of the convenience of mobile handheld devices for information access.

This chapter seeks to explore and discuss the open and proprietary platforms of smartphones, trends of smartphone usage in terms of ARPU, the three criteria of platform categorization, namely the development tools; distribution channel and degree of Integration, trends of adoption by major platform owner as well as value created through complementary.

BACKGROUND

Smart Phone

A little more than a decade ago, the only function that a regular phone can perform was only making phone calls. With the introduction of a hybrid of phone and camera with low-megapixels, a radical change occurred when Smartphone came into vogue with features such as high-end camera, music, video, internet, games, applications and radio et cetera. Jason Langridge, a mobility business manager at Microsoft, defines a Smartphone as "something that combine traditional communication devices and provide rich applications and rich data applications." Gartner, in their glossary page, defines Smartphone as: "A large-screen, voice-centric handheld device designed to offer complete phone functions while simultaneously functioning as a personal digital assistant (PDA)." Tech-faq. com defines a Smartphone as: "A Smartphone is a small, all-in-one mobile device that is used for communication and computing functions. Unlike regular cell phones, Smartphones allow users to choose the applications they want to install and use. It often has PC-like functionality."

Current Market Penetration by Smart Phone

Fox (2006) argues the traditional phone or personal digital assistants are quickly being obsolete in the marketplace by what are called converged, integrated, or multifunctional devices such as smartphone as a result of the market responding to user's demands for convergence and a reduction in the number of separate devices needed to carry around. These devices include but are not limited to phones, music player, cameras, global positioning system (GPS), web browsing, storage; all of these features and functions can be found in a single smartphone.

The worldwide market for mobile phone performed extremely well in 2009 and is expected to continue its performance through 2010 and beyond. According to IDC's Worldwide Quarterly Mobile Phone Tracker, the last quarter of 2009 saw a new record level being set which 54.4 million units were being shipped, an increase of 39% from the same quarter in 2008. The full year saw a total of 174.2 million unit being shipped in 2009, an increase of 15.1% over 151.4 million units in 2008. Of all the units shipped, converged mobile devices or smartphones accounted for 15.4%, a slight increase from 12.7% in 2008.

The potentials for smartphone seems rosy as IDC anticipates that the ongoing demand will drive the smartphone market to a new shipment record in 2010. The additional impetus from the shifting landscape of mobile OS is also expected to increase its demand. Both Google's Android and Palm's webOS, released only in 2009, have revealed new ways to engage the users with their increased functionality. Windows and Symbian are expected to unveil new versions of their respective OS with more advances in 2010. All the mobile OS will compete with a thriving mobile application library, improved intuitiveness and seamlessness to provide user with a compelling experience.

Users will benefit from greater personalization, customization and usability which are likely to drive demands even further.

Gartner expects Smartphone sales to make up 37% of overall mobile devices sales with a value of US$ 191 billion in 2012, up from the current 14%. Overall, mobile device market is booming, especially for Smartphone. The art of the Smartphone is the operation system and its ability to run various types of applications. Therefore, the reasons behind Smartphone market expanding are software and application.

Value Net Framework

The Value Net Framework, also known as Co-opetition is an extension of Porter's Five forces framework, enables organizations to classify the relevant actors in their industry and beyond. This model attempts to understand and influence the behaviour of these actors by incorporating insights from the game theory. Adam Brandenburger and Barry Nalebuff, professors in economics at Harvard and Yale University, argues that cooperation and competition are both necessary and desirable when doing business, unlike Porter's five forces model where the focus is almost exclusively on competition. Cooperation is needed to increase benefits to all players by focusing on market growth whereas competition is required to divide the profits and benefits by focusing on market share.

The game theory can be used to study the interaction between actors and the decisions each actor makes can lead to different outcomes or ending. In the game, the actors are seen as customers, suppliers, competitors (include rivals, threat of new entrants, and substitute product or services) and a new actor, complementor, introduced by Brandenburg and Nalebuff (1996).

1. **Customers:** The actor to whom the company sells its products and services to in return for monetary rewards i.e. buyers and end users of Apple's iPhone or Google's Android phones and application.

2. **Competitors:** There are two perspectives to this actor: From the supplier's perspective, a competitor is an actor where the supplier finds more attractive or beneficial to supply its resources to them over you i.e. supplying Apple with accessories over Nokia. From the customer's perspective, a competitor is an actor where the customers value their product more than yours or when your product is a substitute for a competitor's product i.e., valuing iPhone over Nokia or Black Berry phones or substitute product such as Creative's music player.

3. **Suppliers:** The actor where resources are provided to your company in return for monetary rewards i.e. Parts supplier for iPhone. It can be software suppliers i.e., the content providers such as application developers for Apple's portal; AppStore, and hardware suppliers i.e., product manufacturers.

4. **Complementors:** Similarly, this actor also has two perspectives to it. From the supplier's perspective, a complementor is an actor where the supplier finds more attractive or beneficial to provide its resources to you and other actors than when providing to you alone i.e. Singtel's tied up with Apple to sell iPhone. Both actors stand to gain in market share in their respective industries. From the customer's perspective, a complementor is an actor where the customers value your product more when they also have another actor's product than when they have yours by itself i.e., the numerous applications developed by third party developers and iPhone or Andriod Phones.

THREE CRITERIA FOR PLATFORM CATEGORIZATION

Like any other application development and distribution, smart phone applications require the platform that provides development tool for developers, distribution channel to reach out to customers and integrated device to bundle the services. The platform provider usually provides the Operation System (OS) and bundle with the device that is mobile handheld device. The OS is the main actor which decides which kind of application can be downloaded from where. For the richness of applications, platform providers provide development tools and distribution channel for developers, in the form of either open or close. The level of openness and closeness varies depending on the business model of platform provider.

The Smartphone operation system can be categorized into open and proprietary platform by reviewing three criteria: Development tool, degree of portal centralization and degree of distribution process integration. (Holzer, 2009). Figure 1 shows three components of the smartphone platform and their links to both the developer of applications as well as users.

Development Tools

The core of development tool is its software development kit (SDK), which is the key for third party developer to program applications for the operation system. There can be various ways of sharing SDK in different platform. The ways can be listed as totally open, partially open and partially close and totally close. Totally open type can be found at Linux Approach at which all part of source code of SDKs and OS has been enclosed. Partially open and close type can be found in Google Approach at which enclosing everything except Bluetooth

and Instant Chat Messaging APIs. Apple's favorite approach is totally control at which entire source code of SDK and OS is disclosed.

Distribution Channel: Degree of Portals Centralization

The portal is the channel to deliver applications from developers to consumers. Portal is an important factor in mobile application supply chain as it acts as an intermediary between developer and consumers. There are mainly two types of sale strategy over portal: Centralized which is single point of sale and decentralized which is multiple point of sale (Holzer, 2009). In centralized sale strategy, the portal is the mandatory place where applications are published and downloaded. The portal is linked to the Operation System and developers and customers are forced to go through that particular portal. This restriction enables portal provider a competitive advantages and better control over existing applications. The AppStore and the Android Market are such examples. In decentralized strategy, not much restriction for developers and customers is imposed. Developers can publish their application on any third part portals and customers can download from any of their favorite portal. Decentralized strategy enables the fair competition among portal providers to attract customers and application developers. However, it lacks the ability of consolidated management over existing applications across all portals. Examples of such are Nokia and Microsoft.

Figure 1. Overall smartphone software development and distribution cycle

Platform: Degree of Integration

As shown in Figure 2, the distribution process integration can be further divided into full integration when the company controls every step in the distribution model, portal integration when only the application portal is integrated, device integration when the device is manufactured exclusively, and finally no integration when companies only focus on one core business such as programming the OS. (Gereffi, 2005)

The platform adopts a full integration and has tight control over the whole process of product manufacturing, software development and distribution. Apple and Nokia are such examples. Apple has its own product line, iPhone and Operation system which source code is not released and tightly tied to its own portal of AppStore. Nokia also manufactures its mobile line which is its core business and provides applications and other content via OVI portal which is decentralized. The full integration owns the whole platform and the degree of control over each component varies as it depends on the platform provider's core competencies and business strategy. The portal integration means a tight tie between application development and application sale. Google is the best example of which it provides an Android OS and Android Market. Google's ambition is to reach out to the mobile segment for more advertising space. Although, Google does not manufacture its own phone, it has a vertical partnership with mobile device manufacturer, HTC, which is the strong partnership of win-win situation. Device Integration refers to those platforms that are manufacturing its own device and OS but no application portal is provided. For example, Research In Motion, RIM, who is behind the BlackBerry® brand with its own BlackBerry OS is the proprietary software platform. No integration platform provider refers to those software platform providers, which does not own a product line as well as a portal. Microsoft is the best example as its core business is based solely on developing OS.

Closed Platform for Smart Phone

Totally closed platforms have the following qualities: First, they disclose the code of their SDK and operation system from outsiders so as to gain control over third party applications. Second, their portal is centralized so that there is one main portal to publish applications which gives the provider a distinctive advantage over others. Third, they integrate fully the distribution process by manufacturing the device themselves or by outsourcing to selected OEMs and providing application content exclusively on one portal and contracting MNOs for distribution. The closeness and tightness of control varies depend on the different platform providers. Classic examples of

Figure 2. Platform integration (Adopted from Holzer, 2009)

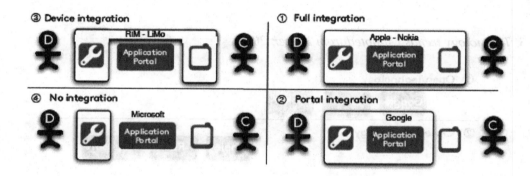

Close Platforms are Apple, Microsoft and RIM. Apple is the most closed and has total control over third party applications whereas Microsoft and RIM are more relaxed when compared to Apple.

Open Platform for Smart Phone

The characteristic of a total opened platform can be listed as follows. Firstly enclose the source of SDKs and Operation System for the benefit of third party developers and all. Secondly decentralize the distribution portal for fair competition among portal providers. Thirdly implement no or loosely platform integration. However, there are a few grey areas in determining open platform for smart phone especially when the entire chain is considered. Most of the platforms may be intermediate by exhibiting qualities both on the closed and open side. For example Google engages an open source technology for application development, while running a centralized portal. On the distribution side, Google approaches both full integration with their Nexus One and no integration by providing their OS to various distributors.

Average Revenues per User (ARPU)

According to the investment website Investorpedia, ARPU is defined as "a measure of the revenue generated per user or unit" (Investorpedia, 2010). Telecommunication companies often use this measurement to survey how much revenue the company makes from the average user. These revenues can be further broken down to indicate which services or products such as data and voice is generating growth or lagging behind. Despite being used widely, ARPU may be misleading, as there is no real link between it and the margins of a telco's business. For example, a telco with high APRU might not be profitable as it could consist of only a small amount of subscribers while a company with low APRU does not mean it is not profitable as it could be encompassing a large customer base. Nevertheless, APRU should not be written off as a way of measuring, as it is a good indicator of how well a telco is doing with its different offerings.

Current Trends in Mobile Application Development and Distribution

Since a few years ago, the once relatively stable smartphone market structure has begun to change. More platforms are moving towards open development tool, centralized portal platform and a higher level of distribution process integration. In the open development tool field, LiMo was the only platform to disclose the source code entirely. Nokia has followed after they adopted Symbian as their OS. Recently, Google with their Android system newly joined the league of open SDK and OS code. This trend is shown in Figure 3. The advantage of an open development tool is that a big pool of third party developers can be assembled and the development and maintenance costs for the OS provider may be greatly reduced.

Apple opened a new market in centralizing the application portal and Google followed this ap-

Figure 3. Technology trends (Adopted from Holzer, 2009)

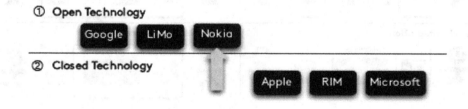

proach. Such a model has proven that with a well organized and review portal, along with its user friendly "one-click" installation, the application market may bring in important revenue. For example, Apple generated revenue of one million a day in its first month of launching AppStore. (Wall Street Journal, 2008) Now, RIM, Microsoft and Nokia has moved or will move to such direction.

Finally, increasing numbers of manufacturers are moving to a more integrated distribution process following Apple. Google has begun to move into full integration by the introduction of Nexus One, Symbian started as a no integration system and moved to portal integration after being acquired by Nokia. With the introduction of OVI they are shifting to full integration. RIM, Microsoft and LiMo are also advancing in such direction, leaving the no integration category empty. Figure 4 and Figure 5 show how various smartphone platforms are moving in terms of centralization and integration strategies.

DISCUSSION AND ANALYSIS

Smart Phone Wave on Developer

The portal centralization affects the developer the most. Previously, third party developers do not have a well-refined platform to publicize their product. Instead, the applications are distributed all over the web through various portals without a comprehensive oversight. This prevented the product from effectively reaching the consumer and might yield the loss of potential customers. In contrast, centralized portals heavily promotes downloads and increase revenues which is a result of a clear user interface as well as systematical advertising. A successful portal catalyzes more developers to program more applications, which broadens the consumer pool, while the increasing demand of consumers conversely stimulates the pool of developers. This is called a two-sided market. (Eisenmann, 2006) The negative side of such portal centralization for the developer is that the platform owner has a great deal of control over

Figure 4. Portal trends (Adopted from Adrian Holzer, 2009, Trends in Mobile Application Development)

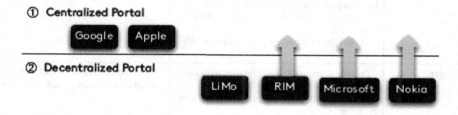

Figure 5. Integration trends (Adopted from Adrian Holzer, 2009, Trends in Mobile Application Development)

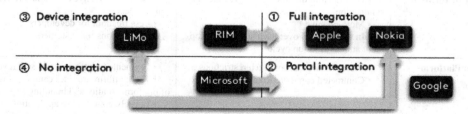

the applications. If they engage a review process of the applications which Apple does, the owner will decide whether the developer's product would be placed onto the portal or not. The developers lose some freedom and are pressed harder to provide high quality applications. Furthermore, some platform owners may apply charges on the developers for selling their products on the portal which yields deducted revenue for the developer. However, as proven by Apple, if an excellent platform attracts many consumers, developers are willing to pay so that their application is publicized by the centralized portal.

The choice of platform for independent developers is also affected by the distribution process integration. The trend towards higher integration makes the development, publishing, purchase and usability of the applications easier by reducing the compatibility issues. In contrast, the developers have to fine tune their programs for each specific device in the heterogeneous systems. Furthermore, developers may be more likely to make revenue through some closed platforms with a strong marketing vision. With an open but poorly organized platform, the developer could make high technical achievements by program-

Table 1. Benefits and potential issues

	Benefits	Issues
Closed Development Tool	• In total control • Trade secret is saved	• Higher Development Cost (labor cost) • Software development restrictions and tools dependency • Lose out Innovative input from independent domain experts • Low contribution to Industry standard • Unable to enjoy the power of "majority trend"
Open Development Tool	• Low development cost • Open opportunity to independent and individual developers • Advancing the open source and standards by contribution from large pool of developers • Manufacturers can reduce their software cost • Benefits of the majority to the better offs for all	• Application battle is heated up • Competitors can also be benefit • Open secret
Portal Centralization	• In total control and insight over existing applications • Gain competitive advantages over its peer competitors • Effective filtering policy	• Complements the "Black" alternative platforms and international grey market problem
Portal Decentralization	• Fair competition among portal providers • More freedom for developers • More options for customers	• No consolidation among portal providers • Repetition can occur among existing applications • Control and filtering policy will be varied
Fully Platform Integration	• Benefit from distribution, aggregation and syndication • More revenue • In total control over each step of development and distribution cycle	• Lack of collective and collaborative work from stakeholders • Less freedom for developers • Less options for customers
Partially or No Platform Integration	• More freedom as not much restrictions • Contracted core competencies	• Segmented platform and lesser revenue • The platform provider cannot enjoy the benefits of platform solidity and bundling services • Loosely control over application or devices • Requires many vertical partnerships

ming based on open source code, but the lack of revenue making distribution channels does not bring in income. Finally, they capture the market, but fail to capture revenue. On the downside of the integrated distribution process, interoperability becomes less, the developers have to make clear-cut choices on which platform they prefer to program. This involves the career criterion. In a fully closed platform, the developer is more likely to be hired by the platform owner. Table 1 summarises some of the benefits and issues of the various strategies available to players.

APRU and Telecommunication Companies

A recent report by Chetan Sharma Consulting (2010) concluded that the global wireless market or data usage continued to grow rapidly in China and India. Amongst the rest, added 30 million new subscribers are added every month. The global subscription penetration was above 68% in 2009. The report also revealed that APRU from voice has been declining steadily since 2004 while APRU from data continues to increase (see Figure 6). APRU from data services contributes almost 50% for some of the leading telecommunication

companies such as NTT DoCoMo and AT&T. In the fourth quarter of 2009, Ericsson reported that the global data usage exceeded the global voice traffic for the first time.

Value Net

With reference to the value Net framework, platform owners create more value for their handsets through complementing each other by going towards with Portal Centralization. As with the case of iPhone and AppStore, the existence and combination of both products add to the value for consumers rather than the standalone of each product. Consumers can leverage on the centralized portal to find an install application, and also survey the popularity of the applications rather than looking everywhere for applications they need such as finding applications for windows mobile handset. The control of application development and approval could be restrictive for developers and the cost of application is likely to be higher for consumers but the quality of these applications is also ensured this way. Telecommunication companies such as AT&T are also considered to be complementary as the existence of these smartphones increased the revenues from the usage of

Figure 6. ARPU trends from 2004-2009 (Adopted from Chetan Sharma Consulting, 2010)

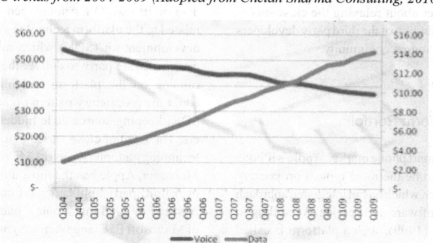

services while at the same time, generate profit for platform owners and handset manufacturers.

SOLUTION AND RECOMMENDATIONS

In order to remain profitable for telecommunication companies, they must revisit their business model to focus on increasing the APRU from data services as researches and trends discussed in earlier sections has shown that voice traffic usage is no longer a viable revenue generating driver. Some of the recommendations would be:

- Pricing the data plans to cater to the mass market and cross the chasm
- Rapidly deploy new products and move from a carrier to a distributor focus
- Innovate new products and services
- Improve market penetration by leveraging on micro segmentation strategies.

For device manufacturers, the trend is going towards software rather than hardware. To stay profitable is depends highly on how it creates alliance with its vertical partners, especially platform providers and content providers. Since the software is what make a difference rather than hardware, the platform providers on close platform might need to consider about relaxing the closeness to enjoy the contribution of the third party developers pool and open source community.

Case Study

Apple's Platform Portfolio

In the current smart phone market, Apple's iPhone is considered to be the most typical proprietary platform adopter, which has an integrated approach to hardware, software and service. According to Eric Raymond (1999), such a platform is called the "Cathedral", while those open ones are called the "Bazzar". It is believed that closed ones have more possibility to be obsolete or suffer from market share dwindling in the future mainly due to the industry standard established and the facilitation of collective work. Many concerns related to Apple's future success or failure in the smart phone market place are based on the history that if lost in the PC war to Microsoft in the 1980s. This is not the first time that Apple has dealt with decisions about open standards. At present, however, whether Apple should be open is no longer an issue because it has already demonstrated its power in leading the smart phone market place. In the current high technology product market, the success of market decision is no longer technology-oriented but user-oriented, especially users' superior experience, which is the crucial factor in the competition in the smart phone market place. Therefore, Apple's decision on its smart phone platform is not based on its lessons drew from history or technology-oriented considerations but how to create a portfolio to balance its maximized profitability, namely value capture, and efficient delivery of wonderful user experience to users that adds on to value creation.

Apple's Closed Technology

Apple's iPhone works on the closed operation system (OS) that only allows applications running on its own OS. Another central component related to the platform technology is the software development kit (SDK) which allows the third party software party to deliver their applications running on the platform and iPhone platform adopt the proprietary pattern on both its OS and SDK, keeping source code hidden from outsiders. The level of close varied among those close technology adopters, such as Microsoft and RIM. Moreover, Apple has the most unlimited control over third party applications. For example, it is reported in 2008 that Apple's planned inclusion of Microsoft Exchange ActiveSync, a technology required to synchronize data directly rather than third-party gateways, gained praise from mobile industry watcher because it offered better secure connections. Besides, some built-in set of APIs, such as Cocoa Touch, was used to handle the user-interface-generated events in Mac OS X provided developers an elegant way to deal with the interface paradigm, thus creating consistent and wonderful user experience.

Apple's Centralized Portal

Apple proposes a single point of sale with its AppStore and it pushed for a unique and exclusive portal with strict application reviewing process (Holzer, 2009). Through the tight control over publishing to the portal, the quality of applications is ensured so that user experience will not be negatively influenced by applications with disjointed components, cluttered interface and content with low quality, which may flooded in those open platforms, and this is the most crucial factor as a 'gate keeper' to guarantee the user experience. iPhone's Appstore facilitates 'one-click' operation directly executable on the mobile device and such convenience encourage downloads and actually increase the pool of potential customers. Besides, the centralized portal serves as a "checkout" point to directly gather the profit from the sales through this platform to ensure value capture.

Apple's Platform Integration

There are several degrees of integration and Apple exhibits a strong degree of integration. It produces the device on its own operation system, namely iPhone, and its own authorized and centralized portal, namely the AppStore. It also works as the content provider with its iTunes. It even signed contract with carriers to create exclusivity to lock in customers and elbow out competitors. Such a wholesome integration covers almost all the parties in the whole supply chain and value net, thus creating a completely consistent user experience and extract profit from each sectors.

Google's Platform Portfolio

Google has been known as Giant Search Engine and its first step to reach out Mobile Market has started by Android, Linux based Operation System application for mobile. From OS to APIs to middleware to applications, everything is built on open source and open standards which can run on any typical modestly powered processors. Since mobile is the new area for Google, it found powerful alliance with different vertical partners. Its alliance consists of 34 companies across all parts of the mobile value chain: chip makers like Intel and Qualcomm, device manufacturer like Motorola and HTC, mobile operators like Sprint Nextel, T-Mobile USA, and NTT DoCoMo; software companies like Nuance Communications and Packet Video; and "commercialization partners" like Wind River (Golvin, 2007).

Google's Open Technology

Since entire Android software stack is distributed under Apache Software Foundation's open source license, it provides free and available platform. The source code of OS and APIs are enclosed and under this licensing scheme, any developers are allowed to contribute in advancing the platform for better use of others. For the security reasons, however, Google refuses to allow access to Bluetooth and Instant Massaging APIs source code (Holzer, 2009).

By implementing the Open Technology, Google provides one option for mobile handhelds makers to reduce their software costs of investing continuously in software customization and optimization with the contributions from pool of open source developers. Developers can also benefit from the open platform to build mobile Internet Applications. Through richness of application, network operators can also benefit from expanding their networks' value on more mobile data usages (Golvin, 2007). Although open source enable benefits of the competitors as well, Google however, believes in its ability to deliver a better experience through its superiority of services (Golvin, 2007). Moreover, Google plans to generate its revenue mainly from highly optimized advertisements. Therefore, Google's real interest is to reach out to more customers.

Google's Portal Centralization

Google adopts the centralized portal strategy in distribution of applications by introducing the Android Marketplace. Initially the portal started to operate "only for free application" and has lately turn on its ability to charge for the applications and more features such as versioning, multiple device profile support, analytics, etc (Hobbs, 2008). Regardless of attempting to own distribution channel, Google still provides freedom for any developers to post any application without any approval process or require certification. By simple registering, Google provides additional help for developers by providing useful dashboard and analytics to help drive business and improve their offerings.

Google's Platform Integration

Currently Google has been listed under portal integration for having both OS and centralized portal. Early 2010, Google announced its first Android Smartphone, Nexus One, powered by HTC and prominently branded "Google". Nexus One is available from Google through its own online sales channel which means it will be the first major Smartphone to be sold exclusively online without any presence in other sales channel (Milanesi &Dulaney, 2010). It can recognize SIM cards from any mobile service provider using the GSM standard and options to be unlocked at higher price or contract plan with network provider at lower price. Google has yet to manufacture its own device but however has its own product line and some potential to migrate into fully integrated platform like Apple. Unlike Apple, Google is

believed to continue its openness through smart integration.

CONCLUSION

This chapter touched on some of the important aspects about smartphones. Although the areas covered are quite diverse, it presents an overall understanding of the smartphone and its general market, trends, issues and opportunities. In general, the manufacturers and platform owner of smartphones stand to gain in the coming years with an even higher sales predicted by researching firms despite its competitive environment. Usage of data services has also outpaced voice traffic and is expected to continue increase in this direction. By opening up the development tools from platform owner to application developers benefit both parties as developers can sell their application for the platform while platform owner can increase demands of its operating system. Centralizing and decentralizing portal has its pro and cons as discussed, but generally, centralizing is more beneficial to the platform owner, and consumers although debatable for developers. Network owners or carriers are increasingly beneficial from the revenues from data usage, to fill the declining revenues from the traditionally profit generating driver of voice traffic usage. The areas being discussed to allow interested parties to analyze the smartphone marketplace on a holistic level, see the connections between the different stakeholders and understand the value they bring to each other.

REFERENCES

Cheng, J. (2010). *Google makes biggest gain in smartphone market share*. Retrieved April 6, 2010, from http://arstechnica.com/gadgets/news/2010/02/google-makes-biggest-gain-in-smartphone-market-share.ars

Chetan Sharma Consulting. (2010). *Global wireless data market - 2009 update.*

Eisenmann, T. (2008, August 11). Strategies for two-sided markets. *Wall Street Journal.* Retrieved on 11th April, 2010, from http://online.wsj.com/article/SB121842341491928977.html?mod=2_1571_topbox

Fox, M. K. (2006). Product pipeline: Megan Fox looks at the latest ebook devices and what they mean for librarians. *Library Journal, 131*, 18–22.

Gartner. (2009, October). Gartner says PC vendors eyeing booming smartphone market. Retrieved March 28, 2010, from http://www.gartner.com/it/page.jsp?id=1215932

Gartner. (2010). *Competitive landscape: Mobile devices, worldwide, 4Q09 and 2009.*

Gereffi, G. (2005). *The governance of global value chains.*

Golvin, C. S., Schandler, T., Delay, E., Lussanet, M., Veen, N., & Lawson, A. (2007). *Google bootstraps an "open" mobile platform: The open handset alliance gives the mobile internet a needed boost. An expert review for strategy professionals.* Cambridge, MA: Forrester Research.

Hello Android. (2008). *Android marketplace officially announced.* Retrieved April 29, 2010, from http://www.helloandroid.com/content/android-marketplace-officially-announced

Hollan, R. (2009). *The ambitions of Android.*

Hollan, R. (2010). *Google Android captures 9% of smart phone market.* Retrieved April 6, 2010, from http://socialmediaseo.net/2010/04/06/google-android-os-market-share/

Hollan, R. (2010). Is Google outsmarting Apple in the mobile market? Retrieved April 6, 2010, from http://socialmediaseo.net/2010/03/31/google-android-apple-iphone/

Holzer, A. (2009). *Trends in mobile application development.*

IDC. (2010, February). *Worldwide converged mobile device market.* Retrieved March 18, 2010, from http://www.idc.com/getdoc.jsp?sessionId=&containerId=prUS22196610&sessionId=B31E48E1535B9E4541C13240420FA03A

Milanesi, C., & Dulaney, K. (2010). *Google's Nexus One takes Android to new level.* Gartner Research Paper.

Chapter 18
Using Web 2.0 Features on Social Networks for Word-of-Mouth Effects

Tan Chee Liang
Nanyang Technological University, Singapore

Chua Kok Seng
Nanyang Technological University, Singapore

Kaung Pye Soe
Nanyang Technological University, Singapore

ABSTRACT

Over the last few years, social networking has established itself to be a significant trend on the Internet. Together with the existence of social networking, Web 2.0 tools have gained much popularity. Internet users around the world are catching the social networking and Web 2.0 bug. According to a study in the UK, 20 percent of online users were regularly logging onto social networking websites like Facebook, MySpace, Orkut, and Friendster. With the growth in the popularity of social networking and Web 2.0 tools, it is only a matter of time before people and businesses become receptive to the commercial possibilities offered by them. We look at one of the popular social networking website, Facebook, and see how these Web 2.0 tools can actually aid in the advertising and promotion aspects through Word-of-Mouth effects.

INTRODUCTION

Business firms today aim to be prominent and noticeable in the global marketplace to advertise their products and services to the consumers. Promotion is an integral part of marketing which includes advertising, sales promotion, personal selling and

publicity. In pre-Web 2.0 days, business firms have to use media promotion through television, radio and Internet as well as sales promotions, marketing campaigns and face-to-face marketing. With the presence of Web 1.0 approach from a decade ago, companies raced to capitalise on Internet advertisements for getting their product information across to the users. However, one critique of Web 1.0 is that it comprises static webpage which

DOI: 10.4018/978-1-61350-147-4.ch018

allows only one way information flow to the user or consumer where the user can find information. In other words, Web 1.0 is constrained by the usage of read-only materials on the website.

Impact of Web 2.0

With the advent of Web 2.0 phenomenon, it is feasible for businesses to enhance their promotion by leveraging social networking sites, video sharing sites, wikis and blogs. Web 2.0 offers rich user experience and it is a two-way information flow between the content creator and users in which the users become the producers of information as well as being the traditional consumers. According to O'Reilly Media, Web 2.0 is the new generation comprising of a spectrum of web-based services that appear to change the way of using the World Wide Web. (O'Reilly, 2005) Web 2.0 facilitates community-oriented sharing, collaboration and interactivity between consumers that allows them to generate, create, organize and share the contents online. The fundamental principle of Web 2.0 is the offering of control to the consumers to generate content. Consumers are able to create content using social networking sites or blogs and post the content as well as distribute them to other websites via syndication such as RSS (Really Simple Syndication). One major advantage to businesses is that companies will benefit from consumer input about their products in the Web 2.0 websites contributing to increase in consumer base.

Role of Social Networking

Social Networking sites such as Facebook, MySpace, Friendster and even YouTube are becoming iconic with the users interacting on Web 2.0 platforms. Social networks allow users connection in order to share each other's contents via social media as well as applying user participation. Hence businesses are able to promote their products by fuelling social media with promotional content and also creating campaigns within the online

social network. Social media boast many upsides to businesses. The first benefit is that it permits the marketers to engage the consumer directly in the creative process which might entail engagement and loyalty of the consumers. Another distinct advantage is that it facilitates viral marketing underpinned by the forces of word of mouth. It is the means of how people convey information about a product on the social networking site. Hence social media in social network brings about efficient market promotion.

The objective of this chapter is to understand how Web 2.0 tools in Social networks brings about or enhances Interactive Digital Media (IDM) promotions. We will use Facebook as a case study to explore the usage of Web 2.0 tools in Facebook for IDM promotion.

Case Study of Facebook

Facebook was launched on Feb 4, 2004. Facebook contains all the information; photos and textual details, about an individual that friends and people in the network can view. Facebook's features include real time news feeds, groups, events, notes, posted items and videos. There are a number of reasons why we use Facebook as a case study:

- It is the leading social networking site based on monthly unique visitors according to comScore.
- Facebook has experienced tremendous commercial interest as well as being a trusted community.
- Marketers are able to build communities in Facebook.
- It serves as form of Customer Relationship Management (CRM) tool for companies selling product and service where communities can be formed around product, service or media.
- Most importantly, there is no subscription fee involved for profile registration.

- Facebook advocates network externalities; end user connects to service with most end users coz there more diverse ways to discover information and content.
- It is perceived as the new generation of marketing.

LITERATURE REVIEW

"Web 2.0" refers to a second generation of web development and design that facilitates communication, secures information sharing, interoperability, and collaboration on the World Wide Web. Web 2.0 concepts have led to the development and evolution of web-based communities, hosted services, and applications; such as social-networking sites, video-sharing sites, wikis and blogs.

A social network, by definition, is a social structure made of nodes that are tied by one or more specific types of interdependency, such as values, visions, ideas etc. Some of the popular internet social communities include Myspace or Facebook, which are examples of Web 2.0 sites. In such communities, customers or users leverage on web 2.0 tools to communicate, create and share contents. This attracts the attention of internet patrons and draws heavy internet traffic to these online communities. Based on such a huge customer base, companies and marketers/ promoters are thus focus more attention to this segment. According to PC Pro, an online magazine, internet traffic to social networking sites has overtaken webmail services in the United Kingdom. The top twenty-five social networking sites according to Hitwise, include Facebook and MySpace account for more than five percent of United Kingdom internet traffic. Such news would attract the advertiser's attention as they realize that this is a new platform for them to advertise and promote their products. They do not need to find the consumers, as the consumers are already hitting upon these social networking sites.

As stated from IDM insights (Martin, 2007), what Web 2.0 offers is the chance to interact with the consumers and other audiences and create a dialog with them. This is attainable via social networking sites. This also explains why big acquisitions that have recently hit the headlines; Google's purchase of YouTube and Yahoo buying Flickr. Marketers will go where the audiences are headed for and in this aspect, the web 2.0 sites. Martin stated that most companies cited marketing and sales as an area where Web 2.0 could help to increase revenues, primarily through customer acquisition and service and Web 2.0 technologies were seen as a way to reduce costs in the areas of customer support, advertising and public relations, and product/service innovation.

However, according to a research study (Clemons et al., 2007), although there have been a rush to acquire social networking websites such as Myspace and YouTube, it is believed that these acquisitions are justified as such websites have great potential to generate enormous profit through advertising. The authors believed that it may not be a rational decision to do so, although some websites may prove to have profound value. Such social networking sites are not actual networks, which create trust and credibility. Users or customers do not visit social networking site primarily for advertising or promotion events and social networking sites will not work as advertising websites.

While discussing trust in online communities (Gayatri et al., 2008), some studies state that when users join social networks to publish and maintain their profiles and establish links to their friends, the resulting social links are evidences of trust between the connected users. The study states that those users who perform business transactions with friends of friends generally obtain significantly benefits in the form of higher user satisfaction. So do social networking sites promote only high volume of internet traffic but low revenue advertising business? According to the New York Times, this statement may be true as those companies who placed their advertisement on social networking sites such as Facebook to promote their products faced difficulties in making such promotion work, mainly due to the fact that members of such social networks want to spend time with their friends and not advertising brands. The members of such sites do not pay any attention to the advertising banner. Companies could only attract consumers by using old promotion methods such as lucky draw or prized contest.

Despite the difficulties encountered by companies who embarked on the advertising campaign on social networking sites, this market segment is still an attractive platform for the advertisers as various studies has proved that people are spending less time on traditional media such as TV, radio or printed materials such as newspapers. Traditional advertising is a one way process and the rules of marketing and promotion have since changed as the web has proved a catalyst in bringing such changes forward and amplifying their scale (Danny, 2008). People are spending more time on new technologies and advertisers are facing great challenges in engaging consumers.

So how do the advertisers increase their engagement with the consumers? One of the ways is through viral marketing and such marketing technique is important on social networking sites. Viral marketing refers to marketing techniques that relies on existing social networks to achieve marketing objectives, such as spreading the news using word of mouth. Such social networking sites, such as Facebook has millions of members worldwide and by implementing such advertising strategy on these social nodes, the outcome could be highly positive to the sales of the product, unlike engaging customers using the traditional methods. In such marketing technique, customer value is important. Customer value is the expected profit from sales to the customers, over the lifetime of relationship between the customer and the company. It is important to the companies because companies would be able to determine how much it is worth is to spend to gain the customer confidence and trust (DOMINGOS, 2005) Traditional advertising methods ignore this fact as they do not take into account that a customer, which is happy with a particular product, would in turn influence others to buy them. This is an example of network value. Thus, advertisers can look for a group of customers with high network value, market to this group of users and gain profits of the resulting wave of word of mouth.

We use a framework shown in Figure 1 to illustrate its effectiveness on consumer marketing.

In the above framework, there are two axes that create customer value in marketing; entertainment and relevance. Relevance may refer to the advertising which is meaningful and relevant to the interest of the users i.e. content and information whereas entertainment refers to advertising as entertainment medium. Why should advertisers need to create value for the customers? The answer is simple. Customers are the ones who decide whether they want your products. They are the ones in control.

In quadrant 1, mass marketing with low relevance and low entertainment value aims to reach as many people as possible. This is different from target marketing aspects as they target at a specific segment of consumers. Mass marketing products could be burgers or fizzy drinks such as coca-cola. Advertising in this segment may not be useful to the customers and there is not much entertaining advertisement as well.

In quadrant 2, local or niche comes with high relevance and low entertainment. niche marketing aims to target a needed segment in a general market and to provide solution and support to that particular segment. Once done, they spread the word on that solution to all using various marketing techniques. One example is Toyota where they create environment friendly cars to a group of environmental friendly conscious customers and they hold the niche market to themselves during that time. In the space of internet marketing, we would be focusing on markets which are not being dominated, such as selling rare books online, instead of competing with the sale of general book with Amazon.com.

Figure 1. Conceptual framework for analysis

In quadrant 3, brand advertising comes with low relevance and high entertainment. Brand advertising mainly refers to advertising with strong emphasis on company logo or brand. Web 2.0 comes into picture for such cases as companies of all sizes can take advantages in adding some internet entertaining media into their marketing campaign. For instance, a company could have invited some customers to play their interactive games for free once they click their advertisement banner on social networking sites. If the customer has had an enjoyable experience in such activities, they would be likely to spread the word on it. More customers will be willing to try and sales will improve.

Quadrant 4 consists of promotion and advertising. This segment has increased values in both relevance and entertainment. But how can advertisers meet this quadrant? Advertisers can combine digital promotions and advertising to achieve increased value on relevance and entertainment.

METHODOLOGY

Social networking is definitely one important aspect of marketing areas with the emergence of Web 2.0. Web 2.0 focuses on user generated content sharing, user collaboration and user interactivity. Promotions and advertisements form part of the marketing mix to promote the product to the consumer. The use of Web 2.0 features, tools and applications has made it feasible to associate the product with consumers in the marketplace as well as endorsing it through the buzz word of mouth. Hence we want to determine the usage of Web 2.0 tools in bringing about IDM promotions in social networks such as Facebook.

First and foremost, we had done an extensive study on marketing and Web 2.0 in order to search for relevant information that provides guidelines for best practices. There are numerous contents on Web 2.0 tools and marketing available on the Internet. We had to organize, filter and consolidate information that would fit into our research object. Next we searched for various frameworks and select one that catered for evaluating the Web 2.0 tools in bringing about IDM promotions in Facebook. Marketing is about creating consumer value and producing brand awareness and engagement through promotion. We had since identified a framework for it.

Framework for Marketing

This framework is about creating consumer value in marketing. This framework dictates that consumer value is measured upon two dimensions namely, relevance and entertainment. By using this framework, we can find out whether the site contents have high consumer value. High consumer value derives from maximum relevant value and maximum entertainment value. Hence Web 2.0 tools will be evaluated on how well they facilitate in creation of such contents.

Once the framework has been identified, we set the main list of Web 2.0 tools on Facebook to be analysed and discussed. These include: (1) Wiki, (2) Blog, (3) User Generated Content, (4) Application Programming Interface (API), (5) Micro-Blogging, (6) Widgets and (7) Really Simple Syndication (RSS).

Equipped with experience in using Facebook and a detailed understanding of the framework being used, we evaluated our research objective.

Data Collection Methods

We used the following 3 data collection methods for our analysis.

Case Study

The nature of our study needs to assess and analyze real world data. Therefore we would be using the case study of a particular social networking site, Facebook. Case study is an intensive study of a single group, incident or community. It is a

qualitative research strategy which involves the intensive study of a real life instance or event. By using a case study, we can grasp the intricate details of the nature and behaviour of an instance. For example we can understand the usage of Web 2.0 in social networking sites such as Facebook and later derive the reasons how Web 2.0 usage in Facebook drive IDM promotions.

Web Search and Database Search

The Internet and database online has comprehensive collection of information on Web 2.0 in marketing and also social networking sites such as Facebook. It is a good provision of a wide variety of reference materials and data for us. Hence we will be able to find best practices, effective methodology and framework for our research study which focus on using Web 2.0 tools to bring about IDM promotions. Moreover, it assist us in writing literature review to uncover what is currently being research upon that is related to our topic.

Observation

Adopting observation method is useful as this is performed in real situation and context where marketing promotions occurs in Facebook Marketplace. We observe the complete process in how the product is being introduced to the consumers, the interaction between the seller and the consumers, and finally selling the product to the consumer. This method provides us with contextual information needed to frame evaluation and justify our data collected.

DISCUSSION AND ANALYSIS

There are various Web 2.0 tools that are available in the market and they are being deployed for different promotion usages. In this section, we discuss on the various Web 2.0 tools that can be found in one of the popular social networking site,

Facebook and we then analyse how these Web 2.0 tools aid in the advertising and promotion aspects for marketing purposes.

Wiki

A wiki is referred to as a collection of web pages that allows people with access to it be able to contribute his or her knowledge to the content or modify the existing content, using a simplified markup language, for instance XML. It is commonly used to create collaborative space and to power community websites. This idea of participation and cooperation help to create a more productive, usable information portal for all its affiliated members. In Facebook, the concept of wiki has been rebranded to be what is known as 'Groups' within Facebook. Within a given group, users are able to start a conversation within a group message, add photos, and provide simple commentary.

From the Figure 2, it can be seen that a general group contains a few description like group name, range of network, the size of the group, the type of common or shared interests and the new members. The concept of 'Groups' is crucial for the existence of viral marketing as part of the internet adver-

tising and promotion strategies. Viral marketing or referral marketing refers to making offers so compelling such that people will pass them around to his or her friends. It takes the advantage of the power of contacts and shared interests to stimulate word of mouth via emails, social networks etc. When people respond to the offer, it enables the business provider to capture both the names and email addresses of the possible customers. As wiki mainly consists of only text and links regarding a particular topic, the level of relevance is high. However the level of entertainment will be low due to lacking presence of dynamics contents like photos and videos. Therefore based on the matrix, wiki will belong to the second quadrant of local or niche marketing which is characterized by high relevance and low entertainment.

Blogs

A blog is a type of website that is mentioned by an individual to record his or her regular entries of commentary, description of events and to post other materials like photos or video to share knowledge, information and make a post about day-to-day observations in their lives. The entries are usually displayed in reverse chronological

Figure 2. Groups in Facebook

order. In Facebook, when a user writes a 'Note', they are actually expressing entries of their daily thoughts or opinions in a given manner. A collection of these *notes*, in reverse chronological order, may be classified as a Weblog or blog in this case (Figure 3).

The concept of having 'Notes' is similar to 'Groups' which uses the advantages of the power of contacts and shared interests to stimulate word of mouth. Through 'Notes', the user can inform his or her fan about recent press mentions or awards, highlight new products and share any other information. Since most blogs are primary textual and personal in nature, the level of relevance is high. However the nature of some blogs can be quite diverse as well, with some focused on art (artlog), photography (photoblog), sketches (sketchblog), videos (vlog), music (MP3 blog) and audio (podcasting), the degree of entertainment can then hence be high too, depending on the context of the usage i.e. what it is being used for. As such, blogs on the whole, can be classified under the fourth quadrant of the matrix, promo-tions and advertising, which is characterized by high relevance and high entertainment.

User Generated Content

User Generated Content is actually a term referring to the various kinds of media content that are publicly available and created by the users themselves. One thing to bear in mind is that the content generated does not belong to any specific production quality. Some examples of User Generated Content include photos, videos, and audio clips. In Facebook, users are allowed to create and post their own contents on what is being known as the 'Wall'. Facebook does not only has an astonishing amount of photos uploaded into its website every day but they provide users a simple, yet powerful video experience. Users are hence placed in constant interaction with User Generated Content, information from within themselves (Figure 4). The 'Wall' is also a public comment board where your friends or fans can

Figure 3. Notes in Facebook

Figure 4. User generated content in Facebook

leave messages that will be visible to everyone who views your Facebook page.

The concept of having User Generated Content on the 'Wall' is similar to 'Groups' and 'Notes' where the purpose is to once again use viral marketing to take advantages of the power of contacts and shared interests to stimulate word of mouth. Through User Generated Content, the user can inform his or her fan about recent press mentions or awards, highlight new products and share any other information which is similar to 'Notes'. The concept of giving the users the ability to generate their own photos, videos and audio clips will naturally lead to high entertainment. However the level of relevance is low due to the lacking presence of related contents (information) found i.e. an user may just post a photo, video or an audio clip without much explanation regarding what is it about. Hence User Generated Content may be classified under the third quadrant of the matrix, brand advertising which is characterized by low relevance and high entertainment.

Application Programming Interface (API)

Application Programming Interface (API) is actually a set of technologies that allows websites to interact with each other using applications like SOAP, Javascript and other web technologies. It is currently a highly and heavily sought after solution to connect different websites in a more fluid and user-friendly manner. API is also a means of letting other users be integrated with your service by tapping into your data. This application programming interface facilitate the use of user generated content to add social context to the application being made by leveraging data such as profile, group, event data and photo.

In Facebook, users are allowed to create their own API for business purposes as it allows others to have the ability to tap into Facebook's database and create applications which can then be added to the system and adopted by users (Figure 5).

The concept of introducing APIs in Facebook will naturally lead to high entertainment due to its highly interactive nature. The level of relevance can be quite high as well due to the increased interaction of websites with one another, hence results in an increased quantity in the information as well as its accuracy. As such, APIs can be classified under the fourth quadrant of the matrix, promotions and advertising, which is characterized by high relevance and high entertainment.

Micro-Blogging

Micro-blogging is actually a form of multimedia blogging that enables the users to send brief text updates of daily events or micromedia like photos and audio clips to be viewed by anyone or by a restricted group which has been granted permission by the user. These messages are usually submitted via the web, e-mail, text, or instant messaging. The difference between the content of a micro-blog from a traditional blog is that a micro-blog generally smaller in size and aggregate file size. A single entry on a micro-blog can consist of a simple single sentence usually consisting of less than 200 characters or a fragment or an image or even a brief ten second video for instance. Users can micro-blog about anything, for example "what are you doing at the moment" to particular business topics like particular products etc. Most of the micro-blogs provide short commentary on a person-to-personal level, shares news about a company's products and services or provide logs of the events of one's encounter.

Figure 5. Application programming interface (API) in Facebook

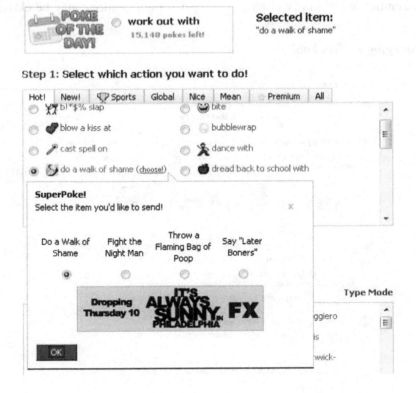

In order to meet demand in this area, Facebook launches 'Status Updates', which is simply another way of rebranding the concept of micro-blogging (Figure 6).

Like the rest of the Web 2.0 tools mentioned earlier, Micro-blogging also uses viral marketing to take advantages of the power of contacts and shared interests to stimulate word of mouth. As mentioned earlier, users can micro-blog about anything, which will indirectly inform his or her friends about news about a company's products and services. Like blogs previously mentioned, the nature of micro-blogging can be quite diverse, depending on the context of the usage i.e. what will it be used for. As such, on the whole, micro-blogs can be classified under the fourth quadrant of the matrix, promotions and advertising, which is characterized by high relevance and high entertainment.

Widgets

From Wikipedia, widgets can be considered to be anything that can be embedded within a web page.

The purpose of widgets is to add some content to the page that provides some level of value to the publisher. Early web widgets provide functions such as link counters and advertising banners. Businesses can hence exploit them for media advertisements as well as viral marketing in social networks. In Facebook, widgets are also known as 'Applications' (Figure 7). Once a user adds a given application, it will appear on their profile page, where other users can see it and interact with it or even add it themselves. This is especially true for developers adopting the business model of developing game applications for Facebook. One example is Playfish who is quite successful in promoting its products through applications like Pet Society and Restaurant City.

The concept of widgets or applications in Facebook provides users the ability to interact with the dynamic contents, hence resulting in high level of entertainment. However the level of relevance is low due to the lacking presence of related contents or information which is rarely available in widgets or applications. Hence widgets or applications may be classified under the

Figure 6. Micro-blogging in Facebook

Figure 7. Twitter widgets or applications in Facebook

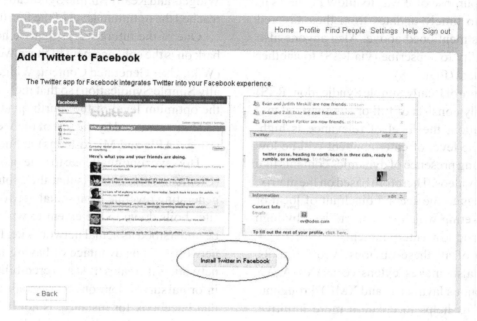

third quadrant of the matrix, brand advertising which is characterized by low relevance and high entertainment.

Really Simple Syndication (RSS)

Really Simple Syndication (RSS) belongs to part of the Web feed formats that are used to publish frequently updated works such as blog entries, news headlines, audio and video. It can contain full or summarized content, including metadata like publishing dates and authorship. It can benefit business publishers by letting them syndicate content from the publisher's website automatically and this will benefit readers who want to subscribe to timely updates from their favourite websites or to aggregate feeds from many sites into one place. RSS feeds are readable by using software called RSS reader, feed reader or aggregator which can be web-based, desktop-based or even mobile-device based. In Facebook, the concept of the 'News Feed' actually acts as an RSS reader

Figure 8. Really simple syndication (RSS) feed in Facebook

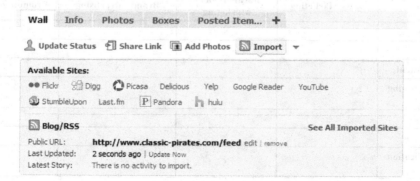

where the purpose of it was to allow the users to subscribe to timely updates from their favored websites as mentioned above. Also anyone also has the ability to subscribe (via RSS) to another user's 'Notes' (Figure 8).

The nature of Really Simple Syndication (RSS) feeds mainly consists of full or summarized text or information, the level of relevance is high. However the level of entertainment will be low due to lacking presence of dynamics contents like photos and videos. Therefore based on the matrix, wiki belongs to the second quadrant of local or niche marketing which is characterized by high relevance and low entertainment.

On top of all these obvious Web 2.0 tools, Facebook also makes extensive use of AJAX (Asynchronous JavaScript and XML) throughout the site. This helps to create a more intuitive, enjoyable user experience when the users are surfing the site (Table 1).

CONCLUSION

It can be seen that most of the Web 2.0 tools that are currently available in Facebook support the aspect of advertising and promotion in one way or another, although it is also noted that some of the Web 2.0 tools (Wiki, User Generated Content,

Widgets and Really Simple Syndication) have not reached the optimum level of the fourth quadrant.

One of the future works that we hope to embark on is the enhancement of these Web 2.0 tools (Wiki, User Generated Content, Widgets and Really Simple Syndication) so that they could reach the optimum level of the fourth quadrant which had been achieved by the rest of the Web 2.0 tools (Blogs, APIs and Micro-blogs) in Facebook.

However one challenge to note in our research (Clemons et al, 2007) is that the central issue in generating revenue from social networking websites boils down to the extent to which they can be understood as actual networks i.e. face-to face networks. One advantage of having face-to face network is it creates trust and credibility. From an informal survey done on college students, it shows that Facebook for instance, is not being seen as trustworthy and credible, largely because anyone can be added to a list of 'friends' or he or she can add him or herself to the list. Users nowadays are very wary of external intrusion of unwanted people and perspectives when they are on the internet and are careful not to place themselves in adverse or potentially dangerous positions. Users in social network websites tend to reserve a sense of control of active participation and advertising can limit the positive vibe. Direct product advertising, even recommendations from his or her virtual friends are seen to be untrustworthy as they can be per-

Table 1. Promotion characteristics supported Web 2.0 tools in Facebook

	Mass Marketing	Local or Niche Marketing	Brand Advertising	Promotion and Advertising
Wiki		X		
Blog				X
User Generated Content			X	
Application Programming Interface (API)				X
Micro-blogging				X
Widgets			X	
Really Simple Syndication (RSS)		X		

ceived as setups. Moreover these virtual friends do not have a history of trustworthiness that is crucial to valuing a product recommendation. Therefore it is necessary for one who plans to advertise and promote their products using social network websites to take into consideration the following "axioms":

- A virtual community is not really a community
- A virtual friend is not really a friend
- Product suggestion from virtual friends may be unwelcomed and not trustful.

See also Table 1.

REFERENCES

Clemons, E. K., Barnett, S., & Appadurai, A. (2007). *The future of advertising and the value of social network websites: Some preliminary examinations* (pp. 267–276). International Conference on Electronic Commerce.

Comscore. (2008). *Social networking explodes worldwide as sites increase their focus on cultural relevance.* Retrieved on April 20, 2009, from http://www.comscore.com

Domingos, P. (2005). Mining social networks for viral marketing. *IEEE Intelligent Systems, 20,* 80–82.

Griffith, D. (2009). *Promotions 2.0 - The future of interactive marketing.* Retrieved on April 25, 2009, from http://www.slideshare.net/dgriffith/promotions-20-the-future-of-interactive-marketing-1008197

Jain, A., & Ganesh, J. (2007). *Harnessing the power of Web 2.0 in online retail,* (pp. 2–8). White Paper.

Karp, S. (2008). The future of online advertising: Entertainment vs. information. Retrieved on April 25, 2009, from http://publishing2.com/2008/04/23/the-future-of-online-advertising-entertainment-vs-information/

Laboy, F., & Torchio, P. (2007). *Web 2.0 for the travel marketer and consumer* (pp. 2–18). White Paper.

Mapping The Web. (2007, July 19). *How Facebook is bringing Web 2.0 mainstream.* Retrieved on April 25, 2009, from http://www.mappingtheweb.com/2007/07/19/facebook-web-20-mainstream/

Marketing Titan. (2008). *What is niche marketing?* Retrieved on April 26, 2009, from http://www.marketingtitan.com/what_is_niche_marketing

MaxFinn.com. (2009). *Facebook 101: The business value of Facebook,* Retrieved on April 22, 2009, from http://www.maxfinn.com/?p=33

Meadows-Klue, D. (2008). Falling in love 2.0: Relationship marketing for the Facebook generation. *Journal of Direct, Data and Digital Marketing Practice, 9*(3).

Needham, A. (2005). Word of mouth, youth and their brands. *Young Consumers, 9*(1), 60–62. doi:10.1108/17473610810857327

New York Times. (2008, December 14). *Advertisers face hurdles on social networking sites.* Retrieved on April 22, 2009, from http://www.nytimes.com/2008/12/14/business/media/14digi.html?em

O'Reilly, T. (2005). *What is Web 2.0 – Design patterns and business models for the next generation of software.* O'Reilly Media Inc. Retrieved on April 20, 2009, from http://www.oreillynet.com/lpt/a/6228

Pro, P. C. (2007). *Social networks overtake webmail.* Retrieved on April 26, 2009, from http://www.pcpro.co.uk/news/135912/social-networks-overtake-webmail.html

Red Bridge Marketing. (2008). *Social network marketing – The basics.* Retrieved on April 25, 2009, from http://www.redbridgemarketing.com/social_networking_the_basics.pdf

Schonfeld, E. (2008). *Facebook is not only the world's largest social network, it is also the fastest growing*. Retrieved on April 25, 2009, from http://www.techcrunch.com/2008/08/12/facebook-is-not-only-the-worlds-largest-social-network-it-is-also-the-fastest-growing/

Swamynathan, G., Wilson, C., Boe, B., Almeroth, K., & Zhao, B. Y. (2008). Do social networks improve e-commerce? A study on social marketplaces. *Proceedings of the First Workshop on Online Social Networks*, (pp. 1–6).

Thackeray, R., Neiger, B. L., Hanson, C. L., & McKenzie, J. F. (2008). *Enhancing promotional strategies within social marketing programs: Use of Web 2.0 social media* (pp. 338–343).

Today, U. S. A. (2005, June 22). Viral advertising spreads through marketing plans. *USA Today*. Retrieved on April 26, 2009, from http://www.usatoday.com/money/advertising/2005-06-22-viral-usat_x.htm

ul-Haq, R. (1998). Marketing and social networking. *Qualitative Market Research: An International Journal, 10*(1).

WebProNews. (2009, March 11). *Facebook can drive more traffic than Google*. Retrieved on April 22, 2009, from http://www.webpronews.com/topnews/2009/03/11/facebook-can-drive-more-traffic-than-google

Section 3
Digital Communities

Chapter 19
The Role of Social Networks in the Viral Marketing of IDM

Bhatt Diptee
Nanyang Technological University, Singapore

Chang Tai Hock
Nanyang Technological University, Singapore

Wang Lihui
Nanyang Technological University, Singapore

Ravi Sharma
Nanyang Technological University, Singapore

ABSTRACT

Social networks are structures consisting of individuals or organizations that enable powerful means of communicating and information sharing. Social networks make viral marketing and word-of mouth (WOM) marketing more effective than before. WOM particularly has received extensive attention in the literature. In this chapter, we discuss the value of social networks in business, especially focusing on the WOM marketing which relies on social ties and preexisting connections to spread marketing messages through a community. We discuss viral marketing using a WOM unit framework. Five qualities of a WOM unit are explained with examples. We illustrate new products and services like the iPhone and relate them with the WOM unit framework. It is recognized that WOM helps businesses spread their marketing message in a cost effective way. We found that WOM marketing plays a vital role in the IDM marketplace and conclude that businesses should actively promote and manage WOM communications using viral marketing methods to achieve desired behavioral response.

DOI: 10.4018/978-1-61350-147-4.ch019

OVERVIEW AND SCOPE

Many are now aware of social networks which have attracted the attention of half a billion users within five years. Millions of hours per day are spent on social networking functions. Social networking is hence is a large and rapidly expanding application on the Internet. The success of social networks shows a dynamic shift in how people use the Internet nowadays. A universe of sites in the networks is created by people for people that enhances new business relationships. The theme of this chapter is to examine if social networks may be leveraged upon as a tool for business development and networking.

Online social networks present an efficient platform for high-tech marketers to spread their marketing messages or promotional schemes without investing more on infrastructure and services. These networks are increasingly being used as an important source of information influencing the adoption and use of products and services. The use of social networks is not to make money directly from the customers, but to harness their marketing potential and to use them in the business. Online communities have a large group of users who can help to increase brand awareness for products and services. With the help of social networks, marketers tap into these communities with advertising tools or content targeting their specific sub-culture and people are likely to get a lot of attention. In this way, social networks create new channels of advertising and thus help marketers in spreading business promotion. For example, companies encourage word of mouth advertising. They offer referral bonuses to current customers who bring in new clients. Hence, social networks make viral marketing and word-of mouth marketing more effective than before.

In this chapter we focus on the value of social networks in business enterprises, and more specifically on word-of-mouth messaging. We explain how it helps marketers leverage customer capital for buying decisions with optimal effort.

BACKGROUND CONCEPTS

Social information-processing theory provides a useful lens to examine the interpersonal influence processes that are the hallmark of viral marketing. It views the social network as an important source of information and cues for behaviour and action for individuals (Wellman et al., 1996). Social network marketing is different from that of traditional marketing. Traditional marketing such as TV and radio force advertisement on the audience and creates interruption in what they are doing. On the other hand, social network marketing is all about marketing with participation. With social networks, businesses can target a large number of audience with low cost per unit.

Word-Of-Mouth (WOM) and viral marketing have received extensive attention in the recent years. For instance, the success of the largest social network Facebook, with 500 million users, has been driven primarily by word of mouth. It has helped Facebook cross a threshold of cultural importance in the sense that what your "friends" think and say influences you more then the opinions and actions of strangers who may be authorities. Most of the literature describes WOM as one of the more powerful tools in the marketplace. This is due to fact that consumers rely more on informal or personal communication sources in making purchasing decisions than commercial sources. In this sense, WOM is highly effective (Bansal & Voyer 2000). Ditcher (1966) suggested the idea of 'aha' experiences which occurs through a WOM exchange. This idea may be a little outdated; however, it provides a view on WOM exchange. Brown and Reingen (1987) investigated the social ties and their influence on WOM. They found that weak-ties are more likely to serve as bridges than strong ties through which WOM referrals flow across groups. Some researchers surveyed online and offline WOM for a group of population and suggested high correlation among them. In their research, online WOM was found to be more pervasive (Bruyn & Lilien, 2004).

In business-to-business contexts, buyers of privately owned firms transmit more WOM as do buyers of smaller firms (File et al., 1992). Marketing professionals believe that WOM is the compelling way to bring in new customers. Contemporary business firms are commonly using Social Networking or Web 2.0 as a mechanism to reach out to and interact with people. They are using web tools such as LinkedIn, Facebook and such. People are interacting using these tools as legitimate business enablers.

Several researchers (cf. Helm, 2000; Hennig et al., 2004) have stated that viral marketing is not an innovative idea. But, viral marketing is subtly different from WOM in several ways such as the expanded scale and scope of influence (Subramani and Balaji 2003). Helm (2000) suggested high categorization between high and low (passive) integration strategies varying in the degree of requiring the consumer's activity in passing on the "virus". Viral marketing is a consumer-to-consumer process and related to WOM, they are different in all other aspects. Subramani and Balaji (2003) suggested that viral marketing is powerful for marketers and recipients to benefit from the innate helpfulness of individuals in social networks. All of these reviews support the tremendous potential of viral marketing for various purposes including business purposes.

FRAMEWORK FOR ANALYSIS

In the new marketing realm, indirect marketing no longer provides a lucrative source in the attempt to influence human behavior into buying power. Direct marketing tactics seem to be a more viable, definable and measurable method.

Unfortunately, no profound methodology has yet been erected from the viral marketing strategies prescribed today. In particular, WOM and its associated interpersonal communicative phenomena have been constantly brought up by researchers in recent years due to the increased complexity and the unstructured nature in the marketing process involved. The Word-of-Mouth Marketing Association (WOMMA) has derived a unified framework defining the dimensions and processes that helped media companies, WOM marketing services firms and brand marketers help to plan, price, buy, and measure WOM marketing campaigns. It provides guidelines, control and standardization into the medium aiding to create a universal platform and common understanding for dissemination between interpersonal subjects. (WOMMA, 2005)

In line skyrocketing Internet usage, most companies have moved their marketing forces into virtual spaces, leveraging on the social contacts created by the networks. Many online social networking sites are built to strengthen the ties between individuals, not only to create a channel for individuals to "voice" out and express their emotions, but also to indirectly establish an ideal place for WOM marketing campaigns.

On January, 2007, Apple's CEO Steve Jobs announced their new product iPhone at the Macworld Expo. Almost 40 major publication articles were printed on the announcement and speculation spread like wild fire on how iPhone would shape the mobile world and, what features and functions might be added on. Almost everyone had an opinion about the device from a consumer's perspective. People were debating what the price would be during its launch. Discussions of Apple's partnership with AT&T were also rampant. Bloggers around the world were "talking" furiously about this game-changing event. During the announcement, Steve Jobs did not show every single function or feature and only 20 units were released before the launch. On June 30, 2007, when iPhone was officially launched, it invited much discussion and speculation from media across different channels, specifically from the Internet. The intensity grew stronger each time every tiny component of the device was discovered. Information was instantaneously propagated through blogs, forums, and gadgets (Balter, 2008).

From the point the announcement was made to the official release, Steve Jobs created a "triangle of urgency" and managed the medium of WOM to near perfection over the span of five months. Firstly, the broad and immediate appeal of the new mobile phone by the prestigious brand created an "air of curiosity". Secondly, instead of making the price more appealing, the tantalizing dash of exclusivity by setting the price high, hinted that only the prestigious ones can afford his new creation. Lastly, by not revealing most of the features and functions of the phone during his previous announcement and releasing only 20 units before the launch, Apple also created an "air of mystery" (Balter, 2008).

How did viral marketing help in all this? The success of iPhone did not happen by accident. Careful planning and thoughtful management were the key factors. By managing the timing of press announcements, following the sequence of ads releases and mastering the time between them had help the product to become the star of talk. The carefully crafted words and fonts that flaunted well together with the demonstrators they hired – their palms were large enough to make the relatively hunky phone look smaller – increased the public's eagerness for a massive transformation of the mobile category (Balter, 2008). We can understand why Apple's word-of-mouth marketing strategy was such a success based on word-of-mouth unit (WOMUnit). A WOMUnit (see Figure 1) describes a single unit of marketing-relevant information in WOMMA framework. It was chosen because it is media-agnostic (WOMMA, 2005). Since WOM takes place both online and offline, WOMUnit is a neutral term that reflects the unique nature of WOM as a cross-medium form of communication (WOMMA, 2005). The WOM unit typically

consists of five qualities: Topicality, Timeliness, Polarity, Clarity, and Depth as shown in Figure 1.

Topicality

Topicality measures the consistency and clarity of the marketing message of a product or service targeting on the pre-defined market segment. The desired marketing message created not only tells what the product or service does, but instead, convinces others to experience it.

In the case of iPhone, Steve Jobs had delivered a clear and concise message to his consumers. For example, one of the marketing messages mentioned in Leslie (2008): "The iPhone is a revolutionary piece of hardware; it is actually much more than a typical smartphone, functioning as both a video and music player". Additionally, it is also powerful and flexible enough to run various applications which were created by both consumers and IT industries (Balter, 2008).

Websites and blogs started analyzing every scrap of news about the iPhone even to its colored wire and materials made boosted new owners' ego to show off their phone to others like friends and colleagues. These owners were driven by a subconscious intent for "bragging rights" and this secured the fit with WOM. Moreover, the business alliance between two giants – Apple and AT&T, created a scene hyped the product's visibility in the social networks.

The efficiency and effectiveness of a message to measure low or high topicality will be determined by two group of factors: sender's credibility, trustworthiness and reliability as an information source (Gilly et al., 1998) and, consequently, the value placed on his or her opinion leadership (Sweeney et al., 2008).

Opinion Leaders

Opinion leaders are the people who interpret the message to lower-end users and, a opinion leader typically has high esteem who can convince oth-

Figure 1. WOM unit characteristics

Quality	Description	Example
Topicality	A measure of the degree to which a desired marketing message is contained in the WOMUnit.	• In a campaign to promote brightly colored PCs, a message about microprocessors would have low Topicality. • A protest campaign about chicken-raising practices against a fast food outlet would have low Topicality for the restaurant, but high Topicality for an activist group.
Timeliness	A measure of whether the WOMUnit arrives in time to be relevant to a specific campaign.	• An email about a retail promotion has low Timeliness if it is forwarded after the sale is over.
Polarity	A measure of the positive vs. negative content of the WOMUnit.	• Participants on a travel web site can post reviews and rate their vacation experiences as positive or negative.
Clarity	A measure that determines if a message is understood by the Receiver as it was intended by the Sender.	• Many customer service web sites now include a link that asks "Was this helpful?"
Depth	The "richness" or amount of visual, written, or verbal information included in a WOMUnit, assuming that these aspects increase message persuasiveness.	• High-production-value video email may be more persuasive than a text email. • An in-depth conversation with a friend is a richer WOMUnit than a casual mention. • A communication that gives specific reasons why a consumer had a positive experience with a brand will usually be more persuasive than a simple recommentation.

ers to accept his/her opinion. 20 iPhone units were distributed to the opinion leaders such as Anandtech (www.anandtech.com) to evaluate and create topical messages to the public. The number of opinion leaders affects the speed with which a message is being distributed. Consequently, a less number of opinion leaders slows down the distribution speed.

Source Credibility

"The source credibility is the believability of a communicator, as perceived by the recipient of the message" (Wikipedia). Malcolm Gladwell noted that each of us has a social network capacity of about 150 people, and the number represents the source credibility (Balter, 2008). The sources are company advocates, experts and peers (Cross et al., 2006), and they are the initial receivers. The credibility of source influences the distribution spread the number of receivers reached by a single sender (WOMMA, 2005).

Timeliness

Timeliness is used to measure whether the message arrives in time to be relevant to a specific campaign (WOMMA, 2005). Most of the time, the launch date of a product or service will be defined and announced by the organizations with the launch date being carefully planned according to R&D and production process management plan. However, it may be adjusted based on consumers' responses. The significant number of demanding loyal consumers may cause the launch date to be ahead of schedule. On the other hand, the power of WOM may deviate from the original features and functions of the product to one that consumers really want and subsequently, postpone the launch date. Take for instance, the game Diablo III, which deferred its launching date for a week.

Before Apple launched iPhone on 27 June, 2007, Steve Jobs had five months earlier announced the phone at Macworld Expo. During this time span, Apple had managed the time for the media of WOM nearing to perfection. People had debated about the price, features and functions before the launch the phone within this five months period; the relevant information seems to generate a "Tsunami" effect on the Internet. Many people waited for days hoping to be among one of the first phone users. "Consumers were dying to start consuming the iPhone through Internet or AT&T" (Leslie, 2008).

Another example that took place recently was the alliance between Apple and SingTel – local Telecom was established to launch iPhone in Singapore. The announcement made on 19 Mar, 2007, declared that SingTel will launch the iPhone in Singapore on 22 August (See Figure 2).

When new product or service is just getting on track, it takes time to build an audience through social networks to make sure that people know where it is and how to find it. The firm could accumulate loyal customers and higher market share over time before launching the product. However, the firms also made fewer incursions into the market such as the imitation of iPhone, the Hiphone, with 99% similarity produced from China.

Polarity

Polarity is a measure of positive versus negative points of the product or service published on blogs or social network websites. The product's reputation was established based on consumer feedback. "One of the earliest and best known Internet

Figure 2. SingTel introduces the iPhone 3G

reputation systems is run by eBay, which gathers comments from buyers and sellers about each other after each transaction" (Resnick & Zeckhauser, 2002). The outcome of polarity measurement on large amount of content could leverage potential consumer decisions. The products or services reputation profiles were predictive though statistic analysis on positive and negative contents.

iPhone's early adopters have had freshness of immediate experience. Many of them have started spreading messages about the goodness of the phone by WOM immediately after using the device. Consumers have felt compelled to become highly vocal advocates. The discussion and speculation grew more intensively through social network on the Internet. There exist thousands of iPhone review websites in different languages on the Internet, iPhone users, sometimes anonymous, were able to post their experiences and thoughts as positive and negative opinions (see Figure 3). The customer reviews encouraged by websites allowed consumers to spread the WOM and share information far more easily than ever before (Bruyn & Lilien, 2004).

In-the-Wild Viral Marketing

The way of spreading positive and negative information of the particular product or services via Internet can be considered as in-the-wild viral marketing. The polar message is perpetuated through whatever the consumers want to share; the most important aspect being that the user can choose to send the message in whichever way they want, such as social network web sites, blog, and forum. This way, it can build tremendous brand equity at a marginal cost, because communication takes place directly between consumers (Quirk, 2007).

Controlled Viral Marketing

Another way of spreading positive and negative information is through e-mail, which can be considered as controlled viral marketing. It has more of a direct outcome in which its success is determined by specific goals. Ultimately, controlled viral campaign should lead to interaction with the newly acquired products that adds value to the organization (Quirk, 2007).

Clarity

This is used to determine if a message is understood by the receiver as it was intended by the sender. For instance, many customer service web sites now include a link that asks "Was it helpful?" (WOMMA, 2005). All the successful brands that grew through WOM had one thing in common:

they delivered clear and understandable messages. Google, iPod, and Starbucks all set out messages to serve a specific need. In fact, they did it better than what consumers had expected.

In the case of iPhone, Steve Jobs's demonstration video about iPhone was placed on YouTube; the video clearly features the phone's design, display, menu, touch screen and features like messaging and e-mails in his usual inimitable way. Predictably, the video began receiving thousands of views and likes and shares every day. A certain percentage of them liked the video so much that they shared it with friends through social and electronic means. The message spreads among friends and the video is embedded on the blogs of friends to be shared. The moderately sized blogs allows visitors to watch the video uninterrupted and this further catalyzes the spread in a day. The ripple effect then continues through varies channels of online social networks. Pandemic Labs (an unknown brand) created a test video that spread due to these very same mechanics and reached over four million views in four months (Meerman, 2008).

The Success of Hotmail

A clear and attractive message of a "free email service that could be accessed through the web" (http://www.hotmail.com) had started to spread the word through Internet and face-to-face. There were 100,000 users registered within two months and by eighteen months they had 12 million subscribers. This is the Hotmail story which started in 1995; Microsoft bought Hotmail for $400 million and as of 2001, there were hundreds of thousands people signing up each day (Wikipedia, 1997).

Depth

Depth is the "richness" or amount of visual, written, or verbal information included with the assumption that these aspects increase message persuasiveness (WOMMA, 2005). An in-depth

Figure 3. iPhone reviews

conversation with others is a richer message than a casual mention.

Steve Jobs's presentation was the high-production-value video which is more persuasive than a text message. This impressive presentation demonstrates to the world a revolutionary device – iPhone. It is the combination of iPod – wide-screen music player with touch screen controls and phone – a revolution phone and break-through internet communications. Steve Jobs had provided positive user experience with a brand rather than a simple recommendation.

7 to 350 Million

For another instance, Harry Potter was a successful case where the richness of information was spread through WOM from a small group of avid fans. Seven of Harry Potter's fans were invited to participate in a top-secret Webcast on May, 2007 in order to create persuasiveness in the message around the world. These seven people were hand-selected from top Harry Potter fan sites by the vice president of new media, who launched the Wizarding World of Harry Potter. These hand-picked influencers propagated rich news to some 350,000,000 fans that are passionate about all relevant information of Harry Potter. The series of books by author J.K. Rowling has been translated into sixty-five languages and has sold more than 325 million copies in more than 200 territories around the world (Meerman, 2008).

KEY FINDINGS AND TAKEAWAYS

As compared to traditional social networks, online social networks have no physical boundaries nor limits. These online networks impart the benefits of the traditional networks and enhance its social and economic advancements across time and space. They accelerate the reach to wider audiences worldwide. These virtual communities in turn utilize new information and communication technologies such as web 2.0 and RSS provided an arena to promote and stimulate commerce and collaboration activities, which consequently enhances business networks (Lea et al., 2005).

Benefits

Social networks bridge the senders (ie organizations and influencers in Gladwell's parlance) with the receivers (consumers) augmenting viral marketing messages or direct marketing to be delivered within strategic benefits. Firstly, social networks allow the releasing of web-only viral materials yet retaining the brand and campaign themes, maintain and boost the level of brand awareness in a cost effective way. Secondly, the release of viral editions of the new marcom (market communication) activity on these social

networks kick-starts to create a buzz before the actual advertising campaign goes to the media, which helps to exploit the exclusivity factor. Lastly, social networks act as an effective standalone marketing tool for brands that cannot afford the premium cost of media broadcasts, or marketing strategy that requires only online distribution to a vast target group. However, social networks are no means to replace the overall marketing strategy. Under these circumstances, online viral marketing messages through social networks are simply an effective of telling a story to the audiences (Bates, 2005).

Online friendships of social networks need not be trusted relationships because of shared experiences and shared needs. Online WOM trust does not have the risk that trust and vulnerability imply in the physical world, and online betrayal does not have the physical risk that real world betrayal does (Clemons et.al, 2007).

In terms of the perceived risk associated with a purchase decision, WOM is more likely to be acted on in case of simpler products or when the importance or value of a product or service is less relative to other purchase decisions (Sweeney et al., 2007).

The trust of WOM is built upon the large number of senders or previous recipients and creators' messages, which are topicality, clarity and depth enough to prove the reputation of a product or service, as well as recipients' reviews or comments posted on the Internet. However, the extent to which online social network such as Facebook and Second Life do not reflect upon actual friendship and participation also determines reputation. In the case of Second Life, online members do not immediately look to each other for advice and support on a wide range on concerns, from product evaluations to life choices (Sweeney et al., 2007).

WOM are credible, reliable and trustworthy through online social network or viral marketing. The receiver's ability is to give feedback and the sender's ability is to deliver tailored or personalized information in which information may be added or filtered or one's own interpretation is added to make it more relevant to the receiver (Lang, 2006). More importantly, WOM has both reach and accessibility compared to unique promotion techniques such as advertising.

Disadvantages

In online communities, information is transferred directly between the users' computers connected to the network (Krishnan et al., 2004). A user can either choose to participate in the network activities or take a free ride. The problem with free riding, however, causes degradation of the network performance (Krishnan et al., 2004) and creates vulnerabilities (loss of privacy, denial of service) for a system where there are risks to individuals (Adar & Huberman, 2000). Another issue to be considered in online networks is information credibility (Fogg & Tseng, 1999), which considers information that is not accurate in the user's perspective. Integrity of the content design and interface design need to be factored in making the network credible (Fogg et al., 2002; Kuo et al., 2004). Furthermore, user's satisfaction with usage and network self-efficacy are also important to effectively retain users in virtual communities (Hsu et al., 2004).

However, another disadvantage of WOM through virtual communities is that they might decrease the social capital of the real community. The members of these communities look for resources in the virtual network to be narrowed to a certain interest, and trade off the physical community bonds. The members thus might pass up opportunities to learn about new interests and topics in the real world (Hales, 2000).

On the other hand, the process of establishing and maintaining a strong social network is time consuming and effort intensive albeit through a traditional social network process. Resulting from this observation, a research project named Innovation Information Infrastructure (I3) has been proposed to develop a social network based on virtual community prototype for entrepreneurs to gain access to critical technology and business assets and, to address his or her social network needs by monitoring, assessing and reporting on the influential factors on social network and their correlation to innovation success of network participants (Lea et al., 2005).

In fact, users are faced with too many choices on the individual types of social media they can tag on and this may lead to confusion and cost them their confidence (Mayfield, 2007). WOM does not necessarily travel from person to person but, to numerous people who may be "impersonal" not listeners. Therefore, WOM has less power and it is less attractive to the propagator where he or she is not instantly rewarded (Callebaut, 2006).

CONCLUSION

Online social networks are gradually being accepted as an important source of information influencing the adoption and use of products and services. These social networks make WOM marketing feasible and effective. WOM marketing leverage existing social networks. WOM marketing tangibly affects how consumers create or distribute marketing relevant information to other consumers.

This chapter discussed the value of social networks in business, especially focusing on the WOM message that affects viral marketing. It narrated how WOM helps marketers to leverage its customers for buying their product with minimal effort. The proposed WOM unit framework included in this article draws attention to a variety of qualities that describes WOM units. This framework reflects the unique nature of WOM as a cross medium form of communication. The qualities provided in the framework are associated with WOM units and highlight the contexts. These are key to explaining WOM in viral marketing. Each quality is specific in nature and measures the topicality, timeliness, polarity, clarity and depth of WOM units. By analyzing this framework we noticed that some campaigns for WOM marketing (e.g. mobile devices) has encouraged business growth. It seems that iPhone has changed the mobile world. The alliance between Apple and SingTel, a dominant mobile network operator in Singapore is a fresh example how iPhone is spreading with WOM. WOM marketing is a powerful means for marketers to benefit from the innate helpfulness of individuals in social networks. Marketers promote and manage word-of-mouth communications by using viral marketing methods to achieve desired behavioral response. Firms can realize the benefits by adopting this type of marketing as compared to traditional way of advertising.

REFERENCES

Adar, E., & Huberman, A. B. (2000). Free riding on gnutella. *First Monday, 5*(10). Retrieved from http://firstmonday.org/issues/issue5_10/adar/index.html.

Balter, D. (2008). *The word of mouth manual* (*Vol. 2*). Developed with the Butman Company.

Bansal, H. S., & Voyer, P. A. (2000). Word-of-mouth processes within a services purchase decision context. *Journal of Service Research, 3*(2), 118–126. doi:10.1177/109467050032005

Bates, K. W. (2005). *An introduction to word of mouth marketing*. Chicago, IL: IT Association Retrieved from http://www.kbates.com.

Bih-Ru, L., Wen, B. Y., & Nisha, M. (2006). Enhancing business networks using social network based virtual communities. *Industrial Management & Data Systems, 106*, 121–138. doi:10.1108/02635570610641022

Brown, J., & Reingen, P. (1987). Social ties and WOM referral behavior. *The Journal of Consumer Research, 14*, 350–362. doi:10.1086/209118

Bruyn, A. D., & Lilien, G. L. (2004). A multistage model of word of mouth through electronic referrals. Research Report, Pennsylvania State University, University Park, PA. *also published in International Journal of Research in Marketing (2008).*

Callebaut, J. (2006). *From word of mouth to word of mouse, or: Are your brands best served by gossip?* Synovate Censydiam Company. Retrieved from http://www.censydiam.com/.

Clemons, E. K. (2007). *The future of advertising and the value of social networks.* The Wharton Program on Global Strategy and Knowledge-Intensive Organizations. Wharton ISE Blog.

Cross, R., Parker, A., & Borgatti, S. P. (2006). *A bird's-eye view: Using social network analysis to improve knowledge creation and sharing.* IBM Institute for Knowledge-based Organization.

Dichter, E. (1966). How word-of-mouth advertising works. *Harvard Business Review, 44*, 147–166.

File, K. M., Judd, B. B., & Prince, R. A. (1992). Interactive marketing: The influence of participation on positive WOM and referrals. *Journal of Services Marketing, 6*, 5–14. doi:10.1108/08876049210037113

Fogg, B. J., Kameda, T., Boyd, J., Marshall, J., Sethi, R., Sockol, M., & Trowbridge, T. (2002). *Stanford-Makovsky web credibility study 2002: Investigating what makes web sites credible today.* Stanford, CA: Stanford Persuasive Technology Lab & Makovsky & Company. Retrieved from http://captology.stanford.edu/pdf/Stanford-MakovskyWebCredStudy2002-prelim.pdf.

Fogg, B. J., & Tseng, H. (1999). *The elements of computer credibility,* (pp. 80-87). Paper presented at CHI'99, Pittsburg, PA, 15-20 May. Retrieved from http://captology.stanford.edu/pdf/p80-fogg.pdf.

Helm, S. (2000). Viral marketing – Establishing consumer relationships by word-of mouse. *Electronic Markets, 10*, 158–161. doi:10.1080/10196780050177053

Hennig-Thurau, T., Gwinner, K. P., Walsh, G., & Gremler, D. D. (2004). Electronic word-of-mouth via consumer-opinion platforms: What motivates consumers to articulate themselves on the Internet? *Journal of Interactive Marketing, 18*, 38–52. doi:10.1002/dir.10073

Hsu, M., Chiu, C., & Ju, T. (2004). Determinants of continued use of the WWW: An integration of two theoretical models. *Industrial Management & Data Systems, 104*(9), 766–775. doi:10.1108/02635570410567757

Krishnan, R., Smith, D. M., Tang, Z., & Telang, R. (2004). The impact of free-riding on peer-to-peer networks. *Proceedings of the 37th Hawaii International Conference on System Sciences*. Retrieved from http://csdl.computer.org/comp/proceedings/hicss/2004/2056/07/205670199c.pdf.

Kuo, H., Hwang, S., & Wang, E. (2004). Evaluation research of information and supporting in electronic commerce web sites. *Industrial Management & Data Systems, 104*(9), 712–721. doi:10.1108/02635570410567702

Lang, B. (2006). *Word of mouth: Why is it so significant?* Manukau Institute of Technology. Retrieved from http://conferences.anzmac.org/ANZMAC2006/documents/Lang_Bodo.pdf.

Lea, B.-R., Yu, W. B., Maguluru, N., & Nichols, M. (2005). Enhancing business networks using social network based virtual communities. *Industrial Management & Data Systems, 106*(1), 121–138. doi:10.1108/02635570610641022

Leslie, S. (2008). *A critical element for both recreational and business wireless communications convergence*. Retrieved from http://www.scribd.com.

Mayfield, A. (2007). *Grabbing attention in the new marketing environment, Head of content and media at Spannerworks*. The Institute of Direct Marketing (IDM). Retrieved from http://www.theidm.com/resources/idm-insights/grabbing-attention-in-the-new-marketing-environment/.

Meerman, D. S. (2008). *The new rules of viral marketing: How word-of-mouse spreads your ideas for free.*

Qurik. (2007). *e-Marketing, viral marketing, chapter 12*. Retrieved from http://www.quirk.biz/cms/812.emarketingone-chaptwelve.pdf.

Resnick, P., & Zeckhauser, R. (2002). Trust among strangers in internet transactions: Empirical analysis of eBay's reputation system. *The Economics of the Internet and E-Commerce, 11*, 127–157. doi:10.1016/S0278-0984(02)11030-3

Subramani, M. R., & Rajagopalan, B. (2003). Knowledge-sharing and influence in on-line social networks via viral marketing. *Communications of the ACM, 46*, 300–307. doi:10.1145/953460.953514

Sweeney, J. C., Soutar, G. N., & Mazzarol, T. (2008). Factors influencing word of mouth effectiveness: Receiver perspective. *European Journal of Marketing, 42*(3-4), 344–364. doi:10.1108/03090560810852977

Terminology Framework, W. O. M. M. A. (2005). *A standard method for discussing and measuring word of mouth marketing*. Word of Mouth Association. Retrieved from http://womma.org/term/womma_term_framework.pdf.

Wellman, B., Salaff, J., Dimitrova, D., Garton, L., Gulia, M., & Haythornthwaite, C. (1996). Computer networks as social networks: Collaborative work, telework, and virtual community. *Annual Review of Sociology, 22*, 213–238. doi:10.1146/annurev.soc.22.1.213

Wikipedia. (1997). *Wikimedia Foundation, Inc*. Retrieved from http://en.wikipedia.org/wiki/Msn_hotmail.

Chapter 20
Review of the Virtual World Community

Reza Y. Azeharie
Nanyang Technological University, Singapore

ABSTRACT

This chapter provides a discussion and an analysis on the virtual world community from the economic and commercial angle to explore further its financial potential. A prominent virtual world called Second Life has been chosen as a proxy of the review. A background section is provided for readers unfamiliar with the concepts and colloquialisms of Second Life, and it is followed by an in-depth discussion of virtual economy and commerce. Understanding the essence of virtual world consumption is seen as necessary to realize the financial potential. It concludes with the need to abide by DRM rights and understand the line between fantasy fulfillment and entertainment when participating in the virtual world.

INTRODUCTION

Within the field of the Interactive Digital Media (IDM) Marketplace, the economic activities that happen within Virtual Worlds have been a topic that meets little attention in the current literature with Castronova (2002), Freedman (2008), Terdiman (2008), and Arts (2009) being some of the notable exceptions. As the name implies, the Virtual World is where experiences are felt and

stay in the mind. Within the Virtual Marketplace, goods and services exist and wealth is created in an unusual manner where most of the consumption may be a mere experience that would only stay in the Virtual World. Sometimes, these become profitable endeavors. For example Terdiman (2008) has noted that in Second Life, a former Chinese language school teacher, Ailin Graef, known as the avatar Anshe Chung has stakes in Real Estate and other businesses with an aggregate value of more than USD 1 million. This new way of creat-

DOI: 10.4018/978-1-61350-147-4.ch020

ing wealth with knowledge therefore deserves a deeper exploration and analysis.

Second Life (SL), developed and operated by Linden Lab Inc. (LL), is perhaps one of the most popular and controversial virtual world platform today as it is a "...3D online digital world imagined, created, and owned by its residents" (Rymaszewski et al., 2007, p.3). According to Rymaszewski et al (2007), SL residents, in the form of avatar (Av), are able to create content within SL using built-in primitives or prims (moldable 3D building blocks), or imported 3D shapes converted into prims. The basic process of content creation covers the manipulation and combination of prims, importing/purchasing media that can be applied on to prims, and/or the behavioral manipulation of prims through the use of Linden Scripting Language (LSL) (Terdiman, 2008). Using these skills, SL residents are able to create and customize their SL experience to one that they have conceptualized in plan or through serendipitous discovery.

The intent of this review is to discuss and analyze the potential of the virtual world as a platform for IDM Marketplace using Second Life, one of the most thriving virtual worlds, as a proxy. The following questions have been constructed: (1) What is a virtual world?; (2) How does Second Life Work?; (3) How does the economy inside the virtual world work?; (4) What are the main business sectors in Second Life?; and (5) What are the essences of virtual world consumption? The first question shall explore the virtual world on a general level. The next two questions shall explore the general setting and economy Second Life respectively. Finally, the last two questions shall explore deeper into the commerce and consumption rationales. This virtual world was one of the first to be created and since 2003 the developer has altered its business models to suit the changing online gaming landscape. Hence a wide range of literature is available for this investigation to take place (Rymaszewski et al., 2007). Moreover Linden Lab's monthly survey

has recorded an average of 216 businesses owned by residents whose profits equal to or greater than USD 5,000 from January to April 2009 (Linden Research, Inc., 2009).

BACKGROUND

In this section conception of the virtual world shall be described and defined in order to maintain coherence in the further analysis and discussion. It will be followed by a description and explanation of Second Life to help reader imagine and understand the specific concepts that are given in the two closing sub-sections namely Virtual World Lands and Virtual World Identities.

The Virtual World

The membership of Second Life is identified to be on a booming trend that grew by 39% in the second quarter of 2009 to around 579 million members, mostly coming from children (Keegan, 2009). Arts (2009) in his paper *The Current State and Future Potential of Virtual Worlds* has provided quite a concise and effective definition of a Virtual World. It is an environment implemented by a computer or network of computers where some (if not all) the entities in the environment act under the direct control of individual people. In this case, the world, in Art's term, can be said to be shared or multi user, and may continue to exist and develop internally without the interactions of its people. Hence this may create the potential for a highly user-generated content albeit this potential is also affected by the developer's attitudes and policies to openness in the virtual world.

Art (2009) has provided three types of virtual worlds namely (1) Game World, (2) The Socializing World, and (3) The Platform World. Game World refers to the virtual world where the players have a predefined goals and rewards defined by the developers such as in the case of the currently popular World of Warcraft. It is possible for the objects created within the virtual worlds to be traded among players whether through a formal or informal market where the latter develops as players interact with each other. The Socializing World refers to those that enable players to develop their own social dynamics which comes in the form of simple text based chat rooms to those with strong visual components such as IMVU (www.IMVU.com). Here the players are seeking social interaction facilitated by the ability to create their own public persona such as avatar forms, gestures, and auto text. Henceforth groups of various sizes and clans can be formed where each has its own cultures, rules, and norms and its own policies with other clans and territories. Finally the Platform World refers to a virtual world that does not have a well defined purpose and can be used for many other purposes—such as Second Life, where players or residents could go into activities beyond gaming and socializing. Here it is possible for virtual entertainment and commerce to thrive (Osborne & Schiller, 2009).

The Platform World is perhaps the most significant and Second Life in particular due to the enormous potential it generates by its massive user-generated environment potential. In this type of virtual of world, generation of content by the user is seen as a way to reduce development cost by the game company (Pearce, 2006) (Tapscott & Williams, 2006). Although only a small number from its 19 million population are still active, Second Life is attempting to grow even bigger by releasing the Open Simulator project that enable users to create their own virtual world (Keegan, 2009) (Arts, 2009).

Entering the Second Life

As of the early 2010, Second Life provides the necessary tools to facilitate and encourage new members to generate content. When an individual registered an account on the main website (www.secondlife.com) they will be able to choose the first and last name of their avatar. The former is fully customizable while the latter is based on a fixed list of last names, presumably to maintain the uniqueness of an avatar name. They will also be able to choose a basic avatar that varies in sex and visual appearance. When the individual logs in to the virtual world for the first time after downloading the client from the main site, they will land on the orientation island where basic navigation tutorials are provided. At this stage, the individual becomes a Second Life 'Resident'. If the individual logs in on main website they will be able to view a dashboard filled with various useful information such as news feed, account financing, link to SLX; the E-bay version of Second Life, event schedules, and hotspots. The same information is also available from the Search Engine inside Second Life itself. The website dashboard and internal Search Engine allow the new resident to seek for information and communities that are relevant to their exploration and goals. As residents transform their imagination into the virtual world, economical and commercial activities come to live.

To achieve their various SL goals, residents are provided with various communication mechanisms so that they could interact with other residents. According to Rymaszewski et al. (2007), the SL client came with a public and local IMs and they are provided to facilitate public, private, and group interactions. In addition, the latest version is equipped with voice chat capability (Schnook & Sullivan, 2007). To communicate to others, residents could fill in their profile page with their purpose in SL, links to their First Life or life outside SL, skills and interest, and the group of interest they are associated with (Tapley, 2008). Residents also have access to an internal search engine where they could search for people, places ranked by Av traffic, advertisement posted by others (ranked by L$ spent), land for sales, and potential groups of interest. The neat organization of the different aspects of the virtual world and efficient communication infrastructure allows residents to interact and socialize with each other, find others with similar interest, perform collaboration, and build organizations and business enterprises within SL.

Rymaszewski et al (2007), thoroughly describe the basic concepts and understanding required for prospective and existing Second Life or SL residents to navigate themselves within SL. The currency used in SL is Linden Dollars (L$) of which can be purchased from LL through the Linden Exchange (Lindex) or others operated by third parties (Freedman, 2008). Each Av is endowed with its own personal inventory where they could store items they have created, purchased, or received from others (Rymaszewski et al., 2007). Images, sound, and animation imported from outside SL will be charged L$10 (Linden Research, Inc., 2008). This can be seen as one of the ways to deter abuse and flooding of unnecessary external content to SL as it cost Linden Lab or LL money to manage each Av's inventory, and the content they create in-world within the Second Life. Content creators who wish to sell their creation have three IP licenses they could impose to content receivers:

1. **Modify:** able to make alteration to the items
2. **Transfer:** able to give it other Avs
3. **Copy:** able to create exact duplicate

Content creators use the combination of licenses to achieve their needs (Rymaszewski et al., 2007). For instance, if a kimono designer wanted to preserve her beautiful kimono as a work of art and at the same time make it a limited edition, the item is likely be put on sale with a Copy license only. Marketplace content creators are able to sell their items in-world and/or on SL Exchange (SLX) (Rymaszewski et al., 2007). In case of the former situation, content creators usually tailor their sales to spot their product, for instance, a weapon seller would sell weapons near combat areas. The latter is the SL version of E-bay where the website (www.xstreetsl.com) is linked to SL client software and provides seamless transaction and virtual goods delivery (also known as XstreetSL).

Virtual World Lands

LL allows Av/s to own a piece of land which can be acquired when a player signs up and they could do so as free member and upgrade to premium member (paid membership) to own a land (Linden Research, Inc., 2009). LL releases land available for purchase through auctions in the in-world search engine and LL website (www.secondlife.com). The membership fees vary according to the size of land owned. The lands are basically divided according to Simulators (SIMs) or LL servers in San Francisco where each SIM can be divided into smaller parcels (land plot) that can be owned or managed separately (Freedman, 2008). Governments, corporations, educators, and huge investors typically purchase entire SIMs of which a customization option from LL is available to suit their purpose. For example Toyota is known to treat SL as their virtual laboratory and have customized their own SIM to suit the purpose (Freedman, 2008). Each land has a default prim (short for primitive) allocation ration and the larger the land, the greater the prim allocation. Prim here is a precious commodity that enables residents to put down or rezz the items they owned inside their inventory whether created or purchased, on their land (Rymaszewski et al., 2007). Renting a land from private owners incurs the purchasers an initial non-refundable down payment plus a daily/weekly fee that is usually cheaper than as if they upgrade to premium membership but incur a risk of owner defaulting or authority abuse such as banning the purchaser from the land (Linden Research, Inc., 2008). Land is constantly in demand and LL therefore releases land on periodic basis to be auctioned in order to keep the land price at a particular level (Freedman, 2008). LL's most recent initiative, as announced on their website, was to offer a standardized building and land for free as long as they are a premium member who has not used their land area ration.

Virtual World Identities

One of the popular application contexts of the communication technologies and land is in Role Playing (RP). RP simply refers to acting a specific character for the avatar that is usually out of the normal avatar life. To recall, a Simulator or a SIM is a server that is configured to host the 3D environment. This can be exemplified by an RP SIM called Toxian City (http://www.toxiancity. com/). For example outside the RP SIM, a male avatar is acted out as ordinary person and a human. However as soon as he enters the RP SIM where he has identified himself as a vampire, he has to follow the vampire community's norms, culture, and behavior. For instance he must stay away from garlic and sunlight. Presumably he must drink blood and does not consume hamburgers and sushi. Hence a resident could be married to another resident, live as a vampire and pursue his RP goal without forgoing the social elements and access to all other non-combat activities. As there is no time restriction on how long a resident could stay in an RP, they are free to leave and enter as they please (needless to say there are protocols to follow). The possibility of having multiple identities in one avatar has enhanced the versatility potential for entertainment, experience creation, and fantasy fulfillment.

RP SIMs can be said to be a MMORPG (Massively Multiplayer role-playing games) that exists inside SL. RP SIMs have their own content that can only be used exclusively in their own SIMs such as a Head-up Display (HUD) DCS2 System that is adopted by the Toxian City community. DCS2 enables participants to level up and install DCS2 equipments for combats with its own battle meter. The website (www.dcs2.org) provides guide for integration of DCS2 for interested SIM owners. Moreover the SIM operator could sell equipments and amours that match the HUD and the role assigned/chosen by the resident participating in that SIM. For instance Toxian City has published weapons that are restricted (even though they are DCS2 based) due to the effect it has on the SIM hardware performance and presumably creates fairness among different combaters. As multiple non-adjacent SIMs can be linked together, there is virtually unlimited potential for these virtual-world-based MMORPGs to further expand and customize.

Based on the above, it can be inferred that the current business model of SL is to allow residents to be what they want to be that they could almost fully design their own storyline, ambience, and level of difficulty progression rate. This is to be contrasted with other virtual world types which have narrow and specific predetermined goals such as to be the top level assassin or hunters. In this sense SL's system is analogues to blank lined sheet of paper that is leased to a particular individual and that particular individual further invited others to write on the provided lines with specific governing rules. In essence SL creates business potential from many angles for interested individuals. The invention of combat system like DCS2 spurs the emergence of innovation from content publishers who used SL as a platform for syndication. This phenomenon therefore requires deeper attention and will be discussed further in the subsequent section.

LOOKING DEEPER INTO THE VIRTUAL WORLD ECONOMY

In this section, virtual world economy and commerce will be discussed and analyzed. The difference between the real and virtual world economy will first be analyzed and this will then be followed by a discussion in attempting to link between the virtual world and other IDM technologies. Thereafter the major business sectors in Second Life will be presented and analyzed in terms of their linkage and contribution to the virtual economy. This section will be closed by a recommendation on exploiting financial potential based on the understanding of the essences of the virtual consumption.

The Real and Virtual Economies

The penetration of the Virtual World in terms of cultural, technological, and business aspects has put into question the relation between the Real and Virtual World Economy. Castronova (2002) has highlighted four important differences in his attempt to look at virtual economy using the conventional economic utility model. These differences shall be discussed in the context of Second Life below.

Firstly, the argument of 'price control is not good' is dispelled by the fact that governments can create and destroy digital goods at zero cost without needing to disturb the price equilibrium. In Second Life for example, Linden Labs pegged the currency exchange rate to roughly 1 USD to 260-300 Linden Dollar, the virtual currency, at least for the past 3 years (Linden Research, Inc., 2009). In the real world, the central bank would need to buy/sell any excess supply and demand of the currency to maintain the fluctuation band but it cost nothing for Linden Lab. Therefore price control to suit a particular goal or objectives can easily be done.

Secondly, the utility of a virtual world is maximized when there is work to do. Work creates entertainment whether done alone or in groups and in its absence boredom would result. Hence the residents must have access to the activities that fulfill their known and unknown desired fantasy.

Thirdly, economic growth is not always desirable. With respect to the above, if the activities can be completed too easily it will lead to boredom as well. This means if it becomes too easy to customize and make one avatar more powerful then the challenge level presented becomes too low and boredom could result. Therefore if the goods within the virtual world are too cheap and/or too easy to acquire, then the effect would be negative. However making it too difficult may drive away

more players. In the context of Second Life, for instance, it can be inferred that the currency peg, among many others, is aimed towards maintaining the balance in the game challenges in terms of acquiring Linden Dollars from outside and inside the virtual world.

Fourthly, the populations and configurations of economic agents or players are not fixed. In Second Life, one of the possible explanations of the former can be explained by the enabling of multi account login by one player in that three accounts could be owned by the same player and allowed to be online all at the same time if the player wishes. Hence it is more accurate to measure economic activities such as rate of consumption as per avatar rather than per account holder. On the latter, the avatar's various configurations can be altered as the player progress and achieve virtual economic wealth whereby abilities, social status, taste, and physical outlook may vary according to the player's mood and thoughts. Accounting for such variability can be a complex task for instance when conducting market segmentation or virtual worldwide census as most variables hardly stay constant.

The IDM Bridge to the Real World

Despite the four differences above, the virtual world and the real world are economically linked due to the availability of various interactive digital media (IDM). In this sense the case goes beyond setting an organizational 3D base or promoting and conducting or promoting real-world product, services, or activities in-world. Rather it refers to the link from the virtual to the real world that leads to meaningful conduct of virtual commerce and economy. The first significant IDM is perhaps the World Wide Web that is linked to SL and therefore allows for data and information to be transmitted between the virtual and the real world. LL has done this notably on the resident information dashboard where they can search for in-world information without being in-world while the SL client software also allows for the reverse. Another example is perhaps the previously mentioned SLX and the Toxian City. However there is perhaps an imbalance between the flow of data and information from versus to the virtual world. For instance it is very difficult to play a Windows Media Player audio stream inside Second Life without the aid of a specially created in-world device and the Second Life client would only export targa (.tga) extension file for snapshots stored in the avatar's inventory.

The second IDM is perhaps the online video based media that are accessible by those who are connected to the internet. Websites such as You-Tube and Machinima.com (www.machinima.com) are able to house Machinima works that can be used by content creators to record their experience in-world. Machinima is a combination of Machine and Cinema and therefore fundamentally can be understood as the production of cinematographic work through the use of computer 3D rendering engine. In the context of SL economy and commerce, this means SL residents could promote their in-world products and services to the real world using Machinima. For instance typing the search keyword "Second Life Machinima Competition" would reveal the works of the contests candidates and in essence the host committee benefits from such activity in terms of marketing and publication. The popularity of Machinima in SL has led to the formation of real world business entity that offers Machinima creation service such as Icarus Studio (www.icarusstudios.co.uk/). Therefore this further shows how different IDM technologies can be combined together to create and communicate value to the real world.

In essence, the presence of these IDMs partially triggered the promotion of in-world economic and commercial activities by distributing information on contents to audiences beyond SL. Furthermore as it does so it also promotes SL as platform for mass collaboration for commercial activity and may lead to real world income creation that real world government can tax. LL has perhaps realized this potential in the earlier stage of their business as they have long advised residents to comply with the tax regulation in their respective jurisdictions. This then demands the further exploration on the potentially fruitful economic activities and this is done in the next section.

The Major Business Sectors in Second Life

In this section the major business sectors in SL is described. A review of several key sources and other resources showed that the significant business sectors are: (1) Real-Estate, (2) Building, (3) Sex Trade, and (4) Fashion. The main literature here was Terdiman (2008) though other sources shall be referenced as appropriate.

The Real Estate business in SL is perhaps best exemplified by the success of a former Chinese school teacher Ailin Graef known as the avatar Anshe Chung (Terdiman, 2008). Anshe was the first land baron in SL who owned 550 SIMs and stakes in other SL businesses with an aggregate value of more than USD 1 million. Her main business was focused on buying and developing custom estates, and renting them to SL residents. Anshe's business is now incorporated in China under the name Anshe Chung Studios (www.anchsechung.com) in Wuhan with more than 30 full-time employees with an additional 20 expected to be added.

From the above, it can be inferred that the profit formulae is similar to the real world buying low- selling high, or renting and leasing. In terms of the former, lands available as listed in SLX varied in terms of themes of Flatland, Hillside, Hilltop, Island, Roadside, Snow, Water, and Waterfront (most highly priced) (Linden Research, Inc., 2009). The listed categories are the results of the customization by the initial buyers who purchased them from LL. To increase the value of their land, land owners typically perform landscaping and put down various building structures with transfer licenses other than holding the land for a period of time.

For renting out, the customization of estates serves to enhance and match a particular resident's experience that tenants can be made to sign covenants such as the types of building allowed. Another example is to create premium rental value in which exotic island estate has set a default theme of beach land with ocean view (Exotic Island Incorporated, 2008).

It can be inferred from the above discussion that building structures are a significant complementary aspect of the Real Estate Business Sector. Judging from the number of buildings listed for sales in SLX, the Building business sector can be said to be very competitive. On 16th May 2009 there were 216,596 items listed in the combined building components, home and garden category, with the price range of L$0-L$83,999 (approximately USD 300) (Linden Research, Inc., 2009) It must noted that the figure of SLX does not represent the entire SL economic activity for a particular business sector nor static as there are shops located within SL and new goods inserted into and taken out from SLX from time to time.

Hence the Building Business Sector should be seen to be consisting not only structures but also gardens - like trees and plants, and furniture. Builders utilize the skills of prims molding, scripting, and various media embedding. In addition they could work in groups of selected people by assigning various licenses together, and build on each other's work. Due to the prim allocation ration that a land has, the best sought building creation therefore are those that correctly balance price, prim efficiency, essential and additional unique features, and aesthetic aspects. The Building Business Sector is critical in enabling residents to create business and organizational facilities such as clubs, casinos, headquarters, and shopping centre; residential structures such as houses and gardens; and furniture such as bed, chair, and bar. One important fact mentioned by Rymaszewski et al (2007) and Terdiman (2008), is that this business

sector as well as others, faces heavy competition from the freebie goods where the virtual goods are free to acquire, however, with varying and questionable quality. This means content creators in SL must work hard to convince buyers to see the value of paying what they have created.

The Sex Trade business represents approximately 30% of the economic activity in SL and treated with age segregation just in real life that its activity is restricted only on SIMs with 'Mature' markings and illegal in the 'Teens' and 'PG' SIMs (Terdiman, 2008). Terdiman breaks down the constituents of the business sector as the following categories: fashion (e.g. clothing set, undergarments, and prosthetic breasts), accessories (e.g. shoes, earrings, and gestures), genitals (usually comes with script and animations), clubs (catered for various sexual orientations and themes), escorts (ranging from geisha style to prostitution), toys (e.g. handcuffs, whips and tails), furniture (e.g. scripted sex beds and lap dance sofas), and animations (e.g. for dance poles, sexual intercourse, and those that complements furniture). In terms of shops, this is best exemplified by the avatar Stroker Serpentine who has made his USD 50,000 from his adult-themed SIM of Amsterdam, a type of shopping centre based on the Dutch's Red Light District, where residents can encounter pornographic materials, sex items, and sex workers (Terdiman, 2008). SLX here would be an alternative option as selling online would target a wider audience.

From the above it can be established that clubs and shops that sells the necessary equipment need buildings and land to operate. For clubs, unlike Land and Building, their success relies heavily on visitors/traffic. Hence just like the financial market, the ideal time to host an event would be when the Asia-Europe-USA time zones overlap or to target the most crowded time zones. The term 'Sex Trade' seems to imply that everything boils down and leads to virtual sexual activity. On broader terms, perhaps it is better understood as the Entertainment Business Sector as virtual sexual activities may not be the absolute end of all or most interactions made within clubs. Similarly, not all clubs are sex clubs or present sexual related content.

According to Terdiman (2008) the Fashion Business Sector can be seen as the biggest business sector and the most competitive. Using the SLX categorical breakdown, the business sector can be broken down as follows: animals, animations, apparel, avatar accessories, avatar appearance, and weapons (Linden Research, Inc., 2009). As this sector is highly related to Av customization, it serves to create the social identity and adaptability of SL residents at individual, group, and organizational levels (Schnook & Sullivan, 2007). It can be further inferred that just like in the real world, the designer will need to skillfully craft his market segments/niche, be sensitive to customer preference awareness, and pay attention to the details. This is perhaps best exemplified by the DCS2 combat system previously mentioned that the HUD and its role as a platform for syndication enables combat-eager residents to express their fantasy together with their own chosen avatar appearances. Hence the Fashion Business Sector permeates and therefore complements other major and smaller business sectors that without it the cyberspace identity creation would not be as effective.

SOLUTIONS AND RECOMMENDATIONS

Knowing the existence of successful commerce within SL, the financial potential hence requires considerable thoughts. In order to unearth, discover, and realize that potential, a solid understanding of the essence of virtual world consumption is therefore a required fundamental. The consumption of virtual goods and services can never be truly felt in the real world that the consumption of such goods only exists in the mind of the purchaser. Nevertheless, the demand for such goods

and services continue to exist. According to Arts (2009) definition, the virtual world investigated comes under the platform world where a well-defined purpose is not present and activities could go beyond gaming and socializing. Meanwhile Castronova (2002) has argued that within games, challenges must be present and it must not be too easy otherwise it will lead to boredom.

In the case of the virtual world, the challenges available vary greatly and come in various forms. Looking at the four thriving business sectors, it can be seen that the most popular challenges enjoyed are those that are closer to real life such as fishing, collecting high-end outfit, and romantic seduction. In this sense the demand for virtual goods and services can be said to have been derived from fantasies where such purchases and therefore consumption could close the gap between the fantasy and reality albeit only in the virtual world. The public display of the purchased goods and services may also serve as sign of accomplishment and can be treated like a trophy for overcoming the challenges. Again this happens only inside the virtual world. Therefore the development of the market for virtual goods and services could possibly be a partial reflection of and consequences from the inability of the real world market to satisfy the real world desire of consumers (Molesworth & Denegri-Knott, 2007).

The challenges can be overcome by accumulating virtual currencies in two ways. The first one is working and/or running a business in the virtual world and the second is by purchasing virtual currencies using real world money. Needless to say the first is more difficult than the second one. The act of purchasing currencies is perhaps comparable to going to the Internet and looking for secret code combinations for infinite life and ammos in console-based games. Henceforth one of the possible motivations for individuals to consume virtual goods and services is the 'psychological experience' in narrowing the fantasy and reality. The term 'psychological experience' is highlighted as the experience of consuming stays within the virtual world. The virtual world is a ground for consumers to mentally negotiate new ways of thinking within the mind such as the consumption of virtual goods and services gradually makes their imagination concrete (Molesworth & Denegri-Knott, 2007). Therefore the value proposition about virtual goods lies within the psychological experience it may create. Such experience could be enhanced in the presence of complementors or made less valuable by substitutors.

The argument for fantasy fulfillment could also be applied to the business owners. This is perhaps more valid for business sectors where imagination and creativity is more intensely involved such as Building and Fashion. Although the vehicle industry has not been investigated, it involves a high degree of similarity as well. In this case, the motivation may be to serve others rather than to profit and the intrinsic reward therefore may be valued higher than the extrinsic. In such an industry, there may be a large gap between the current general level of efficiencies in production and the optimum level of efficiency. For instance some of the encountered have all preferred to produce their own component rather than purchasing. In this case, perhaps the fulfillment of fantasy as a challenge derives pride and higher intrinsic reward when the final product consisted more of the individual efforts. However this does not necessarily mean they completely ignore or second-ranked extrinsic to intrinsic rewards. As such it should be recognized that each individual's motivation to create content varies hence some business owners may not necessarily behave like that as perceived in the real life.

In the path to fulfillment of fantasy and/or creating and running a business in the virtual world, time spent outside the virtual world could also be reduced. This was highlighted in the previous chapter by Lindman (2009) where the refusal to work in teams or delegation may result in one's private life. Tapscott and Williams (2006) further explained that the world today is characterized by a falling cost of collaboration and this is well depicted by Second Life. Nevertheless it can be further argued that an excessive immersion that leads to the addiction in fantasy fulfillment can lead to exploitation of free labor in value creation from the gaming company itself. According to Pearce (2008) Baby Boomers are one of the particular groups of gamers who are able to realize that their life outside the virtual world is a priority. Hence participation activities within the virtual world would require a high level of maturity. For game companies, providing education and limitation on online times to the players in virtual world may seem detrimental to the growth of its community. However such intervention may reduce possible social problems that may be created and backlash and this is where the role of government regulators is required.

FUTURE RESEARCH DIRECTIONS

Based on the preceding discussion and analysis, the future research can be conducted in a more focused manner. Some possible areas for further research are:

- **Pricing Strategy:** This investigates prices and wages in the four industries and how they can be mathematically modelled so that business owners and goods and services creators are able to price their goods more profitably.
- **Optimum SIM Management:** A SIM can be defined as having optimum management if it is able efficiently and effectively manifest the vision of the business owner and management. How this is to be achieved varies from one context to another, however a set of checklist and approaches can be designed to make the process more efficient and effective.
- **Effects of Fantasy Fulfilment:** The effect of Fantasy Fulfilment through psychological experience to the individual's

well being can be investigated. In this case a Virtual World Therapy can be designed. Positive results on this could potentially reduce mental depression and perhaps suicide in society.

- **Optimum Production and Design Process for the Vehicle Industry:** The production of vehicles requires a combination of skills namely prim molding, texturing, programming, mathematics, and understanding of physics. Vehicle builders found often have their products high in prims. An improvement in the production and design process for vehicles could improve the industry's added value in relevance to the entire SL community and tacit simulative capability in the real world.

CONCLUSION

To conclude, consumption in the virtual world therefore can be seen as activities that create fantasy fulfillment through psychological experience. Such psychological experience is stored in virtual goods and services and unleashed when its consumption begins. This has to be done in conjunction with the standard of ethics and regulation. LL may need more direct intervention by actively patrolling for discrepancies and respect international DRM and IP norms. Incentives to set up of intermediary entities to facilitate transparency in the business community may also need to be provided to further accelerate the growth of business in SL.

The very act of fantasy fulfillment is perhaps a controversial issue that has varying social impact. In this light of this possible corollary, perhaps it should be understood that there are different types and extent of fantasy fulfillment. In this sense being associated with a story or a movie to some extent can be associated with fantasy fulfillment as we identify ourselves with one of the actors. At the other end of the continuum there are individuals who use fantasy fulfillment as means of escaping reality where such fantasy can become psychologically unhealthy. Therefore participations in the virtual world should be done with caution and it is important to be able to detect and uncover other's fantasy to reveal their true character.

REFERENCES

Arts, J. M. (2009). The current state and future potential of virtual worlds. In S. Dasgupta, (Ed.), *International Journal of Virtual Communities and Social Networking, 1*(1), 14-22.

Exotic Island Incorporated. (2008). *Second Life island real estate agency with properties and estates for sale*. Retrieved May 14, 2009, from http://exoticislandinc.com/

Freedman, R. (2008). *How to make real money in Second Life*. USA: The McGraw-Hill Companies.

Keegan, V. (2009, July 29). Virtual worlds are getting a second life. *The Guardian*. Retrieved August 2009, 2009, from http://www.guardian.co.uk/technology/2009/jul/29/virtual-worlds

Linden Research, Inc. (2008, March 19). *How do I upload images or sounds?* Retrieved May 14, 2009, from https://support.secondlife.com/ics/support/default.asp?deptID=4417

Linden Research, Inc. (2009). *Xtreet SL real estate new listings*. Retrieved May 14, 2009, from https://www.xstreetsl.com/modules.php?name=Real_Estate

Linden Research, Inc. (2009a). *Second Life, economic statistics (raw data files)*. Retrieved May 14, 2009, from http://secondlife.com/statistics/economy-data.php

Linden Research, Inc. (2009b). *Second Life, Lindex exchange: Market data*. Retrieved May 14th, 2009, from https://secure-web6.secondlife.com/currency/market.php

Linden Research, Inc. (2009c). *XStreet SL marketplace most popular items*. Retrieved May 16, 2009, from https://www.xstreetsl.com/modules. php?name=Marketplace&SearchKeyword=&S earchLocale=0&SearchPriceMin=&SearchPric eMax=&SearchRatingMin=&SearchRatingMa x=&sort=&dir=asc

Molesworth, M., & Denegri-Knott, J. (2007). Digital play and the actualization of the consumer imagination. *Games and Culture, 2*(2), 114–133. doi:10.1177/1555412006298209

Osborne, E., & Schiller, S. (2009). Order and creativity in virtual worlds. *Journal of Virtual Worlds Research, 2*(3).

Pearce, C. (2006). Productive play - Game culture from the bottom up. *Games and Culture, 1*(1), 17–24. doi:10.1177/1555412005281418

Schnook, M., & Sullivan, A. (2007). *How to get a Second Life*. London, UK: Satin Publication Ltd.

Tapley, R. (2008). *Designing your Second Life*. Berkeley, CA: New Riders.

Tapscott, D., & Williams, A. (2006). *Wikinomics: How mass collaboration changes everything*. USA: Penguin Group (USA) Inc.

Terdiman, D. (2008). *The entrepreneur's guide to Second Life: Making money in the metaverse*. Indianapolis, IN: Wiley Publishing, Inc.

Chapter 21
Convenience Prevails Over Homemade:
How Local and Regional Newspapers (Mis)use Online Videos

Marcel Machill
University of Leipzig, Germany

Johannes Gerstner
University of Leipzig, Germany

Sven Class
University of Leipzig, Germany

ABSTRACT

This contribution analyses the online video offer of local and regional daily newspapers. A sample of local and regional landscape press of 15 German newspaper[1] websites offering online videos was investigated. The investigation was carried out with the method of a quantitative content analysis on the basis of an artificial week. The findings show that daily newspapers mainly place purchased videos of external providers (92 percent) in the local and regional area and hardly produced any material by themselves. The videos are themed accordingly: Only 16.2 percent of the videos deal with regional or local topics, and the lion's share is taken by international topics (44.7 percent), while topics related to Germany in any way achieve about one third (31.5 percent). Almost half of the videos can be assorted to the "miscellaneous" desk and, the reporting on political, economic, and social topics, as well as about sports and culture, is less comprehensive. It is also shown that videos are hardly used as a supplement of the remaining editorial offer of the Internet sites and that internal links to other pieces are hardly ever made. In conclusion, online videos are a fixed component of many local and regional news offers of daily newspapers on the Internet, today, but are however hardly used as an addition to the own local reporting competence.

DOI: 10.4018/978-1-61350-147-4.ch021

INTRODUCTION

In the past two years, the moving image became one of the most important information sources in the World Wide Web. Technical progress such as larger band widths of Internet transmission as well as simple and affordable possibilities of production of journalistic providers and recipients leads to an increased offer.

Many local and regional newspapers already use online videos as journalistic contents on their websites.[2] This is supposed to make the offer of information more attractive and to open up new target groups – taking decreasing circulation numbers into consideration. However it must be questioned how newspaper providers use the new possibilities of simpler and more affordable production of the moving image and whether they use these in a targeted manner – in the sense of their local and regional orientation.

Research on online videos with daily newspapers in general and with local and regional daily newspapers in particular is only its forefront. Until now, there are hardly any reliable statements regarding the type and quality of online videos. Existing studies are already very often restricted to the mere description of the offers in general and rarely go beyond qualitative statements about tendencies.[3]

This contribution shows how newspapers in the local and regional area make use of the new possibility of the journalistic transmission of information by means of online videos. In this, it shall not only be considered whether and how many online videos are offered but interest is rather targeted at the length of the videos, the technical and journalistic implementation and integration as well as at the placement of the videos on the websites. Moreover, it will be interesting to see whether the materials are produced internally and/or especially for the respective internet appearance or whether deliveries of external service providers such as agencies dominate the offer. In addition, it will be investigated which topics the videos deal with, from which geographical area such topics stem and how the users are included in the offer. In this, the focus is intentionally not placed on user generated content but on the possibility to assess and comment on professional journalistic contents.

ONLINE VIDEOS: DEFINITION OF TERMS AND CURRENT STATE OF RESEARCH

Online videos, often also referred to as moving image or web videos, are video contents, which are distributed via the Internet and made accessible to the recipient in this way. In connection with the distribution of online videos, there are mainly three forms: online television as streaming offer of a website, video portals and video platforms. IPTV as a pure technical way of distribution will not be discussed here.

Online television is the form of online videos which comes closest to classic television. In this, online television includes streaming offers of individual television providers – i.e. the "reflection" of the programme which can otherwise be received via common ways of transmission – as well as the offer of service providers offering streams of several stations. A stream is the linear non-recurrent transmission of content and thus differs from video on demand. According to Gerhards and Pagel (2009: 14), eleven of the 24 websites of television stations investigated by them offer live streams of their own content at least temporarily (e.g. n-tv[4] or Phoenix[5]). A bundled offer of live streams of several stations is provided by service providers such as Zattoo[6] or Livestation[7]. These offers in general are used occasionally by 18 percent of the online users in Germany according to the study of ARD/ZDF of 2009, while six percent of the online users use them at least once a week and thus regarded as on a regular basis (Eimeren/Frees 2009a: 341 et seqq.). Usually, the offers are free of charge for the user (Siegert 2007: 55 et seqq.).

According to Machill and Zenker (2007: 9), video portals or video hosts[8] are "websites [...] 'broadcasting' short and longer video clips per stream". A difference to the live stream offer is that these videos are available "on demand" and can be viewed an unlimited number of times. Another difference is that the users are actively involved in the composition and provision of the content, either by uploading own videos or by distributing videos of others. Within this frame, the offer includes private videos which satisfy "a communication requirement of the users" and serve for "transmitting a message to others" (Gugel & Müller, 2007: 16) as well as professional contents such as music clips, extracts of movies or TV shows. Examples for such video portals are YouTube[9], Clipfish[10] and MyVideo[11]. The offer of portals serves as a large data base which offers video clips and allows for searching for these clips with key words. 52 percent of the Internet users in Germany currently access such portals "at least occasionally" (Eimeren & Frees, 2009a: 342).

The third form of online video distribution consists in video platforms[12]. They also provide videos on demand but differ from the above mentioned video portals by the fact that the user involvement does not take place and/or is only possible in exceptional cases – and after an editorial process of selection and processing. Examples for such video platforms are media libraries[13]. According to the current study of ARD/ZDF, 17 percent of the Internet users watch TV broadcasts time-displaced in media libraries at least occasionally (Van Eimeren/Frees 2009b: 353 et seq.) and among the group of 14 to 29 year-old persons. This applies also to one third of the Internet users (ARD/ZDF 2009). Gerhards and Pagel (2009: 15) found out that in the meantime, 22 of the 24 websites of TV stations investigated by them offer video on demand.

All the video offers of the local and regional newspapers investigated can be classified as video platforms. They offer videos for repeated retrieval on demand as well as an archive function which is similar to media libraries.

Use and Offer of Online Videos

62 percent of the Internet users in Germany currently access videos on the Internet "at least occasionally" (Eimeren & Frees, 2009a: 342 et seq.) and 34 percent even once every week (Eimeren & Frees, 2009b: 353). This count includes access to all the above mentioned types of online videos. A look at the figures of the past years shows this quick development. In 2008, the value of occasional access amounted to 55 percent (Eimeren & Frees, 2009a: 342 et seq.) and at that time, 24 percent of the interviewees stated that they consumed online videos at least once a week (Eimeren & Frees, 2008: 350 et seq.). In 2006, only seven percent of the Internet users accessed video files online at least once a week. In 2007, this number amounted to 14 percent (Eimeren & Frees 2007: 370).

In total, an average of 25.6 million Internet users watched online videos every month in the first three quarters of 2008 according to a survey of the Federal Association for Information Technology, Telecommunications and New Media (BITKOM). In this, the number of users per month increased by an average of four percent per month during this time. This again demonstrates the increased demand. During this period, the number of clicked videos steadily increased by 13.5 percent to 3.11 billion films. From the first to the third quarter 2008, an increase of the duration from 3:48 minutes to 4:24 minutes could be observed. BITKOM regards this as an indicator for the fact that more and more longer formats are offered and accessed (BITKOM, 2008). In terms of content, according to the W3B study of the business consultancy Fittkau und Maaß, news were particularly popular: 35 percent of the video users watch news videos on the Internet at least once a week, 15 percent watch music videos and 11 percent watch movie and film trailers (W3B, 2007). 62.5 percent of the interviewees of the study Deutschland Online 4 (Germany online) (2006: 58 et seq.)[14] mainly use videos for reasons of information. In this, the main interest is placed on local information (62.1 percent), followed by education (61.2 percent) and sports (52.2 percent). Politics rank on place five, economics on place eight (Deutschland Online 4 2006: 60). In this, the users of online videos are mainly interested in video on demand offers with 48.3 percent. For the future, the study predicts an increase of the number of online video users to 2.6 million in 2010 and to more than seven million in 2015 (Deutschland Online 4, 2006: 55 et seq.).

This increase is recognised by the communicators. Nine out of ten interviewees of a moving image study of the Leipzig University expect an increase of the importance of the moving image content on the Internet (Zerfaß, Mahnke, Rau, & Boltze, 2008: 3 et seqq.). This study also renders information on the type of production. Two thirds of the interviewed journalists said that video production already exclusively or mainly takes place in-house and/or should exclusively or mainly take place in-house. One third prefers the offers supplied by external service providers such as news agencies. When journalists publish videos on the Internet, 70 percent of such videos are complete contributions. In contrast, the amount of user generated content, i.e. videos sent by users, and non-processed raw materials is considerably lower with just above ten percent, respectively. The journalists who do not place moving image offers on the Internet, in most cases they justify this with the big financial efforts and the assumed low interest of the recipients (Zerfaß, Mahnke, Rau, & Boltze, 2008: 34 et seqq.).

Online Videos with Daily Newspapers

Analogous to the increase of the importance of moving image offers in general, the offer of online videos with daily newspapers has also increased in the last years. There are generally very few empirically reliable studies which quantitatively investigated the online video offer of German newspapers and systematically recorded it. What is frequently found are either merely qualitative inventories or statements on tendencies but only rarely descriptive statements.

Katja Riefler (2007: 67) recognises "a clear tendency" towards "video and web TV" with online newspapers. She identifies a preference of local contents on part of the providers in the United States as well as in Europe. Thomas Mrazek (2007: 50) sees "realistic chances to gain a foothold in Internet TV, particularly in the local area" for daily newspapers. According to him, this is due to the fact that in this area, there are only a few moving image offers on the Internet. Holger Kansky (2008: 181 et seq.) sees a tendency with daily newspaper providers to conclude cooperation agreements with TV stations in the past months. He estimates however, the opinion that not only videos of external sources should be bought but that own videos should be offered in order to edge the own profile that has established itself among the publishers. According to this, video clips accompanying local news articles are most widely spread.

Roman Mischel (2006) provided a brief descriptive overview of the video offers on the websites of German daily and weekly newspapers. In this overview, he studies 101 daily newspapers and four weekly magazines and/or weekly newspapers on the basis of a Wiki of Alexander Svensson[15]. He comes to the conclusion that 26 of the newspapers observed offer contributions of the service provider Zoom.in[16]. However, many local daily newspapers already disposed of own rubrics with videos that were self-produced exactly for this at the time of the survey which "partially clearly" differed "in terms of quality [...]" (Mischel, 2006). Mischel describes videos that were placed online without narrator's text and the "informative value [...]" of which was "almost nil" as well as recordings of interviews and of press conferences or local events. He also identifies self-produced news in film and local news broadcasts. In this regard, he finds that there is a clear dominance of bought external contents – especially with nationwide daily newspapers – mainly from the news agency Reuters.

This dominance is also found by Falk Lüke (2008: 51): besides Reuters, he also attests an important role to the service provider Zoom.in. Lüke criticises the offer of Zoom.in as "sometimes questionable" with regard to the editorial quality. In general, he finds that the quality requirements of those making newspapers to their paper cannot be transmitted to moving images with the often small budgets.

Two of the few investigations which study the online video offers of German newspapers empirically in terms of quantity in a more comprehensible form are the studies of Julia Schmid. In her first investigation of the year 2007[17], Schmid investigates a total number of 109 daily newspapers – as Mischel, she bases her work on the Wiki of Alexander Svensson and supplements this with own research. In this, she comes to the conclusion[18] that 52 of these daily newspapers offer videos on their websites (Schmid, 2007).

In another study, Schmid investigated the offer of online videos on the websites of the German daily newspapers again, in 2008. Here, she analysed the online video offer of all 379 German daily and weekly newspapers. Meanwhile, it was discovered that 45 percent of all websites offer online videos. Almost half of them also produces their own video contents which usually concentrate on local or regional aspects. It however also applies that 34 percent of all the providers of videos produce own videos but still buy additional ones from external parties. 70 percent of all newspapers offering online videos are delivered the videos by Zoom.in, 14 percent get their material from classic news agencies such as Reuters and AFP. Eight percent obtain the videos from cooperation's with TV stations or video service providers from the respective region (Schmid, 2008: 5 et seqq.).

The analysis of Gerhards and Pagel (2008: 159 et seqq.) obtains similar findings. In their investigation of 123 regional online newspapers, they found out that 67 of them offer online videos. This corresponds to a rate of 54.5 percent. A big part of the providers of online videos – 80.6 percent – fall back on material from agencies among which Gerhards and Pagel also count Zoom.in in contrast to Schmid. 34.3 percent of the regional newspaper publishers which offer videos also produce videos themselves. 14.9 percent obtain videos from a commissioned multimedia service provider and 7.5 percent also place user generated content on their website. Of the 67 regional daily newspapers with a video offer, 82.1 percent offer national content, 80.6 percent offer international and 50.7 percent offer regional content. As the regional newspaper publishers, the nationwide ones also obtain a big part of the videos, 87.5 percent, from agencies – 75 percent of which come from Reuters. The majority of the nationwide newspapers offering online videos – indeed 62.5 percent – produce online videos themselves. 37.5 percent have others produce videos for them. None of the providers offers user generated content (Gerhards & Pagel, 2008: 169 et seqq.).

STUDY DESIGN AND OPERATIONALISATION

The study period with the data collection for this contribution was one week. To minimise the effects of extraordinary influences, the study was realised on the basis of an artificial week. With this, there is the avoidance of special events dominating for several days that would thus result in a big part of the data collected to become untypical and useless. The collection of data began on Monday, 02.3.2009, and ended on Sunday, 26.4.2009. The regular date of 11.04.2009 according to the template was postponed by one week since this was the Saturday before Easter. With this, the effects of this special constellation (public holiday the day before, public holiday on the next weekday, holiday time…) should be excluded and a usual Saturday should instead be investigated. Therefore, the last day of the collection was also postponed by one week. On every day of the collection, all the videos that were placed on the websites to be investigated within 24 hours were analysed.

The videos were assessed according to formal, journalistic and other criteria whereupon the formal criteria included technical data such as the file format, the length of the video and similar aspects, journalistic criteria related to content and presentation-formative aspects and the other criteria included points such as the embedding of the videos in the site and similar aspects. The individual criteria are listed as Table 1.

METHODICAL APPROACH

The investigation of the online videos was realised with the method of content analysis. In this, a subform of content analysis, a frequency analysis[19], was realised. In this form, text elements – and/or elements of videos in this case – are quantitatively classified and the frequency of their appearance is counted (Schnell, Hill, & Esser, 2005: 408).

Selection of Investigation Units

This contribution is restricted to an arbitrary sample of 15 local and regional daily newspapers. Only newspapers which are published at least six times a week and offer online videos were taken into consideration. Thus, the investigation is an evaluation of 15 individual cases which are however exemplary for the situation of the Federal German local and regional press landscape.

Since there is no scientifically reliable breakdown of all the local and regional daily newspapers as providers of journalistic videos, the list of all the newspapers with an online offer of the Bundesverband Deutscher Zeitungsverleger (Federation of German Newspaper Publishers, BDZV 2009)

Table 1. Criteria for video selection

Length of the videos	**Formal criteria**
Number of videos that were placed online every day	
Advertisement	
Source of video content	
Video player format	
Possibility of assessment by the user	
Localisation of the video on the website	
Presence of narrator text	**Journalistic criteria**
Geographic allocation of topics	
Topics placed/allocation to desks	
Journalistic presentation form of the videos	
Presence of special formats or rubrics	**Other criteria**
Integration in the overall offer of the website	
Sharing/embedding function	

was taken as a basis. For the delimitation between local, regional and nationwide newspapers, the IVW (Information Community to Determine the Reach of Advertising Media) quarter edition III/2008 which was the most topical at that time was taken as a basis. Here, the circulations of German daily newspapers are indicated whereupon nationwide newspapers and tabloids are indicated separately (IVW 2008). In this, all the nationwide newspapers were excluded. In a next step, all weekly newspapers, business newspapers as well as foreign-language and international newspapers were excluded with the help of a list of all the newspapers of the Bundesverband Deutscher Zeitungsverleger (Resing, 2008: 278 et seqq.).

For the draft, a number was allocated to each newspaper title. To get 15 local/regional newspapers offering online videos from the available list by means of a lottery, a total number of 24 draws were necessary. This was due to the fact that nine of the 24 newspaper websites did not offer any video at the time of the draft of the sample. As a result, these were not included in the survey. The following newspaper titles were included in the arbitrary sample: Burghauser Anzeiger, Westdeutsche Zeitung, Hohenzollerische Zeitung, Sünderländer Volksfreund, Kölner Stadt-Anzeiger, Roth-Hilpoltsteiner Volkszeitung. Meinerzhagener Zeitung, Ludwigshafener Rundschau, Vilsbiburger Zeitung, Untertaunus Kurier, Wiesbadener Tagblatt, Eberbacher Nachrichten, Bote vom Untermain, Illertaler Bote, Main-Post.

As it may be that some newspaper titles belong to one and the same journalistic unit. It is thus also possible that different newspaper titles offer a joint online appearance. Despite this, the approach described above was selected since, theoretically, the offer of online videos may vary between different newspaper titles even if they belong to the same journalistic unit.

RESULTS OF THE STUDY

With regard to the following results, it can generally be said that the online video offer of local and regional daily newspapers has not established itself to that extent that a constant situation can be registered in the offer of videos. A continuous development is taking place. For example, the video offers of the Westdeutsche Zeitung and of the Kölner Stadt-Anzeiger changed just after the completion of this data collection. Videos of Zoom. in were completely taken off the websites of both providers. Instead, in addition to the self-produced videos of the publishers, videos of other external providers were included in the offer. With both providers, the conversion also included a change of the design of the video offer and the possibility to place advertisements before the videos is increasingly used here, now.

How Many Videos Are Offered?

On the websites of the newspapers included in this analysis, a total number of 776 videos[20] were placed within the artificial week. It is remarkable that many videos can be found on several websites

and this applies for supplied videos of agencies and in particular for videos of the provider Zoom.in. If one does not look at the number of the cases of all videos but at the number of videos with different content, a total number of 224 [21] independent videos results for the artificial week.

With the local and regional newspapers, which offer videos, 7.4 videos are newly placed every day on average. Almost half of the providers investigated place more than ten videos online every day on average (see Table 2). It is striking that the number of the videos placed at the weekend is lower than the number of those placed during the week with most of the providers. This presumably has to do with the way the online editorial teams that are less staffed on weekends work – as it is the case with all the editorial teams of newspapers. If one looks only at the videos placed from Monday to Friday, an average value of 8.5 videos per day results.

There are big differences between the individual providers regarding the number of videos placed between Monday and Friday – the two days of the weekend are again treated as special cases, here. In contrast, the number of videos placed with one single provider varies only to a minimum extent between the different days. For example, three of the newspapers investigated place the same number of videos every day. In most cases, the number only varies from the average value by a small number of videos.

Who Produces the Videos?

The majority of the videos investigated come from external providers (91.8 percent). The publishers

Table 2. Videos placed with the investigated newspapers per day on average

	Less than 1	1 to 4.9	5 to 9.9	More than 10
Frequency	3	2	3	7

Basis: 15 investigated daily newspapers.

themselves – that corresponds to 61 of the total 776 videos, produced only 7.9 percent of the videos. Only one of the investigated videos user generated content. The large share of supplied videos can be explained by the fact that one video often appeared with several daily newspapers. Since it does not play any role from the point of view of the user, whether a video consumed by the user also appears on other websites, the total number of all the videos observed at different places is analysed – if a video appeared several times, it was counted several times. But even if one subtracted the videos that appear several times from the total number of videos and only considers each video to have been produced once, the resulting value of 82.1 percent for external providers and 16.5 percent for self-produced videos is still high. On average, the individual editorial teams only upload 0.6 own videos per day. The self-produced content thus only make up a very small share of the videos placed online every day. At least, these self-produced videos are offered by 60 percent of the newspapers investigated and only 40 percent exclusively buy videos.

If one looks at the different suppliers of external videos, the picture described above is confirmed. A big part of these videos comes from the providers Zoom.in, AFP and Reuters (see Table 3). In total, these three providers produce almost 90 percent of all the videos supplied. In this, Zoom.in still takes the lion's share of 77.1 percent of all the videos supplied. This might be due to the fact that Zoom.in provides the content free of charge and finances this offer for newspapers with the placing of advertisements in the videos. AFP and Reuters do by far not play such a big role with 8.1 and 3.9 percent, respectively. Other providers

which make up 10.8 percent after all are usually video agencies or local TV stations which exclusively produce contributions for the website of the newspaper or use these as a secondary place to show their contributions.

What is the Duration of the Videos?

While 59.9 percent of the videos supplied have a length of 30 to 90 seconds, about 73.8 percent of the self-produced videos are longer than 2:30 minutes. Thus, supplied contents are relatively short while with the self-produced material, longer contributions predominate. The average length of all the videos is 92 seconds. In this, however, a relatively large range can be observed – the shortest videos are only 27 seconds long while the longest takes more than seven minutes. With 55.9 percent of the videos, a majority ranges in the time span between 30 and 90 seconds (see Figure 1).

If one includes each video found in the investigation only once and subtracts duplicates, the average video length becomes 113.6 seconds. This can be explained by the fact that the relatively short videos of Zoom.in do not carry as much weight as before while the relative weight of the relatively long self-produced videos increases. If one considers the length of the supplied videos without duplicates, an average length of 99.8 seconds results. The average length of the self-produced videos amounts to 177.19 seconds. With these values, the result of the investigation of all the videos according to which self-produced contents are longer than supplied ones is again confirmed. The explanation for this is obvious: the production of every individual video is connected to a certain basic effort. The efforts of

Table 3. Producers of the videos supplied

	Zoom.in	AFP	Reuters	Other providers	Total number of videos supplied
Number	549	58	28	77	712
Percent	77.1	8.1	3.9	10.8	100

Figure 1. Length of the videos (basis: all the videos investigated. N=776)

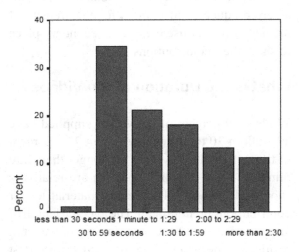

production do not increase proportionally to the length but are relativised. If no journalist with a camera is present on site, it does not take a lot of additional efforts to film longer raw material that can be used in a longer contribution. Thus, the production of a longer contribution is not as complex as the production of several shorter contributions since journey and editorial preparation is not necessary at all times.

Are Videos Used for the Communication of Advertisements?

In 43.8 percent of cases, advertisements are placed before videos – such advertisements are never house advertisings for the respective publisher with the investigated clips but always advertisings of external promotion partners. In case of the remaining 56.2 percent, advertising does not directly take place in the video but this does not however exclude that an advertisement banner is placed next to the video window or that advertisements appear in a pop up window as soon as a recipient clicks on the video.

With regard to self-produced videos, advertisements are only placed before videos in 14.8 percent of the cases while this figure amounts to 46.5 percent with the supplied videos. This high value is mainly due to the videos from Zoom.in: here, advertisements are placed before the videos in 59.9 percent of the cases. These advertisements were not introduced by the respective publishers but directly supplied to the publishers by Zoom. in. In contrast to this, videos of the other two large suppliers Reuters and AFP never include advertisements. Obviously, Zoom.in which provides videos to the publishers free of charge finances itself with these advertisements whereas Reuters and AFP sell their videos to the respective providers.

In Which Format Are the Videos Offered?

All the videos investigated can be directly played on the website and do not have to be downloaded on the hard drive. The videos use either the Windows-Media-Player or a Flash-Player. 29.3 percent of the videos investigated are reproduced with the Flash-Player and 70.7 percent with the Windows-Media-Player that is used by all the clips of Zoom. in. In addition, two of the investigated websites also offer the possibility to directly download the video without using any other programmes.

Thanks to the possibility of streaming videos on the website, they can be used immediately and can be made quickly accessible without any previous downloading and without the waiting times related to this. This low technical effort – no saving and repeated retrieval of the videos – along with the possibility of spontaneous access increase the probability of intense use by the visitors of a website.

What are the Possibilities of the User to Evaluate the Videos?

The possibility for users to evaluate the videos is not widely spread. With only 0.6 percent of the videos, there is the possibility to evaluate them by means of a scale and with another 4.9 percent, the users can express their opinion on the video with a comment function. With the self-produced videos, the user has the possibility to evaluate a video in about 31 percent of the cases. The fact that the share of videos that can be evaluated is low because of the videos of Zoom.in. These make up the majority of the videos investigated and do not dispose of an evaluation function. The user cannot evaluate the videos of AFP and Reuters, either. With other providers, there is a possibility to evaluate the videos in 7.7 percent of the cases.

The large share of the possibility to evaluate the videos with self-produced videos shows that the publishers want to have feedback on their own contents and regard such contents as a fixed editorial component of their journalistic offer. Moreover, the publishers have the possibility to read directly the wishes of recipients from the population and to use their own production possibilities – which are very often limited and cannot be compared to those of external suppliers – in a more targeted way. This is not necessarily the case with most of the supplied videos. The videos of Zoom.in are automatically integrated in the web content without any editorial support.

How Can the Videos on the Website Be Accessed?

49.9 percent of the videos being part of the investigation can be accessed with a video button in the menu and 40.6 percent can be accessed with such a button in a column on the website. 16.2 percent of the videos can be accessed differently – usually with a bar which can be located at different places on the website. With this, it becomes clear that the different providers link their video platforms with different prominence. While a big bar can be easily perceived, the user can easily oversee one button among several buttons and the video offer might not be used.

In addition to this, there is also a video preview on the home page of the provider with 11.6 percent of the videos. This means that an individual image of the video is presented as a freeze frame. This is striking and can serve as an eye catcher for the user. It is even possible to play the video directly on the home page with a simple click on the video in another 6.6 percent of the videos. If one looks at this area from the point of view of the newspapers' websites, it becomes clear that a preview to at least part of the videos is given on the home page with 73.3 percent of the investigated providers. With 20 percent of the providers, the videos can partially be completely played on the home page.

This possibility of quick access and the prominent placement on the home pages of course shall serve for placing the video offer in the foreground in an attractive way. The providers want the contents that are produced with a certain effort or bought to be seen and used by the users.

JOURNALISTIC CRITERIA

In Chapter 4.2, individual videos, not complete videos contributions are taken into consideration. A video contribution is a thematically independent part of a video or a complete thematically independent video. In most cases, a complete video is thus also a video contribution. What is exempted from this within the frame of this investigation are news broadcasts treating several topics. This differentiation between videos and video contributions is necessary in order to cover the different topics like video contributions which appear in a news broadcast (video). The 776 videos included in this investigation consisted of a total number of 820 video contributions.

Which Topics Are Being Dealt With?

If one investigates the topics that are dealt with, this can best be made with the observation of the video contributions. A big part of the total number of 820 video contributions has to be allocated to the "miscellaneous" desk (27.2 percent of the cases). All video contributions dealing with topics from the areas lifestyle, celebrities, animal stories, soft news, automobile/engines and TV are allocated to this area. If one adds the 15.7 percent of cases dealing with accidents and natural disasters as well as the 6.6 percent of cases dealing with topics from the crime area, these three desks make up for a total of 49.5 percent of all the video contributions. Thus, half of the contributions serve the demand for contents that are classically allocated to the tabloids area. Only 15.4 percent of the video contributions come from the area "politics, economy and society" and with 10.9 percent, the share of weather forecasts is high. The culture desk is represented by 10.5 percent and 6.5 percent of the video contributions deal with sports topics (see Figure 2 and Table 4). Any contributions dealing with other topics than those mentioned here would only have achieved low values in independent categories were included in the category "others". This includes topics from the areas of science and aerospace. Moreover, portraits of persons and events that could not be

allocated to one of the above mentioned categories were considered under "others".

There are clear differences between supplied and self-produced videos. It becomes clearer that the supplier Zoom.in places a lot of importance on tabloid topics and the areas crime, accidents and natural disasters. This provider only rarely implements political topics while this area ranks among the first ones with all the others. In contrast to this, sports and culture play an important role with the own productions of the daily newspapers. Maybe local and regional providers count especially on these areas typically because no one else can offer moving images of these. Moreover, moving images deliver an added value in comparison to written texts or photos in these areas.

Which Geographical Connection do the Online Videos Have?

Only 16.2 percent of the video contributions deal with local or regional topics from the respective area of publication of the newspaper. The majority of the video contributions deal with international topics. If one summarises the cases dealing with topics from the EU, the United States and other international countries, a value of 44.7 percent results. In 31.5 percent of the cases, the contents can be allocated to the area of the Federal Republic of Germany. An allocation to one of the categories was not possible in 7.7 percent of the cases (see Figure 3).

If one only regards the self-produced videos, it becomes clear that with 97.1 percent, almost all videos have to be allocated to the local or regional area. With 33.8 percent, a relative majority of these videos deals with topics from the area of politics, economy and society while only 1.5 percent have to be allocated to the crime desk. Of the videos with a national connection, 26.4 percent belong to the desk accidents and natural disasters and here, videos about politics, economy and society are particularly rare.

Figure 2. Allocation of the video contributions to desks

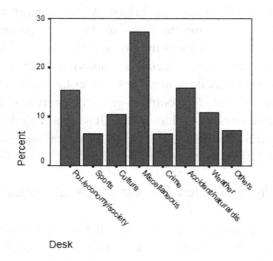

Table 4. Allocation of the video contributions to desks

	All contributions	All contributions supplied	Zoom.in contributions	Supplied contributions without Zoom.in	Self-produced contributions
Politics, economy and society	15.4	12.8	5.8	36.2	33.3
Sports	6.5	4.6	4.7	4.3	17.1
Culture	10.5	9.6	6.7	19.0	17.1
Miscellaneous	27.2	30.1	31.0	27.0	8.6
Crime	6.6	7.3	9.1	1.2	1.9
Accidents and natural disasters	15.7	16.9	21.5	1.2	7.6
Weather	10.9	12.5	15.3	3.1	14.3
Other	7.3	6.3	5.8	8.0	0
Total	100.0	100.0	100.0	100.0	100.0

Basis: all the 820 video contributions investigated. Information is in percentage.

If European topics are dealt with, weather forecasts contribute 35.6 percent and videos from the miscellaneous area 19.5 percent. Culture and crime hardly play a role and videos from the area "others". They do not appear at all. If there are reports about the United States, these are from the desk "miscellaneous" with 51 percent and reports about sports, accidents, natural disasters or the weather were not seen among the investigated video contributions. With regard to international topics, accidents and natural disasters dominate with a value of 26.4 percent of the cases while sports and others are rare.

With the self-produced contributions, the newspapers use their reporting competence on site and mostly even cover the socially relevant topic areas such as politics and economy. With regard to the videos with nationwide topics which are almost exclusively supplied, the area "miscellaneous" with tabloid topics dominates.

How are the Topics Realised? Is There a Narrator's Text?

In general, it is quite usual that online videos are accompanied by narrator's text. Only 2.2 percent of all videos do not have any spoken text, at all. It was understood that the term narrator's text referred to any type of text – whether from the on or the off – which was not given as an original sound, for example by an interview partner. There are differences between supplied and self-produced videos: while only 0.3 percent of the supplied videos are not provided with a narrator's text, this number amounts to 19.7 percent with the self-produced ones. Thus, with the self-produced videos, the efforts of a subsequent scoring are more often refrained from.

Figure 3. Geographical allocation of the video contributions

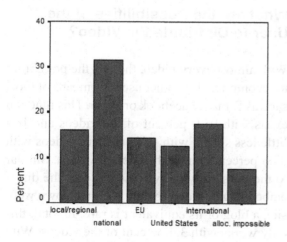

In Which Journalistic Form are the Pieces Presented?

The journalistic form of presentation of the video contributions are mainly reports: 84.4 percent of the investigated cases have to be allocated to this category, followed by read announcements far behind. The value of the latter of 8.3 percent of all the video contributions consists of the Meinerzhagener Zeitung and the Sünderländer Volksfreund which respectively produce a news broadcast with several read announcements on weekdays. 2.1 percent of the video contributions are interviews. Compared to this, other journalistic forms of presentation such as comments, coverage and surveys[22] do hardly play any role. Cut raw materials without any narrator's text is hardly offered.

The report is the form which is most frequently used with self-produced as well as with supplied videos. Eight of the self-produced and nine of the supplied videos are interviews. Read announcements exist only among the self-produced videos of all the videos investigated while trailers were only found among the supplied ones. The online video is thus used mainly in accordance with the function of a report for the quick and topical transmission of information and is supposed to extend the news competence of the respective provider in this way.

OTHER CRITERIA

Are There Any Special Recurring Formats/Rubrics?

With 95.5 percent of the cases, most of the videos do not appear as a part of a recurring format. They thus stand alone as contributions and are not offered within the frame of a thematic or broadcast-related context. The few formats that appear are never video blogs, apart from one exception. 1.3 percent of the videos are news broadcasts and

3.1 percent of the cases are other serials such as daily TV recommendations or a weekly cinema preview. Formats or rubrics exist with six of the 15 investigated websites and thus on 40 percent of the sites. However, only a small share of the videos can be allocated to recurring formats with these newspapers and the possibility of context-related reporting and the offering of certain continuity are hardly used.

How are the Videos Integrated in the Overall Offer of the Website?

The videos offered are hardly embedded in rubrics and only very rarely included in the remaining journalistic offer of the respective Internet site. With only three of the investigated cases, there were references from a video to an article dealing with the same or a similar topic or the video was directly integrated in an article. With regard to the integration in the overall offer, the supplied videos perform particularly poor. None of these refer to a related article or include integration in an article although there are reports on similar topics on the site. The video offer is devaluated because of this lack of embedding. As a consequence, only very few newspapers offer thematic overall complexes and they do not use videos as an addition to their online offer.

What are the Possibilities of the User to Distribute the Video?

With almost every video, there is the possibility to recommend it to other users by means of tools such as E-mail, Facebook or flickr. This function exists with 95.9 percent of the videos and is a little less spread with self-produced videos with 83.6 percent than with supplied videos. Similar to the possibility to evaluate a video, the direct embedding of videos by the user in an own website, a blog or its equivalent is rare. In total, this only works with 3.4 percent of the videos. With self-produced videos, this value is a little higher with 11.5 percent than it is with externally produced ones.

SUMMARY OF FINDINGS AND CLASSIFICATION

The results of this investigation serve for the classification of the commitment of local and regional newspapers in the area of the moving image. This classification is important because concepts in the area of the moving image will gain importance for local and regional newspapers in the years to come. In many cases, efforts – which are often realised tentatively and are only in the stadium of attempts – are already a first step on the way of the newspapers towards becoming multimedia information service providers. However, it will now be decided in the phase of the wider technical spread of online videos, which will acquire the know-how in order to make use of this area in a profitable way in the future. At least a part of the future of the German newspaper landscape that is strongly influenced by regional and local newspapers is decided upon, here.

By now, online videos have become a widely spread phenomenon with local and regional daily newspapers: of 24 daily newspaper titles drawn in the arbitrary sample, 15 offered such videos on their website. With 92 percent, many of the videos offered were not produced in the editorial team itself but supplied. In this, the service provider Zoom.in makes up the biggest part. 60 percent of the investigated newspaper websites offer own videos at least occasionally. This value is remarkable even though these videos only make up a small share in consideration of the total number of the videos offered. Thus, local and regional daily newspapers only use the possibility to extend their reporting competence on site by offering moving images to a moderate extent even though the number of videos is still small. It seems as if some newspapers tried to integrate

this form of transmission first of all with limited efforts on a trial basis.

In the selection of the topics, the desk "politics, economy and society" dominates among the self-produced videos. In general and especially among the supplied videos, the desk "miscellaneous" dominates and the desk of "crime" and "accidents and natural disasters" appear more often here than with the self-produced equivalents. This can mainly be explained by the videos of Zoom. in, which place a strong focus on tabloid topics. Obviously, such topics can be better and wider spread than hard topics. With regard to the forms of presentation, a clear imbalance can be discovered: almost all the video contributions use the form of presentation of reports or news broadcasts.

In total, only 16.2 percent of the video pieces deal with local or regional topics. Since this is exactly the area, which usually is the unique selling point of the investigated newspapers, this number may be considered too low. With regard to the offer of nationwide topics, it will not be possible for smaller newspapers to compete with nationwide competitors in the video offer. The main reason for the low number of videos from the region presumably are the costs: for nationwide videos, more than half of the providers use the provider Zoom.in which is free of charge while local videos have to be produced independently or purchased from another provider who usually has to be paid.

With regard to the takeover of Zoom.in videos, it has to be assumed that many providers can offer videos from the nationwide area thanks to this that would otherwise hardly be possible for them in terms of finance. However, the journalistic and publishing sense has to be questioned: should a local daily newspaper offer nationwide and international videos, at all? Even if a provider answers this question with yes, it is still questionable whether the use of Zoom.in videos does not actually damage the credibility of the provider – even more because the videos of Zoom.in cannot be revised by the editorial team. In addition to this, these videos that are disliked by the recipients according to several studies (e.g. Schmid, 2008: 7 and Mrazek, 2007: 51) and offered in large numbers every day might prevent the users from receiving videos, which were already offered or independently produced in the future.

Recurring formats or rubrics usually do not exist. However, it is exactly these that could allow for recipients to commit themselves to the offer since a regularity of serving certain thematic areas creates a big chance for the users to get used to the regular contributions. Such a habituation, and thus the gaining of regular users, increases the success of video contributions in journalistic terms which has positive effects on the access figures for the Internet offer in total on the one hand and makes online videos more interesting as an advertising field on the other hand.

Currently, advertisements are still only used tentatively, at least with self-produced contributions. Advertisements are only integrated in 14.8 percent of the cases. However, local videos which are accessed particularly often according to Mrazek (2007: 51) would actually offer a favourable advertising field for local companies.

A link of the online video offer to other contents of the website is usually not made. Only in three of all the investigated cases, a video was integrated in or linked to a thematically related article. This corresponds to a rate of 0.4 percent of the videos – supplied videos were always presented without any reference to such an article. Thus, the videos are presented as a separate offer which is detached from the remaining offer of the website. Since some of the topics dealt with in the videos are also shown on the website in text form, an integration into an article or a reference to an article could create a cross-media added value with few efforts which then again could lead to a more interesting offer – with all the advantages described, for example for advertising revenue – as does an integration in rubrics or fixed formats.

After all, it becomes clear that the offer of online videos with local and regional daily newspapers

often has not yet existed for a long time. The video offer of two of the investigated websites was principally changed just after the completion of the investigation. The high rate of newspapers using Zoom.in speaks for the fact that many are still in a finding phase with regard to offering online videos. Added to this is the generally poor integration into other offers of the website. Finally, the growth rates in the offer of online videos in the past years also underline this impression. In order to be able to work in a user-oriented way and to safeguard the future of newspapers as multimedia information service providers, providers have to use more than just third party contents from entertainment journalism which are supplied free of charge. Only if newspapers make the necessary but manageable investments in the technical and personnel area in order to extend their local and regional reporting competence with self-produced video contributions that are consistent and well integrated, they will be able to profit from this in the future.

REFERENCES

W3B. (2007). *Konkurrenz fürs Fernsehen: Immer mehr Online-Nutzer verzichten lieber auf TV als aufs Internet.* Retrieved from http://www.w3b.org/web-20/videos-im-internet.html

ARD/ZDF. (2009). *ARD/ZDF-Onlinestudie 2009: Nachfrage nach Videos und Audios im Internet steigt weiter – 67 Prozent der Deutschen sind online.* Retrieved September 15, 2009, from http://www.ard-zdf-onlinestudie.de/

BDZV. (1995). *Zeitungen '95.* Bonn, Germany: ZV Zeitungs-Verlag Service.

BDZV. (2004). *50 Jahre BDZV – Privater Rundfunk.* Retrieved September 15, 2009, from http://www.bdzv.de/875.html

BDZV. (2009). *Zeitungen Online – Zeitungswebsites.* Retrieved September 15, 2009, from http://www.bdzv.de/zeitungswebsites.html

BITKOM. (2008). *25 Millionen schauen Videos im Internet.* Retrieved September 15, 2009, from http://www.bitkom.org/de/presse/60132_55722.aspx

Breunig, C. (2007). IPTV und Web-TV im digitalen Fernsehmarkt. *Media Perspektiven, 10,* 478–491.

Büffel, S., & Spang, S. (2009). *Studienergebnisse: Zeitungen Online 2008.* Retrieved September 15, 2009, from http://www.media-ocean.de/2009/01/25/studienergebnisse-zeitungen-online-2008/

Deutschland Online 4. (2006). Die Zukunft des Breitbandinternets. Retrieved September 15, 2009, from http://www.studie-deutschland-online.de/do4/DO4-Berichtsband_d.pdf

Eimeren, B. v., & Frees, B. (2007). ARD/ ZDF Online-Studie – Internetnutzung zwischen Pragmatismus und YouTube-Euphorie. *Media Perspektiven, 8,* 362–378.

Eimeren, B. v., & Frees, B. (2008). ARD/ZDF-Onlinestudie 2008 – Bewegtbildnutzung im Internet. *Media Perspektiven, 7,* 350–355.

Eimeren, B. v., & Frees, B. (2009a). Der Internetnutzer 2009 – multimedial und total vernetzt? Ergebnisse der ARD/ZDF-Onlinestudie 2009. *Media Perspektiven, 7,* 334–348.

Eimeren, B. v., & Frees, B. (2009b). Nutzungsoptionen digitaler Audio- und Videoangebote – Ergebnisse der ARD/ZDF Onlinestudie 2009. *Media Perspektiven, 7,* 349–355.

Gerhards, C., & Pagel, S. (2008). Webcasting von Video-Content in Online-Zeitungen . In Zerfaß, A., Welker, M., & Schmidt, J. (Eds.), *Kommunikation, Partizipation und Wirkungen im Social Web – Strategien und Anwendungen – Perspektiven für Wirtschaft, Politik und Publizistik. Neue Schriften zur Online-Forschung (Vol. 2,* pp. 134–153). Cologne, Germany: Herbert von Harlem Verlag.

Gerhards, C., & Pagel, S. (2009). *Internetfernsehen von TV-Sendern und User Generated Content.* Bonn, Germany: bub Bonner Universitäts-Buchdruckerei. Retrieved September 15, 2009, from http://library.fes.de/pdf-files/stabsabteilung/06396.pdf

Gugel, B., & Müller, H. (2007). *TV 2.0.* Retrieved September 15, 2009, from http://www.gugelproductions.de/blog/wp-content/uploads/2007/07/tv20_gugel_mueller.pdf

IVW. (2008). *Quartalsauflagen III/2008 – Zeitungen: Verkaufte Auflage gesamt.* Retrieved September 15, 2009, from http://www.medien-aktuell.de/spezial/ivw_q_zeit.php

Kansky, H. (2008). *Alles von der Zeitung – Bewegte Bilder im Internet,* (pp. 179-186). In BDZV Zeitungen 2008. Berlin, Germany: BDVZ.

Lüke, F. (2008). Fernsehen ohne Fernseher. *Journalist, 7,* 50–52.

Machill, M., & Zenker, M. (2007). *Youtube, Clipfish und das Ende des Fernsehens? Problemfelder und Nutzung von Videoportalen.* Volume 1 of Medien Digital. Berlin, Germany: Friedrich-Ebert-Stiftung. Retrieved September 15, 2009, from http://library.fes.de/pdf-files/stabsabteilung/05044.pdf

Mischel, R. (2006). *Onlinevideo und Zeitungen.* Retrieved September 15, 2009, from http://www.onlinejournalismus.de/2006/12/05/wie-online-redaktionen-in-deutschland-video-einsetzen/

Mrazek, T. (2007). Zeitungs-TV per Videoclip. *Journalist, 2*, 50–51.

Neuberger, C., Nuernbergk, C., & Rischke, M. (2009). Journalismus im Internet: Zwischen Profession, Partiparation und Technik. *Media Perspektiven, 4,* 174–188.

Resing, C. (2008). *Die Zeitungen in Deutschland – Tages-, Wochen- und Sonntagspresse im Überblick*, (pp. 277-296). In BDZV Zeitungen 2008. Berlin, Germany: BDVZ.

Riefler, K. (2007). Der Trend zum lokalen CNN. *Message, 1,* 66–70.

Roth, J. (2005). *Internetstrategien von Lokal- und Regionalzeitungen*. Wiesbaden, Germany: VS Verlag für Sozialwissenschaften.

Schmid, J. (2007). *Analyse von 109 Websites von deutschen Tageszeitungen*. Retrieved September 15, 2009, from http://www.websehen.net/2007/05/29/analyse-von-109-websites-von-deutschen-tageszeitungen/

Schmid, J. (2008). *Bewegte Zeiten – Das Onlinevideo-Angebot von deutschen Zeitungen – Konzepte, Produkte, Erlösmodelle*. Berlin, Germany: BDZV.

Schnell, R., Hill, P. B., & Esser, E. (2005). *Methoden der empirischen Sozialforschung* (7th ed.). Munich, Germany & Vienna, Austria: Oldenbourg.

Schütz, W. J. (2007). Redaktionelle und verlegerische Struktur der deutschen Tagespresse. *Media Perspektiven, 11,* 589–598.

Siegert, S. (2007). Das Ende der Couchpotato. *Journalist, 11,* 54–57.

Svensson, A., Schwarzmann, I., Büffel, S., & Lüke, F. (2007). Spinnweben und Feger. *Medium Magazin, 1*. Retrieved September 15, 2009, from http://www.mediummagazin.de/archiv/2007/01/spinnweben-und-feger/

Zerfaß, A., Mahnke, M., Rau, H., & Boltze, A. (2008). *Bewegtbildkommunikation im Internet – Herausforderungen für Journalismus und PR. Ergebnisbericht der Bewegtbildstudie 2008*. Leipzig, Germany: Universität Leipzig. Retrieved September 15, 2009, from www.bewegtbildstudie.de

ENDNOTES

[1] The following newspapers were analysed: Burghauser Anzeiger, Westdeutsche Zeitung, Hohenzollerische Zeitung, Sünderländer Volksfreund, Kölner Stadt-Anzeiger, Roth-Hilpoltsteiner Volkszeitung. Meinerzhagener Zeitung, Ludwigshafener Rundschau, Vilsbiburger Zeitung, Untertaunus Kurier, Wiesbadener Tagblatt, Eberbacher Nachrichten, Bote vom Untermain, Illertaler Bote, Main-Post.

[2] According to Gerhards and Pagel (2008: 159 et seqq.), 54.5 percent of the regional newspaper providers provide videos online.

[3] This for example applies to the studies of Mischel (2006), Mrazek (2007), Riefler (2007), Kansky (2008) and Lüke (2008).

[4] http://www.n-tv.de/mediathek/livestream/

[5] http://www.phoenix.de/livestream/

[6] http://zattoo.com/

[7] http://www.livestation.com/

[8] In literature, sometimes a difference is made between video hosts as sites which directly offer videos and video portals which only make reference to videos. This contribution follows the argumentation of Machill and Zenker (2007: 9) according to which the term video portals has established itself for providers such as YouTube in colloquial language and video portals are "clearly special search engines" (Machill/Zenker 2007: 9) according to the definition of Gugel and Müller

[9] (2007). Consequently, the terms video host and video portal are used as synonyms, here.

[9] http://www.youtube.com/

[10] http://www.clipfish.de/

[11] http://www.myvideo.de/

[12] This differentiation is not made by some other authors (e.g. Breunig 2007).

[13] As already mentioned above, by now, many TV stations also offer live streams – very often, they use the platform of media libraries for this. Thus, media libraries are somehow mixed forms of online television and video platforms.

[14] This study was released by the Deutsche Telekom AG. The survey was however realised by scientists.

[15] In this Wiki, German daily and weekly newspapers are systematically checked for several criteria and classified accordingly. A current overview of this Wiki can be found here: http://www.wortfeld.de/wiki/index. php/Features_von_Zeitungs-Websites_in_ Deutschland (last access: 15.09.2009). In this connection, it is important to mention that every online user can participate in this Wiki. Despite the mutual control among the users, the data cannot claim to have been collected according to scientific criteria and to be complete. This is a only problem with regard to the findings of Mischel who takes them as a basis since he may thus not claim to have observed the basic population.

[16] Zoom.in is the biggest provider in Europe and produces about 150 news videos in eleven different languages, every day. In this, it is not planned that the respective editorial team further processes the videos (Schmid 2008: 6 et seq.).

[17] The complete study is not freely available (anymore), only a summary can be found on the Internet. The author does not want to provide her complete survey upon reference to the data being outdated, in the meantime.

[18] Since the investigation shows at least a methodical deficiency (definition of the basic population not according to scientific criteria) and the further proceeding is unclear because of quotes from the summary, these results can only serve as pointers. The study is still quoted here due to the lack of comparable studies.

[19] Four common forms can be made out among empirical content analyses. Besides the frequency analysis, there is a valence analysis, the intensity analysis and the contingency analysis (Schnell et al. 2005: 408).

[20] A video is an independent, cohesive file. Since such a cohesive file may partially consist of several thematically independen parts – for example in a news broadcast which presents several topics, the sub-unit of the video contribution was introduced, here. For example, the complete news broadcast is thus a video consisting of different video contributions. This differentiation is particularly important for the analysis in chapter 4.2.

[21] If not specified otherwise, the results presented here always relate to the total number of 776 videos. Thus, videos with identical content are partially included in the investigation several times. This approach has been chosen because, from the point of view of the recipients, it does usually not matter whether a video is also offered anywhere else. Moreover, the sample here was generated from the basic population of all the newspaper websites and not from the basic population of all the different existing videos.

[22] Sometimes, surveys were integrated in contributions and were then allocated to this category.

Chapter 22
Impact of IDM on Healthcare

Lena Stephanie
Nanyang Technological University, Singapore

Thomas Srinivasan
Nanyang Technological University, Singapore

Apurva Deepak Lawale
Nanyang Technological University, Singapore

ABSTRACT

This chapter discusses the impact of interactive digital media (IDM) on the healthcare industry. An overview of the e-health marketplace and business models is provided through a blended approach utilizing two conceptual frameworks, namely ADVISOR and Value Net. Significant macro-environmental forces impacting e-health initiatives are identified through PESTLE analysis for the reason that it is crucial for an e-health firm's business model success and sustainability, to strategize and align itself favorably with these powerful forces of change.

INTRODUCTION

"E-revolution" has transformed the conventional landscape of business and consumerism, as is evident through the successful take-offs of various e-initiatives over the last couple of decades. Today, the Internet has become entwined with most aspects of our day-to-day living, facilitating communication, entertainment, education, banking and a host of ecommerce transactions online. The power of the Internet is so vast that its use has become pervasive and routined in only about 7 years. Comparatively, television took about 26 years to achieve a similar mass penetration among consumers in the US (Chin, 2000).

Despite the Internet having revolutionized most walks of our lives, its foray into healthcare has been relatively tardy (Hill & Powell, 2009). Healthcare is a late arrival to e-commerce, although most analysts agree that the long-term potential for online health is still enormous (Dyer & Thompson, 2001). An estimated 18.3 million US adults purchasing health-related products online

DOI: 10.4018/978-1-61350-147-4.ch022

in 2006, and the rise in the US population looking for health information online from 10 million in 2000 to 100 million in early 2007[1], are testimony to healthcare consumers' insatiable need for easier and greater access to health information and services (Wen & Tan, 2003). Coupled with this is the policy imperative of various governments to reform healthcare through sizable investments in health information technology (HIT) to accelerate improvements in healthcare, (c.f. Clancy et al., 2009). Such healthcare trends are not just confined to the US, but are gaining traction globally, as can be evidenced by the plethora of e-health or telehealth or telemedicine projects that have stemmed worldwide in the recent years[2].

E-health, which is the integration of telehealth[3] or telemedicine technologies with the Internet, is deemed to improve efficiencies, develop new markets, reduce costs, and enhance the quality and value of health services delivery (Wen & Tan, 2003). "E-health is an emerging field in the intersection of medical informatics, public health and business, referring to health services and information delivered or enhanced through the Internet and related technologies" and "encompasses more than just "Internet and Medicine"" (Eysenbach, 2001, p 20). E-health comes with the promise of improved quality of care, reduced costs, reduced medical errors, increased efficiency of information flow and most importantly, empowerment of healthcare consumers in their healthcare decisions.

In this paper, we will attempt to (1) understand the evolving e-health ecosystem, and (2) analyze the impacts of the macro-environment on this "disruptive innovation", which is set to revolutionize the way healthcare will be provided and consumed. To achieve these objectives, our research will focus on the following research questions:

1.   What is the current status of the e-health ecosystem?
2.   What are the impacts of the macro-environmental forces on e-health and their significance?

Finally, in our Conclusion, we will discuss the prospects of e-health gaining acceptance and becoming a way of life eventually.

BACKGROUND

The E-Health Ecosystem

In this section we present a synthesis of key observations made during the course of our review of diverse literature discussing the e-health ecosystem from different perspectives.

Health data will be the asset that drives efficient, high-quality, value-based, evidence-focused medicine (Neupert, 2009). The opportunity for an e-health firm is in evidence-based medicine which is defined as "the conscientious, explicit and judicious use of current best evidence in making decisions about the care of individual patients" (Sackett et al., 1996, p 71). To tap this opportunity, an e-health firm must harness the combined power of technology and the Internet, to create a patient-centric health network that is seamlessly connected for exchange and reuse of health information. A totally "connected" health network is one that encompasses all the key stakeholders and provides a common platform for interfaces and transactions among them.

An e-health ecosystem broadly comprises four key stakeholders namely e-health providers (e.g. hospitals), e-health vendors (e.g. pharmacies), e-health payers (e.g. insurance companies) and e-health consumers (e.g. patients). E-health systems facilitate quick and easy access to information for all stakeholders involved in e-healthcare processes, such as patients, physicians, healthcare providers, healthcare vendors, and healthcare insurers (Wen & Tan, 2003). A typical e-health ecosystem is depicted in Figure 1.

We infer that in terms of information flow, the stakeholders on the e-health network primarily assume 3 roles: while some play the role of "suppliers" of health information to the network, some

Figure 1. E-health ecosystem

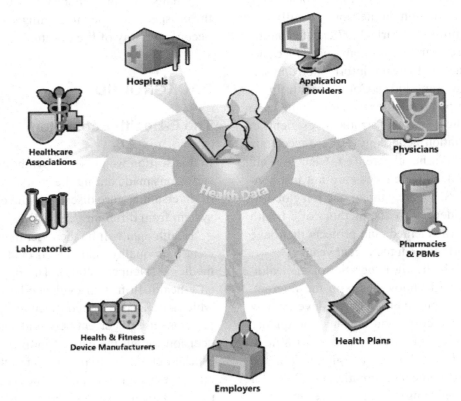

play the role of "consumers" of health information from the network. Yet another role is that of "complementors" played by some stakeholders whose information on healthcare product or service offerings complete the healthcare management continuum for the "consumers" e.g. third-party vendors. These three roles are not mutually exclusive and may often overlap. For example, the information "supplied" by one physician in the form of Electronic Health Records (EHRs)[4] may be "consumed" by another physician in the network, who has also "supplied" health information of some form to the network.

The e-health firm itself plays the role of an infomediary, syndicating[5], aggregating[6] and distributing[7] health information in its central repository to provide added value to its network members. It takes "four forms, each suited to a different purpose and having its own revenue and cost structure. These forms, are portals, connectivity sites, business-to-business applications, and business-to-consumer applications" (Parente, 2000, p 90).

In summing up, we draw the inference that an e-health firm brings together various stakeholders who otherwise would belong to a highly fragmented market place, and facilitates seamless business-to-consumer (B2C), business-to-business (B2B) and consumer-to-consumer (C2C) ecommerce transactions among them. Revenues for the e-health firm may be generated through advertisements, subscription fees, transaction fees, B2C, B2B and / or C2C ecommerce. We list scenarios for each of the possible revenue sources for an e-health firm in Table 1.

Impact of "e" on Healthcare and Significance

Opportunities and Challenges

Presently, health information of a patient is typically recorded on paper which may be scattered across different healthcare providers, and thus be disconnected from the network. There is a serious risk that any updates or changes in any of these records might not come to the attention of the treating healthcare provider, thus compromising the quality of care the patient receives (Middleton, 2008). Even today, many physicians collect and process patient information in "an antediluvian manner" (Hill & Powell, 2009), without the benefit of HIT. However, all this is set to change with the arrival of e-health which promises to put consumers in control of their health information and healthcare management, while creating new business opportunities for all stakeholders on its network through the connectivity it fosters. Rising costs in healthcare, increased global competitions and rapid advances in networking and telecom-

munications promise to close the gaps between digital technologies including e-commerce, and healthcare services delivery (Wen & Tan, 2003). Notwithstanding the promises it brings, e-health, like any other high-technology environment, is not devoid of challenges. "The dawn of health e- commerce presents intriguing opportunities and formidable market barriers" (Parente, 2000, p 101). In Table 2, we have attempted to collate the various opportunities and challenges brought forth by e-health as we believe this will help facilitate an understanding of the implications of e-health on the macro-environment.

Macro-Environmental Scan

In order to understand the multi-faceted implications of e-health, it is necessary to scan the macro-environment in which an e-health firm operates. A good grasp of these implications will enable an e-health enterprise to position itself as a viable business model with benefits for all stakeholders on its network.

Table 1. E-health revenue sources

Revenue Source	A Typical Scenario
Advertisements	The e-health firm may sell web inventory to e-health vendors who wish to promote their products or services to the e-health network members through advertisements e.g. it may charge the vendors on a Cost Per Mille (CPM) basis.
Subscription Fees	The e-health firm may offer premium services to special interest groups on a subscription basis e.g. it may provide updates on new medical technologies to surgeons for a yearly subscription fee.
Transaction Fees	The e-health firm may exact transaction fees when it moves data over the Internet from one network member to another e.g. it may move a patient's medical history from a physician to a pharmacy for a transaction fee.
Business-to-Consumer Ecommerce	The e-health firm may facilitate sale of healthcare products or services by a business on its network to consumers on its network for a commission e.g. it may earn a commission when a patient (consumer) purchases medicines from a pharmacy (business). Additionally, it may also charge the business a listing fee for inclusion in its network.
Business-to-Business Ecommerce	The e-health firm may facilitate sale of healthcare products or services by a business on its network to another business on its network for a commission e.g. it may earn a commission when a hospital (business) purchases refurbished medical equipment from another hospital (business) through online auctions. Additionally, it may also charge the businesses a listing fee for inclusion in its network.
Consumer-to-Consumer Ecommerce	The e-health firm may facilitate sale of healthcare products by a consumer on its network to another consumer on its network for a commission e.g. it may earn a commission when a healthcare consumer purchases a used treadmill from another healthcare consumer through online auctions.

Table 2. E-health stakeholders, opportunities and challenges

E-health Stakeholder	Opportunities	Challenges
Healthcare Consumers (Patients, the ultimate beneficiaries)	• Ubiquitous access to health information • Empowerment to make informed healthcare decisions • C2C business opportunities	• Barriers to access e-health due to the digital divide • Reluctance on account of privacy and confidentiality issues • Loss of "face-to-face" interaction with healthcare providers
Healthcare Providers	• Tele-healthcare delivery • Improved operational efficiencies, reduced costs and enhanced quality of healthcare • New business opportunities created by the e-health network • Improved efficiency in procurement of items	• Reluctance to transition from paper-based to electronic records • Huge IT infrastructure investment costs • Loss of "face-to-face" interaction with patients • Transfer of control from providers to patients in healthcare decisions
Healthcare Vendors	• B2C and B2B business opportunities • Direct access to healthcare providers resulting in decreased marketing costs	• Apprehension about security breaches on sensitive data • Withholding of information to safeguard product /service strategy from competition
Healthcare Payers	• Improved efficiency in payment processing resulting in cost savings • Data aggregation facilitating research and targeted information delivery • Easier implementation of healthcare regulations	• Reluctance to re-engineer processes to adapt to the digital marketplace • Huge IT infrastructure investment costs

At the outset, a country's political climate must favor e-health implementation. "Electronically connecting with patients is a particularly challenging frontier where technical hurdles are generally exceeded by political, legal, workflow, and other barriers" (Joslyn, 2001, p 73). A national-level agenda is mandatory for e-health to become a reality (Hill & Powell, 2009). However, such an agenda from the government will depend on the availability of national resources and the choices of the government in distribution of these resources. Even if an agenda were to exist, successful adoption of e-health may require a firm and controlling role by the government. The project should be imperatively embedded in the existing health structure (Pierre, 2009). A precursor to a government's e-health agenda however, should be a commitment to bridge the digital divide within the nation for successful implementation of the initiative.

An e-health system is touted to improve efficiencies while reducing costs for all stakeholders. With improved efficiencies, the rate of medical errors will reduce, in turn reducing potential litigation costs. However, building such a system calls for huge investments and huge maintenance costs. Moreover, further costs may come in the form of licensing fees and upgrades. Despite the heavy investment, there is no guarantee on returns as there is lack of demonstrable evidence on the long term sustainability of an e-health system. It is impossible to assess the extent to which telemedicine represents a sensible priority for health investment (British Medical Journal, 2002)[8]. Other economic factors influencing the uptake of e-health by providers are the drop in the number of billable events due to improved efficiencies offered by the system, small scale that cannot economically benefit much from the network and finally, the notion of "first mover disadvantage". Whichever health system (A or B) moves first on adoption incurs a higher fixed cost due to implementations of trial-and-error than the second adopter (Hill & Powell, 2009).

Patient engagement is critical to the success and sustainability of an e-health system. "As patients awaken to their role as stewards of their medical information, HIE[9] will only be as good as patients' willingness to allow their data to be shared in ways that clinicians find valuable" (Tripathi et al, 2009, p 435). A deterrent to patient participation in the system is concerned over the security of personal health information – will this sensitive information be safeguarded from co-workers, employers, lenders, marketers, etc. on the Internet? In the words of Antonopoulos (2009), "a lot of the privacy and security we enjoy with respect to our medical records is not just a result of the Health Insurance Portability and Accountability Act – it is a result of the enormous inconvenience imposed by the mounds of paper". Health data being highly sensitive, consumers and healthcare providers will only share it if they trust that the privacy of the data will be protected (Neupert, 2009). Privacy and security of health data should therefore be critical design factors for any e-health system. Another deterrent is the removal of the "interpersonal" component from the doctor-patient relationship. E-health depersonalizes this relationship and removes the physicality and compassion from the healing arts (Wen & Tan, 2003). Other social barriers are the digital divide and users' lack of experience with technologies.

Although the technology behind e-health promises a "connected" way to improve customer experience, reduce costs and increase revenues, its multi-million dollar implementation is an alarming proposition for stakeholders. A further deterrent is the rapidly changing technologies which may render an existing system obsolete and necessitate expensive upgrades. Lack of standards in the industry also poses a challenge to successful technological implementation of e-health, as it is no mean task to get the various disparate systems to talk to each other sans set industry standards. The consequence is a mesh of systems that cannot communicate with one another making sharing of information among the e-health stakeholders difficult, and the ultimate goal of making a national health information system rather distant

(Bulgiba, 2004). Other technological barriers to e-health take-off are lack of success stories demonstrating technological superiority and long term sustainability. It is also imperative for an e-health system to incorporate sound security measures to ensure confidentiality, integrity and availability of health information.

Several ambiguities exist over the legal implications of e-health services. Different countries or regions or states have different privacy laws which make interoperability among healthcare stakeholders a tough proposition. For example, Georgia and Florida have laws that preclude HCPs[10] from viewing results of laboratory tests not ordered by them (Dart, 2006). It may be assumed that e-health, just like any other "e" initiative, would transcend geographical boundaries, but this has serious implications. For example an online pharmacy may be permitted to supply a medicine over-the-counter in one country, but the same medicine could be a prescription drug in another country. Likewise, there are also legal issues surrounding tele-monitoring of patients – who will undertake the quality of service guarantee, the healthcare provider or the monitoring service provider? Data ownership is yet another unresolved issue. What access should patients have to EMRs[11] combined with PHRs[12]? Who will take responsibility for ensuring that PHRs/EMRs contain current information, since the PHRs/EMRs are shared (Vere-Jones, 2005).

With ICT being the main pillar of an e-health firm, and most tasks accomplished online and "tele", one could argue that this is a pro-environment initiative that helps cut down the carbon footprint. However, this advantage is somewhat countered by the green house gas emissions from the use of hardware in data-intensive e-health ventures. Therefore, the Web is not only a crusader but also a culprit when it comes to energy use, with server farms and data centers burning mountains of CO_2, to keep machines cool (Martin, 2008). Therefore the environmental implications of an e-health initiative are highly relevant in the current climate of environmental consciousness, and must be taken into consideration by an e-health firm. Technology giants like Microsoft[13] and Google[14] are instrumental in reversing the greenhouse effects caused by their heavy use of energy, and saving the precious finite natural resources that are rapidly being depleted. E-health firms should take cues from the best practices adopted by these IT giants.

CONCEPTUAL FRAMEWORK

In our Discussion section, we will utilize two frameworks to analyze the e-health marketplace.

Framework I is a blend of the ADVISOR Business Model (Sharma et al, 2008)[15] and the Value Net (Brandenburger & Nalebuff, 1995). The ADVISOR framework is an extension of the VISOR Business Model which was created by the Institute for Communication Technology and Management in the Marshall School of Business at the University of Southern California. ADVISOR adds 2 components namely Adaptations to Consumers and Disruptions, to the VISOR Business Model which in itself comprises five components: Value, Interface, Service Platform, Organizing Model and Revenue/Cost Sharing. The Value Net model is a game theoretic approach to business and focuses on the four principal participants that influence any firm: Suppliers, Customers, Substitutors (Competitors) and Complementors. While ADVISOR focuses on defining the elements of a business model for an interactive digital media (IDM) firm, Value Net focuses on how the four participants in the game of business should shape their strategies.

Framework II is PESTLE, a mnemonic for Political, Economic, Social, Technological, Legal and Environmental, used to analyze the external macro-environment in which a firm operates and to understand its impact on the firm. Such understanding will help a firm strategize to align itself positively with the powerful macro-environmental forces of change.

DISCUSSION

ADVISOR: Value Net Blended Approach

The starting point of this discussion is the construction of the Value Net for an e-health firm focusing on the primary healthcare continuum[16] (P-HCC) market players. At the primary level of the healthcare continuum, the market players use health information to provide patient care directly or indirectly by supporting direct providers of patient care. On the contrary, secondary market players are "users of health information in roles outside of direct and indirect patient care activity. They may include research, monitoring, and respective public and private agency work." (Busch, 2008, p 16). Following these guidelines, the primary healthcare players are defined in Table 3.

The players in the primary healthcare continuum having been identified, and their roles defined, the e-health Value Net is represented in Figure 2.

"Suppliers" are identified as Providers and Payers, who play a direct role in a patient's Financial Case Management and Clinical Case Management during a health episode. "Customers" are identified as Patients, the ultimate beneficiaries of e-health, and "Complementors" as Third-party Vendors. As for "Substitutors", we have identified two categories namely Bricks and Clicks. "Bricks" represents offline Provider, Payer and Third-party entities, while "Clicks" represents online albeit silo or disconnected Provider, Payer and Third-party entities. We have refrained from including "other e-health firms" under "Substitutors" because our objective is to evaluate the e-health initiative per se, as a disruptive innovation.

Table 3. Primary healthcare continuum market players

Players	Role
Patients	Recipients of health services, labeled by their financial status: insured or uninsured, privately or publicly insured, with or without financial assets, etc. for the purposes of Financial Case Management[17] and Clinical Case Management[18].
Providers	Any clinical setting or professional staff that designs, implements, and/or executes any healthcare initiative which may be part of a wellness or illness program
Third-Party Vendors	A large group of diverse market players who play a supporting role to the Providers in their provision of healthcare. These players include medical equipment vendors, pharmaceutical vendors, transportation services, laboratories, legal systems, billing agents etc.
Payers	An entity that processes the claims payment transactions of healthcare episodes on behalf of plan sponsors. A plan sponsor is an entity that funds a health program – private insurance plans, government-sponsored plans, employer-sponsored plans etc.

Information Source: Electronic health records: an audit and internal control guide / Rebecca S. Busch

The next step is to analyze the business models of each of these Value Net players to understand how they bring added value to the e-health network. This will be accomplished by merging the e-health Value Net with the ADVISOR framework described in Section 3 (Table 4).

The E-Health Marketplace: Significant Macro-environmental Forces

Utilizing the PESTLE framework, Table 5 enlists the macro-environmental forces that are bound to have a significant impact on an e-health initiative. An e-health firm must proactively identify these forces, and position itself favorably armed with the right strategies, to ensure longer term sustainability of its business model.

FUTURE RESEARCH

Future research may focus on validating the key players in the e-health ecosystem, and modeling the major digital flows among them. An analysis of the values created and values captured by them on the e-health network would also serve useful to understand if the ecosystem is fair, efficient, stable and therefore sustainable.

Figure 2. E-health value net

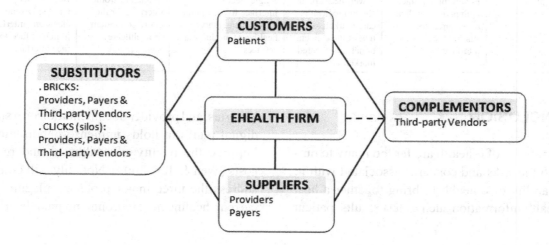

Table 4. E-health: ADVISOR-value net blend

	Suppliers	E-health Firm	Complementors	Customers	Substitutors
Value Proposition	Seamless financial and clinical case management	Ubiquitous healthcare management, patient empowerment	Access to complementary healthcare products and services via a single platform	Personal health records, feedback to system	**Bricks:** Privacy and confidentiality of health information **Clicks:** Privacy and confidentiality of online health information
Interface	E-Health firm's GUI	Web portal with intuitive GUI	E-Health firm's GUI	E-Health firm's GUI	**Bricks:** Face-to-face **Clicks:** Silo, disconnected business portals
Service Platform	IT infrastructure to create health information conforming to recognized interoperability standards	IT Infrastructure that supports secure connectivity among network members	IT infrastructure to support secure connectivity with e-health network members	E-health firm's IT infrastructure	**Bricks:** Physical infrastructures **Clicks:** IT infrastructure (software & hardware)
Organizing Model	B2C and B2B e-commerce	B2C, B2B and C2C ecommerce	B2C and B2B e-commerce	C2C e-commerce	**Bricks:** Offline B2C and B2B commerce **Clicks:** B2C and B2B ecommerce
Revenues	Revenues from targeted sale of healthcare products and services	Ad-revenues, subscription fees, listing fees, data transaction fees, commission from B2C, B2B and C2C ecommerce on the network	Revenues from targeted sale of complementary healthcare products and services	Revenues generated through sale / auction of used healthcare products	**Bricks:** Revenues from sale of healthcare products and services offline **Clicks:** Revenues from sale of healthcare products and services online
Adaptations to Users	Health episode management tailored to a patient's financial and clinical background	Adaptability[19] and adaptivity[20] of health information to network members' needs	Complementary healthcare products and services tailored to a patient's treatment regimen	NA	**Bricks:** Face-to-face, personalized healthcare services **Clicks:** Adaptability and adaptivity of disparate health information without connectivity
Disruptions	Electronic interface with patients in lieu of resource-consuming face-to-face interface	A well-networked electronic healthcare marketplace in lieu of the conventional, fragmented marketplace	Single electronic interface for the gamut of complementary healthcare products and services	Single electronic interface for the entire continuum of healthcare management	**Bricks:** NA **Clicks:** Disparate electronic interfaces in lieu of face-to-face interfaces

CONCLUSION

The benefits of e-health are far too many to outweigh the risks and concerns associated with it. The ability of e-health to bring together a host of health information such as test results, patient histories, and provider documentation on a single digital platform holds immense opportunity to improve the quality of healthcare and reduce costs (Wen & Tan, 2003). Not only will e-health address the three major problems plaguing the current healthcare environment namely acces-

Table 5. E-health: PESTLE analysis

POLITICAL	ECONOMIC
• Availability of national resources • Policy makers' attitude and priorities • Presence of a national-level agenda • Regulatory stance: assertive Vs passive • Commitment to bridge national digital divide	• Heavy IT investment, maintenance, licensing and upgrading costs • Lack of demonstrable evidence of long term economic sustainability • First mover disadvantage • Drop in number of billable events for healthcare providers • Low leveraging potential for small scale healthcare providers
SOCIAL	TECHNOLOGICAL
• Security concerns about personal health information • Depersonalized provider-patient relationship • Digital divide • Lack of experience with technologies	• Heavy investment costs • Rapidly changing technologies • Lack of industry standards • Lack of success stories showcasing technological superiority • Need for stringent security measures in system design
LEGAL	ENVIRONMENTAL
• Disparate privacy laws challenging system interoperability • Cross-border, transnational implications • Ambiguity over access and responsibility levels for EHRs and PHRs • Accountability issues in the event of healthcare lapse	• Greenhouse gas emissions from hardware use • Need for pro-environment research and initiatives

sibility, quality and cost (Hill & Powell, 2009), but will also pave the way for invaluable medical research made possible through the aggregation and exploration of health information (Raghupathi & Kesh, 2009).

Whether e-health will become a reality and realize all these benefits, will, to a large extent depend on a national-level agenda. If such an agenda is non-existent or non-enforceable, "public awareness of the price of failing to develop one may be the best hope of breaking the grid lock" (Hill & Powell, 2009, p 274).

Therefore, the significance of "engaging the trust and willingness of all participants to share and exchange medical records" (Tripathi et al, 2009, p 442) for e-health to gain traction, cannot be emphasized enough. E-health holds great promise for empowerment of patients who are "the largest and most important stakeholder group" (Hill & Powell, 2009, p 270). In the not-too-distant future, healthcare consumers may have complete freedom to make healthcare choices in such a way as to satisfy their unique needs for quality, service, and price (Joslyn, 2001). Opportunities abound for other stakeholders as well who will soon be in a position to realize true value from

e-health by leveraging their massive stores of patient and health information to target and give consumers just the products or services they want via a convenient and easy-to-use interface (Wen & Tan, 2003).

As e-health evolves and its stakeholders reap the benefits and realize success, demand for the platform will emerge making e-health implementations easier and more welcome. It is probably a matter of time before healthcare is consumed the "e" way similar to other precedents like entertainment, education, banking etc.

REFERENCES

Antonopoulos, A. (2009). Digital healthcare brings opportunities, risks. *New World (New Orleans, La.), 26*(12), 20.

Brandenburger, A. M., & Nalebuff, B. J. (1995). The right game: Use game theory to shape strategy. *Harvard Business Review, 73*(4), 57–71.

Bulgiba, A. M. (2004). Information Technology in health care – What the future holds. *Asia-Pacific Journal of Public Health, 16*(1), 64–71. doi:10.1177/101053950401600111

Busch, R. S. (2008). *Electronic health records: An audit and internal control guide.* New Jersey: John Wiley & Sons, Inc.

Chin, T. (2000). The e-impact. *American Medical News, 43*(48), 18–19.

Clancy, C. M., Anderson, K. M., & White, P. J. (2009). Investing in health information infrastructure: Can it help achieve health reform? *Health Affairs, 28*(2), 478–482. doi:10.1377/hlthaff.28.2.478

Dart, B. (2006). *Panel weighs patient privacy rights.* Cox News Service.

Dyer, K. A., & Thompson, C. D. (2001). Medical Internet ethics: A field in evolution . In Patel, V. (Eds.), *MedInfo 2001* (pp. 1287–1291). Amsterdam, The Netherlands: IOS Press.

Eysenbach, G. (2001). What is e-health? *Journal of Medical Internet Research, 3*(2), 20. doi:10.2196/jmir.3.2.e20

Frias-Martinez, E., Chen, S. Y., & Liu, X. (2009). Evaluation of a personalized digital library based on cognitive styles: Adaptivity vs. adaptability. *International Journal of Information Management, 29*, 48–56. doi:10.1016/j.ijinfomgt.2008.01.012

Hill, J. W., & Powell, P. (2009). The national healthcare crisis: Is e-health a key solution? *Business Horizons, 52*, 265–277. doi:10.1016/j.bushor.2009.01.006

Joslyn, J. S. (2001). Healthcare e-commerce: Connecting with patients. *Journal of Healthcare Information Management, 15*(1), 73–84.

Kvedar, J. C. (2008). *Connected health: Using patient-centric technologies to improve quality, access and efficiency.* Presented at Patient-Centred Computing and eHealth: State of the Field, Boston, MA.

Martin, R. (2008). Can the internet save the planet? *Information Week.* Retrieved April 20, 2009, from http://www.informationweek.com/news/internet/showArticle.jhtml?articleID=205601559&pgno=1

Middleton, B. (2008). *EHRs, PHRs, and HIE: Impact on patient safety, healthcare quality and costs.* Presented at Patient-Centred Computing and eHealth: Transforming Healthcare Quality, Boston, MA.

Neupert, P. (2009). Re-inventing healthcare. *Health Management Technology, 30*(3), 8–10.

Parente, S. T. (2000). Beyond the hype: A taxonomy of e-health business models. *Health Affairs, 19*(6), 89–102. doi:10.1377/hlthaff.19.6.89

Pierre, B. (2009). *Assessing the opportunities and the pertinence of e-health in developing countries.* European Commission Information Society and Media.

Raghupathi, W., & Kesh, S. (2009). Designing electronic health records versus total digital health systems: A systemic analysis. *Systems Research and Behavioral Science, 26*, 63–79. doi:10.1002/sres.918

Riva, G. (2000). From telehealth to e-health: Internet and distributed virtual reality in health care. *Cyberpsychology & Behavior, 3*(6), 989–998. doi:10.1089/109493100452255

Sackett, D. L., Rosenberg, W. M. C., Gray, J. A. M., Haynes, R. B., & Richardson, W. S. (1996). Evidence based medicine: What it is and what it isn't: It's about integrating individual clinical expertise and the best external evidence. *BMJ: British Medical Journal, 312*(7023), 71–72.

The Economist. (2005, April 30). The no computer virus – IT in the health-care industry. *The Economist, 375*(8424), 72.

Tripathi, M., Delano, D., Lund, B., & Rudolph, L. (2009). Engaging patients for health information exchange. *Health Affairs, 28*(2), 435–443. doi:10.1377/hlthaff.28.2.435

Vere-Jones, E. (2005, July 14). Confidentiality divides doctors. *Hospital Doctor, 9.*

Wen, H. J., & Tan, J. (2003). *The evolving face of telemedicine & e-health: Opening doors and closing gaps in e-health services opportunities & challenges.* IEEE, HICSS'03.

ENDNOTES

[1] Manhattan Research LLC Survey, 2007

[2] Telemedicine program at BUAP, Mexico; e-healthcare to army in Himalayan mountains, India; Wireless patient monitoring in an ambulance, Japan; Arizona telemedicine network, USA

[3] Telehealth technologies refer to "information and communication technologies for the exchange of health-related information" (Riva, 2000)

[4] An electronic record of health-related information on an individual that conforms to nationally recognized interoperability standards

[5] Syndication: Proactive streaming of digital content to alternate and repeat customers

[6] Aggregation: Collection of digital content from a variety of sources

[7] Distribution: Conveying digital content to consumers' devices

[8] British Medical Journal 324 [15 June, 2002] 1437

[9] Health Information Exchange (HIE) is defined as the mobilization of healthcare information electronically across organizations within a region or community.

[10] HCP: Healthcare Provider

[11] An electronic record of health-related information on an individual that can be created, gathered, managed, and consulted by authorized clinicians and staff within one health care organization

[12] An electronic record of health-related information on an individual that conforms to nationally recognized interoperability standards and that can be drawn from multiple sources while being managed, shared, and controlled by the individual

[13] Source: http://msdn.microsoft.com/en-us/architecture/dd393308.aspx

[14] Source: http://www.google.com/corporate/green/clean-energy.html

[15] Value Frameworks for Interactive Digital Media (forthcoming, to be published)

[16] Healthcare is viewed as a continuum of businesses and services, including research and development, manufacturing, distribution and actual service delivery.

[17] Discipline of creating a financial plan to meet the patient's healthcare needs (Busch, 2008)

[18] Includes current healthcare initiatives and past treatment regimes (Busch, 2008)

[19] User-controlled personalization (Frias-Martinez et al., 2009)

[20] System-controlled personalization (Frias-Martinez et al., 2009)

Chapter 23
Blended Learning:
Using IDM for University Courses

Kevin Anthony Jones
Nanyang Technological University, Singapore

ABSTRACT

This chapter is a personal account of the educational application of eLearning-IDM (eIDM), teaching an upper level software engineering course at Nanyang Technological University. It is combined with face-to-face (F2F) sessions to become a teaching and learning (T&L) approach called blended learning. Blended learning is used in the classroom to address two problems encountered in modern higher education: (1) the digital divide and (2) knowledge glut. It turns out that lectures, the way preferred by teachers (being digital immigrants) of disseminating knowledge, is not aligned with the way students (being digital natives) acquire knowledge. I have developed a ⅓ eIDM and ⅔ F2F blended learning that appeals to the learning needs of digital natives, and satisfies the teaching aspirations of digital immigrants. Current research is on scaling and extending this model, learning resources that align with a student's learning style, and more interactive and conducive interfaces for the eIDM platform.

INTRODUCTION

For some time, IDM has been offered in the curriculum of many universities, yet few have adopted it in their mainstream T&L. Instead, there are teachers here and there who have made

DOI: 10.4018/978-1-61350-147-4.ch023

the leap of becoming early adopters of eIDM in their classrooms.

I expected teaching at university to be an intensely interactive affair, with the lectures generating exciting and challenging discourse that was enjoyable and fulfilling for teachers as well as for the students. To my disappointment, students were distant and disinterested, mostly apathetic to the subject material, and completely passive in their learning. In fact, it was a general problem experienced by most of my colleagues. So, I subsequently attempted several innovations of the material, lectures, and homework review periods (a.k.a., tutorials). However, after several semesters, it was clear that these innovations were ineffective at increasing the students' interactivity with the subject material.

The breakthrough came after I completed a certificate course in higher education. In that course, we studied student interactivity in learning and how it could be increased with eLearning. So, eLearning was the "silver bullet" [1] I sought, but incorporating it effectively into the subject had a price: complete redesign of the existing T&L structure. To fit eLearning into the highly rigid semester schedule in a degree program, unquestionably there would have to be a trade-off with the existing T&L sessions. After exploring all the known factors, including institutional, faculty, and student expectations, I settled on a new T&L that was partly eIDM and partly F2F. Thus came into effect the very first core curriculum blended learning subject in my university (see Figure 1).

When it was first introduced to the students in the first semester of 2008, I was naturally apprehensive, given the glaring fact that the blended learning T&L was unlike anything the students had been exposed to in their degree program up to that point in time. To my relief, the new approach was cautiously though indubitably accepted by the majority of students. Moreover,

Figure 1. The blended learning structure for my subject

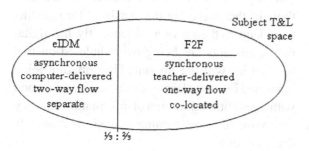

there was a noticeable increase in the students' interactivity in the subject. Since its inception till now, the blended learning has continued to deliver the results I was looking for.

It may well be that in the not too distant future, those teachers who don't adopt eIDM in their classrooms will not be employable as university faculty. That said, it is not an easy undertaking to redesign an entire T&L structure from the ground up to incorporate eIDM; it took me two years to complete the process. Furthermore, my circumstances were somewhat special in that I had been assigned for many years to one subject. Had I been shifted regularly from one subject to the next, it would have been impossible to complete the migration to the blended learning in any of the subjects.

This chapter will explain why eIDM is effective in enhancing the T&L in today's universities, and provide one approach for incorporating eIDM into a university subject, ending with a short look at nascent research into aspects of eIDM.

BACKGROUND

There are several indicators of a serious misalignment of expectations between what the teachers think they are delivering to their students and what their students are actually acquiring from it: (1) significant reduction of the sitting period for end semester examinations, (2) significant moderation upwards of final marks, (3) near-zero interactivity of the students, and (4) too short retention of previous years' subjects' material. For example, in those students' final year projects that I supervise a scant two years downstream from when they had taken my subject, they have forgotten most of its important knowledge. This sentiment is echoed by my colleagues for their subjects.

At the turn of the millennium, sociologists began discussing the "digital natives, digital immigrants" condition. Digital natives go through a deep and profound shaping of their behavior to bring them in sync with the ubiquitous computing technology they have been born into. In contrast, digital immigrants do not sync, but rather adopt the technology similar to taking on a habit. In the context of university, the students are digital natives, and the teachers are digital immigrants.

University teachers have many concerns about adopting eIDM in their classrooms, such as "programming it would be just too much work" or "receiving low teaching feedback if the students didn't like it" or "eLearning would make them redundant" or "eIDM won't work in their subject". Actually, in all the literature from early adopters, none reported that eIDM didn't improve the T&L. Nevertheless, university teachers are not certified like primary and secondary education teachers are, and thus, have the invested authority to adopt whatever T&L approaches they feel are appropriate for their subjects. And for most, lecture is the most appropriate: ponderous PowerPoint presentation with the slides projected in rapid succession during a one hour period. These teachers may think they are following a technique originating in the world's first universities and that has continually proven its effectiveness since. But, I suspect that the lectures of old had far more debate and exchange of ideas than what exists in the modern university lecture theatre. Notwithstanding, even the scheduling standard of one hour for a lecture has no pedagogical justification. Evidence suggests that T&L should be limited to shorter periods to be truly effective.

While their teachers continue to deny eIDM in the classroom, students have eagerly embraced it in their personal lives and more. The enormity of the students' embrace of ubiquitous computing cannot be overemphasized. It is my estimate that a typical university student spends five or more hours a day immersed in the technology for his or her own pursuits. Digital natives expect immediate results in their learning; what they want must be ready when they want it. When acquiring knowledge, they expect it to be in a form such that it can be easily assimilated. Hence, much

of the foundation knowledge or thought pillars behind the information are not accessed. Digital natives consume small "chunks" of knowledge by executing broad-based surface searches and then clicking-to-launch. In other words, they practice interactivity by pushing buttons and manipulating screens in ubiquitous computing devices. I also believe that digital natives are constantly multi-tasking, with multiple computer applications running at once, or several devices operating simultaneously. Despite this, they are surprisingly less productive, with each task being done only superficially. It is not surprising that my expectations of a lot of students are not going to be met by the prevalent lecturing.

Behind this divide between digital natives-immigrants is a knowledge glut arising out of the accelerating growth in technology that we presently enjoy. The amount of knowledge available for transfer to today's student is far beyond what existed 20 years ago, and this is still growing. One would expect that making all this new knowledge available to the learner is a happy problem. However, when coupled with the digital divide, this "cup of knowledge that runneth over" is just too much for most of our digital natives to drink from.

Likely the most disruptive repercussion of knowledge glut in the subject material is the inadequate time given to the learner for knowledge acquisition. A lot of university teachers feel compelled to cram as much as possible into their lectures, lest their students miss out on any of this new and cutting edge knowledge. If asked by management to reduce their subject content, the first things these same teachers cut from the teaching sessions are the foundation topics; it is thought that these are the "easiest" for students to pick up on their own. Consequently, the digital native students are being overwhelmed on two fronts. First with the amount of information being crammed into the classroom sessions, and second with the additional amount of information that they are expected to be learning on their own outside the classroom.

How have the students coped with this situation? The universal response has been to skip the lectures. Attendance rates in the majority of our university's classrooms, and in many universities elsewhere, have taken a serious downturn. In reaction to this situation, many universities offer video recordings of the lectures to the students. Unfortunately, provision of these lectures appears to encourage even more students to forgo the lectures, since videos can be replayed, and viewing is at the time and place of the student's choice, thereby providing reclamation of time otherwise lost in traveling to and from the university.

The disappearance in classrooms of note taking, and teachers not asking questions of the students and vice versa, are the most vivid indicators of the significant decline of interactivity between the teacher and the students. The first indicator is usually attributed to the copious quantities of presentation handouts given to the students. The second may be a combination of several attributes. In large classes, the students' questions and answers (Q&A) would be inaudible without voice amplification. It could also be that certain teachers discourage Q&A by their students. It would eat away the time available for quantitative delivery of knowledge within a fixed-length learning period or lecture.

Finally, the excessive amount of information in standard lectures, delivered at a brisk pace, would be very difficult for even the brightest of students to learn effectively, let alone the normal ones. Hence, to avoid revealing their inability to adequately process information to their peers, most students would forgo asking questions during the learning period, and try to work out their uncertainties with the material in the solitude and safety from ridicule of their living quarters. Recalling that a digital native acquires knowledge by pushing buttons and manipulating screens, it is inevitable that they would simply turn right off in a T&L session where the material came at them as a verbal-visual fire hose. As per their multi-tasking nature, digital natives would conduct other tasks

during such a lecture, like "googling", "texting", and "tweeting". This is not to say that they are not willing to learn. In my opinion it is a case of the digital natives finding that the classroom is not a conducive place for their learning to be optimized. If they were fortunate enough to learn in such a setting, it would be in spite of the mismatch between what they need and what is offered.

A NEW DIRECTION

To bridge the digital divide between themselves and students and effectively deal with the knowledge, teachers have two basic options regarding lectures: (1) replace them entirely, or (2) replace only some F2F. Although eIDM is not the only replacement for F2F, it is the most viable[2]. But not the early eLearning systems - those that were slow, menu-driven, not very scalable or portable, and very passive; essentially, they were triggered to proceed in a fixed step-wise fashion by the human user pushing various command buttons. To meet our objectives, the eLearning system has to be interactive, scalable, and portable in almost any ubiquitous computing platform.

Important considerations when making your choice of option includes: (1) history and tradition of the university, (2) present faculty are digital immigrants, and (3) richness of student experience. History and tradition are cornerstones for the university, and these should be addressed with senior management[3]. It is possible that no T&L approach is as effective and substantial, as the singular authority figure in front of a sea of eager faces espousing insights and imparting wisdom beyond the ages. Universities have been practicing this kind of knowledge dispensing quite successfully for millennia; its merits transcend modernization. A lot of teachers arguing against the adoption of any eIDM in the classroom are highly competent and compelling teachers, so the choice of whether to discard or retain F2F sessions should include and not exclude them. This is especially important in team teaching, where several teachers are assigned to co-deliver the material in a subject. If some F2F T&L is retained, the digital immigrant would have some familiar practice to fall back on. Finally, each student is unique in his/her learning needs, so an effective T&L is one that is as inclusive as possible. A single T&L approach is not as likely to achieve inclusivity like two approaches would. Therefore, the best option is to adopt eIDM for part of the total T&L sessions, and retain F2F sessions for the remainder. For this option to be effective, the two approaches must be combined such that they are mutually supporting, and generate synergetic and seamless interaction.

Mutually supporting means that the two approaches must not be scheduled to operate concurrently. Conduct of the eIDM element is not explicitly scheduled, nevertheless, it must be outside of those timings explicitly reserved for the F2F element. No earnest lecturer could continue for long in a situation where all members of the audience were intently focused, not on the speaker at the front, but on their computer screens, seemingly completely oblivious to all else around them. At the same time, a student would have a tough time concentrating on some eIDM activity in the midst of a verbal presentation reverberating from the lecture theatre walls. Therefore, it is essential that these two approaches be combined as a contiguous sequence, and not concurrently.

Good communication is essential to a synergetic interaction between F2F and eIDM, however, it is conducted quite differently in each approach. In a F2F session, communication is a complex and idiosyncratic amalgamation of verbal cues, body language, and pronouncements on some presentation medium. It is constellates around the presence of the teacher, who assumes the mantle of purveyor of the knowledge. The presentation medium is an aid to the teacher, and it is completely under his/her control; it is not autonomous. Nowadays in universities, that medium is predominantly presentation slides. They overcome a major communica-

tion difficulty associated with large classrooms: equal viewability of the material by all students. In smaller classrooms, slides may be augmented or even replaced entirely by whiteboards, and to significantly lesser extent blackboards[4]. Finally, there is a great degree of leeway in the F2F T&L for on-the-fly re-explaining of any teaching point. That is, the teacher may perform several re-explanations of any part of the lecture, should he/she decide that the concept is not understood by the students. In my opinion, this capability of dynamically assessing knowledge assimilation and taking remedial action is the definitive characteristic of a F2F session.

The act and art of communication is entirely different from eIDM, where the knowledge is offered autonomously to the student, analogous to a store offering its products to a consumer. There is no physical presence of a human purveyor, only the rule-bound effrontery of a machine. So, the eIDM software has to be engineered to broadcast enough of the teacher's presence to have a discernable impact with the students. A typical instance of personification is the aforementioned lecture recordings, but a more impactful archetype of personification is scaffolding. With incisive understanding of teaching and online programming, it is possible to build scaffolding that approached the same dynamic re-delivery inherent with F2F T&L. Another challenge with eIDM is having the learning resources "tell their story" effectively and autonomously. This may still be science fiction[5], however, there is on-going research in my university into learning resources that align to a student's learning preferences, thus being more attuned to the student.

The learning space is an important factor in achieving seamless interaction. In F2F T&L, the learning space is a classroom, meaning a designated and demarcated room, physical or virtual[6], that congregates the students into one location. Naturally, this space is equipped with devices idiosyncratic to the presentation medium. However, as they are purpose-built and cannot all be effectively installed in one room and the devices that are installed serve to demark the room's utilization. Another demarcation coincident with a classroom is time. As the room can only be used by one teacher for one subject at a time, its usage has to be scheduled. In other words, the effectiveness of the T&L is subordinate to the time of day it is scheduled to occur. With ubiquitous computing, the learning space can be anywhere and anytime that the student can access the learning network. The students enjoy better learning when it is anywhere-because it suits their digital native needs.

BLENDED LEARNING MODEL

Blended learning is a mix – where the elements, though combined, still retain their individual identities – of T&L approaches. But it is not just a witch's brew of different approaches thrown into some existing teaching outline. It embodies a synergy of those different approaches into one that is more effective than each conducted separately. There is nothing in the definition that specifically dictates the combined elements are F2F and eLearning (specifically eIDM)[7], however, this is nowadays the most commonly accepted connotation of the phrase. F2F is any session between teacher and students that is synchronous, located in one classroom, helmed by the teacher, and sustains a one-way flow of information from the teacher to the students via a verbal and visual presentation. These F2F sessions can be guest presentations, laboratory experiments, lectures, seminars, and tutorials; they can also be videoconferences and webcasts. eIDM is any session between computer and students that is asynchronous, not located in any common venue, anywhere there is access to the digital learning network, helmed by a computer, and sustains a two-way flow of information.

There is a high risk in being an early adopter, which I mitigated by following a simple and straightforward conversion process. Key tension points were resolved as and when they became evident during each stage of the process. My conversion process consists of four stages. First, set the objectives, conduct, and assessment for the F2F element of the blend, and assign an estimate of learning time required. Second, set the objectives, conduct, and assessment for the eIDM element of the blend, and assign an estimate of learning time required. Third, connect the learning outcomes of the elements in the blend to create a seamless integration. Fourth, build all the learning and control resources to populate and manage the elements in the blend.

In my university, the standard weekly T&L sessions are lecture, tutorial, and lab, with the number of hours allocated to each being respectively three, one and two. Hereafter, I refer to the weekly hour allocation as a tuple having the initial value "{3,1,2}". The learning objectives for these standard T&L session are as follows. The lecture introduces all the concepts and activities, and fixes the breadth of the material that is examinable. The tutorial applies select concepts towards solving a few small problems with fixed input sets; the student is expected to derive the solution prior and present in class. The laboratory practices several concepts towards solving a much larger and open-ended problem; the student is expected to work on the solution in the lab. An online course registration system assigns each of the students in the subject cohort into smaller groups that are loaded into timetable slots for each of the three session types such that they do not clash with any other subjects. So, the initial tension point was ensuring that the new T&L would not impede the operation of the existing registration system. Accordingly, I decided to retain the weekly three-session structure, and have the eIDM element replace one or more of the three sessions. Additionally, this allowed me to declare the blended learning structure in the form of the standard weekly hour allocation tuple, which greatly facilitated my reporting to management at the end of the conversion.

With that, I commenced the conversion process with the first stage being the design of the F2F element. I chose the richest and most interactive activities for the F2F element: analysing concepts in-depth, assessing summatively my students' progress, mentoring, and reviewing. To that end, I assigned the tutorial and lab time to the F2F element – but not the lectures – evaluating the weekly hour tuple as "$\{0,1,2\}$". Now began the detailed shaping of the learning objectives and delivery of the chosen F2F sessions.

The lab went into to the F2F element with no changes whatsoever. Having been completely redesigned a few years earlier, the lab is the most up-to-date and effective T&L session in the subject. The problem in the lab's learning objective is to build a large distributed-processing application that simulates a public bus service. It is conducted in teams comprising five to twelve members, with one member designated as the team leader. Each team is responsible to plan, build, and test one of seven to ten components that make up the distributed software. The formative assessment is weekly, and based on the verbal presentation by select students on the achievements and work in progress of their team. The summative assessment is at the end of the term, and evaluates the student's individual effort in his/her document submissions, plus the team effort in a one hour product demonstration and critique session.

Unlike the lab, the existing tutorial was the least effective T&L session. The students were rarely prepared and passively accepted the stock answer without discussion. So, I created a new T&L session, which I called "seminar", to fit into the one-hour slot originally held by the tutorial. The seminar is a bridge between the F2F and eIDM elements, incorporating both in its conduct. Its F2F part is just-in-time (JIT) T&L and the eIDM part is a wikipedia exercise. In the JIT session, problems are handed to the students when they enter the session room. They brainstorm their resolution in teams, mentored by the teacher, and then present their team's solution to the others. In

the eIDM part, the teams post their solution (including any improvements to it suggested during the in-class presentation), and then write critiques on the correctness, effectiveness, and suitability of the solutions from the other teams. The formative assessment is during the presentation in the class. The summative assessment is at the end of each week, and appraises the solution posting, plus the quality of the peer critique.

The next stage in the conversion was to design the (main) eIDM element. This new eIDM activity would (1) assess formatively the student's competence in the topic, (2) channel the student to the topic material matching his/her competence, and (3) assess formatively the level of learning in the topic by the student. Naturally, the activity would support self-pacing by the student. Thus it would be difficult to specify the time that a student would take to complete his/her learning. However, the apportionment of learning resources was expected to require an average learning completion time of two to three hours at most. A total of thirteen of these activities were designed, one for each week in the semester (Figure 2). In the first version of the activity, the competence formative assessment channeled those assessed competent to bypass the whole activity, thus giving them time to spend on more studies. However, I observed that the students were squandering that time. So, in a second version of the activity, there is a "masters" channel instead of a bypass, with advanced material and a more difficult learning confirmation assessment. In addition to the two formative assessments, there was a summative assessment that tracked the student's participation in the sequence.

A tension point surfaced with respect to conducting an eIDM summative assessment of the student's understanding of the topic. The reliability of such an assessment is low because there are several ways for the student to cheat the system. After further research and deliberation, I decided that it would be best to conduct the summative assessment as a F2F activity. I also concluded that it would be extremely useful to the

Figure 2. Screenshot of custom gateway into weekly eIDM activities

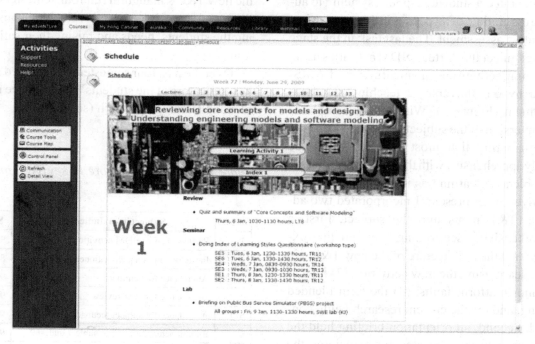

student if the summative assessment were immediately followed by a review to address any class-wide shortfalls in learning revealed in the results of the assessment. So, I decided to create a new one-hour F2F session called quiz-review, for conducting the topic's summative assessment and subsequent revision. The revised the weekly hour allocation tuple for the F2F element is {1,1,2}, and the ratio of eIDM to F2F is ⅓:⅔.

With the elements of the blend designed and their learning time estimated, the next stage was to integrate them. I did this by linking the learning outcomes such that they formed a coherent weekly sequence as follows:

Introduction of topic concepts (eIDM main)

- application of select concepts (F2F seminar)
- critique of solutions (eIDM seminar)
- practice of several concepts in large scale solution (F2F lab)
- assessment of understanding and revision of topic (F2F quiz-review).

This sequence belied a logistical requisite: adjustment of the subject timetable such that the seminar is offered early in the week, the lab to the end of the week, and the quiz-review at the end of the week. The eIDM is not scheduled, but the students are encouraged to start the next week's eIDM activity as soon as the current week's quiz-review is finished.

The final stage in the conversion process was to populate the elements in the blend with all the necessary learning resources and eIDM activity constructs. With respect to learning resources, the comprehensive set of PowerPoint slides used in the lectures were incorporated into the eIDM activities with little or no change. The existing lab resources –manual, briefing, and simulator examples – also needed no changes. The main deficiency in resources was the eIDM activity, seminar, and quiz-review assessments. Two guidelines in their production were adopted: grading had to be as automated as possible, and no repeat questions. Accordingly, I produced 533 multiple choice questions and small problem narratives. I also integrated a student response system [8] to automate the grading of responses in the quiz-review summative assessment. The last task in the stage was to engineer the thirteen eIDM activities using the learning activity management system (LAMS) fielded by our university's teaching standards department (Figure 3). With that, I completed the conversion of the subject to blended learning.

Anticipating that most students would be initially apprehensive with the new T&L activities in the blended learning as it is a one-of-kind in the university at present, I incorporated two additional T&L items into the subject. First, a comprehensive e-scaffolding program that explained: (1) the architecture of the new T&L, (2) how to learn using the new activities, (3) how to fix minor platform faults, (4) the term blended learning, and (5) the current research being conducted. Second, an orientation briefing held the Friday prior to the semester, for explaining the new T&L, and to run a demo eIDM activity. Since

the new T&L's inaugural run four semesters ago, these two items have been invaluable in answering the students' needs and raising their satisfaction.

Over the past four semesters, I measured some key indicators of the students' performance in the blended learning approach (see Table 1).

Table 1. Performance score in key T&L indicators for subject

Ser	Subject T&L Indicator	Score
1	Participation in eIDM activities	92%
2	Participation as a peer critiquer in wikipedia	81%
3	Attendance for seminar	97%
4	Attendance for quiz-review	98%
5	Attendance for subject feedback	98%
6	Exhibit actual learning in subject material	91%
7	Year-on-year change of examination middle mark	+4

Figure 3. Screenshot of authoring view for LAMS activity with masters-journeyman branching

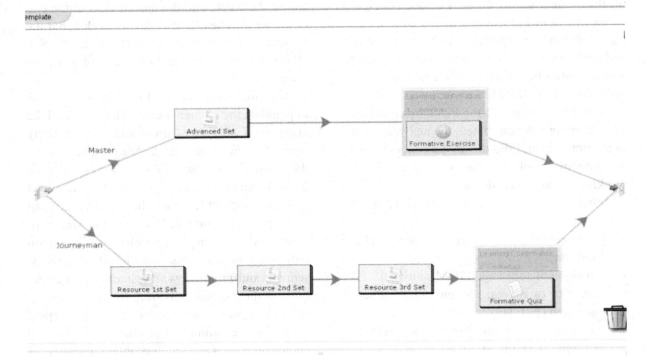

FUTURE RESEARCH DIRECTIONS

Having established a valid, reliable, and acceptable foundation with the blended learning, I commenced research into three associated T&L areas, namely deployability, correlation of learning styles to learning resources, and enhancing the eIDM interface.

The first is to produce a blended learning platform deployable to all schools in the university. The model would have to support all the various subjects being taught in the university (be extensible), and work for any sized classes (be scalable). The present software, LAMS, is highly modular, and provides a large selection of useful learning functions, like resource selection, Q&A, polling, dialog, etc. The setup of a learning activity in LAMS is fairly straightforward, and takes only a moderate amount of time. The real challenge is for the teacher to produce the learning resources that optimize the teacher's eLearning persona and communication of the material to the student. Work is progressing well in producing the deployable platform.

The second is designing learning resources that facilitated better communication with the student. I hypothesized that a direct correlation can be made between a student's learning style and the medium of the learning resource. The first step was to develop thirteen different forms of each learning resource, in mediums that I postulated would each correspond to one of eight major learning styles. This research is in its nascent form right now. The most difficult aspect is designing the eIDM activity such that the student makes their choice according to their preference and not according to factors of familiarity or peer pressure. So far, I have trialed three designs for the resource selection, each proving to be inadequate.

The third is enhancing the eIDM interface to increase the student's interest and performance as a learner. This research is also in its nascent form right now. So far, I have several students conducting their final year projects on simulating various learning management interfaces and testing them with the student cohort in my subject for their feedback.

REFERENCES

Applebee, A. C., Ellis, R. A., & Sheely, S. D. (2004). Developing a blended learning community at the University of Sydney: Broadening the comfort zone. In R. Atkinson, C. McBeath, D. Jonas-Dwyer & R. Phillips (Eds.), *Beyond the Comfort Zone: Proceedings of the 21st ASCILITE*.

Bonwell, C. C., & Eison, J. A. (1991). *Active learning: Creating excitement in the classroom*. Active Learning Workshops. James Rhem & Associates, LLC. Retrieved from http://adminblogs.shc.edu/facdev/Files/IssuesTeach%20Links/ActiveLearningintheClassroom.pdf

Bourne, J., Harris, D., & Mayadas, F. (2005). Online engineering education: Learning anywhere, anytime. *Journal of Engineering Education, 94*(1), 131–146.

Elsasser, G. N., Hoie, E. B., Destache, C. J., & Monaghan, M. S. (2009). Availability of Internet download lecture audio files on class attendance and examination performance. *International Journal of Instructional Technology & Distance Learning, 6*(2).

Felder, R. M., & Silverman, L. K. (1988). Learning and teaching styles in engineering education. *Journal of Engineering Education, 78*(7), 674–681.

Garrison, D. R., & Vaughan, N. D. (2007). *Blended learning in higher education: Framework, principles, and guidelines*. San Francisco, CA: Jossey-Bass, a Wiley Imprint.

Goldhaber, D. (2002, March 10). The mystery of good teaching. *Education Next*.

Hedman, S. (2007). *Achieving success for all students: A statewide initiative on closing the achievement gap.* Retrieved from http://www.webdialogues.net/ctag/studentsuccess

Hovell, M. F., & Williams, R. L. (1979). Analysis of undergraduates' attendance at class meetings with and without grade-related contingencies: A contrast effect. *The Journal of Educational Research, 73.*

Jones, K. A., & Gagnon, P. (2007). New and not so new teaching practices in NTU, 85-BP-A0180. *Proceedings 15th World Conference on Cooperative Education,* 26-29 June 2007, (p. 116).

Kyong-Jee, K., & Bonk, C. J. (2006). The future of online teaching and learning in higher education: The survey says.... *EDUCAUSE Quarterly, 4,* 22–30.

Lodish, H., & Rodriguez, R. K. (2004). Points of view: Lectures: Can't learn with them, can't learn without them. *Cell Biology Education, 3*(4), 202–204. doi:10.1187/cbe.04-07-0054

Pellegrino, J. W. (2006). *Rethinking and redesigning curriculum, instruction and assessment: What contemporary research and theory suggests.* Commissioned by National Center on Education and the Economy for the New Commission on the Skills of the American Workforce. November 2006.

Prensky, M. (2001). Digital natives, digital immigrants. *On the Horizon, 9*(5). NCB University Press.

Rowe, N. C. (2004). Cheating in online student assessment: Beyond plagiarism. *Online Journal of Distance Learning Administration, 7*(2).

Tan, K. H. K. (2007). Is teach less, learn more a quantitative or qualitative idea? *Proceedings of the Redesigning Pedagogy: Culture, Knowledge and Understanding Conference, Singapore,* May 2007.

Vignare, K., Dziuban, C., Moskal, P., Luby, R., Serra-Roldan, R., & Wood, S. (2005). *Blended learning review of research: An annotative bibliography.* Unpublished for ALN Conference Workshop Orlando, Florida.

KEY TERMS AND DEFINITIONS

eIDM: IDM whose primary purpose or theme is learning. Essentially, it connotes an eLearning platform that is definitively interactive with its human user.

eLearning: Software or process that is designed for dissemination of knowledge and activation of learning. Its definitive aspect is its basis in computers, allowing the student to access the material asynchronously and independently.

Scaffolding: Software that assists the user in using the platform.

Ubiquitous Computing: Electronic devices that incorporate an ultra-small digital microprocessor, and are an integral part of everyday objects and activities – so much so that that in the course of the everyday activity, the user may not even be aware of the substance or preponderance of the technology.

ENDNOTES

[1] In his seminal 1987 paper, "No Silver Bullet: Essence and Accidents of Software Engineering", Frederick Brooks was the first to use "silver bullet" in an engineering connotation.

[2] There are at least 50 distinct variants of T&L, some adaptable to a computer platform. For more information, visit www.learning-theories.com, and www.emtech.net/learning_theories.htm.

[3] During a Dean's Mixer Party for Tea/Coffee on 28 November 2008, an informal event

for the College of Engineering faculty in different schools to share ideas and socialize, I discussed my proposal for a blended learning format in my subject. Although supportive in principle, the Dean emphasized that the delivery could not be all eLearning. He stated that a key aspect of the university experience was the traditional F2F discourse between the professor and the student, and in the management's opinion, it is absolutely essential for NTU to retain that for some part of the four years of the degree process.

4 Blackboards are still in use as the primary communication medium. They have a deep-seated sentimental appeal, plus the inconvenience and dirtiness of chalk have been resolved, if you believe a leading manufacturer of this product, Ergo In Demand. See their website About Blackboards – Blackboard Technology and Chalkboard History Advances (2010) from http://www.ergoindemand.com/about_chalkboards.htm.

5 An example is in the 1960 science fiction film "The Time Machine". The protagonist finds the hand-sized "talking rings" in a museum; these are futuristic learning resources. When spun like a top, they deliver an audio recording of past knowledge.

6 An online lecture, held in a virtual classroom, is F2F because it is synchronous, teacher-directed, and one-way flow. Therefore, I do not use online and eIDM synonymously; they connote different variances in computer-based T&L.

7 The common usage of eLearning is not sufficient for our specification of learning, as it often is satisfied with simple one-way flow of information. In this chapter, we make the important distinction that the computer-driven learning must support a two flow of information as per an IDM platform.

8 This is a system comprising of a receiver at some central computer and multiple transmitters in the hands of the audience. When prompted to do so for some question, the audience register their response by "clicking" their transmitter. For more information, see Audience Response in Wikipedia from http://en.wikipedia.org/wiki/Audience_response.

Chapter 24
Online Games for Children

Li Lei
Nanyang Technological University, Singapore

Shen Wanqiang
Nanyang Technological University, Singapore

Edwin Tan Seng Tat
Nanyang Technological University, Singapore

ABSTRACT

This chapter studies the niche market segment of the gaming industry which is the educational games for children aged 3-12. Gaming behaviors including both positive and negative effects of online gaming on children were noted. A framework for developing an online children's educational game is proposed. A prototype is developed to illustrate the use of the framework. Together with the proposed framework (and prototype), the ADVISOR framework has been used to discuss on the product platform, sales, and marketing strategies. The promotion of such online educational games is discussed based on the advertising and promotion strategies. The pricing strategy of the digital product will be discussed using the 3 Cs of pricing framework. Recommendations are suggested to help the online educational gaming industry to cross the chasm. The authors would like to propose the following set of CSR initiatives with alignment to government regulatory.

INTRODUCTION

Since the development of networked computers, online games have become a part of people's life. Modern online games are played through internet connections. There are many digital products and services such as music, movie, games and educational services launched in IDM market with target ranging from children to adults. Particularly for

children, most of what they experienced on the internet is new. Children are keen on searching cartoon characters of their interest and playing simple games online. Older children however are more interested in enjoying the 'cool' experience of interacting with each other through instant messaging, email, blog, social networking web sites and interactive games (Demner, 2001). However, some potential unsafe factors such as violent games might threaten the well being of the children. There are violent games which can be accessed

DOI: 10.4018/978-1-61350-147-4.ch024

on the internet (David, 2007). Therefore, it is necessary for the IDM companies to launch more appropriate digital products such as educational games for children, and government should set regulatory rules to monitor the content produce by the IDM companies.

It has been observed that the numbers of children playing online games are on a globally increasing trend. According to NPD Group 2007 report, a provider of reliable and comprehensive consumer and retail information for a wide range of industries, from toddlers to tweens to teens, more than one-third of kids in the United States are spending more time playing games today than they did one year ago. This trend is particularly pronounced for online game play, according to Kids & Gaming, the most recent report from The NPD Group. The report also reported that although males and older kids are more likely to spend more time per week on gaming, the most significant jump occurs from ages 2 to 5 to ages 6 to 8. At this time, kids become more serious about gaming, reflected by spending 3 more hours a week, or 75 percent more time than they used to (Corporate Social Responsibility, 2008). According to an online article, research shows that the children who played online games were more active and had sharper minds than their other counterparts. Some games have been specifically designed to teach people about a certain subject, expand concepts, reinforce development, understand a historical event or culture, or assist them in learning a skill as they play (David, 2007). However, computer and games also receive much more negative criticism because games are often coined with issues such as mindless entertainment, enhanced social recluse, sexism and consumerism. Research shows that kids who play violent games showed an increase in emotional arousal and a corresponding decrease of activity in brain areas involving self-control, inhibition and attention (David, 2007).

The authors analyze the different requirements of each children group in the game industry and

elaborate the whole business framework of online educational game for children. A framework for developing online educational games targeting at the niche portion of the market i.e. the age group of 3-12 is proposed. The games that are developed through this framework seeks to develop the children in this age group in a positive manner and reduce major negative effects as introduced above. This business model covers the deep analysis of technology platform and product prototype, approach, market strategy, promoting and selling such online educational games, impact on the society and regulatory and policy issues and future trends in the children online educational game area.

BACKGROUND

Choosing the right game software for children will stimulate their interest in learning. Children dislike having to read manuals or even onscreen instructions. The game should have simple and direct visual instructions superimposed in gameplay. It is advisable that the child does not engage in computer games more than three hours a day. Table 1 shows the recommendation game type for different children age group (Demner, 2001).

Table 1 shows that Nursery children need to learn ABCs, how things work and recognize numbers. They are new to interface such as mouse and keyboard. As they are very young, it is recommended that they should not play game for more than 10 to 20 minutes. Kindergarten and lower primary children are hungry to explore the new world. They are curious, and the game type should encourage their interest in mathematics, phonics, reading and spelling. The game should not be more than 20 to 30 minutes. For the upper primary children, they like to be socially involved. They are recommended to play games that encourage critical thinking and those that have build in chat functions. They are recommended to play for half an hour at one stretch.

Table 1. Recommendation game types for kids (adapted from Demner, 2001)

Age	Learning	Games type	Recommendation
Nursery (3-4 years old)	Learn concepts such as ABCs, how things work and how to recognize numbers.	Learn how to point and click with the mouse. Simple typing	Play games not more than 10 to 20 minutes.
Kindergarten (5-6 years old) and lower primary (7-9 years old)	Children hungry to explore new worlds.	Encourage interest in mathematics, phonics, reading and spelling.	Play games 20 to 30 minutes at a go.
Upper primary (10-12 years old)	Tweenies like to get social.	Games that encourage critical thinking and those that build chat functions.	Play games about half an hour at a stretch.

Games created for children should not be restricted with too many rules. Children prefer games that allow them to explore (Digital Life, 2010). The game must be able to arouse the children's interest.

Content need to learn by student is often regarded as being too dry and boring. Kids love to learn when it is not forced upon them (Druin, 1998). Therefore, learning the content through educational game will provide the kids an interesting learning platform. In traditional learning method, the teacher will have to repeatedly teach the kids with the same content twice or more if he does not understand, should there be a need. But the same content can be learnt through playing different educational games. In this way, the kids will not find it boring when learning new content.

The studies have shown that there is difference in learning approach between the left and right brain. The left brain is responsible for logical sequential, analytical thinking while the right brain is responsible for random, creativity thinking. In general, schools tend to favor left-brain modes of thinking while downplaying the right-brain one (Hui, 2009). Most of the games in the market are mostly favor the left-brain modes of thinking. Popular games such as role-playing, strategy and board games require logical and analytical thinking which uses the left-brain modes of thinking.

According to research, there are 97% of adolescents that play video games (Internet Promotion, 2006). Playing violent video games may be related to aggressive behavior (Education Game Development: Partnering with K-12 Schools). Children in primary school treat each other more roughly than a few years ago. One of the main reasons is that children are being confronted more often with violence especially through the Internet (Irina and Jab, 2009).

The internet is a part of a child's natural environment. Most children have access to the Internet at school and/or at home. 99% of the public schools have access to the Internet. Parents and teachers consider Internet to be primarily educational or developmental tool. The Kids.net study showed that children find the Internet easy to use and like to use it for fun, games, e-mail, chat and instant messaging. Two-thirds of the children think that it helps them with their learning, and one-third would like to use it for lessons if they were home sick at school (Karan, 2008).

Figure 1 shows the percentage of kids that consume digital media in November 2000. The kids between 2-11 years old have the least market share of 7.59%. It is a "niche" market which is not taken care of. In an online news article published by New York Times in 2005, it is reported that the sales of educational software to children in this group dropped from an initial sales of $498 million dollars in 2000 to an amount of less than $200 million dollars in 2004 due to competition from free online games and learning sites that are in abundance over the internet (Karen & Katinka, 2006). As this online educational game market takes a dive, the authors in this paper therefore takes a closer look into this market seeking a breakthrough in an effort to cross the chasm.

According to a 2009 market survey research that is based in Hong Kong by AC Nielson, people in Hong Kong continue to be cautious about spending amidst the uncertain economic outlook, yet parents are not holding back when it comes to spending on their children. Figure 2 shows the chart on average monthly expenses per child. Besides school related fees which account for the largest shares (40%), 7 in 10 parents said that they are also spending on additional learning tools and tutorial classes (19%) for their children and parents are willing to spend on their children for their 'well-being' (Rainie & Smith, 2008). Therefore, by demonstrating the benefits and value of what the online educational games can bring for the children, parents will be willing to pay for such a product.

Analyzing the Online Left and Right Brain Games for Children

The authors in this section went to analyze the difference between left and right brain games with through the illustration of 2 actual online games being Gobstopper Gobbler and Strawberry shortcake. They have identified both the weaknesses and strengths of the games, and made recommendations to improve on the weaknesses.

Figure 3 shows the game proposed by left-braingames.com to be a left-brain game. The player has to analyze the best path and control the game character to finish up the points while avoiding being eaten by the monster. The level of difficulty increases as the player completes each level. Analytical thinking is required to complete this game.

Figure 4 shows the game proposed by left-braingames.com to be right-brain game. The player has to control the game character to bake the cake. Player is not required to think of what is right and what is wrong, or the best approach as no analytical thinking is required. Player will need to think creatively and decorate the cake in

Figure 1. Age-gender composition digital media Nov 2000

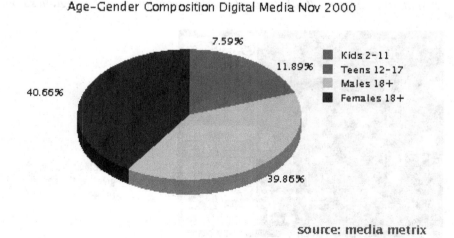

Figure 2. Average monthly expenses per child aged 16 or below. (Information adapted from Rainie & Smith, 2008)

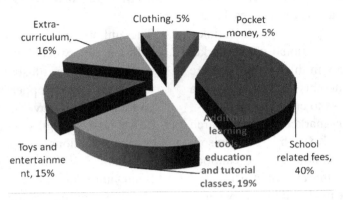

order to complete the game. There is no level involved in creativity game. Creative thinking is required to complete this game. The authors analyze and notice some of the characteristic of children game as shown in Figure 3 and Figure 4.

Gobstopper Gobbler Game

Good Features

1. Simple instructions are given in segment as game progress.
2. Game is accessed from the internet.

Weakness

1. The game has many levels and it will take more than 30 minutes to complete all the levels. It is not recommended to allow children to play games for more than 30 minutes.
   ○ **Recommendation:** The number of level should be reduced.
2. The game is quite restrictive. Player has to follow the set of rules such as moving the characters within the maze, teleporting, avoiding the monsters, eating certain object to gain power to kill the monsters, knowing where the monster will be produce after be-

Figure 3. Screenshot of online game (Gobstopper Gobbler) from http://leftbraingames.com/leftbrain.php

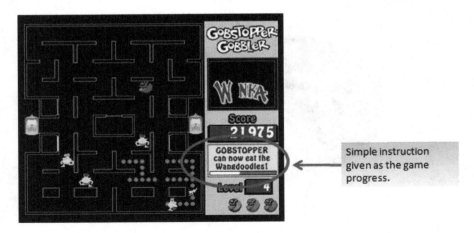

Figure 4. Screenshot of online game (Strawberry Shortcake) from http://leftbraingames.com/rightbrain.php

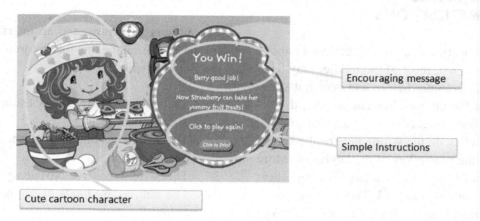

ing eaten, etc. Children may not like it as it is restrictive and it is not easy to play.

○ **Recommendation 1:** The maze should be simplified with more exits so that the character is not easily cornered by the monster.

○ **Recommendation 2:** The produce of monster can be concentrate on only one location.

3. The player has to play the game using the keyboard. Children may not be able to use it effectively.

○ **Recommendation:** Use customized interface devices for children.

4. The game concentrates on left brain training only.

○ **Recommendation:** The game can insert a short bonus level after each level which is creative thinking (right brain game) during the game.

Strawberry Shortcake Game

Good Features

1. It displays encouraging words.
2. Simple instructions are given to player when necessary.

3. Cartoon character is used. Children like cartoon character as it will attract their attention.

4. The game does not have too much restriction. Player can choose any ingredient in any order according to their creativities.

5. The game can be completed in a short time (less than 10 minutes) as there is no level involved.

6. Game is accessed from the Internet.

7. The game concentrates on right brain training only.

Weakness

1. The player has to play the game using the mouse. Children may not be able to use it effectively.

○ **Recommendation:** Use customized interface devices for children.

2. The game concentrates on right brain training only.

○ **Recommendation:** The game can be enhanced with left brain game, e.g. letting the user set customized controls of the oven for baking different type of short cakes. Player has to analyze and set the correct setting for the control of the oven to bake a good cake.

SOLUTIONS AND RECOMMENDATIONS

Creating educational games for children impose a challenge. First, most of the toddler may have not use the computer before and does not know how to use the mouse-click and keyboard. Furthermore, their fingers' actions are not precise. They may click on the wrong area of the screen or type on the wrong key of the keyboard. More than 80% of the games are targeting teenagers above 18 years old Figure 3. There are not much educational games for children; about 7.59% of the games are designed for children age 2 to 11 Figure 3. There are few factors for this trend. It is easier to create games for teenagers as they are more accepting on the rules imposed in the games.

There are uncertainties in catering games for the children. There are risks on the sales because the direct consumer (children) does not have the spending power. Children do not know what they need or want and thus the purchasing decision is base on the parents (Rainie and Smith, 2008). As compared to teenagers, majority of the game (80% - shown in Figure 1) in the market is created for them. It is because they are the direct consumer as well as the purchaser.

According to the research recommendation, children can only spend between 10 to 30 minutes of games at a stretch, depending on the age group (Demner, 2001). The developers face the challenge of maximizing the children learning experience while keeping the game play duration within the recommended duration.

There are some things to consider when designing the educational game for children.

Shown below in Table 2 is a framework proposed by the authors to guide IDM startups in game development.

Proposed Interface Device

The authors have proposed an interface device for the educational game for children. Below are the characteristics.

1. The device dimension is estimated to be 30cmx10cmx2cm.
2. The device has big buttons, about 2.5cm in diameter each.
3. The device is passive. No battery is required.
4. The buttons are made of bright illuminate colors.
5. The device backgrounds are cartoon characters.
6. The device must not have sharp edges.
7. It is able to interface to any type of standard keyboard.

Figure 5 is the prototype design (see Figures 5 and 6).

Table 2. **Proposed framework**

Factors	Recommendation
Interface	Big and colorful (Richtel, 2005)
Back-ground	Cartoon character (Karan, 2008)
Game play	• Non-restrictive (Digital Life, 2010) • Encouraging message (Demner, 2001)
Instruction	• Minimum instructions before game play (Demner, 2001). • Segment instruction and feed to gamers as game progress (Richtel, 2005) • Design instructions to be easy to comprehend and remember (Richtel, 2005).
Target development	Left and right brain
Game time	• < 10 mins (2 to 4 years old child) • <20 mins (5 to 9 years old child) • <30 mins (10 to 12 years old child) (Demner, 2001)
System Configuration	Minimum (Marc, 2003)
Accessibility	Internet-based (Karan, 2008)

Proposed Game Design

A sample of the proposed game is the "number and color game". This game is designed for toddler. Below is the description of the game.

1. The numbers between 1 to 10 and between color yellow, green, blue and red will randomly be displayed on the screen. The toddler will have to press both the button of color and number on the board. Both the left and right brain are being trained within the short time of 10 to 20 minutes. Numbers (logic) will train the left brain and color (creative) will train the right brain.
2. There will not be any instruction when the game starts.
3. There will be short and simple instructions when required at each level.
4. The game will not be restrictive, if the kids press the wrong button, they will not be penalized. Instead, encouraging words will be displayed. If the kids get the correct answer, they will be awarded with praising sentences.
5. The game will have many levels, which will impose challenge to the kid.

Figure 7 is the screenshot of the "number and color game".

ADVISOR MODEL

The authors then look into the advisor model and analyze how the educational games for toddler could fit into the framework.

Value

• Providing intuitive game play to children playing games online. Children will benefit from games that aim to help them develop intellectually and with minimum exposure to undesirable contents provide extra value (Marc, 2003).

Figure 5. Device for educational game for children

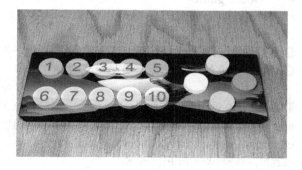

Figure 6. Device attached to the keyboard

Figure 7. Screenshot of the number and color game. The background is the pictures of the cartoon characters that the kids like. There is not much instruction needed to play this game.

- Integrating the game into the education curriculum.
- Offer training services to interested students
- Hiring an experienced teacher on contract basis to help with the content.

Interface

- Self-designed physical interface (big buttons, bright colors, mounted on keypads)

Service Platform

- Internet connection to support game updates
- Online portal to support download of games
- Online portal to support sale and after sales of game titles
- Physical Onsite installation, troubleshooting of problems faced by consumer
- Open platform. Allow others to develop on our platform.

Organizing Model

- Manufacturers to manufacture the hardware device
- Focal company to develop in-house educational games
- Partner software development companies to develop games for us (outsourcing/procurement)
- Distribution: Web portal to for sales by downloading, partnership with payment module companies like paypal, partnership with courier companies e.g. Fed-Ex to provide delivery of game titles, partner companies to provide manpower for physical onsite installation, troubleshooting of problems faced by consumer
- Partnership with schools: bringing the use of IT into education, using the schools'

children feedback to better improvise our lines of gaming products, services

Revenue

- Sales of game titles
- Advertisements on web portal
- Advertisements within the educational games

Adoption

- Parents
- Targeting children or end consumer
- Game developers wishing to develop games on our platform or partners
- Schools; consumer, partners)

Disruption

- Current online children educational games developers
- Educational book publisher
- Board games
- Television programmes

DISTRIBUTION AND SUPPLY CHAIN MANAGEMENT

The authors went on to look into the distribution and supply chain management. Our proposed educational games will have the necessary partnership as shown in Figure 8.

Vertical Partnership

Suppliers

- **Manufacturer**: Companies that help to produce the hardware devices
- **Software Developer:** Companies that help to produce the educational games.

Figure 8. Distribution and supply chain management for educational games for children

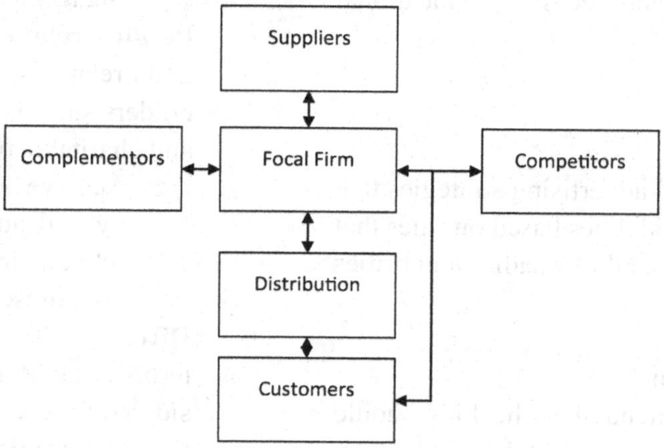

Distribution

- **Distributor:** Software games and device can be sold through 3rd party websites and retailer store. Setting up educational gaming website.

Horizontal Partnership

Customers

- **Consumer:** Educational Centre and schools. Parents may get one for their kids.

Complementors

- Partner with Ministry of Education of government board. Understand and align the country's curriculum guidelines which outline the content for individual subject and grade levels. Target untapped content areas for which there are few (if any) electronic resources available (Marc, 2003).
- Partner with a single school. Target schools that are already investing heavily in computer related instructional programs. Not only do they probably have access to the latest technology, they are also more likely to be receptive to your educational game proposal. It is one of the ways to beachhead into the industry.
- Partnering with one or more teachers in the school who are especially keen on your idea. They will contribute to ideas and content for the educational game development. They will also add as word-of-mouth to promote the products (Marc, 2003).
- Partner with cartoon creating companies and movie maker for licensing of the cartoon characters.

Competitors

- **Syndication:**
  - Partner with other game developing firm to develop games for this device.
  - Aggregate education markets with common needs so developers can bid on a market large enough to justify a major investment in product development (Marc, 2003).
- **Aggregation:** Website sells other products such as educational books, stationary, education centre, tools for parent to monitor kids' activity, etc.

- Partner with education book publisher to create content and ideas for educational games.

Promotion

The authors proposed advertising strategies that adheres to a set of guidelines based on rules that are similar to those set by the Canadian authorities (McCarthy, 1980).

- No exaggeration.
- Do not recommend that the kids should buy the products or should they make their parents buy for them.
- Do not make consumer that they are getting everything that is shown in the commercial.
- Not allowed to show kids or adults doing unsafe things with the product.
- Cannot suggest that using the product will make them better than other kids.
- No brainwashing.

The authors have proposed the list of promotions that are applicable for promoting the digital products (see Figure 9).

- **Media advertising:** prints such as parenting magazine and adult newspaper.
  - **Pros:** Cost efficiency (CPM) in reaching out to mass market, higher frequency of the advertisements, quality of advertisement through the engagement of advertising firms.
- **Public relation/Publicity:** maintaining good relationship with each type of stakeholders such as the government, sponsors, and charitable organizations etc
  - Achieve a good channel to publicity and advertisements such as bus, school, library, Zoo, science exhibition, museum and outdoor events
- **Direct Mail:** this is not so effective in terms of targeting children but can be considered for use for targeting the parents.
- **Sales/Promotion:**
  - Bundle the interface device with the online game services.
  - Partner with ISP Company to bundle with the internet services and the online games services.
  - Partner with movie Company. Bundle the interface device with extra interchangeable background cartoon characters.
- **Personal selling:** focusing on one customer at a time, maybe regular propaganda activities.
  - This is not so effective for targeting children but can be considered for use for targeting the children's parents
  - Can target the school principal to take in as part of the educational course.
- **Internet Marketing:**
  - Word- of-mouth is very effective as well as viral marketing.

Figure 9. Promotional mix hierarchy chart. (Adapted from www.marketing.net [Lachlan et al, 2005])

- ◦ Affiliating with other websites.
- ◦ Search advertisements.
- ◦ Online Advertisements through children website.

Crossing the Chasm

Currently, the educational games for children are still in the early adopter stage. With the usage of the proposed framework, the product development team can seek to cross the chasm to the tornado. In order to take the product into the market, the team will first need to introduce the software to the general market such as the educational institutions, beachhead through a partnership with a school with positive technology adoption. It is important to get the support from the principal and teachers of the school as the principal holds the power of financial decision and the teachers hold the experience in the education syllabus. As such, they will contribute to the software content during enhancement and improvement. They will also provide word of mouth should the adoption of such educational software be successful. The benefits of the educational software and its interfaces will then be demonstrated and trialed with other educational institutions, to build the company's profile as well as doing a concept testing. During the concept testing, feedbacks on the software and its interfaces are to be gathered and further improvised. Success and satisfaction stories from various consumers will be gathered and promoted within the industry. This will lead the product to cross the chasm. As more and more individual consumers and educational institutions see the benefits of such online educational games through their counterparts' educational institution, the tornado effect will take place. To sustain the tornado effect, more educational games titles are being pushed out to the market, keeping a close watch on the market needs and demand. On top of that, it is important for the IDM firm to align themselves with the government education policy and direction. When there is a change in syllabus,

the latest version of the educational game will be published to the market within a short time. Online update for the educational game will be available for consumer within 3 months of purchase. When new improved version of the interface device is launched, the consumers are allowed to upgrade the old set for the new one with portion of the price of the new set (see Figure 10).

Pricing Strategy

Pricing is one of the key factors that we will focus our strategy on. The three Cs of pricing are Costs, Competition and Customers (Figure 11). Setting a very low price is not an option for this context; however the authors would recommend a pricing strategy that concentrates on the customer factor. The authors reference the price according to pricing standard used by customer. The product price will be referenced against the physical board game, educational book, handheld console, online game and game purchase off the shelf. A variety of pricing options is being offered including educational pricing, workgroup and lab pack pricing, and school district wide pricing (Marc, 2003). Parents are willing to pay premium price for product that can help their kids in their education development. They see high value in educational products that have good branding and proven records of effectiveness. Eventually, we will set the price below the consumer judgment on its value (Lachlan et al., 2005).

Having an understanding of the market needs and demand is important. If the market situation is not in favor for marketing the digital product, then the company has to "kill" its product at the early stage to prevent any further sunk cost.

CONCLUSION

In conclusion, the authors have briefly discussed online gaming in general as well as the effects of online gaming on children. Current online games

Figure 10. Crossing the chasm (Adapted from[Rules for advertising to kids])

Crossing the chasm:

- Introducing to general market
- Beachhead with a partnering school
- Demonstration and trial with other educational institutions
- Building company profile
- Perform concept testing to gather feedback and improvise product
- Sharing of success stories and customer satisfaction (from existing customers) with potential customers (educational institutions)

Creating and maintaining the tornado effect:

- Sharing of success stories and customer satisfaction (from existing customers) with potential customers (educational institutions)
- align with the government education policy and direction
- Improved service such as online update of game and upgrading to new device

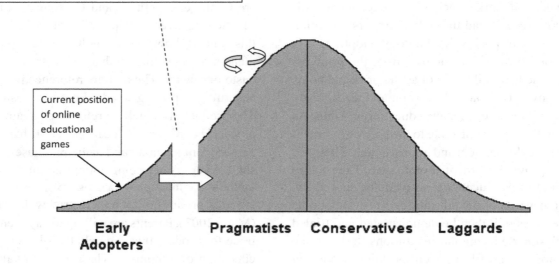

Current position of online educational games

Early Adopters   **Pragmatists**   **Conservatives**   **Laggards**

Figure 11. Focusing on customers of 3Cs of pricing model. (Adapted from [Rules for advertising to kids])

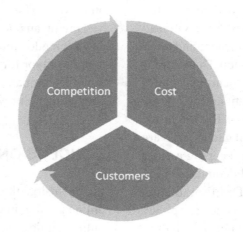

have both pros and cons effects on children, however with cons outweighing the pros according to many research studies. The authors next went on to identify the niche segment of the online gaming market, i.e. children of age 3-12. Using this age group as the target audience, the authors proposed a framework for game developers to develop games for this group of the market segment. The authors supported the framework with a prototype of the interface device as well as the screen interface. The authors next went on to propose the strategies and approaches to market, promote and sell such educational game digital products.

Another area of concern which the authors thought that the firms adopting the paper's framework can look into is Corporate Social Responsibility (CSR). According to definition by Harvard Kennedy School, Harvard University, corporate social responsibility encompasses not only what companies do with their profits, but also how they make them. It goes beyond philanthropy and compliance and addresses how companies manage their economic, social, and environmental impacts, as well as their relationships in all key spheres of influence: the workplace, the marketplace, the supply chain, the community, and the public policy realm (National Summit on Educational Games). Aligning the CSR to the proposed business framework above, the authors would like to propose the following set of CSR initiatives as well:

- The raw material to create the game interface is made from recycle material.
- Encourage consumers to purchase the game by download rather than purchasing it from the DVD by offering much cheaper price for the game purchased from download as compared to DVD.
- Share hosting website resources.
- Explore the economics of developing and marketing simpler, shorter, and less costly to produce "downloadable" educational games (Marc, 2003).
- The background picture of the game interface can be replaced easily as children tend to follow trends in their favourite cartoon characters.
- Provide option for Parent to purchase interface device that are not assembled at a cheaper price. Parent can provide guidance for the kids to DIY the interface device.
- From the upgrade scheme of the interface devices, old devices can be collected from trade ins and donated to more needy children

Figure 12. Serving base-of-they-pyramid markets (adapted from WRI)

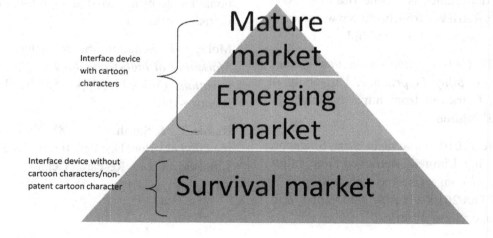

- Segmentation of the market can be done. The interface device can be produced in different variants such as:
  - Interface device with cartoon characters targeting at the mature and emerging market, much more pricey as licensing cartoon characters is involved
  - Interface device without cartoon characters or non-patented cartoon characters targeting at survival market, which can be purchased at a much more affordable price as licensing of cartoon characters is not involved

Figure 12 is a diagram showing the 3 types of market segmentation that is proposed (Lachlan et al., 2005).

The authors noticed that the regulatory and political issues are an important factor to penetrate the product in a country.

All in all, the paper aims to serve as a guideline for new IDM startups to target the niche segment market of the online educational gaming industry which is the age group of 3-12, with the confidence of expanding the market share beyond the niche.

REFERENCES

David, M. (2007). Amount of time kids spend playing video games is on the rise. The NPD Group, Inc. Retrieved from http://www.npd.com/press/releases/press_071016a.html

Demner, D. (2001). *Children on the internet. Universal usability in practice.* University of Maryland. Retrieved from http://otal.umd.edu/uupractice/children/

Digital Life. (2010). *Gaming in class.* Singapore Press Holding Limited. Retrieved from http://global.factiva.com.ezlibproxy1.ntu.edu.sg/aa/?ref=COMPTI0020100330e63v00007&pp=1&fcpil=en&napc=S&sa_from=

Druin, A. (1998). *The design of children's technology.* San Francisco, CA: Morgan Kaufmann.

Harvard University. (2008). Corporate social responsibility initiative. Retrieval on April 14, 2010, from http://www.hks.harvard.edu/m-rcbg/CSRI/init_define.html

Hui, A. (2009). *Parents' spending on their children - It's recession-proof!* Hong Kong: AC Nielson. Retrieved from http://hk.nielsen.com/news/20090819.shtml

Hutchison, D. (2006). *Internet promotion.* Retrieved from http://www.learnmarketing.net/promotion.htm

Irina, V., & Jab, H. (2009). *Computer game design and imaginative play of young children.* IDC Short Papers.

Lachlan, K. A., Smith, S. L., & Tamborini, R. (2005). *Models for aggressive behavior: The attributes of violent characters in popular video games.* US: Communication Studies. Gale Group.

Marc, P. (2003). Digital game-based learning. *ACM Computers in Entertainment, 1*(1).

McCarthy, B. (1980). *4Mat System: Teaching to learning styles with right-left mode techniques.*

Media Awareness Network. (1993). *Rules for advertising to kids.* Retrieved from http://www.media-awareness.ca/english/resources/educational/handouts/advertising_marketing/kids_advertising_rules.cfm

Mohr, J. J., Sengupta, S., & Slater, S. (2010). *Marketing of high-technology products and innovations* (3rd ed.). Upper Saddle River, NJ: Prentice-Hall.

Rainie, L., & Smith, A. (2008). *The internet and the 2008 election.* US: Pew Internet & American Life Project. Pew Research Center.

Richtel, M. (2005, August 22). Once a booming market, educational software for the PC takes a nose dive. *New York Times*. Retrieved from http://www.nytimes.com/2005/08/22/technology/22soft.html?_r=1

Seriousgamesources.com. (2009). *Educational game development: Partnering with K-12 schools*. Retrieved from http://seriousgamessource.com/features/feature_091406_tigc.php

Singh, K. (2008). *Effects of online gaming on kids*. Retrieved from http://www.content4reprint.com/recreation-and-leisure/entertainment/games/effects-of-online-gaming-on-kids.htm

Soeters, K. E., & van Schaik, K. (2006). Children's experiences on the internet. *New Library World*, *107*(1-2), 31–36. doi:10.1108/03074800610639012

The Federation of American Scientists, the Entertainment Software Association, and the National Science Foundation, US. (2008). *National Summit on Educational Games*. Retrieved from http://www.fas.org/gamesummit/Resources/Fact%20Sheet.pdf

Chapter 25
Value Assessment in E-Government

Lai Pek Hia
Nanyang Technological University, Singapore

Lee Shu Wen
Nanyang Technological University, Singapore

ABSTRACT

Governments around the world have implemented or are in the midst of implementing, amid differing levels of progress, electronic government (e-Government). These implementations create different values for the different stakeholders. This chapter examines an e-Government Component Assessment Cube Framework for value assessment of e-Government information technology project implementations. The three main groups are (value) components, stages, and stakeholders.

INTRODUCTION

The rapid global adoption of information technology (IT) has been fuelled by the lowered cost of hardware (i.e. storage and processor) and the availability of communicative infrastructures (i.e. Internet, mobile technology). IT has changed and are still changing the way people interact and communicate with others from around the world and the way corporations perform business internally and externally with their customers, for instance, in e-business and e-commerce.

DOI: 10.4018/978-1-61350-147-4.ch025

In a similar way, governments have been challenged by demands from the public and businesses to employ such technologies to improve service delivery, provide faster response time and productivity. This gives rise to e-government, which changes the traditional way government serves its citizens and the public. After the implementation of e-government, the next step of interest will be to find out the values created for both the government and the people it serves.

Hence this chapter seeks to study and propose a value assessment framework for e-government implementations, which can access a value at a particular stage of implementation and for a particular stakeholder.

BACKGROUND

What is E-Government?

E-Government Definitions

E-Government, an abbreviation for electronic government, is also known as connected government, digital government, e-gov, online government, transformational government (Gronlund & Horan, 2005; King & Cotterill, 2007; Marchionini, et al., 2003).

The European Commission (1998) describes e-government as "an ever-increasing and pervasive use of information and communication technologies in the context of the Information Society, which more and more affects the public sector; the importance of this development is increasingly acknowledged in many countries around the world and experiments are being conducted at all levels of government – local, regional, national and European – to improve the functioning of public services concerned and to extend their interaction with the outside world" (as cited in Vassilakis et al., 2007, pp. 1). As defined by Yoneji Masuda (1980), information society is "a new type of society, where the possession of information (and not material wealth) is the driving force behind its transformation and development [...] (and where) human intellectual creativity flourishes" (as cited in Karvalics, 2007). Likewise, Silcock (2001) states e-government as a new mode of public service where all public organizations deliver an up-to-date, incorporated and seamless service for the general public; it uses a combination of technology, business processes, and human resources to enhance the access to and delivery of government services to benefit citizens, business partners and employees as well as forming partnerships between government and its citizens.

The growth of information and communication technologies has increasingly impacted and challenged the online delivery of government information and services through the Internet and other digital media. It provides with "Everything: Anytime, Anywhere, Anyway" (Deloitte Research, 2003, pp. 23). This non-hierarchical, non-linear, and two-way communication structure is seen as a way to improve service delivery and responsiveness to the general public (West, 2004). Such online services include e-administration, e-citizen, e-collaboration, e-commerce, e-democracy, e-governance, e-management, e-service, and e-society to improve and streamline internal processes and management, connections to citizens and business, electronic exchange of goods and services as well as building partnerships and social developments (Dawes, 2002; Esteves and Joseph, 2008; Yildiz, 2007).

Neal & Cable (2005) defines e-government as "streamlining government by providing efficient and effective services and information to citizens and businesses through advanced technology" (pp. 276). Another definition of e-government is shown on The World Bank's (n.d.) website:

"E-government" refers to the use by government agencies of information technologies (such as Wide Area Networks, the Internet, and mobile computing) that have the ability to transform relations with citizens, businesses, and other arms of government. These technologies can serve a variety of different ends: better delivery of government services to citizens, improved interactions with business and industry, citizen empowerment through access to information, or more efficient government management. The resulting benefits can be less corruption, increased transparency, greater convenience, revenue growth, and/or cost reductions.

As seen, although there are many definitions of e-government in the literature, most point to the same agreement. E-government can thus be summarized as the government using the combination of information technology, business processes and human resources to offer seamless online service delivery. This is characterized by two-way communication, availability and accessibility, to its citizens, business partners, employees and governments.

E-Government Categories

According to Brown and Brudney (2001), the primary delivery model of e-government can be divided into three broad categories, namely Government-to-Government (G2G), Government-to-Citizen (G2C), and Government-to-Business (G2B) (as cited in Yildiz, 2007). G2G represents the backbone of e-government as governments need to have updated systems and procedures for data sharing and conducting electronic exchanges, both intra- and inter-agency; G2B are initiated by both the business community and the policymakers as they seek cost-cutting and efficient use of electronic means for procurement, sales and such activities; G2C aims to provide for citizen interaction with the government as citizens who are familiar with using electronic means in areas such as banking would expect such electronic means of services from the government sector (Seifert, 2007). Additionally, two more groups may be included in the list and they are Government-to-Civil Societal Organizations (G2SC) and Citizens-to-Citizens (C2C), where a G2SC aspect is electronic communication and coordination efforts after a disaster and C2C facilities interaction among citizens as websites incorporate Web 2.0 feature (Yildiz, 2007).

E-Government Stakeholders

The relationships in e-government stated above are defined by various stakeholders. Freeman (1984) stated the Stanford Research Institute (SRI) first defined that stakeholder in 1963 as "those groups without whose support the organization would cease to exist" (pp. 31). Hence it is important for business corporations to serve the interests of and needs of the various stakeholders, in addition to

that of shareholders (Preston & Sapienza, 1990). Likewise, e-governments need to meet the interest of their stakeholders.

The primary e-Government stakeholders consists of six groups and they are: (1) Citizens: They include residents and rights-entitled member of state who interact with the public administration on their civil rights and other democratic processes; (2) Employees: These include all groups of public employees who carry out the daily operations of the agencies and make information based on information from operations; (3) Business. These include both for-profit and not-for-profit companies who interact with the public administration on legal, social, monetary, grant submission and such matters; (4) Governments: These refer to the interaction among different levels of the government, namely local, state and federal who perform planning of operational processes and create legal laws and procedures; (5) IS/IT Personnel: These include hardware and software suppliers, and solutions consultants from both private and public organizations who setups and maintains the e-government environment; and (6) Special Interest Groups (SIGs): These include organized groups in local communities as well as international organization such as non-government organizations (NGOs), civil service organizations (CSOs), European Commission, Organization for Economic Co-operation and Development (OECD), and the United Nations, who build communal voices (Esteves & Joseph, 2008). These stakeholders may be involved in explicit or implicit, recognized or unrecognized contracts (Freeman, 1984; Freeman & Miles, 2002).

Stages of E-Government

As the delivery of electronic services develops, governments will progress through some stages in the transformation towards a higher level of maturity. Three development models from the literature or organization reports, namely, Deloitte

Research six stages model (Deloitte Research, 2000), Layne & Lee four stages model (Layne & Lee, 2001) and Accenture five stages model (Accenture, 2003) are presented in this section.

Deloitte Research (2000) Six Stages Model

According to a report by Deloitte Research (2000), there are six dynamic stages in the transformation of e-government service delivery, and these are:

1. **Information Publishing/Dissemination:** This refers to individual government departments and agencies having their own websites posting information about themselves, the services that they provide and their contacts. These sites offer communication in one direction, with many already in existences;

2. **'Official' Two-Way Transactions:** This refers to the provision of privacy assurance and secure online transaction via the use of digital certificates on individual department's websites. As such, customers are confident to submit personal information and perform financial transactions.

3. **Multi-Purpose Portals:** This refers to the provision of a portal that allows customers via a single point of entry to communicate information, both to and from the organization, and to perform secure financial transactions across a number of departments.

4. **Portal Personalization:** Further to the ability to access a wide variety of services from a single Website, customers are now provided with the means to customize portals with their preferred features. This in turn provides a means for governments to have a more accurate understanding of customer preference for electronics versus non-electronics service options;

5. **Clustering of Common Services:** This is stated as the point where real transformation of government structure occurs, as customers now view the services as groups of transactions via a unified package through the portal. This is achieved by the governments' efforts to group together shared services from individual departments that will also speed up the delivery of shared services;

6. **Full Integration and Enterprise Transformation:** At this stage, 'silo' model of services have been torn down, and technology is integrated further to link the shortened gap between front and back offices. In some cases, previous agencies may be combined and restructured to form new agencies. In some others, there are changing functions of the agencies.

Layne and Lee (2001) Four Stages Model

According to Layne and Lee (2001), the growth model for e-government consists of four-stages as follow:

1. **Cataloguing:** This refers to initial creation of a basic online presence, a 'static' website, with catalogue of presentations of government information. The initiation of this stage may be due to pressure from the media, technology-literate employees and citizens and other stakeholders. Gradually, much information are posted which in turn required an index page so as to facilitate searching and browsing of required information as well as to download required forms. Further on in this stage, websites may include links to other sites. This web presence helps increase citizens' convenience to learn about policies and procedures, location of government services and support while online. From the government's perspective, it helps reduce

the workload of front-desk public staff in answering basic questions about government services and procedures.

2. **Transaction:** This refers to websites with online services and forms, and databases to support transactions, allowing citizens to transact with the government electronically. For example, citizens may pay fines or renew their licenses online. This stage comes about as administrators and citizens comprehend the benefits of using the Internet as another service channel. As this stage progresses, the amount of e-transactions increases where there exists the need for incorporating online transactions directly with internally functioning systems with little or no manual intervention. Additionally, websites provide for interactive two-way communications. This stage allows citizens to save on paperwork, traveling and waiting times as they now can deal with government matters on-line anytime at their own convenience. On the government's side, there are also cost savings and it will be viewed as an active respondent.

3. **Vertical Integration:** At this current and the next few stages, citizens' demands and society's changes are seen to steer governments into looking at the integration of services. This transformation of services takes place in two ways, vertically and horizontally. In vertical integration, it refers to connecting local systems to higher level systems within similar functionalities. An example is the registration of drivers' license at a state system will be updated to national database of licensed drivers. In addition to technological changes, re-conceptualization and permanent process changes of the government organization will also occurred. As this stage progresses, there will be the integration of the current local and scattered systems at the different vertical levels. Likewise, there will

also be integration on different horizontal functions of government services.

4. **Horizontal Integration:** Progressing from the vertical integration stage, this final stage of horizontal integration refers to integration of government functions and services across different functional walls or agencies working in 'silos', such that a transaction in one agency can lead to automatic checks against data in other functional agencies. With this, provides a real 'one-stop' shopping for citizens. Additionally, the functional inadequacy of both the public and private sector will be clearer. For governments to reach this stage, there exists both technical and management challenges. The former includes integration of heterogeneous databases and solution for different system requirements, while the latter concerns the right mindset of decision makers to disregard 'silo' structure of only their department when considering information needs.

Accenture (2003) Five Stages Model

Accenture began its yearly surveys of e-government development in 1999, and stating e-government as a three level of service maturity model, namely publish, interact and transact (Accenture, 2001 & 2003). By 2003, this model has then evolved to five stages as listed below (Accenture, 2003):

1. **Online Presence:** This refers to websites that published online information but with few other available services. These are provided by the early adopter agencies that made early infrastructural investments.

2. **Basic Capability:** This refers to having a central plan and legal framework in place, together with developments in infrastructure and security. With the latter, there is wide online presence and more transaction related services are implemented. This in turn pro-

vide those revenue sectors the opportunity to lead the way, while other agencies learn from the early adopters.

3. **Service Availability:** This refers to the rise of basic portals that aims to provide many possible services and as quickly as possible. At the same time, some complex transaction related services are implemented. There begins cross-agency cooperation and customer focus.

4. **Mature Delivery:** This refers to having intentions-based transactional portals. There is clear ownership and authority. In addition, there are also service clusters and supports for intra-agency relationships and collaborations across different levels of government that aims to add value.

5. **Service Transformation:** There exists the vision to improve customer service delivery, with services take-up rate being a key measure of success. E-Government is now considered as part of a broader service transformation. Furthermore, there is multi-channel integration with organization, process and technology changes across agencies.

Value Assessment of E-Government

As e-government progresses through the stages, multiple projects would have been implemented, one would like to evaluate and understand the value and benefits it brings to its citizens and the society. Research and organizations have studied on the evaluation and improvements in public value and/or e-government projects. A short review of three such models and frameworks, namely REDF social return on investment model (Emerson et al., 2000), value measuring methodology (U.S. Federal CIO Council, 2002), and public sector value model (Accenture, 2004) are presented in this section.

REDF Social Return on Investment (SROI) Model

The Roberts Enterprise Development Fund (REDF) created a cost benefit analysis of social purpose enterprises run by non-profit agency in the San Francisco Bay Area. The Social Return on Investment (SROI) analysis provides non-profit organizations to measure their value.

"For social entrepreneurs operating social purpose enterprises, this value creation process simultaneously occurs in three ways along a continuum, ranging from purely Economic, to Socio-Economic, to Social" (Emerson et al., 2000, pp.1).

The details of the three value factors (Emerson et al., 2000; Emerson & Cabaj, n.d.) are:

1. **Economic value:** This refers to increasing the value of initial inputs that produce a product or service having higher market value at the next level of the value chain; measures include return on investment; for instance, non-profit that employs the school dropouts or the aged represent added value to the local economy;

2. **Social value:** This refers to the combination of resources, inputs, processes or policies to produce improvements in the lives of individuals and society as a whole; for instance, cultural performance, providing greater access to services or improving race relations; it's intrinsic value makes it hard to quantify the actual social value that is created;

3. **Socio-economic value:** This refers to increase value of resource, inputs or processes and thereby generate cost-savings for the public system such as reduction in public expenditure and/or increased in public revenues; this builds on the basis of economic value creation by trying to quantify and include certain elements of social value;

for instance, the provision of job training programs for the unemployed and supported employment programs for the disabled; it is stated this value can be measured using a social return investment metric, social earnings calculations and other metrics.

Value Measuring Methodology (VMM)

In July 2001, cooperation between the United States of America, Social Security Administration (US SSA) and General Services Administration took on a task to develop a methodology to assess the value of e-services. The outcome is a Value Measuring Methodology (VMM) that is "based on public and private sector business and economic analysis theories and best practices" and "provides the structure, tools, and techniques for comprehensive quantitative analysis and comparison of value (benefits), cost, and risk at the appropriate level of detail" (U.S. Federal CIO Council report, 2002, pp. 3).

As presented in U.S. Federal CIO Council report (2002) and by Kevin Foley (2006) of Booz Allen Hamilton, VMM involves developing a decision framework in one of its core steps. The decision framework measures (1) value, (2) risk and (3) cost, both quantitatively and qualitatively and at varying levels of details that aim to maximize value, reduce cost and mitigate risk.

The value measure consists of five factors and they are (1a) Direct User/Customer Value: This refers to the benefits directly achievable and understandable by customers including public employees, other organizations and citizens; for instance, convenient access; (1b) Social/Public Value: This refers to the indirect benefits relating to society as a whole; for instance, trust in the government; (1c) Government Operational/ Foundational Value: This refers to the overall improvements in government operations and processes; for instance, improve response time; (1d) Government Financial Value: This refers to the achievable financial benefits; for instance,

fulfilling organization mission; (1e) Strategic/ Political Value: This refers to the realization of goals in the strategic plan; for instance, reduce cost of correcting errors.

The risk measure consists of two components and they are (2a) Risk Inventory. This identifies risks associated with a plan by considering the five value factors and addresses the mitigation alternatives; (2b) Risk probability and impact scale. This defines the translation of the narrated risk impact to percentages.

The cost measure consists of three steps and they are (3a) Assessment of existing cost element structures; (3b) Assessment with possibility of including business best practices and government lessons learnt; and (3c) Include costs needed to achieve value and risk mitigation.

Public Return on Investment (PROI)

In a paper presented by Cresswell, Burke and Pardo (2006), The Centre for Technology in Government from the University at Albany with sponsorship and guidance from SAP developed a public value framework for evaluating government's IT investment. The result is the Public Return on Investment (PROI) framework that "emphasizes the point of view of the public, not the government, as the basis for the assessment" (pp. 1). This distinguishes this framework from most of the other methods, which focus on economic or financial measures.

Basically, the framework emphasizes on two crucial public values and they are: (1) value that directly benefits individuals and the general public; (2) value that arises from the improvements of the government as perceived by the public. The investment in IT allows the government to deliver a wide range of services more transparently, which provides improve public value. Nevertheless, the total value has numerous measures including savings in cost, improved trust and better service quality.

The public value proposition looks into six different impacts that government IT can have on the interests of its stakeholders and they are (a) Financial: This refers to impacts on current or forecast assets and liabilities; (b) Political: This refers to impacts on individual or business influence on government policies; (c) Social: This refers to impacts on family or public relationship; (d) Strategic: This refers to impacts on monetary or political opportunities for planning and modernization; (e) Ideological: This refers to impacts on moral or ethical on government actions; (f) Stewardship: This refers to impacts on public's trust on the government.

MAIN FOCUS OF THE CHAPTER

Issues, Controversies, Problems

According to our research, the VMM framework (from Section 2.3.2.) has never been applied to other e-governments other than that of the US Federal government. This proved difficulty in verifying the effectiveness of VMM application on other e-governments.

Different stakeholders have different concerns and some of these concerns are the motivations for e-governments. The ability to satisfy them is the main objective of e-government. However, there is not much analysis on the amount of involvement of the stakeholders at the different stages of the e-government.

Solutions and Recommendations

Proposed e-Government Component Assessment Cube Framework

The literature review presented in Section 2 provides us with a good insight on the value elements to be considered for proposing a framework for assessing e-government. From the literature review, we understand the different stakeholders, the various stages in the e-government evolution

process and the different value elements. Based on the result of our analysis, we concluded the following three main considerations that are necessary for performing value assessment of e-government projects, namely (value) components, stages and stakeholders as and they are described in Figure 1.

First, the (value) component is to be determined for the assessment, as it is needed to understand what benefits e-government project brings to the public. The different frameworks, models and definitions have some common value characteristics, although each could be using different value elements, and none of the frameworks covers all value elements of the other. We summarized the common components for value assessment in the earlier study to include the following: strategic, financial, operations and social. In addition, it is viewed that services being offered, including the types, quantity and quality, is an important consideration for the assessment. As such, the final proposed list of components for value assessment is: strategic, financial, operations, social and services.

Secondly, it is seen that e-government projects evolved through various phases towards maturity. Based on analysis results from Section 2, four stages can be summarized, and they are: (1) basic information provider refers to having a website for general information purpose; (2) communicative information refers to having a website that provides for communication to and from the agency; (3) multi-purpose provider refers to having a portal that provides for single logon to some related services; and (4) integrated services provider refers to having a portal that provides for full integration both as seen from the front-end as well as in the back-end.

Thirdly, e-government projects are not successful unless they meet the needs of the various stakeholders, where the latter uses them to perform tasks to the benefits for themselves and/or to others in the community. The six groups of stakeholders are (1) citizens, (2) employees, (3) business, (4) governments, (5) IS/IT personnel and (6) special interest groups.

Figure 1. Proposed e-government component assessment cube framework

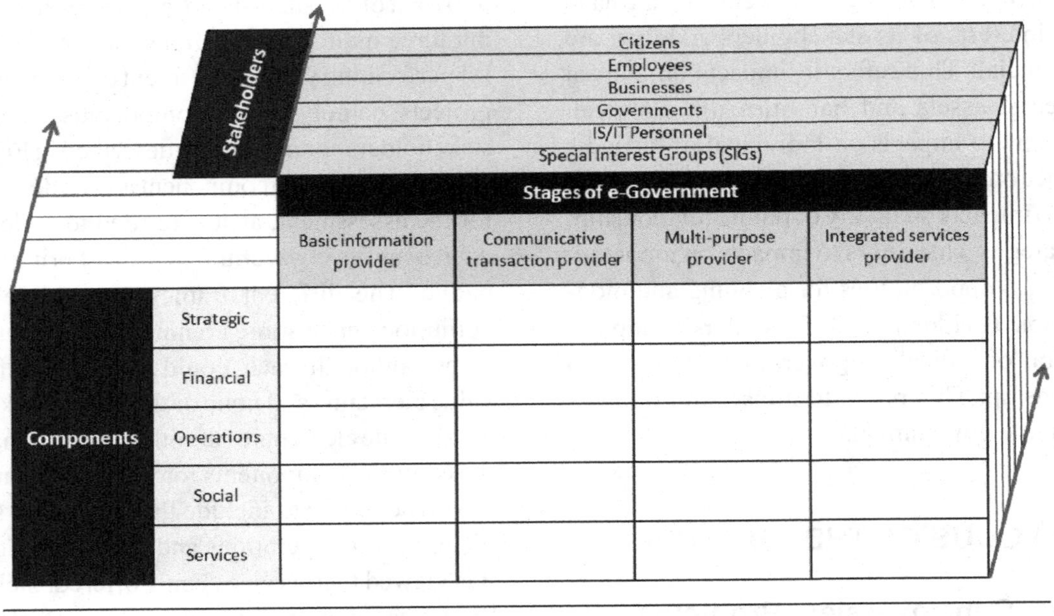

To summarize, we have proposed a three-dimension representation to depict a value assessment framework consisting of components, stages and stakeholders. The outcome is an e-Government Component Assessment Cube Framework as shown in Figure 1. A dicing performed on the three-dimensional cube, results in a sub-cube, presents the actual value offered to the respective stakeholder at a particular stage and for that component under consideration.

Application of the Proposed e-Government Component Assessment Cube Framework

Let us see some of applications of the proposed model on real-life e-government websites.

Case Study on Iraq Ministry of Electricity (Stage1-Citizen-Social)

Electricity was first introduced in Iraq in 1917 (Ministry of Electricity, 2008). The Iraqi Ministry of Electricity was formally established in 2003 (Ministry of Electricity, 2008). At that time, It was faced with badly-damaged transmission and distribution infrastructure that resulted mostly from the Second Gulf War (Farage, 2008). This proved to be a challenge to the Ministry's mission of producing, relaying, and delivering electrical energy in Iraq (Ministry of Electricity, 2008).

In order for most of the major cities' residents to get uninterrupted electricity, more than 70% of these residents own their own power generators (Farage, 2008). A third source of electricity involved unauthorized installation of loose cables on hydro poles supplied by a generation plant (Farage, 2008). However, these three sources is still incapable of meeting the minimum daily electricity demands (Farage, 2008).

With the aid of United States government funded reconstruction programs, Ministry of Electricity began engaging vendors to repair the infrastructure at damaged areas in 2003 (Farage, 2008). Although physical improvements are made, the trust and confidence of citizens in the newly appointed government agency were not gained as smoothly as the progress of the underway repairs.

Supplying progress information on repair efforts and plan details to initiate development of the electrical network for new areas on its e-government aims to achieve transparency with the whole community. Transparency will be able to clear doubts and mistrust among citizens. In turn, this may gain more understanding, support and cooperation from the community.

Case Study on Zambia Department of Immigration (Stage2-Employee-Services)

The Department of Immigration is a part of Zambia's Ministry of Home Affairs (Department of Immigration, 2007). It is in charge of regulating human movements, i.e. incoming and outgoing of the country (Department of Immigration, 2007). It legislates the requirements of travel documents for citizens, immigrants and visitors (Department of Immigration, 2007).

Its e-government website offers detailed information on guidelines, fees, applications of permits and visas. It also offers contact details for their offices in other countries that are available to assist in enquiries on services that are beyond the website. In addition, the website also provides an online feedback form to collect comments on its use.

Making this information available online will free the department's staff from spending too much time and effort in answering commonly and frequently asked questions. This allows the freed-out labour resources to be diverted to concentrate on issues that will require more tacit knowledge and more human interaction. Staff now can specialize in specific duties to perform their best in it. Specialized small number of staff can now be provided with professional trainings that may cost a lot for an individual. This enables the department to focus on improving its level of overall customer services.

The online feedback form being an important feature of a communicative transaction provider not only offers users a convenient channel to express their thoughts about either the website or the department. This brings about valuable inputs for future improvements. To be able to review and make amendments and improvements according to collected suggestions, complaints and compliments is the beginning step towards a user-driven environment. This directive approach will prevent unnecessary wastage of time and effort of staff.

Case Study on Malaysia myGovernment e-Portal (Stage3-Business-Operations)

Malaysia's e-Government kicked off on 24 February 2004 (Ooh, Zailani, Ramayah, & Fernando, 2009). Up to date, it has already reached the third stage of e-Government in our proposed e-Government Component Assessment Cube Framework. Users can login to just one portal to gain access to assorted services offered by different government agencies (myGovernment, 2010).

This website offers services and information not only for citizens but for businesses too. These services and information covers the business process from planning to start-up to maintaining growing stages. At each level, it covers legislative, financial and corporate resources of concern.

This process-oriented approach is particularly useful for new entrepreneurs. It helps to organize and advise on the available resources. This approach prevents inexperienced entrepreneurs from getting information overload by informing them on the appropriate issues and concerns at the right time. This forms a virtual step-by-step guideline and help for these entrepreneurs to start their business operations quickly and easily.

As for established entrepreneurs, this portal will keep them updated about legislative changes, which may sometimes open up potential business opportunities to them. This portal also lists available projects opened for tendering from different government agencies. This makes it convenient for businesses to monitor just one list rather than visiting multiple websites to access the listings of the different agencies.

Case Study on Canada Government of Canada Site (Stage4-SIG-Strategic)

Canada has been taking a very active role in environmental, humanitarian concerns and many more other special interests. These can be seen evidently in the international foreign policy link in its e-government website, Canada Site.

In this section, information and links to policies, projects and subsidiary bodies related to these concerns are listed. These portfolios display the efforts made by the Canadian government with regards to their interest topics. This is especially useful to Special Interest Groups (SIG).

SIGs can easily monitor the progress of their interested projects and what supportive approach is the government adopting. With that, they can determine whether the government can do better in support and whether they should step in to encourage and assist the government further.

As for governments that do not exhibit any effort, SIG can attempt to make connections with them and influence their adoption. In some cases, these countries need the assistance of SIG to improve the quality of life in their countries.

CONCLUSION AND FUTURE RESEARCH DIRECTIONS

In this chapter, we have studied and proposed an e-Government Component Assessment Cube Framework for e-government implementations. This framework looks at three main groups for the assessment, namely components, stages and stakeholders. The components consist of strategic, financial, operation, social and services. The stages consist of basic information provider, communicative transaction provider, multi-purpose provider and integrated services provider. The stakeholders consist of citizens, employees, businesses, governments, IS/IT personnel, and special interest groups.

We evaluated this framework on four countries, namely, Iraq, Zambia, Malaysia and Canada. Each of them represented a different stage of e-government. We presented the values created by e-government with different stakeholders in focus. All of the discussed e-governments have managed to create beneficial values for the different stakeholders.

From the application of our proposed model above, we would like to suggest that one potential research directions that may be done in the future will be to first identify or assemble the value proposition prior to the creation of e-government and thereafter with the aid of our model to evaluate the true values obtained from the same e-government after implementation. By comparing the expected and obtained values, the analysis will be able to determine what the unimplemented but wanted values are. With this, the e-government will be able to develop more targeted improvement plans.

The second research direction that we recommend will be to perform a research on the stakeholders' satisfaction and usability level in comparison to the amount of values created by the e-government. This aims to find out if the e-government has been offering the right services and information to the stakeholders, in other words, has it been user-driven.

The suggestions for further research on this topic include using our proposed model from different perspective and to evaluate the perceived usefulness of the e-government website.

REFERENCES

Accenture. (2003). *E-government leadership: Engaging the customer*. Retrieved April 10, 2010, from http://accenture.com/xdoc/en/newsroom/epresskit/egovernment/egov epress.pdf

Accenture. (2004). *E-government leadership: High performance, maximum value*. Retrieved April 10, 2010, from http://www.accenture.com/ NR/rdonlyres/D7206199-C3D4-4CB4-A7D8-846C94287890/0/gove_egov_value.pdf

Brown, M. M., & Brudney, J. L. (2001). *Achieving advanced electronic government services: An examination of obstacles and implications from an international perspective*. Paper presented at the National Public Management Research Conference, Bloomington, IN.

Dawes, S. S. (2002). *The future of e-government*. Presented to the New York City Council Select Committee on Information Technology in Government's hearing, An Examination of New York City's E-Government Initiatives.

Deloitte Research. (2000). At the dawn of e-government: The citizen as customer. Retrieved April 10, 2010, from http://www.egov.vic.gov.au/ pdfs/e-government.pdf

Emerson, J., & Cabaj, M. (n.d.). Social return on investment. *Making Waves, 11*(2).

Emerson, J., Wachowicz, J., & Chun, S. (2000). *Social return on investment: Exploring aspects of value creation in the nonprofit sector*. REDF box set.

Esteves, J., & Joseph, R. C. (2008). A comprehensive framework for the assessment of e-government projects. *Government Information Quarterly, 25*, 118–132. doi:10.1016/j.giq.2007.04.009

European Commission. (1998). *Public sector information: A key resource for Europe*. Green Paper on Public Sector Information in the Information Society. Retrieved April 15, 2010, from ftp://ftp. cordis.europa.eu/pub/econtent/docs/gp_en.pdf

Farage, T. (2008). Progress amid chaos. *Transmission & Distribution World, 60*(6), 22–28.

Foley, K. (2006). Using the value measuring methodology to evaluate government initiatives. *Proceedings of the 2006 Crystal Ball User Conference*.

Freeman, A. L., & Miles, S. (2002). Developing stakeholder theory. *Journal of Management Studies, 39*(1).

Freeman, R. E. (1984). The stakeholder concept and strategic management . In Freeman, R. E. (Ed.), *Strategic management: A stakeholder approach* (pp. 31–49). Marshfield, MA: Pitman Publishing Inc.

Gronlund, A., & Horan, T. A. (2005). Introducing e-gov: History, definitions, and issues. *Communications of the Association for Information Systems, 15*, 39.

Iraqi Ministry of Electricity. (2008). *The Ministry's mission*. Retrieved April 29, 2010, from http:// www.moelc.gov.iq/pages_en.aspx?id=2

Karvalics, L. Z. (2007). *Information society - What is it exactly? The meaning, history and conceptual framework of an expression*. Retrieved April 30, 2010, from http://www.ittk.hu/netis/doc/ ISCB_eng/02_ZKL_final.pdf

King, S., & Cotterill, S. (2007). Transformational government? The role of information technology in delivering citizen-centric local public services. *Local Government Studies, 33*(3), 333–354. doi:10.1080/03003930701289430

Layne, K., & Lee, J. (2001). Developing fully functional e-government: A four-stage model. *Government Information Quarterly, 18*, 122–136. doi:10.1016/S0740-624X(01)00066-1

Marchionini, G., Samet, H., & Brandt, L. (2003). Digital government. *Communications of the ACM, 46*(1). myGovernment: The Malaysia Government's Official Portal (2010). *About us*. Retrieved April 29, 2010, from http://www.malaysia.gov. my/EN/Site/AboutUs/Pages/myAboutUs.aspx

Ooh, K. L., Zailani, S., Ramayah, T., & Fernando, Y. (2009). Factors influencing intention to use e-government services among citizens in Malaysia. *International Journal of Information Management, 29*, 458–475. doi:10.1016/j.ijinfomgt.2009.03.012

Preston, L. E., & Sapienza, H. J. (1990). Stakeholder management and corporate performance. *The Journal of Behavioral Economics, 19*(4), 361–375. doi:10.1016/0090-5720(90)90023-Z

Seifert, J. W. (2007). A primer on e-government: Sectors, stages, opportunities, and challenges of online governance. Retrieved April 15, 2010, from http://assets.opencrs.com/rpts/RL31057_20020328.pdf

Silcock, R. (2001). What is e-government? *Parliamentary Affairs, 54*, 88–101. doi:10.1093/pa/54.1.88

The World Bank. (n.d.). *Definition of e-government*. Retrieved April 15, 2010, from http://web.worldbank.org/wbsite/external/topics/extinformationandcommunicationandtechnologies/extegovernment/0,contentMDK:20507153~menuPK:702592~pagePK:148956~piPK:216618~theSitePK:702586,00.html

U.S. Federal CIO Council. (2002). *Value measuring methodology: How to guide*. Retrieved April 16, 2010, from http://www.cio.gov/documents/ValueMeasuring_Methodology_HowToGuide_Oct_2002.pdf

Vassilakis, C., Lepouras, G., & Halatsis, C. (2007). A knowledge-based approach for developing multi-channel e-government services. *Electronic Commerce Research and Applications, 6*(1), 113–124. doi:10.1016/j.elerap.2006.07.004

West, D. M. (2004). E-government and the transformation of service delivery and citizen attitudes. *Public Administration Review, 64*(1), 15–27. doi:10.1111/j.1540-6210.2004.00343.x

Yildiz, M. (2007). E-government research: Reviewing the literature, limitations, and ways forward. *Government Information Quarterly, 24*, 646–665. doi:10.1016/j.giq.2007.01.002

Zambia Department of Immigration. (2007). *About us*. Retrieved April 29, 2010, from http://www.zambiaimmigration.gov.zm/zims/About_Us.aspx

ADDITIONAL READING

Amit, R., & Zott, C. (2001). Value creation in E-business. *Strategic Management Journal, 22*(6/7), 493–520. doi:10.1002/smj.187

Andersen, K. V., & Henriksen, H. Z. (2007). E-Government Research: Capabilities, Interaction, Orientation and Values. In D. F. Norris, Current Issues and Trends in E-Government Research (pp. 269-288). Hershey: CyberTech Publishing.

Giuliani, R. W. (2005). Efficiency, Effectiveness, and Accountability: Improving the Quality of Life through E-Government. In E. A. Blackstone, M. L. Bognanno, & S. Hakim, Innovations in E-Government: The Thoughts of Governors and Mayors (pp. 44-55). Lanham, Maryland: Rowman & Littlefield Publishers, Inc.

Gottschalk, P., & Solli-Saether, H. (2009). Stages of E-Government Interoperability. In P. Gottschalk, & H. Solli-Saether, E-Government Interoperability and Information Resource Integration: Frameworks for Algined Development. (pp. 108-123). Hershey: Information Science Reference.

Morphet, J. (2008). Joining-up around customers - the role of e-government. In J. Morphet, Modern Local Government (pp. 74-85). London: SAGE Publications.

Neal, L., & Cable, S. (2005). Transforming E-Government into E-Service. In E. A. Blackstone, M. L. Bognanno, & S. Hakim, Innovations in E-Government: The Thoughts of Governors and Mayors (pp. 276-285). Lanham, Maryland: Rowman & Littlefield Publishers, Inc.

KEY TERMS AND DEFINITIONS

E-Government: Electronic Government refers to refers to the use by government agencies of information technologies (such as Wide Area Networks, the Internet, and mobile computing) that have the ability to transform relations with citizens, businesses, and other arms of government. These technologies can serve a variety of different ends: better delivery of government services to citizens, improved interactions with business and industry, citizen empowerment through access to information, or more efficient government management. The resulting benefits can be less corruption, increased transparency, greater convenience, revenue growth, and/or cost reductions (The World Bank, n.d.)

Information Society: It is "a new type of society, where the possession of information (and not material wealth) is the driving force behind its transformation and development [...] (and where) human intellectual creativity flourishes" (defined by Yoneji Masuda, 1980; as cited in Karvalics, 2007).

Stakeholders: It refers to "those groups without whose support the organization would cease to exist" (Freeman, 1984)

Chapter 26
The Wisdom of the Crowds:
Creating Value with Blogs and eWoM

Zhang Wei
Nanyang Technological University, Singapore

Yang Ke
Nanyang Technological University, Singapore

ABSTRACT

What happens when a classic tool meets the Internet? This is the question that word of mouth (WOM) marketing faces. Word of mouth marketing as the oldest marketing method was completed by oral communication. But since entering the Internet era, and especially with the advent of Web 2.0, the way people share information is more dependent on hands rather than mouth – that is, through the keyboard, mouse, and smart phones – to affect others easily. This chapter will discuss the blogs and eWoM from the business, technical, social, and political aspects to reveal how eWoM thrives in the age of the Internet.

INTRODUCTION

The advent of the Internet makes it possible for consumers to browse and search the review, information and relevant discussion regarding a certain product or service. Moreover, customers are also able to share his or her own purchasing experience, opinion and all knowledge about the product or service—all these adding up together becomes the so called eWoM (electronic word of mouth), the alias of which is online word-of-month or sometimes word-of-mouse.

So what is the motive of eWoM? The basic motive lies in consumer's intention to disseminate positive or negative comments to others, based on his or her own attitude and opinion towards the product or service. In other words, when a consumer is happy and satisfied, he or she is likely to disseminate positive WoM; and when not satisfied, what he or she disseminates will be negative WoM.

DOI: 10.4018/978-1-61350-147-4.ch026

BACKGROUND

Literature Review

Word of mouth (abbreviated as WOM) refers to the process of conveying information from person to person. The traditional kind of WOM happens offline, and it plays a major role the buying decisions of the customers (Richins & Root-Schaffer, 1988).

WOM in a commercial setting means customers share their own opinions, attitudes, experiences, concerns and reactions regarding businesses, products and services with other parties.

With the quick development of Internet technologies, a new type of WOM is now prevailing, it is known as electronic WOM (eWoM). The eWoM communication is now quite vibrant via Web 2.0 applications such as online discussion forums, electronic bulletin board systems, newsgroups, blogs, review sites, and social networking websites (Goldsmith, 2006).

Research shows that WOM, based on social-networks and mutual trust, is quite influential. Interestingly, it seems that people are more likely to trust seemingly disinterested opinions coming from outside their immediate social network (Duana, Gub, & Whinston, 2008).

ISSUES

From the corporate perspective—what is the significance of eWoM? Why should a company know at all about eWoM and why should a company endeavour to implement a smart eWoM strategy?

Here are three ways that eWoM helps with a company's value capture:

Incremental Sales

As mentioned in literature review, it is already a proven fact that positive eWoM would bring in new customers, and eventually generate higher revenue. In the meantime, reduces the costs of customer acquisition.

If the company reacts and respond to the negative eWoM in a proper and timely fashion, it will be able to protect the revenue by minimizing the number of lost customers.

Higher CSI (Customer Satisfaction Index)

During the process of eWoM communication, customers have a chance of self-expression, and such expression happens in an uncontrolled, natural way. Such utterance is valuable raw material for the firm to see what the customer's perception of the products/services is, what the pros and cons are in customers' eyes, what differentiates it from products/services from competitors or substitutes, what else customers are expect from the products/services (features that competitors have).

Facilitates Product Development

Testing takes up a big portion from a company's R&D budget. When launching certain products or rolling out new services, the firm always have to arrange such research activities as interviews, surveys, focus groups and so on.

However, it is inappriopiate to say eWoM could replace surveys or focus groups. Companies could however make good use of eWoM as a tool/approach of market research, because customers contribute to the improvement of products/services through revealing their own feelings and experiences.

Another question comes from the consumer perspective: why should consumers care about eWoM? What value does it create for the consumer community?

Huang and Li (2007) used the concept and theory of "social capital" when discussing eWoM in beauty-care virtual communities in China. This theory of "social capital was firstly introduced in 1980s (Bourdieu, 1986), which, according to later researchers, refers to the "resources embedded within, available through and derived from the network of relationships possessed by in individual or social unit" (Nahapiet & Ghoshal, 1998). The "virtual community" discussed here is a kind of online forum where consumers share their beauty-care knowledge, experience and so on, and it is obviously one of the beauty-care products eWoM platform, since consumers will discuss about different products and services in this category. Actually such a platform/community could be seen as a place to aggregate and syndicate the "social capital".

According to the relevant studies, one of the key effects of social capital is its ability to "pool, create and disseminate knowledge", and some research (Kozinets, 1999; Rheingold, 1993) have demonstrated that many people are willing to exchange and share their "tacit knowledge" regarding their own experiences of products and brands. In this sense, eWoM on a certain platform is basically the syndication pool of consumer-generated content, which helps greatly to reduce the searching cost of novice consumers.

Choosing a Suitable e-WOM Strategy

According to the categorization done by the World-of-Mouth Marketing Association (WOMAA), eWoM could be organic or amplified.

Organic WOM, as the name suggest, occurs naturally when consumers just willingly become advocates, for the simple reason that they are happy with the product or service, thus feel the natural

Table 1. Types of word of mouth

Organic WOM	Amplified WOM
Buzz/Viral Marketing	Community Marketing
	Influencer Marketing
	Cause Marketing
	Brand Blogging
	E-mail Marketing
	Mobile Marketing

(Adopted from PricewaterhouseCoopers & IESE, 2006)

impulse and drive of sharing the their support and enthusiasm with others.

Amplified WOM refers to the situation in which marketers purposefully launch marketing campaigns, encouraging WoM, either in the new community/on the new platform or in the existing community/on the existing platform. (see Table 1)

Selection of Appropriate Platform

When a firm wants to implement a eWoM strategy, it has to take into consideration—where and how? In this era of information and web technologies, we are offered a wide variety of platforms. Table 1 was adapted from the platform classification from the eWoM report co-published in 2006 by the consulting firm PricewaterhouseCoopers and IESE Business School's e-business Center. Seen from Table 2, it is quite obvious why blogs - weblogs and microblogs - have been one of the most versatile and flexible technology platforms to carry eWoM.

The versatility of blogs was categorized by PWC & IESE into three major aspects:

1. In the first place, companies have high level of control over company blogs, since they are able to decide about which discussion topics should appear. Of course, besides maintaining an official company blog, companies can also market through individual bloggers by giving interesting, enticing topics and ideas that bloggers might feel interested to write or blog about. Once the bloggers are genuinely attracted by the company's selected topic or content, they will be very motivated to write about the product, service, or event held by the company.

2. Generally speaking, blogs have gained a remarkable popularity on the Internet. A large number of people have their own individual blogs and are keen on reading other's blogs—and this blogger community is still growing, according to the statistics provided

Table 2. Selection of e-WoM platform

Technology	Purpose of Strategy	Control	Reach	Level of Intrusiveness	In-house/ Outsource
Email	1. Incremental Sales 2. Product Development 3. Higher CSI	High	High	High	Both
Feedback Mechanism/ Product Review	1. Product Development 2. Higher CSI 3. Incremental Sales	Low	Low	Low	Outsource
Online Forum (Virtual Community)	1. Product Development 2. Higher CSI 3. Incremental Sales	Low	Low	Low	Both
Podcast	1. Incremental Sales	Medium	Medium	Low	In-house
Blogs	1. Higher CSI 2. Product Development 3. Incremental Sales	High/Medium	High/Medium	Low	Both

(Adapted from "Electronic Word of Mouth: what do we know about this powerful marketing tool?" e-business Center PricewaterhouseCoopers & IESE, 2006)

by Technorati (Figure 1). This ensures that blogs reach a significant number of readers, who are diffused and possibly cannot be reached effectively via other platform of traditional media (e.g. print ads, TV commercials and etc.)

3. The level of intrusiveness that blogs carry is relatively low, compared to other kinds of eWoM platforms, and at the same time they deliver a quite satisfying user-experience.

With the help of web technologies (HTML. CSS and etc), blogs are very capable of delivering rich multimedia content (in text, audio, video, and even animation other multimedia formats). Blogs also possesses the nice interactivity feature of Web 2.0, allowing the audience to have two-way communication with authors, or even co-authoring some content. Not only can blogs store information chronologically, following the calendar order, but also could it apply new techniques such as taxonomy when organizing

information, making it possible for the audience to quickly and accurately locates the content that arouse their interest.

We also would like to mention the use of RSS (Really Simple Syndication) in blogs, the useful and efficient web feed format that "pull" selected content according to the reader's personal preference, is also an approach to relieve the burden of information overload.

ANALYSIS AND DISCUSSION

To better utilize the eWOM by a company, a eWOM process was developed by Wangenheim and Bayón (2004) to understand the process of effective use of the eWOM. To begin with, the very first step is to match the sender's motivation with the receiver's motivation. Only when the senders want to express themselves to a certain products or service and meanwhile the receiver have the needs to utilize their words to develop, the eWOM could be greatest useful.

Figure 1. Technorati statistics showing rapid increase of weblogs

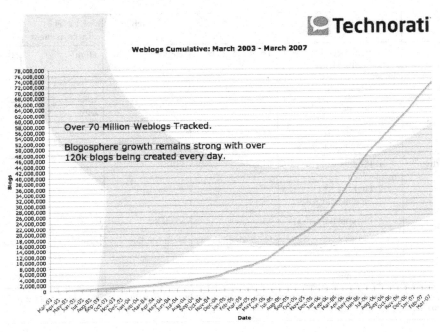

Furthermore, after understanding the needs from both senders and receivers, a well designed strategy chosen from the methods mentioned above should be developed to fulfil their needs. In this process, four elements need to take into consideration. They are copyrighted design, content layout, platform and interactive resource. Also they can use mixed methods for creating the opinions of the products, such as companies affect the consumer needs by giving incentives to the sender like financial compensation and creating positive texts, to serve the purpose of increasing sales. In this step, one thing that could be noticed is that since there is no other close relationship or attachment between the senders and the receivers, because the senders are under the anonymous status, the receivers could only choose to believe the authenticity of the information. However, there are always many people with different intentions to manipulate the opinions or words on the blogs. There are always several common unethical tricks such as stealth marketing, shilling, infiltration or defacement. In order to solve the problem of un-ethical spam, first the Word-of-Mouth Marketing Association gives the definition of unethical "any practice intended to deceive people." Then from nowadays eWOM system we can find that it is naive to believe all the comments and words on blogs but we should see how far the companies go to deceive people or guide people. From this point we see that the tolerance and compromise of the eWOM system today are also existent nowadays.

At last, the company needs to examine the effectiveness of their eWOM strategy. Some quantification or dispersion methods are recommended in this step, so that it could combine with some economic assessment methods to explain the results. For example, from the volume perspective, companies could calculate on how many people express their negative opinion on the products or services and how many are having positive products, and then categorize their complain to tell the level of problems. The question with the largest complaining proportion could be regarded as the most urgent problem needed to solve.

Normally, high-tech companies use the eWOM to develop themselves according to their customer needs and comments that are more targeted, and one of the reasons for them to do so is to simply and directly increase the sales. With the help of eWOM, they can build a community of customers like what Apple does by giving stars to their app on iTunes; they can also recognize key influencers such as the emotion of the users. To achieve the goal of increasing the sales by eWOM, companies could adopt the ways of identifying a social cause and stick to it so that once certain issue appears they will be connected with the users. They can also use email marketing to target their users with special scope and coverage (Figure 2).

According to the Arroyo and Pandey's (2010) study, the blog posts impact the album sales most strongly because the blog articles are usually published by music producer or by music lovers. Moreover, blogs are also obviously the best way to get the free news updates and comments on the music because of the number of viewing people

and the structure of the blog. There will always be fans patronising the sites.

Information overload can occur in the context of eWoM. (Park & Lee, 2008) Normally, the increase of the positive eWOM messages to the products is not considered as information overload. However, Schneider pointed out that information overload happens under the situation of the information is uncertain, which means the message is ambiguous, complex or intense. When people required more effective information for their decision, but the offered information is over sufficient, the information overload will take place. Another study has found that, information with same length but with different content or information type will also cause the information overload, that is to say, not only the quantity of information but the quality of information can also effects the information overload. These studies arise the company's attention to avoid the information overload of their customer and they should prevent it both from quantity and quality aspect. Also, some data mining tool could

Figure 2. Consumer influence model of eWOM

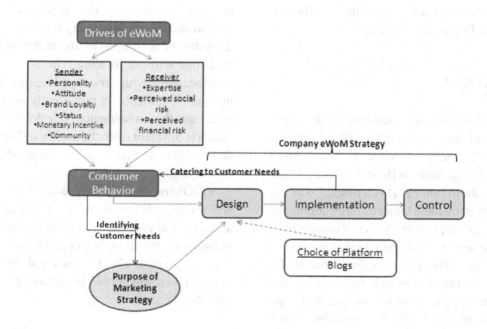

be development point to resolve the problem of information overload.

The electronic advertisement is a subversion of the communication mode of the traditional advertisement. On one hand, the space limitation was broken in information dissemination and the information deliverer need not take the traditional "face to face" form in the process of information delivery; on the other hand, the electronic advertisement surpasses the former oral mode in the content of message, the text, image, video, audio and animation may all be spread by the electronic means. Compared with the traditional advertisement, the electronic advertisement has a wider coverage, a higher accuracy, a faster speed, a lower price, a greater variety in the form and content of the advertisements, more audience and readers, etc. Therefore, the enterprise must pay attention to the marketing function of electronic advertisement in the new communication environment.

Relying on experience marketing blog has shown a more and more optimistic future. The corporate blog, entrepreneurs' blog and online video products can become a platform of experiential marketing on line, and ultimately inspire the costumers' interest and establish an e-reputation for the product brands, corporate brands and entrepreneur brands among them.

CONCLUSION

Online word-of-mouth dissemination is mainly through email, news groups, E-mail list service, listservs BBS, Online forums, Industry Portal Discussion Areas, Bulletin Boards System, MUD and Chat room to realize. It is a mighty way for companies to implement their customer communication strategy. At present, many companies have begun to use eWOM and gain a great success.

To conclude this paper, value creation for customers is created through higher CSI and contribution to product development. Although information overload will be occurred during the eWOM, there will be some tools to reduce the rate of information overload. Also, traditional advertisement is gradually lose its advantage nowadays, eWoM could help the company to gain a greater attention.

Most importantly, there are three main reasons to the motive of WoM. They are increasing sales get new ideas for product development and to improve the level of customer service.

In the process of reaching these goals, companies should be aware of what are the people talking and they are willing to hear their voice. A proper strategy then needs to be adopted to build a bridge between the senders and receivers so that each of them could take what they want. Evaluation is very important to understand the job already done and predict other possibilities at the final stage.

eWOM receiver and sender under the influence of electronic word-of-mouth information, will produce certain cognitive to eWOM, combining the characteristics of network information and reference for the theoretically framework advertising theory, information cognition is divided into four categories, information quality, authenticity, authoritative and interesting. In network environment, the authenticity of information and the quality is very important, because the network is an open platform for information exchange without filtering. Therefore, all kinds of information with varied qualities are provided, the quality authenticity will greatly influence the effect and the consequences of eWOM behavior, which is different from the traditional advertising and the face-to-face word-of-mouth dissemination in reality.

eWOM receivers' value recognition conclusion will produce different effects, it may affect their attitudes and purchase intention and purchasing behaviour towards brands or products in eWOM. For resenders of eWOM, they will not only be affected as receivers but may further spread the eWOM.

REFERENCES

Arroyo, M. M., & Pandey, T. (2010). *Electronic word-of-mouth: Impact on music sales in the American market* (pp. 431–436). China Academic Journal Publishing House.

Bourdieu, P. (1986). The forms of capital . In Richardson, J. G. (Ed.), *Handbook of theory and research for the sociology of education* (pp. 241–258). New York, NY: Greenwood.

Duana, W., Gub, B., & Whinston, A. B. (2008). Do online reviews matter? An empirical investigation of panel data. *Decision Support Systems*, *45*(3), 1007–1016. doi:10.1016/j.dss.2008.04.001

Goldsmith, R. E. (2006). Electronic word-of-mouth . In Khosrow-Pour, M. (Ed.), *Encyclopedia of e-commerce, e-government and mobile commerce*. Hershey, PA: Idea Group Publishing. doi:10.4018/978-1-59140-799-7.ch067

Huang, K., & Li, S. Y. (2007). The influence of eWoM on virtual consumer communities: Social capital, consumer learning, and behavioral outcomes. *Journal of Advertising Research*, *47*(4), 485–495. doi:10.2501/S002184990707050X

Kozinets, R. V. (1999). E-tribalized marketing? The strategic implications of virtual communities of consumption. *European Management Journal*, *17*(June), 252–264. doi:10.1016/S0263-2373(99)00004-3

Nahapiet, J., & Sumantra, G. (1998). Social capital, intellectual capital, and the organizational advantage. *Academy of Management Review*, *23*(April), 242–266.

Park, D., & Lee, J. (2007). eWOM overload and its effect on consumer behavioural intention depending on consumer involvement. *Electronic Commerce Research and Applications*, *7*, 386–398. doi:10.1016/j.elerap.2007.11.004

Richins, M. L., & Root-Shaffer, T. (1988). The role of involvement and opinion leadership in consumer word-of-mouth: An implicit model made explicit. *Advances in Consumer Research. Association for Consumer Research (U. S.)*, *15*, 32–36.

Wangenheim, F., & Bayón, T. (2004). Satisfaction, loyalty and word of mouth within the customer base of a utility provider: Differences between stayers, switchers and referral switchers. *Journal of Consumer Behaviour*, *3*(3), 211–220. doi:10.1002/cb.135

Section 4
Regulatory and Policy Issues

Chapter 27
Saviours and Barbarians at the Gate:
Dilemmas of Regulatory Policies for New Media

Arun Mahizhnan
National University of Singapore, Singapore

ABSTRACT

This chapter is based on the Keynote Speech at International Workshop on Regulatory Policies for New Media at Leipzig on 23-25 September 2009. It addresses the tensions between the inevitable need for some kind of regulation of the new media and the essentially uncontrollable nature of the architecture and the function of the media. State-regulation, self-regulation, and co-regulation have each its own strengths and weaknesses as a regime, and there is no magic bullet for keeping the new media under control. Ultimately, self-control of the end user seems more critical to the outcome than externally imposed control regimes.

INTRODUCTION

A good starting point for discussions of the regulatory framework of new media could be found in the deliberations of the Internet Content Summit held in Munich in 1999. It is the first sentence of the speech made at the Summit by Ira Magaziner, once the presidential advisor on internet policy development in America. This is what he said: "The one thing that we know for sure – and it is the only thing we know for sure about what our policies should be for the Internet – is that we do not know for sure what they should be!"[1] At the

DOI: 10.4018/978-1-61350-147-4.ch027

time of this writing ten years have passed since that statement. Are we any wiser? Are we any surer?

This essay is a response to those questions. It is divided into four parts, each of which would cover one fundamental framework in providing the answer to the quest for the right regulatory framework for the new media. Each part highlights just one or two salient aspects that are particularly contentious in the discussions over the regulation of new media.

The first part will discuss State-Regulation as a policy framework, the second part, Self-Regulation, the third part, Co-regulation, a kind of hybrid system, and the final part, No Regulation – the fond hope of the pioneering generation of internet evangelists.

State Regulation

State-regulation or what some scholars would term as legal regulation has been the most widely engaged site in the continuing debate about regulating and liberating the new media. And it is understandable because historically the state has been the most powerful agent in conceiving, imposing and ensuring compliance with a regulatory regime. Though non-state actors such as private corporations are increasingly becoming powerful in imposing restrictions and conducting surveillance, the state remains the most effective regulator. This is especially so in the maintenance of inter-state regulatory regimes which have become an imperative in dealing with the new media which is essentially a global media.

Twenty years ago when the internet first came into common use, there was a messianic sense of a new media that was not only unprecedented but also, by its very nature, untamable by any kind of shackles. The Internet world was resonating with the voices of Nicholas Negroponte[2], John Perry Barlow[3] and others of the same ilk. The way the internet was developed and how it functioned gave both philosophical and practical demonstrations of a control-free media. However, within a short

time, precisely because of the phenomenal growth of the internet from a network of nerds to the most global of communication channels, governments, corporations and civil society groups began to pay closer attention to the new medium of communication and came to very different conclusions. That is when some saw saviours at the gate and others saw barbarians.

Many governments, though not all, sensed that this technology was both a boon and a bane: boon because it could help in their economic development but a bane because it could unravel their political arrangements and social norms. Thus began a series of actions as well as contentions that brought the state squarely into the internet world. There is some irony in that it was a government – the US Government -- that originally seeded the birth of the internet and yet once the child could stand on its own feet, the one thing that many people did not want it to submit itself to is 'parental' control.

The internet is now a global medium and no government or commercial corporation owns it or runs it. Still, the fact that the US is its native home, the trend that its spiritual leaders are mostly American and the reality that no other country uses the internet more innovatively, together make the American response to internet issues as a standard bearer. Everyone watches what happens in America. On the other hand, China, already the home of the biggest number of internet users on this planet – more than 300 million at the time of writing -- and with the ability to build its own version of internet, coupled with tremendous economic and political power, does have its own special place at the high table of internet rule makers. However, as it happens, the two countries – their governments in particular – have such different attitudes and approaches to the internet and the new media that it would be difficult to put them both in the same frame of state-regulation.

The following two examples illustrate the differences in state intervention between America and China and are also indicative of the wide range of state-regulation that is trying to cope with the new media proliferation across the globe. However, countries such as Myanmar are not reckoned here as most of their people are denied the use of the internet altogether by their governments. The focus here is on countries which have a strong commitment to using ICTs but differ on how to use it.

The first example is one of the most discussed internet laws and probably the first major attempt by the US government to regulate the new media. The US government introduced the Communications Decency Act in 1996[4] and it had two significant provisions: one was to prohibit the spread of indecent materials to children under 18 and the other was to protect online service providers from the illegal activities of others through their services. The very next year, in a much publicised case, known as Reno vs. American Civil Liberties Union, that challenged this piece of legislation, the first provision was struck down by the US Supreme Court on the grounds that it violated the First Amendment right to free speech and the Act has since been amended. The second provision has remained part of the Act. The US Supreme Court decision[5] was celebrated among the libertarian advocates of internet freedom as a victory for the saviours at the gate while much of the world mourned the demise of a provision that it saw as protection against the barbarians at the gate.

The second example is the Green Dam experience in China which has also had wide publicity in the internet world. The Chinese government issued a directive in May 2009 that all personal computers sold in the country should pre-install a special software that can filter out pornographic materials and other "unhealthy information" from the internet, within three months.[6] The software was generally referred to as Green Dam, an allusion to keeping the internet clean of undesirable materials. Though the government claimed the measure was aimed at protecting the public – especially minors -- from pornography and violent content, many outside China believed the measure had more sinister motives and was widely seen as yet

another attempt to strengthen the Great Chinese Firewall. What do not feature in many Western media reports or intellectual discourses are the Chinese public's own views on such measures, partly because the information is not readily available and partly because it is ignored. Be that as it may, in August 2009, well after the deadline passed and most computers remained 'un-damed', People's Daily, one of China's official news sources, reported that according to the minister in charge "it was never the ministry's intention to demand that the software be pre-installed," and that "PC users were to have the final say about whether to use the software or not." The minister added: "We will listen to the public's views before issuing a new directive on Green Dam." According to People's Daily, he declined to set a new deadline for the implementation of the software.[7]

Looking at the two examples of government intervention to regulate the flow of information through the new media, we see two extremely different approaches for probably the same purpose and two extremely different processes in settling the conflicts with probably the same outcome – neither government quite succeeded in what it intended to achieve.

The first point to note here that there is a vast difference in the way media freedom is treated in America and many Western European democracies on the one hand and many other countries in Asia and Africa on the other, even if, in some cases, they are democracies too. This is one reason why state-regulation of even the old media in the West is so different from the rest. The concept of Fourth Estate and the role of the media as a watch dog over government are simply not accepted by some governments and they see the subjugation of mass media to state control as a necessary and unavoidable precondition to economic growth and political stability. Obviously, this is a seriously contested notion even in those countries but the point here is that state-regulation of old media is even more entrenched there than in many Western democracies.

In the US example, it is amply demonstrated that within the US political culture, it is not easy for the state to intervene, no matter how noble the cause appears to be because there are other equally noble causes that must be engaged, debated and settled through due process of law. In many other countries, the processes and, therefore, the outcomes are completely different. There are any number of internet laws abridging the freedom of speech in these countries. Such significant differences among the regimes of state control would make it difficult to reach any consensus over how the global regime for the new media should be shaped. This is why despite a shared network that connects the whole world, there has not been—and highly unlikely to be—a shared state regulatory framework to govern the new media. As Manuel Castells, the scholar who first conceptualized the network society, acknowledges, it would be "made of many cultures, many values, many projects.[8] A Swedish judge—Thomas Carlen-Wendels—is reported to have summed up the dilemma of universal jurisdiction rather succinctly: "As long as different countries have different laws and cultures, there are no good principles for jurisdiction, only less bad ones."[9]

The second point pertains to state-regulation within the state. Here it might be useful to invoke the wisdom of George Santayana, albeit with slight rephrasing: Sometimes we must forget history so we are not condemned to repeat it.[10] Relying on past best practices does not guarantee future success. The US Federal Communications Commission (FCC) has had some significant successes in the past in curtailing undesirable content in the old broadcast media. China certainly has near total control of its vast broadcast media. So do many other countries. The regulatory success with the broadcast media over the last fifty or sixty years seemed to have seduced many governments into thinking of the new media as an extension of the old media. This is, perhaps, the biggest problem in governments dealing with the new media. Despite acknowledging that new media is different from

old media, they seem to think it is not that different from the old ones. If one looks at the number of governments which have lumped internet into the same state agency that regulates broadcast media, this assumption would become self evident. In reality, however, hundreds of millions of people use the internet just the way they use the mobile phone – in fact, thinking of the internet as an extension of the telephone – having conversations, sharing personal accounts, exchanging gossip, and so on. Unlike the newspaper, radio or television, which cannot perform the function of a personal medium, the internet functions both and at once as mass and personal medium. To make things even more complicated, the mobile phone is increasingly used as a mass medium too.

Since old habits die hard, many governments have gone ahead to deploy the same old strategies used for the broadcast media in initiating state-regulation and, in some cases, self-regulation too. As a result they have met with the same degree of success as those who drive by looking at the rear-view mirror or as those generals who fight today's war remembering yesterday's wars. It would be hard to find a single case where the state has been able to retain the same level of control over the internet as it has over the old media. These governments seem to ignore the fact that the new technologies have not merely changed the way we play the game but have changed the game itself.

The third point with regard to state-regulation is that the state alone can no longer succeed in keeping the barbarians outside the gate. It needs the cooperation of the industry more than ever. With the old media, it was possible in some countries to simply dictate to the industry what needs to be done and the industry complied. This approach of state intervention is no longer tenable because the new media is not altogether owned by the so-called "industry" as there are numerous new media outlets that are of anonymous origin and ownership. However, there is some scope for self-regulation of the new media which is discussed below.

Self-Regulation

Self-regulation as a concept of self-governance developed along with the old professions such as medicine, law and accounting. While they all are subject to legal regulation, there is also an extensive body of self-regulatory principles, codes and practices, developed over many decades, if not centuries, in some cases. It is generally accepted that self-regulation is not a substitute for state-regulation, though very often self-regulation is established by consenting parties to avert state-regulation. It is also generally assumed that self-regulation by itself will not be effective if not backed up by state support either through enabling legislation or, at the minimum, through clear and strong signalling that failure to comply with self-regulation would attract state intervention. In the old media domain, the broadcast industries in particular did develop substantial self-governance practices.

Based on such experience, the denizens of the cyberworld too have attempted to replicate or at least adapt those self-regulatory systems. Much work has been done in this area and many good examples could be found in "Protecting Our Children on the Internet" by Jens Waltermann and Marcel Machill Marcel, cited earlier. In analysing the various self-regulation regimes, Waltermann and Machill lay out a schematic of how the self-regulatory concept works in five dimensions: the self-regulation of the internet industry; the self-rating or filtering mechanisms to be developed and applied by various internet producers and consumers; the establishment of hotlines that would be used to flag or eliminate illegal and undesirable content; the integrated structure that will involve the state and the non-state actors in the fight against illegal content; and finally, the ongoing effort at nurturing media literacy for all. This is a commendable effort and reflective of widespread thinking in many other countries. Prior to this, the European Commission itself has done

some spade work through a Green Paper in 1996 on the protection of minors and human dignity.[11]

However, perhaps, the most critical point to remember in all this is that in much of the past practices of self-regulation there was a clear definition and identification of who the "self" was. In the cyberworld, this "self" is a most elusive character to pin down. It is true that, as with the old media, we can identify a large number of new media players who are or can be bound by self-regulation. This would include Internet Service Providers (ISPs), established websites, respected bloggers, and so on. But what about the millions, indeed billions, of other players who may not be identifiable, or made accountable and who certainly are not willing to be part of the collective self? They play by their own rules but are very much part of the same game.

It appears that just as in the case of state-regulation, which followed old habits from the broadcast media, in the case of self-regulation, too, old practices from broadcasting days are being introduced. However, the concept of self-regulation of content in cyberspace is extremely difficult, if not impossible, to implement with even reasonable success.

Second, one critical component in the self-governance structure of the broadcast media was their liabilities as a "publisher" – because they had the ultimate control of what flowed through their channels, they were held directly responsible for the content they broadcast. However, in the cyberworld, the ISPs, which are the conduits of content, have already been exempted in many jurisdictions from any liability as it is virtually impossible to sift through trillions of bits of information going through their channels every day. With the elimination of the "publisher" role, one of the pillars of the old media self-governance structure has been removed.

Third, there is a whole range of questions about even much used terms like "illegal" "harmful" or "undesirable". There is no international or inter-cultural consensus on the meaning of these terms except in a few rare cases such as pornographic materials using children. That is why child pornography is perhaps the most often cited case for state-regulation, self-regulation, rating and filtering. Virtually the entire world is in agreement that child pornography needs to be eradicated. However, it is hard to think of even a handful of other such examples.

Fourth, the rating system is even more problematic as recent experience has shown. The terms used in rating systems have certain values to them and these vary immensely. Just take nudity as an example. Nudity is a perfectly legitimate and necessary condition in certain contexts such as medical or artistic content. Besides, nudity is a culturally loaded practice that would be wholly welcome in some cultures and wholly unwelcome in others. How does the rating help? This is where, it is argued, the "layered cake model" comes in. One can use the filters to calibrate the kind of nudity one wants to allow into the personal screens. The Internet Content Rating Association (ICRA) and other such organisations have developed a descriptive vocabulary to help the rating and filtering processes.[12] However, even the most sophisticated filtering system finds it hard to cope with what kind of nudity is allowed and what is not.

In addition, the American Civil Liberties Union (ACLU) and others have offered other criticisms of the rating and filtering systems. Some advocates of rating systems have likened it to the food labelling system where all the ingredients are spelt out and the consumer knows what she is buying. But this is a misleading comparison. Food labelling is based on objective and verifiable information whereas content self-rating may not be and, often, are not. Besides, the sheer act of self-rating hundreds or thousands of pages by individuals and small groups of people would be very costly or inefficient. However, the advocates have pointed to ratings organisations and agencies which are willing to do this at low or no cost. Then, there is the usual problem of deceptive rating or mis-rating in order to avoid filtering out and that necessitate the need for checking on self-rating by someone else.

Finally, the ACLU has pointed out what is perhaps the most telling criticism: Conversation can't be rated.[13] As the Union points out, most internet users do not run web pages, but millions of people around the world send messages, every day, to chat rooms, news groups and mailing lists. A rating requirement for these areas of the internet would be "analogous to requiring all of us to rate our telephone or streetcorner or dinner party or water cooler conversations."[14] Millions of people around the world have survived for centuries without formal rating of their conversations but through socialisation and self-filtering. So it is suggested that rating is unnecessary. However, the counter argument is that humankind has never before engaged in so many conversations, with so many people, and without the benefit of identity or affiliation. Just as an example, children have always been led astray by adults into sexual abuse but the current scale and scope of this crime, thanks to the cyber facilities, is unprecedented. Thus it is the enormity and velocity of conversational communication that prompt advocates of self-regulation and state-regulation to filter the internet.

It should be noted here that this critique of the rating and filtering system is not to suggest that it should be abandoned altogether. Instead, it brings to the fore the problematic nature of the system and it urges us all to think harder about how to refine the system and implement it more judiciously.

Co-Regulation

This section discusses the third aspect of the regulatory framework—Co-Regulation.

This hybrid model is intended to be the best of both worlds. As we have seen so far, neither state-regulation nor self-regulation by itself would be sufficient, no matter how necessary. State-regulation is constrained by geography and self-regulation by inefficiency. On the other hand, state-regulation is binding and usually predictable. Self-regulation allows for diversity and flexibility. That realization has led many advocates to push for the development of co-regulation in a systematic and sustained manner so that the strengths of each approach could be synergised with the other and they could reinforce each other.[15]

Co-regulation as a model of internet governance is still in its early stages. Many governments are either choosing not to regulate or are unwilling to enforce existing regulation in the hope the market mechanisms and incentives would lead to some kind of self-regulation within the internet industry.

While co-regulation offers a more workable model, there are many challenges in defining the multi-stakeholder structure and the spelling out of each one's role. Even when we succeed in getting the industry and the state to subscribe to the co-regulation system, there remain the multitudes of internet users who belong neither to the government nor to the industry. These users will continue to affect the way the entire internet network functions in keeping the barbarians or saviours outside the gate.

No Regulation

In the final section of this essay, it is worth considering the possibility of placing a moratorium on further regulation. In other words, no further regulation for the time being.

It is not hard to imagine a chorus of opposition to the idea of "no regulation." Again, because of old habits, we find it almost sacrilegious for anyone to suggest that there should be no control of the new media that play such a critical role in our lives – even more so than the old media. However, the argument that the internet does not need any more special regulation than what already exists for the old media is not entirely without merits. This argument is advanced partly because the existing regulations could address some of the

major concerns about the new media and partly because new regulations are not going to make that much difference.

Those concerns relating to pornography, terrorism, incitement to violence, hatred and other such concerns are well covered by existing regulations in many countries. Those found guilty of violating the rules can be dealt with in the same manner as old media users. However, the challenge with the internet is finding them in the first place, before finding them guilty. It is a legitimate worry. What, then, are the solutions?

Unlike the old media, the internet was born global, defying geography and code. It was designed to circumvent disruptions and now provides a high degree of anonymity. The ability to stop every single one of the barbarians at the gate, compared with the old media, is at best limited and, often, non-existent.

It is true that the new media also allows for greater scrutiny, surveillance and identification than in the past but that is not a universal condition. Despite the most sophisticated surveillance system in the world such as in China, hundreds of millions do remain outside such scrutiny. They generate volumes of information that would be much too costly to be processed by any system. Most countries would not be able to bear that kind of cost.

It is true that in most jurisdictions, once someone is targeted it is not impossible to find that person because of sophisticated software. It is equally true that if someone is determined enough, he/she can circumvent that surveillance, thanks, again, to sophisticated software. The technology is developing in such a way that no one can predict when or how this continuous cat-and-mouse game will end.

Therefore, instead of relying on technology, we may do better by re-looking at an easier and certainly a far better tested system that we have had with us for a long time – the social immune system. It will be part of the "new culture of common responsibility" that Waltermann and Machill argued for in their book. Some would prefer the word "responsibility" to "regulation," especially in the context of what is feasible and what is less so. It would seem that in today's internet world the best way to protect our children is to teach them how to protect themselves rather than relying on the nanny state or the socially responsible corporations.

There is such a thing as self-control and if we could invest the time and effort to educate and socialize our younger generation to look out for themselves, the chances of saving our children from harmful content would be much greater. Besides, it might be a sobering thought to those who rely on net-nanny type of filters, many kids under 12 know how to uninstall the software in contrast to those over 40 who do not even know how to install it in the first place. It is for this reason that "media literacy," the fifth element in Waltermann's and Marcel's schematic of self-regulation and centrally placed in that diagram, seems so relevant and so appropriate. Unfortunately, not enough attention has been paid to this element, nor enough resources allocated to the development of internet literacy among the young people. Even governments that spend hundreds of millions of dollars in rolling out the new fiber-optic cables and satellites that would connect them to the cyberworld have not reached out to their own children to properly introduce and socialize them into the cyberworld.

It would be difficult to argue against all regulation nor would it help to view the internet as completely ungovernable. That would be too sweeping and too nihilistic. However, based on the preponderance of evidence, it is arguable that we would be better served by a much more calibrated regulation i.e., high-touch regulation in cases like child pornography or public security because global consensus on that score is high; light-touch regulation in cases like hate speech because there is partial consensus; and no-touch approach in cases where existing analogue regulation can cover the cyberworld too.

The thrust of this essay is deliberately focused on content regulation because it is much more controversial. Issues like ownership and competitiveness require a different perspective and there is much justification for strong regulation. John Thomson has articulated the principle of "regulated pluralism" which is to ensure that "diversity and pluralism are not undermined by the concentration of economic and symbolic power."[16] Governments should take special pains to regulate the concentration of ownership and the narrowing of technological choices because in the long run these tendencies would harm the society on the whole. This is also an area where only regulation – whether state- self- or co-regulation -- could bring about the desired effect. "No regulation" is not the solution here. As a Rand Corporation study done last year for the European Commission by Jonathan Cave and others points out there may be a need for "more regulation in particular policy areas, where the benefits of market-based [self- and co-regulatory organisations] are outweighed by distortions of competition, free-rider problems, lack of compliance incentives, extra costs in self-regulation or other costs."[17]

On the other hand, we also have to be wary of the state appropriating the spaces best left to the public to debate and dialogue, all in the name of political stability or social harmony. Otherwise, the internet is in danger of what Habermas called the 're-fudalization' of the public sphere by the vested interests of governments and corporations.[18]

CONCLUSION

In conclusion, the main arguments with regard to regulation of the new media may be summarized into five points:

1. First, regulate what is regulable. Making false promises about protecting the society may, in the long run, be more harmful than making no promises.

2. Second, the state should intervene with regulation when state intervention is the only option or at least an essential ingredient for solving the problem.

3. Third, self-regulation is more desirable than state-regulation but less efficient in the internet world.

4. Fourth, the best protection for the people is what they can do themselves. New media literacy is more critical than regulation.

5. Fifth and final point: Saviours and barbarians are not mutually exclusive creatures – they are often one and the same but seen from different perspectives. And, by the way, they are not outside the gate but inside. They are us.

REFERENCES

Banerjee, I. (Ed.). (2007). Jurisdictional issues of the Internet and governance. cited by Venkat Iyer in Indrajit Banerjee (Ed.), *The Internet and governance in Asia: A critical reader,* (p. 376). Singapore: AMIC & Nanyang Technological University.

Cave, J., Marsden, C., & Simmons, S. (2008). *Options for and effectiveness of Internet self- and co-regulation* (p. 11). Cambridge, UK: Rand Corporation.

Habermas, J. (1991). *The structural transformation of the public sphere: An inquiry into a category of bourgeois society (Trans. T. Burger with F. Lawrence).* Cambridge, MA: MIT Press.

Machill, M., & Waltermann, J. (Eds.). (2000). *Protecting our children on the Internet* (p. 61). Gutersloh, Germany: Bertelsmann Foundation Publishers.

Thompson, J. (1995). *The media and modernity: A social theory of the media* (p. 241). Cambridge, UK: Polity Press.

ENDNOTES

[1] Jens Waltermann & Marcel Machill (eds) (2000). *Protecting our Children on the Internet.* Gutersloh: Bertelsmann Foundation Publishers. P. 61.

[2] Nicholas Negroponte's famous remark: "Bits don't wait in customs; they flow freely across borders. Just try stopping them." (Wired magazine: Issue 2.09, Sep 1994)

[3] http://homes.eff.org/~barlow/Declaration-Final.html Read Barlow's *A Declaration of the Independence of Cyberspace* to get a sense of the frontier spirit embodied by internet evangelists.

[4] See http://frwebgate.access.gpo.gov/cgi-bin/getdoc.cgi?dbname=104_cong_public_laws&docid=f:publ104.104.pdf for the full Act

[5] http://www.law.cornell.edu/supct/html/96-511.ZO.html

[6] http://www.nytimes.com/2009/06/09/world/asia/09china.html

[7] http://english.people.com.cn/90001/90781/90877/6728816.html

[8] Castells, M. (1996). *The Rise of Network Society.* Oxford, UK: Balckwell Publishing. P. 199

[9] Cited by Venkat Iyer in "Jurisdictional Issues of the Internet and Governance" in Indrajit Banerjee (ed) (2007). *The Internet and Governance in Asia: A critical Reader.* Singapore: AMIC & Nanyang Technological University. P. 376

[10] Santayana had said: "Those who cannot remember the past are condemned to repeat it." http://en.wikiquote.org/wiki/George_Santayana

[11] http://europa.eu/rapid/pressReleasesAction.do?reference=IP/96/930

[12] http://www.icra.org/vocabulary/ Provides a detailed account of the ICRA vocabulary and definitions and guidance on how it should be interpreted.

13   http://www.aclu.org/privacy/speech/15145pub20020317.html

14   Ibid

15   See http://www.iia.net.au/index.php/codes-of-practice/draft-privacy-code/co-regulation.html for example of the Australian Internet Industry Association's views; and http://www.foruminternet.org/telecharge-ment/forum/cp200331_en.pdf for a European example.

16   *Thompson, J. (1995).* The Media and Modernity: A Social Theory of the Media. *Cambridge: Polity Press. p. 241.*

17   Jonathan Cave, Chris Marsden, Steve Simmons, (2008). *Options for and Effectiveness of Internet Self- and Co-Regulation.* Cambridge, UK: Rand Corporation. p. 11.

18   Habermas, Jürgen. *The Structural Transformation of the Public Sphere: An Inquiry into a category of Bourgeois Society.* Trans. Thomas Burger with Frederick Lawrence. Cambridge, MA: MIT Press, 1991.

Chapter 28
Regulation of Violence in MMORPG

Lim Poh Heng
Nanyang Technological University, Singapore

Lu Dong Wen
Nanyang Technological University, Singapore

Tan Huc Huey
Nanyang Technological University, Singapore

ABSTRACT

This chapter looks at the MMORPG market, the impact of prolonged exposure to violent game content on children and reviews the current regulatory measures in Singapore. Complementary strategies, apart from legislation and censorship, empower all stakeholders to manage the risks while promoting the growth of the digital game industry in Singapore are recommended. It is hoped that the range of strategies will adequately ensure that children are protected while they develop the skills and capacity to make responsible choices. With the trend moving towards online distribution of game software, increasing household broadband access to the Internet and increasing connectivity via mobile devices, the extent and frequency with which the young are accessing and engaging with violent game content online in MMORPGs needs urgent attention from the authorities and society at large. Regulatory measures based on the film censorship model should be re-considered to address business models that leverage the ubiquitous outreach afforded by the Internet. The game industry, parents, and the society at large should be more participative in influencing the direction for game content development.

INTRODUCTION

Based on IDA's statistics on Telecom Services, household broadband penetration for internet subscription has reached 99.9% in 2008. This would mean that children and teenagers in Singapore have easy and convenient access to media from multiple channels - television, Internet and mobile devices. 90% of young children (7 - 14 years) had accessed to the Internet over the last 12 months. It is notable that today's youth are constantly tethered to the Web, playing online games, interacting via social networking sites such as Facebook and viewing video clips on YouTube.

DOI: 10.4018/978-1-61350-147-4.ch028

According to the Straits Time article entitled "I Must, I Must Complete my Quest", published on 12 August 2008, Singapore's youth rank high on the online gaming scale. In April 2008, research company Synovate released the results of its yearly Asian youth survey, which ranked Singapore's teens third for time spent playing online games. They averaged 33 minutes daily, behind Thailand's teens (who averaged 39 minutes), and the Taiwanese (who spent 34 minutes). This brings to mind the potential for children and teenagers to be influenced by detrimental contents via the wide range of media services now available to them.

The question we have is how best to protect the young from violent content in MMORPGs which are currently the rage among gamers worldwide. This paper will explore the MMORPG market, the impact of prolonged exposure to violent game content on children and review current regulatory practices.

The MMORPG Marketplace

Massively multiplayer online role-playing games (MMORPG) are online games that involve players from all over the world, in numbers ranging from thousands to millions, logging in simultaneously at any given point of time. These players own characters represented by avatars, assume digital personalities or roles and interact with other characters in a virtual world. MMORPGs commonly involve characters completing missions, such as battling and overcoming monsters and villains, to progress through different levels of difficulty and gain game points or credits.

A survey on Massively Multiplayer Online Game (MMOG) subscriptions market share by MMOGCHART.COM in 2008 revealed that MMORPGs such as World of Warcraft (62.2%), Lineage I and II (12.9%) and RuneScape (7.5%) enjoy a huge following among game players worldwide. Figure 1 shows that MMORPGs account for more than 90% of the entire MMOG market

that also includes other genres such as music or rhythm, e.g. Audition Online, and strategy games.

Player Demographics

At least 50% of game players around the world are located in Asia (includes Australia), another 30% in North America and the remaining 20% in Europe (Feng, 2007). Figures from the Internet Literacy Handbook (Council of Europe, 2008) state that 58% of children online play games on the Internet, 30% of them play at least one day a week with some even going up to seven days a week. 5% of children online play games for ten hours or more per week.

A study in the US revealed that at least 25% of MMORPG players are teenagers. Figure 2 reflects the minutes played per week throughout play history. 60% of players were also found to have played an MMORPG for at least 10 hours continuously.

Growth Potential of MMORPGs

The digital game business today garners USD 5.8 billion in annual revenue from the US market alone, with at least 50% of this amount coming from the Massively Multi-Player Online Games inclusive of role-playing genre, another 22% from casual games e.g. traditional board games, puzzles, word games, trivia and prize-oriented games and the rest from a variety of other genres such as first person shooter (FPS), sports/fighting/racing (SFR), strategy games and children's entertainment (see Figure 3), as quoted by Lakritz (2008).

Lakritz (2008) also cited the forecast by DFC Intelligence that broadband access in households worldwide will reach more than 130 million by 2012 (see Figure 4). This suggests that access to MMORPGs via the Internet will soar to an unprecedented high level. This potential market for such games would definitely be a much relished

Figure 1. The games pie

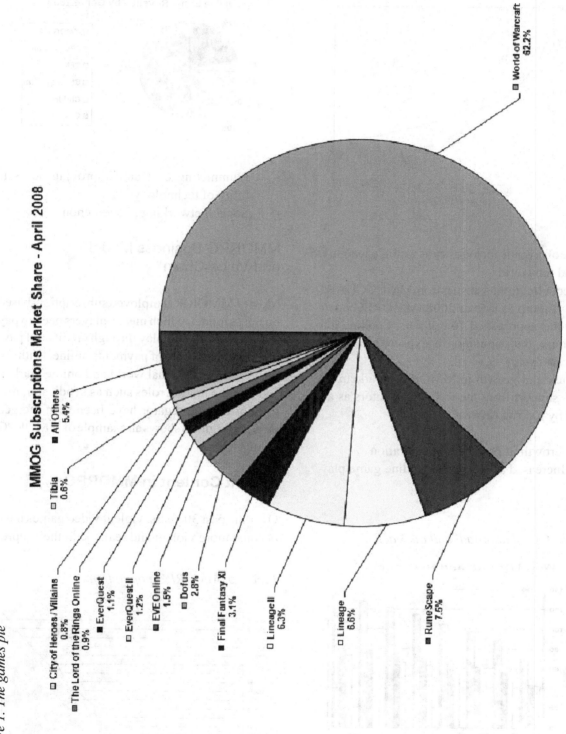

MMOG Subscriptions Market Share - April 2008

☐ World of Warcraft 62.2%

☐ Tibia 0.6%
■ All Others 5.4%

☐ City of Heroes / Villains 0.8%
■ The Lord of the Rings Online 0.9%
■ EverQuest 1.1%
☐ EverQuest II 1.2%
■ EVE Online 1.5%
☐ Dofus 2.8%
■ Final Fantasy XI 3.1%
☐ Lineage II 6.3%
☐ Lineage 6.6%
■ RuneScape 7.5%

Figure 2. A long-term study of a popular MMORPG

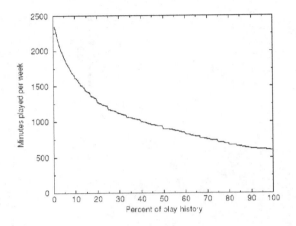

Figure 3. Online game revenue by genre, 2007

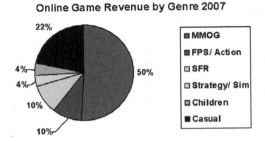

- Plummeting cost and improving accessibility of technology
- Social networking phenomenon

source of revenue for industry as well as economies around the world.

According to the statistics from MMOGCHART. COM (Figure 5) in year 2008, MMORPG population has approached 16 millions. Looking into the future, the population is expected to double every two years.

The rapid growth in MMORPG marketplace draws support from the following factors as advised by Lakritz (2008):

- Growth in broadband penetration
- Increased acceptance of online game play

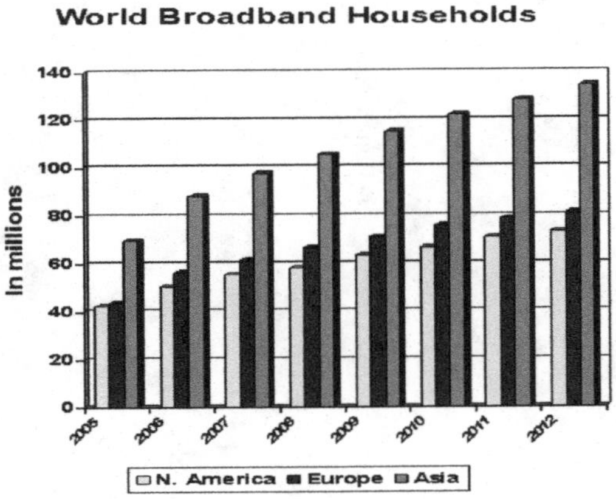

MMORPG Business Model and Value Chain

Most of MMORPG employed subscription-based business model, which means players need to pay for a monthly fee to play through credit card payment or other forms of payments online. With the convergence of virtual world and online market, some of the market roles such as syndicator, distributor and aggregator have been seen merged into one. Figure 6 shows an example of MMORPG value chain.

Violent Content in MMORPGs

Over the past 30 years, violent video games have become more violent and realistic in their repre-

Figure 4. Global broadband outreach

Figure 5. MMORPG population

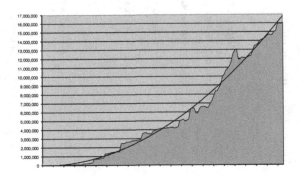

Figure 6. MMORPG value chain

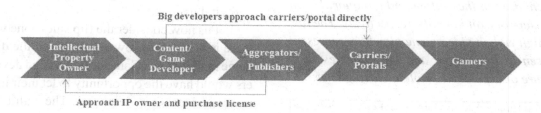

sentation of violence. For instance, the "violent" video games of the Atari Era would be considered less violent or even non-violent today. Starting from the Nintendo Era, however, the violence embedded in video games has become increasingly realistic. Thus, differences in the comparative disparity between the level of violence depicted in violent and nonviolent video games became larger with each successive era.

Video games have long provoked bitter debate between the media industry and society, especially where the content is graphically violent and aggressive. Doom, by Acclaim Entertainment, has gained notoriety on virtue of being played frequently by Dylan Klebold and Eric Harris, the perpetrators of the Columbine High School tragedy in Littleton, Colorado, on April 20, 1999. This incident saw 15 people (including the perpetrators) shot dead with dozens seriously injured or wounded.

In a lawsuit by the estate of Sanders, a teacher at Columbine High School against Acclaim Entertainment in 2002, the courts ruled in the defendant's favor. Citing the First Amendment and elements of causality in dismissing the lawsuit, Judge Thornton argued there was "social utility in expressive and imaginative forms of entertainment even if they contained violence." Such a statement is akin to pouring fuel into the fire of an already fiery debate on violence in video game content.

Nowhere is it more evident of such a phemenon than in an article by Robert F. Howe in Reader's Digest August 2005 issue entitled *"Are kids so hooked on video game violence that it becomes their reality?"*. One Devin Moore, an 18-year-old

accused of the fatal shooting of 3 police officers in Fayette, Alabama, was quoted as saying *"Life is like a video game. You have to die sometime."* Has life indeed taken to imitating "art" with deadly consequences for law enforcement officers, perpetrator, and society alike?

Impact of Violence on Youth

Gentile and Anderson (2003) advises that playing violent video games leads to incremental physiological excitement, aggressive cognitions, aggressive emotions and behaviors while decreasing pro-social behaviors. Pro-social behavior is caring about the wellbeing and rights of others with concern and empathy, and acting in a way that benefits others. The result of the study carried out by Gentile and Anderson (2003) for the percentages of Eighth and Ninth Graders Involved in Physical Fights, Split by Hostility and Violent Video Game Exposure is illustrated in Figure 7.

Given such difference, Kirsh (2006) suggests that it is important to assess the effects of violent video games on youth. Issues of video game violence and children merit serious consideration, especially after Federal Trade Commission findings in September 2000 that youths under the age of 17 were specifically targeted by 60% of all marketing plans developed for 118 M-rated violent video games sampled. In fact, a survey highlighted in Kutner and Olson (2008, p. 94) pointed out 69% of boys and 29% of girls ages 12 to 14 reported playing M-rated games "a lot."

Figure 7. The low and high hostility bars represent children in the bottom and top quartiles on a measure of trait hostility, respectively. The low and high violent video game play bars represent children in the bottom and top quartiles on a measure of exposure to violent video games.

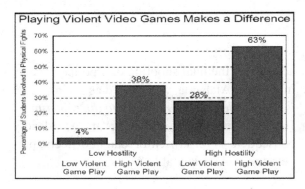

Although no known research to date has conclusively addressed the impact of MMORPG on youthful aggression, the question of how to best protect the youth from accessing violent game content needs to be addressed.

Regulating the MMORPG Marketplace

Imagine a scenario where there is a high degree of regulation of game content and the digital game industry. Game designers and developers would feel stifled by the restrictions—creativity and innovation will lack the space and flexibility necessary for realizing its potential. The high entry barrier due to strict regulations will deter potential game developers from entering the industry. The few existing game developers would likely resort to rehashing game designs to avoid running afoul of the legislation and being unable to recoup on the huge investments involved in game production. Consumers would find the game scene lackluster. Society at large, being aware of regulations in place and totally reliant on the 'safety net' provided by the authorities, would have no concern at all, possibly even exhibiting

signs of apathy, over long-term exposure of youth to digital games.

Let us now consider the flip side—one where there is minimal or low regulation of the digital game marketplace. Game designers and developers would have the opportunity to let their imagination and creativity reign free. The multitude of game genres and choices would seem like paradise to the game consumers or players. However, the youth among them would easily be immersed in pursuit of achieving game mission outcomes through any means available to them, including various forms of violence. Society at large would be surrounded with such a myriad of digital game products that they would be overwhelmed if they were not well informed and able to discriminate between the products available. Figure 8 summarizes the impact of both low and high regulation of game content for its stakeholders, namely, the game industry, consumers of game products and services, and society at large.

Regulatory Measures in Singapore

In Singapore, the Media Development Authority (MDA) plays this regulatory role where the media industry is concerned. A two-prong approach is currently taken to regulate the video game industry.

Legislation and Licensing of Internet Business Entities

Provision has been made for legislation of business on the Internet under the Broadcasting (Class License) Notification in the Broadcasting Act (Chapter 28, Section 9). According to the Broadcasting Act, "class license" means a license determined under section 9 to be applicable to certain licensable broadcasting services, and "class licensee" shall be construed accordingly (MDA, 1996)".

Clause 13 of the Class License specifies that the class licensee is expected use "its best efforts to ensure that its service complies with such Codes

Figure 8. Regulation of game content

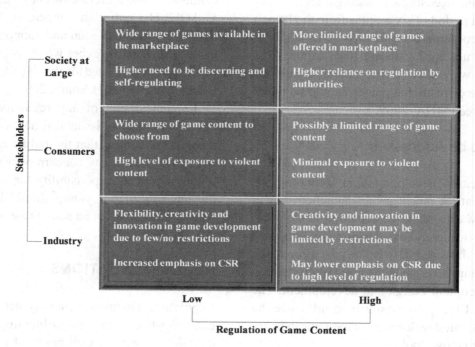

of Practice as the Authority may issue from time to time". Chapter 172 of the Media Development Authority of Singapore Act defines that "a Code of Practice may, in particular, specify the duties and obligations of any person in relation to his business operations in any media industry" (MDA, 2002).

Control and Censorship of Game Content

MDA launched a video game classification system on 28 April 2008. This system defines three categories, M18 (Mature 18), Suitable for 16 & Above (Age Advisory) and Not Allowed for all Ratings (NAR). Overall, games are expected to be screened for the theme or treatment, violence, sex, nudity, language and drug use, racial and religious elements, and threats to public order and national interest or stability (MDA, 2009a, b). The description of the categories by MDA can be found in Appendix 2.

In tandem with the launch of the classification system, a clearinghouse process, much alike the one for films is in place for video games. Businesses that import or distribute video games in Singapore are required to declare the game title via a registration form that is available online for classification. They are also required to complete and submit to MDA a questionnaire that requires them to self-profile the video game based on the genre and Singapore classification descriptors as well as declare the previous rating history of the game under other content rating systems, e.g. Pan European Game Information (PEGI) rating used across European Union (EU) (Interactive Software Federation Europe, 2007a) and Entertainment Software Rating Board (ESRB) system in the United States (US) (Entertainment Software Association, 2009). Candidates for the M18 rating are required to submit copy for evaluation. MDA reserves the right to call for evaluation copies of the video game classified under other categories, where deemed necessary.

However, licensing of video games was deferred for a period of six months from the launch of the video game classification scheme. Businesses did not need a license to distribute M18 games but were advised that general conditions for the sale of restricted games should be noted and followed (MDA, 2009c).

Issues to be Addressed

With increased development in technology, it is noted that the recent games launched show a leaning towards increased depiction of violence. Rather than to merely consider measures for access restriction, it would be wise to take a proactive in addressing the issue at the point of production i.e. game content design and development. The potential of the game designer to influence the direction for the development of the game industry should not be overlooked.

The business model for games, especially MMORPGs, is increasingly shifting towards distribution via the Internet. The two predominant models are hybrid distribution i.e. games are sold on CD through shops but are played online, and direct monthly subscription to the game publisher. A survey and tests involving young volunteers aged between 12 and 16 years conducted by UK's Trading Standards Institute revealed that children were able to illegally buy violent video games through online auction websites. About 90% of the game retailers who sold their products via the online auction channel sold 18-rated games to the volunteers ("Youths 'buy violent games online'", 2008). The measures and process currently mapped out by MDA does not appear to have taken into consideration the trend towards online purchase of games.

Apart from legislative measures, it is necessary to ensure that society at large adequately understand these changes around them and are in a good position to make the right decisions and guide the youth. To this end, it is necessary for sustained outreach and public education programmes to be conducted. The current efforts by agencies such as TOUCH Community appear to be targeted mainly towards remedial and support action for game addicts while cyber wellness programmes seem somewhat limited to schools (National Youth Council and TOUCH Youth, 2005).

Implementation of any regulatory measure has always been an issue. It is necessary to have a one-point contact that the public can relate to whenever there is any concern over violation of regulations. The responsibility for safeguarding the interests of our young should be one that society at large takes an active role in.

RECOMMENDATIONS

Regulation of industry, generally, needs to strike a balance between ensuring profitability and growth of industry and the well being of the public at large. The Government thus has the challenge of nurturing the growth and competitiveness of a new industry in its infancy in Singapore while steering innovations towards a more 'healthy' and positive orientation for public good. Thus, it is not beneficial to all stakeholders to have overly stringent regulatory measures nor overly lax ones. We propose that the perspective taken here should be one of adequately managing risks to children.

While a number of measures are in place to screen the video games, more could be done. These include refining the age classification system and raising awareness of parents about age-ratings and tools available to help control what their children play.

Promoting Design of "Safe" or Non-Violent Games

While the freedom of Internet surfing may have created difficulties for Governments to monitor and control the access to detrimental and inappropriate game content. The most popular MMORPGs however are hosted on a relatively small number of sites. The other sites host a long tail of less popular MMORPGs (see Figure 6). As such, the Government should focus on reducing the availability of violent game content in the most popular sites and encourage the design and production of a larger number of non-violent games.

Possible ways to influence the development of game content towards a more positive direction are:

- **Recognition of quality game software:** Industry players who focus their creativity juices on providing safe game content for the young should be recognized for their efforts in this direction. This can be achieved through awards, e.g. Most Innovative Game for the Young Award, established as a sign of quality (branding in this category of software) and an indicator of corporate social responsibility exercised on the part of the award winner.

- **Incentive scheme for educational game developers:** Setting up an incentive scheme for game developers to add value and enrich education by producing safe yet challenging games that are also embedded with good pedagogies and interesting content for learning. In most of the pedagogical theories, the best way to teach someone from unknown to known is to tweak the task so that it is challenging but not overly frustrating. Video games can satisfy children's interest to learn new skills and confront new challenges. They could be widely used to help teach math, science, logical thinking, readings and help children hone their hand-eye coordination. A study based on six Malaysian secondary school students, aged 16-17 years old, which was conducted by Baki et al. (2008) demonstrated benefits. Based on the students' feedback, the online video games allow the students to experience the impossible in the physical world.

  - ◦ It helps them develop skills for socializing in the virtual world.
  - ◦ It helps them learn about the cultures and lifestyles of the players of different places of the world which is an enhancement to their classroom learning.
  - ◦ It helps them learn skills of trading and negotiation.
  - ◦ It helps them learn skills of management through strategic games.
  - ◦ It also provides them opportunities a chance to learn how to manage finances, resources and humans (e.g. The Sims). The players need to analyze strategically about their position, their opponents' strengths and weakness before executing their own plans.

Regulating Access to Violent Games

Current measures pertaining to this aspect can be complemented with technological solutions that allow parents to actively participate in protecting their children from violent MMORPG content that is easily accessed online. Two possible solutions are the use of parental control software and improvement of online purchase mechanism.

- **Activating parental control software:** From consumer perspective, parents play a dominant role in managing children's access to game content using the parental control technical tools available in the market. Parents should learn how to protect children by setting up parental control software. This means the promotion of a culture of self-regulation and personal responsibility on the part of the parent. In the long run, a more pervasively proactive and self-reliant culture can be developed.

- **Review and revision of the video game classification categories:** Age-rating systems are for the purpose of informing consumers about age-appropriateness of media content for good decision-making. Sadly, the current classification system conveniently views children below 16 as a 'one-size-fits-all' game audience. It is, ironically, the interests of these young children that need to be considered in a more deliberate manner. Piaget's stages of maturation (Hamachek, 995) states that children go through four broad stages of development, shown in Table 1. To better advise and guide parents and children, the current classification categories should address the needs and abilities of children at various stages of development and maturity. See Appendix 2 for age-groupings used in PEGI and ESRB. MDA can consult with child development experts to further refine the current classification system.

- **Online purchase checking mechanism:** As MMORPGs generally require payment for subscriptions via an online mode of payment, this means that youth who would like to gain access to game sites with violent content would need to do so by using an electronic means of payment. This is a leverage point for parents to intervene when any dubious online transaction is in process. When the child attempts to subscribe to a MMORPG that is beyond his age-rating by using his supplementary

Table 1. Piaget's stages of maturation

Stages	Age group	Cognitive development
sensorimotor	birth to 2 years	Sensory development and learning motor skills
preoperational	2 to 7 years	Mainly guided by intuition, not logic
concrete-operational	7 to 11 years	Shifts towards logical reasoning
formal-operational	11 years and older	Able to do hypothetical, trial and error reasoning

credit card, the payment service provider should be able to detect this and return a null transaction. At the same time, an email or instant message is sent to inform the holder of the principal card (logically this is expected to be the parent) regarding the failed transaction.

Increasing Outreach and Public Education about MMORPGs

Parents are concerned about the opportunity costs related to their children's gaming habits and about the content of some games, but they are less aware of the potential risks of online gaming. When it comes to content, parents not only want better information on which to base their decisions—but more importantly, they see it as their role to educate their children what violent game content is, the negative consequences of playing such games and thereby help them have the confidence and skills to enjoy healthy game play. They can take into account the characteristics of their children and the context in which they play. This is reinforced in the research evidence, where context and what the child brings to the gaming experience is the key to understanding potential risks and harms.

Promoting Corporate Social Responsibility

- **Code of Practice for online safety:** In the EU, there is now a PEGI Online Safety Code that provides children engaging in online game activities with a minimum level of safety (Interactive Software Federation of Europe, 2007b). Singapore can certainly benefit the establishment of a similar online safety code of practice. For it to be meaningful, sustainable and put into practice, this code of practice needs to be crafted with the participation of representatives from all stakeholders i.e. government, industry, parents and community at large. Those who are committed to this code of practice can be recognized by the presence of a seal of commitment on their game web site.

- **Game education sessions for families:** Industry partners can offer training sessions for new games at nominal cost to family groups. This builds understanding between the industry and the community as it provides an opportunity for both parties to communicate their goals and concerns related to game activities.

Monitoring Implementation and Effectiveness of Regulatory Measures

- **Appointment of ombudsman with advisory council:** Putting regulations in place do not mean that they will be automatically acted upon. A survey and tests involving young volunteers aged between 12 and 16 years conducted by UK's Trading Standards Institute revealed that children were able to illegally buy violent video games through online auction websites. About 90% of the game retailers who sold their products via the online auction channel sold 18-rated games to the volunteers (BBC News, 2008).

The formation of a Digital Game Council headed by an ombudsman and representatives from the stakeholder groups in advisory capacity can ensure that the interests of all stakeholders are continually noted and safeguarded. Public can also play a more participative role looking after the interests of the young where digital media is concerned by having a channel to communicate their concerns and any observed new developments in this arena.

CONCLUSION

Nowadays, the video games industry is thriving and the popularity of video gaming amongst children and adolescents is prevalent. Games are diverse and developing rapidly, especially with the growth of online gaming. We need to take a multi-faceted approach to managing children's access to games in the context of this diversity and convergence. We also need to recognize that there is no single solution to the problem of children and adolescents playing games that might not be appropriate for them.

Through implementing the recommendations in this paper, the best outcomes would be achieved for the stakeholders: the Government, game industry, consumers and society at large. Children and young people would then be able to:

- explore and play online video games for fun, creativity and development.
- achieve this in an environment where there is a reduced risk of coming across violent game content.
- manage or be able to find the support to manage risks that are age-appropriate should they encounter them.

To Probe Further

An area for consideration is the development of recognition software permitting the recognition of scenes of violence as opposed to merely relying on ratings. Currently, regulatory authority depends on an online declaration from industry player as to the level of violence contained in video games. To remove any element of bias, recognition software can be deployed randomly together with manual inspection according to definite standards of what constitutes violence before permitting any online game entry into Singapore.

REFERENCES

Baki, R., Yee Leng, E., Wan Ali, W. Z., Mahmud, R., & Hamzah, M. S. G. (2008). The perspective of six Malaysian students on playing video games: Beneficial or detrimental? *US-China Education Review*, *5*(11), 11–21.

Council of Europe. (2008). Games. In Council of Europe (Ed.), *Internet literacy handbook*. Retrieved April 21, 2009, from http://www.coe.int/t/e/integrated_projects/democracy/02_activities/03_internet_literacy/internet_literacy_handbook/13_Games.asp#TopOfPage

Entertainment Software Association. (1998-2009). *Game ratings & descriptor guide*. Entertainment Software Rating Board. Retrieved April 15, 2009, from http://www.esrb.org/ratings/ratings_guide.jsp

Federal Trade Commission. (2000). *Marketing violent entertainment to children: A review of self-regulation and industry practices in the motion picture, music recording, and electronic game industries*. Retrieved March 14, 2009, from http://www.ftc.gov/reports/violence/vioreport.pdf

Feng, W.-C., Brandt, D., & Saha, D. (2007). *A long-term study of a popular MMORPG*. Retrieved from http://www.thefengs.com/wuchang/work/cstrike/netgames07_long.pdf

Gentile, D. A., & Anderson, C. A. (2003). Violent video games: The newest media violence hazard . In Gentile, D. A. (Ed.), *Media violence and children*. Westport, CT: Praeger Publishing.

Hamachek, D. (1995). *Psychology in teaching, learning and growth* (5th ed.). Boston, MA: Allyn & Bacon.

Howe, R. F. (2005). Video game violence: Grand Theft Auto/Your America. *Readers' Digest*. Retrieved April 8, 2009, from http://www.rd.com/your-america-inspiring-people-and-stories/video-game-violence/article27207.html

iDA Singapore (2009). *Infocomm usage - Households and individuals*. Retrieved March 25, 2009, from http://www.ida.gov.sg/Publications/20070822125451.aspx#usageHse9

Interactive Software Federation of Europe. (2007a). *PEGI Pan European game information*. Retrieved April 15, 2009, from http://www.pegi.info/en/index/

Interactive Software Federation of Europe. (2007b). *PEGI online*. Retrieved April 15, 2009, from http://www.pegionline.eu/en/index/id/235/

Kirsh, S. J. (2006). *Children, adolescents, and media violence: A critical look at the research*. Thousand Oaks, CA: Sage.

Kutner, L., & Olson, C. K. (2008). *Grand theft childhood: The surprising truth about violent video games and what parents can do*. New York, NY: Simon & Schuster.

Lakritz, D. (2008). *Top global markets for online games (and how to speak to the gamers)*. ION 08 Game Conference, Refining Online, May 13-15 2008, Seattle, WA.

Media Development Authority. (2009a). *Media development authority – Video game guidelines*. Retrieved April 10, 2009, from http://www.mda.gov.sg/wms.ftp/videoGames/Video_Games_Guidelines.pdf

Media Development Authority. (2009b). *Singapore introduces video games classification system*. Retrieved April 21, 2009, from http://www.mda.gov.sg/wms.www/thenewsdesk.aspx?sid=862

Media Development Authority. (2009c). *Media development authority – Video game development policies*. Retrieved, April 29, 2009, from http://www.mda.gov.sg/wms.www/devnpolicies.aspx?sid=137#1

National Institute of Education Singapore. (2008, August). I must, I must complete my quest. *Straits Times*, B10. Retrieved March 14, 2009 from http://www.nie.edu.sg/nie_cma/attachments/topic/1442c80437tH/12_Aug_08_ST_I_Must_I_Must_Complete_my_Quest.pdf

National Youth Council and TOUCH Youth. (2005). Youths in cyberspace: What are they doing. *In The offline guide for the online generation.* Retrieved March 30, 2009, from http://www.nygr.org.sg/cyberwellness

News, B. B. C. (2008, June 23). Youths buy violent games online. *BBC News*. Retrieved, April 15, 2009, from http://news.bbc.co.uk/2/hi/business/7470328.stm

Sanders v. Acclaim Entertainment, Inc., 188 F.Supp.2d 1264 (D. Colo. 2002). In 1st Amendment Online. Retrieved from http://1stam.umn.edu/archive/fedctapp/sanders.pdf

Woodcock, B. S. (2008). MMOG subscriptions market share – April 2008. In *An analysis of MMOG subscription growth: Version 23.0.* Retrieved April 22, 2009, from http://www.mmogchart.com/Chart7.html

APPENDIX A

Singapore's Video Game Classification Categories

Table 2

Suitable for 16 & Above (Age Advisory)	M18 (Mature 18)	Not Allowed for all Ratings (NAR)
Violence • Moderate level of violence. This refers to realistic but not excessively graphic violence with depiction of blood which may be included in the gameplay. Sex • Portrayal of implied sexual activity. Nudity • Nudity without details, e.g. no nipples, genitalia or pubic region (includes hair). • Still or moving images which may be mildly suggestive may be featured, e.g. scantily-clad women in bikinis or lingerie. Language • Coarse language should generally be limited to the use of words like "fuck". Drug Use • Depiction of illegal drug use which is incidental to the game and not realistic. Content of the game does not encourage drug use.	Theme • Treatment and exploration of mature themes appropriate to 18 years and above. • Content that requires the player to engage in illegal activities or play the role of a criminal so long as it does not contain detailed instructions for committing crimes. • Some homosexual content, provided it does not glamorize the lifestyle or is exploitative. Violence • Depictions of realistic violence, such as killing, maiming or causing other serious injury to humanoid characters if the violence is not sadistic, cruel and abhorrent. Sex • Portrayal of sexual activity with some nudity, both topless and frontal, if not detailed. • Homosexual activity should be limited to kissing and hugging. Nudity • Depiction of topless nudity or occasional full frontal nudity, if not exploitative. Nudity should not titillate or be the main feature of the game. • Still or moving images which may be sexually titillating (but does not contain nudity), e.g. scantily-clad women shown in a manner that is sexually suggestive, if not excessive or gratuitous. Language • Frequent use of strong, coarse language. • Drug Use • There may be realistic depiction of illegal drug use, but portrayal should not include instructive details. Games should not glamorise or encourage drug taking or the primary intent of a game should not be to encourage the consumption of drugs to achieve success, e.g. kill the enemy or complete a level.	• Content which denigrates any race or religion, or undermines Singapore's national interest. • Content that glorifies deviant sexual behaviour or activities such as paedophilia or bestiality. Games dealing with alternative lifestyles such as sadomasochism and group sex. • Clear instructional details of criminal activities, such as step-by-step guide to making a bomb. • Detailed and bloody depictions of sadistic and cruel violence, including horrific, brutal or repulsive depictions of death, injury, dismemberment or torture. • Depiction of sexual violence, including rape. • Content where the primary purpose is for the players to engage in sexual activity. • Detailed and frequent depiction of sexual activity, such as depictions of actual sexual intercourse including content which depicts explicit sexual activity where genitals may not be visible. • Exploitative and excessive depiction of nudity. This refers to male and female nudity where genitalia are clearly depicted. This would include content where the presentation of nudity is exploitative and nudity is a constant feature of the game. • Coarse language which is religiously offensive and denigrative. • Content that glamorises or encourages the use of illegal drugs. Or serve as a step-by-step guide to preparing and consumption of illegal drugs.

Source: Media Development Authority. (2009a). Media Development Authority – Video Games (http://www.mda.gov.sg/wms.ftp/video-Games/Video_Games_Guidelines.pdf)

APPENDIX B

ESRB Categories

Figure 9. **Early childhood.** *Titles rated EC (Early Childhood) have content that may be suitable for ages 3 and older. Contains no material that parents would find inappropriate.*

Figure 10. **Mature.** *Titles rated M (Mature) have content that may be suitable for persons ages 17 and older. Titles in this category may contain intense violence, blood and gore, sexual content and/or strong language.*

Figure 11. **Everyone.** *Titles rated E (Everyone) have content that may be suitable for ages 6 and older. Titles in this category may contain minimal cartoon, fantasy or mild violence and/or infrequent use of mild language.*

Figure 12. **Adults only.** *Titles rated AO (Adults Only) have content that should only be played by persons 18 years and older. Titles in this category may include prolonged scenes of intense violence and/or graphic sexual content and nudity.*

Figure 13. **Everyone 10+.** *Titles rated E10+ (Everyone 10 and older) have content that may be suitable for ages 10 and older. Titles in this category may contain more cartoon, fantasy or mild violence, mild language and/or minimal suggestive themes.*

Figure 14. **Rating pending.** *Titles listed as RP (Rating Pending) have been submitted to the ESRB and are awaiting final rating (This symbol appears only in advertising prior to a game's release).*

Figure 15. **Teen**. *Titles rated T (Teen) have content that may be suitable for ages 13 and older. Titles in this category may contain violence, suggestive themes, crude humor, minimal blood, simulated gambling, and/or infrequent use of strong language.*

ESRB Content Descriptors

Alcohol Reference: Reference to and/or images of alcoholic beverages.

Animated Blood: Discolored and/or unrealistic depictions of blood.

Blood: Depictions of blood.

Blood and Gore: Depictions of blood or the mutilation of body parts.

Cartoon Violence: Violent actions involving cartoon-like situations and characters. May include violence where a character is unharmed after the action has been inflicted.

Comic Mischief: Depictions or dialogue involving slapstick or suggestive humor.

Crude Humor: Depictions or dialogue involving vulgar antics, including "bathroom" humor.

Drug Reference: Reference to and/or images of illegal drugs.

Fantasy Violence: Violent actions of a fantasy nature, involving human or non-human characters in situations easily distinguishable from real life.

Intense Violence: Graphic and realistic-looking depictions of physical conflict. May involve extreme and/or realistic blood, gore, weapons and depictions of human injury and death.

Language: Mild to moderate use of profanity.

Lyrics: Mild references to profanity, sexuality, violence, alcohol or drug use in music.

Mature Humor: Depictions or dialogue involving "adult" humor, including sexual references.

Nudity: Graphic or prolonged depictions of nudity.

Partial Nudity: Brief and/or mild depictions of nudity.

Real Gambling: Player can gamble, including betting or wagering real cash or currency.

Sexual Content: Non-explicit depictions of sexual behavior, possibly including partial nudity.

Sexual Themes: References to sex or sexuality.

Sexual Violence: Depictions of rape or other violent sexual acts.

Simulated Gambling: Player can gamble without betting or wagering real cash or currency.

Strong Language: Explicit and/or frequent use of profanity.

Strong Lyrics: Explicit and/or frequent references to profanity, sex, violence, alcohol or drug use in music.

Strong Sexual Content: Explicit and/or frequent depictions of sexual behavior, possibly including nudity.

Suggestive Themes: Mild provocative references or materials.

Tobacco Reference: Reference to and/or images of tobacco products.

Use of Drugs: The consumption or use of illegal drugs.

Use of Alcohol: The consumption of alcoholic beverages.

Use of Tobacco: The consumption of tobacco products.
Violence: Scenes involving aggressive conflict. May contain bloodless dismemberment.
Violent References: References to violent acts.

Online Rating Notice

Online-enabled games carry the notice "**Online Interactions Not Rated by the ESRB.**" This notice warns those who intend to play the game online about possible exposure to chat (text, audio, video) or other types of user-generated content (e.g., maps, skins) that have not been considered in the ESRB rating assignment.

APPENDIX C

PEGI Age-Rating Information

Figure 16. 3+

The content of games given this rating is considered suitable for all age groups. Some violence in a comical context (typically Bugs Bunny or Tom & Jerry cartoon-like forms of violence) is acceptable. The child should not be able to associate the character on the screen with real life characters, they should be totally fantasy. The game should not contain any sounds or pictures that are likely to scare or frighten young children. No bad language should be heard and there should be no scenes containing nudity nor any referring to sexual activity.

Figure 17. 7+

Any game that would normally be rated at 3+ but contains some possibly frightening scenes or sounds may be considered suitable in this category. Some scenes of partial nudity may be permitted but never in a sexual context.

Figure 18. 12+

Videogames that show violence of a slightly more graphic nature towards fantasy character and/or non graphic violence towards human-looking characters or recognisable animals, as well as videogames that show nudity of a slightly more graphic nature would fall in this age category. Any bad language in this category must be mild and fall short of sexual expletives.

Figure 19. 16+

This rating is applied once the depiction of violence (or sexual activity) reaches a stage that looks the same as would be expected in real life. More extreme bad language, the concept of the use of tobacco and drugs and the depiction of criminal activities can be content of games that are rated 16+.

Figure 20. 18+

The adult classification is applied when the level of violence reaches a stage where it becomes depictions of gross violence and/or includes elements of specific types of violence. Gross violence is the most difficult to define since in a lot of cases it can be very subjective, but in general terms it can be classed as the depictions of violence that would make the viewer feel a sense of revulsion.

Descriptors shown on the back of packaging indicate the main reasons why a game has received a particular age rating. There are eight such descriptors: violence, bad language, fear, drugs, sexual, discrimination, gambling and online gameplay with other people.

Figure 21. **Bad Language**. *Game contains bad language.*

Figure 22. **Discrimination**. *Game contains depictions of, or material which may encourage, discrimination.*

Figure 23. **Drugs**. *Game refers to or depicts the use of drugs.*

Figure 24. **Fear**. *Game may be frightening or scary for young children.*

Figure 25. **Gambling**. *Games that encourage or teach gambling.*

Figure 26. **Sex**. *Game depicts nudity and/or sexual behaviour or sexual references.*

Figure 27. **Violence**. *Game contains depictions of violence.*

Figure 28. **Online game play**. *Game can be played online.*

Chapter 29
Is DRM the Great Spoiler in the IDM Marketplace?

Ilyas Balgayev
Nanyang Technological University, Singapore

Phng Jia Shyan
Nanyang Technological University, Singapore

Kaung Myat Win
Nanyang Technological University, Singapore

ABSTRACT

Digital Rights Management (DRM) has been a popular option employed by firms to deal with piracy issues. The rationale of DRM, the expected benefits for firms, and their implications in the Interactive Digital Media (IDM) marketplace are presented. Using the VISOR framework, the chapter also analyses the impacts of DRM based in the IDM marketplace, and to suggest if DRM is the great spoiler in the IDM marketplace. Studies have shown that the advantages brought by DRM to firms go beyond what would be needed for an efficient provision of digital goods. The chapter concludes with some recommendations and suggestions whether DRM is the great spoiler in the IDM marketplace.

INTRODUCTION

With the advent of modern information technologies, the wealth of information provided by digitization devices e.g. desktop computers, laptops, MP 3 players, iPod players, PSP players, Nintendo, IP TVs, has grown dramatically. The contents of digital information in the form of sound and multimedia e.g. video shows, video clips, video games, digital music, as well as still images, e-books etc. offer many advantages to the users as they are able to enhance human-machine interaction in many areas. Owing to the usefulness and many advantages offered by this digitized contents, they have been turned into digital goods for sale over the computer networks. The emergence of this new form of business is known as the content industry.

Within the content industry, e-commerce is becoming a primary distribution channel for the interactive digital media (IDM) marketplace. The IDM marketplace consists of three groups of

DOI: 10.4018/978-1-61350-147-4.ch029

intermediaries i.e. syndication, aggregation and distribution who come between the producers and consumers of digital media products and services. The relationships amongst all the various participants of this IDM eco-system can be complicated as many issues e.g. selling of digital content over computer networks remain unresolved.

As digital content can be easily altered, copied or even distributed to a large number of recipients or consumers, the extent of consumers' piracy can undermine the growth and viability of the vendors in this industry. This is because piracy can cause revenue loss to these media companies (Qiong Liu et al., 2003). Sony, for instance, has blamed digital piracy for eroding its profit at its music business posted a loss of 10.3 billion yen (US$160 million) in 2002 (Suzuki, 2002).

To prevent unauthorized access to digital content and manage content usage rights, one of the most common solutions is the introduction of Digital Right Management (DRM) technologies. In this aspect, supporters of DRM systems believed that they could help to provide a secure distribution of digital content. In addition, DRM enables the firms to gain additional strategic advantages e.g. switching costs, consumers lock-in, and barriers to entry, absence of second-hand market, and collection of information on the consumers' behavior. It can also help the firms appropriate extra revenues (DRM allows the high-tech firms to charge consumers several times for the usage of the same digital goods at different locations e.g. car, home, workplace etc.) (Rayna et al., 2007).

The opponents, however, argue that DRM infringes private property rights, prevents the legitimate users to take full advantage of the digital media and that such moves restrict users' activities.

This chapter presents an overview of the current state in DRM and its role in the IDM marketplace. It also discusses the rationale of DRM, the theoretical framework of Visor as well as analyze its impact on IDM marketplace e.g. high-tech firms, consumers and society with real life examples using the Visor framework. With the in depth

analysis of the DRM and its impact, this chapter seeks to find out if the DRM is the great spoiler of IDM marketplace.

DIGITAL RIGHTS MANAGEMENT

As music and films are becoming more and more popular for consumption via the Internet, this is exactly where DRM plays its role by providing a secure environment for transactions of copyrighted content in the networked world to be sold and purchased (Sensarkar, 2007). DRM is a generic term for a set of technologies for the identification and protection of intellectual property in digital form (Sensarkar, 2007). There is no big difference between the electronic and the common meaning of the term "copyright" (Rao, 2003). The term 'e-copyright' came from the time of Napster, peer-to-peer file-sharing service. It gave an opportunity to users to illegally distribute and exchange digital music files. File-sharing is a highly dynamic field with variety of publication platforms and access tools. New tools like torrent networks appeared on the horizon that sequentially substitute file-sharing services (Wolf et al., 2007). The challenge is to prevent access to content without an authorization, in other words, consumer's usage rights must be explicitly expressed so that content providers do not lose out on generating their revenue.

In order to protect copyrighted work and prevent unauthorized usage, a number of mechanisms were developed such as allowing identification of security and control of the content so as to avoid economical losses for copyright owners as well as their moral rights (Fernandez-Molina & Peis, 2001). Various systems like ECM (Electronic Copyright Management), DRM (Digital Rights Management) and ERM (Electronic Rights Management) allow methods of protection of property used in various sectors but which may not be obvious in the digital environment (O'Rourke, 1998). For instance, "Regulation by law" is different from the "regulation by code" or through a technology (Lessig, 1999). In fact, technology makes it possible to follow the stream in order to prevent certain behaviours (Reidenberg, 1998). With DRM system in place, it is noted that content cannot be moved to a file-sharing network. However, when users break the mechanisms and remove the restrictions, it can result in an unprotected and freely distributable file (Wolf et al., 2007). Thus, unprotected content after it was obtained, can be distributed and used in any manner, bypassing the DRM system. Another role of the DRM systems is to prevent the duplications of unauthorized copies as it has a mechanism by which copies can be detected and traced (Lin et al., 2005).

It is therefore important that collaborations among systems and technologies allow copyright owners to control the access to their works, with permissions of usage; and mechanisms helping to identify digital works used to manage delivery of materials to customers. DRM aims to secure exchange of intellectual property, such as copyright-protected music, video, or text, in digital form over the Internet or other electronic media. It also allows content owners to distribute content to authorized recipients as well as giving them control over the distribution chain (Hartung et al., 2000). Figure 1 presents a DRM framework consisting of the well-known PEST categories.

Figure 1. DRM framework

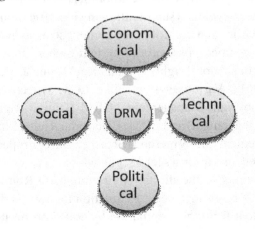

Political Aspect

The political aspect is important as regulations and legislations play an important role in the implementation of DRM. The Motion Picture Association (MPA), part of the Motion Picture Association of America (MPAA), claimed US $2.2 billion losses because of piracy in 1997 and $3.5 billion annually in the years of 2002, 2003, and 2004. Despite various legal regulations supporting DRM, piracy still is an increasing issue. The Digital Millennium Copyright Act (DMCA), developed in 1998, is an American law implementing the 1996 World Intellectual Property Organization (WIPO) Copyright Treaty (WCT) and the WIPO Performances and Phonograms Treaty (WPPT) (The Library of Congress, 1998). European Union came up with the European Union Copyright Directive (EUCD) in 2001, with implementation of the WIPO treaties (Lohmann & Seltzer, 2006). The Australian Copyright Amendment Act (DACA) proposed in 2000, is similar to the DMCA. Consumer Broadband Digital Television Promotion Act (CBDTPA) was introduced to the U.S. Senate in 2002. It proposed that anyone selling, creating, or distributing "digital media devices" must include government-approved security to prevent illegal copying of protected data (Emmanuel & Kankanhalli, 2005).

Economic Aspect

Considering that the IDM marketplace is relatively new, Amberg & Schröder (2007) propose various new business models to ensure the viability of the business as follows:

1. **"Pay-per-download" (independent of the technology of the supplier):** customer permitted to download music in data file and has to pay per downloaded song or album. File is not restricted to any hardware and could be played everywhere.

2. **"Pay-per-download" (dependent of the technology of the supplier):** the same case as for previous one, but difference is that downloaded file is in a format that could be played only using technology of the supplier.
3. **Flat rate or monthly fees:** where a customer has to pay a subscription fee but in return allowed to have unrestricted scale access, with regard to downloading and listening.
4. **Consumer's low-rated commission for every selling:** The incentive to use the offer of these models is the opportunity to earn money by reselling the content.

Social Aspect

Societal norms of fair use are laid in the DRM. Education organizations that are non-profiteering are allowed to use and use copyrighted materials, and others should pay for it. Act of giving gifts, loaning a digital video to a friend, making a backup copy of questions remain. Education of consumers for the risks associated with using the pirated content is one of the responsibilities of social aspect of DRM. Education on how a copyrighted material should be used, penalties associated with the breaking of a copyright agreement stand for regulatory functions.

Technical Aspect

In order to support business models and legal issues, technical standards and information architecture should be established. Hardware and software protection mechanisms are to be considered when we speak about technical infrastructure and architecture. Cryptographic and watermarking, fingerprinting, trading protocols, rights language, and content descriptors and identifiers are common techniques.

The following discussion presents two case studies that show the impact of a DRM implementation in the media industry.

Internet Radio

According to the DMCA, many Web radio stations must pay royalties to record labels and artists, but the radio stations claimed that with this initiative they would have to pay out more in royalties each year than they could make in advertising. Unfortunately, SomaFM had to shut down, and many, more were expected too (Cherry, 2002). Artists and record labels were unhappy at the reduction in rate, while small Webcasters predicted bankruptcy for all but the largest Internet broadcasters (Zacks, 2002). "That would be the end," said Jon Buck, CEO of Dublab, a small Internet radio station in Los Angeles. "We're not making any revenue now. No one is. We would owe US$17,000, according to the CARP plan. There is no way we could pay. What we would like to see is a flat fee on revenue".

Song sharing associated with the copright infringer maybe true from one hand, but on the other hand it helps to boost CD sales (Santini, 2003).

Video Broadcasting

In 2007 Viacom (Media conglomerate, owner of MTV and Comedy Central) complained to YouTube which is owned by Google about infringing the use of their content, particularly "The Colbert Report", "The Daily Show" and the "South Park" TV shows. Viacom tried to force Google to delete these unauthorized videos that violated the copyright act. These were videos that had resulted in YouTube's increased popularity, which in turn drives their advertising revenues. "There is no question that YouTube and Google are continuing to take the fruit of our efforts without permission," said Viacom. "Therefore we must turn to the courts to prevent Google and YouTube from continuing to steal value from artists and to obtain compensation for the significant damage they have caused" (Medeiros, 2009). As a result, Viacom won the battle over YouTube and Google who were then forced to remove all the inappropriate materials. However Viacom failed to do so. Google had then claimed that the situation is no longer under their control. Every attempt was unsuccessful; the online community posted almost every video back up again. It had become a situation whereby if the company closes down all the video facilities, it may also close down popularity of its service. One of the solutions was that Viacom was allowed to track what people watch on YouTube. However, potential question of privacy violations arose. What if Viacom uses the information to track down and sue all the people who watched copyrighted video clip on the site? Moreover, this victory can bring down many YouTube like companies such as Flickr, eBay or even MySpace; companies that built their success on so-called networked effect.

ANALYSIS OF DRM'S IMPACT ON IDM THROUGH VISOR FRAMEWORK

In the emerging IDM marketplace, there are often new products and services, new partners and new IT-based delivery, hence, new forms of business model. That is especially the case in the networked digital industry where new e-Commerce channels, comprising syndication, aggregation and distribution, are becoming a primary distribution channel for the interactive digital media marketplace. The three participants, together with content providers and consumers, have created a complicated business relationship within this new business model in the IDM marketplace. The introduction of DRM into the IDM marketplace has further made this relationship even more complex. In view of this complex interactions, it is, therefore, not practical for us to directly delve into DRM issues and their impact on IDM marketplace without first analyzing the underlying framework i.e. the VISOR (Value, Interface, Service Platforms, Organizing Model and Revenue/Cost) framework needed to understand the e-business model in the IDM marketplace.

The VISOR framework (El Sawy et al., 2005), first described by Professor Omar El Sawy and his co-workers at the Marshall School of Business (University of Southern California), is a business framework developed to articulate how companies can act, evaluate and capitalize on the emergence of new technology or service offering in the IDM marketplace (Figure 2).

Figure 2. The VISOR framework

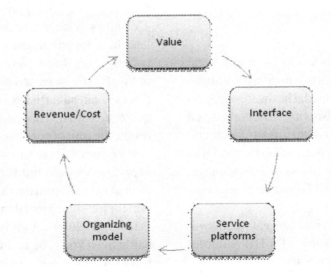

Value

In IDM marketplace, both content and device producers can only retain their copyrights if they can control over the replication and reproduction of the products. Therefore, it is critical that DRM brings the value proposition for such IDM content and device players. The case of Sony BMG CD copyright in 2005 helps to illustrate the point.

Sony BMG implemented DRM enforcement software Extended Copy Protection (XCP user, a piece of software that prevents consumers from copying the content of a CD more often than the three times allowed. XCP not only recognizes and registers the CD that is played on a computer, identifies the IP number of the computer, it is also able to monitor and report user behavior back to the firm, manipulates parts of the computer memory, crashes applications or the entire Windows operating system, interferes with file copying software and other media players and, accidentally, offers shelter for viruses, worms and other nasty things. Attempts to remove the software can lead to system crashes, malfunctions, un-usability of the CD driv) technology, to protect unauthorized copying. Sony BMG's XCP installs, unnoticed by the e and other damage at consumer's computers (Russinovich 2005a). On November 15, Sony BMG backed out of its copy-protection software, recalled unsold CDs from all stores, and offered consumers to exchange their CDs with versions lacking the software. Unfortunately, Sony faced multiple lawsuits for invasion of privacy and breaking spyware laws.

Interface

For digital media products (such as iPod) device interface and usage are the key attractions to the customers. However, even innovative products as iPod has been sued for an infringement case at a high value of US$612.5 million by Creative Technologies in the US District Court seeking an injunction and damages for Apple's "willful infringement" of Creative's self-termed Zen Patent. Creative's patent was filed in January 2001 and was awarded US patent 6,928,433, the "Zen Patent," a method for browsing and sorting files based upon metadata. Subsequently Apple's 2002 submission was denied which leads to a lawsuit of a hugh sum of payouts.

Service Platform

In the IDM marketplace, content producers, service providers and device manufacturers should work together to achieve the common goal. This is because if one party fails to comply with or honor the basic fundamentals of DRM, there will be repercussions along the supply chain. For example, if one makes changes to the computer hardware, Windows Media Digital Rights Management system may not work, hence, one may not be able to play the protected content, for instance, the songs that one purchases and are downloaded from an online store (cf. Microsoft 2004). The reason for this is that users have to authenticate the computers they want to use to play the music they have purchased. Therefore, while this prevents the user from illegally swapping files, it may also prevent the user from swapping hardware components, as legitimately purchased property might become inaccessible. This specifically includes crucial components such as the central processing unit or motherboard. This practically means that the user has to backup all DRM licenses. If this is not possible, legitimately purchased files might be lost, unless there is support from the distributor. In case there is more than one distributor, things can get even more complicated. Thus, Microsoft's DRM licensing system and authentication policy can make the replacement of hardware an annoying task, probably resulting in the loss of content.

Organization Model

In IDM marketplace, various parties ranging from producer to distributors need to cooperate to protect their assets and profits. Unfortunately, in the Digital Media Marketplace, many organizations and partnerships tend to be disconnected with numerous conflicts. Microsoft has enhanced a lot of the core operating system to add copy protection technology for new media formats like HD-DVD and Blu-ray disks. Certain high-quality output paths are reserved for protected peripheral devices. Microsoft put all those functionality features into Vista to establish a standing point in the entertainment industry. While it may have started as a partnership, Microsoft eventually ends up locking the movie companies into selling content in its proprietary formats. If Vista is firmly entrenched in the marketplace, Sony's Howard Stringer will not be able to dictate pricing or terms to Bill Gates. This is the similar case, as Apple pulled it on the recording industry. First iTunes worked in partnership with the major record labels to distribute content, but soon Warner Music's CEO Edgar Bronfman Jr. found that he was not able to dictate a pricing model to Steve Jobs. Partnerships and organizations are broken along the way, as organizations are not properly structured.

Revenue/Cost

Cost sharing to increase revenue is crucial in the IDM marketplace for both the content and service providers. In the music business, casual downloading and peer-to-peer networks are responsible for 3.6 billion songs illegally downloaded each month in the United States. In the UK, predicted sales of £1.5bn on recorded music between 2002 and 2004, were reduced to £858m due to illegal downloading. 1.2 billion Illegal music discs were sold in 2004 – 34 percent of all discs sold worldwide. Sales of pirate music exceed the legitimate market in a record 31 countries in 2004 - including China

(85% of sales are pirated copies), India (56%), Indonesia (80%), Mexico (60%), Pakistan (59%) and Russia (66%).

In 2007 February, Steve Jobs mentioned that DRM is not efficient and effective among the cosmic amount of music industry. Finally, in 2009 January, Apple's Vice President Phil Schiller announced that Apple has finally struck deals with all the major music labels, making songs sold via the iTunes Store free of digital rights management. Up to date, iTune has sold 6 billion songs and cost of removing DRM is 30cents per track. 18 billion dollar cost or removing DRM known as "*Music Tax*" is the revenue aspect of DRM being spoiler in IDM marketplace.

CONCLUSION

In this chapter, we have touched on the architectures, underlying infrastructure primitives and implementations, laws and standards. The introduction of DRM seems to be good news for digital content providers who want to develop digital content and services without fear of losing control over their digital assets. However, to deploy a successful digital online service, cryptography itself is not sufficient. (Qiong Liu et al., 2003)

A graphic presentation of DRM's impact on the IDM marketplace can be illustrated in Figure 3. It is believed that a stronger implementation of DRM will provide a higher impact in the marketplace. This is because if there is likely the increase with the additional DRM components, there will be greater regulations in the market for enforcement on its compliance, and hence the content and service owners would not be deprived of their economic gains.

Security technologies can certainly help to make it more difficult to defeat the protection scheme. However, the crucial factors that determine successful deployment of the new protection services do not depend on security alone. Some essential issues have to be considered:

Figure 3. Graph of the IDM dependency

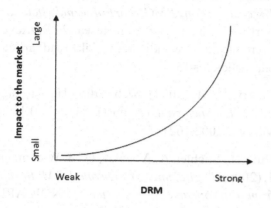

1. Will consumers be willing to play by the rules? Some comments or even criticisms about limitations of DRM e.g. inconveniences, incompatible platforms and dilution of fair use rights raise alarm that a restrictive and complicated DRM system may not be valued by consumers. (Liu et al., 2003)
2. Government intervention by legislating laws to back DRM is important to prevent large-scale illegal distribution. The court ruling to shut down Napster's illegal distribution system is one such example (Lara 2000).

DRM provides firms with some strategic advantages:

1. Helps companies to strengthen their market position. Thus, it is can be a useful tool to create corporate value. However, DRM can have a destructive power as well.
2. Allows the firms to obtain increased market power and to adopt anti-competitive behaviour.
3. Reduce the durability of digital goods.

Meanwhile, DRM has certain limitations:

1. The restrictions imposed by DRM strongly decrease the value of digital goods. This has made protected digital goods very poor competitors as compared to unprotected legal/illegal digital goods.
2. From a social point of view, the absence of standard among DRM systems and their incompatibilities is likely to decrease social welfare even further. (Rayna et al, 2007)
3. DRM is a very powerful tool, and it could enable firms to achieve near-first degree price discrimination. Since this price discrimination requires a costly reduction of the quality of digital goods, it is expected that DRM systems are wasteful and socially undesirable. (Thierry Rayna et al., 2007)
4. As opposed to the objective of implementing DRM, law-abiding consumers are, in fact, punished for their honesty: The digital goods they have paid for have fewer features than pirated ones. (Thierry Rayna et al., 2007)
5. Inappropriate use of DRM softwares e.g. DRM enforcement software Extended Copy Protection technology (XCP) in Sony BMG has, indirectly, become a malware itself and caused inconvenience to the consumers and distributors.
6. Some DRM tools such as Microsoft's Windows Media Digital Rights Management system and copy protection technology for new media formats like HD-DVD and Blu-ray disks have been implemented to move towards monopolizing the IDM marketplace much more than purely used for copy-right protection.

Is DRM the Great Spoiler in the IDM Marketplace?

Content creators/owners are facing a dilemma, either to protect their content or lose customers by instilling strict DRM systems. Although it is not the psychological intention of content owners is not to use such schema (Berman, 2004), however, it appears that the service providers seem to control DRM and content creators/owners. Thus, if the content owners want to be in the game, they have to play by the service provider's rules and pay royalties.

Network providers have different goals: cable and satellite companies take their revenue from the limiting of view window and the number of views, so they strongly support DRM; ISPs generate revenue from the traffic, mostly they do not have strong DRM, but they do not want to be on the other side of the law, moreover they adapted to have benefits from DRM Manufacturers' (DVD or MP3 players) revenue depends on content availability. They apply DRM in order to protect content.

A number of studies on a perception for restrictions of digital content have been done, with a result that the majority of respondent do not accept restrictions (Amberg & Schröder, 2007; Fetscherin, 2003; Duft et al., 2005). DRM more often stands for Digital Restrictions rather than for Digital Rights Management. "R" should stand for rights, not for restrictions.

REFERENCES

Amberg, M., & Schröder, M. (2007). E-business models and consumer expectations for digital audio distribution. *Journal of Enterprise Information Management, 20*(3), 291–303. doi:10.1108/17410390710740745

Baker, M. (2005). *Aegis DRM*. DRM White Paper I. Retrieved from http://www.aegisdrm. com/information/AegisDRM%20White%20 Paper%20I%20-%20Preventing%20Piracy%20 in%20Music%20and%20Video.pdf

Berman, S. (2004). Media and entertainment 2010 scenario: The open media company of the future. *Strategy and Leadership, 32*(4), 34–44. doi:10.1108/10878570410699627

Bohn, P. (2005, November 24). *Intrusive DRM: The cases of Sony BMG, StarForce and Microsoft*. Berlin, Germany: Berlecon Research. Retrieved from http://www.indicare.org/tiki-read_article. php?articleId=155

Cherry, S. M. (2002). Web radio: Time to sign off? *IEEE Spectrum*, (August): 53. doi:10.1109/ MSPEC.2002.1021955

Duft, N., Stiehler, A., Vogeley, D., & Wichmann, T. (2005). *Digital music usage and DRM: Results from a European consumer survey*. INDICARE, July. Retrieved from www.indicare.org/tiki-page. php?

Emmanuel, S., & Kankanhalli, M. S. (2005). *Multimedia encryption and authentication techniques and applications* (pp. 353–382). Auerbach Publication.

Fetscherin, M. (2003). Evaluating consumer acceptance for protected digital content. In Becker, E., Buhse, W., Günnewig, D., & Rump, N. (Eds.), *Digital rights management: Technological, economic, legal and political aspects* (pp. 301–320). Berlin, Germany: Springer.

Gutmann, P. (2007). *A cost analysis of Windows Vista content protection*. Retrieved from http://www.cs.auckland.ac.nz/~pgut001/pubs/ vista_cost.html

Hartung, H., & Ramme, F. (2000). Digital rights management and watermarking of multimedia content for m-commerce applications. *IEEE Communications Magazine*, (Nov): 78–84. doi:10.1109/35.883493

Helberger, N. (2006). The Sony BMG rootkit scandal. Retrieved from http://www.indicare.org/ tiki-read_article.php?articleId=165

Jobs, S. (2007, February 7). *Thoughts on music*. Retrieved from http://www.apple.com/hotnews/ thoughtsonmusic/

Klowden, T. (May 15, 2006). *The Zen patent: Creative sues Apple over media player interface.* Retrieved from http://arstechnica.com/old/content/2006/05/6838.ars

Lin, E. T., Eskicioglu, A. M., Lagendijk, R. L., & Delp, E. J. (2005). Advances in digital video content protection. *Proceedings of the IEEE, 93*(1), 171–183. doi:10.1109/JPROC.2004.839623

Liu, Q., Safavi-Naini, R., & Sheppard, N. P. (2003). *Digital rights management for content distribution.* Australasian Information Security Workshop (AISW2003), Conferences in Research and Practice in Information Technology, vol. 21.

Medeiros, N. (2009). Smack down: Copyright cases head to court (part 2). *OCLC Systems & Services: International Digital Library Perspectives, 25*(1), 5–7.

Microsoft. (2007). *The Windows Media digital rights management system may not work after you perform a system-restore operation.* (Article ID: 936621 - Rev. 1.2). Retrieved from http://support.microsoft.com/kb/936621/

Rayna, T., & Striukova, L. (2007). *Digital rights management: White Knight or Trojan horse? The consequences of DRM for consumers, firms and society.* Retrieved from http://pubs.doc.ic.ac.uk/drm-white-knight-or-trojan-horse/drm-white-knight-or-trojan-horse.pdf

Reisinger, D. (January 8, 2009). *DRM-free iTunes store to haunt Apple?* Retrieved from http://news.cnet.com/drm-free-itunes-store-to-haunt-apple/

Santini, S. (2003). Bringing copyright into the information age. *Profession,* (August): 102–104.

Schonfeld, E. (January 6, 2009). *The price of going DRM-free: Apple's hidden $1.8 billion music tax.* Retrieved from http://www.techcrunch.com/2009/01/06/the-price-of-going-drm-free-apples-hidden-18-billion-music-tax/

Sensarkar, N. (2007). The potential impact of digital rights management on the Indian entertainment. *Industry Journal of International Trade Law and Policy, 6*(1), 45–55. doi:10.1108/14770020780000549

Subba Rao, S. (2003). Copyright: Its implications for electronic information. *Online Information Review, 27*(4), 264–275. doi:10.1108/14684520310489050

von Lohmann, F., & Seltzer, W. (2006). Death by DMCA. *IEEE Spectrum,* (June): 24–30. doi:10.1109/MSPEC.2006.1638041

Wolf, P., Steinebach, M., & Diener, K. (2007). Complementing DRM with digital watermarking: Mark, search, retrieve. *Online Information Review, 31*(1), 10–21. doi:10.1108/14684520710731001

Zacks, M. (2002). Party's over: Bills come due for internet radio. *IEEE Internet Computing,* (July-August): 12–13. doi:10.1109/MIC.2002.1020320

Chapter 30
Television in Flux:
Emerging Strategies for the Online Distribution of Television Programs

Steven S. Wildman
Michigan State University, USA

Han Ei Chew
Michigan State University, USA

ABSTRACT

The television landscape is in a state of flux. In this new environment, profit-driven media companies have to balance tradeoffs between traditional and new channels of video distribution to optimize returns on their investments in content generation. This chapter describes the challenges traditional television service providers face in adapting their strategies to an environment in which the internet is playing an increasingly prominent role as a new distribution channel. In the short to intermediate run there is the challenge of finding ways to monetize an internet audience without cannibalizing profits earned through traditional distribution channels. The longer-term challenge is adapting to a distribution technology that embeds a fundamentally different economic logic for video market organization. In this chapter, we describe and analyze current trends in the internet television market and traditional television industry players' efforts to respond to the opportunities and threats posed by internet distribution.

INTRODUCTION

When YouTube turned five in May 2010, the company celebrated its anniversary with a proclamation of its newest milestone on its official blog (YouTube, 2010). According to the YouTube Team, the website exceeds two billion views a day. YouTube is currently the top video destination on the World Wide Web (Nielsen.com, 2010). The salience of digital media in everyday life is also underscored by other telling statistics such as the 41% year-on-year growth of video streams viewed in the U.S. to almost 11.5 billion monthly streams by August 2009 (Nielsen.com, 2009). The

DOI: 10.4018/978-1-61350-147-4.ch030

popularity of YouTube and other sources of online video is a telling indicator that the market for consumer video services is morphing rapidly. For decades, video was almost synonymous with TV services (networks and TV stations) that delivered programs in "pre-arranged schedules via one-way channels of communication." (Wildman, 2008). While home recording technologies beginning with the video cassette recorder (VCR) and now digital video recorders (DVRs) have given viewers more freedom to decide when they will watch their favorite programs, the internet and other modes of distribution that allow viewers to select from programs stored on video servers offer viewers much more interactive and (self) customizable ways to access video content while at the same time altering the technological and economic logics that shaped the traditional television industry.

The nature of video audiences has also undergone a metamorphosis in recent years. While even fairly recently it was fashionable to think of the difference in consumption patterns between audiences for online content and traditional media in terms of generational differences, new market research is revealing that shifts in consumption patterns transcend generational differences. Market researchers are finding that viewers, young and old, are increasingly turning to online sources for some portion of their video consumption. Three years ago, the Pew Research Center estimated that 57 percent of online adults had used the internet to watch or download video and 19 percent were doing so on a daily basis (Madden, 2007). Now, more than 81 percent of total online users in the U.S. have used the internet to watch or download video. In April 2010, 178 million U.S. internet users watched online videos according to the comScore Video Metrix service, a total that had increased by 15 percent per annum over the previous two years (from 136 million in June 2008 and 157 million in June 2009) (comScore Inc, 2010, 2009, 2008). A then all-time high of more than 25 billion videos viewed online was reported in September 2009, but only six months

later that number had increased 20 percent to 30 billion videos according to an April 2010 report from comScore (comScore Inc, 2010).

For the still dominant suppliers of traditional television service, the growth of the internet and other forms of video delivery that allow viewers to pull content from network-based video services has created a strategic dilemma. While it appears that the future of television will be shaped by the new technologies, programs delivered through traditional "linear" channels still account for most of their viewers and totally dominate their profits. The internet appears to offer opportunities for incrementally adding to the audiences and revenues for programs today's networks and TV stations already distribute, but it has become increasingly apparent that internet revenues may be gained at the expense of earnings through traditional channels, and, if not managed properly, the losses may substantially overshadow the gains. Based on decades of experience, networks and stations understand at an intuitive level the logic of service provision and the nature of competition in traditional channels, but video on the internet is a still-evolving competitive space where new, though yet to be determined, rules will almost certainly apply. The challenge is to manage what likely will be a years-long transition in a manner that leaves them strongly positioned in the emerging new video marketplace while preserving the profits from positions hard won in that portion of the television market that still relies on traditional delivery technologies.

Of course the television industry is made up of a heterogeneous mix of firms occupying niches of dramatically varying sizes. In this chapter we focus on the most visible and powerful suppliers of programming services in current television industry in the United States—the four major broadcast networks whose prime time programs still dominate in audience ratings. In doing so we emphasize that the basic analytical perspective and conclusions drawn are not specific to the United States. The U.S. networks have counterparts in other countries with market-based television systems and they too must look for ways to address the threats and opportunities posed by the internet.

The remainder of the chapter is organized as follows. The next section identifies critical differences between traditional television distribution technologies and the internet and other server-based means of distributing video content and explains why a server-based television industry can be expected to structure itself and its services in a dramatically different fashion than the industry does currently. The following section builds on this background to identify the short- and long-run challenges the internet poses to the television industry, describes the industry's early and more recent attempts to respond, and speculates on further evolution of competitive strategies and industry structure as the internet continues to reshape the nature of television service. Basic lessons and insights from our analysis are summarized in the conclusions section.

BACKGROUND

Traditional Television: Linear Schedules, Appointment Viewing, and Windowing

Television programs have traditionally been delivered to viewers via spectrum using channels. This is most obviously true for terrestrial broadcasters, who utilize government-designated radio frequency bands to send electromagnetic signals from broadcast towers to antennas connected to viewers' television sets. The more spectrum, or bandwidth, allocated to these services, the more channels of programming they can deliver to viewers. This is also true for cable television, where the spectrum utilized is encased in coaxial and fiber optic cables and for the newer IPTV subscription services offered by major telephone companies in the U.S. Program content for each channel is delivered at the same pace at which a viewer

would consume it, with one program delivered per channel. A viewer selects a program by tuning her receiver to the channel currently carrying the program she most wants to watch among those currently being broadcast on the channels reaching her television set.

This system has a number of consequences for the nature of television service. Perhaps most obvious is that the number of viewing options is limited to the number of channels reachable through a viewer's television set. This number is limited by the amount of spectrum governments allocate to terrestrial and satellite broadcasters, by the costs to terrestrial and satellite broadcasters of operating their channels, and by the costs to cable and IPTV services of increasing bandwidth on their networks. Because incremental cost of bandwidth on wire-based networks is nontrivial and governments must consider a number of valuable alternative uses for spectrum, the number of channels available to viewers is quite limited compared to what would be required to deliver to viewers all the programs (both old and new) that theoretically might be made available.

The fact that the number of programs that might be broadcast exceeds considerably the supply of channels available to broadcast them means that in effect there is competition among program suppliers for access to available channels. The end result is that the programs that networks and stations choose to carry are those that generate the audiences that channel operators find most profitable due to their value to advertisers, or to the amounts that viewers are willing to pay for access to particular types of content (or, in the case of premium channels, to enjoy commercial free programming). Channel operators thus function as gatekeepers determining which programs are or are not made available to viewers. Because channel capacity is limited, it is also valuable in the sense that the opportunity cost in terms of revenue lost when programs with limited audience appeal or appeal to limited audiences are carried can be substantial. Networks and stations thus devote considerable resources to the selection and scheduling of the programs they carry.

Of considerable importance to our analysis is that many prerecorded programs retain some of their initial audience appeal after they are first broadcast. This may be because some members of their potential audience were not able to watch them at their scheduled broadcast times - a constraint eased somewhat by home video recorders, because there are viewers who might have liked these programs but were not aware of them when they were first broadcast, or because serious fans enjoy watching episodes they have already seen after sufficient time has elapsed since they first watched them. This residual appeal, combined with the fact that production costs are sunk at the time that a second or subsequent showing of a program is contemplated, means that once a sufficient number of episodes have accumulated, a popular network program can profitably be sold in syndication for second (or subsequent) run showings to lower ranked television stations which are typically independent stations not affiliated with networks or, increasingly, to cable networks whose programming also attracts smaller audiences than the major broadcast networks. For popular network programs, syndication revenues can run to the hundreds of millions and even billions of dollars and constitute a significant fraction of their total earnings over time.

Pre-recorded network programs typically enter syndication after their third or fourth year in a network's prime-time schedule, when they have accumulated enough episodes to be run on a daily basis in a cable network's or independent station's Monday-Friday schedule (a practice known as stripping) without subjecting viewers to excessive repetition of the individual episodes. A popular network program's life in off-network syndication can last decades as it slowly migrates to more niche venues that attract increasingly smaller audiences. The profits earned by popular network programs thus accumulate over many years and investments in the production of these programs are appropriately viewed as investments in durable assets that slowly depreciate over time. The practice of licensing television programs to successively less popular and more niche channels (including DVDs) over time is known as windowing, a term that is also applied to the release of motion pictures through a well-defined sequence of distribution channels following their initial releases to cinemas.

The finances of the major broadcast networks and the independent stations and cable networks that carry their programs in syndication are thus linked and made interdependent by windowing. Cable networks and independent stations depend on off-network programs to anchor their programming schedules, and, because they anticipate subsequent syndication earnings, program producers are willing to license their programs to the major broadcast networks for substantially less than their production costs. When Owen and Wildman (1992) examined this relationship in the late 1980's, they found that network licenses fees averaged about 85 percent of production costs for comedies and approximately 79 percent of production costs for dramas.

Internet Video: The Very Different Economics of Server-Based Content Distribution

With channel-based distribution, channels that specialize in showcasing the big-budget programs that attract the largest audiences schedule new first-run programs one after the other, and those of their programs that prove popular enough to have subsequent runs do so on other channels whose business models are built around serving smaller number of viewers looking for a narrower range of program types. This pattern of migration of programs across channels over time that is a prominent economic feature of traditional television is itself a consequence of reliance on channels to deliver programs. If popular programs on major networks are to have second lives, it must be on other channels because each channel can show but one program at a time.

The technology and cost constraints that shape internet video services are entirely different. Videos and other content are delivered to a broadband internet user through what is effectively a single virtual channel that can be redirected to different sources of online content at the user's discretion. Because the bandwidth from of a single channel is sufficient to access content from a potentially unlimited number of internet sources, there is no need to add channels or bandwidth beyond a minimum threshold to give a user access to more content. Rather, because content that might be accessed resides on servers somewhere in the internet cloud, the binding economic constraint on content supplied via the internet or content stored on servers generally is server capacity. Compared to the cost of adding channels, the cost of expanding server capacity is extremely low. Thus YouTube can offer its users a choice among hundreds of millions of videos posted by both amateurs and professionals, some of which use the service simply to share personal videos with family and close friends. Similarly, we see FaceBook hosting simultaneously the postings of several hundred million subscribers along with content and applications supplied by a growing array of commercial services that make use of the FaceBook platform.

Because server capacity is cheap and channel capacity is not a material constraint, the economic incentives governing the design of online video services or server-based video services generally are quite different from those that shaped traditional television. Where by necessity television networks and stations have always had to restrict their content offerings to one program at any given time and the number that might be delivered in sequence with a single channel over any longer period of time such as a week or a month, the incentive for internet service providers is to continually increase the number of content offerings from which viewers might choose. Where the need

to send programs one-by-one in sequence down a one-way channel to viewers forces traditional television services to pay close attention to what is available on a channel and when, everything hosted by a online video service can be accessed at any time and the focus is on making it easier for viewers to search among the many options available. Finally, once a program or other video has been posted to a video service, there are no binding cost or capacity constraints that compel the host service to remove it. A unit of content could potentially stay on an internet video service's servers forever. Thus there is no obvious reason why giving viewers repeated access to older programs over time would have to be accomplished by anything analogous to windowing if the internet were the primary delivery technology for television.

The Challenge to Traditional Television Service Providers

Balancing Tradeoffs

The challenge of the internet to suppliers of traditional television services is to balance the internet's promise of expanded audience reach against the threat that profits from audience gains realized through internet distribution will be more than offset by losses in traditional distribution channels. The basic tradeoffs have already been identified in Wildman (2008). From the individual network's perspective, the plus side of internet distribution is the possibility of attracting larger audiences for popular programs as viewers who would like to watch their programs but don't because the broadcast times are inconvenient or perhaps conflict with other programs they want to watch and watch them later on the web. As long as advertisers will pay for access to a program's internet audience, this aspect of internet distribution makes a positive contribution to profits. Viewers added to a network program's initial audience through internet distribution who later want to watch that program in syndication or view old episodes on the web would amplify this gain.

There are also potential profit downsides to internet distribution that are both immediate and longer term. Most immediate is the likelihood that some, and perhaps most, people who watch a network's programs online would otherwise have watched them at their scheduled broadcast times on television. This reduces the size of the broadcast audiences networks can sell advertisers. Whether this diversion of viewers to the internet is a net financial loss to a network depends on whether advertisers pay more or less for internet viewers than they do for viewers in broadcast audiences. There are also potential financial losses due to audience diversion if the network make past episodes of their programs available online. For popular network series in a fifth or subsequent year of their network runs, previous seasons' episodes are already being broadcasted by cable networks or by independent television stations. Back episodes available online could thus cut into the programs' audiences in these second round venues for as many years as they are broadcasted. In recent years networks have been releasing new episodes of their prime-time programs for DVD sales and rentals at the end of each television season. So posting back episodes online could cut into DVD earnings as well.

The best strategy for dealing with these trade-offs is by no means obvious, and it will undoubtedly change over time as the internet channel for video distribution continues to develop. Thus it is not surprising that networks' online offerings are different today from what they were even a couple of years ago, or that these strategies continue to evolve.

Evolving Online Strategies: Present and Past

When they first started experimenting with web distribution for their programs, there were some network executives who believed that success

would be achieved by making their programs available to internet users at websites scattered broadly throughout the internet. This was reflected in an initial move by some networks, most prominently CBS, to seek broad internet distribution for their programs (Catone, 2007; Gray, 2005). Thus, based on a 2008 search for internet access to the then popular Fox Network program Prison Break, Wildman (2009) could write that the program could be "streamed from Fox's website and websites maintained by a large number of Internet services, including Yahoo!, Hulu, AOL.com, Veoh, and Fancast, to name just a few."

By 2009 the networks' online strategies had changed considerably and further changes are clearly foreshadowed by more recent developments. During the summer of 2009 we systematically catalogued the availability of the four major U.S. broadcast networks' prime-time programs in their summer schedules on websites maintained by each of the networks to showcase their own programs - which we will refer to as their official sites and eight of the most popular video-oriented websites maintained by other internet services: Hulu, Fancast, Veoh, Sling, YouTube, Joost, TV.com, and IMDb.[1] (See Appendix 1 for a list of the programs). A review of the same websites in spring 2010 showed the situation little changed from the previous year.

We found that by summer 2009 the networks had for the most part limited direct web access to their programs to their own official websites and typically one or two other authorized internet video services. Four web hosting services, Hulu, TV.com, Fancast, and Sling stood apart for their ability to enable streaming of broadcast network programs from their websites. Each offered access to a substantial number of prime-time network programs from their sites. Two of these sites had one or more network owners, ABC, NBC, and Fox all have significant ownership stakes in Hulu; CBS owns TV.com and Fancast is owned by Comcast, the largest U.S. multisystem cable operator and owner of a number of popular cable networks.

Table 1. Availability of programs by genre

	Number of shows	Availability on network sites	Availability on alternative sites
Animation	5	4 (80%)	4 (80%)
Comedy	13	6 (46%)	6 (46%)
Current Affairs	3	2 (66%)	2 (66%)
Drama	45	39 (86%)	41 (90%)
Game Shows	7	5 (83%)	5 (83%)
Reality	16	9 (56%)	7 (43%)
Total	89	65 (73%)	65 (73%)

The degree of sharing observed among these three services, and especially Hulu and TV.com, may reflect recognition of mutual dependence if each is to offer truly broad based online access to the most popular television programs. While Sling is not a major supplier of content, it is owned by EchoStar, the owner of the Dish Network, the second largest subscription satellite TV service in the United States. With a subscriber base of approximately 14 million, it too is a major television service distributor. The other six services, although offering direct access to programs and videos from other sources, were largely relegated to offering short clips for current network programs. Degrees of access to the four networks' programs through Hulu, TV.com, Fancast and Sling is described in Table 1. Access to the networks' prime time programs on their official sites and the few approved other sites broken down by program genre is described in Table 2.

As can be seen from Table 1, Fancast and Sling do not have access to as many network programs as the two services with network owners. Hulu and TV.com also discriminate against each other to a degree by making it possible to stream their own networks' programs directly onsite while requiring that the competing service provide online access to these programs via links that take the viewer back to the program originating networks' official sites. Thus, while CBS content is listed on Hulu, users follow web links from Hulu back to the CBS website and are unable to stream CBS programs directly from the Hulu site. Likewise, on TV.com users are unable to stream programs from Fox, ABC, and NBC directly from the website. This arrangement developed after CBS acquired TV.com in 2008 (Mills, 2009).

The networks' decisions to withhold their programs from most websites in which they do not have an ownership interest undoubtedly reflects a fuller recognition and reevaluation of the tradeoffs between online distribution and distribution through traditional channels described earlier in this chapter. Perhaps most important was a realization that while online episodes were starting to attract audiences, they generated little revenue directly and, to the extent online viewers would have watched the same programs on TV, the online line audience was generated at a substantial cost to net profits. Of all the online video sites, Hulu generates by far the most advertising revenue, yet

Table 2. Availability of programs by outlets

	Availability				
	Networks' official websites	Hulu.com	TV.com	Fancast.com	Sling.com
Fox (21)	16	18	17	9	16
CBS (26)	8	6	14	7	7
NBC (21)	15	14	10	10	8
ABC (21)	15	10	15	8	8
Total (89)	54 (60%)	48 (53%)	49 (55%)	34 (38%)	39 (44%)

even here the per viewer yield from the sale of ad time pales in comparison to what advertisers pay for access to broadcast audiences. Much of this disparity reflects the fact that advertisers simply are not willing to purchase as much commercial time in programs streamed online as they do when the same programs are broadcast. Programs that occupy an hour of network broadcast time typically run about 45 minutes as webcasts, with the reduction in ad time sales accounting for most of the difference. As hour-long network programs usually have 17-18 minutes of commercial time, the fall-off is on the order of 80 percent. Of course some of the ad time in the programs networks broadcast is used to promote other programs in their lineups, but time is reserved for self-promotion because it generates a return at least as large as earnings on ad time sold to outside advertisers (Shachar & Anand, 1998).

The same strategic concerns are behind the reduction over time in the number of program back episodes networks make available through their own and partner websites. At one time it was not unusual to find a full season's back episodes available on the web. At the time of our survey, it was more typical to find four or five back episodes.

What is Next?

In the near future it seems likely that some form or perhaps several forms of pay-to-play will become an important feature of the online video marketplace. The industry has already taken several steps in that direction. For example, Hulu now offers its Hulu Plus service, which for $9.95 per month gives subscribers access to all the back episodes, current and previous seasons for all the network shows it carries, offers a high definition picture, and provides access through a growing array of mobile devices. Netflix, which built its business by mailing internet-ordered rental DVDs to subcribers now allows its subscribers to stream the videos they order directly to their personal computers or directly to their TV sets using a variety of interface

devices, including the Xbox and Playstation video game players, the Roku Digital Player, a TiVo digital video recorder, and Blu-Ray players from a number of manufacturers. TV Everywhere, an initiative promoted by Comcast and Time Warner Cable, the two largest U.S. cable operators, seeks to make online access to cable networks' original programming available only to individuals with access codes verifying their status as a subscriber to a pay TV service, whether cable, satellite, or IPTV. TV Everywhere's sponsors are also encouraging participation by the traditional broadcast networks, which, due to rapidly rising retransmission consent payments from cable and satellite services, are now seeing their financial futures increasingly tied to the fees subscribers pay to these multichannel service providers.

The motives and objectives behind these strategic moves are several and somewhat intertwined. First, advertising sales associated with online video remain anemic as described above. This is undoubtedly due in part to the fact that there are no online audience measurement services with acceptance among advertisers comparable to the well-established services that have served their needs for traditional television for decades. This deficiency will undoubtedly diminish over time as online measurement services improve and advertisers and agencies gain experience with them. Second, it is quite clear that the convenience of online access to television programs is of substantial value to some portion of the internet audience, and this fact by itself creates a strong incentive to develop a pay model that woud allow programming services to collect some portion of this enhanced value to viewers.

Third, in its current form online video is more of a threat than an opportunity for television services whose revenues depend in part on viewer payments. Cable networks and the cable, satellite, and IPTV suppliers of subscription multichannel television service obviously fall in this category, but so increasingly do the U.S. broadcast networks due to rising retransmission consent fees. Free internet distribution of TV programs undermines subscription TV services in two ways. Most direct is the loss of subscribers who find watching television over the internet to be an adequate substitute for a subscription TV service, a phenomenon known as cord cutting. While the magnitude of cord cutting is debated, the devices and services described above that facilitate accessing long form video via the internet certainly make it more appealing. As more television sets are manufactured with internet ports built-in and as new initiatives, like Google TV (The Official Google Blog, May 20, 2010), designed to make the internet a television-friendly environment take shape, this appeal will only increase. But even if few pay TV subscribers opt for the pure internet alternative, the fact that this option exists reduces perceived value added of pay TV service, and thus indirectly, reduce pay service revenues.

If successful, TV Everywhere would bolster the finances of traditional TV services in two ways. First, it would reduce the appeal of cord cutting by putting the most popular television programs behind a pay wall. Second, it would allow pay services to collect on the convenience value of accessing TV programs over the internet via a variety of devices by factoring this benefit into their subscription charges. What is currently a downside of making their content available online would then become a way to grow revenue.

Even if successful, these pay initiatives are likely only the next step in the evolution of a television industry that in the long run will be radically restructured by forces unleashed by the internet and perhaps other forms of server-based content distribution. As we argued earlier, the structural logic of an internet-based video service differs dramatically from a television industry build around the logic of multiple one-way channels. We can even see this difference in the broadcast networks' online offerings. While Hulu is a partnership of three of the four major U.S. broadcast networks, for all practical purposes the distinctions betwen the networks disappear on the Hulu website. The historic pattern for services built on new distribution technologies is that they start out as new ways to distribute content created by established service providers, but as they grow they become important sources of original content in their own right. For example, cable television was originally developed to retransmit broadcast TV stations to viewers too distant for their signals to reach. Today cable networks are important suppliers of original programming. As the internet becomes established as a consumer friendly means of delivering video content to television sets, we should not be surprised to see this facet of video history repeated.

The relative importance of a pay component to internet-based television in the long run is also uncertain. With internet delivery, the targeting capabilities of internet advertising can more easily be applied to television commercials, with the potential to dramatically increase revenue from sales of television advertising time. Kim and Wildman (2006) show that profit-maximizing video services should respond to this development by reducing subscription fees to increase the size of the audience that can be sold to advertisers.

CONCLUSION

The internet poses significant challenges to the traditional television industry. In the immediate term, there is the challenge of finding synergies between giving viewers online access to their favorite programs and distribution through traditional channels. On the one hand, by making it feasible for viewers to access their content at new times and in places where television viewing was previously not possible, it promises opportunities to increase revenues by charging viewers for expanded access to content and advertisers for expanded access to viewers. On the other hand, online distribution has yet to generate to generate substantial revenues and it threatens to divert viewers from the still profitable traditional channels. Solutions, other than pulling television programs from the internet, lie in finding ways to better monetize internet viewing, whether by charging viewers for online access or by improving the quality and reliability of internet audience measurements services.

In the longer term, the challenge is more substantial. The economic logic inherent in server-based internet distribution of video is very different from the costly channel-based logic that has shaped the traditional television industry. In the long run an internet-based television industry will almost certainly look much different than the industry that is confronting the internet challenge today.

REFERENCES

Catone, J. (May 18, 2007). *CBS' new online video strategy: Court Web 2.0*. Retrieved July 30, 2010, from http://www.last100.com/2007/05/18/cbs-new-online-video-strategy-court-web-20/

CNN.com. (February 6, 2009). *More turning to Web to watch TV, movies*. Retrieved July 30, 2010, from http://www.cnn.com/2009/TECH/02/06/internet.tv/index.html?iref=allsearch

ComScore Inc. (2008). *11 billion videos viewed online in the U.S. in April 2008*. Retrieved July 30, 2010, from http://www.comscore.com/Press_Events/Press_Releases/2008/06/ US_Online_Video_ Usage

ComScore Inc. (2009). *Major news stories drive June surge in U.S. online video viewing to record 157 million viewers*. Retrieved July 30, 2010, from http://www.comscore.com/Press_Events / Press_Releases/2009/8/Major_News_Stories_ Drive_June_Surge_in_U.S._Online_Video_Viewing_to_Record_157_Million_Viewers

ComScore Inc. (2010). *ComScore releases April 2010 U.S. online video rankings*. Retrieved July 30, 2010, from http://www.comscore.com/Press_Events/Press_Releases/2010/6 /comScore_Releases_April_2010_U.S._Online_Video_Rankings

Gray, T. (December 27, 2005). *Yahoo to stream CBS programs on Web: Networks continue to blur lines between TV and the Web*. Internetnews.com. Retrieved July 30, 2010, from http://www.internetnews.com/ec-news/article.php/3573676/Yahoo-to-Stream-CBS-Programs-on-Web.htm

Kim, E., & Wildman, S. S. (2006). A deeper look at the economics of advertiser support for television: The implications of consumption-differentiated viewers and ad addressability. *Journal of Media Economics, 19*(1), 55–79. doi:10.1207/s15327736me1901_4

Madden, M. (2007). *Online video*. Pew Internet & American Life Project. Retrieved July 30, 2010, from http://www.pewInternet.org/Reports/2007/Online-Video.aspx

Mills, E. (February 17, 2009). *Hulu pulls content from TV.com*. Retrieved July 30, 2010, from http://news.cnet.com/8301-1023_3-10166467-93.html?tag=contentMain;contentBody;1n

Nielsen.com. (September 15, 2009). *Total online video streams up 41% from last year*. Nielsenwire. Retrieved July 30, 2010, from http://blog.nielsen.com/nielsenwire/online_ mobile/total-online-video-streams-up-41-from-last-year/

Nielsen.com. (May 14, 2010). *Top online video sites in U.S. for April*. Nielsenwire. Retrieved July 30, 2010, from http://blog.nielsen.com/nielsenwire/online_mobile/top-online-video-sites-in-u-s-for-april-2010/

Owen, B., & Wildman, S. (1992). *Video economics*. Cambridge, MA: Harvard University Press.

Shachar, R., & Anand, B. N. (1998). The effectiveness and targeting of television advertising. *Journal of Economics & Management Strategy, 7*(3), 363–396. doi:10.1162/105864098567452

The Official Google Blog. (May 20, 2010). *Announcing Google TV: TV meets Web, Web meets TV*. Retrieved August 1, 2010, from http://googleblog.blogspot.com/2010/05/announcing-google-tv-tv-meets-web-web.html.

Waterman, D. (1985). Prerecorded home video and the distribution of theatrical feature films . In Noam, E. (Ed.), *Video media competition: Regulation, economics, and technology.* New York, NY: Columbia University Press.

Wildman, S. (2008). Interactive channels and the challenge of content budgeting. *International Journal on Media Management, 10*(3), 91–101. doi:10.1080/14241270802262401

Wildman, S. (2009). Delivering media content in a new technological environment: An exploration of implications for television policy . In May, R. (Ed.), *New directions in communications policy* (pp. 137–150). Durham, NC: Carolina Academic Press.

Youtube.com. (May 16, 2010). At five years, two billion views per day and counting. *The Official Youtube Blog.* Retrieved July 30, 2010, from http://youtube-global.blogspot.com/2010/05/at-five-years-two-billion-views-per-day.html

ADDITIONAL READING

Albarran, A. B. (2009). *Management of electronic media.* Boston, MA: Wadsworth.

Albarran, A. B., Chan-Olmstead, S. M., & Wirth, M. O. (Eds.). (2006). *Handbook of media management and economics.* Mahwah, NJ: Lawrence Erlbaum Associates.

Noam, E. Groebel, J. and Gerbarg, D. (eds.) (2003). Internet television. Hillsdale, NJ: Lawrence Erlbaum Associates.

Owen, B. M. (1999). *The Internet challenge to television.* Cambridge, MA: Harvard University Press.

Vogel, H. L. (2001). *Entertainment industry economics* (5th ed.). Cambridge, U.K.: Cambridge University Press.

Zotto, C. D. and van Kranenburg, H. (eds.) (2008). Management and innovation in the media industry. Cheltenham, England: Edward Elgar.

KEY TERMS AND DEFINITIONS

Distribution Strategies: Strategies such as syndication and windowing traditionally used to maximize profits on the investments in content production. These strategies are changing with the advent of IPTV.

Hulu: U.S. based website offering commercial-supported streaming video of TV shows from NBC, Fox and ABC.

IPTV: Internet Protocol Television is a system through which video content is delivered over the internet.

Online Video: Full length television programs that are available on the internet (in the context of this chapter).

Television Networks: The major players in the U.S. include ABC, CBS, FOX and NBC.

YouTube: A subsidiary of Google Inc., YouTube is a video sharing website on which users can upload and share videos.

ENDNOTE

[1] YouTube, being the pioneering and foremost online video outlet, was included due to the huge amount of traffic its videos generate. Hulu, Sling, Veoh and Joost were listed as four of the most popular Internet video websites by CNN.com (February 6, 2009). Fancast is a subsidiary of Comcast Corporation and was one of the first major forays into the provision of online content by a cable company. TV.com was previously independent, but was acquired by CBS when it purchased CNET in June 2008. IMDb is an online database of information related to

movies, actors, and television shows and was acquired by Amazon.com in 1998. Traditionally, IMDb offered only information and links to DVD sales on Amazon.com, but it has recently started to offer streaming videos.

It should also be noted that YouTube stands apart from the other services examined for its emphasis on the user-generated content for which it is best know.

APPENDIX 1

List of Prime Time Programs Tracked

Table 3.

FOX	Genre	CBS	Genre
The Simpsons	Animated Series	60 minutes	Current Affairs
King of the Hill	Animated Series	The Amazing Race	Reality
Family Guy	Animated Series	Cold Case	Drama Series
American Dad	Animated Series	The Unit	Drama Series
Terminator: The Sarah Conner Chronicles	Drama Series	The Big Bang Theory	Drama Series
Prison Break	Drama Series	How I Met your Mother	Drama Series
House: MD	Drama Series	Two and a Half Men	Comedy
Fringe	Drama Series	Worst Week	Comedy
Bones	Drama Series	CSI:Miami	Drama Series
Til Death	Comedy	NCIS	Drama Series
Do Not Disturb	Comedy	The Mentalist	Drama Series
Hole in the Wall	Gameshow	Without a Trace	Drama Series
Kitchen Nightmares	Reality	New Adventures of Old Christine	Comedy
Are You Smarter than a 5th Grader?	Gameshow	Gary Unmarried	Comedy
Don't Forget the Lyrics	Gameshow	Criminal Minds	Drama Series
Cops	Reality	Survivor	Reality
America's Most Wanted	Reality	CSI	Drama Series
24	Drama Series	Eleventh Hour	Drama Series
American Idol	Reality	Ghost Whisperer	Drama Series
Hell's Kitchen	Reality	The Ex List	Drama Series
Mental	Drama Series	NUMB3RS	Drama Series
		48 Hours Mystery	Drama Series
		Rules of Engagement	Comedy
		Flashpoint	Drama Series
		Harper's Island	Drama Series
		Million Dollar Password	Gameshow

Table 4.

NBC	Genre	ABC	Genre
Chuck	Drama Series	America's Funniest Home Videos	Comedy
Heroes	Drama Series	Extreme Makeover: Home Edition	Reality
My Own Worst Enemy	Drama Series	Desperate Housewives	Drama
The Biggest Loser	Reality	Brothers & Sisters	Drama
Law & Order: Special Victims Unit	Drama Series	Samantha Who	Drama
Knight Rider	Drama Series	Boston Legal	Drama
Deal or No Deal	Gameshow	Opportunity Knocks	Reality
Lipstick Jungle	Drama Series	Dancing with the Stars	Reality
My Name is Earl	Comedy	Eli Stone	Drama
Kath & Kim	Comedy	Pushing Daisies	Drama
The Office	Comedy	Private Practice	Drama
30 Rock	Comedy	Dirty Sexy Money	Drama
ER	Drama Series	Ugly Betty	Drama
Crusoe	Drama Series	Grey's Anatomy	Drama
America's Toughest Jobs	Reality	Life on Mars	Drama
Life	Drama Series	Wife Swap	Reality
Dateline NBC	Current Affairs	Super Nanny	Reality
Howie Do It	Comedy		
Medium	Drama Series		
Southland	Drama Series		
Most Outrageous Moments	Comedy		

Chapter 31

Investigating the Demise of Radio and Television Broadcasting

Wong Chuling (Luwen)
Nanyang Technological University, Singapore

Chow Min Hua
Nanyang Technological University, Singapore

Chua Jit Chee
Nanyang Technological University, Singapore

ABSTRACT

Since the emergence of the Internet and Web 2.0, the possible decline and eventual demise of traditional radio and television (TV) broadcasting has been highly debated among many experts of the industry. This chapter seeks to identify the patterns in consumers' behaviors and the evolution of radio and TV broadcasting brought about by Web 2.0 to prove the validity behind this topic, through understanding these changes. We will then propose a modified product life cycle for radio and TV broadcasting in which its decline phase is replaced by an evolution phase due to the Internet. The implications of these findings will be discussed, along with suggested prescriptions on how to avoid the problem of facing demise.

INTRODUCTION

Radio and TV broadcasting have been around since 1920s and 1940s respectively (Hilmes, 2002), and have saturated the mainstream market till today. With the introduction of Internet

and Web 2.0 which focuses on being consumer-centric, applications catering specifically to the demanding consumers' needs and adding of value to consumers becomes the main objective of web retailers. With this change in the marketplace, consumers are now offered a wider range of options to choose from. This result in a change in consumers' behaviors, coupled with a spike in

DOI: 10.4018/978-1-61350-147-4.ch031

consumer created content which brings about an imperative concern about the possible demise of radio and TV broadcasting.

Our take on this topic, however, is that the demise of radio and TV is being an overly exaggerated claim. In order to support our argument, we will review the current product life cycle and analyze how it is no longer valid in today's context.

Research on the current trends of consumers' behavior in today's Web 2.0 era, and how radio and TV has sought to fulfill this need will be conducted showing an integration of technology as an extra distribution channel to broaden their audience base. This leads to the development of our proposed product life cycle which takes evolution into consideration replacing the decline stage and making it more suitable for use in current rapidly changing dynamic marketplace of today.

Towards the end of this paper, problems faced by radio and TV during the evolution stage of the lifecycle will be discussed along with recommendations on future studies areas, which can be further looked into.

BACKGROUND

The widespread adoption of radio and TV broadcasting can be observed in our current surroundings; however, radio and TV broadcasting faces new challenges due to changes in consumer behaviors and the introduction of Web 2.0.

In this section, the traditional product life cycle, current consumer behavior trends and the evolution of radio and TV broadcasting brought by Web 2.0 along with crossing of the chasm are discussed.

Review on Traditional Product Life Cycle

The traditional product life cycle has been around since half a century ago and is widely used and recognized in the marketing sector (Tibben-

Lembke, 2002). It is believed that every product or service goes through a life cycle taking on the analogy of human beings' life cycle and how this is handled affects its survival in the market (Grantham, 1997). For a product or service to successfully take off, the crossing of a chasm has to be considered.

Chasm in Traditional Product Life Cycle

"The Chasm" is an invisible barrier arising from the saturation of early market and the lack of adoption of mainstream market (Mohr, Sengupta & Slater, 2010). This is identified to be apparent at the transition between the introduction phase and the growth phase. It is a gulf between the visionaries and the pragmatists adopters and is usually overcome with a change in marketing strategy as different adopters requires different selling techniques addressing different buying motivations. Organizations have to cross this chasm in order to capture the mainstream market.

The traditional product life cycle typically consists of sequential phases namely "Development", "Introduction", "Growth", "Maturity" and "Decline" and the most common portrayal of the cycle is with an S-shaped curve as shown in Figure 1 (Marklew, 1985).

Figure 1. Typical product life cycle

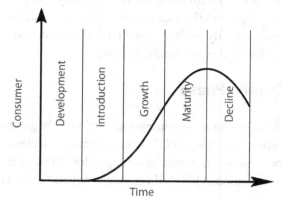

Development Phase

Development phase is the period before marketing when the product or service is being created (Marklew, 1985). There is no consumption during this phase and a considerable amount of investment might be required depending on the type of product or service.

Introduction Phase

This phase involves the initial introduction of the product or service into the market (Marklew, 1985). When it is first introduced, the growth of consumption is usually slow and substantial investment could be required due to the need to cross a chasm and reach over from the visionaries to the pragmatists' adopters.

Growth Phase

According to Marklew (1985), during this phase, sales and profits increase greatly as the market begins to accept the product or service showing a crossing of the chasm. The substantial investment spent to get to this phase is usually offset by the increase in consumption.

Maturity Phase

Maturity phase is when most of the customers who have bought or used the product or service are now also covering the late majority category of consumers (Marklew, 1985). The trend in this phase usually leads to a gradual decline in demand as the market is already saturated.

Decline Phase

At this phase, consumption rate will begin to drop (Marklew, 1985), with the rate of decrease becoming prominent, resulting in loss of the market position. This could be due to several reasons including the change of customers' preferences or competitors gaining market share.

Issue with Traditional Product Life Cycle

According to Dhalla and Yuspeh (1976), a product life cycle is often a dependent variable which is determined by market actions and not a natural trend with prime reasons appearing to be product developments and motivations that are of a non-technical nature. Wood (1990) concurs by pointing out that the "dynamic markets of the eighties, bore little resemblance to the relatively simply defined and stable markets of the early sixties", bringing to question the reliability of the current product life cycle.

In today's fast paced high technology marketplace, if companies do not plan ahead and seek to avoid the decline stage, they will not be able to cope with the changes and evolve, hence resulting in self-prophesize demise. According to Hiam (1990), "maturity simply reflects saturation of a specific target market with a specific product form" and if the form of product is enhanced, expanding the target market, new growth is possible and it is only "a myth that products have a predetermined life-span".

Review on Chasm of Radio and TV Broadcasting

The crossing of the chasm of radio and TV Broadcasting can be observed in our current surroundings with every household owning 2.86 television sets (Nielsen, 2010) and every car having a radio set installed as a standard feature.

Radio

Hilmes (2002) discusses the timeline of the radio industry in America highlighting that during World War II, the radio brought about national unity during the times of social and economic uncertainty allowing information to be delivered to the mass public faster than printed newspaper could. The radio era during this period was also considered to have hit its peak saturating the consumer market and successfully capturing the vast majority of the Americans to tune in on the radio for information and entertainment. Statistics gathered by Sterling (1979, table 670-A) also shows that by 1953, nearly 60% of all automobiles in the US already had radios installed.

Television

Shortly after, in the 1940s, television was the new medium that was introduced incorporating aural and visual elements. Television programs started off by having the most successful radio programs transferred to its medium. It was only during the late 1950s that television was able to cross the chasm when it started to deviate and differentiate itself from the traditional radio by hosting a wide variety of programmes ranging from documentaries to sports shows, quiz shows. By the 1960s, a generation of TV-stars and producers emerged further distinguishing the association between radio and television (Hilmes, 2002; Davie & Upshaw, 2006).

Review on Consumer Behavior Trends in Web 2.0 Era

Humans are social creatures as they are always "changing social habits, and creating new ones, upsetting staid political practices, affecting tastes in all forms of entertainment, building unprecedented demand for products and services never before so widely distributed" (Chester, Garrison & Willis, 1978, p. 3).

The reason behind such human behavior is a complex matter and changes that happen may be due to internal and external factors that are dependent on the individual's culture, environment they were brought up with, people they surround themselves with, the media, and so forth.

In the case of the introduction of Web 2.0, it brought about new consumers' behaviors associated with user participation, interaction and communication through easy to use technologies that allows user to generate their own content, control the use of the web portals and share information easily (Chen, 2008; Riegner, 2007). There is a clear adoption seen through the widespread use of social networking sites such as Facebook, video sharing sites such as YouTube, online journals that consist of a user perspective on a particular subject known as Blogs and episodic; downloadable; programme-driven digital audio or video file known as Podcasts. To suit individuals' preferences, all applications are capable of being personalize-based to cater to differing needs (Chen, 2008).

The Internet had provided a digital platform in allowing media convergence made possible with the introduction of Web 2.0 which emphasizes on participatory culture, collective intelligence and interactivity. The Internet influences the economy and the definition of value creation changes from value created by the business model itself to a consumers centered model (Avi Dan, 2006).

Mobile technologies can act as a medium for Web 2.0 generated information (Hardey, 2007) as users are accessing Internet using mobile devices and also retrieving location based information through the wireless connections and global positioning system technologies (GPS).

A summary on the consumer behavior trends due to Web 2.0 is shown in Table 1.

Review on the Evolution of Radio and TV Broadcasting with Web 2.0

Brendon (1988), Coyle and Vaughn (2008) states that it is only the techniques of communication that changes basically highlighting the fact that through time only the medium evolves. In the 1990s with the emergence of the Internet, the digital generation came by storm where Montgomery claims that it would be the "epicenter of major tectonic

Table 1. Consumer behavior trends

Consumer Behavior Trends in Web 2.0
User generated content
Control
Interactivity and Participatory Culture
Information on the move

shifts... [and it transformed] the media landscape" (p.2). Flanagin and Metzger (2001) study shows that radio and television stations on the Internet deliver the content by streaming it online which is similar as broadcasting it to reach the listeners and viewers.

With media convergence allowing "flow of content across media platforms" and "cooperation between media industries" (Jenkins, 2001, p.93), it brought about the idea of merging different services into one place, allowing consumers to be able to choose and perform multiple tasks at one time (Dominick, Sherman & Messere, 2000). This affected radio and TV by giving it more capabilities where activities such as promotions could be done concurrently or even allow listeners or viewers to provide comments and feedbacks when they heard their favorite song played or when the viewer saw their idol on television. In a way it gave the consumers more control in the media they choose to use.

Evolution of Radio

With the introduction of the radio on the internet, consumers are no longer limited to just hearing what is available on their country terrestrial dial but that of other stations around the world (Doyle, 2001; Sterling, 2008) fulfilling a unique but grow-ing niche in today's shrinking world (Crisell, 1994). It addressed a wide range of consumer's niche interests. Internet radio also removed cer-tain restrictions set by the federal regulations for broadcasting which would have been encountered through broadcasting (Riismandel, 2002).

Besides having to stream large files there was also podcasts available which allowed the idea of time shifted radio. Consumers would then be downloading radio shows of what they wanted to hear and listening to it at a later time when they wanted to (Richter, 2006).

Through the Internet, listeners are offered options of "subscription radio" and commercial radio because of the electronic music formats used (Internet Online radio, 2009). An added feature of readily available song information is also provided to the consumers as many people will have encountered a situation where a great song is heard on the radio but the track name and artist was missed (Phil, 2010).

It is also more efficient when tuning to a new station as there is no longer the need to twiddle the dial to get the best signal as all stations have their names shown (Phil, 2010). The consumer will be able to know exactly which channel they are tuned to. They could also use other devices such as mobile phones that could connect to the Internet to stream the radio.

Evolution of Television

In his dissertation work at the Department of Journalism, Media, and Communication, Jakob Bjur (2009) studied social viewing and noticed the growing trend on how consumers are being more and more individualistic in TV choices. Social viewing went down from 45% in 1999 to 37% in 2008. He also lists out several key changes on the evolution of television.

With technological advancement, multiple devices like PCs and mobile phones allows media to be portable and consumed anywhere, anytime. Digital Video Recorders (DVRs) such as TiVo, Video On Demand (VOD) and Internet video sites also allows the freedom of choosing to watch shows over leisure time instead of specific time blocks like in the past. The syndication companies would be the ones offering VOD, and Internet videos hoping to profit by selling the shows that the consumers wanted to see in their own time. The idea of interactive television (ITV) with the audience by using Tele-texting and Videotext (Davie & Upshaw, 2006) sparked off as well.

Due to the digitalization of the terrestrial network, the amount of available viewing content has dramatically increased with channels available to cater to specific interests. The niche strategy was thus adopted. It targets market segments that are less vulnerable to substitutes or where a competition is weakest to earn above-average return on investment (Porter, 1980) as well as catering to the long tail (Anderson, 2006).

ISSUES OF RADIO AND TV BROADCASTING

In this section, the relationship between consumer behavior trends in Web 2.0 and the evolution of radio and TV broadcasting will be analyzed showing the adoption of the Internet platform, further supporting the notion on how exaggerated the demise of radio and TV broadcasting is. A proposed product life cycle for radio and TV broadcasting will then be introduced and the issue of crossing a second chasm will then be discussed.

Consumer Behavior and Evolution of Radio and TV in Web 2.0

From literature review gathered, we established an association between consumer behavior trends caused by Web 2.0 and the evolution of radio and TV, shown in Table 2. Consumers are beginning to contribute and create their own content and radio and TV have evolved to support such needs. For example, podcast content can be generated by users themselves.

Furthermore in the Web 2.0 era, consumers want more control and radio and TV have responded by allowing users to watch TV or listen to radio on a time shifted basis and providing readily available information regarding the content

Table 2. Comparison between consumer behavior and evolution

Consumer behavior trends in web 2.0	Examples of supporting evolution of radio and TV
User created content	• Podcast
Control	• Time shifted radio and TV
Interactivity and Participatory Culture	• Interactive features such as discussion board Tele-texting • Videotext
Information on the move	• Mobile devices such as mobile phone with Internet connectivity as a medium for radio and TV

being played such as song information. Consumers are also provided with more interactive features catering to a participatory culture such as discussion board for comments and feedbacks. Lastly, consumers need for information on the move is met by catering of media formats to work on mobile devices.

As seen from Table 2, the relationship shows a need for evolution. The following section will show the current market trends and the evolution that is currently on-going.

Market Trends of Radio and Television Broadcasting

Radio and TV have evolved from traditional broadcasting medium to use other ways to reach the public (Hauger, 2008). The following statistics shows the shift currently occurring in today's marketplace.

Radio Trends

In Benson and Perry's study (2006), statistics from the UK taken from the Radio Joint Audience Research (RAJAR) in 2004 shows that "radio has a 90% reach" where 13% of adults are listening to the radio over the Internet while 27% are listening via their digital television." This reveals that users are adopting alternatives ways of retrieving the same content.

A further analysis into RAJAR statistics of 2004 (Figure 2) and 2009 (Figure 3 and Figure 4) of the UK population, shows an increase of the UK population tuning to radio on the Internet where it grew from 9.3% end of 2001 to 16.3% at the end of 2004 (Figure 2).

In looking at the most recent statistics of RAJAR (2010) for the UK of the fourth quarter of 2009, Figure 3 shows that when comparing statistics of December 2008 and December 2009, people who listen to radio on the digital platform have increased by 2.6%.

Figure 2. People listening to the radio in the UK (©2004, RAJAR, p. 2)

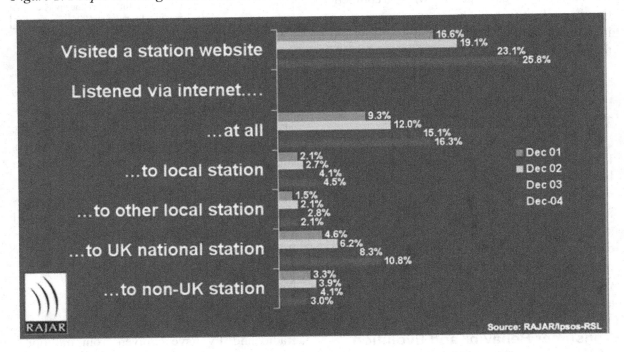

Figure 3. Different platforms people listen to the radio on in the UK (©2010, RAJAR.)

All Radio Listening - Share Via Platform (%)

AM/FM	68.6	66.1	66.6
All Digital	18.3	21.1	20.9
DAB	11.4	13.3	13.7
DTV	3.2	3.6	3.4
Internet	2.0	2.2	2.1
Digital Unspecified *	1.7	2.0	1.7
Unspecified *	13.0	12.8	12.5

Figure 4. People listening to radio via the mobile phone in the UK (©2010, RAJAR.)

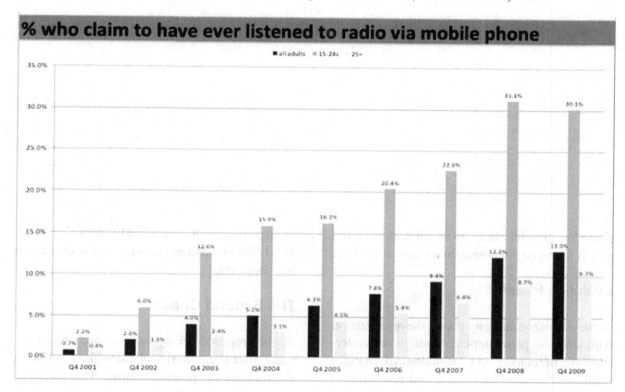

Figure 4 goes on to reinforce the trend of use of different mediums in listening to radio by showing that there is a general increase in people using their mobile phones to listen to radio.

Television Trends

Based on the 2008 and 2009 statistics gathered by the Nielsen Company (2009) on the viewership usage of the television in the US, watching television at home has maintained the overall number of users which is also the highest number of users i.e. 284,396,000 users in 2009 (Figure 5).

Even though that is the case, there is a huge percentage increase in overall viewership using different platforms such as mobile phones which increased by 70% and time shifted television which increased by 32.2% as shown in Figure 5.

According to Figure 6, people spend on average 141 hours per month in 2009 watching television at home. There is a growing trend in the popularity of people watching videos on the Internet. It has grown by 45.5%, with time shifted television ranking second which increased by 19.5%.

This information reflects that there is an obvious trend in people adopting time shifted television and also shows that perhaps consumers are starting to use mobile phones to access the Internet to watch videos more often.

Proposed Product Life Cycle

Based on the discussion in the preceding section, a strong need for evolution is proven and based on section 2.1, Issues with Traditional Life Cycle; we see that the traditional product life cycle is no longer relevant. This section will provide an overview of our proposed product life cycle which is shown in Figure 7 below. It encompasses the evolution of products by providing an evolution

Figure 5. Overall usage of television in the US (©2009, Nielsen Company, p.2.)

Overall Usage Number of Users 2+ (in 000's) – Monthly Reach				
	2Q09	1Q09	2Q08	% Diff Yr to Yr
Watching TV in the home°	284,396	284,574	281,746	0.9%
Watching Timeshifted TV°	82,297	79,533	62,240	32.2%
Using the Internet**	191,035	163,110	159,986	19.4%
Watching Video on Internet**	133,962	131,102	119,164	12.4%
Using a Mobile Phone^	233,722	230,436	221,651	0.5%
Mobile Subscribers Watching Video on a Mobile Phone^	15,267	13,419	9,004	70.0%

phase in a product life cycle which is more suited as it is a proven phenomenon as seen in Table 2.

Evolution Phase

At the end of the maturity phase, the organization with strategic plans in place through the understanding of market and technological changes would move on to this phase and reach out to a greater market including those at the long tail resulting in a higher consumption level avoiding demise.

Adopting a proactive market orientation, companies through the gathering of anticipatory intelligence would be able to figure out latent and future needs of its customers and cater to these needs before they are even aware that they need it.

Taking the mobile phone companies as an example, most of it evolved to provide added features beside its sole ability to communicate through voice as they reached the maturity phase. This hence avoids demise and results in an increase in consumers.

The Second Chasm

In our proposed life cycle, a second chasm appears after the maturity phase with its crossing determining the product demise. This chasm is identified as it is also based between the same categories of adopters, which are the visionaries and the pragmatists. As the product will be seen to evolve through the use of different distribution channels or newly available technology, different strategies have to be used to get the majority to accept it. From the statistics gathered, radio and television are shown to have already targeted the visionaries and the early adopters who use the Internet as the medium of access.

Figure 6. Monthly time spent in watching television in the US (©2009, Nielsen Company, p.2.)

Monthly Time Spent in Hours:Minutes Per User 2+					
	2Q09	1Q09	2Q08	% Diff Yr to Yr (2Q09 to 2Q08)	Absolute Diff Yr to Yr (2Q09 to 2Q08)
Watching TV in the home*	141:03	153:27	139:00	1.5%	2:02
Watching Timeshifted TV*	7:16	8:13	6:05	19.5%	1:11
Using the Internet**	26:15	29:15	26:29	-0.9%	0:14
Watching Video on Internet**	3:11	3:00	2:12	45.5%	0:59
Mobile Subscribers Watching Video on a Mobile Phone^	3:15	3:37	3:37	-10.0%	0:22

Figure 7. Proposed product life cycle

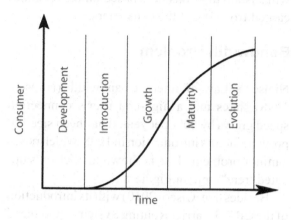

Crossing of the Second Chasm

Due to the emergence of Web 2.0 which serves to offer complementary services and resulted in a shift in consumer behavior trends, radio and TV make use of the Internet as an upcoming distribution channel.

However it has yet to successfully cross the chasm despite the fact that there is a continuous growth occurring. This can be seen when comparing figures of the usage between analog and digital mediums as shown in our findings.

The gulf here can be countered by attracting consumers who are unable to fit radio and TV programs with traditionally fixed schedules into their daily lives. The new channel's ability and flexibility in providing consumers with customization can be marketed in areas that includes content, time and mobility.

There is however difficulties encountered by radio and TV themselves in adopting of this new distribution medium.

Problems Encountered with the Evolution

The following are problems that are being encountered by radio and TV due to the evolution of broadcasting medium.

Difficulties in Earning Revenue

According to Miller (2008), it is hard for web radio to earn revenues even if the royalties that webcaster have to pay record companies fall in US. This is because in order for webcaster to earn from advertisements, they need larger audiences. Having larger audiences however would mean larger fees as well. Smaller web radio stations have even resorted to pleading for public donations to survive as it is hard to find advertisers.

On the other hand, the idea of ITV was successful in France and UK. When it reached the US, however, it failed as net profits were insufficient (Davie & Upshaw, 2006).

Bandwidth Problem

Another issue raised when using the Internet to stream information online is the issue of bandwidth . It requires huge bandwidth and servers hosting information may only be able to serve and support a certain amount of users simultaneously as compared to broadcasting where its only limit is when users are too far and cannot receive the signal (Riismandel, 2002).

Internet service providers in the US have even slowed down traffic online and started charging users based on how much they use on their bandwidth. They have also capped their usage in an attempt to discourage consumers to help fix the bandwidth problem (Bertolucci, 2008; Johnson 2009). YouTube, one of the most popular online video communities has already stopped streaming to certain locations primarily because the consumption of bandwidth has exceeded usage (Johnson, 2009). Even though Internet has advanced so much that it is now more accessible, the reach of Internet to listeners and viewers is however restricted by technological limitations.

RECOMMENDATIONS

This section will be suggestions on ways to overcome problems encountered when attempting to cross the second chasm as mentioned in the preceding section.

Earning Revenue

To counter revenue concerns faced by radio and TV broadcasting after its evolution, we recommend Internet radio and TV to adopt the use of "Freemium" pricing, a term coined by Fred Wilson, which suggests making the basic version of the Internet radio and available to all the users for free and Anderson's (2008) suggestion of the 1% rule, whereby 1% of the consumers pay for the 99% who uses the basic version.

These pricing methods are used for web software, services and content providers, making it also suitable for Internet radio and TV. If users wish to access advance functionalities such as discussion boards and members only content, they have to pay a fee. Internet radio and TV will sustain their business based on the revenues earned from 1% of the consumers.

Bandwidth Problem

Nielsen's Law of Internet bandwidth (Nielsen, 1998) states that a high-end user's connection speed grows by 50% per year. It has been steadily proven since its introduction in 1998, which poses a minor problem. This is shown in Nielsen's updated trend table in Figure 8.

Besides that, Cisco (2010) with its introduction of the CRS-3 Carrier Routing System, announced a major advancement in the Internet infrastructure. The capacity of its predecessors is now tripled and able to handle more than 12 times the traffic capacity of the current system available now.

CONCLUSION AND FUTURE RESEARCH DIRECTIONS

In conclusion, we have shown an evolution of traditional radio and TV adapting the use of Internet as a new distribution platform, thus prov-

Figure 8. Empirical data mapped against the exponential growth curve (©2010, Nielsen's Law)

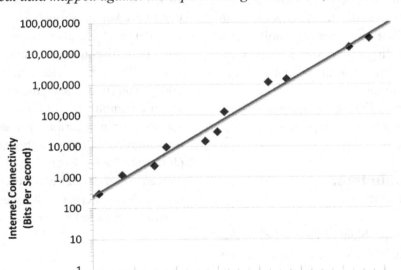

ing that the hype on the demise of TV and radio broadcasting is overly exaggerated.

Recent changes in technology are refinements in enhancing the efficiency of transmission to communicate to people at lower costs. If traditional radio and television broadcasting companies are inflexible and resistant to technological changes, these organizations will struggle to survive. In addition, after companies shift to Internet radio and TV, they have to continue to find other means to earn revenues to sustain their businesses through added value given to their consumers.

It is important to anticipate the progress of Internet radio and TV broadcasting in order to prevent a further possible demise of TV and radio, hence future research areas could be in media content provided to consumers. This could be done in relation to collective human intelligence with focus being on the study of consumer media choices and its trend with regards to Web 3.0.

REFERENCES

Anderson, C. (2006). *The long tail: Why the future of business is selling less of more*. New York, NY: Hyperion.

Anderson, C. (2008). Why $0.00 is the future of business. *Wired*, (pp. 140-149). Retrieved April 21, 2010, from http://www.wired.com/techbiz/it/magazine/16-03/ff_free.

Avi Dan. (2006). Transcend function and focus on the visual. *Advertising Age*. Retrieved April 12, 2010, from http://www.avidanstrategies.com/library/2006/3/6/transcend-function-and-focus-on-the-visual.html

Benson, A., & Perry, S. D. (2006). The influence of humor in radio advertising on program enjoyment and future intent to listen. *Journal of Radio Studies*, *13*(2), 169–186. doi:10.1080/10955040701313198

Bertolucci, J. (2008). ISP bandwidth limits make a comeback. *PC World*, *26*(9), 41–42.

Bjur, J. (2009). *Transforming audiences. Patterns of individualization in television viewing*. Department of Journalism, Media and Communication, University of Gothenburg.

Brendon, P. (1988). Primal urge. *Columbia Journalism Review*, *27*(3), 60–62.

Chen, H. (2008). *Understanding content consumers and content creators in the Web 2.0 era: A case study of YouTube users*. Conference Papers -- International Communication Association, (pp. 1-34). Retrieved from Communication & Mass Media Complete database.

Chester, G., Garrison, G. R., & Willis, E. E. (1978). *Television and radio* (5th ed.). London, UK: Prentice-Hall.

Cisco (2010, March 09). *Cisco introduces foundation for next generation Internet: The Cisco CRS-3 carrier routing system*. [Press Release]. San Jose, CA: Cisco Systems Inc.

Coyle, C. L., & Vaughn, H. (2008). Social networking: Communication revolution or evolution? *Bell Labs Technical Journal*, *13*(2), 13–18. doi:10.1002/bltj.20298

Crisell, A. (1994). *Understanding radio* (2nd ed.). London, UK: Routledge.

Davie, W. R., & Upshaw, J. R. (2006). *Principles of electronic media* (2nd ed.). Boston, MA: Pearson.

Dhalla, N. K., & Yuspeh, S. (1976). Forget the product life cycle concept. *Harvard Business Review*, (Jan-Feb): 1976.

Dominick, J. R., Sherman, B. L., & Messere, F. (2000). *An introduction to modern electronic media* (4th ed.). United States of America: McGraw-Hill.

Doyle, A. (2001). *The future of radio*. Retrieved April 5, 2010, from http://digitalcontentproducer.com/mag/video_future_radio/

Flanagin, A. J., & Metzger, M. J. (2001). Internet use in the contemporary media environment. *Human Communication Research, 27*(1), 153–181. doi:10.1093/hcr/27.1.153

Grantham, L. M. (1997). The validity of the product life cycle in the high-tech industry. *Marketing Intelligence & Planning, 15*(1), 4–10. doi:10.1108/02634509710155606

Hardey, M. (2007). The city in the age of web 2.0: A new synergistic relationship between place and people. *Information Communication and Society, 10*(6), 867–884. doi:10.1080/13691180701751072

Hauger, D. (2008). *The future of radio broadcasting*. Retrieved April 3, 2010, from http://www.associatedcontent.com/article/954263/the_future_of_radio_broadcasting.html

Hiam, A. (1990). Exposing four myths of strategic planning. *The Journal of Business Strategy*, (September/October): 23–28. doi:10.1108/eb060082

Hilmes, M. (2002). Rethinking radio . In Hilmes, M., & Loviglio, J. (Eds.), *Radio reader: Essays in the cultural history of radio* (pp. 1–40). New York, NY: Routledge.

Internet Online Radio. (2009). *Internet radio stations offer free online streaming music*. Retrieved April 10, 2010, from http://www.articlesbase.com/music-articles/internet-radio-stations-offer-free-online-streaming-music-1076093.html

Jenkins, H. (2001). Convergence? I diverge. *Technology Review, 93*. Retrieved March 30, 2010, from http://web.mit.edu/cms/People/henry3/converge.pdf

Johnson, J. T. (2009). The Internet sky really is falling. *Network World*. Retrieved April 10, 2010, from http://www.computerworld.com/s/article/9132638/The_Internet_sky_really_is_falling

Marklew, A. (1985). The product life cycle – Fact or myth? *Education + Training, 27*(2), 39–41. doi:10.1108/eb017099

McCauley, M. P. (2002). Radio's digital future . In Hilmes, M., & Loviglio, J. (Eds.), *Radio reader: Essays in the cultural history of radio* (pp. 1–40). New York, NY: Routledge.

Miller, C. C. (2008, October 27). Even if royalties for Web radio fall, revenue remains elusive. *The New York Times*. Retrieved April 20, 2010, from http://www.nytimes.com/2008/10/27/technology/internet/27radio.html?pagewanted=1&sq=radio&st=Search&scp=8

Mohr, J., Sengupta, S., & Slater, S. (2010). *Marketing of high-technology products and innovations* (3rd ed.). Upper Saddle River, NJ: Prentice-Hall.

Montgomery, K. C. (2009). *Generation digital: Politics, commerce and childhood in the age of the Internet*. Cambridge, MA: MIT Press.

Nielsen, J. (1998). *Nielsen's law of Internet bandwidth*. Retrieved April 21, 2010, from http://www.useit.com/alertbox/980405.html

Nielsen Company. (2009). *A2/M2 three screen report, volume 5, 2nd Quarter 2009*. Retrieved April 10, 2010, from http://blog.nielsen.com/nielsenwire/wp-content/uploads/2009/09/3ScreenQ209_US_rpt_090209.pdf

Porter, M. E. (1980). *Competitive strategy: Techniques for analysing industries and competitors*. New York, NY: Free Press.

RAJAR. (2005). *2004 Q4 DTV and Internet listening*. Retrieved April 10, 2010, from http://www.rajar.co.uk/docs/2004_09/2004_Q4_DTV_Internet.ppt

RAJAR. (2010). *2009 Q4 all radio listening and all radio listening via platform*. Retrieved April 10, 2010, from http://www.rajar.co.uk/docs/2009_12/2009_Q4_Listening_via_platform.pdf

RAJAR. (2010). *2009 Q4 listening to radio via a mobile phone*. Retrieved April 10, 2010, from http://www.rajar.co.uk/docs/2009_12/2009_Q4_Mobile.pdf

Richter, W. A. (2006). *Radio: A complete guide to the industry*. New York, NY: Peter Lang.

Riegner, C. (2007). Word of mouth on the Web: The impact of Web 2.0 on consumer purchase decisions. *Journal of Advertising Research, 47*(4), 436–447. doi:10.2501/S0021849907070456

Riismandel, P. (2002). Radio by and for the public . In Hilmes, M., & Loviglio, J. (Eds.), *Radio reader: Essays in the cultural history of radio* (pp. 423–450). New York, NY: Routledge.

Sterling, C. H. (1979). Television and radio broadcasting . In Compaine, B. M. (Ed.), *Who owns the media? Concentration of ownership in the mass communication industry* (pp. 61–125). New York, NY: Harmony.

Sterling, C. H. (2008). Slow fade? Seeking radio's future . In Keith, M. C. (Ed.), *Radio cultures: The sound medium in American life* (pp. 321–329). New York, NY: Peter Lang.

Tibben-Lembke, R. S. (2002). Life after death. *International Journal of Physical Distribution & Logistics, 32*(3), 223–224. doi:10.1108/09600030210426548

Wood, L. (1990). The end of the product life cycle? Education says goodbye to an old friend. *Journal of Marketing Management, 6*(2), 145–155. doi:10.1080/0267257X.1990.9964122

Chapter 32
The Future of Television

Xu Mingqing
Nanyang Technological University, Singapore

Xu Wenjing
Nanyang Technological University, Singapore

Zeng Junming
Nanyang Technological University, Singapore

ABSTRACT

The TV industry grew exponentially after World War II. In 1962, the percentage of American homes with a TV set reached ninety percent. Today the television not only brings entertainment but also serves as a form of cultural transportation. Furthermore, viewers have turned to watching digital content on a personal computer rather than watching programs on television. We believe in the near future, television will integrate more elements of information technology rather than vanish in the history. We use the ADVISOR model to define the scope of future television. We also use it to find how television in the future may create value, seize value, and add value into the service and products they provide. Finally, we find TV has become more than just an appliance for viewing broadcast programmes. It has become an important and integral part of the interactive digital media industry.

INTRODUCTION

A picture is worth a thousand words. Moving images provides even more information. With video and audio, the television has come a long way since its development started in the nineteenth century (Wikipedia, 2010). In this report, we give the reader snippets of the television's early beginnings, current situation and future trends.

Next, we apply the ADVISOR framework to discover how the TV industry creates value in order to understand viewers' needs and pass better services to viewers.

The Early Days of the Television

The TV industry took off after World War II (Baughman, 2002). Supported by military research, companies strived to create devices that were capable of receiving clear image and sound

DOI: 10.4018/978-1-61350-147-4.ch032

signals over the air. In the United States, although expensive for the average consumer, companies began to put up TV sets for sale. At the same time, broadcasting networks offered programming to TV stations.

Enabled by a strong economy after the war, coupled with an increase in marriages and child-bearing, young adults in the United States typically had their own homes. Hence, this made the television an affordable device for home entertainment. Factors such as having a generous income and later the size of the family became strong predictors of whether a home owned a TV set.

In 1962, the percentage of American homes with a TV set reached ninety percent (TV History, 2010). Outside of the United States, the television soon became a common household item. However, the ownership of TV sets spread slowly in less developed countries. This was because of reasons such as high costs, lack of infrastructure for electricity and lack of common standards for producing TV sets.

In the United States, advertisers held control over programs during the early days of the television. Because of demand for programs, advertisers were at an advantageous position over broadcasting networks and TV stations. Usually, programs were entirely sponsored and blended with the advertisers' products. Advertisers also targeted their programs at the largest audience possible by seeking popular program genres.

Over the years, power shifted from advertisers to broadcasting networks and TV stations as they started to produce their own programs. As a result, programming decisions were made not by advertisers but by broadcasting networks and TV stations. Together with an extensive increase in advertising demands, many programs began to have various different sponsors during the 1960s decade.

Americanized TV was largely rejected in other countries (Baughman, 2002). Because of political or religious reasons, the development and production of TV sets were tightly controlled in third world countries. Hence, the television could be used as a device for governmental control and propaganda. Country leaders only changed their minds due to market pressure from citizens who experienced choice.

Additionally, unlike the United States, Britain formed a broadcasting authority (i.e. BBC) that received television taxes instead of advertiser fees. This was adopted by by African and Asian countries in the Commonwealth right up to the 1980s. Commercial TV in the United Kingdom was also under the influence of many regulations in contrast to greater freedom in the United States and Japan (i.e. NHK). As a result, commercial TV companies had to pay large taxes.

During the 1980s, entertainment serials in the United States such as action and humor were tremendously popular. This was brought forth by having excellent production facilities as well as having actor and director talents. Successful serials were syndicated and distributed to national cable operators and overseas broadcasting networks. Katz and Wedell (1977) state that over half of all programs in the third world were imported from the United States.

Although entertainment serials were popular, news became the next most valuable source of revenue for broadcasting networks and TV stations in the United States. Initially, newscasts were unpopular with over half of all citizens not watching them during a fortnight period. However, in the 1970s, CBS's 60 Minutes, with its unique exposes and features, captured a large portion of news viewership.

With the success of 60 Minutes which is still continuing today, many similar imitations on other broadcasting networks began to surface. Evening and nightly newscasts ignited advertiser interest and generated more revenue than entertainment serials as they were less costly to produce. By creating a less serious atmosphere for news, a large portion of viewership could be captured, thus this blurred the difference between entertainment and news.

The Screen in the Home

From black and white TVs to color ones and from cathode ray tubes to liquid crystal displays, the television has evolved to become the largest household screen in everyone's home (Safran et al., 2008). Alternatively, the television can also be considered as the primary viewing screen in the home.

Looking further than the wide range of programs shown, the television not only brings entertainment but serves as a form of cultural transportation (McKenney, 2008). Although the television offers viewers a glimpse of what is happening at multiple locations, it threatens to isolate and alienate them (Arnheim, 1957). This form of divide is caused by the lack of interactivity between viewers and whatever is happening at a particular place.

Today, the main aim of media companies is to make their programs as accessible to the largest audience as possible. This is achieved through mobility and flexibility. Mobility allows individual viewers to consume programs without being bound to their home TV sets. Flexibility enables programs to be viewed across a multitude of alternative viewing devices and platforms. Through mobility and flexibility, the significance of watching television has been altered altogether. Viewers have begun to view programs on their mobile devices such as smartphones or portable video players.

The eco-system in television has three key players: producers, broadcasters and advertisers (Kompare, 2005). Through the continuous flow of content, all three players always attempt to keep the audience viewing from one program to the next and so on (Williams, 1975). However, viewers are being freed from the flow imposed by traditional TV viewing. New technologies such as video on demand, digital video recorders, online video websites, movie DVDs etc. allow viewers to create their own flow without being constrained by regular programming.

As the flow is disrupted, uninterrupted consumption of programs is broken up into separate segments (McKenney, 2008). For example, a movie trailer can be downloaded onto a computer and viewed separately from its accompanying movie that is about to be broadcasted on television. This segmentation of content in turn enables new forms of marketing strategies to be taken by media companies.

While increasing the mobility and flexibility of television, distribution methods and business models have been changing. Entire episodes of a program can be purchased online through credit card payment while bypassing centralized broadcasting networks. As a result, niche audiences can be supported. Thus, media companies adopt the Long Tail strategy by selling many niche titles in small quantities while offering few popular titles in large quantities to maximize profits (Anderson, 2006).

The implications of digital or time shifted content are such that advertisers are threatened as their advertisements can be skipped over altogether. Digital piracy threatens producers as programs can be illegally shared and downloaded online thus causing a dent in revenue. Although Digital Rights Management exist as a means to protect content, viewers see few benefits as media companies charge prices above marginal costs. Furthermore, protected content limits sharing or reselling (Rayna & Striukova, 2007). Media companies can instead stream their content or activate self destruct mechanisms for downloaded content after a fixed time period to prevent digital piracy.

Instead of broadcasting networks, media companies have come to rely on cable operators for distribution (McKenney, 2008). This switch allows media companies to cut production costs, decrease risk of low viewership and encourages programmers to take up niche programs (Lotz, 2007). Cable operators find it advantageous to set up programming that matches the interests of niche audiences as they will pay for content they like instead of programs they just watch to pass time.

FUTURE OF TELEVISION

Watching television will become an individual activity rather than a family experience (Safran et al., 2008). This is because in recent years, viewers have turned to watching digital content on a personal computer rather than watching programs on television. Interest in video websites such as YouTube and portable media such as DVDs or Blu-ray discs is growing. Such competitive substitutes should not surpass the television but take on supplementary roles in content viewing.

Additionally, supporting the theory that television watching is becoming an individual activity, Safran et al. discovered through their survey that college students tend not to have a TV set in their dormitories. Instead, they rely on their personal computers or laptops to view content. Similarly, teenagers do the same while their parents watch television in the living room.

The television will become overlooked as the number of activities that can be performed on it increases (Safran et al., 2008). Firstly, the television can be connected to a set top box for cable television hosting a wide variety of content. Secondly, the television can be connected to a DVD or Blu-ray disc player for high quality playback of movies. Thirdly, the television can be connected to a console for gaming purposes. Lastly, the television can be connected to a digital video recorder for capturing video for time shifted playback.

The television will become interactive with viewers (Jensen, 2005). Traditionally, the television permits the viewer only to turn it on or off, modify volume settings or switch channels. With interactive television, the viewer can interact with the content directly. What follows are eight interesting examples of interactive television. As shown below, the significance of watching television will further change in the coming years.

Electronic Program Guide

An electronic program guide quickly scans through available cable channels for interesting current or upcoming programs that the viewer may want to view. This may incorporate search engines to search through the hundreds of channels, viewer preferences or reminders that inform the viewer of must-watch programs.

Enhanced TV

Enhanced TV is defined as overlaying interactive content on traditional content. Enhanced content is synchronized with the program and allows the viewer to access accompanying information associated with it. This may include TV synopses, sport statistics or news alerts.

Video on Demand

With video on demand, the viewer can receive content based on individual orders. This time shifted playback allows the viewer to watch content at his/her convenience. Video on demand usually involves pay per view content and the viewer is immediately billed by the cable operator upon viewing.

Personalized TV

Personalized TV incorporates a digital video recorder. As a result, personalized TV allows the viewer to rewind or fast forward a program during broadcasting. For example, the viewer may rewind to see a goal in more detail during a live soccer match or fast forward to skip over advertisements during commercial breaks.

Internet TV

This is a marriage between the television and the personal computer. Internet services can be accessed through the television by the viewer without the need for a computer. As a result, the viewer may read or write emails, participate in instant messaging or surf the Internet using the television.

Interactive Advertising

Interactive advertisements take the concept of conventional advertisements further by overlaying additional information. An interactive advertisement provides triggers which allow the viewer to acquire more information about the product or service, retrieve a brochure or make a comment.

Television Commerce

This is a hybrid of the television combined with e-commerce. This allows the viewer to perform a transaction through the television and acquire a product or service upon viewing its advertisement. As a result, viewers become consumers and can perform home shopping.

Games

Viewers may play games through the television. For example, such games can be broadcasted and different viewers may compete against one another. Game inputs take the form of SMS messages where the player specifies his/her command. The game is updated accordingly when every player's command is received.

THE ADVISOR FRAMEWORK

Nowadays, the television market need a new model to show how value added into their products after mixing with the information technology. The advisor model can help us to define future television services' scope with which service we should pass to our customers, how can we add value into our services and make them become much more competitive. Furthermore, ADVISOR can also help us to position what's our customer's need and if it is possible for us to create value for our customer or changing their watching habits. With the assistance of ADVISOR model, we can easily find the television's future applausive to interactive, variable and highly integration. These three elements help the television service suppliers to get a closer understanding with their customers' need and pass much more attractive service to their customers.

Value Proposition

Companies are also starting to realize that they have to provide "value for money" for their customers in the face of the fast changing technological evolution of the interactive media.

Video-on-demand (VOD) programmes are very popular as they let the customer elect what they like to watch and the price they need to pay. However, having just VOD alone is not sufficient to let the company stay competitive. Good quality programmes in high definition are fast becoming the choice of consumers.

Another variant of the VOD is the pay-per-view (PPV) programmes. Such programmes are usually "one-off" programmes, such as a sporting final, a musical concert, or telecast of natural disasters, etc.

Pricing strategies will become increasingly important as the consumers become more sophisticated in their choices of the wide range of services available.

Advertisers are also not immune to the changes taking place in this industry. These advertisers on regular television programmes are being compelled to change their strategies in recognition of the fact that consumers can now shift their viewing with ease from one programme to another during commercial breaks, or, in the case of PPV programmes, there are no commercial slots. Many advertisers are now participating in so-called branded entertainment, where their brand names or products are financially involved in the specific content creation in the programme. One example is a sporting equipment manufacturer sponsoring a sporting programme where their brand name and logo are occasionally superimposed on the programme itself.

Interface

Many programmes are now being made in high definition as the technology for high quality compression and transmission is available. As market studies had shown, the primary criteria of choice for a home television set is predominantly picture quality, followed by widescreen and, of course, pricing.

As a result, makers of television are turning out High Definition Television (HDTV) at great speed in various forms such as plasma, LEDs and LCDs. These are getting cheaper as production costs go down and will become increasingly affordable. Broadcasting or cable TV providers are also providing more programmes in high definition due to the better picture qualities.

Television will still remain the core-viewing hub of many households, and thus will continue to remain a very lucrative market for manufacturers. Equipment or home entertainment manufacturers are now designing equipment or components revolving around the television set. Home entertainment, with the central widescreen TV, DVD or Blu-ray disc players, audio/video multi-channel system with HD upscaling connected by HDMI cables, and set-top boxes capable of connecting to internet line are now becoming the norm.

Following the success of the 3-D (three dimensional) movie, Avatar, hardware manufacturers are keen to catch on the wave. Some leading manufacturers such as Sony and Samsung are already marketing new 3-D TV. Even 3-D Blu-ray disc players are already available in the market. However, they are limited at the moment by the lack of a wide selection of genuine 3-D programmes. It is not impossible to foresee that 3-D technology in the future will not be confined only to cinemas

and TVs, but perhaps also to the computers and mobile phones.

As broadband penetration and coverage grow, so will IPTV. PC makers will have to design both hardware and software on new PC models to stay relevant in the growing market of IPTV. For example, upscale PCs now come provided with handheld remote controls that work almost like a regular TV's remote control to enable comfort viewing of IPTV programmes. Screen monitors of PCs are also now being made in widescreen formats to follow the picture aspect ratio of normal movies.

To tap into the market of mobile TV consumers, mobile phone makers are continuously trying to roll out new models with feature-packed functions, bigger and better screens with higher resolutions and battery packs with longer life in between charging. 3-G network operators are upgrading their infrastructure to provide wider coverage.

Service Platforms

IPTV will become a common platform for systems where television and/or video signals are distributed to subscribers or viewers using a broadband connection over Internet Protocol (Shin, 2007). That means with the swift development of technique, broadband has become an important contributor for IPTV development. Broadband helps IPTV to handle with the problem of network jam and improve the quality of video. Compare to the traditional cable TV service providers, IPTV service provider can pass much more high quality products via the broad band's support.

Allowing other firms to contribute to your platform can be a brilliant strategy, because those firms will spend their time and money to enhance your offering (Gallaugher, 2008). This theory is also adapted in the IPTV standardization platform. As we know if IDM products have a widely accepted standard, this kind of product development will become swifter than others which do not have a common standard. Different brands products with a standard platform will strength the cooperation between different suppliers in complementary aspects.

Nowadays, BBC has developed its own platform for IPTV which name is Iplayer. This platform can enable the content providers easily to launch their service in internet TV service. We consider this action as the bargaining with the suppliers and users.

Iplayer provides a standard, high quality input protocol to their content providers with a relatively lower cost. On the other hand, Iplayer enable their users with the function of watching highlight instantly, sending clips to their friends, easily monitoring what's being said on twitter, accessing the archive and using 3rd part applications and services. Such functions can adding much more value into their service and platform attracting much more new users and strengthen their relationship and brand loyalty with their customers.

Organizing Models

The various content contributors are the key elements to the IPTV. They supply various products to the IPTV content. Variable content will attract more users. On the other hand, because of the development of information technology, the presenting of the rare content at any time becomes possible. In the long tail theory, one grocery can not prepare all sorts of products to meet different demands from different groups of people, so the profits from seizing the demand in the tail are really unbelievably huge. IPTV provider can merge different contents from any place in the earth. It can meet any odd demand as much as possible. Such characteristics improve the competitive force of IPTV. Their user will finally find that they can access most of which they want in the IPTV, and in their mind, IPTV becomes the symbol of everything and key elements. This future inspire IPTV supplier to do much better in meeting the demand of their customers.

Internet will complement future TV. Internet can help users to access much more various resources. Compared to the internet, IPTV has a robust performance on videos, but sometimes users require much more information and not only the videos. So the internet can help them to access much more resources that IPTV can not provide. But we do not believe television will vanish in the future, we think it will integrate with internet services. This will be further introduced later.

IPTV can prevent the phenomena of free-riding effectively because of the license. User can only access to the service after applying it. It is impossible to receive any service data without the authority from the supplier. Just like using the broadband. Supplier benefit from this characteristic and get an almost 0 profit lost.

Revenue or Cost Sharing

We believe that television's revenue will be affected by the network effect in the future. More users equate to more value. Exchange, staying power and complementary benefits often work together to reinforce one another in a way that makes the network effect even stronger (Gallaugher, 2008). We can also use this theory to explain the revenue model of IPTV.

Without doubt, web2.0 exhibits us new understandings on how value comes from exchanging. For example, most of the supplier will share a recommend list of their content. The recommend list includes the hottest, newest one. Much more users click and watch the hottest one will lead the fact that it becomes much hotter. The network effect can be found in the recommend list.

As we mentioned in the organizational model, supplier satisfied their user with various value added services which can strengthen their users' brand loyalty. If their users are the stable followers of their products, the switching cost will be higher and higher. This is really good news to the supplier because that's means they can invest much more money on seizing users rather than looking for users.

A key reason for companies to invest in IPTV solutions is to increase the revenue they get from each subscriber – providing a broader range of services to which customers can be cross-sold is a clear way to increase revenue potential.

Adoption by Customers

Recent studies had shown that a sizeable percentage of television and media broadcast consumers are now spending more time on the internet on some sort of online social networking sites as well as gaming sites. Additionally, with the shift of transmission and programme media from analogue to digital, from dial-up modem to broadband on cable or optic fibre, this is changing the way consumers spend their time, whether in front of the television or online on their PCs, or simply using mobile devices, such as mobile phones, to access information and news.

Penetration of broadband access is affecting conventional TV usage in households, and this have to be acknowledged by the conventional media broadcasting companies. The media companies, including satellite and cable television broadcasters, have to transform themselves to stay relevant and recapture, and then expand on their share of the consumer market. Conventional TV broadcasters like digital-terrestrial television (DTT) are being challenged by cable TV with on-demand availability of many titles in the library. Thus such operators are always staying competitive by providing a wider selection of services, such as telephony and internet services. Likewise, cable providers are also encroaching into programme distribution. The lines between these different players are becoming less and less distinct as the market changes.

Expectations of better quality programmes on high resolution formats are also creating a huge influence on the way companies are now selling their products, be it HDTV, 3-D TV, IPTV or mobile TV.

Disruptive Innovation

It is therefore vital that these conventional media broadcasters, or TV companies, innovate, not just to maintain, but also to expand on their share of the consumer base in the challenge of the broadband service providers.

Examples of some of these innovations are:

- Pay-per-view (PPV) programmes
- Video on demand (VOD)
- Personal video recorders (PVR)
- Interactive gaming and/or gambling via Set-Top-Boxes (STB)

To capture a wider range of consumers, and their diversities or preferences, in some cases, merging and acquisitions (M&A) of such companies will help them expand their platform and diversity to offer a wider range of services such as bundled packages with cable TV, broadband internet access, telephony and mobile phone services. Traditional media broadcasters are now even utilizing broadband as a platform to sell their video selection as an online media for such programmes.

Another significant emergence due to digital TV and broadband penetration, especially in more mature markets, is the IPTV (Internet Protocol TV). This service has the advantage over traditional mass broadcasting in that the individual customer can elect when and what programmes he or she would like to watch at their own convenient time.

With IPTV, the companies can expand their revenue per customer by offering a wider range of services, including unicasting and broadcasting.

The Mobile TV is also becoming an increasingly popular means of access to entertainment and broadcasts via existing 3G telecommunications network. Although mobile TV is not a direct competitor of mainstream television programmes, however, mobile TV can provide consumers with the freedom of access wherever they go. Potential revenue from advertisers on the mobile consumer market cannot be ignored by these telcos.

This is also providing device manufacturers with intense competition to produce handheld devices or mobile phones with bigger and better quality screens, packed with more features and at low costs such as Apple's iPhone.

Can you imagine the day when you can use text to communicate with other users to interact your opinion and other information while watching the television? We can find some surveys on media uses (e.g., Miller, 2005) show that SMS (Short Message Service) texting and other user interactions in response to TV programs have gained a lot of popularity recently as part of the viewing experience. Nowadays users' desire on communicating and interacting becomes stronger and stronger. If the service supplier can provide such value added functions to their users via IPTV in the near future, we think this integration will lead an evolution in the traditional idea on television revenue model.

CONCLUSION

As we can see, television will still remain important in the future, but the big change will be in the way the TV is being used as the interface to bring visual and audio to the viewer. Instead of waiting for a particular time for a particular programme to be broadcasted to the TV, viewers now have the versatility or choice of watching available programmes at his or her own time, with high definition or even 3-D pictures, whether through cable or optic fibre, but also through broadband without the need to navigate with a computer. Such services are already available, and it is going to be a continuous challenge for the TV media and IP service providers to constantly innovate and upgrade their programmes or services to the consumers.

Expectations of more and more sophisticated consumers can no longer be ignored by big TV media companies as competitions from other sources such as internet service providers who not only offer much more interactive entertainment, but are becoming cheaper and readily available. These TV companies can no longer operate as conventional broadcasting companies, but are forced to expand their range of services to stay relevant and alive in the future.

TV manufacturers are also keeping a parallel watch on technological advances of programme transmission as well as contents available on internet to produce TV sets not only capable of reproducing the available picture and sound quality, but also capable of features for interactive entertainment (such as online gaming).

Personal computers are no longer just machines for use such as word processing, data storage and retrieval, but they are increasingly being widely used not only for accessing digital media, and interactive information sharing, but also for audio and visual entertainment viewing.

Thus we can see that the TV has become more than just a machine for viewing broadcasted programmes. It has become an important and integral part of the interactive digital media industry.

REFERENCES

Anderson, C. (2006). *The long tail: Why the future of business is selling less of more*. New York, NY: Hyperion.

Arnheim, R. (1957). A forecast of television . In Arnheim, R. (Ed.), *Film as art* (pp. 188–198). London, UK: University of California Press.

Baughman, J. L. (2002). Television: History . In Smelser, N. J. (Ed.), *International encyclopedia of the social and behavioral sciences* (pp. 15579–15583).

Crosbie, T. (2008). Household energy consumption and consumer electronics: The case of television. *Energy Policy, 36*(6), 2191–2199. doi:10.1016/j.enpol.2008.02.010

Jensen, J. F. (2005). Interactive television: New genres, new format, new content. *ACM International Conference Proceeding Series, 123*, 89-96.

Katz, E., & Wedell, G. (1977). *Broadcasting in the third world: Promise and performance.* Cambridge, MA: Harvard University Press.

Kompare, D. (2005). Acquisitive repetition: Home video and the television heritage . In Kompare, D. (Ed.), *Rerun nation: How repeats invented American television* (pp. 197–220). New York, NY: Routledge. doi:10.4324/9780203337387_chapter_8

Lotz, A. D. (2007). Revolutionizing distribution: Breaking open the network bottleneck . In Lotz, A. D. (Ed.), *The television will be revolutionized* (pp. 119–151). New York, NY: New York University Press.

McKenney, B. (2008). The future of television. *Comm-entary: The University of New Hampshire Student Journal of Communication*, 66-75.

Rayna, T., & Striukova, L. (2007). *Digital rights management: White knight or Trojan horse?* (pp. 1–19). Bristol Economics Discussion Papers.

Ryu, H., & Wong, A. (2008). Perceived usefulness and performance of human-to-human communications on television. *Computers in Human Behavior, 24*(4), 1364–1384. doi:10.1016/j.chb.2007.07.011

Safran, N., Ask, J., Meyer, L., & Fogg, I. (2008). *Evolution of the television: From passive consumption device to the entertainment center of the home. Digital Home, 1.* Jupiter Research.

Shin, D. H. (2007). Potential user factors driving adoption of IPTV: What are customers expecting from IPTV? *Technological Forecasting and Social Change, 74*(8), 1446–1464. doi:10.1016/j.techfore.2006.05.007

TVHistory. (2010). *Number of TV households and percentage of USA homes with television – 1950 to 1978.* Retrieved April 11, 2010, from http://www.tvhistory.tv/Annual_TV_Households_50-78.JPG

Wikipedia. (2010). *Television.* Retrieved April 9, 2010, from http://en.wikipedia.org/wiki/Television

Williams, R. (1975). *Television: Technology and cultural form.* New York, NY: Schocken Books. doi:10.4324/9780203450277

Chapter 33
The Future of the Printed Book

Lee San Bao Elizabeth
Nanyang Technological University, Singapore

Noriahni Ismail
Nanyang Technological University, Singapore

Ma Saw Zarchi Tun
Nanyang Technological University, Singapore

ABSTRACT

The printed book was widely believed to be "dead" in the 1990s, but sales continue to remain brisk till today. Studies have shown that the advent of e-books will pose as a threat to the printed book; however, despite the increase in sales of e-books, readers still believe that printed books will never become extinct. This chapter aims to examine the various alternatives to the printed book, and explore the implications of the future for the book publishing industry and other players. The shift of physical books into digital content format has resulted in a significant change in perspectives of business models in the book publishing industry. In addition, as with any paradigmatic shift in technologies, there are implications and strategic reactions to the impact on the various affected players in an industry's eco-system.

INTRODUCTION

The printed book was widely believed to be "dead" in the 1990s, but till today sales of printed books continue to remain brisk (Staley, 2003). However, the scenario of the end of the printed book is still a possibility in the future, with the increasing usage of digitisation. The Internet allows for the choice of online versions and electronic books, with the benefit of updated versions and revisions to be easier and more cost-effective to implement (Publishing Industry Profile, 2009).

Book publishers are increasingly utilising the Internet as part of their business by diversifying their products to customers in other media formats,

DOI: 10.4018/978-1-61350-147-4.ch033

and reaching out to new target markets (Publishing Industry Profile, 2009). It is indeed more cost-effective to produce online versions of text or books, as information online can be shared by two or more people and used at the same time at the same costs. In fact, the cost to reproduce the same e-book for all readers is next to nothing, as opposed to the print version. Furthermore, digital technology can allow "artists, writers and other creators of content to maintain greater control of their work, and keep more of the proceeds from it" (Staley, 2003). Thus, with digitisation, making e-books cheaper and easier to reproduce and distribute simultaneously to all readers, will the future of printed books be at risk?

On the other hand, computers and other new technologies may boost the ability of book publishers to produce and distribute printed books, which ensures the future of printed books. According to Staley (2003), computers may change the production and distribution of printed books but they will have little effect on the physical appearance. With the print-on-demand technology, for example, although the written text is kept electronically, when a customer wants a copy, it can be printed and bound, and then shipped to the customer as a printed book. Staley (2003) believes that printed books will be part of the future; it would simply be "idle in electronic form until ready to be made material in the printed book form". In addition, according to Staley (2003), if information remains an intellectual property, then "authors and publishers will continue to maintain control over this property via the best available technology: the printed book".

This paper aims to examine the various alternatives of the printed book, and explore the implications of the future for the book publishing industry and other players. The first part will cover the literature review of the printed book's alternatives. We will explore the shifts of the business models in the book publishing industry in the second part, followed by its impacts on the book publishing eco system. The paper will conclude in whether there is a future for the printed book, or will it be replaced by its other alternatives.

BACKGROUND

Literature Review

Many people are still using books in print since centuries ago because they believe that the printed book is more traditional and convenient in terms of effectiveness in usage (Zahda, 2007). Ventura (2005) states that his "central point here is that we are using the electronic environment to find the books we want, but we will not replace books with electronic, digitized reading. It is uncomfortable to read from screen for any length of time". Reading a printed book is more comfortable, convenient and sensual for readers.

Our daily lives started to change to become more digitized because of the advancement of Internet and computer technology. This has increased the diversity of many digital products available in the interactive digital media (IDM) market (Zahda, 2007). E-books are one aspect of these technologies and it can be defined as "text in digital form, or book converted into digital form, or digital reading material, or a book in a computer file format, or an electronic file of words and images displayed on a desktop, notebook computer, or portable device, or formatted for display on dedicated e-book readers" (Rao, 2003).

Oghojafor (2005) highlights that e-book publishing can help save money for both the authors and the consumers. From the perspective of the authors, they can correct any mistakes at any time without costs. Moreover, consumers can obtain any updates of the book and supplementary contents. E-books also have more attractive features such as images, animation, audio, video and hyperlinks than the printed books, and readers can zoom in and out of the e-book pages.

Zahda (2007) notes that the physical storage space for e-books is quite different from printed books. At present time, everyone can store hundreds of e-books on a single thumb drive. In this innovative era, almost all digital devices have the power to connect to the Internet and download e-books from libraries or online sellers. Thus, customers can have a portable library with different contents that is available at the touch of their fingertips, no matter where they are. E-books are non-rival goods; so there is no issue of limited available copies for distribution and they can support translation services to be interoperable with the e-readers.

Many organizations and prominent companies that are heavily involved with e-publishing, such as Google and Open Content Alliance, have started to convert printed books into electronic books (Zahda, 2007). Moreover, many education institutions and universities all over the world have started to switch from using printed books to e-books in their curriculum (Zahda, 2007). Villano (2005) notices that "textbook sales continue to sag and their prices proceed to rise, thus colleges and universities are increasingly turning towards electronic publishing as an affordable alternative". As a result, the sales of printed books are sinking dramatically and the sales of e-books are increasing day by day. For example, "according to the IDPF (International Digital Publishing Forum), e-book sales have grown from around $6 million in 2002 to around $33 million in 2007 -- still less than 1% of the book publishing business" (Herther, 2008).

Even though e-books have several advantages and the percentage of sales is increasing, the e-book users and non-users still believe that the printed books will never become extinct. Zahda (2007) points out that "some consider the phenomenon of e-books as a temporary one since printed books proved to be the main medium of education and knowledge transfer". When it comes to printed books, there are two questions: "Will the printed books still be alive in the future, and will e-books actually replace the printed books?" Zahda (2007) also mentions that "many bookworms cannot imagine themselves reading books without flipping their pages. It is kind of impossible for them to read books without touching their papers and turning the pages". Furthermore, Ardito (2000) contemplates the enjoyment of the sound of a flipped page, which provides the feeling of being immersed in books and the simple enjoyment of real reading. Sifton (2009) adds on to say that his reading on the web is of a completely different order from his reading of or in a book, and it would be even more so if he hadn't already put in decades of bookish exertion.

According to the academic literature papers, we can consider printed books to have a strong future even though e-books have many advantages compared to them. However, it is to be noted that there remains the possibility of e-books replacing printed books to some extent, but not all. Bodomo (2003) reports that the majority of students (77%) in Hong Kong universities preferred printed materials. Snowhill (2001) describes that some academic librarians also felt the role of e-books is not to replace printed materials but to serve as a duplicate copy. Helfer (2000) states that "the users use e-books just as a reference tool to get the answer they needed and they could or would buy a physical copy of it if they wanted or need the book on an ongoing basis". By looking at these studies, it is almost certain that e-books would face a great challenge in attempting to replace the traditional printed books.

The next section focuses on the shift of the business models of the book publishing industry, with increasing digitisation.

BUSINESS MODELS

Definition

The term "business model" became widely used as an essential business practice only in the 1990s (Lawrence *et el*, 2003). There is no one definition of the term "business model". The diversity in definitions makes it difficult to clearly state the nature and components of a good business model, and what constitutes a good model. According to Morris, Schindehutte and Allen (2002), this also leads to confusion in the terminology as "business model, strategy, business concept, revenue model, and economic model" are often used interchangeably.

There is a wide range of perspectives on the nature and definition of business models in the literature. The review of related literature on the definition of business models by Shafer, Smith and Linder (2005) have uncovered 12 definitions in established publications during the years 1998 – 2002. However, they found that none of the definitions have been utilised fully in the business community, as these definitions come from different perspectives like strategy, business and technology, and thus they have come from different viewpoints and lenses. In fact, they found 42 different components of business models from these 12 definitions, in which some components like creating value, capturing value, strategic choices and value network, appear in most definitions, while others like cash flow, customer interface, culture, are found in only 1 definition. From the above findings, Shafer, Smith and Linder (2005)

came up with a new definition of business model, which is "a representation of a firm's underlying core logic and strategic choices for creating and capturing value within a value network". Their "affinity diagram" which summarises the components of a business model can be seen in Components of a Business Model (Figure 1).

The above definition includes four key terms: core logic, strategic choices, creating and capturing value. Shafer, Smith and Linder (2005) explains that the core logic suggests that a "properly crafted business model helps to articulate about the cause-and-effect relationships, and the internal consistency of strategic choices". For companies to remain viable in the long term, they must create and capture value. It was added that the definition is not restricted to the online world (Shafer, Smith and Linder, 2005).

Another study on business models by Morris, Schindehutte and Allen (2005) shows that the most frequently cited components from established publications from years 1996 – 2002 are the "firm's value offering, economic model, customer interface/relationship, partner network/roles, internal infrastructure/connected activities and relationships, and target markets". It was noted that there are few insights on what makes a business model appropriate, existence of generic

Figure 1. Components of business model affinity diagram. Taken from Shafer, Smith & Linder (2005).

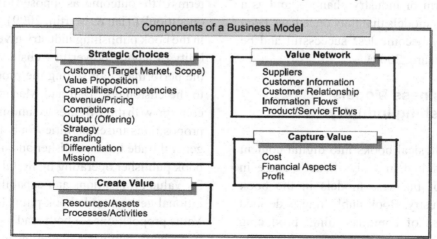

models, and methodologies to evaluate the model quality, among other questions. Thus, based on their findings and theoretical roots, Morris, Schindehutte and Allen (2005) developed a standard framework to characterise a business model. The proposed framework consists of 3 specific levels of decision making; "foundation, proprietary and rules" levels. In addition, at each level, there are 6 basic decision areas to be considered. The foundation level defines the basic components; the proprietary level is to create unique combinations and the rules level is to establish guiding principles. This proposed framework allows users to "design, describe, categorise, critique and analyse" a business model for any type of firms, including online businesses, and to strategically adapt the basic elements of a business (Morris, Schindehutte & Allen, 2005).

Picard (2000) states that "there is no one formula to create a successful arrangement within the interests, and different firms and technologies seek different business models for transferring the potential of technologies into successful business enterprises". It is important to understand the business models operated by the different firms or businesses, and it becomes especially crucial when new products or services are developed, or the industry in which they operate in changes significantly. The factors or components that support a business model change as the environment of the firm or industry changes, and as a result, business models that may once have been successful may become less successful and be abandoned. (Picard, 2000).

Shift in Business Models: Book Publishing Industry

The shift of physical books into digital content format has resulted in a significant change in perspectives of business models in the book publishing industry. Book publishing is defined as "the process of commissioning, producing and distributing books for sale" (Tian & Martin,

2009). According to Tian and Martin (2009), the key players in both the production and distribution channels have increased. This is in spite of the notions that the uptake of digital technologies would result in "disintermediation of the value chain" for book publishing, as authors can now become publishers by potentially implementing all roles, from content creation to publicity of the end product. Technology has allowed businesses to reach out to a large number of customers at minimal cost, but only in the context of viable business models (Kinder, 2002).

As mentioned above, there are many different interpretations and descriptions of business models. Using Shafer, Smith and Linder (2005)'s definition, a business model can be summarised into the categories of strategic choices, value network, create and capture value. This paper will focus on two important elements; the firm's value propositions, to create and capture value; and the capabilities like strategic choice of the book publishers. Firms' value proposition is fundamental to remain viable in the long term, and it is thus important to understand the reasons customers purchase their products instead of others, and the value of the publishers. Bagchi and Tulskie (2000) explain that the "value propositions offered by a firm are generated by a set of internal capabilities", which is the ability of the firm to "perform functions that are described in terms of the outcome, as opposed to the method of operation" (Tian & Martin, 2009). One example in the book publishing industry given is the capability of having powerful websites, which helps the performance of selling the products directly to the customers. Tian and Martin (2009) have come up with three figures to summarise the value propositions and capabilities for both a traditional general trade book publisher and a general trade book publisher operating in digital mode. Figure 2 - Value propositions and capabilities for a traditional general trade book publisher; Figure 3 - Value propositions for both readers and a general trade book publisher operating in digital mode and Figure 4 - Capabilities required for a general trade book publisher operating in digital mode, list the important value propositions for both the customer and a general trade book publisher in traditional and digital models.

Figures 2 to 4 show that there is a difference in the value propositions and capabilities of book publishers when they move from traditional to digital modes. The value propositions for the customer and book publisher, as well as the capabilities of the publisher, increase with the use of digital formats. This indirectly shows a shift in the business models. However, according to Tian and Martin (2009), despite the changes, the methods for selecting or constructing business models remain the same. The firm still needs to customise its value propositions to meet the needs of its external parties, as well as to align with its existing internal capabilities (Tian & Martin, 2009).

In their study of the business models in digital book publishing in Australia, Tian and Martin (2009) found that in the context of increasing digitisation, book publishers in general have acknowledged the importance of considering new and more appropriate business models. It is interesting to note that although the book publishers are already engaged in constructing appropriate business models to accommodate to the digital era, most of them continue to operate as both providers and recipients of value. Traditional players continue to operate familiar and profitable business models, while "implementing or participating in hybrids which allow for the activities of additional players and the impact of digital technologies" (Tian & Martin, 2009). One example is the multi-channel distribution model that most of the book publishers are still implementing, where they use both traditional and electronic channels to sell their products. This multi-channel distribution model can also be customised to suit various products or services. Although the study was done in Australia, the findings do align with evidence, reflecting the existence of similar trends and issues in other countries (Tian & Martin, 2009).

Despite the shift in business models and the emergence of hybrid models, book publishers today are still producing and selling printed books,

Figure 2. Value propositions and capabilities for a traditional general trade book publisher. Taken from Tian & Martin (2009).

Traditional general trade book publishing	
Value proposition for readers	Value proposition for publishers
High quality printed books	*Content*
Wide range of content	Access to quality content
Opportunities for interaction with authors, publishers and other readers	*Relationships*
	Access to leading authors and agents
	Strong relationships with other key stakeholders (distributors, booksellers, printers) to achieve high quality content creation, efficient distribution, successful marketing and sales
Capabilities required for publishers	Ability to develop good relationships with various partners on the chain
	Ability to identify readers' interests and needs regarding content
	Ability to source content quickly to meet customer requirements

Figure 3. Value propositions for both readers and a general trade book publisher operating in digital mode. Taken from Tian & Martin (2009).

Digital publishing for general trade books	
Value proposition for readers	Value proposition for publishers
Content	*Content*
Superior quality, increased choice, reduced cost and multiple choice format	Provision of high quality and customized content
	Provision of a wider range of resources
Facilities	Provision of multi-format options for increased customer choice
Simple access to complex market and product information through easy-to-use interfaces	More effective provision of data on information use by readers
Facility for searching content from a wide range of sources	*Facilities*
Products	Digital storage and archiving to enable content re-use
Increased supply of new products	Enhanced facility for communication and interaction
Faster access to and delivery of products	*Products*
Customer management	Faster introduction of new and improved products
More interactivity (not just with publishers but with other authors, readers and special interest groups)	*Marketing*
	Expansion into new geographic territories
Lower transaction costs for order and delivery	Enhanced interactivity, with the potential to attract more readers
Broader and advanced service availability (any time and any place) and service customized to the requirements of reader	Ability to offer differentiated pricing based on customer expenditure levels
Enhanced communication including alerts and reminders for specific events and community forums	*Distribution and sales*
	Choice of lower cost distribution channels
Recommendations and promotions tailored to readers' interests	More targeted promotions and cross-sells (for customers)
Single publisher point of contact	*Management*
	Better management of uncertainty and variability in partner relationships and processes
	Increased organizational learning
	Increased cost effectiveness in primary and support services
	Reduced need for inventory functions due to new technologies
	Ability to outsource general operational (but non-strategic) tasks
	Enhanced collaboration including the sharing of information and ideas between business partners and between publishers and reader communities

Figure 4. Capabilities required for a general trade book publisher operating in digital mode. Taken from Tian & Martin (2009).

	Capabilities required for general trade books in digital mode
Technologies	More powerful, stable, interacting and customized website and interfaces
	Ability to generate and present personalized customized information
	Ability to provided secure and private information transmission/transaction facilities
	Ability to monitor user actions and identify user preferences for prediction of user behavior
	Ability to synthesize and integrate market data (readers, suppliers, etc.) through use of data mining, filtering and advanced search techniques
Management	Design of new (automated) business processes that integrate and interoperate with external business systems
	Ability to reproduce information items at close to zero cost
	Ability to develop structure and organization for knowledge management, including knowledge search and retrieval techniques
	Ability to maintain a high level of security and privacy
	Ability to manage rights in resources, access, distribution content and information
	Ability to link all parties electronically for product inventory and ordering information
	Logistics management

although there are multiple formats to choose from. The next section will cover the impact of this change to the book publishing eco-system.

IMPACT ON THE ECOSYSTEM

As with any paradigmatic shift in technologies, there are bound to be impacts on the various affected players in an industry's eco-system. The implications and strategic reactions to these impacts are the focus of this section. For the purpose of this paper, we have identified the following affected players in the publishing industry eco-system: publishers and authors or suppliers, bookstores/booksellers, online bookstores and libraries or distributors, and customers.

Publishers and Authors (Suppliers)

Most certainly, this is the group of players that is significantly impacted by the online revolu-

tion going on. From gaining of sales revenue to points of distribution, it can be said that publishers greatly need a thorough rethinking of their business strategies. Their organisation priorities and objectives may have to be realigned in order to better deliver to end customers. Authors are also given a jolt of awakening, with regards to the copyrights and intellectual property of their produced work. If it is expected that everything on the Internet should be priced free, is there any more incentive for them to create more materials for publishing? These challenges are just a mere glimpse into the multitude of issues facing this group of players. Below, we highlight a few of the more pertinent issues.

From the literature review and business models discussed, it should become apparent to publishers that it is the content and not the medium that is crucial. If much rhetorical debate were spent on deciding between print and digital formats, and neglecting the bigger implication of the book as an asset, perhaps it would be the wrong track of thinking to follow. "It is important for publishing companies to not think in terms of books vs. Internet, but to realize that their value is their content, in whatever form it is distributed." (Marlow, 2006)

Costs management has always been an important aspect of any organisation. For publishers, the cost savings that book alternatives would bring about heavy involvement fuel and paper costs. Theoretically, logistics would become smoother and environment conservation could be implemented as well. However, there may exist higher hidden cost, such as in terms of digital storage and archive management of electronic books and implementation of digital rights management. If a partnership is reached with an initiative such as Google Book Search, does this signify that there is an implicit handover of all copyrights to Google?

Furthermore, the publishing industry does not have a homogenous nature, i.e. different specialising publishers catering to different book market segments. Thus, the business strategies will naturally differ for each segment, from academic publishing to literary publishing. Academic publishing of university textbooks may be more suited to promoting electronic materials, as University of Texas has illustrated with its pilot trial of textbooks on Amazon Kindle, Sony e-readers and laptops. Because students consume these textbooks differently, e.g. skimming and searching for useful materials, rather than reading end to end, this pilot trial proved promising results for all textbooks in the University of Texas to be rolled out in electronic format within 5 years (Butler, 2009). On the other hand, romance novels are consumed and marketed differently. In 2006, Harlequin (2006) developed "a successful cell phone e-book strategy for its romance novels that allows for downloading serialized romance titles and some mystery titles to cell phones. It also offers users optional games or a service that teaches users how to write their own romance novel." (Herther, 2008)

In Figure 5 - Evolving science content value model, Marlow (2006) uses the flow and publishing of academic scientific materials as a model

for the content value. Within one arena of the publishing world, there are already eight levels of information and publishing solutions, which most probably can imply eight different levels of distribution points. Such complexity in the nature of published information can only point to being absolutely clear about customer needs and the value add required in the products or services being offered. For each different market segment, publishers have to seriously consider how to best deliver their content via convenient and economical distribution points, whether it be print or electronic format.

The electronic revolution has enabled easier methods of publishing materials for authors, allowing them to self-publish on platforms such as blogs. This movement of self-publishing can indicate greater control over creative materials and signal the end of publishers as intermediaries. This is only because, the reach of such self-publishing platforms is wide, i.e. the world is the audience. However, the threat of piracy and plagiarism would remain. Even with the usage of Creative Commons, authors may still need to tackle intellectual property issues.

With new information and knowledge platforms around, there are greater means for related creative collaborations among authors for book promotion, e.g. video trailers of book, online games based on book, working with other authors on a book. The landscape of book promotion has changed from the traditional medium of promotional posters and advertisements. Electronic word of mouth, peer recommendations and online social media are some of the potential promotional strategies that can be utilised for greater reach and effectiveness by authors.

Bookstores / Booksellers, Online Bookstores, and Libraries (Distributors)

In the face of drastic technological and readership pattern changes, the brick and mortar bookstores and libraries have to evolve accordingly or risk

Figure 5. Evolving science content value model. Taken from Marlow (2006).

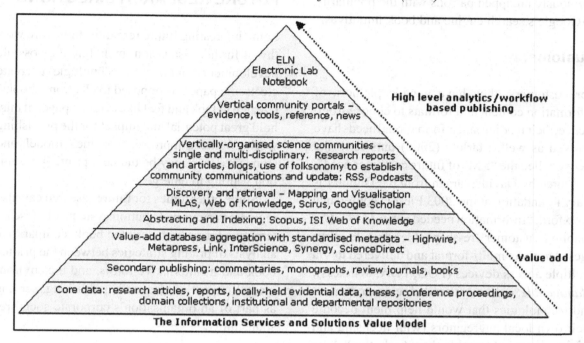

extinction. According to Doug Armato, director of the University of Minnesota Press in Minneapolis, "If you're not investing in eBooks, you're crazy" (Alexander, 2010). But, the decision to go digital or not depends also on the nature of the books being sold. In particular, niche bookstores may find that an Internet presence may not be profitable at all. "The owner of a small, specialty bookstore focusing on African-

American titles reported that the store actually shut its Web site down after 3 years of operation: "The site was removed after 3 years because it generated $300.00 in total sales. We may put it back up for advertising only" (Kaarst-Brown, 2004). As for libraries, they face great challenges as well, from heterogeneous patrons with diverse reading needs to selecting suitable materials in various formats, priced affordably for maximum usage.

Again, the major impact on this group of players heavily involves cost savings. Bookstores can economise on shelf space and excess inventory, as can libraries. They can even implement print-on-

demand technology as another enhanced method of gaining more revenue. This technology, "which makes printing short runs of physical books more economical, should help them squeeze more money out of the old-fashioned format." ("Technology driving publishing revolution", 2010) But, the hidden costs should also be considered, e.g. annual subscription fee for electronic journals, electronic archive and storage upkeep, and training of users / readers to read from a different platform / medium.

Partnerships and alliance strategies for these players may also have been changed greatly. Working in unions, trade organisations or with other major conglomerates make good business sense; collaboration towards a common goal with competitors would play an important part in keeping customers engaged. Amazon and Google are good examples of synergy at play, with bookstores and libraries respectively. Linking book products with Amazon can potentially gain wider reach for smaller bookstores and libraries may find previously untapped patrons with the popularity of Google's search engine and book initiatives.

Customers

For customers, they have a wide plethora of information content and formats to choose from. Hence, their reading and informational needs have evolved as well. Marlow (2006) puts forth the theory called the "5 Ms of future customer need", presented by David Seaman from the Digital Library Foundation at the 2003 Fiesole conference in Oxford. "Information needed to be; *Malleable*: enabling customer 're-shapeable' data & packages; *Multiple*: multi-format and delivered to/via multiple access devices (POD, PDA, Wireless); *Manageable:* customers needed access to content and technologies that would help them become their own local aggregators (with licensing and pricing that would enable them to do this); *Mixable:* content (and technology) that encouraged users to mix, match and manage differing content types and 'research in progress', integrated with and into their 'home grown'/'home collected' personal and personalized content libraries; and finally, *Massive*: more information required, more easily found, linked, identified, verified, communicated . . . and 'in context'." (Marlow, 2006)

However, this model of customer needs may result in the cultural attitude of taking information subsidies for granted, e.g. paying a flat fee to Internet service providers and having accessible information at your fingertips. This can perpetuate user expectations of information being priced at zero, when it is not really free in reality. If customers can become accustomed to paying $0.69 for music, nothing can stop them from demanding a price no less than free for books, creating little monetary incentive for authors to innovate and produce.

FUTURE RESEARCH DIRECTIONS

Some interesting future research studies are worthy of further discussion, including the possible development of innovative technologies to create electronic paper, as opposed to electronic books. Created to look and feel like original paper, it may hold great potential and impact for the publishing world. With the appropriate business models and strategies, they may be the next printing revolution waiting to emerge.

Some other topics for future research can also include: various distribution systems of these alternative forms to the printed book, comparative analysis of pricing strategies between the printed book and its alternative forms, and the environmental impact of electronic publishing, serving as part of an organisation's corporate social responsibility.

CONCLUSION

The world of publishing has endured its share of setbacks and criticisms since the invention of the printing press. From censorship to profit maximisation, the major aspects of publishing, book marketing and distribution, and reader consumption have been examined in much literature. This paper has analysed the future of the printed book, in relation to the digital interactive media aspect. The shift in business models due to the advent of interactive technologies was discussed, along with the various impacts on the different players in the publishing industry eco-system.

The printed book was once an innovative technology, one that survived for seven centuries and counting. While there may be reports of growing financial revenue from electronic and alternative formats of the book, industry players still predict that the printed book will remain a formidable player. Gall (2005) states that it is a myth to view books and electronic books as competitors, and von Bubnoff (2005) proposes that "having a mix of e-books and real books could be the answer". No matter what format or platform it comes in, the book is here to stay.

REFERENCES

Alexander, S. (2010, 16 August). Publishers like the look of e-book profits: The book business is starting to go electronic - And local publishers are embracing the trend, in part because e-books are just as profitable. *McClatchy - Tribune Business News*. Retrieved April 10, 2010, from ABI/INFORM Dateline. (Document ID: 1832186591).

Anonymous. (2010, April 3). Technology driving publishing revolution - companies scramble to adapt to online world. *Winnipeg Free Press*.

Ardito, S. (2000). *Electronic books: To E or not to E; that is the question*. Retrieved from http://www.infotoday.com/searcher/apr00/ardito.htm

Bagchi, S., & Tulskie, B. (2000). *E-business models: Integrating learning from strategy development experiences and empirical research*. Paper presented to the 20th Annual International Conference of the Strategic Management Society, Vancouver. (pp. 15–18).

Bodomo, A., Lam, M.-L., & Lee, C. (2003). Some students still read books in the 21st century: A study of user preferences for print and electronic libraries. *The Reading Matrix, 3*(3). Retrieved from http://readingmatrix.com/articles/bodomo_lam_Lee/article.pdf.

Butler, D. (2009). Technology: The textbook of the future. *Nature, 458*(7238), 568–570. .doi:10.1038/458568a

Datamonitor. (2009). *Publishing Industry Profile: Asia-Pacific, 1*.

Gall, J. (2005). Dispelling five myths about e-books. *Information Technology & Libraries, 24*(1), 25–31.

Helfer, D. S. (2000). *E-books in libraries: Some early experiences and reactions*. (Internet/Web/Online Service Information). Information Today. Retrieved from http://www.finarticles.com/cf_0/m0DPC/9_8/66217098/p1/article.jhtml?term=-e-books

Herther, N. (2008). The ebook reader is not the future of ebooks. *Searcher, 16*(8), 26–40.

Ismail, R., & Zainab, A. N. (2005). The pattern of e-book use amongst undergraduates in Malaysia: A case of to know is to use. *Malaysian Journal of Library & Information Science, 10*(2).

Kaarst-Brown, M., & Evaristo, J. (2004). Perceived threats and opportunities: A preliminary model of the book retailer internet presence decision. *Journal of Organizational Computing and Electronic Commerce, 14*(4), 269–283. .doi:10.1207/s15327744joce1404_3

Lawrence, E., Lawrence, J., Newton, S., Dann, S., Corbitt, B., & Thanasankit, T. (2003). *Internet commerce digital models for business* (3rd ed.). Milton, Australia: Wiley.

Marlow, M. (2006). E-volution of revolution: Some observations on emerging trends in content, technology and service provision. *Information Services & Use, 26*(2), 191–197.

Morris, M., Schindehutte, M., & Allen, J. (2003). The entrepreneur's business model: Toward a unified perspective. *Journal of Business Research, 58*, 726–735. doi:10.1016/j.jbusres.2003.11.001

Oghojafor, K. (2005). *E-book publishing success: How anyone can write, compile and sell e-books on the Internet*. Oxford, UK: Chandos Publishing Oxford Limited.

Picard, R. (2000). Changing business models of online content services: Their implications for multimedia and other content producers. *The International Journal on Media Management, 2*(11).

Rao, S. S. (2003). Electronic books: A review and evaluation. *Library High Tech, 21*(1), 85-93. Retrieved from www.emeraldinsight.com/0737-88831.html

Shafer, S., Smith, H., & Linder, J. (2005). The power of business models. *Business Horizons, 48*, 199–207. doi:10.1016/j.bushor.2004.10.014

Sifton, E. (2009). The long goodbye? *The Nation.* Retrieved from http://live.thenation.com/archive/detail/39983861

Snowhill, L. (2001). E-books and their future in academic libraries. *D-Lib Magazine, 7*(7/8). doi:10.1045/july2001-snowhill

Staley, D. (2003). The future of the book in a digital age. (Cover story). [Retrieved from Academic Search Premier database.]. *The Futurist, 37*(5), 18.

Tian, X., & Martin, B. (2009). Business models in digital book publishing: Some insights from Australia. *Publishing Research Quarterly, 25*(2), 73–88. .doi:10.1007/s12109-009-9115-1

Ventura, M. (2005, January). The future of books. *Technology Review.*

von Bubnoff, A. (2005). Science in the web age: The real death of print. *Nature, 438*(7068), 550–552. .doi:10.1038/438550a

Zahda, S. A. A. (2007). Electronic books: Fad or future? In *Building an Information Society for All: Proceedings of the International Conference on Libraries, Information and Society,* Malaysia. ISBN 9789834349103

ADDITIONAL READING

Attanasio, P. (2006). The impact of technology on European small and medium-sized publishers. *Information Services & Use, 26*(2), 109–113.

Barnes, M., Clayborne, J., & Palmer, S. S. (2005). Book pricing: publisher, vendor, *Collection Building, 24*(3), Retrieved from http://www.emeraldinsight.com/10.1108/01604950510608258 doi: 10.1108/01604950510608258

Brown, D. J., & Boulderstone, R. (2008). *The Impact of electronic publishing: the future for publishers and librarians. Müchen: K. G. Saur.* doi:10.1515/9783598440137

Cope, B., & Phillips, A. (Eds.). (2006). *The Future of the book in the digital age.* Oxford: Chandos.

Darnton, R. (2007). Old Books and E-Books. *European Review (Chichester, England), 15*(2), 165–170. doi:10.1017/S106279870700018X

Darnton, R. (2009). *The Case for books: past, present, and future.* New York, N.Y.: PublicAffairs.

Davidson, L. (2005). The End of Print: Digitization and Its Consequence—Revolutionary Changes in Scholarly and Social Communication and in Scientific Research. *International Journal of Toxicology (Taylor & Francis), 24*(1), 25-34. doi:10.1080/10915810590921351.

DONATICH, J. (2009). Why Books Still Matter. *Journal of Scholarly Publishing, 40*(4), 329–342. doi:10.3138/jsp.40.4.329

Forman, S. (2005). Textbook Publishing: An Ecological View. *The Journal of American History, 91*(4), 1398–1404. doi:10.2307/3660180

Godinho, F. (2006). The Other Side of the Coin: Alternatives for the Sustainable Growth of the Book Market in Brazil. *Publishing Research Quarterly, 22*(4), 37–48. doi:10.1007/s12109-007-0004-1

Kempe, J. (2007). BookStore – Strategic options of a publisher-driven service. *Information Services & Use, 27*(4), 167–171.

Liu, Z. (2008). *Paper to digital: documents in the information age*. Westport, Conn.: Libraries Unlimited.

Magda Vassiliou, & Jennifer Rowley. (2008). Progressing the definition of "e-book". *Library Hi Tech, 26*(3), 355-368. Document ID: 1564044441.

Meckes, R. (2007). Pricing in Academic Publishing: A wake-up call to the online era. *Information Services & Use, 27*(4), 221–228.

Nelson, M. (2006). The Blog Phenomenon and the Book Publishing Industry. *Publishing Research Quarterly, 22*(2), 3–26. doi:10.1007/s12109-006-0012-6

Robinson, L., & Halle, D. (2002). Digitization, the Internet, and the Arts: eBay, Napster, SAG, and e-Books. *Qualitative Sociology, 25*(3), 359–383. doi:10.1023/A:1016034013716

(2005). The Future of Books. *Technology Review, 108*(1), 60–63.

Young, N. (2009). How Digital Content Resellers are Impacting Trade Book Publishing. *Publishing Research Quarterly, 25*(3), 139–146. .doi:10.1007/s12109-009-9122-2

KEY TERMS AND DEFINITIONS

Book Publishing: Process of production and distribution of information or literature in the form of printed or other formats like electronic media.

Business Model: A framework that shows the components of a firm and how it creates delivers and captures value within its value network.

Capabilities: Skills, knowledge or competencies that are applied by the firm to achieve the success and in this case, its value propositions.

E-Books: Conventional books that are converted into digital format, and sometimes restricted with digital rights management system. It is also known as digital book.

Eco-System: A complex set of relationship among the suppliers, distributors and customers, in the book publishing industry.

Value Network: Formation of several firms' value chains into a network, where they work together to create social goods. Each firm plays a role in contributing to the total value chain.

Value Proposition for Publishers: Primary benefit or value that a product or service offers to the firm or in this case, the publishers.

Value Proposition for Readers: A unique value that a firm offers to its customers and one that separates it from its competitors.

Chapter 34
The Future of Newspapers

Antonius Ruddy Kurniawan
Nanyang Technological University, Singapore

Kok Wai Mun Mervin
Nanyang Technological University, Singapore

Zhang Qiushi
Nanyang Technological University, Singapore

ABSTRACT

Newspapers have been around for many years. The London Gazette was the first true newspaper in English in 1666, but since the development of the internet in 1990, newspaper circulation and readership keep sinking. Print advertising revenues are weakening, and investors under heavy pressure approved the sale of Knight Rider, one of the industry's most respected companies. Most of them believe this is the beginning of a long-term decline of newspaper industry.

There are many challenges faced by newspaper companies to gain competitive advantage over the internet and increasing digital media consumption. How do newspaper companies face these challenges? How can they refine and strategize their business model to remain competitive? What are the issues that newspaper industries face? With all these questions, this chapter discusses key areas and conceptual models of future newspapers' strategy framework and supply chain management through literature review and analysis of technologies and innovations.

INTRODUCTION

The development of internet has affected the way in which most business work. Among these activities, newspaper industry across the world is undergoing significant changes. There has been a decline in the printed editions of newspapers,

replaced by digital versions. Furthermore, market research has indicated that reduction in advertising revenues of newspapers have significantly declined due to the switch of advertising from printed newspapers to Internet. These changes have prompted suggestions that there will be necessarily major changes to newspaper supply chains (Currah, 2009; Economist, 2006, pp. 57-59). For instance, a rapid decline in reader numbers has

DOI: 10.4018/978-1-61350-147-4.ch034

been observed in regional newspapers: sales of UK regional newspapers declined from 2.1 billion in 2000 to 1.7 billion in 2005. This decline is predicted to continue so that, by 2010, sales will have fallen to 1.4 billion copies (Graham and Smart, 2010). Many newspapers are losing their market share and disappearing, while others are moving almost inevitably to online and digital formats. However, it has been difficult to find ways of profiting from the digital ventures (Ihlström & Henfridsson, 2005), which creates several issues during the transformation of newspapers industry.

Digitalization has indeed created new consumption habits. Today, younger people essentially consume news in a steady stream of information bites (Elizabeth, 2009). Breakthrough innovations of internet technology have allowed new channels of information sharing through social networks. People are now constantly connected to internet through computers and mobile devices which allow them to gain multiple digital resources at the same time.

With the transformation of newspapers industry and increasing online and digital consumption, challenges are also raised for newspaper companies to refine their business strategies and supply chain management to re-gain value proposition.

In this paper, the following questions would be addressed:

- What are the major Internet technologies and their roles to influence users' consumption of information?
- What are the fundamental disruptive issues in the newspaper industry?
- How do we refine the business model in the future of newspapers?
- How do we define a new model of supply chain management of newspapers industry under the impact of Internet technology?

With these questions in mind, the key areas are reviewed and conceptual models of future newspapers' strategy framework and supply chain management are proposed with future research recommendations.

BACKGROUND

Emerging new technologies followed by demand from early adopter prompted the press industries to create online or digital version of printed newspapers. Newspaper, being the source of information for news and articles, have been around for ages, has now been challenged by services invented with new technologies. In this section, we will review the current technologies' impact and different types of innovations they have brought to the newspapers industry.

The review of technology and networked information economy and sustaining innovation vs. disruptive innovation addresses our first and second question in the paper.

Technology and Networked Information Economy

With the advent of Web technology, Web 2.0 services are becoming more and more popular. Web 2.0 services mainly fall into 3 categories, information push/pull, information retrieval and information exchange (Chua et, al., 2008). Typical online services include Blogs, Wikis, Social Networking Sites, Social Sharing Sites, Mashups, Social Tagging and RSS. Web 2.0 has changed the traditional Web by providing more interactive and collaborative features which greatly improves the effectiveness in communication. By emphasizing peers' social interaction and collective intelligence, Web 2.0 presents new opportunities for leveraging the Web and engaging its users more effectively (Murugesan, 2007). Since Web 2.0 came out, the Internet has been stepping toward the concept of communities online. The first web of 1990s was only the conversion of printed content into digital formats in the form of web pages, and now with collaboration and interaction involved, Internet is becoming a platform for information sharing and exchange within communities with almost zero cost. More and more information are digitalized, and they are slowly forming a network with low cost. The network comprises what Benkler (2006) calls the networked information economy. Benkler describes how a digital networked media enables: (1) the production and distribution of information through nonproprietary processes much like those in the arts, education and sciences; (2) a blend of market and nonmarket mechanisms for making information available to the public; (3) large-scale, cooperative efforts that generate output from many providers, e.g. wikis.

Networked information economy has provided several features (Mulhern, 2009):

- **Infinite reproduction and sharing:** Due to the digitalization, contents are no longer restricted with physical formats. Now information can be copied and shared online with either low or no cost, and they do not suffer from the loss of quality as printed content. Sharing of the contents no longer requests a transfer of physical items, but through online channels provided by Web 2.0 services which is faster and in a more collaborative manner.
- **Modularity of content:** Traditional media content are bundled by editors and products into relevant packages such as newspapers, advertisements and deliver to users. In digital age, users are receiving media as information, which can be unbundled and delivered individually to users who are interested to particular content. The packages are cut into pieces of information and offered to users in the online network.
- **Consumer networks:** With networked information economy, we are forming communities and networks online. Traditionally, the interaction and collaboration between consumers cannot be tracked due to no existing network. Therefore,

individuals are making decisions purely on themselves and the limited amount of information they could acquire through their private network. With online communities, consumers are no longer blind. The centrality of the individual decision maker will give way to meaningful social clusters that make purchase decisions and effectively constitute the target audiences for advertisers (Barabasi, 2003).

- **User controlled content production:** Technologies now empower consumers to control what information they would like to receive, and also produce information for others in the same manner. Therefore, contents are customized and users can decide what information they would like to share among the communities. With networked information economy, market has shifted towards consumer oriented, where the services and information are highly customized according to consumers' needs (Gal-Or & Gal-Or, 2005).

As a media content, digital newspapers have inherited all these features in networked information economy. Because of the different nature, the supply chain of newspapers has been affected and gone through a paradigm shift.

Sustaining Innovation vs. Disruptive Innovation

Innovations are always presented in newspapers industry. Traditionally, sustaining innovation, which refers to incremental improvements of products, is adopted widely in the industry. The actions taken in the newspapers industry include adding new sections, redesigning, building new press to meet advertisers' color demands and adding video or audio to news websites (American Press Institute, 2006, pp. 11). Dr. Christensen (Christensen & Raynor, 2003) has demonstrated this type of innovation in Figure 1.

As we can see from Figure 1, the blue line shows the performance of sustaining innovations on product improvements over time, and the red line shows the average customers' expected performance over time which they can actually use. There is always a gap between product innovation and customer satisfaction. Customers always desire a wide range of products, however few of them can benefit from all of them, while most customers' needs are very specific towards one product. As a result, incremental innovations are always rising faster than average customers' needs to make sure all customers' needs are met.

However, due to the new technologies and networked information economy presented in the previous section, a new type of innovation is seen to be occurring: disruption innovation, which is also illustrated by Dr. Christensen in Figure 2 (Christensen & Raynor, 2003). Disruptive innovations are often triggered by new technology's presence; it does not just offer incremental improvements but fundamentally changes the business strategy. Typical new products with disruptive innovations are providing lower performance along some traditional dimension, but it offers those factors with new benefits such as simplicity, convenience, ease of use and ease of access.

According to Figures 1 and 2, incumbents have a significant advantage because they have the resources and existing market shares to make investments in sustaining innovation. However,

this leads them to overlook the needs of average users, as the figure shows only a certain level of product improvements will be actually used. While sustaining innovations by keeping incumbents stay alive in the game, they do not realize the capitalization of disruptive innovations on the over-improvement. Disruptive innovation does not provide the same power as these incumbents; however it does provide a good enough level of satisfaction to average consumers, where their narrowed solutions may fit into specific requirements for users. For example, social media cannot replace newspapers' role in authorized information distribution and generate the same amount of revenue from advertisement, it provides a community to make the information flow much faster and effective than newspapers with almost zero cost, which satisfies people who want easy access to information better. Craiglist also offers an example of Christensen's principle of disruptive innovation. The site began as a self-service online classified solution for San Francisco Bay area residents. Overtime, the site's creators have refined its functionality in response to users' expressed needs, and it has become a preferred alternative to print and online classifieds in many major metro markets (Sterling, 2008).

Due to new technologies and networked information economy, firms are facing a paradigm shift of their business strategies in the newspapers industry. Although established firms have more resources to invest in sustaining innovations which

Figure 1. Sustaining innovation (Christensen and Raynor, 2003)

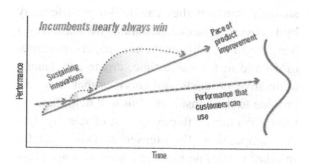

Figure 2. Disruptive innovation (Christensen & Raynor, 2003)

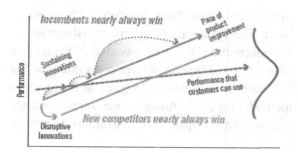

bring them competitive advantages, they could not ignore the effect of disruptive innovations brought by new technologies over the Internet. Newspaper firms suffer from the loss of reader population and advertisement revenues need to corporate with disruptive innovations and refine their business strategy to fit these innovations into their business blueprint, as this is the root cause of the issues they are facing.

DISCUSSION

After reviewing the impact and innovations brought by new technology to the newspapers industry, we have seen fundamental shifts of business strategy occurring in the industry to accommodate the new challenges. In this section, a new conceptual model is introduced to battle against the disruptive innovation; a model on business strategy and a model on supply chain management are proposed to facilitate and leverage on the impacts of disruptive innovation.

The proposed strategy framework and supply chain management model addresses the third and fourth questions in our paper:

- How do we refine the business model in the future of newspapers?
- How do we define a new model of supply chain management of newspapers industry under the impact of Internet technology?

The Newspaper Next (N2) Innovation Methodology

In the American Press Institute's "Newspaper Next: The Transformation Project, Blueprint for Transformation" Report released on 27 September 2006, API and Innosight have recommended the N2 Innovation Methodology as an innovation methodology for the American newspaper industry to counter the impact and invasion of disruptive

innovators that technological advancement has brought about (Sterling, 2008).

The proposed N2 Innovation Methodology consists of four key steps and they are as follows (Sterling, 2008):

- **Step 1:** Spot Opportunities
- **Step 2:** Develop Potential Solutions
- **Step 3:** Assess Approach
- **Step 4:** Test, Learn and Adjust

Steps 1 and 2 are Phase 1, which is the initial product development phase, and Steps 3 and 4 are Phase 2, which is the evaluation and improvement cycle. Finally, after going through the four recommended steps, the innovative solutions are ready to be launched (Sterling, 2008). Figure 3 depicts the N2 innovation Methodology.

According to Step 1 of the N2 Innovation Methodology, before newspaper companies are able to spot opportunities, they must first conduct the "jobs to be done" research (Sterling, 2008). In order to be successful, newspaper companies have to do things differently to adapt to changes and new forces in the marketplace, and invest in building new capabilities. In addition, they can no longer survive, grow and prosper alone. In other words, they need to collaborate in the networked economy (Christensen and Davis, 2010).

Hence, the "jobs to be done" research requires a shift in mindset and it starts with the way newspaper companies look at the consumers. Traditionally, newspaper companies will try to increase their readership levels by convincing readers to read their newspapers. However, they should be analyzing on how they can do things differently by discovering the indispensable information jobs that consumers will hire the newspaper companies to do and at the same time, create and launch innovative products and services that they can provide to the consumers that will help them do those jobs more effectively and efficiently than the competition (Christensen & Davis, 2010). In other words, newspaper companies are play-

Figure 3. The N2 innovation methodology (American Press Institute, 2006, pp. 5)

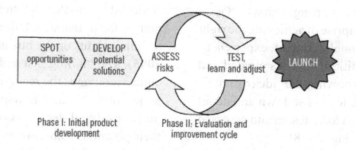

ing a new role as solution providers or problem solvers to consumers, who currently do not read newspapers. Thus, newspaper companies need to build and create new capabilities to support the execution of the solutions. For instance, newspaper companies need to explore new ways of tapping into the collective wisdom of the community and building data warehouses for data mining. In addition, newspaper companies can tap on the growth, reach and popularity of social networking and Web 2.0 technologies to create the necessary platforms for the building of virtual communities (Christensen & Davis, 2010).

Besides looking at the consumers differently and approaching those who do not currently read newspapers differently, newspaper companies should also do the same for advertisers who do not currently advertise on newspapers (Christensen & Davis, 2010). In fact, the most direct path to new growth for newspaper companies is for them to focus on non-readers and non-advertisers (Sterling, 2008). Hence, it is time for newspaper companies to re-look into their traditional business models and revenue streams, mainly from display and classified advertising. One very common misperception is that the problem that the businesses seek to solve is to advertise (Christensen & Davis, 2010). However, this is not true because survey and research have shown that those businesses that do not advertise on newspapers are interested in building long-term and sustainable relationships with customers, and creating brand awareness and corporate image (Christensen &

Davis, 2010). In addition, their main focus is on how to attract good people to join them as employees, and to simplify and make their back-end operations more effective and efficient. In fact, these are the real jobs that need to be done and not the misperception of solving problem through advertising (Christensen & Davis, 2010).

Hence, newspaper companies can add value to both businesses and consumers that do not advertise by helping them to address these issues or rather "jobs to be done" by offering them both online and offline innovative solutions, such as paid search, consumer direct, niche publications, lead generation, special events and targeted advertising (Christensen & Davis, 2010). Thus, newspaper companies are able to reach out to the segment of customers, both businesses and consumers made possible by innovative solutions that they previously have no inroads. Nevertheless, new capabilities need to be invested, created and built, in order to be equipped to provide the potential innovative solutions. Alternatively, newspaper companies can collaborate and form strategic alliances or partnerships with other industry players and niche players from other industries that can complement their innovative solution offerings (Christensen & Davis, 2010).

After spotting opportunities in Step 1, newspaper companies will have to develop potential solutions in Step 2 to address the "jobs to be done" or rather the needs that have been identified in Step 1. It is recommended for newspaper companies to develop "good enough" solutions for a start, which will improve over time with the help of sustaining innovation (Sterling, 2008). "Good enough" solutions comprise of achieving the right mix and match of channels, content, experiences and frequency. In addition, API has created and offered a simple tool, known as the "idea resume", for newspaper companies to list down and detail their potential solutions to be tested and assessed in Steps 3 and 4 (Sterling, 2008).

In Steps 3 and 4, the N2 Innovation Methodology provides the capability for newspaper companies to assess the risks involved and at the same time, to challenge the assumptions made during the development of their potential solutions (Sterling, 2008). Steps 3 and 4 are crucial because the steps allow newspaper companies to assess and test the potential solutions that have been developed in Step 2, so that only viable and tested solutions will be launched. In addition, Step 4 allows newspaper companies the opportunity to learn and adjust the potential solutions in accordance to the outcome of the assessment and testing before launching them into the marketplace (Sterling, 2008). In other words, Steps 3 and 4 allow newspaper companies to ascertain the feasibility, viability, sustainability and robustness of the potential solutions that they have developed based on the findings and spotting the appropriate opportunities in Step 1 (Sterling, 2008).

Steps 3 and 4 are based on three guiding principles that have been adapted from the book authored by Christensen and Raynor (2003), in which they have identified 14 patterns of disruptive success factors, which have been embedded in Steps 3 and 4. The three guiding principles are as follows (Sterling, 2008):

- "Invest a little, learn a lot"
- "Failing fast and failing cheap"
- "Be patient for growth, but impatient for profits"

The "invest a little, learn a lot" principle encourages learning to be achieved after risk assess-

ment has been carried out. This objective can be achieved by challenging the assumptions and by putting the potential solutions to the test, in order to gain insights on the business models (Sterling, 2008). The "failing fast and failing cheap" principle encourages the recognition of risks as early as possible, so that newspaper companies can make informed decisions on whether to launch their potential solutions or not after risk assessment, in order to prevent expensive failures. This principle also encourages cheap and quick testing and challenging of the assumptions to be carried out (Sterling, 2008). The "be patient for growth, but impatient for profits" principle encourages newspaper companies to start small and grow organically and progressively. However, they should stop any ventures that do not meet the planned profit goals and performance expectations as soon as possible to minimize losses (Sterling, 2008).

The Strategic Framework

The newspapers today are facing a dilemma, as its public audience are decreasing in numbers year after year as individual are moving to a faster and cheaper solution for information. But in every threat in the industries there will always be an opportunity and this in itself is not an exception to newspaper industries as well.

In this section, we will cover the newspaper strategic framework taken from American Press Institute's "Newspaper Next: The Transformation Project, Blueprint for Transformation" Report released on 27 September 2006, of how the media industries should expand their horizon and look beyond the new audiences for the new type of business customers and new business models (Figure 4).

This framework is not a magic formula that has to be followed because we believe that every newspaper has a unique internal circumstances and unique market characteristics, and there is no fixed formula could address them all. This framework provides a flexible plan or strategies that

Figure 4. Newspaper strategic framework (American Press Institute, 2006, pp. 4)

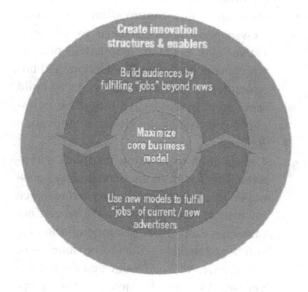

Figure 4. Newspaper strategic framework (American Press Institute, 2006, pp. 4)

can be shaped to suit each company and community.

Maximize Core Business Model

At the centre of the framework is to maximize the core business model. Companies must maximize their existing core products, such as product that rely primarily on display for example classified and advertisement. These core products are proven winners that generate revenue and make money in familiar ways, using existing business models, content, sales, and production and distribution resources.

Build Audiences by Fulfilling Jobs beyond News

Nearly half of baby boomers do not regularly read the newspaper, the numbers are even higher in younger generations. Furthermore, among all age groups, non-consumption of newspapers has become popular.

How do newspaper companies reclaim the readership despite this phenomenon? The com-

pany needs to shift their focus from products and services to the lives of consumers.

What can the company do to begin building the new audiences? First the company needs to discover the unsatisfied consumer jobs beyond the news. Second, the company must recognize the content of the article that goes beyond the written words and professionally done photograph.

User News Models to Fulfill Jobs of Current/New Advertisers

As a dominant player and being information providers, newspapers in the past had attracted many user populations especially businesses who wanted to reach large population. Newspapers then enjoyed a healthy margin through selling subscriptions, display advertising and classifieds. Their online presence promises more revenues and audiences, but the growth is not quick enough to offset the softening revenue from printing, advertising and subscriptions.

Some of the recommendations include the following:

- **Identify important, unsatisfied advertiser/business jobs to be done in their markets.** The quest for innovation begins with understanding the jobs that current and potential customers cannot adequately solve with current solutions. Seeking out important, unsatisfied jobs of current and potential advertisers yields an important insight. While many businesses and individuals advertise, the job they are trying to get done is never advertising. Advertising is a means to an end.
- **Offer new models that get these identified jobs done better than traditional solutions.** The good news for newspaper companies is that new technologies allow them to fulfill existing and potential advertisers' jobs better than ever. Putting together the right solutions can increase revenue

by delivering new value to their best customers, and by serving new non-customers including small businesses and individuals for whom the newspaper is too broad, expensive or difficult to use. If newspaper companies were to collaborate effectively on a national level, they also could use these new tools to serve national advertisers who long ago rejected newspapers as too expensive and too difficult to buy

Create Innovation Structures and Enablers

Companies should have in place structures that enable users to make innovation a regular and repeatable part of day-to-day operations. The following are the four specific actions that newspaper companies can take to create structures and enablers that help them master innovation and transformation:

- **Build a common language:** Newspaper companies need to break out of deep-rooted habits of thought and limits on imagination. This is by opening eyes to a new way of thinking and a new way of seeing opportunity. The company also needs to teach these concepts to the management team and across the company and this will generate new ideas and create new excitement. By allowing them to be a constant part of the organization's internal communications, the concepts can be cemented and lead to real organizational change.

- **Dedicate resources to innovation:** Newspaper companies needs to appoint innovation champions that will be tasked with spotting and seizing new growth opportunities. He or she ideally needs to be a champion in innovation and should spend a substantial portion of their time on innovation. On top of that, the company should also allocate "just-enough" money to help champions develop early-stage opportunities.

- **Develop an innovation process:** Newspaper companies need to be innovative and develop innovation process which need not always be random and unstructured. There are many ways to build innovation processes. In fact some newspaper companies already have innovation processes.

- **Create jobs-to-be-done feedback channels:** This has been the trend among newspaper companies, which carry out research on readers and advertisers. However, not many have any processes for exploring the wants and needs — jobs to be done — of non-readers or businesses that do not advertise. As a result, large realms of opportunity for new products and services remain invisible.

Lastly, to fuel the innovation process, newspaper companies need consistent mechanisms to constantly gather knowledge about the jobs non-consumers and consumers are trying to do.

Supply Chain Management of Newspapers

A supply chain encompasses all the activities associated with the flow and transformation of goods from the raw-materials stage, through to the end user, as well as the associated information flows (Handfield & Nichols, 2002). The design of a supply chain involves four over-arching design decisions: (1) the choice of actors; (2) the choice of governance mechanisms; (3) the structure (sequencing order) of activities; and (4) co-ordination structures (Graham & Smart, 2010). Supply-chain management aims to procure the correct inputs; raw materials, components and capital equipment, convert them into finished products and dispatch them to their final destinations (Bowersox & Closs, 2007).

The Regional Newspaper Industry Supply Chain model (Graham & Smart, 2010) as shown in Figure 1, developed from Clemons and Lang(2003), synthesizes previous work on value chains, media convergence, digital economics and societal influence. This model has been proved to have strong theoretical underpinnings and shown to be internally consistent (Graham & Hill, 2009). Figure 5 presents 4 different stages in value creation activities along supply chain. It is influenced by societal, technological and commercial factors. With networked information economy, social media also becomes one of the factors that influence production and distribution. The number of readers of newspapers have declined rapidly due to the fact that potential news audience have shifted to social media such as blogs and social networking sites to acquire news and information, instead of reading newspapers. Therefore, newspapers are undergoing two trends: first, accessing of news is enabled on Internet with multiple devices (Bird, 2009); second, advertisers are placing increasing emphasis on on-line news and non-news (Domingo et al., 2008). The digitalization of newspapers industry has eventually lead convergences in media and devices. Therefore, news is produced in many formats including printed, online, mobile versions. They are also pushing to news to communities instead of individual users to allow faster information sharing and reduce the cost of distribution by letting the information reproduce and flow itself on the Internet.

The disruptive innovation from social media and technology has promoted the digital age of newspapers. To be able to corporate and leverage on these innovations, the proposed model has changed the traditional supply chain model to Figure 5 with the integration of the Internet; it also has changed the way of value creation of newspapers. Traditionally, newspapers are produced in printed formats; old stories and news are very hard to reproduce and distribute due to the high cost. On the other hand, digital newspapers have a much lower reproduction and distribution cost compared with printed newspapers. As a result, Digitalization allows the recreation of value on newspapers' archives, thereby effectively capturing the value in long tail (Anderson, 2004).

The process innovation of supply chain management can be mapped into our conceptual model according to the 4 stages in Figure 3.

Spot Opportunities

Internet media and device convergence, which can be known as the major impact to newspapers industry supply chain, also provide firms opportunities to explore their benefits on lower cost of production and distribution. Therefore, supply chain process should leverage on these opportunities in production and distribution of newspapers.

Develop Potential Solutions

The disruptive innovation of technology has generated services such as social media and online social network websites have influenced the way news are created, distributed and produced. Newspapers firms should accommodate these innovations into their supply chain process, news creation is no longer only a job for professional journalists, and instead it has become part of a collaborative and interactive activity with communities and readers. Potential solutions can be developed based on these impacts, while the technology has shifted its focus on collaboration, why should newspapers firms not do the same?

Assess Approach

After implementing the supply chain process, the approach of leveraging on innovation and technology should be assessed to make sure that it does not bring a negative impact to the core business. Value flow between the supply chain process and impacts from innovation and technology should

Figure 5. Regional newspaper industry supply chain model (Graham and Smart, 2010)

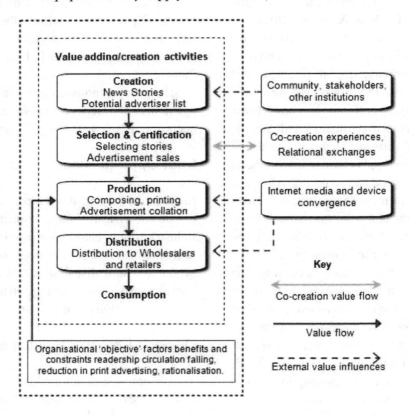

be favoring the newspapers firm; therefore new value proposition can be acquired.

Test, Learn, and Adjust

Although this model has proven to be theoretically strong, it does not suggest the details to leverage on innovation and technology. Therefore, firms adopting the model need to constantly re-evaluate their supply chain process using either qualitative or quantitative analysis to verify the investments and direction of current model. According to different situational factors, the same model can be applied to firms in a very different manner.

CONCLUSION

Clayton Christensen and Andrew Davis (2010) strongly believe that it is possible for newspaper

companies to remain successful. In fact, there still exists a massive growth potential for the newspaper industry, even after so many market leaders have stumbled due to the emergence of game changing disruptive innovators in the newspaper industry. They have made this claim based on the outcome of their research. In fact, the core content is the real assets that continue to generate revenues and profits for newspaper companies. Ironically, the core content is also the driving force behind the emergence of the disruptive innovators, such as news reporting on the television, blogs, and news on Search Engines, such as Google and Yahoo. Without the core content produced and provided by newspaper companies, the emergence of disruptive innovators in the newspaper industry will not be possible. In order to counter the invasion of disruptive innovators successfully, newspaper companies need to adapt to the changes in the industry innovatively and evolve by fully tapping on the innovation potential.

Last but not least, the important role that newspaper companies played in society as the sole and responsible providers and processors of primary sourced news and information cannot be overemphasized. For instance, most of the secondary news channels and providers, such as news-related blogs, online news aggregators, radio news and television news, obtain their news content either wholly or partially from the original reporting of newspaper companies (Sterling, 2008).

REFERENCES

American Press Institute. (2006). *Blue print transformation*.

Anderson C. (2004).The long tail: Why the future of business is selling less of more.

Barabasi, A.-L. (2003). *Linked: How everything is connected to everything else and what it means*. New York, NY: Plume.

Bird, S. E. (2009). The future of journalism in the digital environment. *Journalism, 10*(3), 293–295. doi:10.1177/1464884909102583

Bowersox, D. J., & Closs, D. J. (2007). *Logistics management: The integrated supply chain process*. New York, NY: McGraw-Hill.

Christensen, C. M., & Davis, A. B. (2010). *The next act for newspaper companies*. Retrieved from http://www.docstoc.com/docs/35815845/The-next-act-for-newspaper-companies

Christensen, C. M., & Raynor, M. E. (2003). *The innovator's solution*. Harvard Business School Press.

Chua, A., Goh, D., & Lee, C. S. (2008). The prevalence and use of Web 2.0 in libraries. *Proceedings of the 11th International Conference on Asian Digital Libraries* (ICADL), *Lecture Notes in Computer Science, 5362*, (pp. 22–30). December 2-5, Bali, Indonesia.

Clemons, E., & Lang, K. (2003). The decoupling of value creation from revenue: A strategic analysis of the markets for pure information goods. *Information Technology Management, 4*(2-3), 259–287. doi:10.1023/A:1022958530341

Currah, A. (2009). *What's happening to our news. An investigation into the likely impact of the digital revolution on the economics of news publishing in the UK*. Oxford, UK: Reuters Institute of Journalism, University of Oxford.

Domingo, D., Quandt, T., Heinonen, A., Paulussen, S., Singer, J. B., & Vujnovic, M. (2008). Participatory journalism practices in the media and beyond: An international comparative study of initiatives in online newspapers. *Journalism Practice, 2*(3), 326–341. doi:10.1080/17512780802281065

Elizabeth, S. (2009). The future of journalism in the digital environment. *Journalism, 10*(3), 293–295. doi:10.1177/1464884909102583

Gal-Or, E., & Gal-Or, M. (2005). Customized advertising via a common media distributor. *Marketing Science, 25*(5), 241–253. doi:10.1287/mksc.1040.0092

Graham, G., & Smart, A. (2010). The regional-newspaper industry supply chain and the Internet. *Supply Chain Management: An International Journal, 15*(3).

Handfield, R., & Nichols, E. L. (2002). *Supply chain redesign: Transforming supply chains into integrated value systems*. London, UK: FT Press.

Holland, M. (2008). Historical British newspapers online. *Library Hi Tech News, 25*(7), 18–20. doi:10.1108/07419050810921319

Hurter, A. P., & Van Buer, M. G. (1996). Newspaper production/distribution problem. *Journal of Business Logistics, 17*, 85. Retrieved on March 11th, 2010, from http://findarticles.com/p/articles/mi_qa3705/is_199601/ai_n8741053/

Ihlström, C., & Henfridsson, O. (2005). Online newspapers in Scandinavia: A longitudinal study of genre change and interdependency. *IT & People, 18*(2), 172–192. doi:10.1108/09593840510601522

Mulhern, F. (2009). Integrated marketing communications: From media channels to digital connectivity. *Journal of Marketing Communications, 15*(2-3), 85–101. doi:10.1080/13527260902757506

Murugesan, S. (2007). Understanding Web 2.0. *IT Professional Magazine, 9*(4), 34–41. doi:10.1109/MITP.2007.78

Sterling, J. (2008). A plan for a US newspaper industry counterattack against disruptive innovators. *Strategy and Leadership, 36*(1), 20–26. doi:10.1108/10878570810840652

Wruck, P. (2006). Newspaper distribution today. In *Proceedings of Managing Distribution Conference*, Madrid. Retrieved on March 11th, 2010, from http://www.ifra.com/website/News.nsf/All /499649365D99DFC0C1257187004B0ACB/$F ILE/Ifra_Distribution06_WruckP.pdf

About the Contributors

Ravi S Sharma is an Associate Professor at the Wee Kim Wee School of Communication and Information at the Nanyang Technological University since 2004. He is the Principal Investigator of an NRF-funded project on Interactive Digital Enterprises. He spent the previous 10 years in industry as Asean Communications Industry Principal at IBM Global Services and Director of the Multimedia Competency Centre of Deutsche Telekom Asia. He has (co-) authored over 100 technical papers in various journals, conferences, trade publications, and the broadcast media.

Margaret Tan is an Associate Professor at the Wee Kim Wee School of Communication and Information, and Deputy Director of the Singapore Internet Research Centre at Nanyang Technological University. Her research focuses on knowledge management and mobilization, electronic trust and security, data protection and privacy, e-Government, and the digital societies. She has published widely over 100 articles in various scholarly journals and conferences, including two books, "The Virtual Workplace," and "e-Payment: The Digital Exchange."

Francis Pereira is the Director of Industry Research at the CTM, Marshall School of Business, University of Southern California. His research focuses on business issues in telecommunications, particularly the adoption rates of E-commerce in the small and medium size enterprises, and business models in new multimedia environment and the effects of emerging technologies on these models. Francis has published papers in journals that include the *Journal of Communications Networks* and the *Journal of the Institution of British Telecommunication Engineers*.

* * *

Nisha Alexander has a B.Eng (Electrical and Electronics Engineering) and MSc (Information Systems) from Nanyang Technological University. Her professional experience is in application development.

Ankit Bansal has a degree in Business Studies from Delhi University and MSc (Knowledge Management) from Nanyang Technological University. Currently, he is spearheading knowledge management initiatives at Jones Lang LaSalle, India. His research includes corporate memory, knowledge architecture, and organizational learning.

Aditya Budi holds a double Bachelor in Computer Science and Statistics from Bina Nusantara University, Indonesia. Currently he is pursuing MSc (Information System) at Nanyang Technological University while working as a Research Engineer in software system and data mining at Singapore Management University.

Sven Class holds a Bachelor in Politics and Management from the University of Constance, Germany and Master in Journalism at the University of Leipzig. He is a journalist for the German public media stations ZDF and WDR.

Chow Min Hua has a B.Com (Information Technology) from Curtin University of Technology, Australia and is currently pursuing M.Sc (Information Systems) at Nanyang Technological University. A Kauffman Global Scholar in Entrepreneurship in 2011, he has training at the Kauffman foundation, Stanford, Harvard, and MIT University and worked with VML, Inc., a digital marketing agency during her Global Scholars Internship.

Chua Jit Chee has a B.Eng (Computer Engineering) and MSc (Information Systems) from Nanyang Technological University, Singapore. She is a Research Engineer at A*STAR Institute for Infocomm Research. Previously, she was a systems analyst on software design and development in the telecommunications industry.

Omar El-Sawy is Professor of Information Systems at the Marshall School of Business of the University of Southern California. He specializes in IT-enabled business strategy in turbulent environments, and business models for digital platforms. He is the author of over 100 papers, serves on several editorial boards, and is a six-time winner of the Society for Information Management's Annual Paper Award. Prior to joining USC, Professor El Sawy worked as an Engineer at NCR Corporation, and as Manager of computer services at Stanford University, served as an Advisor to the United Nations Development Programme in Egypt, and was a Fulbright scholar in Finland.

Fan Jing has a B.Arts (English Literature and Education) and MSc (Information Studies) from Nanyang Technological University, Singapore. She is currently marketing and promoting a payment aggregator product in the emerging mobile market.

Johannes R. Gerstner is a Researcher at the Institute of Communication and Media Science of Leipzig University. His research interests include cross media, web TV, and online communication. He also teaches TV journalism, TV planning, and inter-media forms of journalism and media-scientific methods. Johannes has a journalism and sociology diploma at Leipzig University.

Gaurav Gupta is a Gold Medalist at the M.Sc (Information Systems) at Nanyang Technological University. Has has a B.Eng from Visveswaraiah Technological University, India.

Goh Kok Min has a B.Computer Science with Business as well as MSc (Information Systems) at Nanyang Technological University, Singapore.

Han Ei Chew is a Doctoral student of the Department of Telecommunication, Information Studies and Media at Michigan State University. He received his MA in Communication Studies from Nanyang Technological University. His research interests include information technology for development (ICT4D) and social capital theory.

Joshua Ho is a Software Engineer who has spent most of his early career designing and building software in the process automation and defense industries. In 2006, he discovered the Web as a powerful medium for creating interesting and useful applications. Rallying a few friends, he started his 1st Web startup and has not looked back since.

Tahani Iqbal holds a Master in Public Policy from the National University of Singapore, and a BSc in Economics and Management from the London School of Economics. She was a Research Associate at the Singapore Internet Research Centre, Nanyang Technological University. Her research interests include ICT policy and regulation, infrastructure and urban policies, and public sector reforms.

Noriahni Ismail is a graduate of the Master's of Science in Information Studies programme at Nanyang Technological University. She has been a Librarian in the Public Libraries, National Library Board Singapore, since 2006 and has an interest in the research of printed books. Noriahni also holds an undergaduate degree in Bachelor of Business from Nanyang Technological University.

Fan Jing is a recent graduate of the Master of Science in Information Studies programme at Nanyang Technological University. Her research interest in the smartphone platform and trends has led her to write a paper *"Smartphone Application Wave and Trends on Different platforms"* during the course *"Interactive Digital Media Marketplace"* under the supervision of Professor Ravi S. Sharma. Fan Jing also holds an Undergraduate Degree of Bachelor of Arts in English Literature and Education. She is currently working in an innovative start-up company as a marketing professional promoting a payment aggregator product to the emerging mobile internet market.

Keshav Kamat has a Bachelor's degree in Computer Engineering and MSc (Information Systems) from Nanyang Technological University. Previously, a Senior Software Engineer at Siemens Information Systems, Bangalore, he is currently a corporate planner for Intel-Micron Flash, Singapore.

Niazi Babar Zaman Khan is a Senior Software Engineer in a multinational engineering consultancy. He has completed his Master's of Science in Information Studies at Nanyang Technological University. Prior to this, his professional experience was in software development and architecture. Babar also holds an undergraduate degree in Computer Engineering.

Khin Mu Yar Soe is currently pursuing his MSc (Information System) at Nanyang Technology University. She holds a BSc in Information System Management. Her professional experience includes web developing, software engineering, and project management.

Satish Kumar is an IT consultant in a major software firm. He has completed his Master of Science in Information Systems at Nanyang Technological University. Prior to this his professional experience was in the area of software development and training.

Apurva Lawale has a M.Sc (Information Systems) at Nanyang Technological University. Working as a Program Manager in a software company, he also has interest in artificial intelligence and natural language processing.

Lee Shu Wen has a Bachelor of Computer and Mathematical Sciences and a MSc (Information Systems) from Nanyang Technological University, Singapore. Her experience includes data management and market analysis – particularly in identifying and assessing elements that influence the failure and/or success of businesses, product and services.

Elizabeth Lee is a graduate of the Master of Science in Information Studies programme at Nanyang Technological University. She has been a public librarian at the National Library Board of Singapore since 2005 and has interest in research on printed books in the library industry. Elizabeth also holds an undergraduate degree in Computer Science from the National University of Singapore.

Marcel Machill holds the Chair of Journalism II at the University of Leipzig in Germany. He was also a McCloy scholar at Harvard University in Cambridge, USA. He holds academic degrees from three countries: a Master of Public Administration (MPA) at the John F. Kennedy School of Government, an M.A from the French Journalism Institute Centre des Formation des Journalistes, and a diploma ("with honors") from the University of Dortmund, and a PhD ("summa cum laude") that was honored by the University of Dortmund with the 1997 prize of "outstanding thesis of the year."

Arun Mahizhnan is Deputy Director of Institute of Policy Studies at the National University of Singapore. He is also concurrently Adjunct Professor at the Wee Kim Wee School of Communication and Information at the Nanyang Technological University. His research interests include policy issues pertaining to new media and its impact on society.

Marcus Mansukhani is an English teacher working in Bandung, Indonesia and is a part time postgraduate student studying an MA in Education (Applied Linguistics) at The Open University, UK. He previously studied at London Guildhall University and Nanyang Technological University, Singapore.

Goh Kok Min has a B.Computer Science with Business as well as MSc (Information Systems) at Nanyang Technological University, Singapore.

Miguel A. Morales-Arroyos received his PhD in Information Science at the University of North Texas through a Fulbright scholarship. Currently, he is a Researcher at the Institute for Research in Applied Mathematics and Systems at the National University of Mexico. Previously, he taught at the School of Communications and Information at Nanyang Technological University where he was also a Research Fellow.

Bakrudeen Nizam has completed his Master of Science in Information Systems in the year 2010. His interest in Digital Media Marketplace has led him to study the IDM course in his Master's programme. He submitted a paper on *"Profiting from IDM Innovations: Learning from Amazon.com & iTunes"* for his final project. Bakrudeen Nizam is currently working as a Technical Manager in a European Company.

Penny Peng is currently an Executive in a media and publishing company. She was previously a Research Assistant at SIGIDE. She earned a B. Eng (1st class honours) in Electrical & Electronics Engineering from Nanyang Technological University and is currently pursuing post-graduate qualifications.

Kristy Shi is currently a doctoral candidate at Ball State University in the United States. She was previously a Research Associate with SIGIDE. She has a Master's of Mass Communication from Nanyang Technological University.

Sander Myint Shwe is a recent graduate of the Master of Science in Information Systems programme at Nanyang Technological University. Her research interest in the business model has led him to pursue a critical inquiry information system during the course of study in the area of "Developing Online Tool for Business Modeling of Interactive Digital Media Marketplace" under the supervision of Professor Ravi S. Sharma. Prior to this, her professional experience was in Cost and Management Accounting after she finished her professional certification in LCCI Level III. Sander also holds an Honour degree of Bachelor of Computer Technology from University of Computer Studies, Yangon, Myanmar.

Lena Stephanie is currently a doctoral candidate at Nanyang Technological University, Singapore, with research interest in e-health business models. A certified Project Management Professional (PMP), she has successfully managed several research and IT projects in her career of over twelve years. Lena also holds a B.Eng from PSG College of Technology, India, and a MBA from Anna University, India.

Tan Chee Liang graduated with a Master of Science in Information Systems from Nanyang Technological University (NTU) in 2010. His research interest in the area of social media and marketing has this led his team to come out with a paper on the effect of Web 2.0 Features on Social Networks for viral marketing. His professional experience is in Information Technology where he currently heads the Technology and Services team in one of the local polytechnics. Chee Liang also holds a Bachelor degree in Engineering from NTU with a minor in Business.

Daniel Tan is an analyst at Credit Suisse. He holds a BSc in Information & Computer Science from the University of California, Irvine and MSc (Information Systems) from Nanyang Technological University. As an undergraduate, he worked as a Research Assistant at The Center for Research on Information Technology and Organizations (CRITO).

Edwin Tan Seng Tat has a B. Computer Science, and is pursuing the MSc (Information Systems) at Nanyang Technological University. Currently, he is a senior engineer at the High Performance Computing Centre at Nanyang Technological University. His professional experience includes end to end software application projects and website development, efficient automation, and reporting to manufacturing operations.

Kelvin Tan Yuean Soo holds both a B.Business (Accountancy) and MSc (Information Systems) from Nanyang Technological University.

Tan Huc Huey has a BSc (Hons) in Computing from Staffordshire University and a MSc (Knowledge Management) from Nanyang Technological University. Prior to his graduate studies, he was an administration assistant, librarian, sales executive, retail trainee, and customer service in the retail, education, and gift industry in Malaysia.

Srinivasan Thomas has a BSc in Chemistry and Master in Public Administration from Madras University, India as well as a MSc (Information Systems) from Nanyang Technological University. He is a project manager and an aspiring information technology architect. His interests include interactive digital media, particularly in e-health.

Steven S. Wildman is the James H. Quello Professor of Telecommunication Studies and Director of the James H. and Mary B. Quello Center for Telecommunication Management & Law at Michigan State University. He holds a PhD in Economics from Stanford University and a BA in Economics from Wabash College. He is well known for his research and publications on economics and policy for communication industries.

Luwen Wong Chuling has a B.Sc in Information Systems and Management from University of London and a M.Sc (Information Systems) from Nanyang Technological University.

Harley Wu Sze Wei holds a MSc (Information Systems) from Nanyang Technological University and a Bachelor of Information Technology from the Australian National University. An Internet proprietor and software developer, Harley designs and develops solutions for the Internet.

Yang Ke is a graduate of the M.Sc (Information Studies) at Nanyang Technological University. Her curiosity is in the eWOM marketing led her to research in "*The wisdom of crowds: Creating value with blogs and eWoM.*" She is now working with eWOM as a purchaser.

Yang Yi is completing her MSc by research at the Wee Kim Wee School of Communication and Information from the Nanyang Technological University. She also has another MSc from RSIS at Nanyang Technological University. She did her undergraduate at the China Foreign Affairs University. Her research interest is in the area of strategic analysis of digital and social media.

Irvine Yeo is pursuing her Master of Science in Information System at Nanyang Technological University. He holds an MBA from University of Strathclyde as well as a Bachelor with double major in Mass Communication and Marketing. Professionally, he is a project manager and IT strategist in technical infrastructure.

Reza Azeharie Yudaputra holds a BSc in Information Systems and Management and a MSc (Knowledge. Management) from Nanyang Technological University. His previous experience included risk management in Commercial Insurance.

Zeng Junming holds a B.Computer Science and a MSc (Information Systems) from Nanyang Technological University. Currently, he is a research officer at Agency for Science, Technology and Research.

Zhang Wei holds a MSc (Information Studies) at Nanyang Technological University and a Bachelor of Law in International Economic Law. Her professional experience included eCommerce and ITO/BPO industry. Currently she works in Singapore as the Business Development Manager of an online gaming/SNS company.

Kaung Myat Win is a recent graduate of the Master of Science in Information Systems program at Nanyang Technological University. Kaung also holds an Undergraduate degree of Bachelor of Science (Hons.) in Computer Network Systems from Coventry University.

Index